Edutainment *Comes Alive!*

William P. Mann

SAMS PUBLISHING

201 West 103rd Street
Indianapolis, Indiana 46290

For Patti and Jennifer, who make it all worthwhile.

Copyright © 1994 by Sams Publishing
FIRST EDITION

All rights reserved. No part of this book shall be reproduced, stored in a retrieval system, or transmitted by any means, electronic, mechanical, photocopying, recording, or otherwise, without written permission from the publisher. No patent liability is assumed with respect to the use of the information contained herein. Although every precaution has been taken in the preparation of this book, the publisher and author assume no responsibility for errors or omissions. Neither is any liability assumed for damages resulting from the use of the information contained herein. For information, address Sams Publishing, a division of Macmillan Computer Publishing, 201 W. 103rd St., Indianapolis, IN 46290.

International Standard Book Number: 0-672-30450-3

Library of Congress Catalog Card Number: 93-86959

97 96 95 94   4 3 2 1

Interpretation of the printing code: the rightmost double-digit number is the year of the book's printing; the rightmost single-digit, the number of the book's printing. For example, a printing code of 94-1 shows that the first printing of the book occurred in 1994.

Composed in Goudy and MCPdigital by Prentice Hall Computer Publishing

Printed in the United States of America

Trademarks

All terms mentioned in this book that are known to be trademarks or service marks have been appropriately capitalized. Sams Publishing cannot attest to the accuracy of this information. Use of a term in this book should not be regarded as affecting the validity of any trademark or service mark.

Cover art reproduced courtesy of the following companies. All rights reserved.
    Dr. T's Music Software; Conexus; 7th Level;
    Discovery Communications; Ebook, Inc.;
    Science for Kids; Paramount Interactive;
    Davidson & Associates; Apogee

CD-ROM label art from Kid CAD, the Amazing 3-D Building Kit, by Davidson & Associates

Publisher
Richard K. Swadley

Associate Publisher
Jordan Gold

Acquisitions Manager
Stacey Hiquet

Managing Editor
Cindy Morrow

Acquisitions Editor
Grace Buechlein

Development Editor
Keith Davenport

Production Editor
Jodi Jensen

Editorial and Graphics Coordinator
Bill Whitmer

Editorial Assistants
Sharon Cox
Lynette Quinn
Carol Ackerman

Technical Reviewer
Peter Scisco

Marketing Manager
Greg Bushyeager

Cover Designer
Jay Corpus

Director of Production and Manufacturing
Jeff Valler

Imprint Manager
Juli Cook

Manufacturing Coordinator
Paul Gilchrist

Book Designer
Alyssa Yesh

Production Analysts
Mary Beth Wakefield
Dennis Clay Hager

Proofreading Coordinator
Joelynn Gifford

Indexing Coordinator
Johnna VanHoose

Graphics Image Specialists
Tim Montgomery
Dennis Sheehan
Sue VandeWalle

Production
Nick Anderson, Carol Bowers, Mona Brown, Cheryl Cameron, Elaine Crabtree, Kimberly K. Hannel, Angela Judy, Jamie Milazzo, Shelly Palma, Ryan Rader, Marc Shecter, Tonya Simpson, Susan Springer

Indexer
Charlotte Clapp

Overview

Foreword xvii

Introduction xxi

PART I   Edutainment and the Basic PC   1

  1   What Is Edutainment? 3
  2   The Capabilities of the Basic PC 15

PART II   About Edutainment Products   29

  3   Drill-and-Practice Products 37
  4   Multimedia Reference Materials 49
  5   Simulation Programs 73
  6   CD-ROM Storybooks 91
  7   Preschool Products 105
  8   Creativity Tools 121
  9   General Edutainment Products 133

PART III   Upgrading Your System for Edutainment   157

  10   Sight and Sound 161
  11   CD-ROM Drives 177
  12   Edutainment and Windows 189
  13   Upgrades for Users with Special Needs 205
  14   Troubleshooting DOS and Windows 213
  15   Troubleshooting CD-ROM Drives and Sound Cards 231

PART IV Edutainment in the Future 243

16　Trends 245

17　Interviews 255

APPENDIXES

A　The Companion CD-ROM 267

B　The Basics of Telecommunication 285

C　The MPC Specifications 305

D　Resources 311

　　Glossary 319

　　Index 327

Cont

Contents

Foreword xvii

Introduction xxi

PART I Edutainment and the Basic PC 1

1 What Is Edutainment? 3
A Working Definition 4
Why Is Edutainment Important? 5
    Low Test Scores of U.S. Students 5
    Lectures Don't Work for Everyone 5
    Interactivity and Empowerment 6
    Kids Love Edutainment Software 6
Does It Work? 6
    Similar Activities in Other Settings 6
Types of Edutainment Products 7
    Drill-and-Practice Products 7
    Multimedia Reference Materials 8
    Simulation Programs 9
    CD-ROM Storybooks 10
    Preschool Products 11
    Creativity Tools 12
    General Edutainment Products 12
Summary 14

2 The Capabilities of the Basic PC 15
The Operating System 16
How to Determine Which Version of DOS You Have 18
The Microprocessor 18
    The 8088 Microprocessor 18
    The 80286 Microprocessor 18
    The 80386 Microprocessor 18
    The 80486 Microprocessor 19
    The Pentium Microprocessor 19
How to Determine the Type of Processor in Your Machine 19
Memory 20

Read-Only Memory (ROM) 20
Random-Access Memory (RAM) 20
How to Determine the Quantity
and Type of RAM in Your System 22
Video 22
    The Monochrome Display Adapter 23
    The Color/Graphics Adapter 23
    The Hercules Graphics Card 23
    The Enhanced Graphics Adapter 23
    The Video Graphics Array 24
How to Determine What Type of Video System You Have 25
Audio 25
Mass Storage 26
How to Determine the Size of Your Hard Drive 27
Summary 28

PART II   About Edutainment Products   29

3   Drill-and-Practice Products 37
Common Features 38
Unique Features 38
Using a Drill-and-Practice Product—
Math Blaster: In Search of Spot 39
What's Available? 40
    Math Programs 41
    Other Subjects 45
Summary 47

4   Multimedia Reference Materials 49
Common Features 50
Unique Features 51
Using a Multimedia Encyclopedia: Encarta 52
What's Available? 53
    Multimedia Encyclopedias 53
    Other "Traditional" Reference Works 57
    Health and the Human Body 60
    Space 64
    Prehistoric Life 67
    Art and Music 69
Summary 72

5	**Simulation Programs**	73
	Common Features	74
	Interesting Variations	75
	Using a Simulation Program: The Oregon Trail	76
	What's Available?	78
	Traditional Simulations	79
	Other Types of Simulation Products	84
	Summary	89
6	**CD-ROM Storybooks**	91
	Common Features	92
	Variations on a Theme	93
	Using a CD-ROM Storybook: Arthur's Teacher Trouble	95
	What's Available?	96
	CD-ROM Storybooks for Young Children	97
	CD-ROM Storybooks for Older Readers	99
	Summary	103
7	**Preschool Products**	105
	Common Features	106
	Unique Features	107
	Using a Preschool Product: Sierra On-Line's Early Math	107
	What's Available?	110
	Number and Math Skills	110
	Letter and Reading Skills	112
	Other Products	114
	Summary	119
8	**Creativity Tools**	121
	Common Features	122
	Other Features	124
	Using a Creativity Tool: Print Shop Deluxe	125
	What's Available?	126
	Kid CAD	126
	Kid Works 2	127
	Creative Writer	128
	Storybook Weaver and My Own Stories	130

   Print Shop Deluxe CD Ensemble 131
    Announcements 2.0 for Windows 132
  Summary 132

9 **General Edutainment Products** **133**
  What's Available 134
   Social Studies 134
   Animals and Ecology 138
   Language and Music 144
   Brain Teasers 148
   Math 151
  Summary 155

PART III Upgrading Your System for Edutainment 157

10 **Sight and Sound** **161**
  Types of Video Cards 162
   Types of SVGA Cards 162
   Features to Look For 163
  Monitors 168
  Sound Cards 168
   Features of Sound Cards 168
  Speakers and Microphones 174
  Summary 174

11 **CD-ROM Drives** **177**
  Introduction to CD-ROM 178
  What Is a CD-ROM System? 181
   The Drive 181
   The Interface 182
   CD-ROM Device Driver 182
   Microsoft CD-ROM Extensions 182
  Types of CD-ROM Drives 183
   Features to Look For 183
  Summary 186

12 **Edutainment and Windows** **189**
  Why Windows? 190
   Ease of Use 190
   Device Independence 190
   Memory Management 190

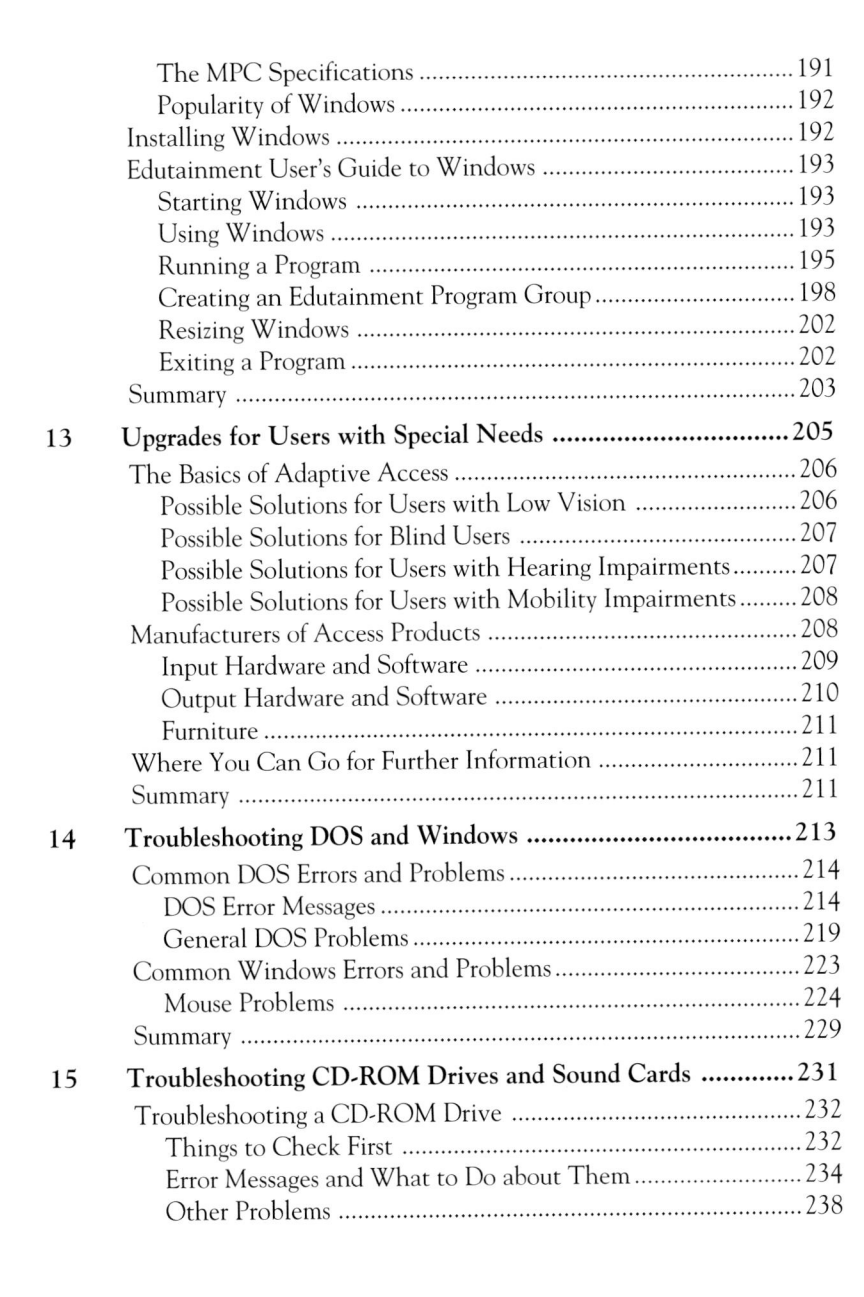

	The MPC Specifications	191
	Popularity of Windows	192
	Installing Windows	192
	Edutainment User's Guide to Windows	193
	Starting Windows	193
	Using Windows	193
	Running a Program	195
	Creating an Edutainment Program Group	198
	Resizing Windows	202
	Exiting a Program	202
	Summary	203
13	**Upgrades for Users with Special Needs**	**205**
	The Basics of Adaptive Access	206
	Possible Solutions for Users with Low Vision	206
	Possible Solutions for Blind Users	207
	Possible Solutions for Users with Hearing Impairments	207
	Possible Solutions for Users with Mobility Impairments	208
	Manufacturers of Access Products	208
	Input Hardware and Software	209
	Output Hardware and Software	210
	Furniture	211
	Where You Can Go for Further Information	211
	Summary	211
14	**Troubleshooting DOS and Windows**	**213**
	Common DOS Errors and Problems	214
	DOS Error Messages	214
	General DOS Problems	219
	Common Windows Errors and Problems	223
	Mouse Problems	224
	Summary	229
15	**Troubleshooting CD-ROM Drives and Sound Cards**	**231**
	Troubleshooting a CD-ROM Drive	232
	Things to Check First	232
	Error Messages and What to Do about Them	234
	Other Problems	238

Troubleshooting a Sound Card 239
　　Things to Check First 239
　　Other Problems 239
Summary 241

PART IV　Edutainment in the Future　243

16　Trends 245
Hardware 246
　　Processing Power 246
　　Memory 248
　　Hard Disk Drives 249
　　Video Cards 249
　　Sound Capabilities 250
　　CD-ROM 250
　　Edutainment-Ready Machines 250
Software 250
　　The Move to Windows 250
　　Larger, More Power-Hungry Products 250
　　Many Different Approaches 251
　　Lifelike Characters 251
　　Speech Recognition 251
Other Trends 252
　　Other Distribution Channels 252
　　On-Line Edutainment 253
Summary 254

17　Interviews 255
The Interviews 256
　　Greg Bestick, VP and General Manager Infotainment,
　　　Creativity, and EA*Kids Electronic Arts 256
　　Douglas M. Brannan Vice President of
　　　Sales Software Marketing Corporation 257
　　Jeff Braun, CEO Maxis 258
　　Karen Crowther President, Redwood
　　　Games Director, Alliance Interactive Software 259
　　Bill Dinsmore, President and CEO
　　　The Learning Company 260

Elon Gaspar Founder, Bright Star Technology, Inc.
VP of Research and Development Sierra On-Line. 260
Bill Gross, Chairman and Founder Knowledge
Adventure 262
Dale LaFrenz, President and CEO MECC 263
Scott Miller, President and
Founder Apogee Software, Ltd. 264
Ian R. Wade, Director of Marketing Waterford Institute 264
Summary 265

APPENDIXES

A The Companion CD-ROM 267

Overview of the CD-ROM 269
Installing and Running the DOS Software 269
    The Opening Page 269
    The Category Pages 270
Installing and Running the Windows Software 271
Company and Software Information for DOS Products 271
    Devasoft 271
    Electronic Arts 272
    GameTek 272
    Humongous Entertainment 272
    Impressions Software 273
    Interplay Productions 273
    MVP Software 274
    Paramount Interactive 274
    Epic Megagames 274
    First Magnitude 275
    ImagiSOFT, Inc. 276
    Software Creations 276
Company and Software Information for Windows 276
    7th Level 276
    Conexus 277
    Davidson & Associates 277
    Discovery Channel, The 277
    Dr. T's Music Software 278
    EBook, Inc. 279
    Morgan Interactive 281

	MVP Software	281
	Paramount Interactive	281
	Science for Kids, Inc.	282
	Waterford Institute	282
B	**The Basics of Telecommunication**	**285**
	Telecommunication and Edutainment	286
	Modems	287
	Types of Modems	287
	Modem Features	288
	Sending Information over Phone Lines	291
	Special Considerations	294
	Communication Software	294
	Types of Communication Programs	294
	Features of Communication Programs	294
	Dialing Directory	295
	Who Do You Talk To?	298
	Bulletin Board Systems	298
	Community Networks (Freenets)	298
	On-Line Information Services	298
	The Internet	299
	Downloading an Edutainment Product	300
	Setting Up Windows Terminal	300
	Calling and Logging On	302
	Searching for Files	303
	Downloading a File and Exiting the System	304
C	**The MPC Specifications**	**305**
	Multimedia PC Specification 1.0	306
	Hardware Specifications	306
	System Software	307
	Minimum Full-System Configuration	308
	Minimum Upgrade Kit Configuration	308
	Multimedia PC Specification 2.0	308
	Hardware Specifications	308
	System Software	310
	Minimum Full-System Configuration	310
	Minimum Upgrade Kit Configuration	310

D	**Resources**	311
	Books	312
	Magazines and Newsletters	312
	On-Line Services and BBSs	313
	Mail-Order Catalogs	313
	Edutainment Product Providers	314
	Glossary	319
	Index	327

Forex

Foreword

What is the most seductive entertainment medium today? Television. What is the most compelling productivity tool today? The personal computer. A class of computer software known as *edutainment* has facilitated the congruence of the PC and television. This congruence has led to the rapid embrace of the PC as a significant learning tool. *Edutainment Comes Alive!* is an in-depth analysis of this class of software. It helps establish edutainment software as the catalyst for a new paradigm in learning.

Edutainment software titles make the computer monitor look less like a data-entry screen and more like the engaging television screen we've all grown up with. The screen display of edutainment software is vibrant, colorful, and action-packed. The edutainment learning experience more closely resembles a video game than it resembles the obsolete drill-and-practice experience of educational software just a few short years ago. By integrating education and entertainment, edutainment titles make learning fun.

Two characteristics of edutainment titles render them potent in forming a new paradigm in learning. The first characteristic is the notion of interactivity. By allowing the user to determine the pace and the direction of the learning process, the student is central and in control. The student's actions determine the flow of the learning experience, which engages the student as an active participant—much as he or she is a participant when playing a video game. Lectures or passive TV instruction often fail to hold a student's attention. By empowering the student to be an active explorer, however, rather than a passive sponge for information, interactive edutainment titles guarantee a captive, involved audience.

The popularity of CD-ROM as a publishing medium is the second aspect of edutainment software that renders it potent as a teaching tool. The vast size of the CD-ROM disc (equivalent to more than 600 floppy disks of information) enables color pictures, animation, video footage, and stereo audio to enhance the richness of the software and bring it to the level of a satisfying multimedia experience. The multimedia and interactive characteristics of edutainment software engender a seductive learning environment. In this way, computer technology, television, and video games converge to create the new learning paradigm.

With edutainment titles, software engineers have created a Trojan horse that brings this new paradigm for learning into home, school, and business environments. By looking like TV and video games, edutainment titles prevail over the problem of the short attention span. The encyclopedia becomes a friendly, fun tool. Your research on bears lets you read about bears, see a color picture of a bear, view a video of a bear running, and hear the sound of a bear growling. Titles such as *WHERE IN THE USA IS CARMEN SANDIEGO? Deluxe Version* lift geography—a sedating subject matter for many students—to a captivating learning experience. Disguised as a game, it teaches US geography, history, and culture.

Simulation programs are a perfect application of edutainment's nature as interactive multimedia. Presenting the student with believable worlds that have their own sets of rules can make it easy to teach difficult social, cultural, and managerial concepts. By creating the illusion of real interaction with equipment and actors, simulations can train airplane pilots, lead nuclear reactor personnel to anticipate emergencies, and teach managers supervisory skills.

In the traditional lecture-and-read learning environments, the student's attention is often distracted by daydreams, secondary activities, or just plain boredom. When you observe a student using a compelling edutainment title, you can see the same intensity of concentration as when that student is playing a video game. A dialogue is taking place between the software and the user. It is this interactive engagement that makes edutainment software powerful as a learning tool. Edutainment is the educational paradigm of tomorrow.

Vahé Guzelimian
President
EDUCORP Multimedia

Acknowledgments

I would like to thank everyone who contributed to this book. The following people in particular deserve mention: Grace, Jodi, Keith, Marlaina, Patti, and Tom. Each of you added something special to the project.

About the Author

William P. Mann is the chief (and only) programmer at his company, Desert Frog Software. Bill is the developer of a number of shareware and retail software products, including two that would now be considered edutainment. This is his second book for Sams Publishing.

A graduate of the University of Rochester, Bill spent more than 10 years working on military and commercial flight simulators. Now a full-time writer and software developer, he lives in Arizona with his wonderful wife Patti, and his daughter Jennifer, who just loves her edutainment programs.

Introduction

Edutainment is a popular buzzword these days. As often happens with terms coined to describe new situations or new technology, the term *edutainment* means different things to different people. The word seems to be used wherever it sounds good and is applied to all sorts of products. There is no "official" definition of the term, so this book uses my definition:

> **Edutainment**—*Software that integrates education and entertainment elements, with each element playing a significant role.*

Defined this way, the term edutainment can apply to almost any good educational product. In this book, the focus is, of course, on edutainment products for IBM PCs and compatibles. The convergence of a number of factors makes this the start of a new era in PC edutainment products.

The primary driver for this new era is hardware, and the home computer is undergoing a massive hardware transformation. Unbelievably powerful processors are controlling high-quality video and audio systems that draw massive amounts of sound and numerous images from CD-ROMs with immense storage capacities. Where once you had to settle for low-resolution, static images accompanied by beeps and clicks, you now can have full-color, full-motion, cinematic displays accompanied by near-CD-quality stereo sound! The personal computer is changing from a number-cruncher to a mind amplifier.

Unfortunately, very few PCs contain all the hardware and software you need to take advantage of the wealth of edutainment products. One of the primary goals of this book is to help you convert your present PC into a powerful edutainment system.

The other goal of this book is to teach you something about the kinds of edutainment products available. I have defined seven broad categories of edutainment: drill-and-practice products, multimedia reference materials, simulation programs, CD-ROM storybooks, preschool products, creativity tools, and general edutainment products. Each category has its own chapter in Part II. Grouping the products this way lets you explore the common elements of each category and makes it easier for you to decide which types of edutainment products you are interested in.

Who Should Read This Book?

This book is for anyone who wants to take advantage of modern PC edutainment products. If you are worried about the quality of your children's education, or if you want to help them explore a favorite subject in more depth, PC edutainment programs can help. If you want to let them use the computer, but you don't want them playing violent games all the time, edutainment products offer an alternative. And if you just want to give your child a head start on a lifetime of learning, edutainment products offer an educational experience that is fun and under your child's control.

If you wrote off educational computer programs in the past, you really might want to take another look. The newer programs are incredible, with capabilities that were unavailable just a couple of years ago. These products have moved beyond simplistic imitations of workbooks and flash cards, and can help your child learn new things, instead of simply practicing what she already knows. Today's programs are also much more engaging, thanks to the high-quality audio and video now possible.

What This Book Covers

This book is designed to teach you about edutainment software and the equipment you need to use it. It is divided into four parts: "Edutainment and the Basic PC," "About Edutainment Products," "Upgrading Your System for Edutainment," and "Edutainment in the Future." A description of each of these four parts follows.

Part I, "Edutainment and the Basic PC"

Part I introduces you to some things you need to understand before you read the rest of the book. First, Part I provides some background information on the concept of edutainment itself. Chapter 1 answers the question "What is edutainment and why should I care about it?" and also introduces the seven categories of edutainment products.

Chapter 2 takes a look at the capabilities of the basic PC. Edutainment products demand a great deal from a PC, so knowing the capabilities of a basic machine helps you to understand what upgrades are required to make your basic machine into an edutainment system.

Part II, "About Edutainment Products"

Part II is the heart of *Edutainment Comes Alive!* Here you explore each of the seven categories of edutainment products and (hopefully) increase your understanding so that you can decide which products are right for you and your family.

Part II includes Chapters 3 through 9, with one chapter devoted to each product category. Each chapter examines both the common and the unique features of the products from that particular category. In most chapters, a short walk-through of a representative product from the category gives you an idea of what it's like to actually use that kind of program. The remainder of each chapter is devoted to specific products within the category. I make no attempt to rate these products, but I was able to install and run every one of them.

The opening pages for Part II contain useful information that didn't quite fit anywhere else in the book. These pages contain a section on alternative sources for edutainment products. Far more edutainment products are available than can fit on the limited shelf space in a typical computer store, so finding the program that you want may take a little digging. A short section is also included that discusses the few edutainment products that make explicit accommodations for users with special needs.

Part III, "Upgrading Your System for Edutainment"

Part III pulls you back into the real world after exploring all that great edutainment software. The chapters in Part III get serious about upgrading your machine so that you can run the products you want to run.

The coverage of upgrades begins with hardware in Chapters 10 and 11. A CD-ROM drive, SVGA video, and a sound card are all virtual necessities for an edutainment system. This part of the book tells you what capabilities to look for and teaches you enough about these devices to enable you to shop intelligently.

Although DOS programs will still be developed for a few more years, Windows is the future of edutainment. If you bought your PC in the last year or so, you probably already own a copy of Windows—even if you haven't ever run it. Chapter 12 can help you get started with Windows and even walks you through installing and running a Windows edutainment product.

Chapter 13 is dedicated to users with special computing needs. It examines hardware and software that can make edutainment titles more accessible to these users.

And finally, Chapters 14 and 15 give you advice on what to do when things go wrong. You learn basic troubleshooting techniques that could save you a costly service call.

Part IV, "Edutainment in the Future"

Part IV looks to the future. The computer industry as a whole is marked by rapid, often chaotic change and growth. The edutainment portion of the industry is not much different. Rapid change is certain, driven mainly by the development and adoption of new technology.

Part IV is designed to give you an idea of where things are headed in edutainment. It is divided into two chapters: Chapter 16 describes the current trends in edutainment and where they are taking us; Chapter 17 lets the people who create, publish, and distribute edutainment products tell us where they think things are headed and how their companies fit into the big picture.

Appendixes

This book includes four appendixes that provide additional information. Appendix A examines the CD-ROM that is attached to the inside back cover of this book. This appendix describes the interactive demos, shareware, and retail products included on the CD-ROM. We have made every attempt to find interactive demos—so that you can play with and experience the products—

rather than ones that simply show you a canned demonstration. I think you will find that the software on the CD-ROM alone is worth the price of the book.

Appendix B provides information on telecommunications. Telecommunications will become increasingly important to edutainment users as the information superhighway becomes a reality. Telecommunications is already important to shareware users, who find that the newest versions of the best products are normally available on-line weeks, or even months, before they show up in other locations.

Appendix C contains the Multimedia Personal Computer (MPC) specifications. These specifications define the equipment your PC needs to qualify as a multimedia PC. In most cases, you only have to look for the MPC logo to know that the equipment is appropriate for edutainment use, but this appendix provides the complete specifications in case you want to review them.

Appendix D offers a resource guide. Here you can find the names, addresses, and telephone numbers of companies that produce edutainment products. This appendix also lists other sources of information on edutainment and on upgrading your PC, including books, magazines, on-line services, and alternative sources for hard-to-find products.

Summing Up

To help you get the most out of *Edutainment Comes Alive!*, you'll find this icon scattered throughout the book. This symbol signifies that a demo version of the product being discussed appears on the *Edutainment Comes Alive!* CD-ROM accompanying this book. As an additional marker, a smaller version of this same icon appears under figures that show products featured on the CD-ROM. Be sure to load the CD-ROM and try out these demos!

I hope you enjoy reading *Edutainment Comes Alive!* The field of PC education is undergoing massive change, and edutainment products are at the heart of that change. I honestly believe that these products, and the ones that follow them, can revolutionize the way our children learn. Read on and see if you agree.

EDUTAINMENT & the Basic PC

Part I

Welcome to Part I of *Edutainment Comes Alive!* In this first section, you are introduced to some of the fundamentals you will want to understand before you read on.

The first concept you need to grasp is the definition of *edutainment*. What is it? Why is everyone talking about it? What can it do for you and your family?

Second, you must have a good understanding of your PC's capabilities so that you can effectively use edutainment software. Many edutainment products push PCs to their limits, and they often require specialized hardware to work correctly.

These two topics are covered in detail in Part I of the book, which consists of two chapters. Chapter 1 deals with the concept of edutainment, and Chapter 2 discusses the capabilities of the basic PC.

Chapter 1, "What Is Edutainment?"

Chapter 1 provides an introduction to the world of PC edutainment software. It begins with a definition of edutainment as it applies to personal computers. Much hype surrounds the subject of edutainment, and depending on who you talk to, the term *edutainment* may be applied to various products. I present my definition of edutainment, which determines the types of products discussed in this book.

The remainder of Chapter 1 explains why I think you should be interested in edutainment software. It shows why the concept is important and provides evidence that edutainment works. It also divides the universe of edutainment products into seven categories, each with unique characteristics. Each category is presented in its own chapter in Part II.

Chapter 2, "The Capabilities of the Basic PC"

The best edutainment products demand more from a PC than is demanded by either a word processor or a spreadsheet. With digitized speech and music, as well as colorful animation or video clips, edutainment products push every part of your system to the limit. Many products require additional equipment you might not even have, such as a sound card and a CD-ROM drive. To get as much punch as possible out of your edutainment software, you may have to upgrade your system.

Before you can upgrade your system, however, you have to know what capabilities it already possesses. This chapter takes a look at the elements contained in basic PCs and then examines the way these elements work together to give your PC its processing power.

Besides looking at a PC's general capabilities, Chapter 2 also contains several tricks to help you determine the capabilities and characteristics of your machine. Armed with this information, you can decide what upgrades make sense for your system.

Chapter 1

What Is Edutainment?

Edutainment—it's one of the hot new computer buzzwords of the '90s. The word generates strong emotions for many people. Some love it, and some hate it. Some folks feel it will be the salvation of American society. Others fear it will trivialize education and de-emphasize reading and writing skills. Some people feel that edutainment is just another passing fad; others believe it will profoundly transform the way people learn. Edutainment is hot, and it is also controversial.

Marketeers and publishers see edutainment as a hot growth market. Over 700 edutainment products are on the market today, with hundreds more being added every year. Indeed, most of the available home education software falls into the edutainment category. According to the Software Publisher's Association, sales of educational programs grew nearly 50 percent in 1992 and 66 percent in 1993. The growth shows no signs of slowing, either. Fourth-quarter 1993 sales were up 73 percent over the same period in 1992! These figures make educational products the fastest-growing software category today.

Many professional educators are worried about all the hype surrounding edutainment software. They fear edutainment will lead to another attempt to integrate computers into the school curriculum. Previous attempts to computerize classrooms have generally failed, leaving our schools filled with underpowered and underutilized equipment.

Even when quality equipment is available, teachers and staff often lack the skills or interest to use the equipment effectively. I know of schools in which the students are only allowed to use the machines to type their assignments before submitting them. Using a $2000 multimedia PC as a glorified typewriter is a horrible waste.

Some teachers fear the results if edutainment software *does* become part of the curriculum. These folks feel that the act of making education more game-like may trivialize it. They also worry about the impact of visually oriented, computerized education on traditional reading and writing skills. If edutainment becomes an important part of education, it will transform the profession; teachers will have to learn new skills and new ways to relate to students.

Many people, particularly technologically literate baby boomers, see edutainment as a way to make up for perceived shortcomings in their children's educations. With one or more PCs already in the home, and with the obvious attraction children have for television and video games, the advantages of fun, educational software seem obvious. After the boomers see how well children take to the new crop of multimedia edutainment programs, it is quite possible that they will begin demanding major reform of our educational system.

It's obvious that I approve of the concept of edutainment—that's why I'm writing this book. Because you are reading it, you probably at least have an open mind about the subject. The rest of this chapter introduces you to the concept of edutainment and gives you background information to help you understand why so many people are so worked up about it.

The following topics are discussed in this chapter:

- A working definition of edutainment
- Why the concept of edutainment is important
- Evidence that edutainment works
- The seven types of edutainment products

I hope that this introduction to edutainment can convince you that edutainment software can play an important role in your child's (or your own) education. The remainder of the book gives you the information you need to turn your PC into a powerful edutainment system, and it also provides a survey of the edutainment products currently available. The edutainment software industry has something for everyone. This book can help you take advantage of what's available.

A Working Definition

It makes sense to start learning about edutainment by looking up the definition of the word. Let's pull out that trusty dictionary. Now, take a look after the word *education* and, hmmm, it's not there. Well, how about that big, unabridged dictionary in the library? Nope, not there either. This is part of the reason the term *edutainment* is so controversial.

Edutainment is a hybrid word, created by combining the words *education* and *entertainment*, and you can combine education and entertainment in several ways. The way in which the two are combined in particular products is a large part of what excites the edutainment enthusiasts and upsets the critics.

Education with a little entertainment thrown in defines one end of the spectrum. Entertainment that educates defines the other. Any conceivable blending of education and entertainment lies somewhere in between. In the broadest sense, this entire spectrum is edutainment. Is it any wonder that people look at edutainment in so many different ways?

Defining edutainment so broadly does no one any good. A more exact definition makes the subject easier to grasp. Because this is a personal computer book, I define edutainment in terms of personal computer software:

> **Edutainment:** *Software that integrates education and entertainment elements, with each element playing a significant role.*

Let's look at this definition piece by piece. The first half of the definition is "software that integrates education and entertainment elements." The key to this phrase is the word *integrates*, which necessitates education and entertainment working together reasonably well. This interpretation rules out drill-and-reward programs in which the entertainment aspect is simply tacked on to the end of a lesson. This type of program just doesn't capture the spirit of edutainment. Neither does an arcade game that adds a math problem at the end of each level.

The second part of the definition is equally important. The phrase "with each element playing a significant role" is meant to rule out those programs with marginal educational or entertainment value. Any reasonably complex game can teach you something, and some people enjoy browsing through reference works, but by my definition, neither activity can be considered edutainment.

This definition of edutainment is broad enough to cover most of the software people think of when they use the term, yet not so broad as to be useless.

Why Is Edutainment Important?

Now that you know what edutainment is, you may be wondering what all the fuss is about. Why is edutainment suddenly so hot? Does learning really need to be more like play? Will these products really help children learn better and faster?

I think edutainment is important and necessary. Judging by the booming sales figures for edutainment products, many people agree with me. People are embracing the concept of edutainment for many reasons, including the following:

- Concern about low achievement test scores in the U.S.
- The belief that current teaching methods are not right for everyone and are out of sync with much of the rest of the world
- A desire to empower students
- Kids love this stuff

The next several sections take a look at these reasons in more detail.

Low Test Scores of U.S. Students

If you read the papers or watch the news, you have certainly heard about the poor performance of U.S. students on standardized tests. SAT scores are down. Functional illiteracy is up. American students score near the bottom when compared to students in other countries. Businesses spend huge sums training employees in basic skills. The list of woes goes on and on.

Although the root causes of the problem are open to debate, it is abundantly clear that American children are not learning the skills they must have to become productive citizens. Society is responding to the problem in many different ways. Education reform bills are under consideration in state legislatures across the country. Parents are demanding school choice—the right to choose which schools their children attend. Some are even opting out of the public school system altogether, scraping up the money to put their kids in private schools or even teaching them at home. And computer-literate parents are looking to edutainment software to give their kids a leg up.

Lectures Don't Work for Everyone

Not all children (or adults) are suited to the teaching methods used in most schools. Some people are verbally oriented and respond well to classroom lectures. Others are more attuned to visual information and can learn better from images and graphics. Still others seem to need the stimulation of a multimedia presentation to sustain their interest.

From their earliest days, children are exposed to television. The TV has a powerful attraction for both children and adults, and many spend a significant part of each day watching it. They learn that information comes in the form of interesting or entertaining images on a screen, with accompanying sound and special effects.

Most of modern society is visually oriented, as is television. It seems likely that the lecture-based education system found in today's schools will become relevant to fewer and fewer students as time goes on.

Interactivity and Empowerment

Unlike television, edutainment software is interactive. The user can, and must, actively participate in what is happening. Even the traditional classroom, in which an instructor is present to answer questions, is much less interactive than an edutainment product.

The interactivity of edutainment products is a large part of their appeal. As in a video game, a good edutainment product puts the user in control. This control, coupled with the computer's infinite patience, enables a user to learn at his or her own pace, explore what he or she wants to explore, and generally take charge of the learning experience.

Giving a student control of, and responsibility for, the learning experience empowers the student. As U.S. businesses have learned, empowering employees makes them happier and more productive workers. Empowering students can have the same results.

Kids Love Edutainment Software

Kids (and many adults) love this stuff. Just about anyone involved with edutainment has stories about its appeal to the user. My daughter, Jennifer, who is only three, spends some time playing with edutainment software every day. We don't force her to play with it or even suggest that she do so. Every morning, after the usual hugs and kisses, she asks for one of her edutainment programs. They are a normal part of her life, just like her toys, games, and puzzles. The only problem is, I usually have to chase her off the machine. Left to her own devices, she would spend hours playing with this software!

Does It Work?

The reasons people like edutainment seem reasonable. But does the concept actually work? Do people learn better with edutainment software than by traditional methods? Will you just be throwing your money away on this stuff? Although I would like to be able to cite a slew of reports showing huge improvements in skills and knowledge, I can't. Very little concrete evidence is available that shows that edutainment products

work. I know of only one study, commissioned by the Software Publishers Association, which did indeed show that edutainment products significantly increased the speed at which users learned.

Even without scientific proof, many people are convinced that combining education and fun is a more effective way to teach. Think back to the filmstrips and slide shows of your school days. Professional educators know that adding pictures and sound to their lectures keeps the student's interest high. Edutainment software can replace these audiovisual aids and add interactivity at the same time. Rewarding good performance with a game or other fun activity is another tried-and-true teaching method.

Games and stories can teach, often without the players or audience even realizing it. Since language was first developed, mankind has used fables and parables to teach the young. Epic poems and bard's tales were once the primary repository of western history, and the Chinese still use shadow puppets to pass along their culture and myths. Although sometimes frowned upon by today's teachers, entertainment has always been a large part of education.

Similar Activities in Other Settings

When you move beyond its use at home and in school, you can find further evidence that edutainment can be effective. Businesses and the armed services spend large amounts of money on training. Each year, more of their training budgets are going to computerized training systems that have features in common with edutainment products. Especially with businesses, increased spending is a good indication that these systems work. Driven by the changing business climate, companies are desperately trying to do more with less. Only those things that improve the productivity and skills of workers are funded.

The following sections illustrate a couple of areas in which edutainment-like training systems are proving their worth outside homes and classrooms.

Simulation Equipment

Every year, governments and industry spend hundreds of millions of dollars on simulation equipment. Flight simulators are the most widely known type, but everything from nuclear power plants to the phone system has been simulated. In each case, the money is spent because the simulations provide a faster, more efficient, and more cost-effective way to teach people what they need to know.

Although these systems lack the game elements of many edutainment products, they resemble edutainment programs in their multimedia approach to teaching.

Interactive Training in Business

Businesses are finding that interactive training systems are the best way to train employees. Surveys by the Institute for Defense Analysis indicate that students finish interactive training courses 31 percent faster than traditional courses. Many companies find that the multimedia aspects of the training appear to make a stronger impression on the students, increasing their retention of the material. If nothing else, students seem to enjoy interactive training more than traditional lectures, so they pay closer attention.

Interactive training systems have some of the same features as the edutainment products in which you are interested. They combine sight and sound with user interaction to engage the student's attention. Some systems make the process more like a game, with students able to post their high scores on the system for all to see.

Types of Edutainment Products

You can divide the spectrum of edutainment products into several different categories. From my perspective, six primary categories stand out from the general mass of edutainment products. These categories are as follows:

- Drill-and-practice products
- Multimedia reference materials
- Simulation programs
- CD-ROM storybooks
- Preschool products
- Creativity tools

If you include the remaining products on the market in a general category, you have a total of seven categories of edutainment products.

Dividing the products into categories simplifies our discussion of them. Products in the specific categories all share certain features, whereas those products in the general edutainment category differ in some significant way from those in the specific categories. The following sections describe each of the categories in more detail and point out the features that make them distinct.

Drill-and-Practice Products

Most early edutainment software was drill and practice. These programs typically require the user to solve a set of equations or answer a series of questions. After the user has successfully completed that task, he or she gets to play some kind of game or receives some other sort of reward. The reward at the end motivates the user to complete the drills.

The world's best-selling math program is Math Blaster, a drill-and-practice program from Davidson & Associates. Combining colorful graphics, sound effects, and music—all with an adventure theme—the Math Blaster series keeps children interested enough to work through large numbers of math problems. The following figure shows a drill scene from Math Blaster: In Search of Spot, the latest in the Math Blaster series.

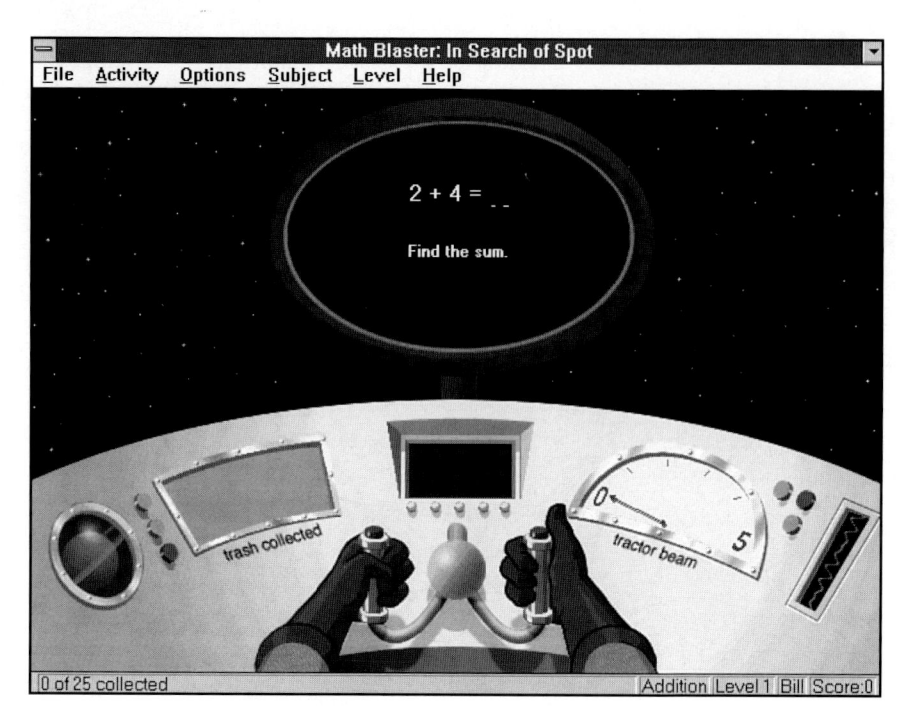

▲ *Math Blaster: In Search of Spot.*

Two features distinguish a drill-and-practice program from other edutainment products. The first distinguishing feature is its obvious educational orientation. The primary focus is the educational aspect of the program. Anyone using a drill-and-practice program can plainly see that the program is trying to teach some specific skills.

The second distinguishing feature of a drill-and-practice program is the distinction it makes between the drill-and-practice portion and the entertainment portion of the program. This distinction is both a strength and a weakness.

The strength in this approach is the fact that it is clear to everyone involved that this program is a learning tool and that the games are a reward for completing the work. This technique is analogous to the real world, where normally you must do the work before you can reap the rewards.

The weakness in this approach is really the same as the strength. It is clear to users of a drill-and-practice product that they are doing work. It may be a lot more fun than completing a workbook, and the game at the end may be better than a gold star, but it is still work.

Multimedia Reference Materials

Although an encyclopedia isn't the first thing you might think of when someone says the word *fun*, the new multimedia reference materials really can be fun to use. Taking advantage of the huge storage capacity of CD-ROMs, the best of these products rise far above a printed document.

Surely you have used an encyclopedia before. Suppose that you are researching space flight. You pull down the *S* volume and find the reference to space flight. There is all sorts of useful stuff here—perhaps even a picture of a space craft. From this point on, you chase references, pulling the appropriate volumes and copying down the information you need. "What was that little speech Neil Armstrong gave on the moon?" you wonder. Perhaps it is in there somewhere. I'm sure you remember the routine now.

Moving the contents of an encyclopedia to CD-ROM certainly simplifies things. Pull the encyclopedia off the shelf and insert it into your CD-ROM drive. Yes, the entire encyclopedia is on one tiny plastic disc. The space savings alone make this an exciting product. Start the program, and tell it you want to search for the phrase *space flight* (the exact details of how you initiate the search differ from program to program, so I'll keep it general). What's this? The program generates a list of every reference to space flight in the entire encyclopedia. The following figure shows the results when this search is performed using the New Grolier Multimedia Encyclopedia. To find related topics, you simply browse through the list (this certainly can speed things up). To refer to one of the listed topics, simply select it. Within seconds, the appropriate reference is on the screen. All this is a giant step forward, but it hardly qualifies as *fun*.

The fun of multimedia reference works comes from additional features that no paper encyclopedia can match. Still curious about Neil Armstrong's speech? A multimedia encyclopedia probably contains the speech. Not a transcription of the speech, but a recording of the actual speech! It may even contain a video clip of his first step on the moon, complete with voice! This is where multimedia reference works blow away their printed predecessors. Multimedia means pictures, sound, and video clips. Even after it stores the entire text of an encyclopedia, a CD-ROM has plenty of room for all these added features. Research becomes fun when the text is accompanied by sights, sound, and motion.

Besides encyclopedias, a wide variety of multimedia reference works is available. A partial list includes atlases, medical references, literary guides, history books, guides to plants and animals—the list goes on and on. It's likely that, before long, most reference works will be available on CD-ROM.

The key feature that sets multimedia encyclopedias and the rest apart from other edutainment products is that they are, first and foremost, reference materials. They may take advantage of the possibilities offered by multimedia and CD-ROM storage, and they may be fun to use, but at the heart of it, they are intended to be used for reference.

Simulation Programs

Simulations are an exciting type of edutainment product. A simulation is an imitation, or model, of something. The thing being simulated may be a system—such as an aircraft, a city, or the weather—or an event—such as the Battle of the Bulge or a moon landing. A simulation imitates certain aspects of the system or event. As a simulation becomes larger and more powerful, it can model more aspects with increased accuracy.

Some simulations—for example, weather models—enable the user to predict real-world events based on the simulation. Others, such as flight simulators, teach the user to understand the responses of the simulated system or event.

Simulations used for PC edutainment model both systems and events. The goal of an edutainment simulation is to help the user understand the simulated system or event. To do this, a potentially dry model is turned into a game.

The classic edutainment simulation is SimCity, by Maxis. This product simulates a city, and the player assumes the role of mayor of the city. As mayor, the player must allocate resources to create

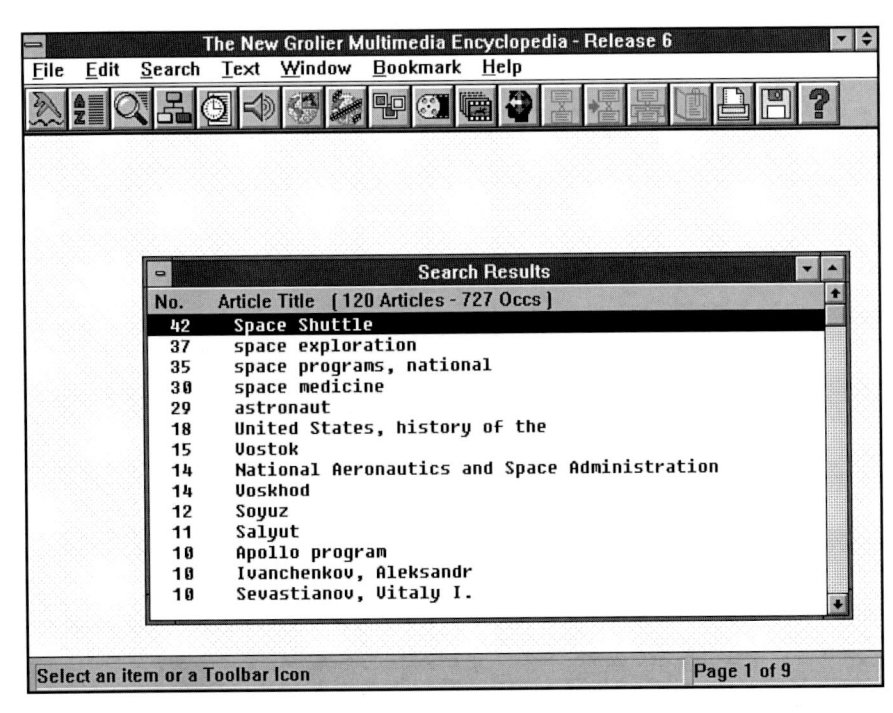

▲ *A search using the New Grolier Multimedia Encyclopedia.*

and maintain the city. In each turn, the player is presented with the kind of problems a real mayor might face: Do I build a new police station to reduce crime or develop more land to increase my tax base? Should I build a subway or an airport? Should I fund a new sports stadium or a fire station?

While facing these decisions gives the user a better understanding of modern urban planning, it also sounds a lot like work (and could be kind of dull). The simulations that work well as edutainment, however, turn work into play simply by the way they are presented. Again, SimCity is a perfect example. Whatever the player builds actually appears on the screen. Little dots (representing vehicles) move from place to place within the developing city. Houses go up and roads develop traffic jams. Jets fly overhead and ships sail the rivers. Fires appear and consume buildings. Floods and tornadoes occur, wreaking havoc on the city. Through the use of sound and graphics, a living, breathing world takes shape, drawing the player into the experience.

As you can see, modern simulation programs can contain an incredible amount of detail. What you can't see, and what you won't really understand until you spend some time playing with simulation programs, is the depth and realism they contain. A good simulation product lets you understand the situation and feel a part of it. These programs can be truly addictive.

Simulations stand apart from the other types of edutainment products because they convert a model of a complex, real-world system into a fun, stimulating game.

CD-ROM Storybooks

At first blush, a computerized storybook seems like a horrible idea. Sitting upright in front of a monitor, with a cooling fan humming in the background, just isn't the same as curling up with your child and her favorite book for a bedtime story. Even so, CD-ROM storybooks have some advantages and capabilities that no printed book can match.

CD-ROM storybooks use the power of modern multimedia PCs and the storage capacity of CD-ROMs to enhance the original story. Most offer a human narrator to read the story—complete with appropriate background music. The figures on the screen might act out the scene as the narrator reads it. Click the mouse on a toy car in one of the illustrations, and it may drive right out of the picture! These products have incredible power to draw a child into the story.

Often, CD-ROM storybooks include features that are more specifically educational in nature. The highlighting of words or phrases as they are pronounced can help the child associate words and their sounds. On-line dictionaries and glossaries

▲ *A scene from SimCity 2000. (Courtesy of Maxis)*

help with unfamiliar terms used in the story. Some CD-ROMs provide complete text and narration in foreign languages.

Arthur's Teacher Trouble, by Broderbund, is a good example of this genre. The CD-ROM takes the original printed story and enhances it with sound and animation. Notice the "thought bubble" on the upper-right side in the following figure. This image appears in response to something one of the characters says. Accompanied by spooky music, the appearance of this image makes abundantly clear what is going through Arthur's mind.

Touches like these abound in CD-ROM storybooks and can make them captivating for children.

Although CD-ROM storybooks will never replace printed books, they add a new dimension to the stories these books contain.

Preschool Products

Preschool products, sometimes called *totware*, are edutainment programs aimed specifically at the needs and abilities of children as young as two. They use interactivity, bright colors, music, and sound effects to keep little children interested while they introduce them to basic concepts. These programs usually contain friendly animated characters that youngsters can relate to.

The products in this category address a wide range of skills and concepts. Some products stress letter and word recognition, while others help with counting and problem-solving skills. Still other products explore shapes, colors, or the animal kingdom. And all of these products aim to make the child more familiar and more comfortable with the computer itself.

Although this class of products as a whole covers a wide range of skills and concepts, individual programs are sharply focused on specific ages or skill levels. The goal is to provide appropriate content for the user: not so easy as to be boring, and not so difficult as to be frustrating. In most cases, there are no wrong answers. Every action by the child results in some positive outcome.

Most of these programs take full advantage of the high-quality sound and video found on newer PCs. Many of the product lines have consistent cartoon characters that inhabit the programs. This provides a way for children to relate to the program and makes other programs in the line instantly familiar. Some products, such as those from Disney Software, feature famous characters like Mickey Mouse.

Although preschool products cover a range of subjects, they share a focus on exposing young children to basic concepts in a fun and non-threatening way.

▲ *Arthur's Teacher Trouble.*

▲ *A scene from Mickey's 123's.*

Creativity Tools

Creativity tools are a relatively new category of edutainment product. These products use the power of the computer to help the user explore a creative medium. Children love to make things, and creativity tools help them do it. The programs in this category have no right or wrong answers, so there is nothing to prevent users from experimenting to their heart's content.

The dominant creativity tool is Print Shop, by Broderbund. Print Shop, and its descendant, Print Shop Deluxe, are simple publishing programs. They enable the user to create signs, cards, and banners, complete with a variety of fonts and images. The incredible popularity of the Print Shop series is a testament to the potential of creativity tools.

A wide variety of new creativity tools has appeared in the last year or two. Besides other publishing programs, the genre has expanded into new areas. Painting and story-creation products are now available, such as Broderbund's KidPix and Davidson's Kid Works. These products allow the user to create pictures and then build stories around them. The newest version of Kid Works, Kid Works 2, adds speech to the mix, enabling the computer to read aloud the stories created by the child.

For older kids, there are products that come closer to the tools that adults use, but which still encourage creativity and exploration. The new crop of creativity tools even includes word processing and computer-aided design programs.

These new tools are stripped down to the basics and then enhanced with interfaces and features suitable for the target audience. The result is a functional product that is fun to use.

Creativity tools stand out from other edutainment products in the way that they encourage the user to explore a creative medium.

General Edutainment Products

The general edutainment category is a catch-all for products that don't fit into one of the other six categories. A wide variety of products can be included in this category, and they cover the spectrum from primarily educational products with some entertainment value, to primarily entertainment products with some educational value. General edutainment products cover a full range of subjects from archaeology to zoology, and everything in between. The following paragraphs describe a few of the products in this category.

General edutainment includes such products as Broderbund's Carmen Sandiego series. These

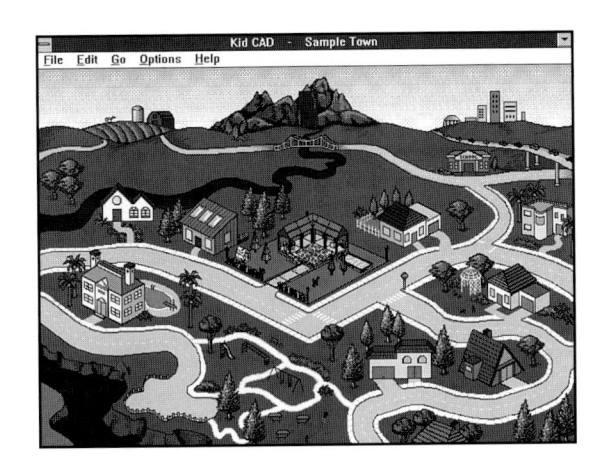

What Is Edutainment?

▲ *A scene from Davidson's Kid CAD.*

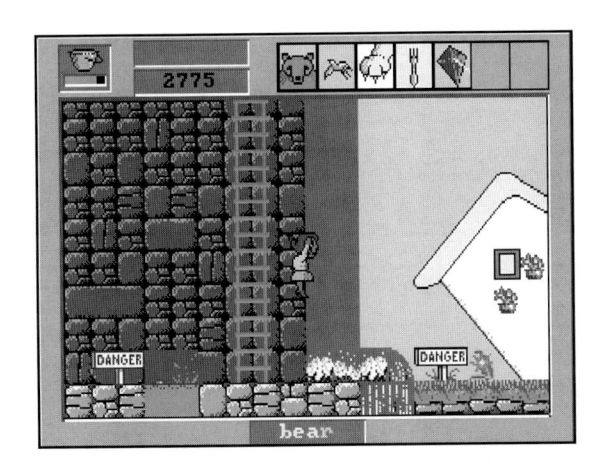

▲ *A typical screen from Broderbund's WHERE IN THE USA IS CARMEN SANDIEGO?*

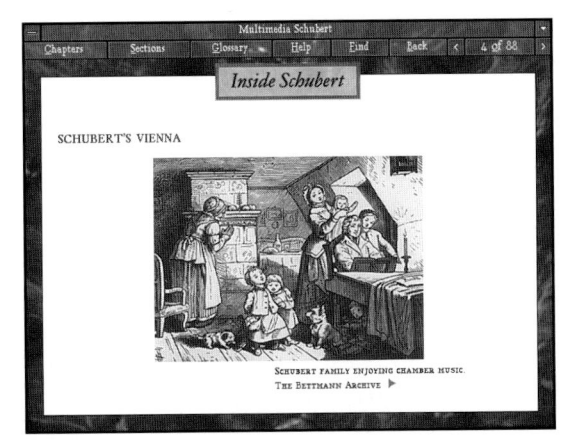

▲ *A scene from Apogee's Word Rescue.*

▲ *Multimedia Schubert, from Microsoft's Multimedia Composer series.*

wildly successful programs combine research and problem-solving skills with a detective adventure.

Many general edutainment products place heavy emphasis on action. Products such as the Rescue games from Apogee have the look and feel of a video game. The player's character jumps and dodges through scrolling scenes, avoiding monsters, gathering treasures, and solving math or word problems. The adjacent figure shows a typical scene from Word Rescue, which offers you a glimpse of what this type of game is like.

A completely different type of product is represented by the Multimedia Composer series from Microsoft. These products use the storage space and audio capabilities of CD-ROM to explore the works of the great composers. The user can explore the life and times of the composer to get some insight into the motivation behind the composer's work. The music itself can be examined and analyzed—and of course listened to in full digital sound.

Another CD-ROM-based general edutainment program is The San Diego Zoo Presents…The Animals!, published by Arnowitz, Inc. and The Software Toolworks. The program takes the user on a tour of the San Diego Zoo, one of the top zoos in the world. Filled with photos, video footage, and sounds from the zoo, as well as additional background information, this product lets the user study the animals and explore their habitats.

As you can probably tell from even these short descriptions, general edutainment products are not inferior or lacking in value just because they don't fit into one of the other categories. The Carmen Sandiego series is so successful that it has spawned events in schools across the country. There are even two Carmen Sandiego TV shows! The Rescue programs are the best-selling shareware education programs of all time. The Multimedia

▲ *The main map of the San Diego Zoo from The San Diego Zoo Presents…The Animals!*

Composer series is spectacular, and it provides new methods for us to use to look at the lives and works of our greatest composers. The Animals! is the next best thing to actually visiting the San Diego Zoo.

Summary

This chapter introduced the concept of edutainment as it applies to personal computer software. With a controversial topic like this, it is important to work from an explicit definition. In the context of this book, an edutainment product is software that integrates education and entertainment elements, with each element playing a significant role.

You learned that the broad spectrum of edutainment products can be divided into seven categories: drill-and-practice products, multimedia reference materials, simulation programs, CD-ROM storybooks, preschool products, creativity tools, and general edutainment products. Each of the first six categories has unique characteristics that separate that category from the others, while general edutainment covers all the remaining types of products.

The beginning of this chapter defined and categorized edutainment software, and the second part explained why you should care how the term is defined and categorized. The basic concept of edutainment—education combined with entertainment—has been with us since the dawn of history. This chapter introduced you to edutainment by showing how the concept is applied in a variety of settings. I hope that you are beginning to see the potential of edutainment software as a teaching tool.

If you have begun to see the value of edutainment software, you certainly will want to put some edutainment products to use. Before you can do that, you have to know something about the capabilities of your PC. Most edutainment software puts heavy demands on a computer, and many products require such items as a CD-ROM drive and a sound card.

Chapter 2 takes a look at the capabilities of the basic PC and gives you the information you need to choose edutainment products that will run on your current system.

Chapter **2**

The Capabilities of the Basic PC

All PCs have certain fundamental capabilities. They can accept information from you through the keyboard, process it, store it, and provide information to you through the monitor or printer. Although these capabilities make a PC useful for many kinds of tasks, they don't make a PC into a modern edutainment machine. To take full advantage of the edutainment products currently available, as well as those that will become available in the future, a PC has to do more than just the basics.

Before you can decide which capabilities to add to your PC to make it into an edutainment system, you must have a solid understanding of what your PC can do now. This chapter takes a look at some of the elements of basic PCs. These elements, working together, give PCs their various capabilities. By learning about them, you should better understand your machine.

This chapter gives you basic information about the following aspects of the PC:

- The operating system
- The microprocessor
- Memory
- Video
- Audio
- Mass storage

To help you relate to all the technical mumbo-jumbo you are about to see, I have created a generic System Requirements Label that resembles those that you see on any software package. A copy of this label, with the relevant information shown in bold type, is provided near the beginning of each section in which a feature from this label is discussed.

```
IBM PC or compatible
-----------------------------------
Requires:
• DOS 3.1 or greater
• 20 MHz 386 or better
• 640 KB of RAM
• EGA or better video
• Sound Blaster compatible sound card
• Hard drive

Recommended:
• VGA video
• EMS or XMS memory
```

▲ *The generic System Requirements Label.*

As you read about the elements of a PC, you also learn several tricks that can help you determine the specific capabilities and characteristics of your personal machine. This information is invaluable when the time comes to decide how to convert your machine to a more powerful edutainment system.

The Operating System

The operating system is the program that coordinates your computer's activities. It controls the microprocessor, and it handles the information coming in through the keyboard and other input devices, as well as the information going out to the monitor and other output devices. Unless you are using some kind of menu program or DOS Shell, or unless your system is set up to go directly into Windows, you eventually end up at the DOS prompt when you start your PC. The DOS prompt typically looks something like this:

C:\>

When you type a command at the DOS prompt, you are communicating directly with the *command processor*—the part of DOS that accepts input from you.

```
IBM PC or compatible
-----------------------------------
Requires:
• DOS 3.1 or greater
• 20 MHz 386 or better
• 640 KB of RAM
• EGA or better video
• Sound Blaster compatible sound card
• Hard drive

Recommended:
• VGA video
• EMS or XMS memory
```

▲ *Operating system requirements.*

MS-DOS, the disk operating system sold by Microsoft, serves as the operating system for the vast majority of PCs. Throughout this book, I use the term DOS to mean any and all versions of MS-DOS, as well as any of the custom versions of DOS created for PC manufacturers.

DOS is the most important program in your machine, and which version of DOS you have strongly affects what your machine can do. The following sidebar (see "Common DOS Versions") provides some information on the most common DOS versions, one of which is almost certainly installed on your machine. If you are not interested in this information, skip ahead to find out how to determine which version of DOS your machine is using.

Common DOS Versions

DOS 3.3

DOS 3.3 was the standard DOS version from its release in 1987 until the release of DOS 5.0 in 1991. It could support both high- and low-density, 3 1/2-inch and 5 1/4-inch floppy disks, as well as multiple 32M hard disk partitions.

DOS 4.0 and 4.01

DOS 4.0 came out in 1988. Although it had some powerful features, such as the DOS Shell (a graphical menu program) and the capability to support lots of expanded memory and huge hard disk partitions, it also was big and had many problems. Users experienced unexplained crashes and odd behavior, which led many people to either skip the upgrade or return to DOS 3.3.

Microsoft tried to remedy the situation by releasing DOS 4.01 later that year; but by then, DOS 4 had developed a bad reputation. Apparently, most users decided to wait for DOS 5.0.

DOS 5.0

After a huge test program designed to alleviate the fears caused by DOS 4.0, DOS 5.0 became available to the general public in 1991. The test program was successful, and DOS 5.0 became a hit.

DOS 5.0 introduced many new and powerful features. To make more conventional memory available, PCs with extended memory could move part of DOS into something called the high-memory area. This action frees a significant amount of conventional memory for user programs—potentially increasing their speed and efficiency.

Running DOS in the high-memory area also enables Microsoft Windows to run multiple DOS programs faster and more efficiently.

On PCs with an 80386 or better microprocessor, DOS 5.0 allows certain programs and device drivers to run in the upper-memory area. This feature provides the same advantages as moving DOS to the high-memory area.

DOS 5.0 supports hard disks with partitions of up to 2G (gigabytes) in size and includes many useful utility programs that previously were available only from third-party vendors.

DOS 6.0 and 6.2

DOS 6.0 arrived on the scene in March 1993. Like DOS 5.0, this new version was the product of a massive test program involving thousands of test sites. The most impressive feature of DOS 6.0 is DoubleSpace, a disk-compression program that is part of the DOS 6.0 package.

DoubleSpace can increase the apparent size of your hard disk by 50 to 100 percent by compressing the data on the disk. Several companies provide disk-compression utilities, but each one is unique. The big difference with DoubleSpace is that it is integrated into the operating system.

Unfortunately, DoubleSpace problems started appearing as soon as DOS 6.0 shipped. People who were using DoubleSpace began to experience random data loss and other unusual occurrences. These problems prompted Microsoft to release DOS 6.2 at the end of 1993.

DOS 6.2 addresses data loss concerns with the addition of DoubleGuard, a DoubleSpace feature that constantly checks for data errors, and ScanDisk, a utility that can repair many DoubleSpace errors.

Of particular interest to people interested in edutainment, DOS 6.2 contains a new version of the disk-caching program, SMARTDrive. Disk caches speed up hard-disk access by reading extra data from the hard disk and holding it in memory, where it can be read very quickly. With DOS 6.2, SMARTDrive was upgraded so that it can cache CD-ROM drives as well as hard drives. This enhancement can make your CD-ROM drive seem much faster and can improve the quality of the audio and video it provides.

DOS 6.2 seems to resolve the problems found in version 6.0 and is the current DOS version of choice. Unfortunately for Microsoft, just as they got the technical problems with DOS under control, they were hit with legal ones.

In 1993, Stac Electronics, a leading supplier of data compression products for personal computers, sued Microsoft for patent infringement. The suit claimed that Microsoft infringed two of Stac's patents in DoubleSpace. In February of 1994, a jury found in favor of Stac and awarded the company $120 million in damages. As a result of this suit, Microsoft can no longer sell versions of DOS that contain DoubleSpace.

As of this writing, Microsoft is shipping DOS 6.2.1, a new version that doesn't contain DoubleSpace.

How to Determine Which Version of DOS You Have

It's easy to determine which version of DOS your system is running by using the VER command that has been included with DOS since Version 2.0. You can enter **ver** at any DOS prompt, and the program responds with the DOS version number in use on that machine. The following figure shows the results I received when I ran the VER command on my PC.

```
C:\>ver
MS-DOS Version 6.20
C:\>
```

▲ *Using the VER command.*

As you can see, it can't get much easier than that!

The Microprocessor

The microprocessor is the "brain" of your PC. This complex integrated circuit processes instructions stored in the computer's memory. Every program you run on your PC consists of huge numbers of these instructions. By processing these instructions, and with the help of the other components in your computer system, the microprocessor does the work necessary to run your programs.

```
IBM PC or compatible

Requires:
• DOS 3.1 or greater
• 20 MHz 386 or better
• 640 KB of RAM
• EGA or better video
• Sound Blaster compatible sound card
• Hard drive

Recommended:
• VGA video
• EMS or XMS memory
```

▲ *Microprocessor requirements.*

The majority of microprocessors that run PCs are produced by a company called Intel. When IBM created its original personal computer in 1981, it used an Intel microprocessor called the 8088. Personal computers have evolved rapidly since then. Intel drives this evolution by continually introducing new microprocessors—each one more powerful than the last, yet each still capable of running preexisting software.

It sometimes seems that a million different microprocessors have been produced by Intel for use in PCs. In truth, however, Intel has produced only about a half-dozen basic types. Each type can contain many variations, based on speed, power consumption, and other details. The following paragraphs provide short descriptions of each of the basic microprocessor types.

The 8088 Microprocessor

The 8088 processes information internally 16 bits at a time; it transfers information to other parts of the system 8 bits at a time. The 8088 can access 1M of memory. Much of the newest software will not run on a PC powered by an 8088 microprocessor.

The 80286 Microprocessor

The next generation of Intel processor to power an IBM PC was the 80286. The 80286 microprocessor (often just referred to as the "286") accesses memory more efficiently than earlier microprocessors, both processing and transferring 16 bits of information at a time. The 286 can address more memory than an 8088, runs faster, and provides various technical advantages over its predecessor. The full potential of the 286 is seldom used. Instead, most of the time the 286 is used as little more than a faster 8088. Most new edutainment products won't run on this processor either. Any machine with less that a 386 processor is obsolete for edutainment use.

The 80386 Microprocessor

The 286 family was followed by the 386 family. The Intel 80386 processors are far superior to the 80286 family. In addition to processing instructions faster and more efficiently than earlier processors, a 386 handles data 32 bits at a time. The DX-series of 386 processors moves data between the processor and the rest of the system 32 bits at a time, whereas the SX-series moves data around the system only 16 bits at a time. A processor that can transfer data 32 bits at a time is inherently faster than one that moves data 16 bits at a time. Computers based on SX chips, consequently, are generally slower and less expensive than DX-based systems.

Possibly the most important feature of the 80386 processor is that it can support *multitasking*. Multitasking enables the microprocessor to execute multiple programs simultaneously by very rapidly switching between them. Microsoft Windows takes advantage of this feature. When you are running Windows in enhanced mode, you can be writing a chapter of your new book while your communications program downloads a file from CompuServe. In fact, I am doing that as I write this!

The 80486 Microprocessor

Not surprisingly, the 386 family was followed by the 486 family. The 80486 adds several new hardware features, but for most of us, the biggest advantage of the 486 is greater speed. Improved instruction execution and greater raw speed make the 486 noticeably faster than the 386.

Like the 386, the 486 has a DX-series and an SX-series. Both the 486DX and 486SX communicate with the rest of the system 32 bits at a time. The main difference is that the 486SX lacks the math coprocessor built into the 486DX.

The Pentium Microprocessor

After the 80486 came the Pentium. Intel chose the name Pentium because of problems with trade marking the numbers 586. As with the transition from 386 to 486, the most important thing about the arrival of the Pentium is its increased processing speed. The Pentium moves and processes data 64 bits at a time, while running faster and more efficiently than the 486.

As of this writing, PCs with Pentium processors are the top of the line. Although other processors are available that may be faster than a Pentium, the most powerful mainstream PCs use the Pentium microprocessor. For a concise overview of the differences between the processors just described, see Table 2.1.

How to Determine the Type of Processor in Your Machine

Having a powerful processor is something of a status symbol for many PC users, so you may already know what type of microprocessor is in your system. If you don't know its type, you can use any of several methods to find out. The easiest method is to run Microsoft Diagnostics (MSD). This program, which comes with DOS 6.0 (or later) and many other Microsoft products, gathers together all sorts of useful information about your computer.

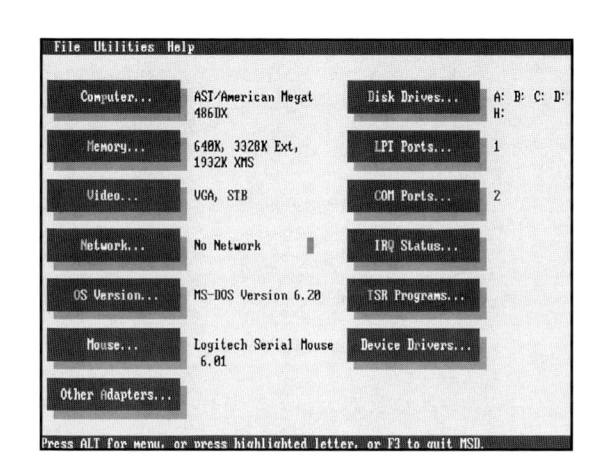

Table 2.1. Comparison of the common Intel microprocessors.

| | | | Processor | | |
Feature	8088	80286	80386	80486	Pentium
Data moved	8 bits	16 bits	32 bits	32 bits	64 bits
Data processed	16 bits	16 bits	32 bits	32 bits	64 bits
Memory addressed	1M	16M	4G	4G	4G

▲ *The Microsoft Diagnostics main screen.*

The first item on the MSD screen, labeled `Computer...`, is of particular interest to us in this discussion. It shows that my PC has a 486DX processor. You can click the word `Computer...` to display more detailed information.

You have to be at the DOS prompt to use MSD. Type the following command and then press the Enter key:

`\dos\msd`

If the computer displays a `Bad command or filename` message, you do not have MSD on your system. If MSD is on your system, a screen similar to the preceding figure is displayed, and you can determine your processor type from there.

If you cannot run MSD, you have to resort to other methods to determine the type of processor in your system. On some systems, the processor type is displayed shortly after you turn on the power. Press the Control, Alt, and Delete keys simultaneously (Ctrl+Alt+Delete) to restart your system. Carefully watch the messages that appear on-screen, and you may get your answer.

> **Caution:** If you press Ctrl+Alt+Delete while a program is running, you will lose everything you have done in that program since you last saved your work! It is always safest to exit all programs and return to the DOS prompt before you press those three keys simultaneously!

Another way to determine your processor type is to look on the front of your computer. Many manufacturers work the processor type into the text that they place there. For example, my machine has a little raised emblem right below the power switch that contains the characters *4DX*. These characters indicate that the machine has a 486DX microprocessor.

My wife's PC has a rectangular logo that says *DATA-386*; this designates that it contains a 386 processor. Although you can't tell from the logo, the processor is a 386DX. You can usually assume that if there is no mention of DX or SX, the machine has a DX-series microprocessor.

If these methods fail, you can usually find the processor type somewhere in the manuals that came with your machine.

Memory

```
IBM PC or compatible
--------------------------------
Requires:
• DOS 3.1 or greater
• 20 MHz 386 or better
• 640 KB of RAM
• EGA or better video
• Sound Blaster compatible sound card
• Hard drive

Recommended:
• VGA video
• EMS or XMS memory
```

▲ *Memory requirements.*

PC memory is a confusing subject. When people talk about PC memory, they usually are *not* referring to the amount of space on the computer's hard disk. Instead, they are referring to the extremely fast, relatively expensive memory circuits built into the machine. This memory either is installed directly on your computer's main circuit board or on separate circuit boards that plug into the main circuit board.

The two types of memory chips in your PC are RAM and ROM. RAM (*random-access memory*) chips are the temporary storage areas of your machine's memory and are where programs normally reside when they are running. ROM (*read-only memory*) chips are permanent storage areas. Neither you nor the computer can change the information stored in them.

Read-Only Memory (ROM)

The ROM holds various information and programs that are vital to the operation of your system. The programs and information in these chips are not something you normally need to worry about. Just ignore the ROM, and you will do fine.

Random-Access Memory (RAM)

The RAM is very important to you as a user. In general, the more RAM you have, the better. This is especially true if you are using Microsoft Windows. The speed of the RAM is also important. In the case of RAM, the speed refers to how fast you can get information into, or out of, the chips themselves. For any given processor speed, there is an optimum RAM speed. RAM that is too slow for your processor can slow the processor down. RAM that is too fast for your processor does nothing to speed up the machine, and it will be more expensive than slower RAM that may be more compatible with your machine. If you ever decide to add memory to your machine, you should talk to the memory supplier about the appropriate speed of memory to buy.

The RAM in your machine can be divided into four types: conventional memory, extended memory, expanded memory, and the upper-memory area. Table 2.2 contains some memory-related definitions and abbreviations that you may find useful in this discussion of RAM.

Table 2.2. Memory-related terms.

Term	Abbreviation	Size in Bytes
Kilobyte	K or KB	1,024
Megabyte	M or MB	1,048,576
Gigabyte	G or GB	1,073,741,824

Conventional Memory

Conventional memory is available on every PC and is the portion of the RAM in which most programs normally run. Your machine may contain as much as 640K (kilobytes) of conventional memory.

Many different programs use your PC's conventional memory at the same time. DOS uses some conventional memory, as do the various device drivers and terminate-and-stay-resident (TSR) programs you may be using. Your edutainment programs can use any conventional memory that is left over.

More and more frequently, new software expects your PC to contain the full 640K of conventional memory. If your machine does not, you won't be able to run some of the newer edutainment programs. Even if your machine does have the full 640K of conventional memory, it is still possible to run out of usable space. See Chapter 14, "Troubleshooting DOS and Windows," for tips on making more memory available for your edutainment programs.

Extended Memory (XMS)

Extended memory (also known as XMS) is a type of memory that exists beyond conventional memory. The memory addresses occupied by extended memory begin at the 1M point. Extended memory provides an efficient way for programs to access a vast amount of memory. Much of the power of Microsoft Windows comes from its ability to use extended memory. Extended memory can only exist on PCs with an 80286 processor or better.

A special program called an *extended-memory manager* is required to give programs access to extended memory. An extended-memory manager coordinates access to the extended memory and provides a standard interface to it. DOS 5 and 6 come with an extended-memory manager called HIMEM.SYS. HIMEM.SYS conforms to a specification promoted by some of the major PC software and hardware companies. Any program you are likely to run into will work with HIMEM.SYS if it uses extended memory.

Expanded Memory (EMS)

Expanded memory (EMS) is the third type of RAM you may have in your machine. It consists of an expanded-memory manager and an expanded-memory board. The expanded-memory manager is similar to an extended-memory manager, in that it provides a standard interface between the EMS board and the programs that want to use EMS. The EMS board is a circuit card that contains the memory chips that make up the expanded memory. You can install expanded memory in almost any PC, even those that use the lowly 8088 processors.

> **Note:** Some extended-memory managers can simulate expanded memory (EMS) by using extended memory (XMS). With memory managers such as QEMM, from Quarterdeck, the memory manager can automatically give your programs the kind of memory they want. HIMEM.SYS does not have this capability.

The Upper-Memory Area

The upper-memory area is a 384K area of memory located just above (after) the 640K of conventional memory in a PC. This area normally is reserved for devices such as video cards. Expanded-memory managers may also be able to use some of this space.

If your PC has an 80386 processor or better and is running DOS 5.0 or later, you may be able to move some of your device drivers and TSRs into the upper-memory area, which frees more conventional memory for your programs to use. Consult your DOS manual for instructions.

How to Determine the Quantity and Type of RAM in Your System

It is quite useful to know the type and quantity of memory available in your machine. When you buy an edutainment product, the package lists certain hardware requirements. The program will not run on machines that do not meet these minimum requirements. The list may specify a certain minimum amount of conventional, extended, and, sometimes, expanded memory for operation. If your PC has DOS 5.0 or later installed, it is easy to determine the quantities of the various types of memory installed in your system.

At the DOS prompt, type **mem** and press Enter. DOS provides a screen of information about the memory in your system. The following figure shows the results of the MEM command executed on my 486 PC, which is running DOS 6.2.

```
C:\>MEM

Memory Type         Total  =   Used   +   Free
----------------    -----      ----       ----
Conventional        640K        23K       617K
Upper               128K       127K         1K
Reserved            128K       128K         0K
Extended (XMS)    7,296K     2,464K     4,832K
                  ------     ------     ------
Total memory      8,192K     2,741K     5,451K

Total under 1 MB    768K       149K       619K

Total Expanded (EMS)          7,760K (7,946,240 bytes)
Free Expanded (EMS)           4,832K (4,947,968 bytes)

Largest executable program size     617K (632,208 bytes)
Largest free upper memory block       1K     (704 bytes)
MS-DOS is resident in the high memory area.

C:\>
```

▲ *Results of the MEM command.*

The resulting table provides some interesting information. The first line of data indicates conventional memory. In the case of my PC, it shows that I have a full 640K of conventional memory, with 23K being used by DOS, device drivers, and TSRs.

The second line shows that 128K of the upper-memory area is available for use, and all but 1K of it is in use. On my system, this 128K contains drivers for actual hardware, such as my CD-ROM drive and mouse, as well as drivers for such things as the SMARTDrive disk-cache program and the Stacker disk-compression program. Stacker is similar to, but more capable than, the DoubleSpace program that comes with DOS 6.0.

The third line in the table shows that 128K of memory is reserved and not available for me to use. The operating system set aside these memory addresses for ROM and for the memory on the video card. Each of these occupies 64K, yielding the 128K total.

The fourth line contains information on the extended memory. My machine has just over 7M of extended memory, of which a little more than 2M is in use. If my system had expanded memory, the table would include a similar line for it.

The Total Memory line shows that I have 8,192K of memory (since 1024K = 1M, this is equal to 8M). Of that 8,192K, 2,741K is in use, and 5,451K, mostly extended memory, is still available.

The Total Under 1MB line indicates that of the 1024K of possible memory, 768K is accessible. Of that, 149K is in use and 619K is still available.

Because QEMM can use XMS to simulate EMS, two lines show the amount of total EMS and free EMS. The total EMS is 7,760K and the free EMS is 4,832K.

That 619K shows up on the next two lines where the size of the largest executable program that can run in conventional memory (with the current system configuration) is shown as 617K, and the largest free upper-memory block is 1K. The numbers do not add up to 619K because there are surely some small pieces of unused upper memory that eat into the last 1K.

And finally, the last line generated by the MEM command shows that part of DOS is running in the high-memory area.

Video

```
IBM PC or compatible
-----------------------------------
Requires:
• DOS 3.1 or greater
• 20 MHz 386 or better
• 640 KB of RAM
• EGA or better video
• Sound Blaster compatible sound card
• Hard drive

Recommended:
• VGA video
• EMS or XMS memory
```

▲ *Video requirements.*

The video systems in PCs have been advancing continually since the first IBM PCs appeared in 1981. These advances have resulted in several generations of video systems, each more powerful than the last. With all the different video systems available, it is no wonder that video is one place where basic PCs vary enormously.

The obvious part of your PC video system is the monitor. The monitor is similar to a television display. On very basic systems, the monitor may actually be a TV set. The monitor on your system determines the quality of the video image your PC can display. No matter how good the rest of the video system is, the number of colors you see and the amount of information visible at one time are limited by the monitor.

The monitor displays the images you see; the video card supplies the image that the monitor displays. The video card contains the hardware that actually generates the image you see on your monitor. It may be useful to know a little about the available mainstream video cards.

The Monochrome Display Adapter

When the IBM PC was first introduced, it had a text-only video card—called the Monochrome Display Adapter (MDA)—connected to a monochrome monitor. This card could display only 80 characters of text on 25 lines. Very few MDA video systems are still in use.

The Color/Graphics Adapter

Shortly after IBM introduced the MDA, it brought out the Color/Graphics Adapter (CGA). CGA cards are capable of generating color and graphics, as the name implies. Like the MDA, the CGA can display 80 characters and 25 lines of text, but it can do so in 16 colors. Unfortunately, the quality, or *resolution*, of the characters is not as great as those generated by the MDA. This makes the text display of the CGA harder to look at for extended periods than that of the MDA.

Although the CGA can display graphics, the quality of the image it produces is quite poor. Although some programs still support CGA graphics, the vast majority ignore this card, making it effectively obsolete.

The Hercules Graphics Card

The first major PC video card created by a third party was the Hercules Graphics Card (HGC). This card is completely compatible with the MDA. It provides the same 80-character-by-25-line video mode and the same resolution. As far as the PC can tell, the HGC is an MDA card.

Beyond compatibility with the MDA, the HGC provides reasonably high-resolution monochrome graphics. Although the resolution is good, being limited to monochrome is a serious handicap. If your machine is more than a few years old and has a monochrome display, it quite likely is equipped with a Hercules video card.

The Enhanced Graphics Adapter

With the introduction of the Enhanced Graphics Adapter (EGA), IBM set a new standard for video performance. The EGA supports all the video modes of the MDA and CGA. Any software that worked with either of these earlier cards works just fine with the EGA. The EGA also has several more modes that provide various mixes of higher resolution, more colors, and more video pages. Multiple pages of video memory enable programs to be drawing an image on one page while displaying a different image. After the image is drawn, the program can tell the video card to display the new page, and the new image appears on the screen instantly. Multiple pages are almost a necessity for good animation.

When used with an EGA monitor, an EGA card can display 16-color text or graphics images with resolution approaching that of the Hercules card. The 16 colors come from a possible set of 64. In text mode, this card can display 43 lines of 16-color text, as well as the standard 25 lines found on earlier cards.

The EGA also can display custom character sets, or fonts. Word processing programs in particular can take advantage of this capability. Word processors enable words to appear in bold or italics, or to have other typographic characteristics. Custom fonts enable these characteristics to be visible on-screen rather than just in printed form.

The EGA works with a monochrome monitor, replacing the MDA or HGC in many systems. If your system provides color graphics and was built more than a couple of years ago, it probably contains an EGA card.

The Video Graphics Array

The Video Graphics Array (VGA) provided the next big leap in video capabilities for PCs. This card retains full compatibility with the earlier cards while once again adding new modes of its own. Virtually all new computers being sold today have *at least* VGA-level video.

A VGA card provides sharper, clearer text than an HGC card, and does so in 16 colors. For applications in which it is important to have as much text as possible on-screen, the VGA can display up to 50 lines of text.

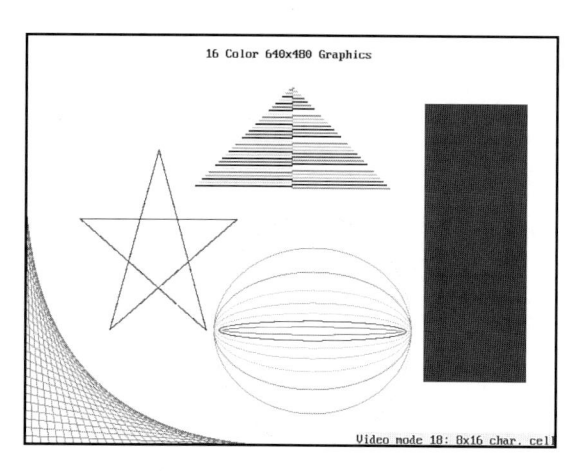

With a maximum graphics-mode resolution of 640 pixels horizontally by 480 pixels vertically, the VGA provides a sharper graphics display than the HGC, while still allowing up to 16 colors. In a VGA system, those 16 colors can come from a set (*palette*) of 262,144 colors (also known as 256K colors)!

When color is more important than resolution, the VGA provides a mode that has 320 pixels horizontally and 200 pixels vertically—and can display 256 colors simultaneously. Once again, these 256 colors come from a palette of 256K colors. The next figure shows the same sample displayed in 256-color mode.

> **Note:** Because the figures in this book are, for the most part, presented in black and white, you can't actually see the 256 colors. Like an old black-and-white TV set, however, the various colors show up as different shades of gray.

The 256-color mode is inferior for displaying simple geometric shapes. However, this mode, and certain non-standard derivatives of it, have become extremely popular. If used wisely, the greater number of colors in this mode can more than compensate for the reduced resolution, and images seem much more realistic. Many products use the 256-color modes to display scanned photographs of real-world objects and scenes.

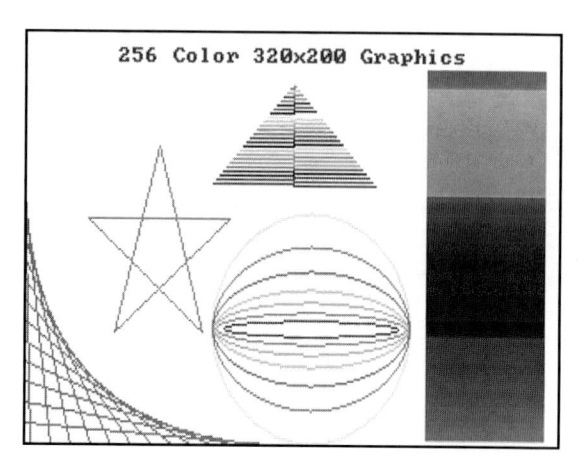

▲ *An image displayed in the high-resolution VGA video mode.*

▲ *The same image displayed in 256-color VGA video mode.*

Although 256-color images are not photographic quality, they certainly are usable for many applications. The following figure demonstrates this fact with a scanned photograph of my daughter, Jennifer.

▲ *A scanned photo of Jennifer Michelle Mann in 256-color mode.*

Many edutainment products utilize the official 256-color mode, or one of its non-standard variants, so an edutainment system with less than a VGA video system is at a severe disadvantage. Many of the hottest game developers have already abandoned sub-VGA video completely, and more than a few non-game developers are thinking about it. As time goes on, fewer and fewer non-VGA edutainment products will be available.

How to Determine What Type of Video System You Have

If your machine is running DOS 6.0 or later, you may be able to use Microsoft Diagnostics (MSD) to find out what type of video system is installed in your PC. To activate Microsoft Diagnostics from any DOS prompt, enter the following command:

`\dos\msd`

If a message such as `Bad command or filename` is displayed, MSD is not on your system.

Assuming that your system does have MSD, you should see a display similar to the one you saw earlier in this chapter. The third heading on the left is labeled `Video...`. Next to this heading, MSD lists the type of video it thinks your machine has. If you refer back to the figure, you may notice that MSD thinks my machine contains a VGA video card manufactured by a company named STB. In actuality, the video card in my machine was produced by STB Systems Inc., but it is a Super VGA card, not a VGA. Even so, MSD was able to give me some useful information. If MSD says you have VGA video, you can be confident that you have *at least* VGA.

Another way to determine what kind of video you have is to carefully watch the messages that appear on-screen when you first turn on your computer. The video card displays a message identifying itself at this time.

If you are running Microsoft Windows, you also can look at the `Display:` section of the Windows Setup dialog box and find out the video mode in which Windows is running. If you see that EGA is listed as the display, you know that your machine has at least EGA video.

Finally, the documentation that came with your video card should tell you all you need to know.

Audio

```
IBM PC or compatible

Requires:
• DOS 3.1 or greater
• 20 MHz 386 or better
• 640 KB of RAM
• EGA or better video
• Sound Blaster compatible sound card
• Hard drive

Recommended:
• VGA video
• EMS or XMS memory
```

▲ *Audio requirements.*

All PCs have a built-in speaker. This speaker generates the beeps and tones you hear coming from the machine every now and then. With appropriate programming, the speaker can even generate crude music and speech. Here's how it works.

The PC speaker can be turned on or off by either hardware or software. Turning it on moves the cone of the speaker. Turning it off enables the cone to move back to its original position. That's it. All the sounds your machine makes come from rapidly turning the speaker on and off.

Turning the speaker on and off one time produces a click. Turning the speaker on and off repeatedly causes the cone of the speaker to oscillate, or swing back and forth. These oscillations produce sound waves of a particular frequency. The frequency (number of oscillations per second) of the sounds generated by the speaker can cover the full range of human hearing, and far beyond. By adjusting the rate at which the speaker oscillates, sounds with the frequencies of the various musical notes can be created.

Although the PC speaker can generate sounds that have the same frequency as musical notes, music played over the speaker is not of very good quality. There are many reasons for this poor quality, starting with the speaker itself.

If you were to open your PC and look inside, you would see that it contains one small, inexpensive speaker. Compare this to your home stereo system with its two large, relatively expensive speakers.

Because the PC has only one speaker, it can't produce stereo sound. Stereo requires two speakers. Because the speaker is small, it can't put out as much sound as the monsters hooked up to your home stereo. And finally, because the PC speaker is inexpensive, it can't reproduce sound as well as your stereo speakers.

> **Caution:** Unless you are comfortable working on electrical and electronic equipment, I recommend that you just take my word for what you will find inside your PC. Inside that cover is a confusing jumble of sensitive components, fragile mechanical devices, and a high-voltage power supply.

Even if PCs somehow came equipped with two large, high-quality speakers, the sound from your basic PC would *still* be low quality. Why? Because high-quality sound is produced in a fundamentally different way than by turning a speaker on and off.

Turning the speaker on and off can capture the frequency of a sound, but it completely ignores the amplitude, or level of a sound. Real-world sounds have a constantly varying amplitude that must be reproduced to create high-quality sounds. No matter how good the speaker in the PC, there is no way to provide it with the amplitude signal it requires for high-quality sound.

You can, however, add a sound card to get high-quality sound from your PC. These devices, when attached to an appropriate set of speakers, can make your PC sound nearly as good as your stereo system. Sound cards are covered in detail in Chapter 10, "Sight and Sound."

Mass Storage

```
IBM PC or compatible

Requires:
• DOS 3.1 or greater
• 20 MHz 386 or better
• 640 KB of RAM
• EGA or better video
• Sound Blaster compatible sound card
• Hard drive

Recommended:
• VGA video
• EMS or XMS memory
```

▲ *Mass storage requirements.*

Currently, the general-purpose mass-storage device on most PCs is a hard drive. The hard drive consists of one or more rotating disks coated with a magnetic material and an arm that holds read/write heads. The read/write heads are similar to the heads in a tape recorder: either sensing the magnetic field of the area beneath the head or modifying it. By moving the arm in or out over the rapidly rotating disks (usually faster than 3,000 revolutions per minute), the hard drive can position the read/write heads over any spot on the disk quickly and accurately. Hard drives are capable of holding huge amounts of information, and drives larger than 1G are available.

Although hard drives have a more technical side, with buzzwords such as SCSI, MFM, IDE, and the like, you don't really have to concern yourself with this side. If you are curious about what these buzzwords mean, read the following sidebar (see "Hard Drive Jargon"). A hard drive's most important features are its speed and storage capacity.

The storage capacity of a hard drive is pretty obvious because hard drives typically are described by their storage capacities.

When you talk about the speed of a hard drive, the relevant value is not disk rotation speed, but *average access time* (also known as *seek time*). The average access time is the amount of time it takes the hard drive, on average, to find a piece of information. This time is measured in milliseconds, and the smaller the number the better.

You can improve the average access time of your current hard drive dramatically if you use a disk-cache program. A disk-cache program stores data from the hard disk in a piece of your RAM, called a *cache*. The RAM in a PC is immensely faster than the fastest hard disk, so retrieving data from the cache speeds up access. Microsoft has included a disk-cache program, SMARTDrive, with all versions of DOS since 5.0.

Paradoxically, as hard drives gain more storage capacity, they tend to become faster. This occurs because the physical size of the drive doesn't increase with storage capacity; instead, more data is crammed into the same, or even a smaller space. With more data in the same space, and the disks in the drive spinning just as fast, it takes less time to access data.

Hard Drive Jargon

Hard drives are associated with various buzzwords, and the following list gives you some of the definitions of those buzzwords:

ST506—The identification number for a type of hard-drive controller manufactured by Seagate. Early PC hard drives worked with this controller, but it has been replaced by SCSI and IDE in newer equipment.

ESDI—Enhanced Small Device Interface. An advanced version of the ST506, which, like the ST506, has been replaced by SCSI and IDE.

SCSI—Small Computer System Interface. A standard for the way that peripheral devices talk to a computer. SCSI-2 is the latest version of the standard.

IDE—Imbedded Drive Electronics. IDE drives have a controller built right into the drive. Some PCs have a connector for an IDE drive cable built in, which eliminates the need for an interface card.

FM Recording—Frequency Modulation Recording. An early method for storing data on a hard disk. Seriously limits the capacity of the disk.

MFM Recording—Modified FM Recording. A more efficient method of storage than FM.

RLL Recording—Run Length Limited Recording. A storage method that is as much as 50 percent more efficient then MFM.

Multiple-Zone Recording—Fits more data onto the disk by increasing the number of sectors in the outer tracks. Requires more sophisticated drive electronics than earlier methods.

Interleave—Describes how data is arranged on the tracks of the disk. Interleave is not a concern on SCSI or IDE drives.

FAT—File Allocation Table. An area on the hard disk used to keep track of where files are stored on the disk. You normally do not have to worry about the FAT.

A large, fast hard drive is becoming a necessity for an edutainment system.

How to Determine the Size of Your Hard Drive

The easiest way to determine the size of your hard drive is to use the CHKDSK (check disk) command. This command creates a status report for a disk drive that contains, among other things, the apparent size of the disk. You can run CHKDSK from any DOS prompt by entering the following command:

```
\dos\chkdsk
```

```
C:\>\dos\chkdsk
Volume Serial Number is 0CD3-0535

   192,602,112 bytes total disk space
     1,064,960 bytes in 9 hidden files
     1,875,960 bytes in 226 directories
   167,632,896 bytes in 5,405 user files
    22,028,288 bytes available on disk

         8,192 bytes in each allocation unit
        23,511 total allocation units on disk
         2,689 available allocation units on disk

       655,360 total bytes memory
       516,944 bytes free

Instead of using CHKDSK, try using SCANDISK.  SCANDISK can reliably detect
and fix a much wider range of disk problems.  For more information,
type HELP SCANDISK from the command prompt.

C:\>
```

▲ *A CHKDSK status report.*

The following figure shows the results of running CHKDSK on my hard drive.

The second line of the report states that my hard disk has 192,602,112 bytes total disk space. This is equivalent to approximately 184M of space on the disk. Earlier, I told you that I have a 120M hard drive. DoubleSpace is the cause of this discrepancy. Because my hard drive is compressed, it appears to be bigger than it actually is.

Although it might be nice to know how much physical space your hard drive has, what is really important is how much *usable* disk space you have. This is the information that CHKDSK provides.

The preceding figure includes a message about SCANDISK across the bottom. Although SCANDISK is superior to CHKDSK for most purposes, it does not generate the kind of report CHKDSK does, so it is of no use in determining disk size.

Summary

This chapter gave you an overview of the elements of a basic PC. Taken together, these elements give a PC its characteristics and capabilities. All software requires a PC to have a certain set of capabilities before it can run well, or at all. Edutainment products typically demand more from your machine than other types of software, meaning that the machine that works fine with your word processor or spreadsheet may be woefully inadequate for a new edutainment product. Understanding the capabilities of a basic PC in general, and your PC in particular, puts you in a position to choose wisely when, and if, you decide to upgrade your machine to become a better edutainment system.

Through a variety of methods you have learned about *your* PC. Of particular use are utilities and commands such as VER and CHKDSK. Even more useful, if it is installed on your system, is Microsoft Diagnostics (MSD).

Now that you know something about the elements of your PC, you are prepared for Part II, "About Edutainment Products," in which the various categories of edutainment products are covered in detail.

About EDUTAINMENT Products

Part II

Part II takes an in-depth look at the various categories of edutainment products, with one chapter devoted to each of the categories introduced in Chapter 1. Each chapter provides more information about the category in general. Then each chapter looks at some of the common features and some of the unique features of the products in the category. In most cases, I take you on a short walk-through of a product so that you have an idea of what it is like to use that kind of program.

The remainder of each chapter is devoted to specific products in the category being discussed. I have made no attempt to rate these products, but I was able to install and run every one of them. Some of the products have won the prestigious Parent's Choice Award, and this honor is noted in the product's description. Interactive demonstrations of many of the edutainment products discussed in this book (and many products not discussed here) are included on the *Edutainment Comes Alive!* CD-ROM that accompanies this book.

Where Can You Get These Products?

Getting your hands on edutainment products can be harder than you might expect. Most software stores only devote a fraction of their shelf space to educational products, which means that many good products are only on the shelves for a short time—if they ever get there at all.

Fortunately, alternative sources exist for most edutainment products. The first is, of course, the publisher. Publishers normally take credit card orders from the public, but in most cases, they prefer that you buy through their normal distribution channels and will charge you the full list price if you buy from them.

Another alternative is mail-order companies that specialize in educational products. One such company is Educational Resources. The Educational Resources catalog is filled with hundreds of edutainment products. Most of the products discussed in this part of the book are available through them, as well as many products not mentioned. You can request a free catalog by calling (800) 624-2926.

If you have added a CD-ROM drive, another source of products is EDUCORP. The EDUCORP catalog contains a full range of CD-ROMs, ranging from general interest to desktop publishing and multimedia. Although its primary focus is on the Macintosh, most of EDUCORP's edutainment CD-ROMs are available for the PC as well. You can request a free catalog by calling (800) 843-9497.

Some companies are experimenting with new ways of distributing software on CD-ROM. One method is to include a collection of full retail products on a disc, but to "lock" these products. If a customer decides she wants to purchase one of the locked products, she can call an 800 number, pay a fee by credit card, and receive a special code. With this code she can unlock the software and use it.

The Parent's Choice Foundation

Parent's Choice is an operating non-profit service organization that was founded in Newton, Massachusetts, in 1978. The foundation provides information to parents so that they can help their children continue learning outside the classroom.

Parent's Choice is involved in a number of projects that examine and review all types of children's media. The project that is relevant to this book is the Parent's Choice Awards, an annual event started in 1981. Publishers are invited to enter their products in the competition. (Publishers pay an entry fee that helps to fund the awards project). The products are then evaluated by parents, teachers, and other experts, as well as children in the target audience. Parent's Choice uses kids in after-school computer programs as reviewers for software. This gives them access to the opinions of a large number of kids and enables those kids to spend a significant amount of time with each product.

Club KidSoft publishes a monthly CD-ROM of locked edutainment products. Each disc contains locked products, demos, a video news program by and for kids, and a Club Room filled with fun activities. One track on the disc is recorded in audio CD format, so it plays on an audio compact disc player.

Part of the Club KidSoft CD-ROM is given over to an electronic catalog. The catalog contains useful information about the products on the CD-ROM. For any given product, the catalog entry may include screen shots or even full demos. All products have a brief synopsis and a list of hardware requirements.

> **Note:** Like many of the products it contains, the Club KidSoft CD-ROM has somewhat stringent system requirements. It requires an 80386 processor (or better); Windows 3.1; CD-ROM drive (double-speed preferred); sound card with Windows driver; at least 4M of RAM; SVGA video card with 640 x 480, 256-color or better Windows driver; and a mouse.

In addition to the CD-ROM, club members can also receive the *Club KidSoft* magazine. The magazine is full of stories and product reviews, many written by kids. You can reach the Club KidSoft Subscriptions Department at (800) 354-6150.

As you read through Part II, you will notice that some of the products are marketed as shareware. Shareware products are available through a number of sources, including mail-order catalogs,

▲ *The Club KidSoft CD-ROM is colorful, fun, and full of "locked" edutainment products.*

on-line services, electronic bulletin-board systems (BBSs), and retail stores. One source I am partial to is The Software Labs. They are probably the most popular mail-order source, with more than one million customers. You can request a free catalog by calling (800) 569-7900.

Another source of edutainment shareware is the Educational Software Cooperative (ESC). The ESC is a group of authors who have banded together to further the sales of educational shareware. One of their activities is the publication of a CD-ROM containing their products. You can order a copy of their CD-ROM by calling 216-529-1888.

Now that you have some sources for products, here is a breakdown of what is covered in each chapter. Please note that with each product description provided, I include the equipment requirements for that product. In the case of products with

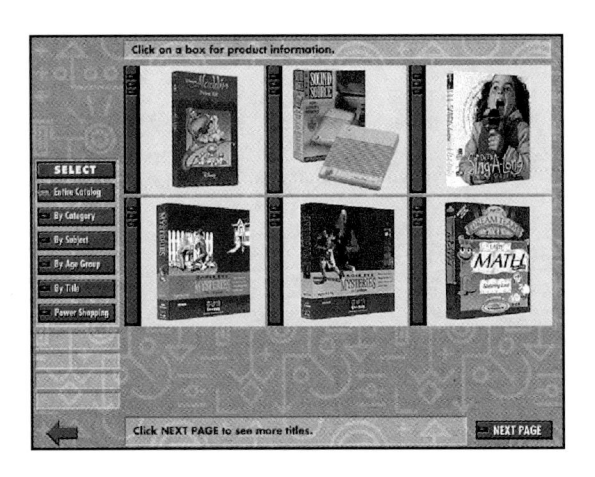

▲ *An on-disc catalog lets the user browse the products available on the Club KidSoft CD-ROM.*

▲ *The Club KidSoft catalog contains enough information to assist users in making their buying decisions.*

multiple formats (DOS versus Windows, or floppy disk versus CD-ROM), I was not always able to include the system requirements for each version of the product. You should always check the current system requirements before you buy a product; this is especially important when you buy a format different than the one I describe.

Chapter 3, "Drill-and-Practice Products"

Drill-and-practice products were the first type of educational software available for home use. Originally little more than computerized versions of written exams and flash cards, they have evolved significantly. Current products provide rewards for successful completion of tasks and often contain music, sound effects, and colorful graphics.

This chapter explores drill-and-practice programs. It begins with a look at the common features of these products, and then moves on to other interesting features. Following that, I take you on a short walk-through of the number one drill-and-practice program of all time: Math Blaster.

The rest of the chapter looks at particular drill-and-practice programs. Math programs are the most common type of drill-and-practice program and are discussed together. Subjects such as typing and language skills are also well suited to this approach, and you find examples of each here.

Chapter 4, "Multimedia Reference Materials"

The phrase *multimedia reference materials* conjures up images of products such as Microsoft's Encarta—an attractive CD-ROM encyclopedia. Although few people would consider a printed encyclopedia to be much fun, a multimedia encyclopedia is an entirely different animal. By enhancing the contents of a printed encyclopedia with graphics, sound, and motion, the developers have created products that are more fun and also can teach more at the same time.

Although encyclopedias are the most visible representatives of the category, there is much more to multimedia reference works. This chapter is designed to let you explore some of the diversity of the category. Because they are so important, a large portion of the chapter is devoted to the three major multimedia encyclopedias. The chapter also contains a discussion of common and unique features of these multimedia reference programs and a walk-through of Encarta.

The rest of the chapter covers some of the other types of multimedia reference works available. From medical references to explorations of extinct life forms (including dinosaurs!), some of the best products available are showcased so that you can get a feel for the size and variety of products in this category.

Chapter 5, "Simulation Programs"

A simulation is an imitation, or model, of something. An edutainment simulation usually models some real-world system, such as a city or an airplane. It helps the user learn about the system by involving him in the complex interactions and occurrences that make up the real world.

This chapter introduces edutainment simulations. It looks at common features of these products, as well as those features that make certain products stand out. A walk-through of SimCity 2000 helps to illustrate the depth and complexity of these products.

The last part of the chapter provides coverage of individual simulations. Although most people think of Maxis and MECC when they think of edutainment simulations, I have included a number of products that have definite edutainment value, yet are seldom thought of in an educational context. After you read the descriptions, I think you will agree that these products deserve to be called "edutainment."

Chapter 6, "CD-ROM Storybooks"

CD-ROM storybooks are computerized renditions of children's picture books. Although this might sound like a silly idea at first, by the end of this chapter, I think you will agree that it is actually a brilliant idea. As with multimedia reference works, the key to the success of CD-ROM storybooks is *multimedia.*

The multimedia capabilities of modern PCs, combined with clever programming, animation, and music, turn the best of the CD-ROM storybooks into a wonderful experience. Whereas a printed storybook is static and unchanging, a CD-ROM storybook is "alive" and interacts with the user.

This chapter provides lots of information about CD-ROM storybooks. It looks at the common features of the programs, as well as the unique ones. It takes you on a short tour of Arthur's Teacher Trouble, my daughter's first CD-ROM storybook. And it describes two different kinds of CD-ROM storybooks: those for young children and those for older children through adults.

Chapter 7, "Preschool Products"

Preschool products are edutainment programs designed for very young children. These programs teach basic pre-math and pre-reading skills. Some are designed to encourage a child's creativity. The programs incorporate interactivity, bright colors, music, and sound effects to keep a child interested. I believe that this particular category is especially important. Showing children the joy of learning at an early age carries over into the rest of their lives.

This chapter is structured like the previous chapters and begins by looking at the common features of preschool products. From there, it moves on to examine the interesting and unique features of the various products.

Next, I take you on a quick walk-through of Sierra On-Line's Early Math (by the time you read this, the name of this program is slated to be changed to Loid's Math Planet). This tour exhibits many of the common features of this category, and should give you an idea of just how fun these programs can be for kids.

Following the walk-through comes the descriptions of specific products. Some pre-reading and pre-math products are discussed, along with a number of other products. Most of these other products take a broader approach, covering pre-reading and pre-math skills, as well as creativity—all in one package.

Chapter 8, "Creativity Tools"

Creativity tools are programs that enable, or even challenge, the user to exercise her creative impulses. As befits a subject as open-ended as creativity, a number of different types of creativity programs are available. These products range from specialized paint programs, to writing tools, to storybook creators.

This chapter introduces you to this exciting category of edutainment products. Although these products are diverse, they still have some common features that are examined here. The unique features are also discussed before I present a walk-through of Print Shop Deluxe, the best-known of all the creativity products.

The remainder of the chapter is devoted to a number of other creativity tools. Whether your child wants to create her own story or experiment with computer-aided design, you can find a creativity tool that is right for the job.

Chapter 9, "General Edutainment Products"

The previous chapters each covered one broad category of edutainment product. This chapter is different. The general edutainment category is the place for products that don't really belong in any of the other categories, yet are still obviously edutainment. This category is the largest, and contains some of the most popular and innovative programs.

It made no sense to look for the common (or unique) features of the products in this category. In the same way, a walk-through of a particular product would tell you little about any other product. This being the case, Chapter 9 is merely divided into five groups. The common feature of each group is its subject matter. In style and technique, the programs in each category may be, and usually are, very different.

Although the products here don't fit into any of the other categories, they certainly aren't low-quality or unknown products. General edutainment contains programs such as the Carmen Sandiego series, a perennial best seller. There are also products such as Math and Word Rescue, the best-selling shareware educational programs ever, and Berlitz Think & Talk German, a top-of-the-line language learning system that comes on nine CD-ROMs!

Support for Users with Special Needs

Only a few of the available edutainment products contain any features that make them accessible to users with special needs. This is a shame. In my opinion, children that use edutainment products have a big advantage over those who do not. I believe they grow up to be better, faster, and more motivated learners than children who do not take advantage of these products. It's important that these products be accessible to all users.

It is important to recognize those products that contain features that make them more accessible to users with special needs. Such special features are discussed within the product descriptions, but I acknowledge them here, as well.

Products from Edmark provide support for single-switch forms of command entry (scanning). A dialog box in the Adult Section lets the parent enable single-switch input, select the type of scan progression, and adjust the scan rate.

Mental Math Games, from the Waterford Institute, contains a utility that enables you to change the overall speed of the activities in the program. This feature is designed to allow the parent to adapt the program to learners who are gifted or challenged.

Microsoft provides products and services that make computers easier for people with special needs to use. These products include a set of keyboard layouts for users who type with one hand, AccessDOS, and the Access Pack for Microsoft Windows.

AccessDOS adds features to DOS to support users who are movement or hearing disabled. AccessDOS contains, among other features, utilities that

- Allow single-fingered typing of key combinations
- Ignore accidental keystrokes
- Control the mouse pointer through the keyboard
- Provide a visual cue when the machine makes sounds

The Access Pack is the Windows equivalent of AccessDOS, and provides most of the same features and capabilities.

Microsoft's multimedia encyclopedia, Encarta, has a feature that may be useful to users with low vision. Each topic in Encarta can consist of text and multimedia elements. The text takes up

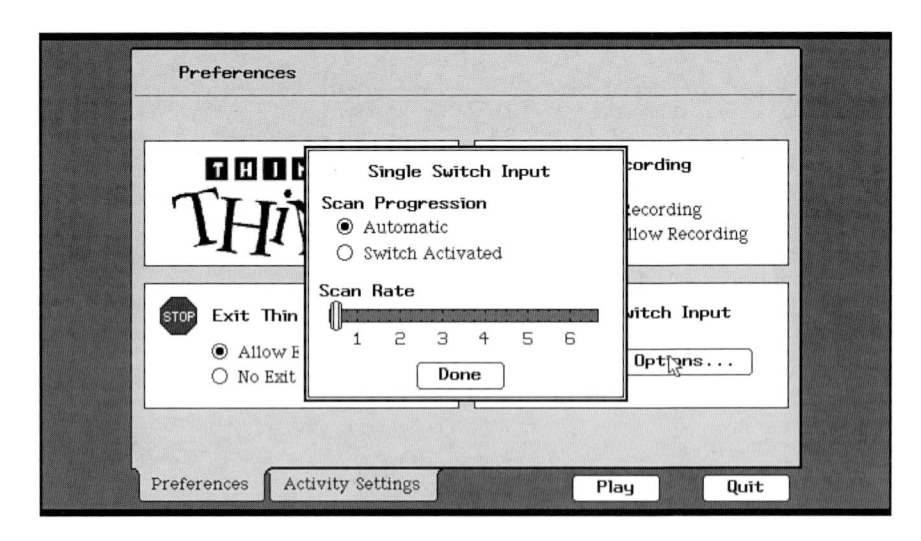

▲ *Edmark products contain single-switch input support.*

approximately the right two-thirds of the screen and is in an average-sized font. The program includes a Zoom Text feature, however, that increases the size of the text so that it occupies the full window, making it easier to read. Many of the photographs can also be zoomed, with similar results.

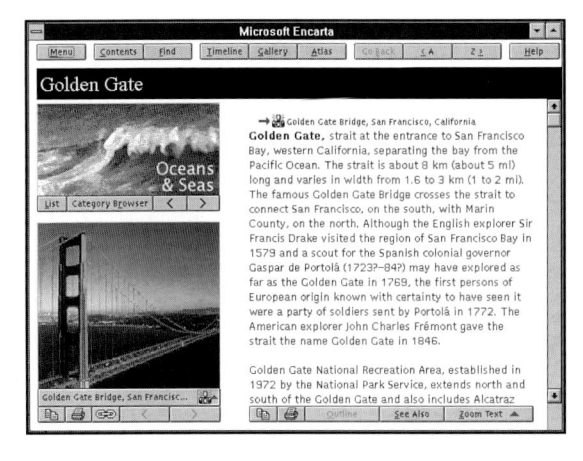

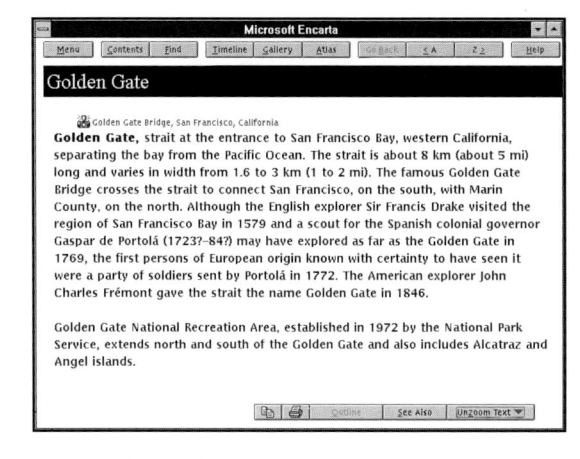

▲ *Zoomed text of the same Encarta topic.*

▲ *An Encarta topic.*

Chapter **3**

Drill-and-Practice Products

At one time, drill-and-practice products were the primary type of PC educational programs. They were nothing more than computerized versions of written tests, with the only real advantage being that the computer graded them and kept records for the instructor.

From this first stage, developers began to add rewards to the programs. If students passed the test, they would see a congratulatory message or get to play a game. Adding these incentives caused the students to work harder and longer at their drills in order to win the reward.

Current drill-and-practice products are more sophisticated descendants of those earlier programs. They contain music, sound effects, and colorful graphics, and they often present the problems in more varied forms. Even modern drill-and-practice products, however, still focus on repeated drills.

The following topics are discussed in this chapter:

- Common features of drill-and-practice products
- Unique features
- A walk-through of Math Blaster: In Search of Spot
- Available math products
- Other available products

Common Features

The current drill-and-practice programs do have some common features. First, like other edutainment products, they take advantage of the sound and video capabilities of newer PCs. The higher-end products, such as Sierra On-Line's Kid's Typing, often include digitized speech and animation.

The other common feature of these products is repeated drill. The presentation varies from product to product, but they all provide a large number of exercises or problems. Math programs in particular contain hundreds or thousands of problems to solve.

Unique Features

Publishers add various features to improve the value of their products and to make them stand out from the crowd. HyperGlot's Learn to Speak Spanish strengthens its teaching with digitized speech and full-motion video of actual people and places.

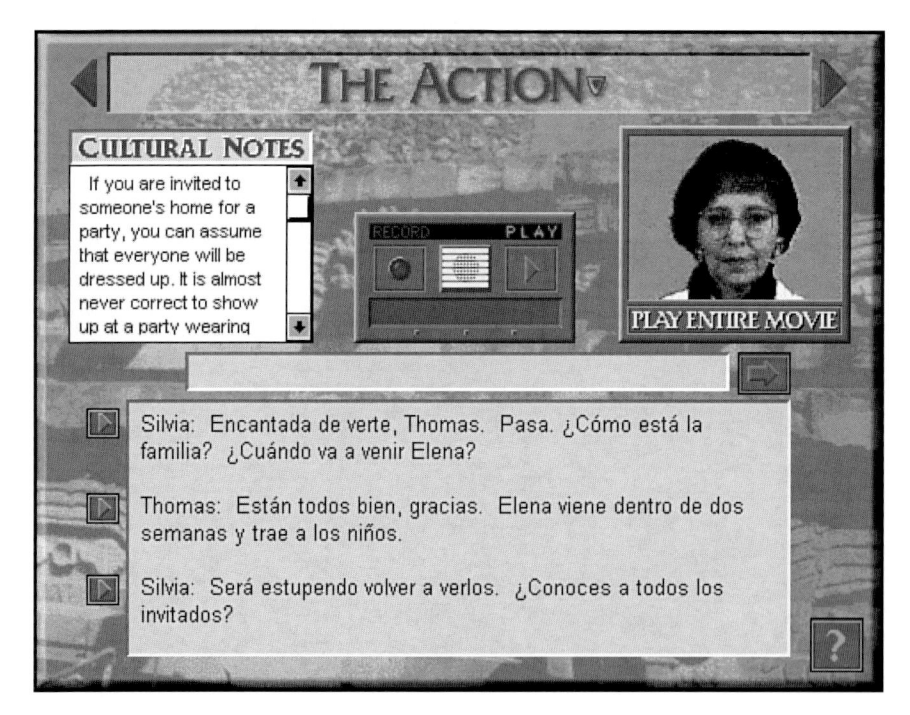

▲ *Digitized speech and full-motion video in Learn to Speak Spanish.*

Mental Math Games, from the Waterford Institute, contains problems related to 635 educational objectives in four categories. One of the categories prepares the user for standardized tests, such as the Stanford Achievement Test and the Iowa Test of Basic Skills. Davidson's Math Blaster: In Search of Spot covers nine subject areas with a total of more than 50,000 different problems!

Math Blaster comes with a Problem Editor. The editor enables the parent or child to change the problems and difficulty at each level of the game.

Mental Math Games does not include a separate editor, but it does have a utility that lets the player adjust the speed of the games to accommodate users with special needs. Another unique feature of this product is its selection of mental math tips. Tips appropriate to the objective the child is working on are available at any time.

Super Solvers OutNumbered!, from The Learning Company, keeps a lifetime score for you. As you accumulate points, you can move up through the Super Solver ranks—from Trainee all the way to Champion. Each rank brings new challenges, with more difficult game play and math problems.

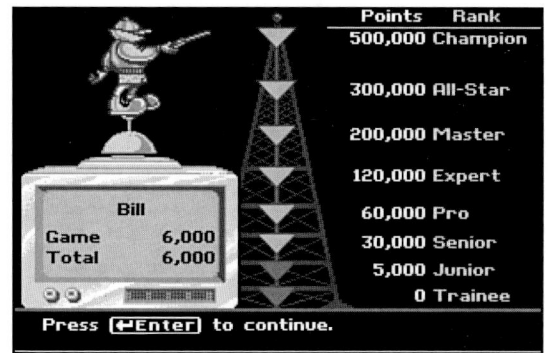

▲ *Super Solvers OutNumbered! keeps track of your score and rank from game to game and increases the difficulty as you advance.*

Using a Drill-and-Practice Product—Math Blaster: In Search of Spot

As you may know, Math Blaster is one of the best-selling series of edutainment programs available. It is also very much a drill-and-practice program. Some of the games in the latest episode, In Search of Spot, deviate from the standard "drill-first-and-then-play" format. Even so, it is a good example of a modern drill-and-practice program. The next few paragraphs take you on a short tour of Math Blaster: In Search of Spot.

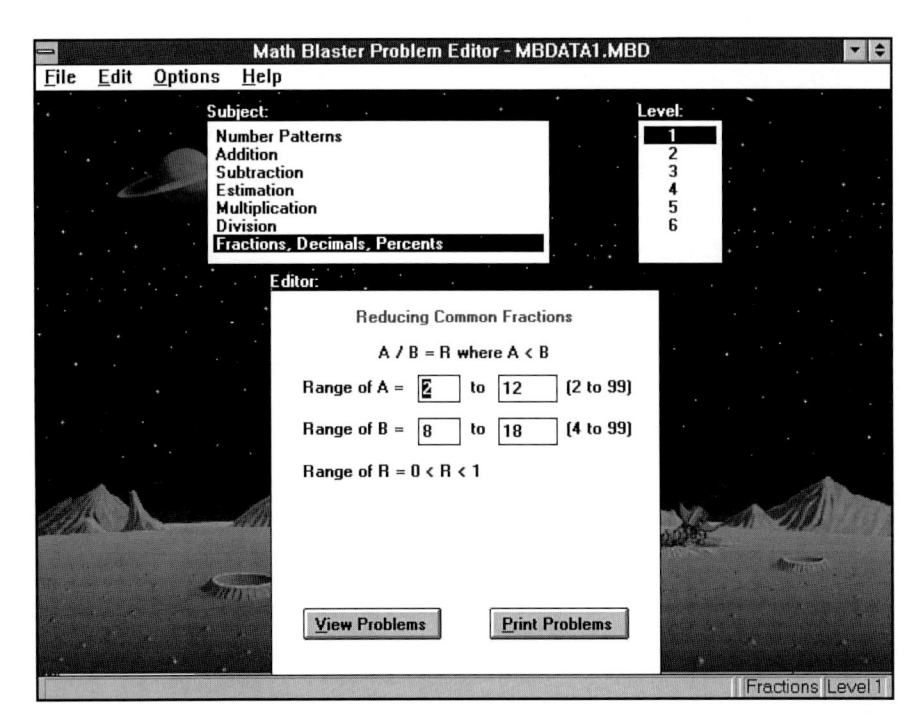

▲ *The Math Blaster Problem Editor.*

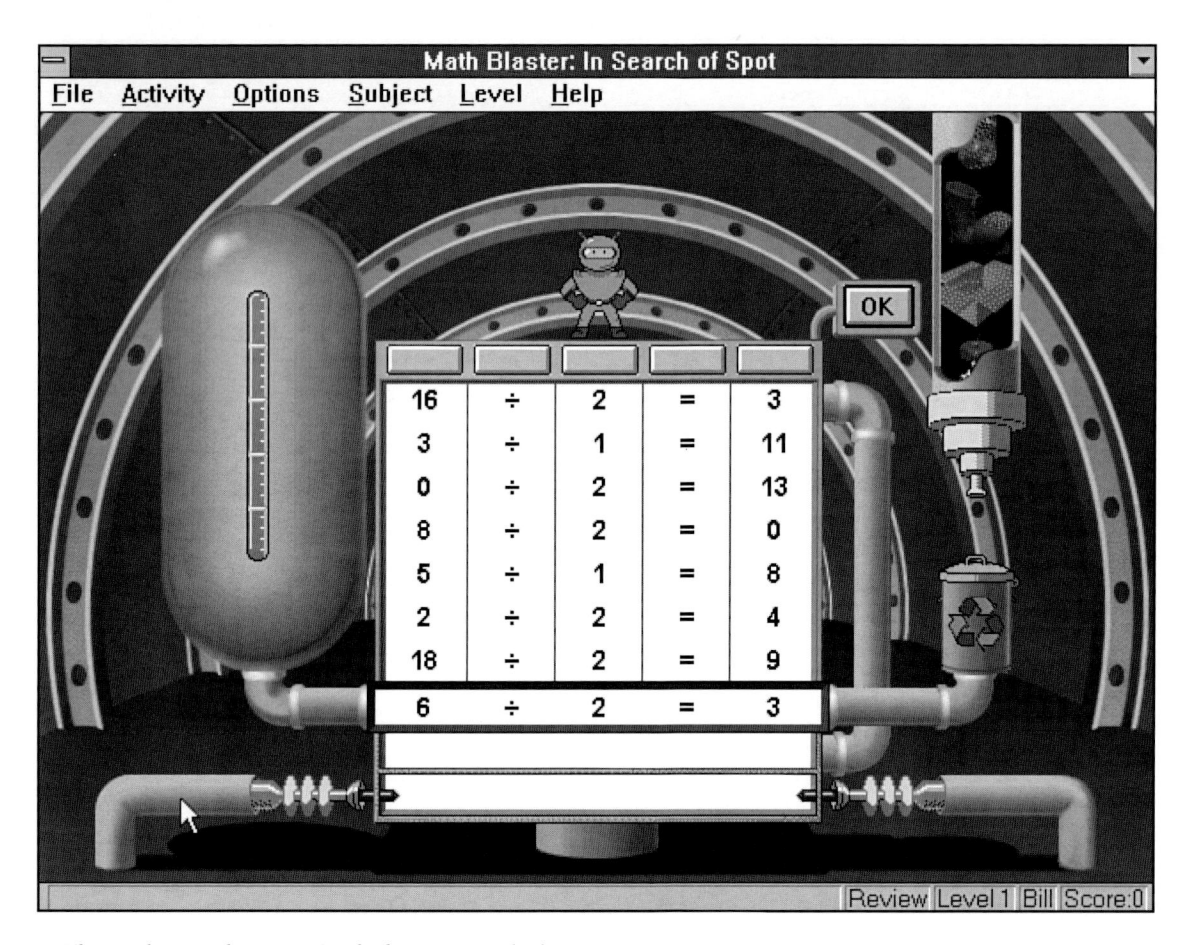

▲ *The Number Recycler game in Math Blaster: In Search of Spot.*

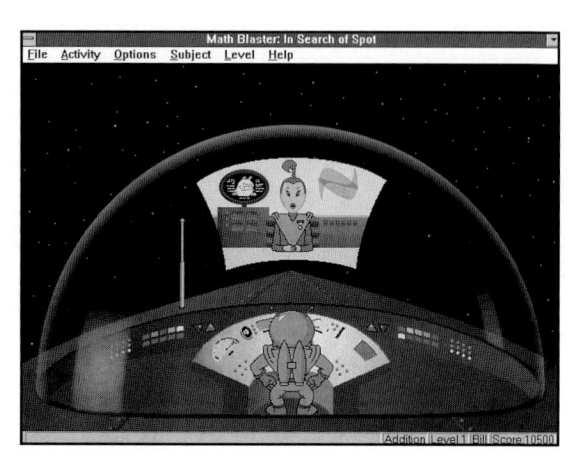

▲ *A transition between games.*

You can play the program two different ways: the first method is to play individual games only, and the second method is to play the entire mission. You can choose from nine subjects and four games. Trash Zapper requires you to solve problems before you get to play a shoot-the-trash game. Number Recycler requires you to create valid equations. Cave Runner and Math Blaster both integrate mental math skills into arcade-style games.

When you choose to go on a mission, you actually encounter each of the individual games. Successful completion of the stages of the mission is rewarded with fun transition segments.

When you complete an entire mission, your score is recorded, and you are rewarded with a certificate that you can print.

What's Available?

Drill-and-practice products seem to be declining in popularity. Most of the new edutainment products appear to be moving away from drill and practice and toward a more integrated approach. These new products tend to disguise the learning aspects of the program—combining them more subtly with the game aspects. Even products such as Math Blaster show some signs of this by mixing problem solving into the play of games, such as Cave Runner, instead of requiring you to solve the problem before you can play the game.

It is still quite possible to find drill-and-practice programs. For some subjects—in particular math, typing, and language skills—new drill-and-practice

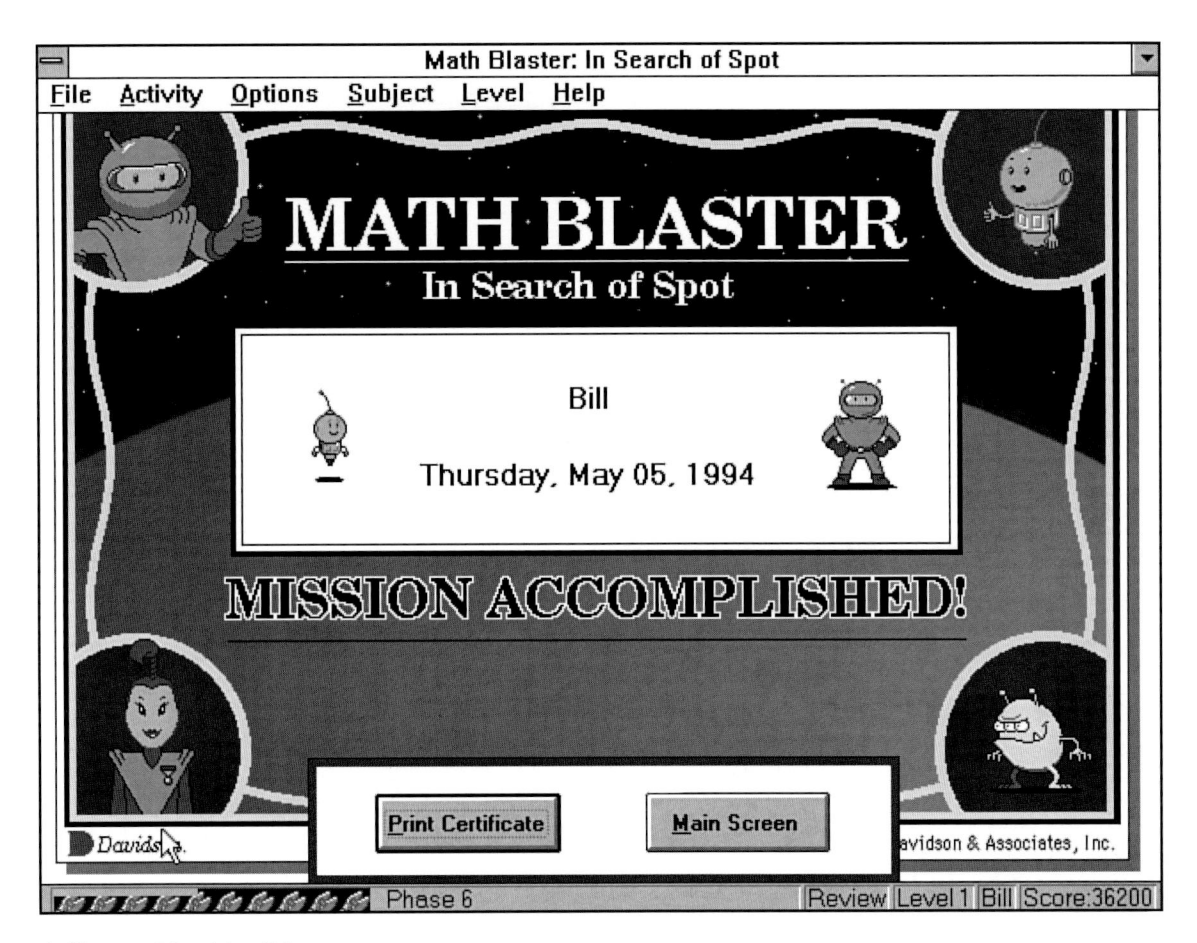

Drill-and-Practice Products   41

▲ *The reward for a job well done.*

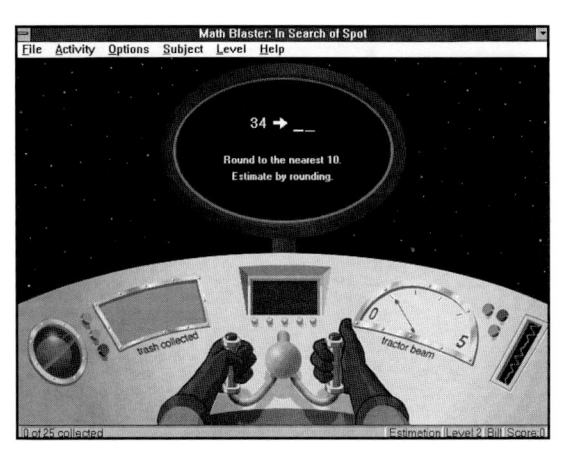

▲ *Testing estimation skills with the Trash Zapper game in Math Blaster: In Search of Spot.*

Math Blaster: In Search of Spot

Davidson's Math Blaster series has been the best-selling line of math programs in the world for more than ten years. DOS and Windows versions of this product (including a Windows CD-ROM) are available. Designed for children between the ages of 6 and 12, Math Blaster: In Search of Spot is the newest version of Math Blaster and won a Parent's Choice Award in 1993.

The program is designed to teach problem solving and mental math skills as part of an exciting adventure game. The program covers a broad array of subjects, including number patterns and estimation and, all told, can generate in excess of 50,000 different problems. Each of the nine different subjects can be run at any of six difficulty levels.

products continue to appear. The following sections describe some of the products that are available.

Math Programs

Math skills remain a popular subject for drill and practice, and four products are discussed in the following sections. Two of them are standard, full-price products from major publishers. One is a low-cost product, and one is free! I think that math drill-and-practice programs will tend to become the province of low-cost and shareware publishers because they are easier and less expensive to develop than other types of edutainment products.

Math Blaster: In Search of Spot features four games: Trash Zapper, Number Recycler, Cave Runner, and Math Blaster. The games contain colorful graphics, music, sound effects, animation, and digitized speech. Any of the subjects or difficulty levels can be used with any of the games.

The games can be played independently or as part of the larger quest to rescue Spot. All of the games in this package require the child to solve a set of math problems before going on to the next level or the next game.

In Search of Spot can track the performance of each child. The program records up to 100 scores in the Record Keeper. These scores can be reviewed by the child or the parent. The Goal Setter can automatically increase or decrease the difficulty of an activity, based on the child's success with that activity. If the child is having trouble with a particular subject, the program displays a relevant math tip.

In Search of Spot comes with a Problem Editor. The Editor enables you to create your own problem sets, which you define by specifying a range of numbers or by setting parameters. Custom problem sets can be saved, restored, viewed, and printed.

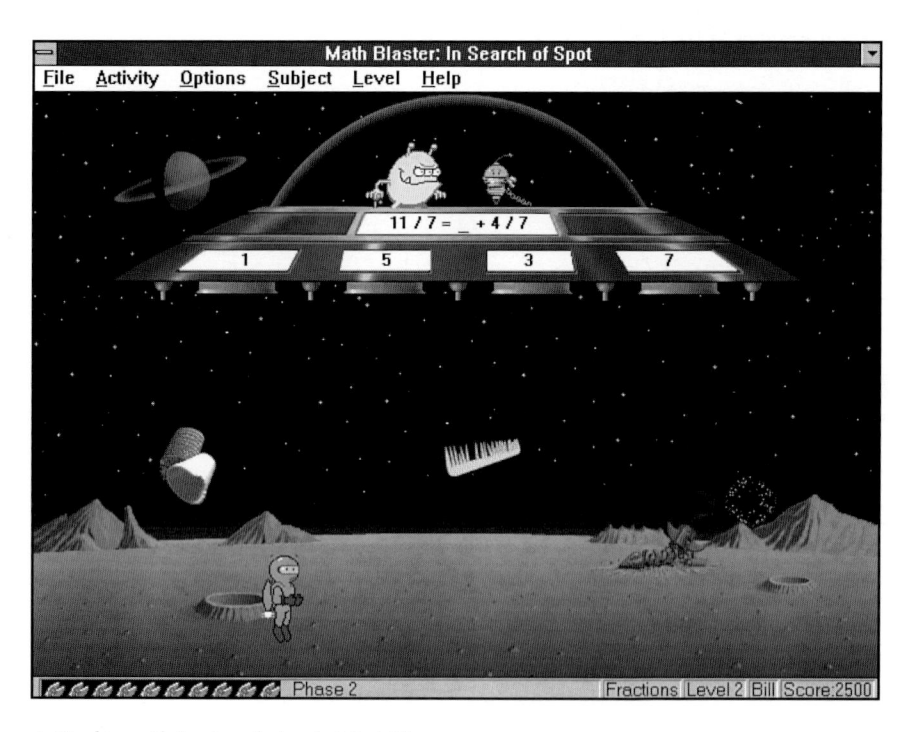

▲ *Working with fractions during the Math Blaster game.*

Required Equipment
- Windows 3.1
- 16 MHz 80386 processor (or higher)
- VGA video (or better)
- At least 4M of RAM
- Sound card with Windows driver
- Microsoft-compatible mouse

> **Note:** You can find out more about the items in the equipment lists by looking in Chapter 2 for general information, Chapter 10 for SVGA video cards and sound cards, Chapter 11 for CD-ROM drives, and Chapter 12 for Windows information.

Super Solvers OutNumbered!

Super Solvers OutNumbered! (SSO) is a DOS product from The Learning Company. Designed for children between the ages of 7 and 10, it is a drill-and-practice program disguised as an adventure game. In this game, the player must prevent Morty, the Master of Mischief, from taking over the Shady Glen Television Station (SGTV). The only way to stop him is to explore the TV station and find Morty's hideout before it is too late. The only way to do that is by solving math word problems and equations.

SSO can be played in two ways. The child can either try to stop the takeover of SGTV or use the Drill for Skill option. When playing to save SGTV, the child explores the TV station searching for clues. At the same time, Telly the robot

Drill-and-Practice Products

and LiveWire, Morty's henchmen, try to steal the child's energy and keep her from saving the station. Telly contains the secret code that is used to locate Morty. The child gets pieces of the code by zapping Telly with her zapper and solving a series of equations. The player discovers clues in the rooms of the TV station by solving math word problem challenges. Matching up the room clues with the secret code enables the child to guess which room Morty is hiding in.

When playing with the Drill for Skill option, the child doesn't deal with Morty or SGTV. Instead, she solves problems. The type and difficulty of the problems can be adjusted to suit the child. Drill for Skill is designed to enable the child to work on her weaker skills or to learn new ones without the distractions of the full game.

SSO has a number of other features, including New User Messages that provide advice and tips for Trainees just learning the game, and an on-screen calculator that can help the child calculate the answers to math challenges quickly and accurately. The problems can be customized so that their difficulty automatically increases as the child moves up through the ranks.

Required Equipment
- EGA or VGA video
- At least 640K of RAM
- DOS 3.3 or higher

(*Note:* A sound card is recommended.)

Mental Math Games

Mental Math Games was created by the Waterford Institute and is distributed by Broderbund. It is a DOS math program for children between the ages of 6 and 14. Mental Math Games contains seven different games that employ the usual spectrum of sound, graphics, and animation found in modern edutainment products. This product won a 1993 Parent's Choice Award.

Some of the games in the package are classic drill and practice, which require the child to solve a set of problems before being rewarded with an animated scene. Others, such as Moon Flight, integrate the problems into the function of the game.

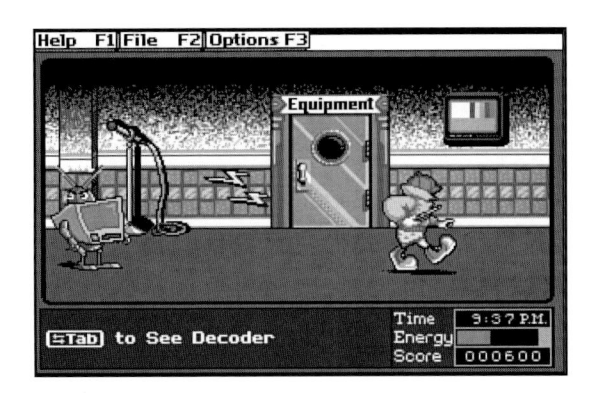

▲ *Exploring the Shady Glen Television Station while being pursued by Telly the robot is part of the fun in The Learning Company's Super Solvers OutNumbered!*

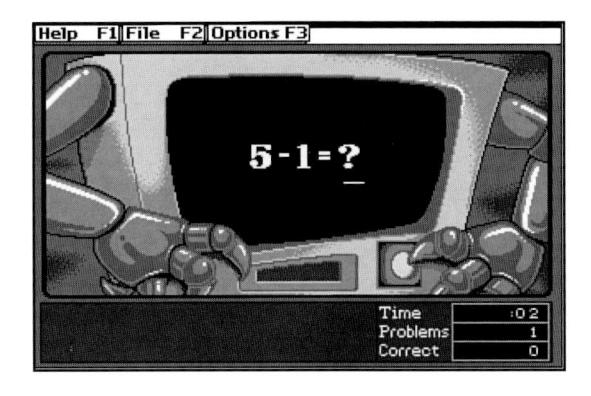

▲ *Super Solvers OutNumbered! has a Drill for Skill mode that lets the child solve problems without the distractions of the full game.*

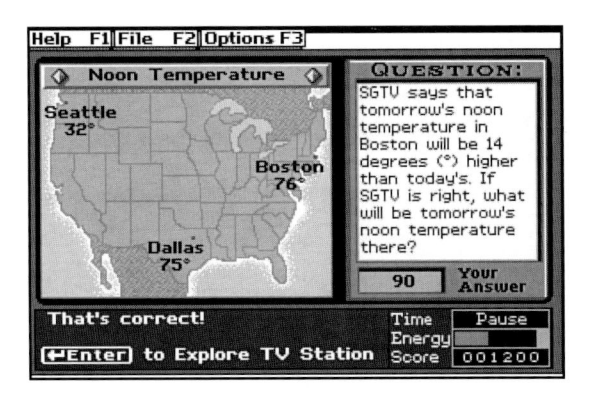

▲ *The child must solve math challenges like this one to win at Super Solvers OutNumbered!*

Moon Flight in Mental Math Games.

The program provides hundreds of objectives for the child to achieve. Achieving these objectives develops mental math skills in four different areas (sequences). One sequence is arithmetic skills involving addition, subtraction, multiplication, and division; another sequence covers skills required for certain standardized tests; the third sequence works with fractions, decimals, and percentages; and the final sequence requires the child to create valid equations (rather than solving existing ones) using addition, subtraction, multiplication, and division.

Each objective has a mastery time. The child must solve the problems in less than the mastery time in order for the program to give him credit for mastering that objective. The product comes with a utility that enables a parent to change the mastery time for all games simultaneously.

Note: The Time Limit Utility is specifically designed so that Mental Math Games can accommodate users with special needs.

With its various games and objectives, Mental Math Games could potentially be a confusing product to use. Waterford handles that problem, however, by providing a main menu screen that centralizes all the options.

The main menu provides access to all the games, objectives, and sequences. From this menu, the child can enter his name so that the program can record the child's progress. The child can also call up mental math tips, which provide help with the math and are keyed to the sequence and the objective currently selected.

Required Equipment
- VGA or MCGA video
- At least 640K of RAM
- DOS 3.1 or higher

(*Note:* A sound card and mouse are recommended.)

Math Flashcards

Math Flashcards is a DOS flash card program from Dinosoft. It is an old-style drill-and-practice program with some additional features. The program covers addition, subtraction, multiplication, and division; it also works with number and object matching, as well as the concept of odd and even numbers.

Math Flashcards tracks each player by name and records the player's scores for each section of the program. A Progress Report for the current player can be printed (but not viewed on-screen). The

▲ *The Mental Math Games main menu.*

▲ *Matching numbers and objects in Math Flashcards.*

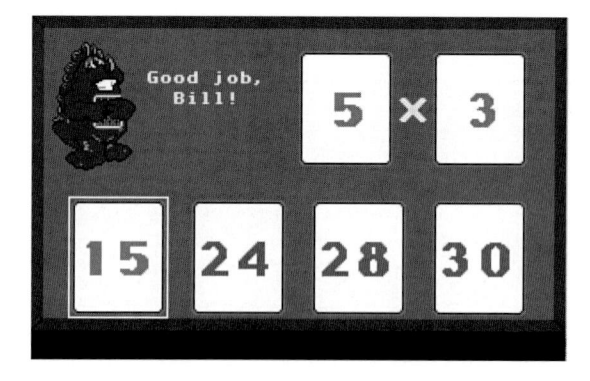

▲ *A message similar to this one appears when you solve a multiplication problem correctly in Math Flashcards.*

program can print worksheets that the player can use for practice away from the computer, and it can also print pictures of the Dinosoft dinosaurs that can be colored. A Parent's Page (actually many pages) provides information on each section of the program and offers suggestions on ways to use the program.

Required Equipment

EGA or better video. (*Note:* A sound card and printer are recommended.)

Beat the Bomb

Beat the Bomb is a timed addition drill program for DOS. It differs from the other products discussed here in that it is a freeware program. This means that you can keep Beat the Bomb without paying for it! First Magnitude, the publisher, hopes you like the freeware version of the program so much that you will invest a little money and purchase the enhanced version. The enhanced version includes the rest of the basic arithmetic operators, additional graphics, and more options.

> **Note:** Along with Beat the Bomb, the freeware version of another math product from First Magnitude—Math Sampler—is available in the Drill-and-Practice section of the *Edutainment Comes Alive!* CD-ROM.

Like other drill-and-practice products, Beat the Bomb uses graphics and sound effects to keep the child interested as he solves sets of equations. In addition to displaying the equation to be solved and the remaining time, the program provides a set of keys displaying possible answers.

The child must solve all the equations within the time limit. Besides the display of the time remaining, the program provides animated graphics, such as bombs, snails, and castles, that indicate how much time is left.

Beat the Bomb provides a Setup screen that enables the child or parent to change almost everything about how the program works. Some of the more useful options are the number of problems per test, the problem orientation (horizontal or vertical), and the location (in the equation) of the number being determined.

Required Equipment

- EGA video (or better)
- At least 512K of RAM
- DOS 2.1 or higher
- Microsoft-compatible mouse

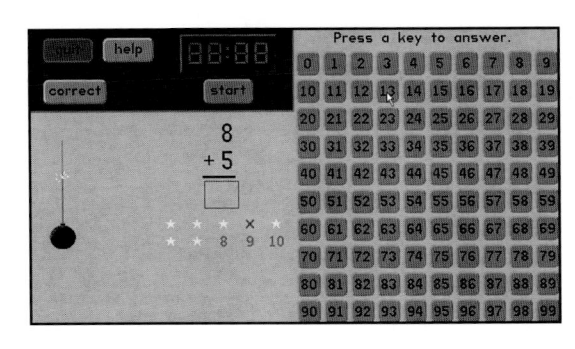

Doing addition in Beat the Bomb.

Other Subjects

Two other subjects lend themselves to the drill-and-practice approach: typing and language skills. In each case, a student must master a large number of individual items—keystrokes or words—and a great deal of practice is required. One product from each of these two categories is discussed in this section.

Kid's Typing

Kid's Typing is a Windows typing program for children between the ages of 7 and 10. Published by Sierra On-Line, the program is part of its Dream Team series of edutainment products. The Dream Team programs use talking, animated characters to teach the subject matter. In Kid's Typing, the character is Spooky, a friendly ghost with an odd sense of humor.

The program alternates hand-and-key-position drills with games that focus on speed, rhythm, and accuracy. The drills occur in the attic.

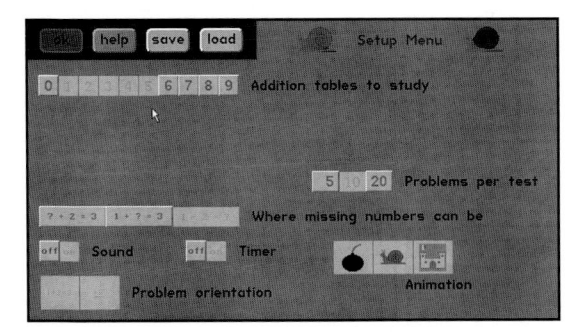

Configuring Beat the Bomb in the Setup menu.

The program automatically creates new drills based on the child's typing accuracy and speed.

The games take place in any of five rooms. Each game is designed to strengthen one of the child's weakest keystrokes. Playing a game in a room causes spooky things to happen. The faster the child types, the greater the effect on the room. In the kitchen, for example, the blender runs faster as the child types faster.

The final room in the house is the library. Reached from the attic, the library contains a bookcase full of interesting stories that a child can use to practice his typing. At the bottom of the bookcase is an encyclopedia set containing 26 books. One book is devoted to each letter of the alphabet. Choosing one of these books yields text that concentrates on that letter.

Kid's Typing records the child's statistics as each game or drill is completed. The statistics include the number of words per minute, the accuracy (percentage of characters typed correctly), the amount of time needed to complete the lesson, and more. One key statistic is the highest number of words per minute ever recorded by the child. The program can print a certificate for this session of Kid's Typing, and the certificate contains the child's name, the date, the current speed, and the accuracy percentage. The documentation provides suggestions for non-computer activities to reinforce what is learned on the PC and also includes a short ergonomics guide.

Required Equipment
- Windows 3.1
- 80386SX processor (or better)
- SVGA video card with 640 x 480, 256-color Windows driver
- At least 4M of RAM
- Mouse
- Sound card with Windows driver

Learn to Speak Spanish

Learn to Speak Spanish is a Windows language drill program on CD-ROM from HyperGlot. Designed for beginning and intermediate students, the lessons are based on real-life situations in Spanish-speaking countries. The CD-ROM combines full-motion video with recordings of nine native speakers of Spanish. The course consists of 30 chapters, and each chapter begins with an Introduction Screen.

The Introduction Screens contain a short movie that sets the scene for the chapter. All footage (except one shot of an aircraft leaving the airport in Tennessee) was shot in Mexico City to provide a visual cultural background for the chapter.

▲ *Practicing keyboard techniques in the attic in Kid's Typing.*

▲ *Typing for accuracy in the kitchen in Kid's Typing.*

▲ *Setting the scene in Learn to Speak Spanish.*

The background music further enhances the atmosphere.

From the Introduction Screen, the action moves to the Vocabulary Screen where new vocabulary words are introduced. The words are pronounced by the program, and then you can view a video clip that uses the words in context. One interesting feature of this product is its capability to record your pronunciation of words. After the program pronounces a vocabulary word, you can record that same word (if your PC has a sound card with a microphone). The program then plays back its own pronunciation of the word, followed by your pronunciation. This process can be repeated as many times as necessary until you get the pronunciation right. A Vocabulary Drill Screen tests your knowledge of the written and spoken forms of the vocabulary words.

The Story Screen uses the vocabulary words in normal Spanish speech. This screen helps with comprehension of spoken Spanish, speaking Spanish sentences, and pronunciation. A video clip of a native Spanish speaker enables you to see the words being spoken. As with the Vocabulary Screen, you can speak the sentences and compare the recording to the correct pronunciation. Other screens in the product include the Action Screen, where several speakers carry on a dialog, and the Listening Skills Screen that tests your understanding and provides writing practice.

Learn to Speak Spanish contains a large workbook, which includes vocabulary and grammar instruction as well as written tests. The CD-ROM

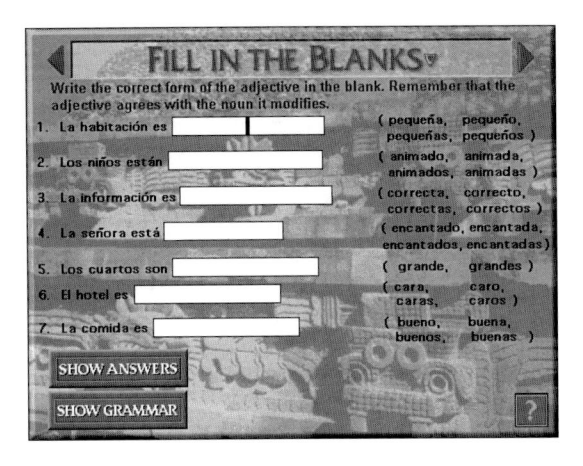

▲ *Fill in the Blanks—one of several types of drills.*

provides a set of Exercise Screens that test your grammar skills. The Exercise Screens come in several different forms, including Fill in the Blanks, Drag and Match, Word Jumble, and Communication Skills.

Required Equipment
- CD-ROM drive
- Windows 3.1
- 33 MHz 80386DX processor (or better)
- SVGA video card with 640 x 480, 256-color Windows driver
- 4M of RAM
- Sound card with Windows driver
- Microphone

Summary

This chapter discussed drill-and-practice programs—products that represent the evolution of one of the earliest forms of computerized educational software. Although the current crop of programs is much more sophisticated and fun than their predecessors, their origins as computer replacements for flash cards and worksheets are still visible.

Drill-and-practice programs remain a popular way to teach certain subjects, such as math and typing. Besides providing the intensive practice that these subjects require, the programs make monitoring the student's progress relatively easy. Some of these products track the child's performance and use that data to design problems that can strengthen the weakest skills.

Drill-and-practice products encourage learning by rewarding the user with fun and games in exchange for hard work. Another category of edutainment product also rewards the user—not with games, but with the form in which information is presented. This category is multimedia reference materials.

Multimedia reference materials use the power of multimedia PCs to make information itself more interesting. Although a paper encyclopedia can tell you all about lions, and may even contain a picture of one, a multimedia encyclopedia may have a video clip of a lion playing with its cubs—complete with a digitized soundtrack.

Encyclopedias are undoubtedly the best-known type of multimedia reference work and also one of the most fertile fields in edutainment. A huge number of titles, covering a vast range of subjects, is being created every year. Turn to Chapter 4 to learn more about multimedia reference materials.

Chapter 4

Multimedia Reference Materials

You may wonder what multimedia reference works are doing in a book on edutainment. They certainly have educational value, but do they have significant entertainment value? Aside from the fact that some people find browsing an encyclopedia fun, several additional aspects of these products make them fun to use.

One of the less enjoyable aspects of using traditional reference works is finding anything. If you know the topic you are looking for, it is just a matter of thumbing through the right volume until you find the appropriate reference. Now suppose that you find a reference to another article related to the one you are reading. You must mark your page, lay down this volume, pull down another volume, and start thumbing. Multimedia reference works eliminate these tedious search situations because they chase down all the references for you, often finding connections to subjects you would never even think of. They usually contain computerized bookmarks or other methods to keep track of every article you examine.

These features are part of why multimedia reference works can be easier and more pleasant to use than printed reference works, but that still doesn't make them fun. The real fun in these products comes from their multimedia nature.

Take the subject of space flight. A printed encyclopedia surely has a large article on the subject and even a few pictures (probably black and white). Look up the same subject in a multimedia encyclopedia, and you also see text and some pictures—but these pictures are in full color!

And text and pictures are only the beginning. Depending on the particular product, you may find audio tracks, such as Neil Armstrong's speech from the surface of the moon, animation, such as models of orbital dynamics, and even full-motion video clips, such as the launch of a space shuttle. These are the things that really make multimedia reference products fun!

Multimedia reference works include a wide variety of products besides encyclopedias. A partial list includes atlases, medical references, historical works, and guides to music and art. It is only a matter of time before most reference works will be available on CD-ROM.

This chapter lets you explore some of the diversity of the multimedia reference category and focuses on the three major multimedia encyclopedias. These products are extremely valuable, and every computer user should have one.

This chapter also introduces some of the other types of multimedia reference works now available. From weighty medical tomes to colorful explorations of the life and times of the dinosaurs, these works showcase some of the best products available and highlight the size and variety in the multimedia reference works category. The following topics are discussed in this chapter:

- Common featuress
- Unique features
- Using a multimedia encyclopedia: Encarta
- Some of the products that are available

Common Features

All multimedia reference works have a few characteristics in common, including the fact that they all are computerized reference works that use multimedia elements such as audio and video clips. Beyond these very general characteristics, it makes sense to look for common features among the various products. The following paragraphs describe some of the common features of the reference works included in this chapter.

The three major multimedia encyclopedias share a number of common features. They each contain the text of a major printed encyclopedia; they each include articles with photos, sound and video clips, and other multimedia elements; and they each include a timeline. The timelines enable you to see how events relate chronologically.

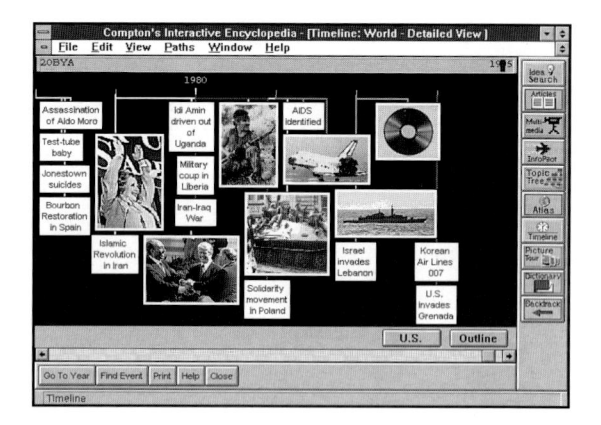

▲ *All three major multimedia encyclopedias have a timeline so that you can see how events relate chronologically.*

Multimedia Reference Materials 51

A common feature of many health-related products is an anatomy section. In this section, color images and video clips are included to provide all sorts of useful information about the human body.

The reference works dealing with prehistoric life feature the most spectacular creatures ever to walk the Earth: the dinosaurs. In particular, both contain animated movies of dinosaurs in action. While no one knows for sure exactly what dinosaurs looked like, or exactly how they hunted, the animation hints at what it must have been like to live with those incredible beasts.

Unique Features

With so many different types of products in the multimedia reference category, listing the unique features of each type would be impractical. A more feasible method is to examine some of this category's unique features.

Multimedia encyclopedias contain tremendous amounts of information; the more ways the user has to access and explore this information, the more useful the product. The InfoPilot feature in Compton's Interactive Encyclopedia shows you how one topic relates to others.

The Knowledge Explorer in the New Grolier Multimedia Encyclopedia provides a narrated overview of subjects.

Microsoft has added the game MindMaze to its Encarta encyclopedia. The player chooses an area of interest. From this area, the game asks the player questions based on topics found in the encyclopedia. When the player answers incorrectly, the game offers the chance to view the relevant topic.

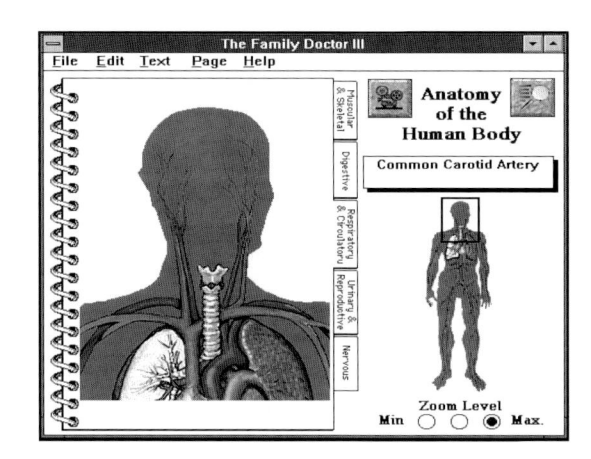

▲ An anatomy section is a common feature of health-related reference works.

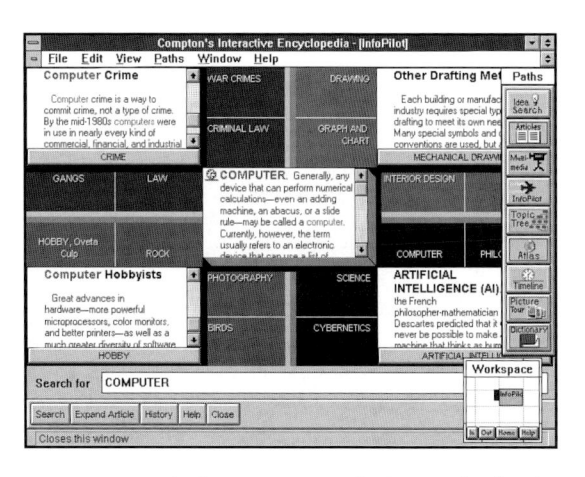

▲ Compton's InfoPilot creates a network of topics related to the original topic.

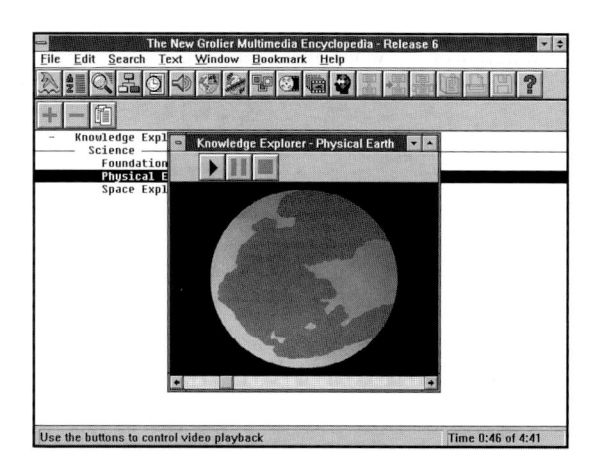

▲ Grolier's Knowledge Explorer gives narrated, multimedia overviews for a number of subjects.

▲ Answering questions based on Encarta topics is the only way to successfully navigate MindMaze.

Using a Multimedia Encyclopedia: Encarta

Here is a real-world example of how a multimedia encyclopedia can help you answer life's everyday puzzles. My wife and I decided to go bicycle riding in Arizona's Usery Mountain Park. While we were there, we encountered a huge eagle. It flew near us for several minutes, and at one point it passed directly overhead—probably no more than 50 feet off the ground. The bird's wing span had to be at least six feet! Needless to say, we were very excited, and we resolved to find out more about the creature when we returned home.

When we arrived home, we fired up Encarta and began our search. We first had to decide how to look for more information. Encarta, like Compton's and Grolier's, has multiple ways to search. Convinced that any bird the size of the one we saw had to have been an eagle, we decided to use Encarta's Find Wizard.

The Find Wizard generates information searches based on questions it asks you. Because we were sure that we were looking for an eagle, we told the Wizard that we were looking for the word *eagle*. We also told it that we were looking for references to the eagle only in the Life Science interest area. I then clicked on the Find button and let Encarta run the search.

As a result of the search, Encarta displayed a window with a list of 15 topics in the Life Science area that contained the word *eagle*. When I double-clicked *Eagle* in the list, the program displayed the article on that topic.

From the pictures and descriptions in the article, we concluded that what we saw was a Golden Eagle. Encountering such a majestic creature in the wild is something we will always remember. Learning more about the bird afterward enhanced the experience.

▲ *Encarta's opening screen offers several paths and options.*

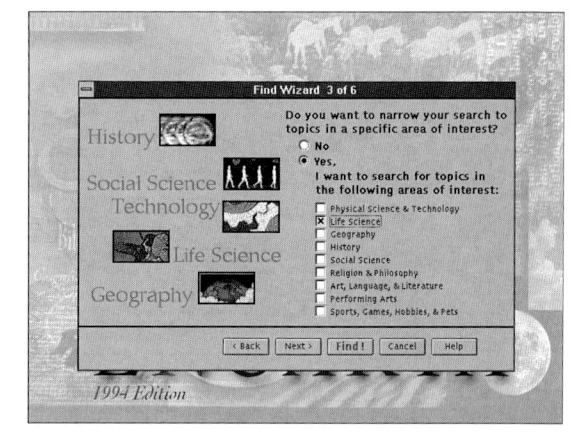

▲ *Narrowing a search by limiting the area of interest.*

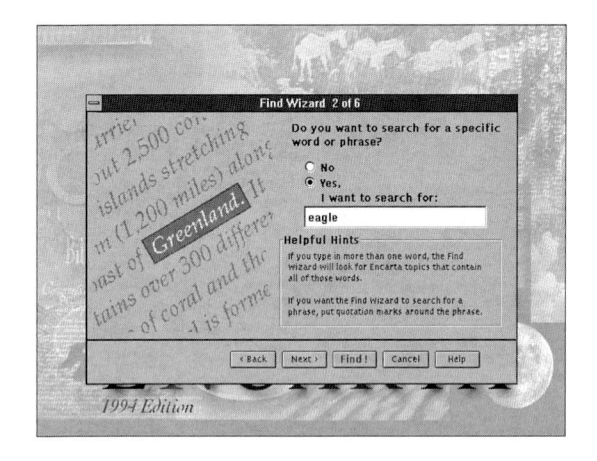

▲ *Using the Find Wizard to search for a particular word in Encarta.*

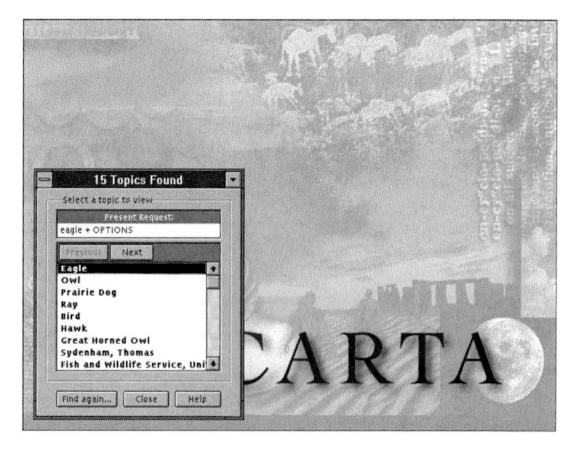

▲ *The results of a search show up in a box like this one.*

Multimedia Reference Materials

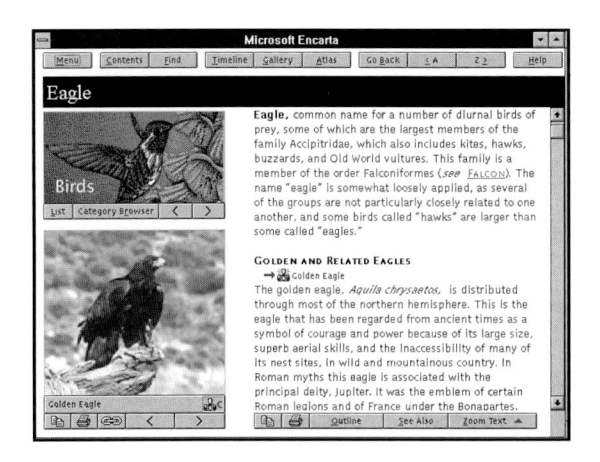

▲ *The Eagle article in Encarta.*

What's Available?

Literally hundreds of multimedia reference materials are available. They cover a huge range, from encyclopedias and other "traditional" reference works, to health and medical works, history, and more. Most likely, multimedia reference works are available for any major subject you can name.

To give you an idea of the diversity and capability of the available products, I have included a few works from each of several different subject areas, including some of the best-known multimedia reference products.

Multimedia Encyclopedias

When I think about multimedia reference materials, I immediately think of the three big encyclopedias: Compton's Interactive Encyclopedia, the New Grolier Multimedia Encyclopedia, and Microsoft Encarta. Each of these products puts an entire encyclopedia set—and more—on one CD-ROM. All the text and graphics of the printed versions are there, plus sound, music, animation, and videos that bring the information to life.

Besides including more information than their printed counterparts, each program contains new and powerful tools for searching and using this information. These multimedia encyclopedias are spectacular examples of how computers can make information more useful. How I wish I had had one when I was in school!

The following sections provide more detail about each of these three encyclopedias. You should realize that with products like the encyclopedias—even more than with most other edutainment products—I can only touch on some of the high points. I hope that the information you find here, though limited, encourages you to check out these products yourself.

Compton's Interactive Encyclopedia

Compton's Interactive Encyclopedia (Compton's) is a Windows CD-ROM published by Compton's New Media. Compton's Interactive Encyclopedia is, of course, based on the 26-volume *Compton's Encyclopedia*. With nine different ways to access the information contained in the over 33,000 articles on the disc, Compton's is designed to suit every learning style.

The encyclopedia contains more than 200 multimedia clips that accompany and illustrate its entries. The clips include full-motion videos, animation, sounds, and slide shows. In addition, Compton's has over 7,000 images on the disc.

Some articles in Compton's have links to other articles. Icons in an article's left margin indicate when links to other articles are available, as well as indicating when multimedia clips or photographs accompany the text. Clicking a word in an article triggers a search for that word in the accompanying dictionary and thesaurus.

As in the other major encyclopedias, Compton's has a timeline feature: in fact, it actually has two timelines: one for U.S. history and one for world history. Each timeline can be displayed in Outline or Detailed view. When you use the Detailed view, the timelines contain event boxes and pictures of people or events.

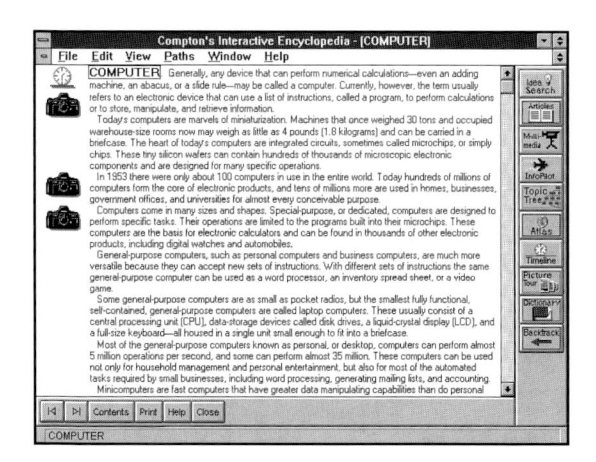

▲ *The computer article in Compton's Interactive Encyclopedia contains links to other articles and multimedia elements.*

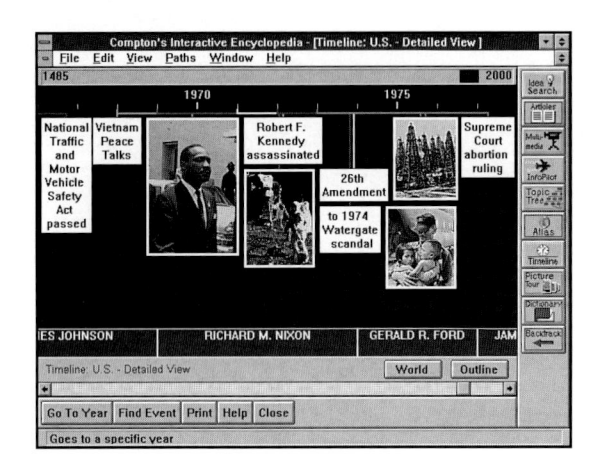

▲ *Compton's Interactive Encyclopedia has two multilevel timelines with graphical details.*

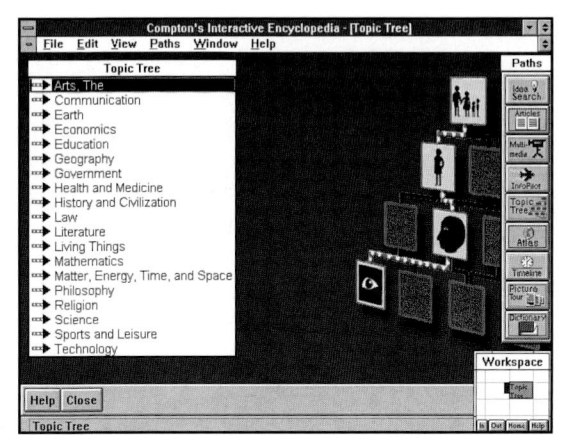

▲ *Many of the articles in Compton's Interactive Encyclopedia are organized into topics and subtopics by the Topic Tree.*

Another interesting approach to the acquisition and display of information is the Topic Tree. Selecting Topic Tree from the path bar (along the right side of the window) causes the program to organize information by topics. When you choose a topic in the tree, its subtopics are listed. Choosing one of these subtopics causes its subtopics to appear, and so on. Double-clicking any of these topics or subtopics causes the corresponding encyclopedia article to appear. By creating these paths, Compton's gives you new ways to look at information.

You can use InfoPilot to expand your research to topics related to the current topic. The InfoPilot (refer again to the figure showing the InfoPilot earlier in the chapter) displays the current article, known as the *focus article*, at the same time it displays other related articles. Between these articles are the titles of still other related articles.

This graphical way of presenting the articles makes it easier to handle related material.

The Compton's Interactive Encyclopedia is more than just an encyclopedia. Integrated into the program are other reference tools, such as a dictionary, thesaurus, and atlas. To make room for all the things you can do in Compton's, the program has a feature called the Virtual Workspace. The Workspace simulates a gigantic Windows desktop, where you can spread out your work and still keep everything just a few mouse clicks away. The Workspace and the items spread across it can be saved as a layout. This enables you to return to the point at which you stopped, so you don't have to manually restore everything.

Required Equipment

- CD-ROM drive
- DOS 3.1 or higher
- Windows 3.1
- 16 MHz 80386SX processor (or better)
- SVGA video card with 640 x 480, 256-color Windows driver
- At least 4M of RAM
- Sound card with Windows driver
- Mouse
- MSCDEX 2.2 or higher

(*Note:* A printer is optional.)

Note: MSCDEX 2.2 is version 2.2 of the Microsoft CD-ROM Extensions for DOS. MSCDEX enables DOS to talk to CD-ROM drives. (MSCDEX is explained in more detail in Chapter 11.)

You can find out more about the other items in this equipment list by looking in Chapter 2 for general informaion, Chapter 10 for SVGA video cards and sound cards, Chapter 11 for CD-ROM drives, and Chapter 12 for Windows information.

The New Grolier Multimedia Encyclopedia

The New Grolier Multimedia Encyclopedia (Grolier) is a Windows CD-ROM published by Grolier Electronic Publishing. It is based on the 21-volume *Academic American Encyclopedia* and contains 33,000 articles. The product is designed to be an unparalleled resource for serious and effective research.

Articles in Grolier consist of the text of the article and an icon bar across the top of the article window. The icon bar indicates the media clips or other special features associated with the article. These features can include photos, animation, movies, and sounds (a set of indexes, accessible from the main toolbar, lets you have more direct access to any of these items). If a word or phrase in the text has its own article in the encyclopedia, it is shown in all capital letters. Double-clicking such a word or phrase brings that article to the screen.

One of the interesting features in Grolier is the Multimedia Maps. These maps are animated and enable you to watch events such as the migrations of prehistoric man or the rise and fall of the Roman Empire.

The Knowledge Explorer contains audio-visual essays on a variety of subjects. These essays consist of narrated collections of images related to the subject, as well as a list of cross-references for further research.

The Timeline in Grolier begins at 40,000 B.C.—the dawn of human prehistory—and is totally text-based. When you double-click an event shown in the Timeline, the program displays a list of relevant articles. If you type a date while the Timeline is displayed, the program takes you to the Timeline event closest to that date.

I have to say that this product gave me some problems. The first problem was an error message that popped up frequently and stated that an image was in an inappropriate format. I resolved this problem by calling the technical support line and having a technician walk me through the modification of an initialization file. Modifying the file took care of the error message.

The second problem occurred whenever I tried to use one of the Multimedia Maps. Whenever the animation reached a particular spot in the map of the Gulf War, it would halt with a `General Protection Fault` error. This problem is fixed in the newest revision of the product, release 6.04. The technical staff at Grolier was courteous and helpful when helping me work through these problems and replaced my disc with the latest version.

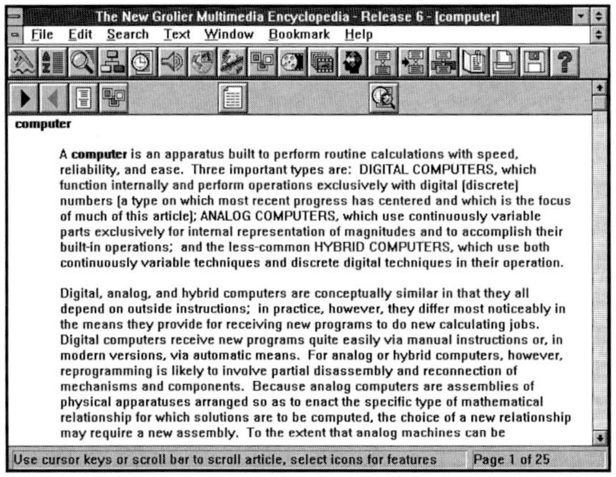

▲ *The computer article in the* New Grolier Multimedia Encyclopedia.

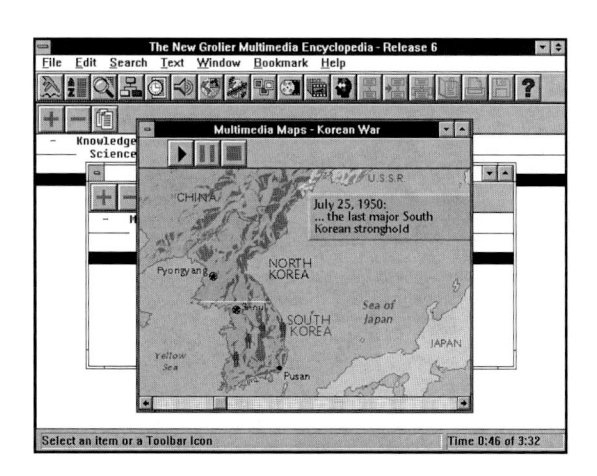

▲ *Multimedia Maps places historical events in a broader perspective in the* New Grolier Multimedia Encyclopedia.

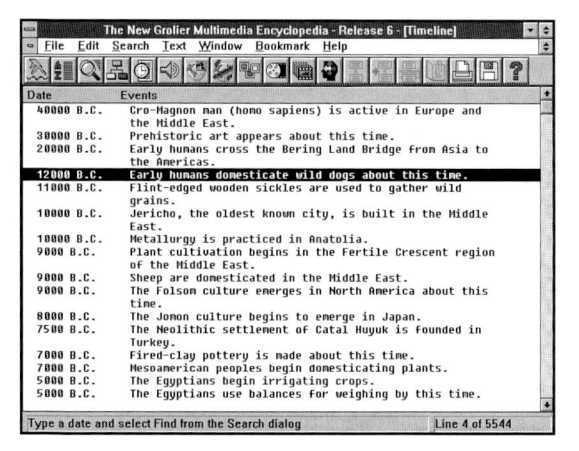

▲ *The text-based Timeline in the* New Grolier Multimedia Encyclopedia.

Required Equipment

- CD-ROM drive
- DOS 3.3 or higher
- Windows 3.1
- 80386SX processor (or better)
- VGA video (SVGA recommended)
- At least 4M of RAM
- Sound card with Windows driver
- Mouse
- MSCDEX 2.21 or higher

(*Note:* A printer is optional.)

Microsoft Encarta

Microsoft Encarta (Encarta) is a Windows CD-ROM encyclopedia based on the 29-volume *Funk & Wagnalls Encyclopedia*. In addition to the information contained in *Funk & Wagnalls*, Encarta adds more than 1,000 articles, hours of sound, language samples, and much more. The program aims to take your family on a never-ending learning journey.

Encarta is divided into three main parts: the Encyclopedia, the Atlas, and the Timeline. Each part provides a different way to look at the information stored in the program's database, but they all eventually lead to an article's main window.

Encarta contains more than 25,000 topics, and each topic includes articles with associated sounds, images, maps, or charts. The maps, sounds, and so on are called *gallery items*. All topics appear on-screen in the same basic form. The upper-left side of the main window contains a Category frame. Topics in Encarta are grouped into 93 different categories. The Article frame is on the right side of the window and contains the text of the article for the current topic. Underlined text in the article serves as *hypertext links*, which, when clicked, take you to that topic. Icons in the article are linked to the article's gallery items. The Gallery frame is beneath the Category frame and provides a place for the gallery items associated with the article to be displayed.

In an article's main window, you also have the option of displaying an outline of the current article, copying it to the Windows Clipboard, and printing it. You can use the See Also button to display a list of related topics, and you can use the Zoom Text button to enlarge the text of the article (as well as some of the gallery items) so that they are easier to see or read.

▲ *The computer topic in Microsoft Encarta.*

You can use the Gallery Browser to view all of the gallery items included in Encarta. You can access the items in a number of different ways, based on a number of different criteria. Any item can be printed or copied to the Clipboard, and a slide show can display every image, audio clip, animation, chart, table, and map in the package! Just click the Gallery button in the main button bar to start browsing.

The Atlas helps you explore the world. It can display any part of the world, and can zoom in to examine particular features. The topic that deals with the current area can be called up, or sights and sounds from that location can be displayed. The program also can pronounce the name of the area, print information about it, and copy that information to the Clipboard.

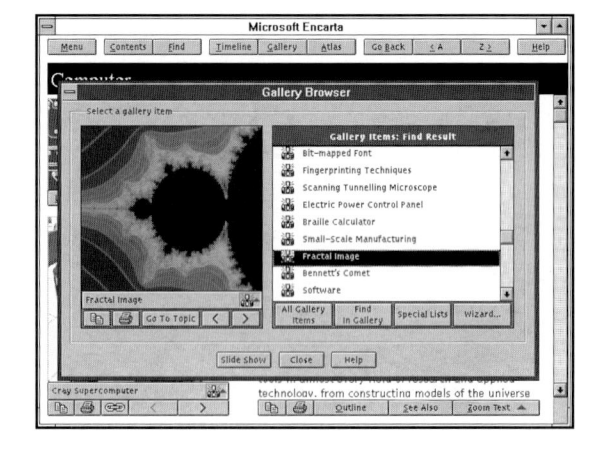

▲ *All of Encarta's gallery items are available through the Gallery Browser.*

The Timeline is illustrated and shows how epochs, civilizations, and events are related. When you click text or an image in the Timeline, the appropriate topic is displayed. The Find an Event button lets you search the Timeline by date or by the name of the event you are interested in.

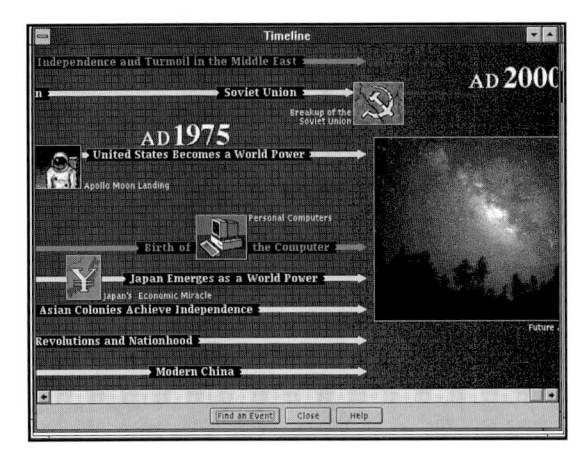

▲ *Encarta's illustrated Timeline.*

Encarta even has Wizards. The Find and Gallery Wizards are special dialog boxes that guide you through a search. The Wizards make it easy to limit searches by area of interest, type of item, and other important criteria.

Required Equipment

- CD-ROM drive
- DOS 3.1 or higher
- Windows 3.1
- 80386SX processor (or better)
- VGA video (SVGA recommended)
- At least 4M of RAM
- Sound card with Windows driver
- Mouse
- MSCDEX 2.21 or higher

(*Note:* A printer is optional.)

Other "Traditional" Reference Works

Encyclopedias are not the only "traditional" reference works to have found their way onto CD-ROM. Almanacs, dictionaries, and atlases are some of the others that are now available as multimedia reference works. Two of these "traditional" products are covered in this section.

20th Century Video Almanac

The 20th Century Video Almanac (Video Almanac) is a five-disc CD-ROM reference work from The Software Toolworks. Running under DOS, this package contains thousands of photos, hundreds of video clips, and hundreds of thousands of words of text about the 20th century.

The first CD-ROM in the package provides a general overview of the century. It contains stills and video footage from such events as the Normandy invasion, John F. Kennedy's inauguration, and the first moon landing.

The other four CD-ROMs take a more in-depth look at the century. Each focuses on a special topic: Sports, Politics, War & Disaster, Science & Technology, and People.

All the discs have the same basic form, and all the text and images on each disc are divided into four sections: Timeline, On This Day, Where in the World?, and Library. As with the encyclopedias discussed earlier, providing different approaches to the information on the discs lets you access the data in the manner most appropriate for the current task.

Timeline lets you explore the events chronologically. You can step through the Timeline frame by frame, or skip forward and backward by decades. An image from the currently selected event is always visible in the center of the screen, and you can click the file cabinet next to the image to display the article associated with the event.

The On This Day section of the package lets you pick any day of the year and see the events that occurred on that day. You select events using a scrollable list of small images, and when you point at one of these images, a one-line description of the image is displayed. Clicking an image causes it to be displayed full size.

The Where in the World? feature lets you select a geographical location and display all the events that occurred in that location.

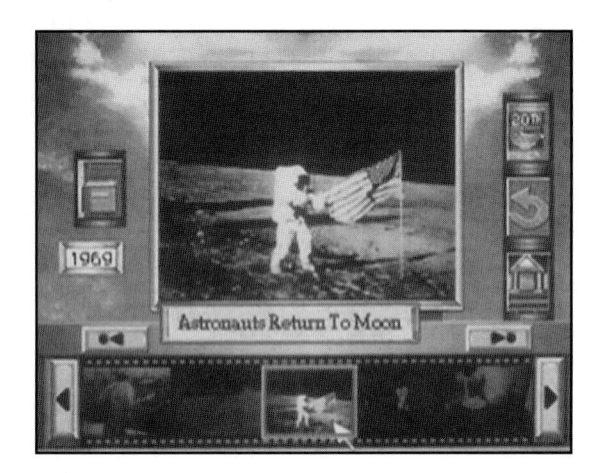

▲ *The Video Almanac's Timeline lets you explore the 20th century chronologically. (Courtesy of The Software Toolworks)*

▲ *Articles are associated with every event in the Video Almanac and provide varying amounts of background information. (Courtesy of The Software Toolworks)*

▲ *Using the On This Day feature in the Video Almanac. (Courtesy of The Software Toolworks)*

Required Equipment

- CD-ROM drive
- DOS 5.0 or higher
- 16 MHz 80386SX processor (or better; 33 MHz 80386DX or better, recommended)
- VESA-compliant SVGA video card with 640 x 480, 256-color mode
- At least 1M of RAM with at least 580K free
- Sound card
- MSCDEX 2.2 or higher

(*Note:* A mouse is recommended.)

Microsoft Bookshelf '94

The 1994 edition of Microsoft Bookshelf (Bookshelf '94) is a CD-ROM multimedia reference set for Windows. It includes seven complete reference books and adds multimedia capabilities to them. This product turns a PC into a general-purpose reference library, replacing an entire shelf full of books.

The program contains updated versions of these best-selling reference works: *The American Heritage Dictionary*, *The Original Roget's Thesaurus*, *The Columbia Dictionary of Quotations*, *The Concise Columbia Encyclopedia*, *Hammond Intermediate World Atlas*, *The People's Chronology*, and *The World Almanac and Book of Facts 1994*. You can access these books by clicking the Bookshelf '94 icon in the appropriate program group or you can reach them from within any application by using the QuickShelf feature.

QuickShelf places a floating toolbar on the screen, thereby making Bookshelf '94 available at the click of a button. The toolbar consists of a variable number of buttons, located at the top of your Windows display, near the left edge. The buttons represent the books in Bookshelf '94. When you click a button, QuickShelf opens the corresponding book. If you highlight a word in any program

Multimedia Reference Materials

and then click a toolbar button, QuickShelf looks for the word in the Table of Contents of the book. If you click on a button with a magnifying glass, QuickShelf does a full text search for the word.

Bookshelf '94 is full of useful features. Four book tabs (the Contents Tab, Find Tab, Gallery Tab, and Back List Tab) help you search for information in various ways. When you specify a word, the Contents Tab searches for the word in the Table of Contents of the selected book; the Find Tab searches for the word in the full text of the selected book (or books); the Gallery Tab lets you search all the articles that have multimedia elements (you simply choose the type of media you are interested in and then browse the displayed list); and the Back List Tab displays a list of the articles you have examined since you opened Bookshelf '94. (You can open a particular article again by clicking the article in the list.)

Bookshelf '94 makes good use of pointing and clicking. Clicking the right mouse button on a word in an article opens a menu of choices. You can open the dictionary to get a definition of the word, or you can search for it in any of the seven books. Clicking the left mouse button on a hypertext link opens the article that goes with that link. Clicking a figure or illustration triggers any multimedia features that figure might contain.

Bookshelf '94 contains other features that make it easy to use. For example, you can add notes to any article in any book. These notes can also serve as bookmarks, because every note is included in the Note list (which you reach through the Edit menu). You can also copy text, pictures, and audio from a particular article to the Windows Clipboard and use these items later in documents and reports, or you can simply print the entire article. If you use Microsoft Word, you can copy directly into a Word document, bypassing the Clipboard completely. If you use Windows, you will want to own Bookshelf '94.

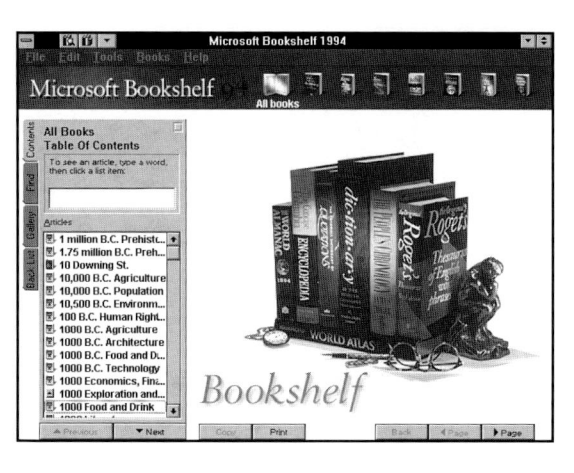

▲ *Microsoft Bookshelf '94 replaces an entire shelf of reference works.*

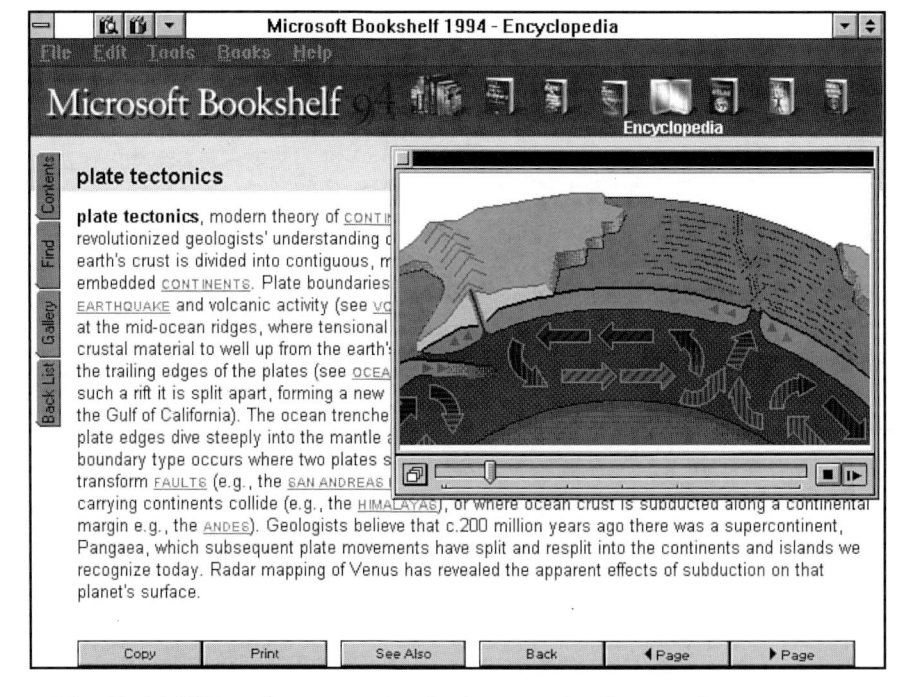

▲ *Many Bookshelf '94 articles contain multimedia elements, such as this narrated animation.*

Required Equipment
- CD-ROM drive
- Windows 3.1
- DOS 3.1 or later
- 25 MHz 80386SX processor (or better)
- VGA video (SVGA with 640 x 480, 256-color Windows driver recommended)
- At least 4M of RAM
- Sound card with Windows driver
- Mouse

Health and the Human Body

Health and the human body are popular subjects for conversion to CD-ROM. Multimedia gives these products some exciting features, such as the capability to display animation of joints flexing or the heart beating. Also exciting for a field filled with unusual-looking words is the capability of some programs to pronounce the words.

BodyWorks 3.0, CD-ROM Version

The BodyWorks 3.0 CD-ROM (BodyWorks) is a Windows anatomy product published by the Software Marketing Corporation; it is an enhanced version of the non-CD-ROM product that has been available for some time. BodyWorks is designed to let you explore the systems and structures of the ultimate machine—the human body.

BodyWorks contains a large database of text and graphics for every function, structure, and system in the body. The graphics and text appear together on a screen divided into four areas. The picture view box contains the current image. The item list is to the right of the picture view box and contains a list of topics that is relevant to the current image. Clicking a word in the item list causes a human narrator to give the proper pronunciation of the selected item. This is a very useful feature in a subject filled with words like *iliohypogastric*, *coccyx*, and *gastrocnemius*. A text box below the item list contains the text for the selected item. A set of control buttons runs across the top of the screen and enables you to choose new topics.

Highlighted words in the text represent hypertext links. Some links bring up a glossary that defines the selected word or phrase. Other links access additional information about the highlighted word. Sometimes there are multiple related items, and the program displays a list for the user to choose from.

A number of other features in the program make BodyWorks even more useful: detailed animation and videos show the complex functions of the body; magnified views and cutaways yield clearer, more revealing views of different systems; a *smart search* feature can help you find a particular subject, even if you aren't sure how to spell it; three-dimensional rotating views of many body tissues and structures enable you to examine these items from different perspectives.

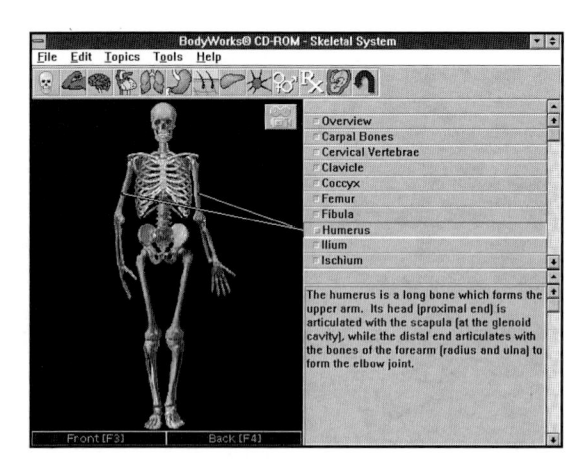

▲ *Learning about the anatomy of the human body is easy with the BodyWorks 3.0 CD-ROM.*

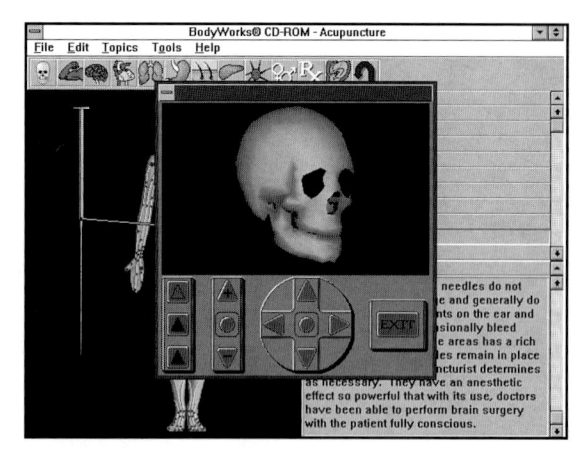

▲ *The BodyWorks 3.0 CD-ROM lets you use 3-D rotating views to explore body structures.*

Multimedia Reference Materials

BodyWorks includes features that can assist in learning and research. The program contains a set of lessons covering many parts of the body, and quizzes to ensure that the lessons stick. The program also makes it easy to transfer text and images to the Windows Clipboard for use in documents and reports.

Required Equipment
- CD-ROM drive
- Windows 3.1
- VGA video (SVGA card with 640 x 480, 256-color Windows driver recommended)
- At least 4M of RAM
- Sound card with Windows driver
- Mouse

The Family Doctor, 3rd Edition

The Family Doctor, 3rd Edition (Family Doctor III) is a Windows medical reference on CD-ROM. Authored and edited by Allan Bruckheim, M.D., FAAFP, it is designed to be a comprehensive medical reference. Family Doctor III is published by the Creative Multimedia Corporation.

Dr. Bruckheim is a nationally known syndicated medical columnist. In putting together this product, he gathered the answers to the 2,300 most commonly asked questions concerning more than 280 medical conditions. Questions and their answers can be accessed by descending through ever-more-specific lists or by searching for key words.

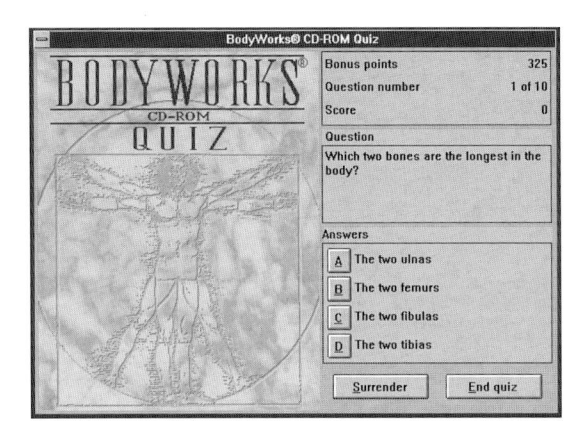

▲ *Lessons and quizzes help you to get the most out of BodyWorks.*

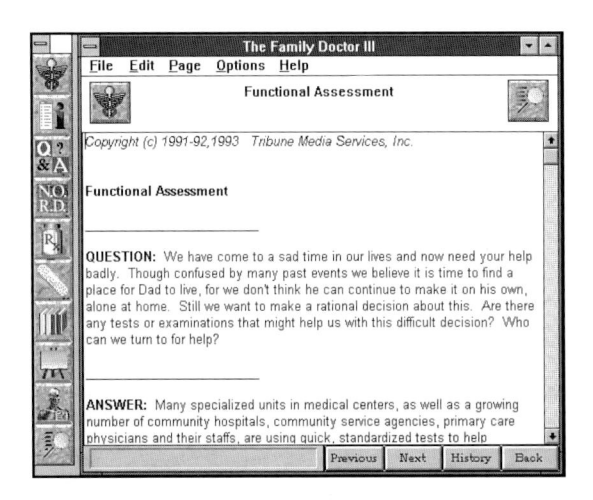

▲ *The Family Doctor III contains answers to 2,300 commonly asked medical questions.*

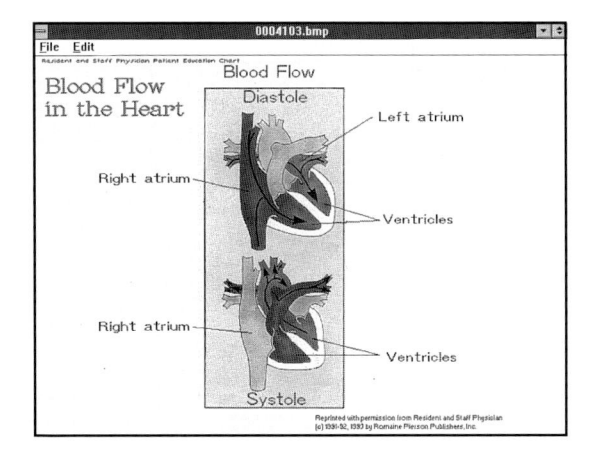

▲ *Full-color illustrations, sound, animation, and video clips help make the information in Family Doctor III easier to understand.*

The text is enhanced with a variety of media clips and 300 full-color illustrations. Sound, including digitized speech, animation, and video clips help to make the information easier to understand.

Family Doctor III has several other features of interest: an animated guide to first-aid; a prescription drug guide with information on 1,600 products; special information on 900 rare diseases (supplied by the National Organization of Rare Disorders and available from the main menu); and an anatomy section containing text, illustrations, and full-motion video of body parts in action.

To assist in research work, the program enables you to capture text to the Windows Clipboard or to print it directly from the program. This feature gives you the opportunity to create a personal medical file. If you can't find the information you need in the program, a Resources section is accessible from the main screen. This section contains the names and addresses of organizations that can provide additional information.

Required Equipment
- CD-ROM drive
- Windows 3.1
- 80386SX processor (or better)
- SVGA card with 640 x 480, 256-color Windows driver
- At least 2M of RAM
- Sound card with Windows driver
- Mouse

Mayo Clinic—Family Health Book

The Mayo Clinic—Family Health Book CD-ROM (The Family Health Book) is a Windows CD-ROM from IVI Publishing. Created with contributions from hundreds of experts at the Mayo Clinic, the program is adapted from the 1,378-page *Mayo Clinic—Family Health Book* and is designed to be a complete and authoritative family-health resource.

The Family Health Book program is divided into a number of parts. Five of these correspond to the five parts in the book of the same name. Each part is composed of chapters containing articles on particular subjects, and you can print the entire text of an article (but not just portions of it.) Articles may have hot links to other articles or to the built-in dictionary. Clicking a highlighted word or phrase opens a window containing the definition. Clicking an underlined, highlighted word or phrase moves you to an article on that subject.

Other parts of the product represent enhancements beyond what is available in the printed book. The Color Atlas of Human Anatomy contains anatomy illustrations, as well as animation and pictures created with modern medical imaging techniques.

The Photographic Guide to Common Skin Disorders is exactly that: a collection of scanned photographs of skin problems. Each photograph is accompanied by a narration, and the narrator pronounces the name of each condition and then provides a brief description. A button enables you to jump to the relevant sections in the text.

Other features are available as buttons across the bottom of the screen and can help you to store and retrieve information: a built-in notepad lets you manually record information displayed by the program; a Search button enables you to find topics directly; and the Trail and Back buttons help you retrace your path through the data.

Required Equipment
- CD-ROM drive
- DOS 3.1 or higher
- Windows 3.1
- 80386SX processor (or better)
- SVGA video card with 640 x 480, 256-color Windows driver
- At least 4M of RAM
- Sound card with Windows driver
- MSCDEX 2.2 or later
- Mouse

▲ *The CD-ROM contains the entire text of the Mayo Clinic—Family Health Book and includes hot links between articles and to the built-in dictionary.*

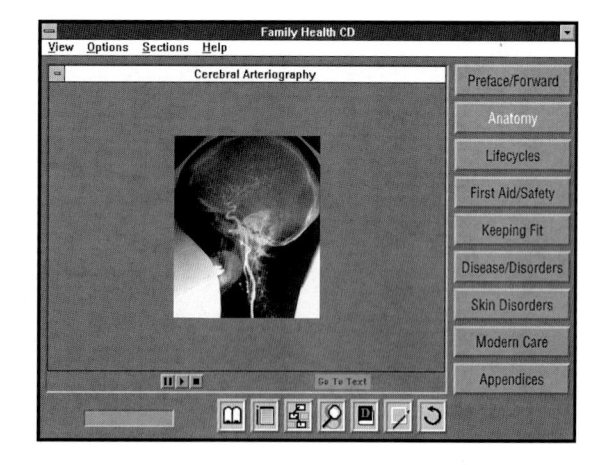

▲ *The Mayo Clinic—Family Health Book contains images such as this Cerebral Arteriography.*

PharmAssist

PharmAssist is a family health reference from the Software Marketing Corporation. The primary focus of the product is drugs, but the Windows CD-ROM version discussed here contains expanded features that cover other health-related subjects.

The program contains an extensive database of prescription and non-prescription drugs. Pictures of commonly prescribed dosages for approximately 600 brand-name drugs are shown, and a narrator pronounces the name of the drug when it is selected. A mass of information about each drug is readily available, including such things as generic name, interactions, and amount of time to take effect.

As you know, drug abuse is one of our society's major problems. The PharmAssist Abused Drug database can help parents educate their children about abused substances and their effects. Information in the database includes pictures of the substances and the paraphernalia used with it. Street names and technical names are listed, as are signs of abuse, federal penalties, and an alphabetical listing of abuse hotlines.

An assortment of special databases enables you to find out more about drugs. Everything from the cost of brand-name versus generic drugs, through their sexual side effects and impact on people over 60 can be found in these databases.

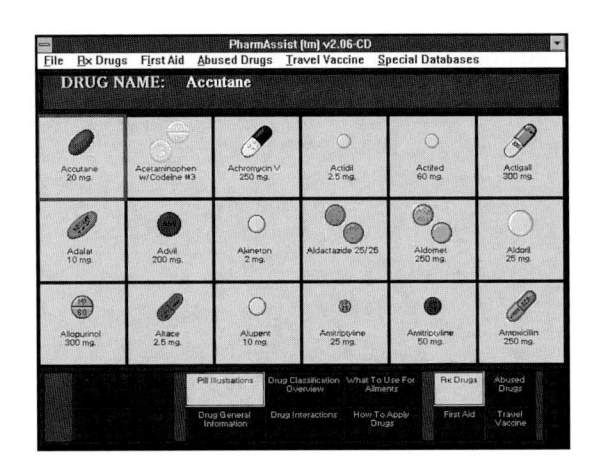

▲ *The PharmAssist image database helps users identify drugs and find out more about them.*

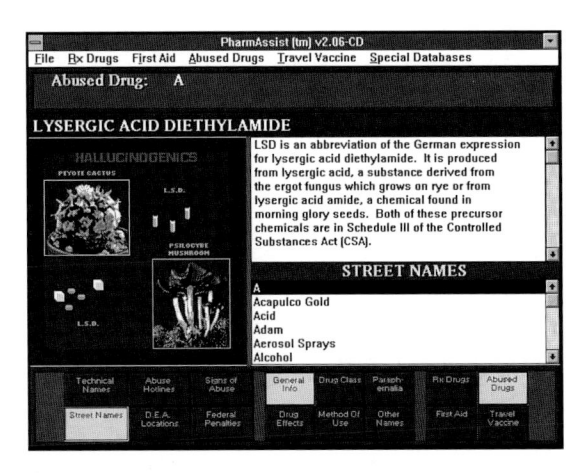

▲ *Information about abused substances can help parents educate their children about the dangers of these products.*

Drugs are not the only thing addressed in PharmAssist. The program contains an illustrated first-aid tutorial. The tutorial is also designed to be used as an aid during emergency procedures. In this case, the steps can be followed by an assistant to the first-aid practitioner, to ensure that no steps are skipped during the procedure.

PharmAssist enables you to print text directly and to copy graphics to the Windows Clipboard. A Travel Vaccine section provides information on worldwide travel requirements, health alerts, and vaccines.

Required Equipment
- CD-ROM drive
- Windows 3.1
- VGA video
- At least 2M of RAM
- Sound card with Windows driver
- Mouse

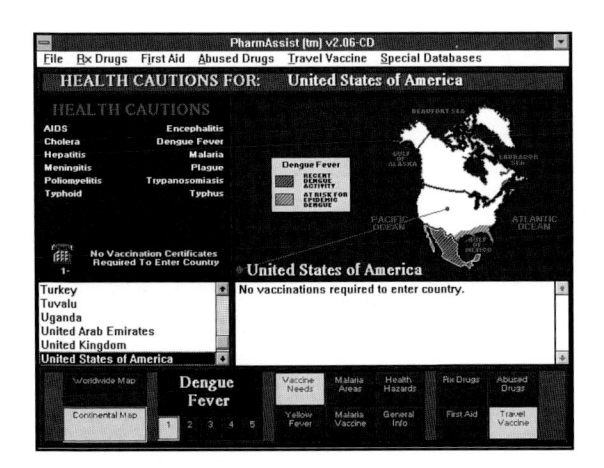

▲ *The Travel Vaccine section of PharmAssist is a comprehensive reference for international travelers.*

Space

Space has always fascinated us. It is the last great frontier, endless and hostile, yet containing innumerable wonders. We have studied the heavens for centuries, and now we have some reasonable ideas about how things work. Although we have never left Earth's neighborhood, our probes have traveled throughout the solar system. These spacecraft have returned spectacular pictures of the planets and have greatly increased our knowledge.

Multimedia space references are designed to make the information that has been gathered available and accessible to the average person. They contain incredible pictures, as well as illustrative animation. Three multimedia space products are discussed in this section.

Beyond Planet Earth

Beyond Planet Earth is a Windows CD-ROM produced by The Discovery Channel. The CD-ROM draws from shows from the channel and contains high-quality media clips from it as well.

This product aims to address the most urgent questions about space exploration and planetary science. To address these questions, the disc holds hundreds of photographs, videos from the Discovery Channel television shows, text, and interviews with space experts. The program is divided into four sections: The Planetary Theater, The Solar Gallery, Mission to Mars, and Space Experts.

The Planetary Theater is a collection of all the videos on the CD-ROM. Selecting a video clip from the theater brings up that video, as well as any associated text. Some words in the text are highlighted in blue. This indicates that they are listed in the Glossary, where you can see their definitions and hear them being pronounced. Any article can be printed or copied to the Windows Clipboard. A Related Topics button displays a list of items related to the current topic.

The Solar Gallery is a comprehensive study of our solar system. It is divided into eight sections. The sections contain video and still images and the text that goes with them. The screens are structured the same as in the Planetary Theater.

Mission to Mars looks at the next great space adventure: a manned mission to Mars! Four topics in this section provide information on the red planet itself, past missions there, missions planned before the year 2000, and the steps necessary to make a manned mission a reality. Each topic is displayed in the same manner as those in the Solar Gallery.

The Space Experts section lets you ask questions of four top experts on space. You ask a question by clicking one of the questions in a list and then clicking one of the experts. Any question can be answered by any expert, so you can compare the answers of the experts by asking them the same question.

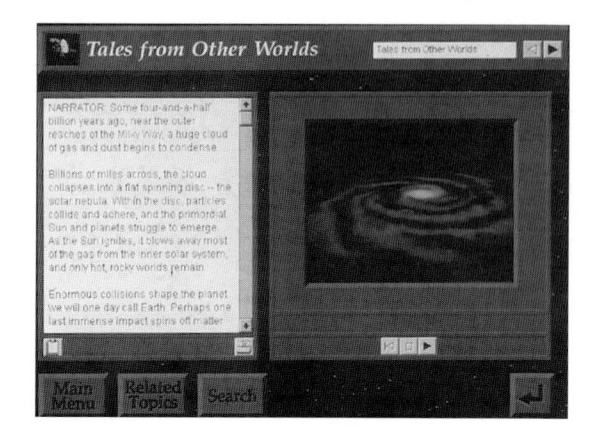

Viewing a topic in Beyond Planet Earth's Planetary Theater. (Courtesy of the Discovery Channel)

Space experts answer tough questions in Beyond Planet Earth.

Required Equipment
- CD-ROM drive
- DOS 3.1 or higher
- Windows 3.1

Multimedia Reference Materials

- 80386SX processor (or better)
- SVGA video with 640 x 480, 256-color Windows driver
- At least 4M of RAM
- Sound card with Windows driver
- MSCDEX 2.2 or later
- Mouse

Journey to the Planets

Journey to the Planets is a Windows CD-ROM from Multicom Publishing. It is called "the complete multimedia guide to extraterrestrial exploration" and is an encyclopedia of the planets and other bodies in our solar system.

The main menu for this program contains a picture of the solar system, and you can get information about any object in the picture simply by clicking the object. For each planet, the information is divided into areas such as Data, Moons, Planetary Tour, and Exploration.

The Data area contains all the vital statistics of the current object, such as mass and diameter, orbital characteristics, surface features, and even weather. Some of this information is presented in the form of animation or video clips, while other information is in the form of text and photographs. When the information is presented in the form of a photograph, you can click the photo to display a full-screen close-up of it.

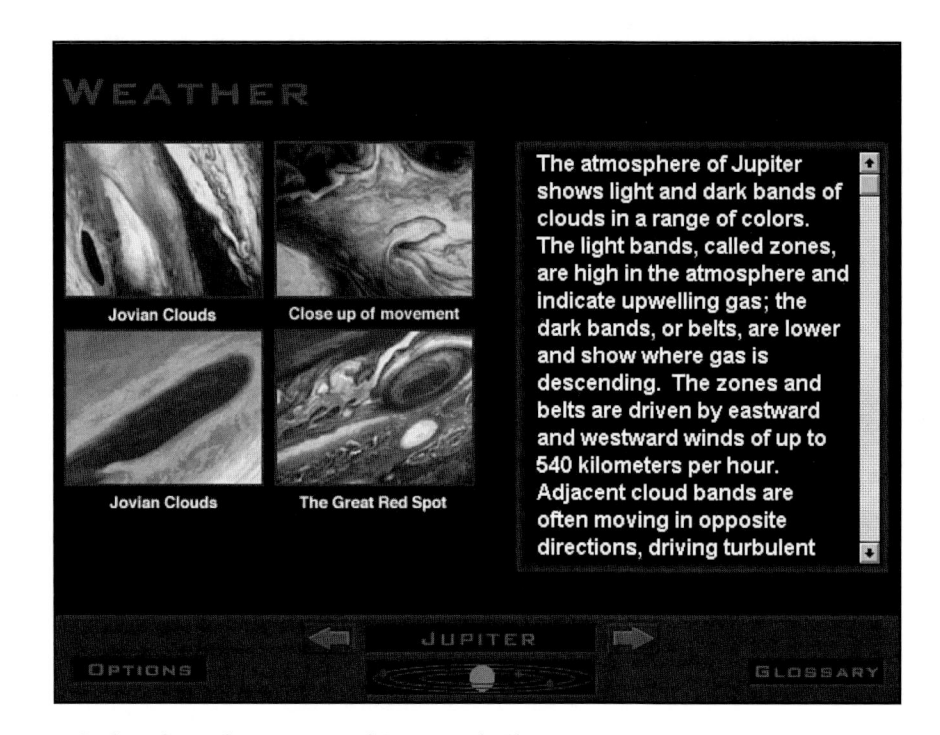

▲ *Studying the weather on Jupiter with Journey to the Planets.*

▲ *Clicking a picture displays a full-screen close-up in Journey to the Planets.*

When you choose the Planetary Tour area, you get a tour of the interesting surface features of the selected object. Features are described in text and with photographs or other real-world images. Some features include *fly-throughs*, computer-generated movies that show what it would be like to fly through, around, or over the surface features.

The video clips and animation in the program are accompanied by either narration or dramatic music. A Glossary contains definitions of the terms used in the text, and a Summary, which you can choose to print, contains the most important statistics about the object.

Required Equipment

- CD-ROM drive
- DOS 3.1 or higher
- Windows 3.1
- 25 MHz 80386SX processor (or better)
- SVGA video with 640 x 480, 256-color Windows driver
- At least 4M of RAM
- Sound card with Windows driver
- MSCDEX 2.2 or later
- Mouse

Small Blue Planet

Small Blue Planet, subtitled "The Real Picture Atlas," is a Windows CD-ROM from Now What Software. This program is a picture atlas of the Earth. It is included in the Space section because of its spectacular pictures—most of which were generated from satellite imagery.

The interface for this program is unusual, and it takes some getting used to. It also helps if you keep the documentation handy. The main screen, called The Grid, contains four large images with a set of smaller ones arrayed below. The four large areas represent different parts of the program. Moving counterclockwise, these four parts represent the Global Relief Map, the World Political Map, the Chronosphere, and the USA Relief Map. The group of images below the large ones represents the fifth part of the program—the Satellite Gallery. To reach a particular part, you can click the button that is visible in the image (or images) representing that part.

Each part of the program contains a different kind of information. The Global Relief Map uses data from National Oceanographic and Atmospheric Administration (NOAA) sources to display a color-coded global relief map. The World Political Map in my version represents the world political situation as of January 1, 1993. The Chronosphere displays the changing patterns of day and night as they play across the globe. It also provides accurate time and date information for anywhere on the planet. The USA Relief Map is a relief map of the United States, created by the United States Geological Survey (USGS). The Satellite Gallery is a collection of images, sorted by the type of remote sensor (see following Note) that was used to create the image.

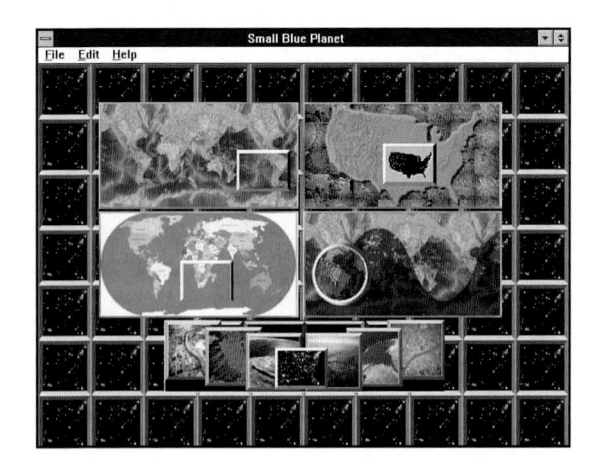

▲ *The Small Blue Planet provides an unusual user interface.*

Note: You may be wondering what a *remote sensor* is. Remote sensors are devices that gather information from a distance. Two of the remote sensors used to gather the images in the Small Blue Planet are MultiSpectral Scanners and Advanced Very-High Resolution Radiometers.

After you select the part of the program you want to explore, you are presented with a menu of images. The images are small replicas of the actual images, so it is easier to find the image you want. When you select the image you want to view, the image appears, along with the Control Panel. The Control Panel contains a number of unusual controls that enable you, among other things, to zoom in on images, display background information, and even annotate the images yourself. Fortunately for the folks at What Now, the images contained in Small Blue Planet make figuring out the user interface worth the effort.

Required Equipment

- CD-ROM drive
- Windows 3.1
- 80386 processor (or better)
- 256-color SVGA video
- At least 4M of RAM

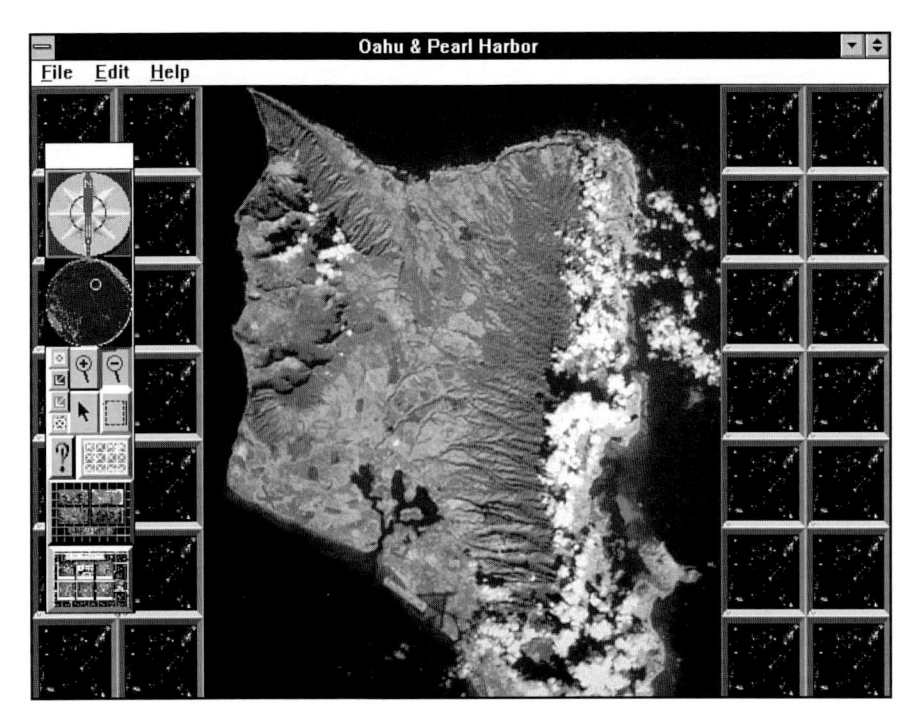

▲ *A Landsat MultiSpectral Scanner image of Oahu and Pearl Harbor, displayed by Small Blue Planet.*

Prehistoric Life

Through fossils and other indirect evidence, we have discovered much about the world in the time before any humans were around to keep historical records. Incredible creatures have roamed the Earth, filling the land, the sea, and the air. Though all of these creatures are fascinating, the ones that have captured the most attention are the dinosaurs. This section introduces two multimedia reference works that deal with prehistoric life, including the dinosaurs.

Microsoft Dinosaurs

Microsoft Dinosaurs is a Windows CD-ROM all about dinosaurs. The program combines features of an encyclopedia and an atlas with fun features such as screen savers and animated movies.

The program is divided into four sections: Atlas, Timeline, Families, and Index. Each section takes a different approach to the data contained on the disc. The screens, however, still have certain features in common. For example, red text is *hot text*. Hot text may display a window with additional information, or it may take you to a related article in the database. Most screens also have a related-article button in the upper-right corner of the screen that, when clicked, takes you immediately to a related article. In addition, each animal article begins with a Facts button. You can click the Facts button to get a summary of facts about the selected animal, and you can also print this summary.

Across the bottom of almost every page in this program is a row of buttons that provides access to the principal options. Clicking the Atlas button, for example, takes you to a map of the world as it is today. When you select a continent, the program shows you a picture of the creatures whose fossils have been discovered on that continent. When you click the small speaker icon next to the name of the continent, a narrator begins to read the text associated with that atlas page.

You can click the Timeline button to see events from the entire spectrum of the Earth's history. The Timeline's focus is on the age of dinosaurs, so the coverage of the non-dinosaur eras is much less extensive. In the Mesozoic Era (the time of the dinosaurs), the Timeline takes you to one of three periods: the Triassic, Jurassic, or Cretaceous. Each screen displayed by the Timeline gives you access to articles containing information about the inhabitants and events of that era or period.

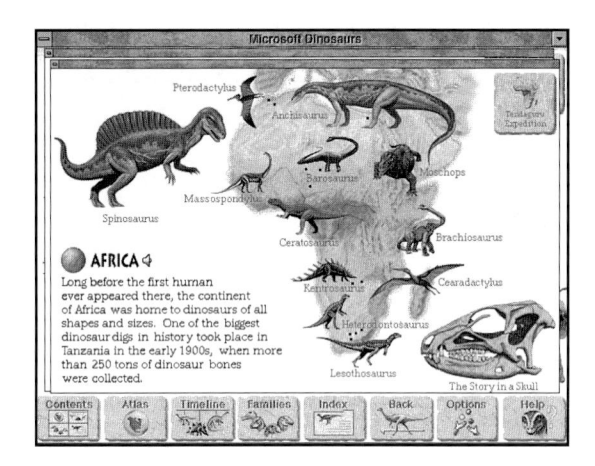

▲ *The Dinosaurs Atlas shows what fossils were discovered on a particular continent.*

You can click the Families button to trace the family history of dinosaurs. It takes you through the two great orders (Saurischians and Ornithischians) and down to individual representatives of each type within each order.

And finally, clicking the Index button displays the Index list box. This box contains all the articles in the program, in alphabetical order. It also contains a Find feature that can help you locate articles containing information about particular topics.

Working through the different sections of the program eventually leads you to the individual articles. Each article consists of a picture of the creature in question and text with a spoken description. The articles are filled with hot-text links to additional information about the creatures.

Dinosaurs has quite a few other features and goodies. Guided tours (available from the Contents screen) are led by a noted dinosaur expert and delve into any of 16 different topics. A collection of six movies illustrates topics with near-full-screen video. Each package of Dinosaurs contains a set of dinosaur stickers and a copy of *Dino Times*, a newsletter from the Dinosaur Society.

▲ *Colorful illustrations help bring Dinosaurs to life.*

Required Equipment
- CD-ROM drive
- DOS 3.1
- Windows 3.1
- 80386SX processor (or better)
- VGA video (SVGA with 640 x 480, 256-color Windows driver recommended)
- At least 4M of RAM
- Sound card with Windows driver
- Mouse

Prehistoria

Prehistoria, A Multimedia Who's Who of Prehistoric Life, is a Windows CD-ROM from Grolier Electronic Publishing. Most programs in the same vein as Prehistoria focus on the 160 million years when the dinosaurs ruled the Earth. Prehistoria, however, looks at over 500 animals that lived in a span of one-half billion years—from 250 million years before the dinosaurs until just a few thousand years ago.

The first thing you see when you start Prehistoria is the Features screen. The program is divided into six major Features: Gallery, Time Tracker, Search, Grolier Museum, Classifications, and Creature Show. The Gallery is where similar types of prehistoric creatures are grouped. These groups include all the major types of creatures, such as fish, birds, and mammals. Clicking one of these groups brings up another screen that contains more specific groups of creatures. Eventually, you can navigate your way down to the information screen for each individual species.

You can click items in the main screen to display additional windows of information. These windows contain all sorts of information about the species—from text describing it in more detail, to

Multimedia Reference Materials 69

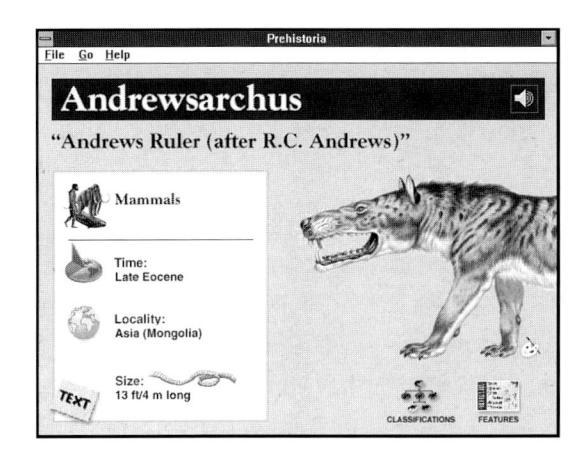

▲ *The main screen for each species in Prehistoria resembles this screen.*

its size relative to a man, to its place in the zoological classification system. Clicking the speaker icon causes the program to pronounce the creature's name, and clicking the Features icon takes you back to the main menu. If you choose, you can also print the information relating to a creature.

You can use the Time Tracker to find out which creatures lived in particular geological periods. If you select one of the 11 time periods, you can see what the Earth looked like in that period. After you select a period, you can click the type or types of creatures in which you are interested. When you click the Search button, the program brings up a list of the creatures that match the search criteria.

The Search feature in Prehistoria uses traditional search techniques to find specific creatures. You can perform simple word searches, or you can perform more complex searches using *and*, *or*, and *not*.

The Grolier Museum lets you explore some of the issues that surround prehistoric creatures. The museum is divided into eight rooms, each dealing with one or more topics. Within the rooms, videos, text, and Knowledge Explorer essays (like those in the New Grolier Multimedia Encyclopedia discussed earlier in the chapter) answer your questions about these topics.

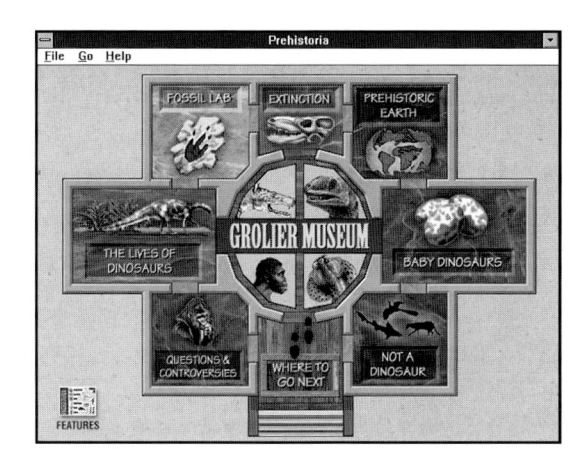

▲ *The Grolier Museum in Prehistoria uses video, text, and Knowledge Explorer essays to answer questions about the prehistoric world.*

The Classifications Feature shows each creature's place in the zoological hierarchy. It provides the creature's class, order, and family, and leads to the main screen for that creature.

The Creature Show Feature randomly browses through all the creatures in the database. It displays the main screen for each creature (for a length of time that you specify) and then moves on to the next one.

Required Equipment
- CD-ROM drive
- DOS 5.0 or greater
- Windows 3.1
- 20 MHz 80386 processor (or better)
- SVGA video with 630 x 480, 256-color Windows driver
- At least 4M of RAM
- Sound card with Windows driver
- MSCDEX 2.21 or later
- Mouse

(*Note:* A printer is recommended.)

Art and Music

Until recently, art and music references on a PC would have been a joke. Low-resolution displays with few colors made viewing visual art a joke, while the ten-cent speaker in most machines could do little more then beep and click. In addition, the storage requirements for quality music and images are such that most PCs could not store them even if they could display them.

With the advent of multimedia PCs, however, the rules have changed. These powerful video systems and their sound cards let PCs reproduce sound and images successfully, and the availability of CD-ROM drives solves the storage problem. This section introduces two products that take advantage of the power of multimedia PCs to create art and music reference works.

Microsoft Art Gallery

Microsoft Art Gallery is a Windows CD-ROM that contains paintings and background information from one of the world's great art collections. The disc holds reproductions of 2,000 works found in the National Gallery in London.

You can experience the artwork included on this CD-ROM through any of the five different features: Artists' Lives, Historical Atlas, Picture Types, General Reference, or Guided Tours. The Artists' Lives feature focuses on details of the artist's life. Biographical information can be presented on each artist, along with thumbnail sketches of his or her works. As with other Microsoft reference products, clicking highlighted text leads you to related articles or causes the program to display additional information about the highlighted term.

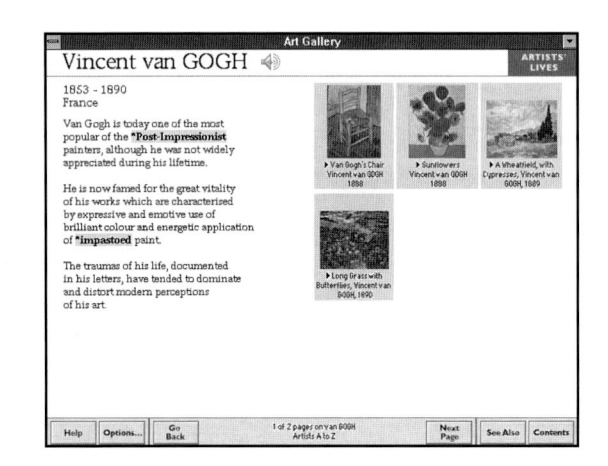

▲ *Microsoft Art Gallery contains biographical data for each artist whose works are included on the CD-ROM.*

You can use the Historical Atlas to find information based on an artist's relationship to selected geographic locations. Screens about cities or other locations contain links to the appropriate artist.

The Picture Types option organizes the pictures on the CD-ROM on the basis of what type of work they represent. The types of work are broken into six categories: Religious Imagery; Narrative, Allegory, and the Nude; Portraits; Everyday Life; Views; and Still Life. Choosing one of these categories leads you eventually to a screen that contains representative works from that category.

All the paths in the program eventually lead to individual works of art. Each work is accompanied by information about the piece and about the artist who created it. The screen for each work also provides a number of options. One option enables you to copy the information you see on-screen to the Windows Clipboard or send it to a printer. Other buttons enable you to display related topics in each category, to move one page forward or backward, to return to the previous screen, or to return to the Contents page. One icon found on most screens resembles a four-sided arrow located to the right of the artwork. Clicking this icon causes the picture to be enlarged to nearly full-screen size.

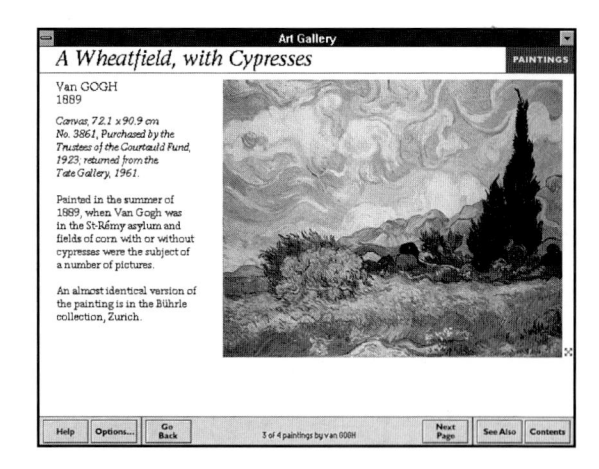

▲ *Van Gogh's "A Wheatfield, with Cypresses," as shown in Art Gallery.*

Multimedia Reference Materials

video, and music to take the user from the origins of jazz to the present day.

The program is divided into three sections: Text, Music, and Pictures. The Text section contains the written descriptions and commentary, the Music section provides access to all the music on the disc, and the Pictures section does the same for stills and video clips.

All three sections are organized in a similar manner. Text is displayed on the right side of the window, and small thumbnail images sometimes appear in the left margin of the window. You can click these thumbnails to play a music or video clip, or to display a photograph.

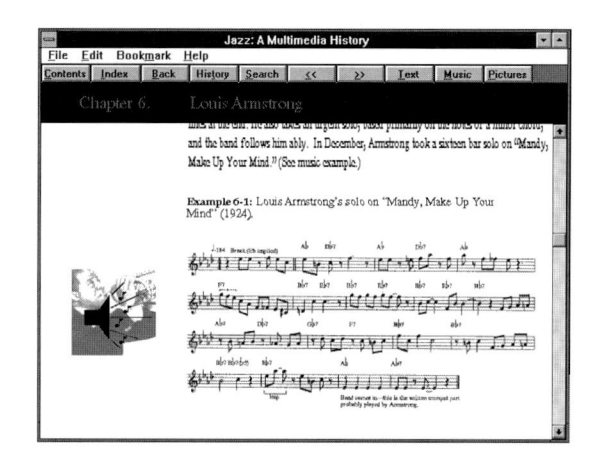

▲ *Art Gallery enables the user to enlarge any painting for better viewing.*

Required Equipment
- CD-ROM drive
- DOS 3.1 or later
- Windows 3.1
- 80386SX processor (or better)
- SVGA video with 640 x 480, 256-color Windows driver
- At least 4M of RAM
- Sound card with Windows driver
- Mouse

Jazz

Jazz is a Windows CD-ROM that covers the history of Jazz. It was produced by EBook and published by Compton's New Media. Jazz is subtitled "A Multimedia History" and uses text,

▲ *The Text section of Jazz can contain media clips, as in this example of the music of Louis Armstrong.*

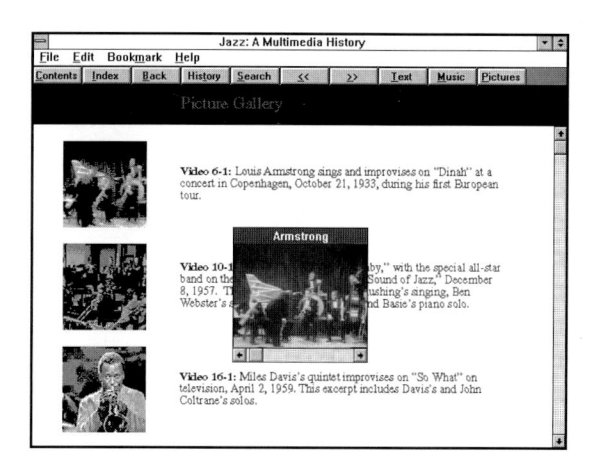

▲ *The Pictures section of Jazz provides easy access to all the photos and video clips on the CD-ROM; the Music section does the same for audio clips.*

Many of the video clips contain audio and video footage from actual performances by jazz greats such as Louis Armstrong, Duke Ellington, and Miles Davis. Some of the photographs contain a magnifying glass icon in the upper-right corner. This icon indicates that the photograph has an enlarged view associated with it. You can click portions of the main photograph to display these enlargements.

Jazz has a number of other features. You can have it sort the text, music, and pictures in its database by the artist's name, date of the performance, or order of its appearance in the text. It can also search for words or phrases. Jazz includes a Glossary, Bibliography, Index, and Discography. Finally, many of the music clips can be played on a standard audio CD player.

Required Equipment
- CD-ROM drive
- DOS 3.1
- Windows 3.1
- 12 MHz 80386SX processor (or better)
- SVGA video with 640 x 480, 256-color Windows driver
- At least 2M of RAM (4M recommended)
- Sound card with Windows driver
- MSCDEX 2.2 or later
- Mouse

Summary

This chapter looked at one of the largest and most important categories of edutainment products: multimedia reference materials. These products take the contents of printed encyclopedias, atlases, and other works, and move them onto one (or several) CD-ROMs. But they do more than just replicate a printed document. Multimedia reference works do things that no printed document can do.

Learning is much more fun—and more effective—when multiple senses and multiple presentation styles are involved. Thanks to the multimedia capabilities of modern PCs, multimedia reference works can stimulate more of the senses and utilize various presentation styles. With animation, audio clips, and full-motion video, these products really come to life.

Although most people think of encyclopedias when they think of multimedia reference works, this category actually offers a wide variety of other products. This chapter contained only a sampling of what is available. Most of these products are designed to run under Windows and are available on CD-ROM. If you (or your child) want to do much work with multimedia references, you will need an MPC-compatible PC (see Chapter 12, "Windows and the Multimedia PC," for more information on MPC compatibility).

Multimedia reference works provide information; they often enable you to see, hear, and move this information, as well. Multimedia reference works also make it easy for you to follow references and explore related topics. Even so, for many kinds of learning, hands-on experience is crucial. This is especially true when the subject involves a complex system, such as the operation of a city or the ecology of a coral reef. For these situations, the complex interplay of factors is best understood by direct experience and manipulation of the system.

Although it is impractical to have every child manage New York City for a few years, simulation products let them do the next best thing. A simulation enables the user to experience (and experiment with) some of the complex interactions that compose most systems. Chapter 5 introduces you to some simulation products and discusses their value as edutainment tools.

Chapter 5

Simulation Programs

Chapter 5

A simulation is an imitation, or model, of something. A good simulation has many of the characteristics of whatever is being simulated. That thing can be a system, such as an ecosystem or an aircraft flight-control system, or it can be an event or series of events. Examples of things that might be simulated include the pioneer's journey across the American West, a space flight, and any number of battles and wars.

Simulations can be used to predict real-world events, such as the weather or a crop harvest. Such simulations tend to be very large and complicated and usually are run on mainframes or supercomputers. This kind of simulation is a powerful tool and falls outside the realm of edutainment.

Edutainment simulations work to increase the user's understanding of whatever is being modeled. The simulation enables the user to experience some of the complex interactions and occurrences that make up most systems and events. A city simulation, such as SimCity 2000, models such things as the relationship between population growth and crime or between taxes and business activity. A simulation of life on the Great Barrier Reef models the relationships between predators and prey as well as the relationship between a creature's size and its energy consumption.

Dealing with the complex relationships of interdependent processes and activities may sound boring, but edutainment simulations can make it quite a lot of fun. The key to making the simulation fun is an easy-to-use graphical interface, and publishers provide this interface using many of the same tools that other edutainment products use. Music, sound effects, graphics, and animation are used to present information in a form that the user can enjoy.

The following topics are discussed in this chapter:

- Common features of simulations
- Variations between products
- A short walk-through of a typical product
- Descriptions of available simulation products

Common Features

Simulations have a number of features in common, but most of these features are "under the hood" and invisible to the user. The most visible common features are user interfaces that make these complex products usable by normal people. All the simulations I reviewed do a fine job of organizing and presenting large amounts of information. Sound effects, graphics, and animation turn dry equations and statistics into a multimedia presentation.

Another feature found in most simulations is depth. Many of these products have various levels of complexity. At the basic levels, much of the complexity of the simulation may be glossed over or eliminated in the interest of playability. Without being overwhelmed by information and details, new players can get started and learn how the program works. The advanced levels then add in more information and complexity to challenge experienced players.

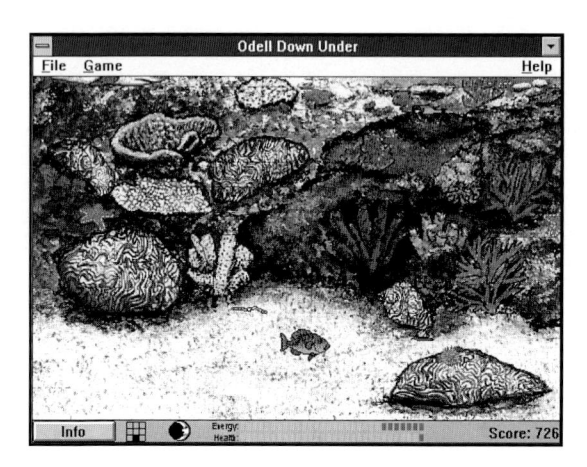

▲ *Although complex, the Odell Down Under simulation drives an animated display that a child can use.*

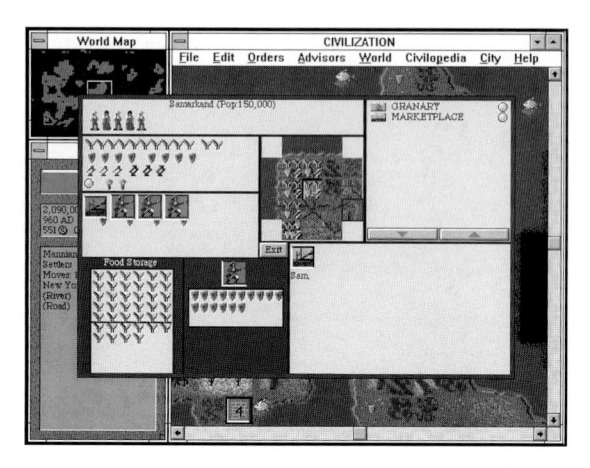

▲ *The skillful use of graphics helps to present a great deal of information in Civilization.*

A final common feature to consider is the commitment these products demand. You may be able to begin playing one of these simulations without too much preparation, but to become really competent takes time and effort. Players often spend hundreds of hours with a favorite simulation, increasing their understanding of the model and developing more control over it. I don't even want to think about how long it took me to be able to play Civilization at the most difficult level. Simulations are not for those with short attention spans.

Except for the products from MECC, which are designed for younger users (10 years and up for The Oregon Trail; 8 to 14 years for Odell Down Under), simulations come with hefty manuals. The manual for SimCity 2000, at 140 pages, is one of the smaller ones, whereas the manual for Flight Simulator is more than 280 pages! The large size of these manuals is due in part to the depth and complexity of the product, but also because extensive background and reference sections are included. Much of the educational value of simulations is derived from this material.

Interesting Variations

Maxis is the most innovative and prolific of the companies creating simulations. The Maxis product line runs the gamut from SimCity, an extremely well-done, addictive, and fanciful city simulator to wild creations such as SimEarth, a world simulation inspired by James Lovelock's Gaia hypothesis, and SimLife, in which you create simulated life forms using the precepts of the new science of artificial life.

Microsoft Flight Simulator is another interesting case. Before becoming an author, I built flight simulators for a major simulation company. My responsibilities included all aspects of the simulation—from hardware and software design through FAA and customer approval. In my opinion, Flight Simulator is in some ways superior to the

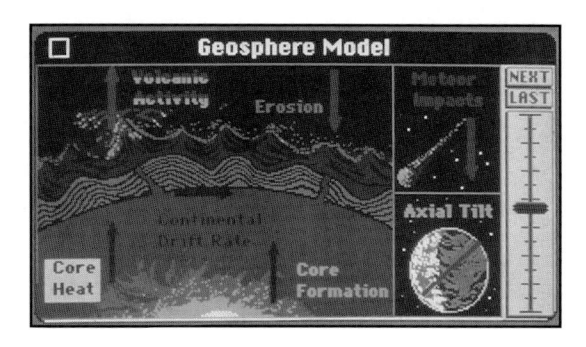

▲ *SimEarth asks: "Is the entire planet a single living organism?" (Courtesy of Maxis)*

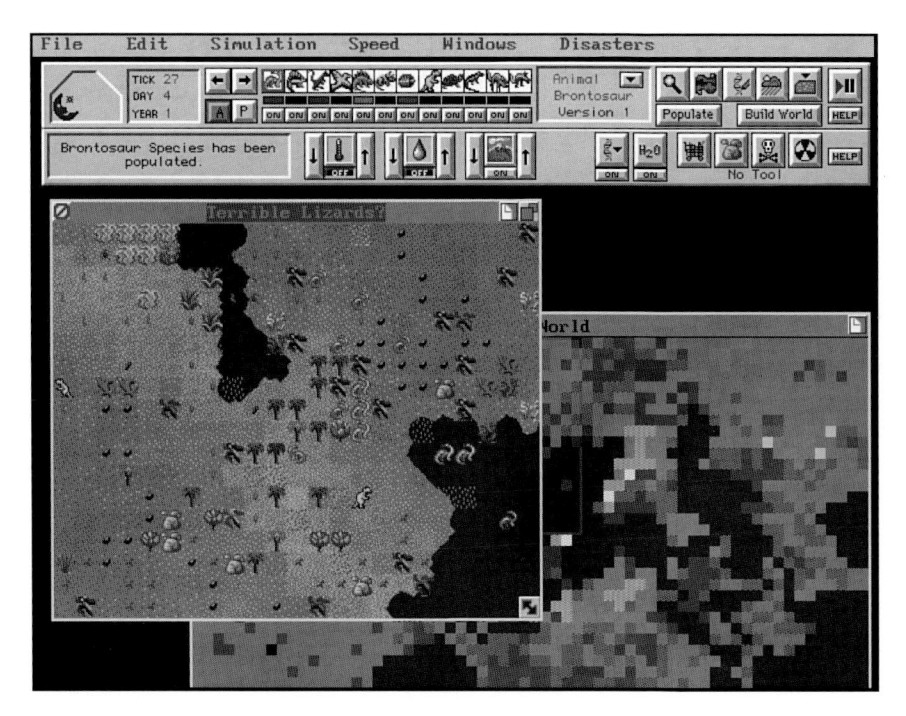

▲ *Artificial life forms run amok in SimLife.*

Chapter 5

▲ *The visual system of Flight Simulator Version 5.0.*

simulators I worked on. Its visual system, in particular, blows away the systems on the commercial and military simulators I was involved with. And those simulations ran on multiple mini-computers! The existence of such a sophisticated simulation on a PC says something about the innovation, drive, and talent of the folks working on PC simulations.

MECC publishes simulation products (The Oregon Trail and Odell Down Under) that are designed for a younger audience than other products available in this category. The complexity of these simulations has been reduced to a level that can be understood by this younger audience. Consequently, the products are simpler to use—and the manuals are smaller! The following section offers a walk-through of The Oregon Trail simulation program.

Using a Simulation Program: The Oregon Trail

The Oregon Trail is one of the most famous of all PC simulation programs. It is a simulation of the nineteenth-century journey across the American West to the Willamette Valley in Oregon.

The first order of business is to select your party. The occupation you select for your character determines the amount of money the party starts with and also regulates the actions that you can perform while on the trail.

After the party is selected, it must be equipped for the journey. You purchase initial supplies in the general store. Within limits, you can choose whatever equipment you wish. The store owner has a digitized voice and provides suggestions for the appropriate equipment to take along.

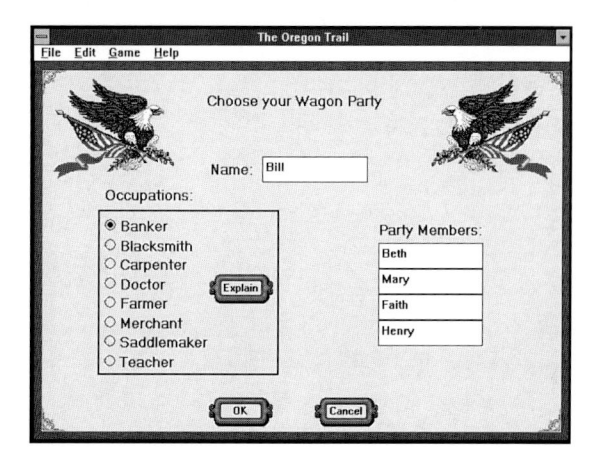

▲ *Many decisions must be made before starting out along the Oregon Trail.*

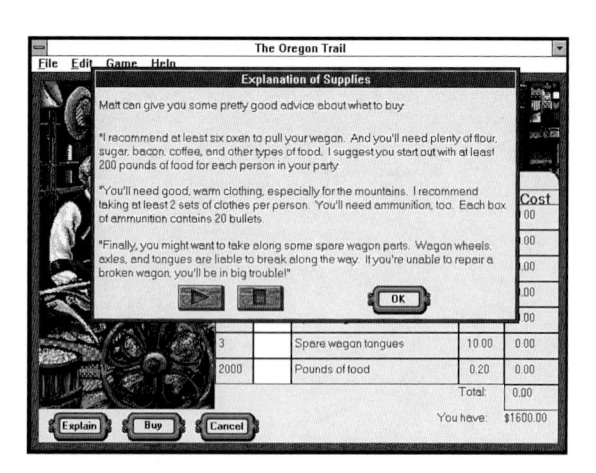

▲ *On-line help makes Oregon Trail easier to use.*

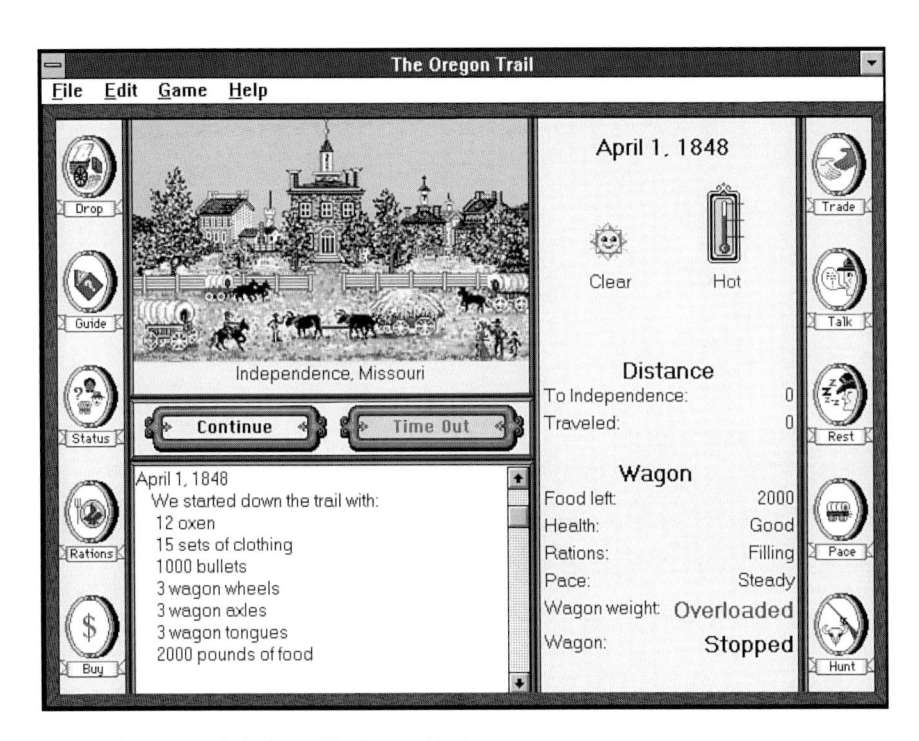

Simulation Programs   77

▲ *An information-rich display in The Oregon Trail.*

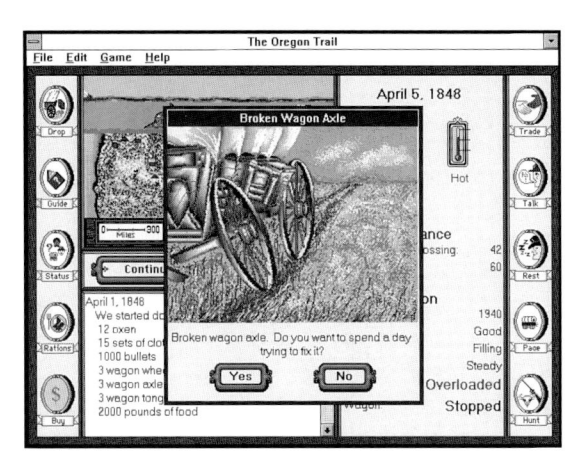

▲ *Random events can disturb the best-laid plans.*

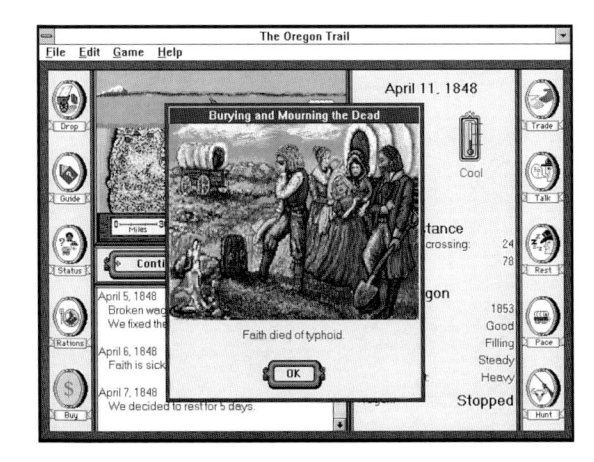

▲ *Not everyone who embarked on the Oregon Trail lived to see the Willamette Valley.*

After you have made the preliminary decisions, the program switches to an information-rich display. One window shows your party's current location, and another window displays a continuous log of your party's experiences. The most important status information is visible at all times, and you can click buttons to access game controls and other status information.

You encounter random events as the party travels along the trail. Illness is a frequent problem; it forces you to choose between resting to help the sick recover and pushing on before supplies run out or the weather turns bad. As you quickly learn, many who set out on the Oregon Trail failed to reach the other end.

Luckily, you don't have to make all the important decisions alone. Clicking the Talk button results in a conversation with another member of the party (when on the trail), or with an inhabitant of one of the forts (when at a fort). These opinions are presented both in text and in digitized speech.

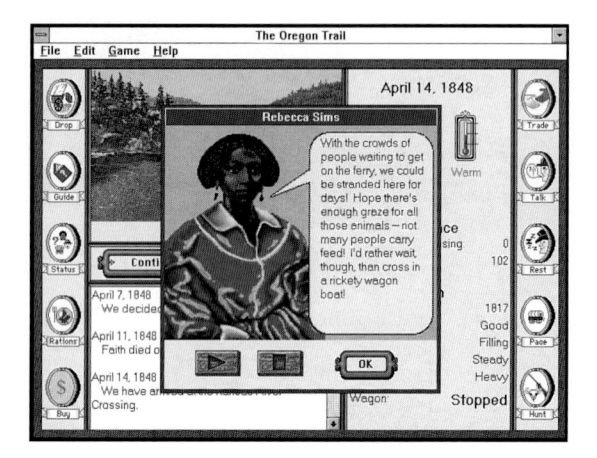

▲ *The party debates a river crossing using text and digitized speech.*

▲ *Forts along the Oregon Trail provided rest and amenities.*

▲ *Hunting for food along the Oregon Trail.*

The Oregon Trail tests your arcade-game skills when it comes time to hunt for food. Hunting for additional food was important along the trail and is also important in the simulation. A simple shooting gallery type of game forces you to try to pick off moving animals. Every shot uses up more of your party's precious bullets.

Despite all the hardships and random events, if you are skilled and make wise decisions, your party eventually makes it to the end of the trail.

What's Available?

Simulation is one of the smaller categories of edutainment products, which isn't a reflection on simulations or the people who create them. I believe that simulations are perhaps the most sophisticated and difficult to create of all edutainment products. Modeling even part of the real world on a PC is, in itself, difficult. Adding requirements for exciting sound effects and graphics complicates things even further. Include the final (and most important) requirement—fun—and you can see that a good edutainment simulation is difficult to create.

Fortunately, a few companies have risen to the challenge and have created some superior simulation products. Two different groups of products are discussed in the sections that follow.

Traditional Simulations

Traditional simulations are not simulations designed the way our forefathers designed them. The field of PC simulations is only a few years old—far too young to have those kinds of traditions. When I use the term *traditional* here, I mean the kinds of products people immediately think of when they think about educational simulations.

Two companies, Maxis and MECC, dominate the field of traditional PC simulations. Some products from each publisher are discussed in the following paragraphs.

The Oregon Trail

MECC's Oregon Trail is one of the classic simulation products, and the latest version is a Windows CD-ROM. The Oregon Trail is a simulation of the pioneers' nineteenth-century journey across the American West.

You assume the role of a pioneer leaving Independence, Missouri, for the Willamette Valley in Oregon. From choosing a name and occupation, to provisioning the wagon, to fording flooded rivers, you have to make the right decisions if your party is to reach the Willamette Valley safely.

As your party travels westward, it encounters many people and events. Forts along the way provide places to rest and to buy or trade for supplies.

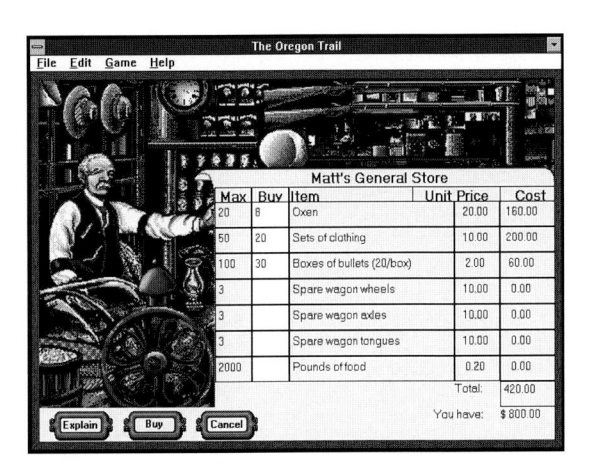

▲ *Buying supplies before hitting the Oregon Trail.*

Random events, such as blizzards, breakdowns, and disease challenge your party at every turn.

By creating a multimedia CD-ROM version of The Oregon Trail, MECC was able to significantly enhance the product, and it now contains thousands of images. Sound effects and more than an hour of music provide a pleasing background while your party travels between historic landmarks such as Forts Boise and Kearney. Using digitized speech, other pioneers tell of their journeys west, and the program also keeps a trail log containing information about significant events that occur along the way.

> **Note:** The Oregon Trail originally was a disk-based product. Disk-based versions are still being created and sold, enabling users without a CD-ROM drive to experience the Oregon Trail.

▲ *A blizzard along the trail. (Courtesy of MECC)*

The Oregon Trail is designed to fulfill many educational objectives. The constant decision-making required helps to improve problem-solving skills. The text descriptions and map displays increase reading and map-reading skills, while the adventure itself teaches about the westward expansion and the settling of the American frontier.

Required Equipment
- CD-ROM drive
- Windows 3.1
- 80386 processor (or better)
- SVGA video with 256-color Windows driver
- At least 4M of RAM
- Sound card with Windows driver
- Mouse

Note: You can find out more about the items in the preceding equipment list by looking in Chapter 2 for general information, Chapter 10 for SVGA video cards and sound cards, Chapter 11 for CD-ROM drives, and Chapter 12 for Windows information.

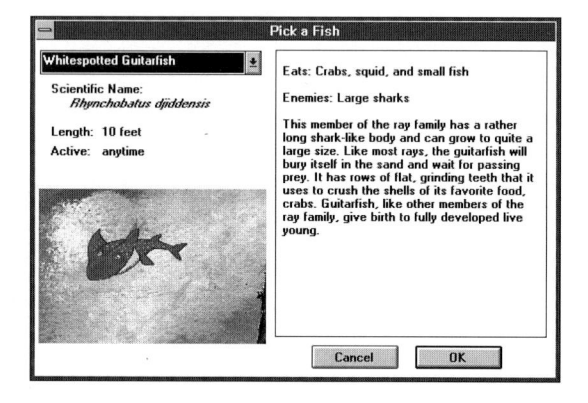

▲ *Choosing a fish in Odell Down Under.*

Odell Down Under

Odell Down Under is a simulation of life on a coral reef. Published by MECC, this Windows product is designed for children between the ages of 8 and 14. The child takes on the role of one of the more than 70 different life forms that inhabits Australia's Great Barrier Reef. The goal is to move up the food chain, playing the role of all the different inhabitants of the reef.

The child must first learn about his fish. The Pick a Fish dialog box gives the child the name of the

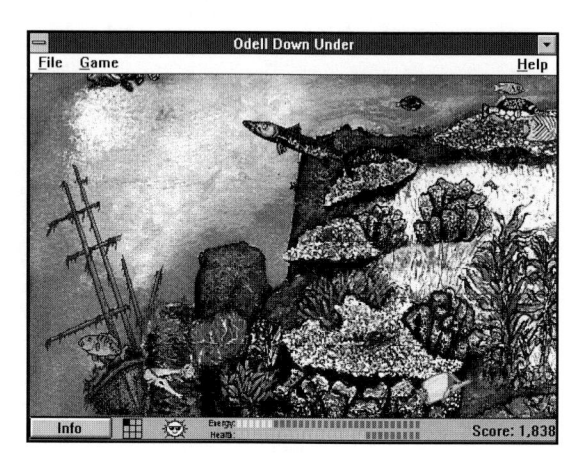

▲ *Life on the Great Barrier Reef.*

fish and shows it in action. Other information crucial to the fish's survival is also shown here.

After a fish has been selected, the action moves to the Great Barrier Reef. Here the child must survive in a real-time simulation of life on the reef. The child must guide his fish to find food, avoid predators, and practice other aquatic survival skills. Important status information is available on-screen at all times, which enables the child to plan his actions based on the fish's current needs.

Odell Down Under offers four levels of play: Challenge, Tournament, Create-A-Fish, and Practice. The Practice level enables the child to play any of the fish or other reef dwellers that are simulated. The child can use his fish to explore the reef—eating and avoiding being eaten. A new fish can be selected at any time.

The Challenge and Tournament levels let the child advance up the food chain. In Challenge, the program chooses four fish for the child. Starting with the smallest fish in the group, the child must survive long enough to advance to the next largest fish. If he gets a high enough score while surviving all four fish, he may be able to add his name to the Reef Rulers high-score display. The Tournament level challenges him to start as the smallest fish on the reef and work up the entire food chain to the role of Great White Shark.

The Create-A-Fish level enables the child to design his own fish. Characteristics such as size, speed, endurance, and special abilities are adjustable, so he can create a fish that is just right for him. After the new fish is created, it appears on the reef, where it can be tested in a game similar to the Practice level.

Odell Down Under uses life on the Great Barrier Reef to teach children about ecological balances and the coral reef ecosystem. It stimulates the child to exercise problem-solving and role-playing skills as well as deductive reasoning and reading comprehension.

Required Equipment
- Windows 3.1
- 80386 processor (or better)
- SVGA video with 256-color Windows driver
- At least 4M of RAM
- Sound card with Windows driver
- Mouse

SimCity 2000

SimCity 2000 is a city simulator from Maxis. The successor to the famous SimCity, SimCity 2000 builds on and enhances the original. You assume the role of mayor and city planner for either a brand new or an existing city.

By controlling zoning and the placement of infrastructure elements, such as power and water, you try to manage the growth and development of the city. If the city is a nice place to live, you find that the population increases, which causes new problems. You can choose to build schools, libraries, stadiums, and many more structures, and you can open new areas to development by building roads and laying railroad tracks. One new feature of SimCity 2000 is the addition of an underground level for the city. Here you can run subways and other utilities to improve the aesthetics of the city.

The graphics in this product are spectacular. As people (known as *Sims* in the game) move into an area, new buildings rise and cars start to travel to and from work. Boats sail the rivers, while aircraft fly overhead. Sports stadiums fill and empty as events occur.

SimCity 2000 features a multilevel user interface: the basic controls are easily accessible, but more depth is readily available when you are prepared for it. Information about the city is provided in a number of ways. Many charts, graphs, and reports

▲ *A scene from SimCity 2000. (Courtesy of MECC)*

shed light on various aspects of the city's operation, such as the budget.

Newspapers contain vital information pertaining to current events, inventions, and public-opinion polls. By reading the newspapers, you can keep track of what citizens think is important.

SimCity 2000 offers many other interesting features, including the following:

- Inventions that enable you to incorporate new technologies into the city, such as desalinization and fusion power plants.
- A selection of scenarios that lets you try to deal with challenges such as the 1991 Oakland fire and Hurricane Hugo.

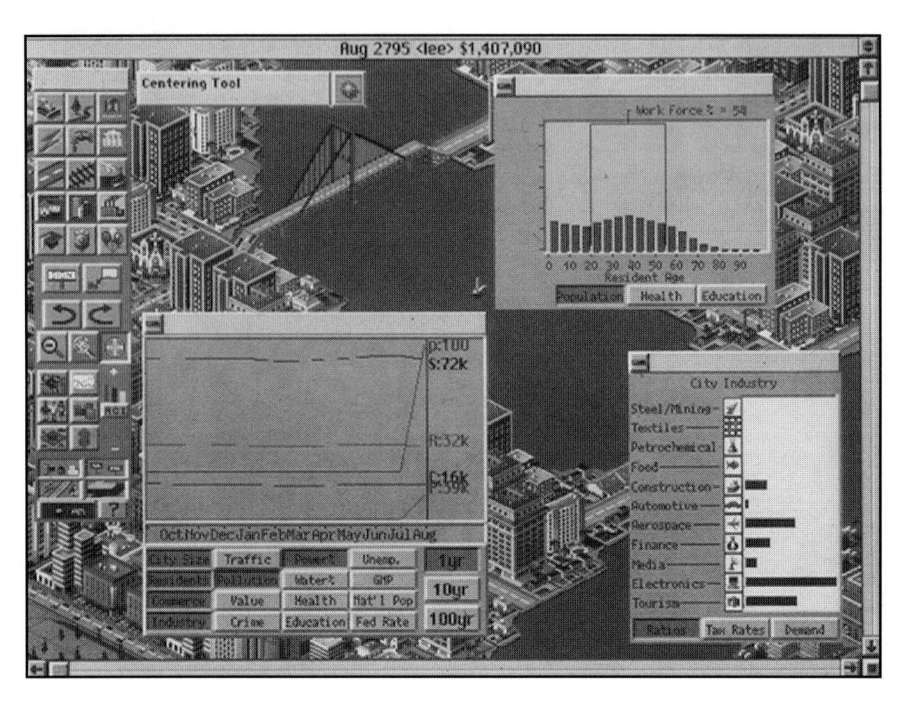

▲ *Charts and graphs provide vital information in SimCity 2000. (Courtesy of MECC)*

▲ *Keeping track of events with a local newspaper in SimCity. (Courtesy of MECC)*

- Natural and unnatural disasters: fires, floods, earthquakes, tornadoes—even monsters and aliens!

Required Equipment

- DOS 3.3 or later
- 80386 processor (or better)
- SVGA video with 640 x 480, 256-color mode
- 4M of RAM
- Mouse

(*Note:* A sound card is recommended.)

SimFarm

SimFarm is SimCity's "country cousin." This DOS program comes from Maxis and won a 1993 Parent's Choice Honors Award. In SimFarm, you are a farmer, and you are just starting out on a plot of land somewhere in the USA.

You begin with some land, some money, and a run-down old farmhouse. Where you go from there is up to you. SimFarm gives you the freedom to run a small family farm or a huge agribusiness. All the options are in your hands—from using the latest chemicals to running a trendy organic farm. When to plow, plant, and harvest the crops are just a few of the decisions you have to make. As in the real world, weather, crop rotation, and soil depletion all affect the crop yields.

Raising livestock is also an option. Of course, after you buy the animals, you have to take care of them and make sure that they get food and water. If the animals are well cared for, they grow to marketable size and are ready for the livestock auction. If you forget to feed or water them, well, at best, they break out of their pens looking for food. At worst, they all die.

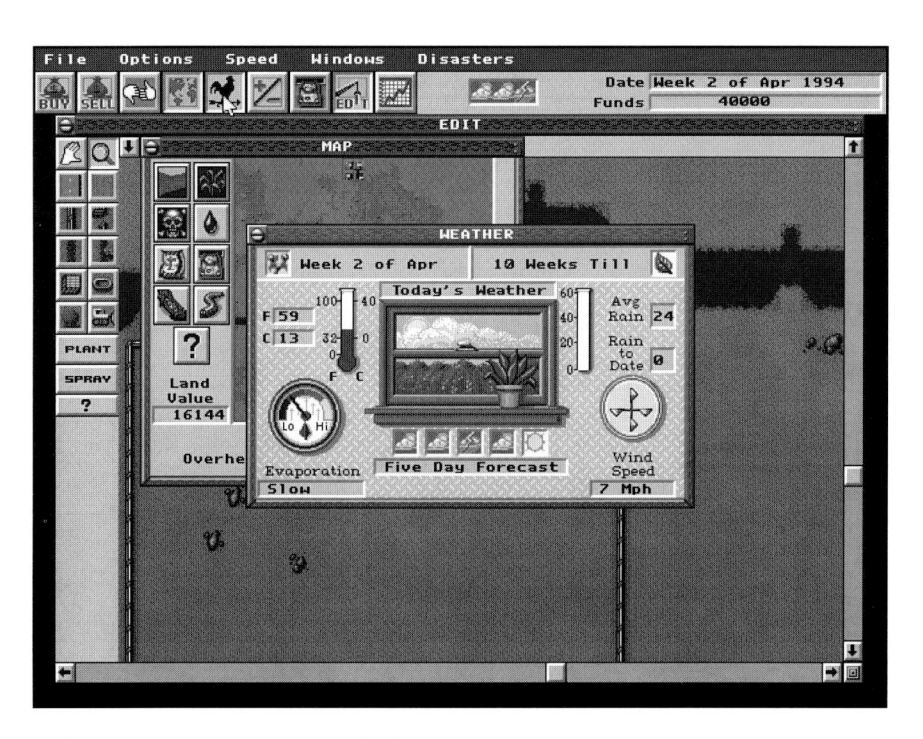

Simulation Programs

▲ *Good weather is vital for a thriving SimFarm.*

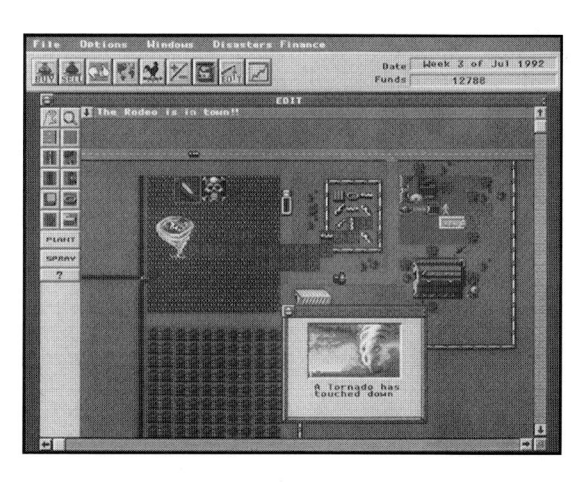

▲ *Natural disasters can strike a SimFarm just as they can a real one. (Courtesy of Maxis)*

After the crops are in and the animals have grown, they must be sold. With any luck, this will be at a high enough price to earn a profit. Crop prices fluctuate, and taxes must be paid, which makes farming as risky in the game as it is in real life. You can use any profits to buy new equipment, to restock supplies, or to buy more land.

Your taxes go to the local town. If you run a successful farm, you see the town thrive, with renovation of old homes and buildings and eventual expansion. Occasionally, you get to vote on town development issues. Just as the success of the farm affects the town, the course of development in the town affects the farm. Unfortunately, the townsfolk don't always agree with you on the best course of action, and the vote may go against you.

As if dealing with normal events isn't challenging enough, SimFarm has a full repertoire of disasters. Tornadoes, floods, and droughts are only a few of the disasters that can wreak havoc on a carefully designed and managed farm. Players who have enough trouble dealing with day-to-day farm life can disable these disasters.

The SimFarm manual includes an interesting 40-page guide to real farms. It covers the history of farming from the present day to our best guesses about the first farms, planted somewhere around 11,000 years ago.

Required Equipment
- 12 MHz 80286 processor (or better)
- EGA video (or better)
- 640K of RAM (EMS recommended)

(*Note:* A sound card is recommended.)

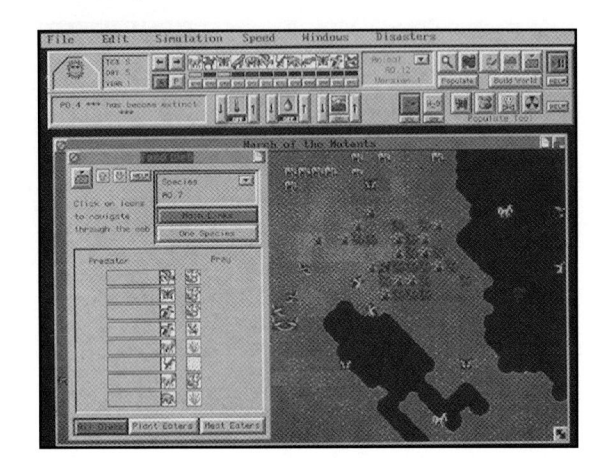

Chapter 5

▲ *Manipulating the food chain in SimLife. (Courtesy of Maxis)*

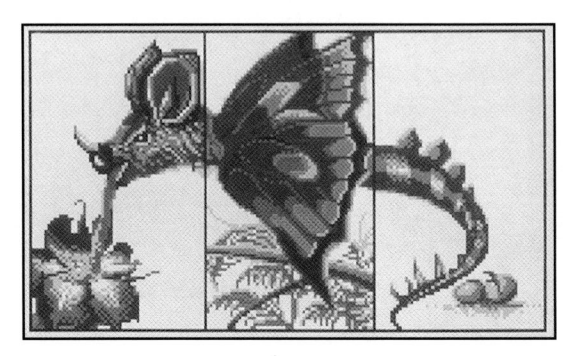

▲ *An animal designed with the flash cards. (Courtesy of Maxis)*

SimLife

SimLife, subtitled "The Genetic Playground," is another innovative simulation from Maxis. Available in both DOS and Windows versions, SimLife enables PC owners to create (simulated) life.

SimLife gives you the opportunity to build an ecosystem from the ground up. You can design plants and animals at the genetic level, thereby influencing their physical characteristics, behavior, and evolutionary potential. Ecological factors, such as the food chain, can also be manipulated.

One way to modify life forms is to use the Biology Lab. The Lab enables you to inspect, modify, and create creatures. A quick way to do this is to use the life form flash cards.

Choosing different combinations of flash cards results in plants and animals with various characteristics.

To exert more control over life forms requires direct manipulation of their *genomes*. Luckily, you can deal with the genomes in terms of high-level characteristics and behavior. By varying the genome, you can create just about any kind of creature.

> **Note:** The SimLife manual defines a *genome* as "the total genetic information in an organism's nucleus." In other words, SimLife lets you directly manipulate a life form's genetic makeup.

After life forms have been introduced into the environment, they try to survive. They also mutate! These mutations tend to change a species over time and are one key to survival in a changing world.

You have the ability to alter almost everything about the world that the creations live in. Land forms, climate, time—even the laws of physics—can be changed. Disasters such as fires, floods, and civilization can be introduced into the environment to test a life form's adaptability.

SimLife contains six specific scenarios. Each scenario has objectives that must be achieved in order for you to "win" the scenario. The program can be treated as a laboratory—and you can work towards personal goals—or as a toy, to be played just for fun.

Required Equipment

- 16 MHz 80386 processor (or better)
- VGA video
- At least 2M of RAM (4M recommended)
- Mouse
- Sound card

Other Types of Simulation Products

Some simulation programs, such as the ones from Maxis, are not sold specifically as educational or edutainment products. Even so, most would agree that these products clearly belong in the edutainment category. Some additional products not normally considered edutainment also fit into the simulation category. One such product is Microsoft's Flight Simulator.

Flight Simulator Version 5.0 provides some of the thrills of being a pilot and has incredible educational value as well. The instrumentation in the simulated cockpits is digitized from actual aircraft and is adequate to fly by FAA instrument flight rules (IFR) and visual flight rules (VFR). The program can give basic and advanced flight training, with excerpts from the applicable FAA documents. Flight Simulator is certainly edutainment.

Some simulation programs that qualify as edutainment come from even further afield. Many strategy games and war games are actually historical simulations. They usually place the player in the role of a leader in one of the great military conflicts of history. Part of the educational value comes from experiencing the decisions and challenges faced by generals and rulers throughout history. The rest of the value is in the support materials provided.

Most historical simulations seem to be created by history buffs. They tend to be packed with background information on the events covered in the game. Two examples of this kind of product are described in the next two paragraphs.

Civilization, from Microprose, turns the player into the leader of a tribe at the time of the founding of the first cities—6000 years ago. As the leader guides the tribe through history, the player contends with the kinds of problems and dilemmas that leaders throughout history most likely have faced. The player and her computer-controlled opponents vie to discover new technologies: from the wheel and writing, to recycling and robotics. As technologies are discovered, background information is provided, and the effects of the discoveries are felt throughout the game.

Kingmaker, from the Avalon Hill Game Company, places the player in the role of the leader of one of the factions vying for the throne of England during the War of the Roses. The program captures the flavor of that chaotic and bloody time. The documentation includes an 80-plus page historical manual that tells about the people, places, and events involved in that war.

Each of these products is covered in more detail in the following sections. By the time you finish reading these sections, I think you will agree that these products all qualify as edutainment.

Flight Simulator

Microsoft's Flight Simulator Version 5.0 is the latest incarnation of the company's popular product. Flight Simulator is a DOS-based, real-time flight-simulation program. By combining detailed graphics with realistic simulation models and sound effects, Flight Simulator turns a PC into the cockpit of an aircraft. To provide greater realism than might otherwise be possible, the instrument panels are digitized images from real cockpits.

▲ *An example of the photo-realistic instrumentation in Flight Simulator.*

The instrumentation meets the minimum VFR and IFR requirements specified by the FAA. The terrain is a three-dimensional model created from satellite photographs. The graphics-display system of the program uses the terrain information to create photo-realistic views from the cockpit of the simulated aircraft. Other aircraft are sometimes visible, as are buildings, bridges, and even a nuclear-powered aircraft carrier! The simulation provides realistic time-of-day visual effects, with the sun rising or setting as you fly.

This product has many other powerful features packed into it. Authentic sound effects are heard throughout the flight, including the sound of cockpit instruments and even crashes. Four different aircraft cockpits are simulated, a Cessna, a Learjet, a Schweizer sailplane, and a Sopwith Camel.

▲ *Flying the Learjet.*

▲ *A young and expanding empire in Civilization.*

The program provides basic and advanced flight instruction using excerpts from the official FAA Flight Training Handbook. A "Land Me" feature causes the simulation to land itself, which enables beginners to fly without having to master the difficult task of landing safely. In-flight failures test your knowledge of emergency procedures, while wind, clouds, and turbulence add realism to everyday flying. An instant-replay feature lets you analyze your performance.

Special fun features include a two-player mode, formation-flying with a computer-controlled aircraft, and a timed crop-dusting game. Five flying adventures are included, with scenarios such as "To Paris with Lindbergh" and "San Francisco Tour in the Sopwith."

Required Equipment

- DOS 3.2 or later
- 80386 processor (or better)
- EGA video (or better; SVGA recommended)
- At least 2M of RAM
- Mouse

(*Note:* A sound card is recommended. Program is compatible with a joystick and a flight yoke.)

Civilization

Civilization, published by Microprose, is a strategic simulation of grand scope. Available in both DOS and Windows versions, Civilization asks you to guide a tribe through the entire course of history.

Starting with the founding of the first cities 6,000 years ago, you must build an empire that can stand the test of time.

If the empire is to thrive, the tribe must deal with many different challenges. An initial challenge is for you to find suitable locations and build cities, as the cities serve as the basis for civilization.

Resource allocation is crucial. You must decide whether to build city improvements, such as granaries and marketplaces, or raise troops to defend those resources already held. Should taxes be increased to raise more money, or should money be spent on luxuries to keep the populace happy? Should more money be spent on research? Should the people live with lower taxes and fewer luxuries?

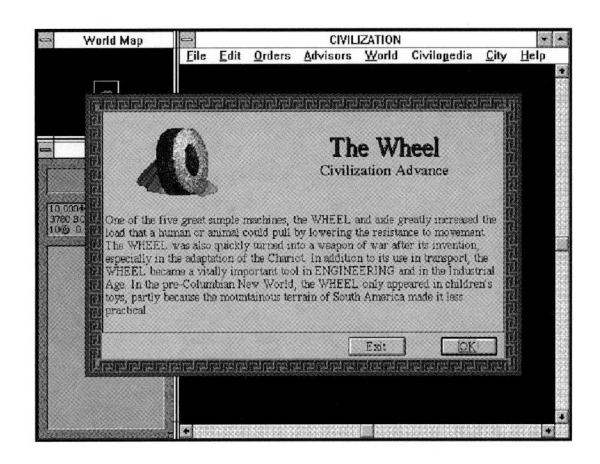

▲ *The wheel: One of the great Civilization advances.*

As if these problems weren't enough, you must also contend with up to seven other empires. Each of the computer-controlled opponents is modeled after a great historical leader: Napoleon, Genghis Khan, Gandhi, and Abe Lincoln, to mention just a few. Managing relations with the other empires is a key to your success. Just as in real life, trade, diplomacy, and conquest all are options.

Developing new technology is vital. Without advances, you find that you begin to fall behind your opponents. Advances in civilization range from the discovery of the alphabet to the harnessing of fusion power. Whenever a new kind of technology is discovered, a window containing historical information appears.

The description of the technology provides important background information about many of mankind's greatest discoveries. Beyond that, every discovery has some sort of impact on your empire. Some discoveries, such as bronze working and flight, enable you to create new military units. Others, such as banking and recycling, grant you the ability to create new kinds of city improvements. Still other discoveries give you the means to choose new forms of government or to build Wonders of the World.

Wonders of the World are awe-inspiring achievements or objects. Each Wonder can be created after a civilization discovers the requisite technology. The Wonders are some of our own greatest achievements, and when you develop one, the program displays important historical information about it. Each Wonder also has effects in the game that show the kind of impact such a spectacular achievement might have had in the real world.

The Civilization manual contains an informative article on the dynamics of civilization. It also contains short biographies on the famous leaders that control opposing civilizations in the game.

Required Equipment

DOS version:

- EGA video (or better)
- 640K of RAM

(*Note:* Mouse and sound card are recommended.)

Windows version:

- Windows 3.1
- 16 MHz 80386SX processor (or better)
- At least 4M of RAM
- Mouse

(*Note:* SVGA video with 256-color Windows driver and sound card with Windows driver are recommended.)

Kingmaker

Kingmaker is a DOS historical simulation program from the Avalon Hill Game Company. In Kingmaker, you lead one of the political factions involved in the War of the Roses. With civil war raging across the countryside, the throne of England is up for grabs.

Kingmaker employs high-quality graphics and digitized speech to portray the chaos and destruction of this period of English history. You must gain the support of other nobles and choose which royal heir to the throne to support. The goal is to control the last of the royal heirs from the houses of Lancaster and York.

You maneuver your forces across the map of England (and through part of France) to seize cities, defeat the forces of opposing factions, and capture royal heirs. Combat can be resolved quickly, with the program determining results based on the size of the opposing forces. You can also take a more direct hand in combat. The

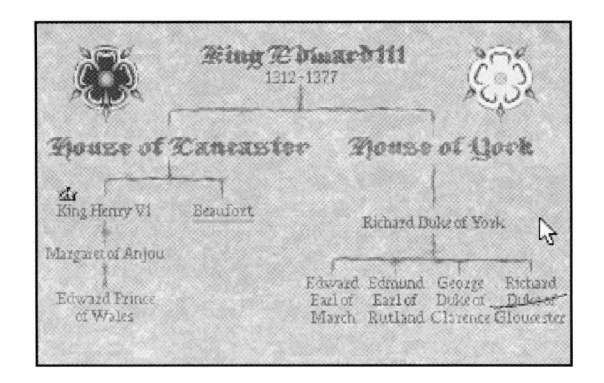

▲ *Claimants to the throne in Kingmaker.*

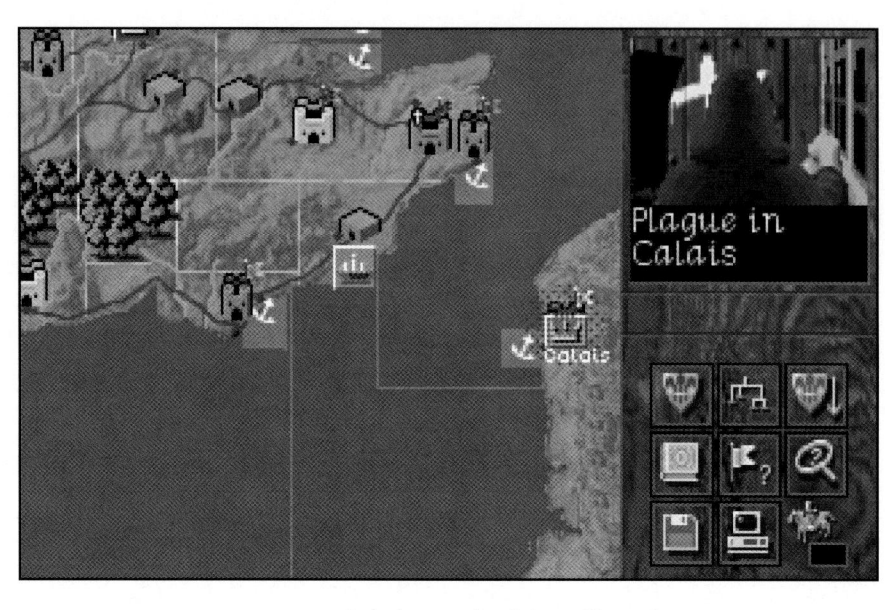

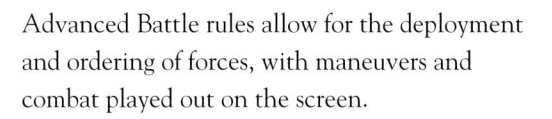

▲ *A plague strikes Calais in Kingmaker.*

Advanced Battle rules allow for the deployment and ordering of forces, with maneuvers and combat played out on the screen.

Although the action in Kingmaker is primarily military, politics does come into play. A faction must get its heir crowned if it hopes to succeed in taking the throne. One possibility is for England to have two crowned kings at the same time—one from the Lancasters and one from the Yorks. When only one ruler is crowned, he or she may be called to meet embassies from other countries. As a title is vacated (usually due to the death of the noble holding the title), Parliament may be convened to reallocate the title. The ransoming of royal heirs and the possibility of secret supporters for the factions adds to the intrigue.

Random events further complicate things. Mercenary troops may return to their homelands, leaving a noble without an army. Storms at sea can force a faction's ships into the hands of the enemy. Raids, revolts, and pirate attacks force nobles to pull their forces out of an army and return home to meet the threat. Plague strikes indiscriminately, killing any royal heirs or nobles in the affected city.

Kingmaker lets you learn about the War of the Roses by making you a participant. To further increase your understanding, Kingmaker includes an 85-page historical manual. This manual provides information on the origins of the conflict, the participants, and the actual course of the war.

In addition, the manual contains details of the art of war as it was practiced at that time, as well as reports on the major battles that occurred and the genealogies of the major families involved.

Required Equipment
- DOS 5.0 or higher
- 80286 processor (or better)
- VGA video
- At least 640K of RAM, with at least 600K free
- Sound card
- Mouse

Summary

A simulation program models something. That something can be a system or an event, such as an ecosystem or the pioneers' journey across the American West. An edutainment simulation aims to increase the user's understanding of whatever is being simulated by allowing the user to interact with it and see the effects of that interaction.

This chapter examined some of the simulations available for edutainment use. Common elements of simulations were identified, such as their sophisticated, highly graphical interfaces. And some of the unique features of various products were also explored.

This chapter also offered a walk-through of MECC's Oregon Trail. Although each simulation is uniquely adapted to the thing it is simulating, the walk-through gives you some idea of how a simulation works.

The rest of the chapter dealt with some of the simulation products currently available. The products covered went beyond the products people generally point to as edutainment programs. These products demonstrated that quality simulations with real educational value are available from unexpected sources.

Simulations are generally complex, demanding products designed for older children or adults. Mastering a simulation may take tens or even hundreds of hours of play.

Chapter 6 looks at another category of edutainment products that is almost the exact opposite of simulations in terms of difficulty and target users: CD-ROM Storybooks.

Most CD-ROM Storybooks are designed to be used by young children. They are simple to use, and it usually takes a child about five minutes to become comfortable in controlling one. CD-ROM Storybooks tend to be bright, colorful, and full of music and sound. If you have small children, or if you know someone who does, you will want to read Chapter 6.

Chapter 6

CD-ROM Storybooks

CD-ROM storybooks are computerized renditions of children's picture books, which may not sound like a very sensible idea to you. Taking the text and illustrations from a good book doesn't enhance them in any way; if anything, it may diminish them. Computerizing these books has other disadvantages besides the impact on the appearance of the book. You can't curl up in front of the fireplace with a CD-ROM, and it's impractical to haul your PC into your child's room for a bedtime story. Even so, CD-ROM storybooks are popular. They offer more than a copy of a book on a CD-ROM. They offer interactivity.

As you know, a CD-ROM can hold huge amounts of information. All the text and illustrations from a large picture book fill only a small portion of a disc. Fortunately, a CD-ROM storybook contains far more than just the text and illustrations from the original book. Some discs are the equivalent of a small children's library and hold numerous stories. The most interesting discs, the ones that exemplify what people think of when you say the words *CD-ROM storybook*, contain only one story. The bulk of the space on the CD-ROM is dedicated to a variety of enhancements to that story.

This chapter presents information about CD-ROM storybooks, discusses what features you should expect to find in these products, and provides information on which publishers produce the products you may find interesting.

The following topics are discussed in this chapter:

- Common features of CD-ROM storybooks
- Variations among products
- A short walk-through of a typical product
- Some of the storybooks available for young children
- Some of the storybooks available for older children and adults

Common Features

CD-ROM storybooks share certain defining features. They are modeled after a child's picture book and feature on-screen either one page (as shown in the following figure) or two facing pages (as shown later in the My Silly CD of ABC's figure).

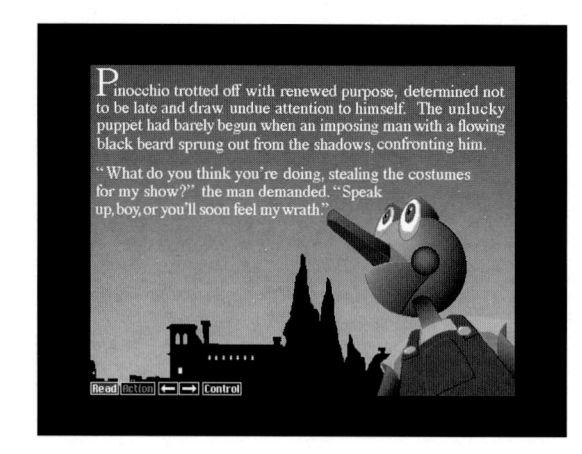

▲ *A typical CD-ROM storybook page, taken from The Adventures of Pinocchio.*

The child can page forward or backward, as if the program were a book. Many of the products use a symbol representing a turned-up page corner that even small children can quickly understand.

▲*Turned-up page corners in The New Kid on the Block.*

Like picture books, most CD-ROM storybooks are heavily illustrated and contain only a limited amount of text. Some discs include exact reproductions of the artwork in the original book, as you can see in the figure showing an illustration from The Tale of Peter Rabbit.

The illustrations on The Tale of Peter Rabbit CD are identical to those in my daughter's paper copy of the book. Other discs contain artwork specially created for the CD-ROM.

CD-ROM storybook products also share features that take them beyond a simple re-creation of a printed book. Taking advantage of a CD-ROM's capability to store large amounts of sound, all the stories are fully narrated. In most cases, words or phrases on a page are highlighted as the narrator speaks them. This feature helps children associate the printed word with the spoken word. Most of the products also let the user disable the narrator so that they can read at their own pace.

Variations on a Theme

Beyond variations in subject matter, each publisher includes a different set of features and capabilities in its CD-ROM storybooks.

Many of the products enhance the basic story with on-screen *hotspots*. A hotspot is an area of the screen that, when clicked with the mouse, triggers some kind of special activity. Several publishers fill each page of their storybooks with hotspots. Some, like Discis, use them to provide the spelling and pronunciation of the item clicked.

Others add sound effects, music, or elaborate animation that combines sight and sound. In Broderbund's Living Books series, virtually everything on a page has some associated animation. One of my favorites has to be the singing cookies in Arthur's Teacher Trouble.

Some products enable the child (or his parents) to specify how text will be highlighted. Individual words, phrases, or even entire lines can be highlighted. Highlighting larger chunks of text emphasizes word groups that are more meaningful than individual words. In many cases, the child can also click individual words to hear the pronunciation.

Many of the storybooks use the available storage space on the CD-ROM to include the entire text of the storybook in one (or more) languages besides English. Select Spanish, for example, and the English text is replaced by the Spanish equivalent. The narration changes to the new language as well.

Multiple languages make the products accessible to many more people, and they can also help those wishing to learn another language. Seeing two or three sentences in your native language and then pressing a key to see them in another language should aid the learning process.

Most of the products provide some way to move through the story other than flipping through the pages in sequence. Pinocchio, distributed by Orange Cherry New Media, has a Go To option that lets the child jump directly to any page. The Living Books series provides a small picture of each page that the child can quickly flip through to find the one he wants. The Annabel series, from Texas Caviar, lets the child place a bookmark that he can instantly return to.

A few CD-ROM storybooks have features that are oriented toward more traditional study. Some contain on-line dictionaries and glossaries to help the child with unfamiliar terms used in the story. In the stories from the Kids Can Read! series from Discis, words that the child had trouble with (the

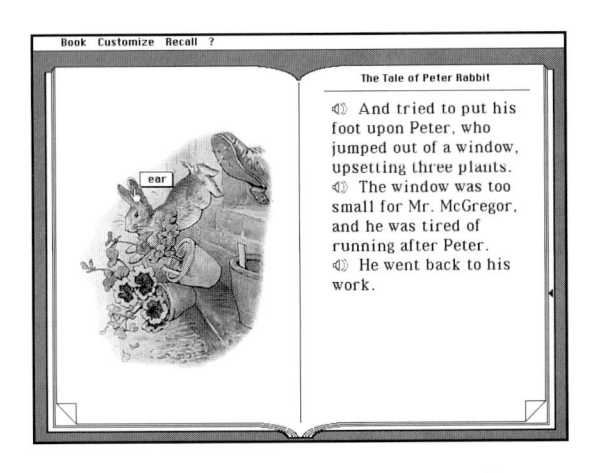

▲ *Reproduced illustrations from* The Tale of Peter Rabbit.

▲ *Singing cookies in Arthur's Teacher Trouble.*

ones that the child clicked for more information) are recorded and saved in a recall list. The child or parent can then review this list and work on words that caused problems.

T.J. Finds a Friend, published by Media Resources, includes a unique Resource Guide. T.J. is a fund-raising project for the National Center for Missing & Exploited Children (NCMEC). The Resource Guide provides a mini-encyclopedia for each page in the story.

This encyclopedia provides information about the items and topics covered on this page. It also contains valuable information about national help agencies such as the NCMEC.

Other products provide a search function that lets the child enter words and see how they are used in the story. Seeing the word in context helps the child determine its meaning.

Various discs include either a parent's guide or a learning guide. In some cases—Ebook's Christmas Carol, for example—the guide is on-line, and accessible from within the storybook. In other cases, such as Discis's My Silly CD of ABC's, the guide is a small paper booklet. Whatever form these guides take, they are full of useful information on how to help your child get the most out of the disc. These guides usually include suggestions on how the parent can work with the child, away from the computer, to extend the skills learned into everyday life.

▲ *The text of Broderbund's Just Grandma and Me in Japanese!*

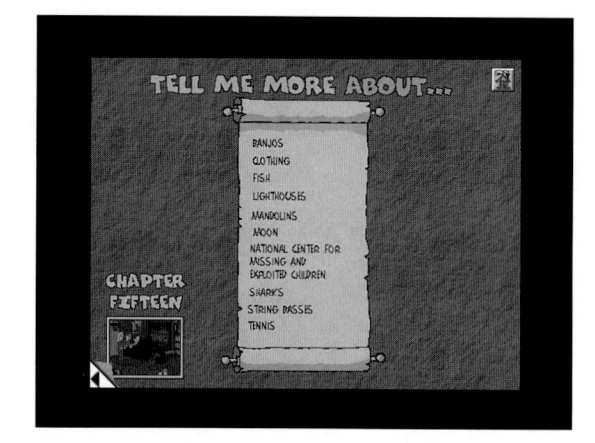

▲ *A mini-encyclopedia page from T.J. Finds a Friend.*

The school versions of products from Texas Caviar (the Annabel series and Whale of a Tale) are particularly rich in non-computer activities. They include songs and dances to perform, pictures to print and color, and assorted other activities.

CD-ROM Storybooks

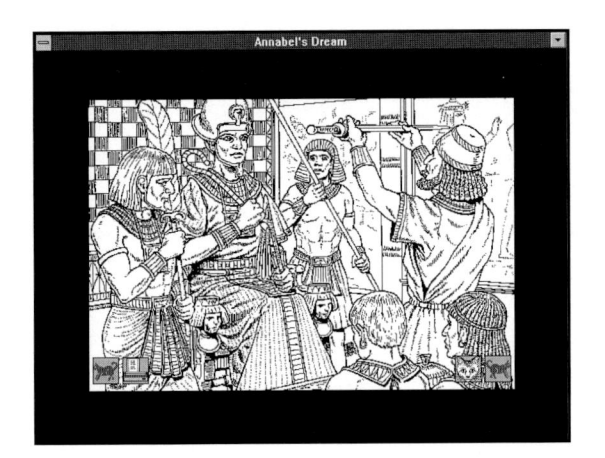

▲ *A printable picture from Annabel's Dream of Ancient Egypt.*

▲ *The control page for Arthur's Teacher Trouble.*

▲ *Highlighted text on page one of Arthur Teacher's Trouble.*

Using a CD-ROM Storybook: Arthur's Teacher Trouble

Arthur's Teacher Trouble was the first CD-ROM storybook I ever used. It is also my three-year-old daughter's favorite edutainment product, and it won a Parent's Choice Award in 1993. To give you a better idea of what a CD-ROM storybook is like, this section walks you through a session with Arthur's Teacher Trouble (Arthur, for short).

Arthur, like many other CD-ROM storybooks, can run directly off the disc. This is handy because it doesn't use up valuable space on your hard disk. After you get past the introductory material, you see the control page.

This page is used to set the story language (English or Spanish) and other features. If the child selects the Read To Me box, the program reads the story straight through. It does not allow any interaction by the child. If the child chooses Let Me Play, the program reads the text on each page and then stops to let the child explore it. The Options button is discussed a little later, and the Quit button lets the child do just that.

For this example, I chose the Let Me Play option. The control page fades away and page one of the story appears. The program immediately begins to read the text of page one in English, Arthur's default language. The program highlights phrases as they are spoken. The following figure shows page one with the phrase *but Room 13* highlighted.

The text highlights are not the only things synchronized with the narration. Animated characters on-screen enact the activities mentioned by the narrator. In the next figure, you can see the children filing out of Room 13 slowly, in alphabetical order.

▲ *Animation enacts the story in Arthur's Teacher Trouble.*

After the narrator reads all the text on the page, the program stops and waits for the child. Clicking either of the turned-up page corners changes the page as in a paper book. Clicking the objects on the screen generates a wide variety of responses. Bells ring, doors open, and blinds rise. The ballerina on the "Dance Class" notice dances. Mr. Ratburn, the teacher, changes outfits. The lost cat on the poster sings and cries, while a bug on the bulletin board scurries around the screen. All the action is accompanied by appropriate sound effects and music, making each page a multimedia adventure for kids (and their parents). At some point, the child will want to stop play and move on, and the easiest way is to click the page number at the bottom of the screen.

If the child remembers that page number, or just what the page looks like, she can come back later and pick up where she left off. Instead of flipping through each page, the child can use the Options page to go directly to the desired point in the story.

The Credits button on the Options page displays the program credits. The credits are done as a little movie and are actually worth watching once. The Previews button shows previews of other products in the Living Books series. The collection of items in the upper-right portion of the page helps the child quickly find the page where she left off last time she used Arthur.

▲ *The Options page from Arthur's Teacher Trouble.*

The left and right arrows change the page. The numeral between the arrows shows the current page number. The image shows a small replica of the page. With both the page number and the image to go by, it is easy for the child to find her place again. Clicking the OK button takes the child to the current page.

Although each CD-ROM storybook has unique features, I hope that this quick walk-through helped you understand how this kind of product works.

What's Available?

A variety of CD-ROM storybooks are available, and more are being created every day. The subject matter of these storybooks includes classic tales and fables, as well as works of contemporary authors and stories specifically designed for CD-ROM. The rest of this section contains information about some of the products currently available. In addition, the *Edutainment Comes Alive!* CD-ROM contains samples from some CD-ROM storybooks.

CD-ROM Storybooks for Young Children

Most of the CD-ROM storybooks on the market seem to be aimed at small children. According to one of the publishers I spoke to, their discs are purchased primarily for pre-readers and early readers. Many parents purchase these products specifically to improve the reading skills of their children. The following sections contain information about some of the young children's CD-ROM storybooks that I was able to review.

Annabel's Dream of Ancient Egypt

Annabel's Dream of Ancient Egypt is published by Texas Caviar and is aimed at children ages 6 and older. It is an original story about Annabel the cat. It is the story of Annabel's successful attempt to come to terms with her annoying sisters. Inspired by the music of the opera *Aida*, Annabel dreams of life in ancient Egypt. There, she learns to cope with anger and her teasing sisters.

Annabel's Dream has many interesting features. The child can insert an electronic bookmark into the text and later resume reading at that spot. The disc provides a glossary that contains all the words in the story. When a word is selected in the glossary, its definition is displayed and the narrator pronounces it.

The illustrations are attractive line drawings that include spot animation.

▲ *A page from Annabel's Dream of Ancient Egypt.*

The initial images are in black and white, but when Annabel begins to dream, the pages appear in color. The program controls can be visible on the screen, as in the preceding figure, or hidden.

Some of the best features of Annabel's Dream are not even part of the story. The disc contains a variety of supplemental articles and activities and includes introductions to ancient Egypt and the opera *Aida*. An earlier figure in this chapter shows one of the many pictures that can be printed from this program and colored.

With adult help, the child can even learn to make paper! The many additional supplemental features of this product give it lots of educational value.

Annabel's Dream of Ancient Egypt and the other CD-ROM storybooks from Texas Caviar (Annabel's Dream of Medieval England and Whale of a Tale) come in both classroom and home versions. The home versions are less expensive, but they do not include some of the supplemental material included in the classroom versions.

Required Equipment

- CD-ROM drive
- Windows 3.1
- 80286 processor (or better)
- EGA or VGA video
- 640K of RAM
- Sound card with Windows driver
- Mouse

> **Note:** You can find out more about the items in this equipment list by looking in Chapter 2 for general information, Chapter 10 for SVGA video cards and sound cards, Chapter 11 for CD-ROM drives, and Chapter 12 for Windows information.

My Silly CD of ABC's

My Silly CD of ABC's is part of the Kids Basics! series from Discis. They combine fun and learning to teach young children basic concepts. This disc introduces the letters of the alphabet through the antics of an assortment of animals.

The book contains a set of facing pages for each letter in the alphabet. Clicking different portions of the screen provides the spelling of the name of the object, as well as its pronunciation. The drawings themselves are cartoons that illustrate the text on the visible pages.

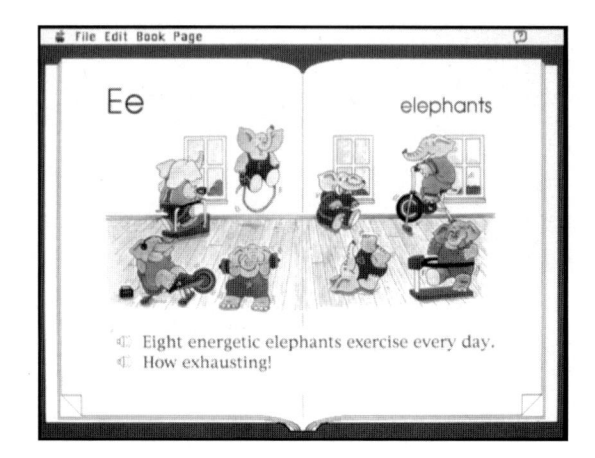

▲ *A page from My Silly CD of ABC's. (Courtesy of Discis Knowledge Research Inc.)*

The child can move through the book by jumping to multiple bookmarks, so he never has to lose his place. A unique feature is the triangular marker visible on the right edge of the book. Moving the marker up or down lets the child travel directly to any page in the book.

My Silly CD of ABC's has a variety of features that enhance its educational value. A Recall List keeps track of the words that the child clicked for additional information. This list can be used to guide a review session. The program can be configured so that when the child clicks a word, it is pronounced either in English or Spanish. An Options page enables a parent to change the reading rate and vary what happens when the child clicks an object.

Some of the Discis Kids Can Read! series CD-ROMs are also suitable for young children.

Required Equipment

(*Note:* Discis CD-ROMs can run under DOS or Windows.)

- CD-ROM drive
- Windows 3.1 (if used under Windows)
- 80386SX processor (or better)
- DOS 5.0 or later
- At least 2M of RAM
- SVGA video card with 640 x 480, 256-color mode
- Sound Blaster or 100 percent-compatible sound card with Windows sound driver
- Mouse

The Tortoise and the Hare

The Tortoise and the Hare is part of Broderbund's Living Books series. It is a CD-ROM retelling of Aesop's fable of the same name. Designed for children between the ages of 3 and 8, it tells of the race between the slow-and-steady tortoise and the slightly hyper hare.

This disc provides text and narration in either English or Spanish. The child can choose to let the program read to her, or she can read and play at her own pace. The child can choose to play in any page, instead of being required to go through them sequentially.

Broderbund's Living Books stand out because of their interactivity. They include clever animation, with music and sound effects, on every page.

Every one of the characters on this page has its own animated sequence, and a mouse click is all that is required to activate a sequence. The characters talk, dance, and sing, accompanied by appropriate music and sound effects. Even the windows, doors, and smokestacks do something! The program also comes with a paperback copy of The Tortoise and the Hare.

▲ A page from The Tortoise and the Hare.

Required Equipment
- CD-ROM drive
- Windows 3.1
- DOS 3.3 or greater
- 80386SX processor (or better)
- At least 4M of RAM
- SVGA video card with 640 x 480, 256-color Windows video driver
- Sound Blaster, Sound Blaster Pro, or 100 percent-compatible sound card with Windows sound driver
- Mouse

CD-ROM Storybooks for Older Readers

Some publishers have extended CD-ROM storybooks beyond their original target audience of young children. A sampling of these products is presented in the remainder of this section. These products generally are aimed at readers age 7 or older, although some products are targeted at teens and up.

A Christmas Carol

A Christmas Carol, from EBook, is part of a large family of CD-ROM story books. Recommended for ages 12 to adult, the text has a sixth-grade reading level. The disc contains the unabridged, original tale, just as Charles Dickens wrote it. It tells the story of Ebenezer Scrooge, who discovers the true meaning of Christmas. He does this through the intercession of the ghosts of Christmas Past, Present, and Future.

The pages of this storybook are mainly text, with 27 color and black-and-white illustrations. The story is fully narrated. A set of control buttons is always available across the top of the screen.

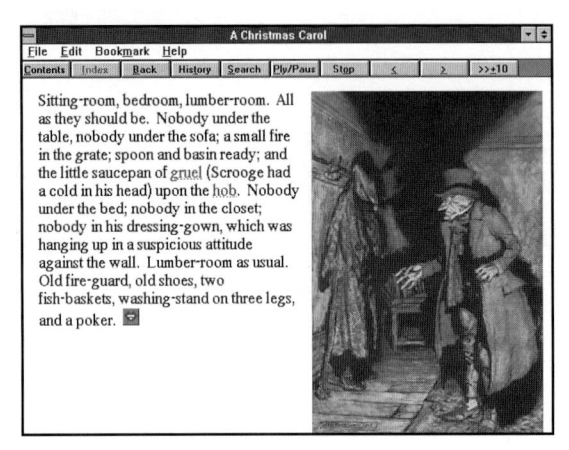

An illustrated page from A Christmas Carol.

Supplemental material in A Christmas Carol.

In the preceding figure, you may notice that two words on the page, *gruel* and *hob*, are underlined. They are also a different color than the other words on the page. When you click one of these words, the built-in dictionary displays a small box with the word's definition.

You can move through the story in several ways: you can use multiple bookmarks, you can page forward or backward, or you can move ten pages at a time in either direction. The program also maintains a history of the pages you have been to, which enables you to go back to pages you have recently viewed. In addition, you can click the Back button to jump back to the page you were last on, and you can use the Search feature to jump to a page that contains a particular word.

The disc contains some supplemental materials. You can access these materials through the menu shown in the next figure.

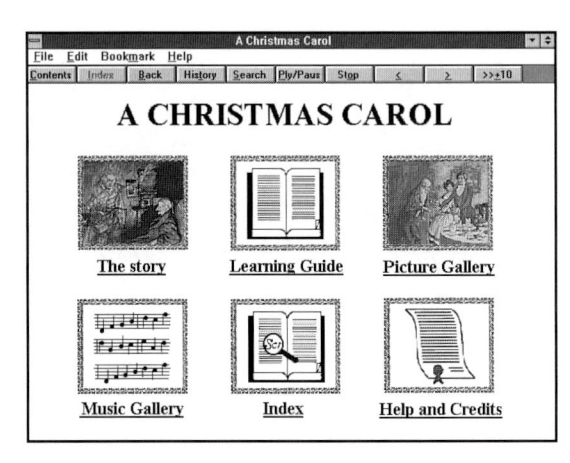

The Learning Guide has suggestions for increasing the educational value of the disc and provides insight into the design of the product. The Music Gallery and Picture Gallery give you direct access to the music and illustrations used in the story.

Required Equipment

- MPC-compliant CD-ROM drive
- Windows 3.1 (or Windows 3.0 with multimedia extensions)
- MSCDEX 2.2 or later
- 80386SX processor (or better)
- At least 2M of RAM
- SVGA video card with 640 x 480, 256-color Windows video driver
- MPC-compliant sound card with Windows sound driver
- Mouse

The Adventures of Pinocchio

The Adventures of Pinocchio is distributed by Orange Cherry New Media. It is a new adaptation of the famous story of Pinocchio, the puppet who wants to be a real boy. This version of the story adds new adventures and new characters to the classic fairy tale.

Although some CD-ROM storybooks contain about 20 pages, The Adventures of Pinocchio has 20 chapters with a total of 270 pages! The pages are full-color and fully narrated. Many of the pages contain animation, sound effects, and music.

Three special Living Pages are interspersed between the regular pages. The Living Pages are full-screen illustrations with hotspots that trigger animation. The publisher thoughtfully provided a way to reach the start of each chapter, as well as a Go To function that enables you to pick up where you left off.

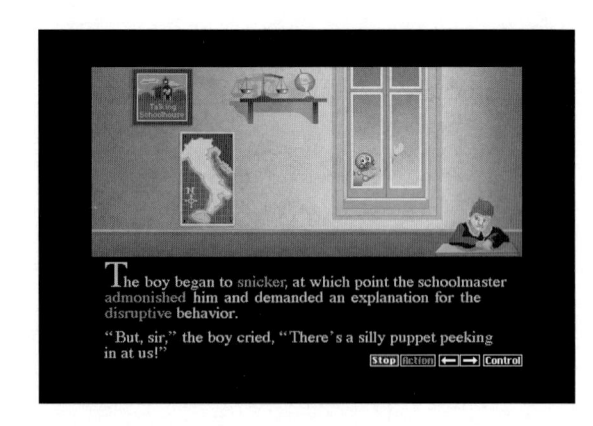

▲ *A page from The Adventures of Pinocchio.*

CD-ROM Storybooks

Pinocchio includes an on-screen glossary with over 450 definitions of words encountered in the story. Words that you can find in the glossary are a different color than the rest of the words on the page.

The disc includes a Question section that contains four questions for each chapter. The quizzes combine complete-the-sentence questions (containing multiple-choice answers) with relevant scenes from the story that offer helpful reminders.

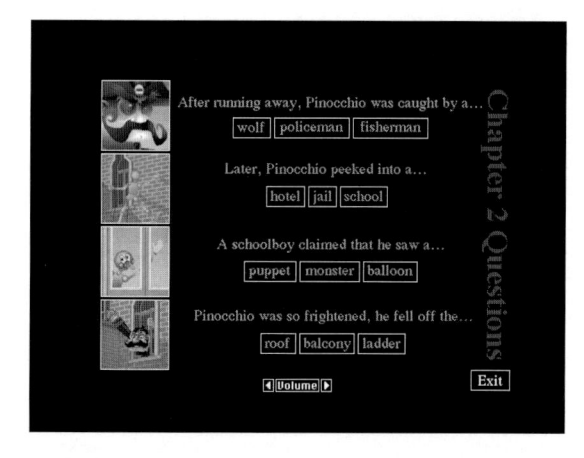

▲ *Questions for Chapter 2 of The Adventures of Pinocchio.*

The quizzes help you retain more of what you read, and they provide a useful break between chapters.

Required Equipment
- CD-ROM drive
- Windows 3.1
- 80386 processor (or better)
- 4M or more of RAM
- SVGA video card with 640 x 480, 256-color Windows video driver
- Sound Blaster, MPC-compatible sound card with Windows sound driver
- Mouse

Scary Poems for Rotten Kids

Scary Poems for Rotten Kids is part of the Kids Can Read! series from Discis. The series contains books for all different ages, some for children as young as 3, others for children age 9 and up. Scary Poems for Rotten Kids is a book of funny (and a touch scary) poetry for kids age 7 and up.

Clicking different portions of the screen provides the spelling of the name of the object that was clicked, as well as its pronunciation. The drawings themselves are cartoons that illustrate scenes from the poems. Each poem contains one illustration, which is the same on all the pages of that particular poem.

The child can move through the book by clicking the name of a particular poem in the Table of Contents. A marker on the right side of the book enables the child to quickly move to any page. The program also allows multiple bookmarks, so that the child never has to lose her place.

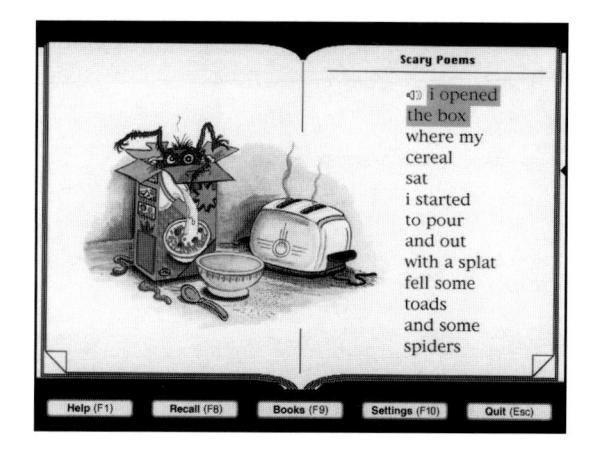

▲ *A page from Scary Poems for Rotten Kids. (Courtesy of Discis Knowledge Research Inc.)*

Like other Discis products, Scary Poems has a variety of features that enhance its educational value. A Recall List keeps track of the words the child clicked for additional information. This list can be used to guide a review session. Optionally, the disc provides Spanish-language support. When the child clicks a word, she hears it pronounced either in English or Spanish depending on which options are selected.

This product and its siblings are very flexible. The Options page enables you to change the reading rate and vary what happens when the child clicks an object.

Discis has also come out with a series called Discis Multimedia. The discs in this series are intended for teenagers through adults.

Required Equipment

(*Note:* Discis CD-ROMs can run under DOS or Windows.)

- CD-ROM drive
- Windows 3.1 (if used under Windows)
- 80386SX processor (or better)
- DOS 5.0 or later
- At least 2M of RAM
- SVGA video card with 640 x 480, 256-color mode
- Sound Blaster or 100 percent-compatible sound card with Windows sound driver
- Mouse

T.J. Finds a Friend

T.J. Finds a Friend is a product with a mission. Distributed by Media Resources, it was produced by Artists for Multimedia as a fund raiser for the National Center for Missing and Exploited Children (NCMEC). Twenty percent of the proceeds from the sale of this product go directly to the NCMEC for discovery and educational programs.

The story is designed to teach children (and their parents) lessons about everyday life. The main focus of the story is on preventing the abduction of children. I suspect that this will not be the last CD-ROM storybook created to benefit a specific cause.

The pages of the story consist of colorful cartoon scenes, such as the one shown in the figure.

▲ *A page from T.J. Finds a Friend.*

The text appears only long enough to be read; then it is removed to allow for animated activity on the screen. The child can use this product in three different ways: the program can present the story straight through, with narration and no interaction; the child can go through the story with no narration, playing as long as he likes on each page; or the two other modes can be combined, with each page being narrated before the child gets to play. Each page contains hotspots that trigger animation.

The child can also choose to go directly to a particular page and start the narration at that point. Each page has an underlying mini-encyclopedia. The mini-encyclopedia contains information about topics and objects found on that page of the storybook. The mini-encyclopedias also contain valuable information about national help agencies. The mini-encyclopedia for page two (called Chapter 2 on this disc) was shown in a figure earlier in this chapter.

This product has a known bug. On my machine, each time I tried to access a mini-encyclopedia page, the program displayed an error message. The error never prevented me from going on with what I was doing, and it apparently is not a surprise to the manufacturer; the documentation for the product contains a note warning that the message may appear.

Required Equipment
- MPC-compliant CD-ROM drive
- Windows 3.1 (or Windows 3.0 with multimedia extensions)
- MSCDEX 2.2 or later
- At least 4M of RAM
- SVGA video card with 640 x 480, 256-color Windows video driver
- MPC-compliant sound card with Windows sound driver
- Mouse

Summary

This chapter took a close look at one of the major categories of edutainment products: CD-ROM storybooks. This is a relatively new type of product. Only in the last year or so have the necessary CD-ROM drives and multimedia capabilities become available on desktop PCs.

The chapter contained information on what is common in CD-ROM storybooks and what varies from publisher to publisher. It took a good look at the available features and the advantages they provide for the user. A walk-through of a representative product enabled you to see first-hand (almost) what using this type of product is like.

The chapter also gave you a look at some of the CD-ROM storybooks currently available. By dividing these products into those aimed at young children and those intended for seven-year-old children through adults, it gave you the information you need to start your search for the appropriate products for you and your family.

Many of the products discussed in this chapter are aimed at young children. This class of user has its own unique needs and requires software designed especially for this age group. Products aimed specifically at the preschool crowd make up a rapidly growing category of edutainment software. Preschool products are the subject of Chapter 7.

Chapter 7

Preschool Products

Preschool products are edutainment programs designed for very young children. These programs teach basic skills that are important precursors to math and reading. Many preschool products also try to encourage a child's creativity. The programs rely on bright colors, music, and sound effects to hold a child's attention. Most important of all, preschool products provide interactivity and give young users a measure of control that they don't often have in other parts of their lives. Commonly, programs make the computer a more comfortable place for youngsters by including friendly, animated characters they can relate to.

You can now find preschool products that address just about any skill a young child might need. Some stress letter and word recognition. Others explore shapes, colors, or the animal kingdom. Still others teach problem-solving and counting skills. Several products include creativity activities geared for a young audience. And using any of these products makes the child more comfortable with the computer.

Although preschool products as a group cover the full range of skills and concepts, most publishers try to make it easy for the parent to tell which programs are right for their children. Products have appropriate age ranges clearly marked, and they frequently spell out the skills to be learned right on the package. The goal is to challenge the child without frustrating her. Many of the products are designed so that there is no "wrong" answer; every action by the child has a fun or interesting result.

The best programs take full advantage of the high-quality sound and video systems found on newer PCs. Many of these programs won't run on my wife's machine, a 20 MHz 386 with 2M of RAM, VGA video, and a basic Sound Blaster card. Usually either the processor is too slow or the program wants SVGA video. If those two items aren't a problem, and the program runs under Windows, 2M of RAM isn't enough. It is paradoxical: the youngest, least sophisticated users require the biggest, most sophisticated computers.

The following topics are discussed in this chapter:

- Common features of preschool edutainment products
- Unique features
- A walk-through of a preschool product
- Number and math skills products
- Letter and reading skills products

Common Features

Several characteristics are common to most preschool edutainment products. The most apparent is the use of bright colors and sound to catch and hold the attention of young children. A decent sound system is equally important; many of the programs depend on spoken messages from the computer to the child.

Less visible, but more important than sight and sound, are interactivity and control. Unlike simply watching TV, the child is actively involved in what is going on when she uses a preschool edutainment product. The interaction with the program and the control that interaction brings keep the child's attention and interest. The products sometimes include a parent's guide that tells how to reinforce what is learned on the PC with non-computer activities.

Many of these products interact with the child through some kind of cute, friendly playmate. These animated characters make the program less intimidating for the child. One good example is Loid, the animated, talking character who inhabits Sierra On-Line's Early Math.

▲ *Loid, a friendly playmate and teacher in Early Math.*

These characters are endlessly patient, assist the child when necessary, and never criticize her.

These products have one more common feature you should remember. Good preschool products make it easy for the child to use the computer. Most use both the mouse and keyboard. This easy introduction to the use of the PC eliminates the fear and discomfort that so many adults feel when they confront a computer. A child who grows up with preschool edutainment products is likely to be right at home on a PC for the rest of her life.

Unique Features

As with other types of software, publishers try to make their products stand out from the crowd by adding unique or unusual features. This section looks at some of these unique and unusual features. Although only a few of the products available are covered here, you can see the innovative thought being applied to preschool edutainment products.

Some kind of kid's mode is a very useful feature. When a program is running in kid's mode, access to the rest of the system is limited. Products with this feature run under Windows and remove system menus and other means of returning to Windows. The parent gets to define a secret combination or key code that lets him end the program and return to Windows.

Most preschool products contain more than one activity. These activities are tied together with a central menu or main screen. The next logical step is to tie families of products together with one common access program, which makes these products easier for a child to use. Such features are particularly useful in DOS, which doesn't have program groups and icons to organize and simplify access. Electronic Arts uses this technique with its edutainment products. The common access program is the EA*Kids Theater. The Theater provides access to all the EA*Kids products on the hard disk, as well as demos of products.

▲ *Families of products are sometimes tied together with common access programs, such as EA*Kids Theater.*

Children love TV and videos. It only makes sense that preschool products use this fact to help kids learn. One approach to this is taken by the Waterford Institute. Their Rusty & Rosy Read With Me products each include a videotape. These tapes reinforce what the child is learning with the software.

Knowledge Adventure's Kid's Zoo provides full-motion video as part of the program. The product contains a number of video clips of animals in action. With full-motion video and stereo sound, these clips are like mini-movies for the kids.

Cute, friendly cartoon characters make programs more interesting to small children. The ultimate expression of this brings famous characters into the computer. Disney is a leader in this, with Mickey Mouse and his friends appearing in several Disney edutainment products.

Disney is not the only company to feature its characters in edutainment products. Electronic Arts is producing games featuring Sesame Street characters, and Broderbund has made arrangements to use Dr. Seuss characters.

A trend that seems to be sweeping the country is karaoke. Karaoke is basically a form of sing-along, in which songs are played without their lyrics. The participant (player? victim?) sings along and his rendition of the lyrics is mixed into the song. Dr. T's Music Software has taken the karaoke concept and applied it to teaching children to read and sing. Dr. T's Sing-A-Long Kids' Classics turns your PC into a karaoke machine for young children.

Animation keyed to the music makes the program even more fun for young users. And the lyrics are displayed as the child sings them, which helps the child relate the words and their sounds.

Using a Preschool Product: Sierra On-Line's Early Math

This section takes you on a quick tour of Sierra On-Line's Early Math. It embodies most of the common features of preschool products that were mentioned earlier. Early Math also happens to be my three-year-old daughter's favorite program in this category.

▲ *Mickey Mouse in a Disney edutainment product.*

▲ *Dr. T's Sing-A-Long Kids' Classics.*

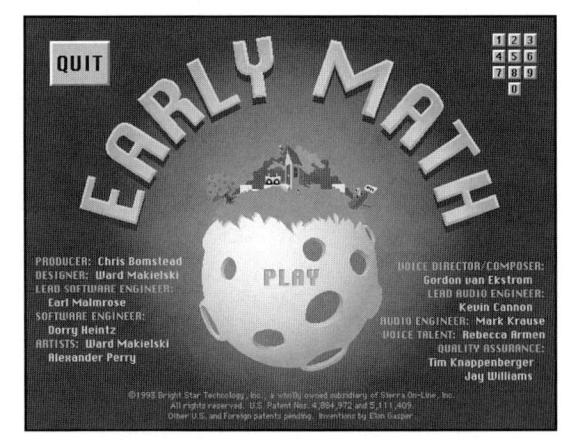

▲ *The Early Math opening screen.*

Clicking the asteroid in the center of the screen takes you to the games. Clicking the keypad in the upper-right corner takes you to the Parent's Screen.

The Parent's Screen lets a parent or other adult configure the game and monitor the child's progress in various activities.

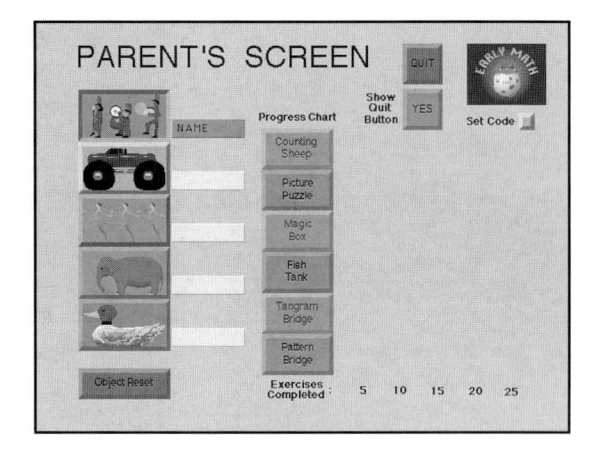

▲ *The Parent's Screen in Early Math.*

Each of the buttons (game pieces) on the left side of the screen can be assigned a child's name. The program keeps statistics on a child's performance in each activity by tracking the use of the game pieces.

The Progress Chart shows the number of exercises completed for each activity and is based on which playing piece is selected. The Show Quit Button option lets an adult put the program into Kid's mode. When the Quit button is not visible, the child has no way to exit the program and get into

Windows. The Set Code button lets you enter a four-digit combination. From that point on, you must enter the combination before you can gain access to the Parent's Screen.

If the child chooses Play in the opening screen, he must then select a game piece from the Game Piece Selection screen.

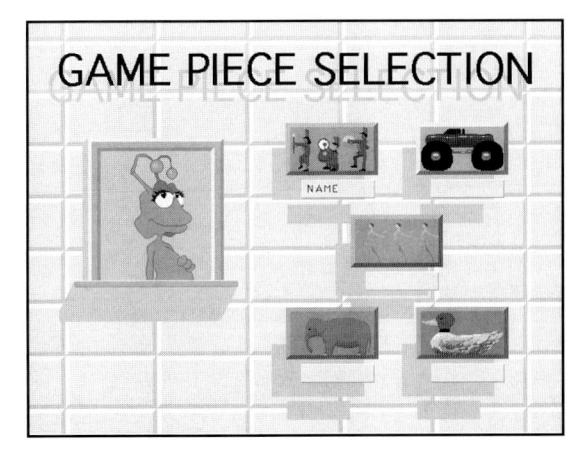

▲ *The Game Piece Selection screen in Early Math.*

All statistics on what happens in the current play session are recorded under this game piece. After a game piece has been selected, the action moves to the surface of the asteroid. The surface is one of two screens that gives access to the activities included in the package.

▲ *The surface of the asteroid in Early Math.*

The child can reach two activities from this screen: Tangram Bridge and Pattern Bridge. If the child selects the car, he accesses Tangram Bridge; if he selects the bucket, he accesses Pattern Bridge. Loid, the friendly little alien who inhabits this asteroid, can be seen entering his house in the center of the screen.

Loid's house is underground and consists of two levels and four more games.

▲ *Loid in his house.*

The four games in Loid's house are Counting Sheep (lower level, left side), Complete the Picture (lower level, right side), the Magic Box (upper level, left side), and the Fish Tank (upper level, right side). Each game works on one or more important math skills for young children.

▲ *Counting Sheep in Loid's house.*

To choose another game, the child can return to the inside of Loid's house simply by clicking the little picture of it in the upper-right corner of the screen.

The program allows the child to roam from game to game easily. The games were reviewed by an education specialist and provide fun and challenges for children between the ages of three and six. Throughout the child's visit to the asteroid, Loid keeps up a continuous stream of encouragement, spoken in his childlike voice.

What's Available?

The number of preschool edutainment products is increasing rapidly. Preschool products are one of the hottest edutainment categories right now. The rest of this chapter looks at some of the products you can buy today.

Number and Math Skills

One popular goal for preschool products is teaching pre-math and basic math skills. Pre-math skills include such things as number recognition, the ability to discriminate between quantities, and recognition of geometric shapes. The following paragraphs describe two products that focus on math and pre-math skills.

Early Math

As you learned during the walk-through, Early Math is a Windows-based math and numbers learning program from Sierra On-Line. It is part of the company's Dream Team series and is designed for children between the ages of 3 and 6. Like the other products in the series, it uses an intelligent, talking cartoon character as a teacher and companion. In this program, the character is Loid, a purple alien who lives on an asteroid.

Early Math offers six games that a child can play. The games utilize different sets of skills and provide a progression of learning activities. Four of the games are accessed from the inside of Loid's house. Counting Sheep is the easiest game. It teaches counting and other basic skills and introduces the child to addition and subtraction. Complete the Picture teaches recognition of geometric shapes. Magic Box deals with place value and carrying.

Fish Tank teaches about addition and subtraction, as well as one-to-one correspondence. The goal is to feed hungry fish by counting out the correct amount of food.

▲ *The Fish Tank game in Early Math.*

The fish all open their mouths when the right amount of food has been counted out, to provide the child with feedback. The equation appears next to the fish and the food to help the child relate the equation to the physical representation of the problem.

The child accesses Early Math's final two games from outside Loid's house. Tangram Bridge is the easier of the two. It teaches basic geometry skills.

The goal of the game is to fill a pit with geometric shapes so that Loid can drive his car over it. As the child successfully completes each level, the shapes become more complex.

▲ *Building the Tangram Bridge.*

Each game increases in difficulty as the child masters the initial level. Throughout Early Math, Loid provides verbal feedback and support. All players choose a unique playing piece, which enables the program to keep track of each child's performance. In the Parent's Screen, a child's performance can be reviewed, and some options can be set. The manual includes suggestions for playtime activities that reinforce what the child has learned.

> **Note:** Early Math is scheduled to be rereleased as Loid's Math Planet by the time you read this.

Required Equipment
- Windows 3.1
- 20 MHz 80386SX processor (or better)
- SVGA card with 640 x 480, 256-color Windows driver
- At least 4M of RAM
- Sound card with Windows driver
- Microsoft-compatible mouse

> **Note:** You can find out more about the items in the equipment lists by looking in Chapter 2 for general information, Chapter 10 for SVGA video cards and sound cards, Chapter 11 for CD-ROM drives, and Chapter 12 for Windows information.

Mickey's 123's

Mickey's 123's is one of several preschool edutainment products from Disney Software. These programs are for children between the ages of 2 and 5 and run under DOS. Mickey's 123's is designed to introduce children to such basic concepts as number recognition, counting, quantities, and sequencing.

The program is very supportive of exploration and experimentation, and no answer is ever wrong. Any number key that the child presses results in an interesting outcome every time. A section of the manual provides suggestions for non-computer activities that reinforce what is learned with the program.

The program is filled with visually exciting images, such as the scene in which Mickey is manufacturing a toy. The machine is full of action—lights flash, things move, dials and wheels spin.

The program provides many opportunities for a child to work on his counting skills. In one example, Mickey is throwing a party for one of his friends. As each guest arrives, the program counts them and encourages the child to do the same. The program offers many similar opportunities throughout.

As you might expect with a Disney program, other Disney characters make guest appearances. The child can invite a total of nine different characters to Mickey's party. Seeing familiar characters on the screen and hearing them speak helps to hold the child's attention.

Required Equipment
- CGA video card (or better; VGA is recommended)
- 8 MHz 8086 processor (10 MHz 80286 or better is recommended)
- DOS 3.3 or later
- At least 640K of RAM with at least 516K free

(*Note:* Sound card and expanded memory are recommended.)

▲ *A toy being manufactured in Mickey's 123's.*

▲ *Improving counting skills with Mickey's 123's.*

Letter and Reading Skills

If one major goal of preschool software is teaching math and pre-math skills, surely the other is teaching reading and pre-reading skills. These skills include such things as letter recognition and picture-to-word association, as well as actual reading. The remainder of this section covers some products that focus on reading and pre-reading skills.

Rusty & Rosy Read with Me Volumes 1 and 2

Rusty & Rosy Read with Me, Volumes 1 and 2 are Windows products from the Waterford Institute. The Institute is a nonprofit research center dedicated to helping children learn through the effective use of computers. The Institute operates a 650-student school in Utah. New software is developed and tested with the help of the students at this school.

Volume 1 of the series aims to teach letter recognition and basic readiness skills such as colors, shapes, and sizes. The package combines two educational games, Catch-A-Match and Coloring Box, with a video about letters. The games engage the child with songs, stories, pictures, and near-human-quality speech. Coloring Box is a simple paint program; Catch-A-Match is a matching game that teaches letters, shapes, numbers, and colors. The following figure shows a scene from Catch-A-Match, in which the child must catch all the fish that match the number shown.

Preschool Products 113

Playing Catch-A-Match with Rusty & Rosy, Volume 1.

Volume 2 of the series deals with more advanced material. In addition to basic readiness skills, the program teaches letter and sound awareness (how the sounds of different letters combine to make words) and language skills.

The two games included in this volume are Treasure Hunt and Word Traveler. The accompanying video uses songs, chants, and nursery rhymes to teach vocabulary skills. Treasure Hunt is a matching and memorization game similar to the game Concentration.

Word Traveler helps the child learn about words by playing with the sounds that make up words (*phonemes*). The game encourages children to create words by pronouncing the sounds associated with letters entered by the child. When the child creates a real word, he is rewarded with a treasure.

The program has a 60,000-word dictionary of English words. When 10 words are created, the child travels to a new location. The following figure shows the Word Traveler at work in Egypt.

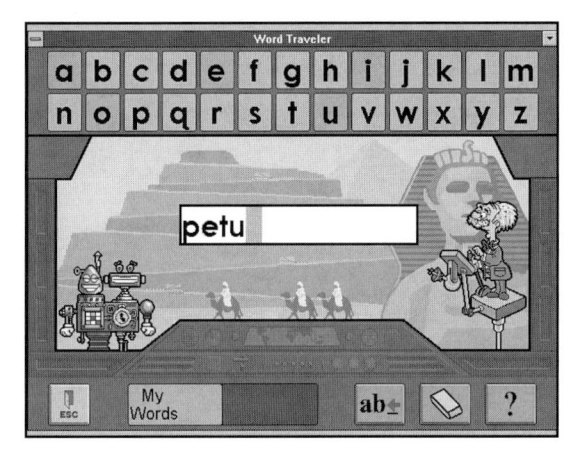

▲ *Making words in Word Traveler.*

Required Equipment
- DOS 3.1
- Windows 3.1
- 80386 processor (or better)
- VGA video
- 4M of RAM
- Mouse

(*Note:* Sound card with Windows driver recommended.)

Mickey's ABC's

Mickey's ABC's is another DOS-based Disney Software product for preschoolers. It is designed to teach children between the ages of 2 and 5 about letters and words while increasing their vocabularies.

The program is designed so that pressing any letter key always causes something to happen. In this way, the program encourages exploration. The child can't do anything wrong or make mistakes. A section of the manual provides suggestions for non-computer activities that reinforce what the child learns with the program.

With Mickey as her surrogate, the child explores Mickey's house and the local fairgrounds. When the child presses a letter key, the program causes some sort of activity that relates to the letter just pressed. In the following figure, you can see what happens when the child presses the C key inside Mickey's house.

▲ *Matching words and objects in Mickey's ABC's.*

While Mickey shows the child a cookie, the word *cookie* appears on the screen. This shows the child that the word *cookie* begins with the letter C, and it also builds an association between the word and the object.

The program can display words in either uppercase or lowercase. It pronounces words and letters as they are used, aiding the child in learning the correct pronunciation. Mickey's ABC's includes guest appearances by Minnie Mouse, Donald Duck, and other famous Disney characters. Seeing and hearing these familiar characters helps to hold the child's attention.

▲ *Mickey's friends appear at the fair.*

Required Equipment
- CGA video card (or better; VGA is recommended)
- 8 MHz 8086 processor (10 MHz 286 or better is recommended)
- DOS 3.3 or later
- 640K of RAM with at least 512K free

(*Note:* Sound card and expanded memory are recommended.)

Other Products

Although many preschool products focus on one subject, usually reading or math skills, others take a broader approach. Such products may teach both reading and math skills. At the same time, these products may address other areas, such as music and creativity. The remainder of this section describes products that explore a number of subjects in a single package.

Kid's Zoo

Kid's Zoo is part of the Interactive Books series published by Knowledge Adventure. The program, subtitled "A Baby Animal Adventure," runs under both DOS and Windows and is designed for children from the ages of 3 to 12. Both floppy disk and CD-ROM versions are available.

Interactive Books has a different feel than most edutainment products. According to the documentation, one goal of the product is to link seemingly isolated facts in a manner that makes them more interesting, understandable, and memorable. The primary goal is to empower the child with a sense of control over her entire learning experience.

Kid's Zoo consists of eight different activities and an encyclopedia, with the common feature being the subject matter: baby animals. The various activities use digitized speech; full-screen, full-motion video; music; and sound effects to enhance the learning experience. The documentation includes a short learning guide.

With an age range of 3 to 12, not all of the activities are useful to preschool children. One activity that is appropriate, however, is the Picture Dictionary. In this activity, the child clicks pictures of animals to see their names spelled and to hear the names pronounced. Clicking a letter on the alphabet bar (across the top in the following figure) causes the dictionary to pronounce the letter and then display the page that contains animals with names that start with that letter.

Another activity suitable for preschoolers is the Movie Theater. Here, the child gets to choose movies of baby animals in action. Clicking one of the small animal pictures at the bottom of the screen tells the program to show that movie.

One of the nice things about Kid's Zoo is its wide range of activities targeted at a wide range of ages. It takes quite a while for a child to outgrow the product. The Talking Storybook is accessible to the youngest users, while activities such as Where Do I Live? and the Kid's Zoo Encyclopedia appeal to older children. The variety of activities also enables the child to explore the subject from various directions, thereby utilizing different skills.

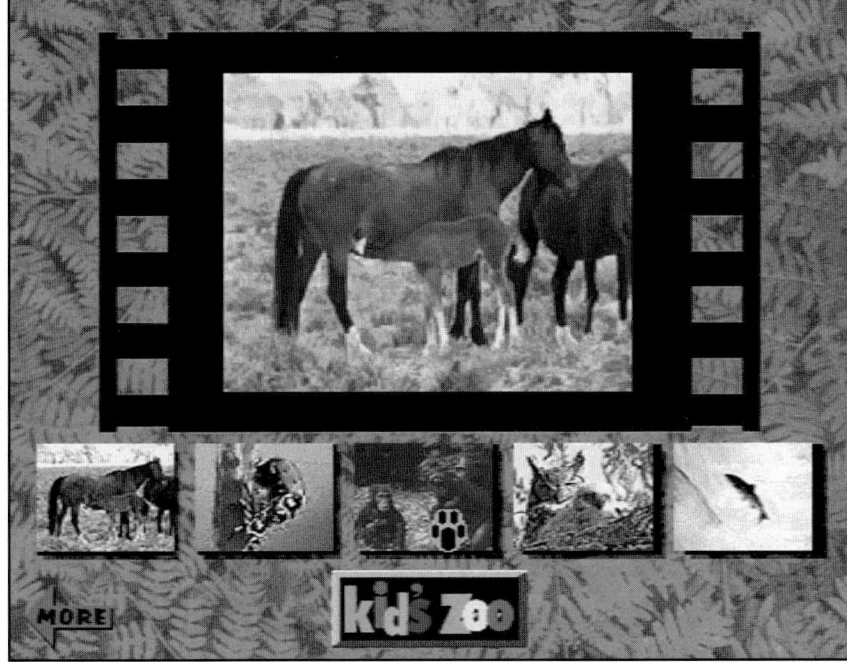

▲ *Viewing the Kid's Zoo Picture Dictionary.*

▲ *A visit to the Kid's Zoo Movie Theater.*

Required Equipment
- CD-ROM drive
- Color VGA or SVGA video
- DOS 3.1 or higher
- At least 640K of RAM

(*Note:* Sound card and mouse are recommended.)

Fun School Learning Adventures with Teddy Bear

Fun School Learning Adventures with Teddy Bear (Fun School Teddy) is a DOS program from Europress Software. Designed for children between the ages of 4 and 7, Fun School Teddy has six different educational games. These games cover a broad range of skills, including pre-reading, vocabulary, counting, estimation, and creative thinking.

Children love to sing, and Fun School Teddy takes advantage of that with Teddy's Karaoke. This game lets the child choose songs and then sing along by following the bouncing ball.

Singing along while the ball bounces on the words builds early reading skills. As the child progresses through the levels of the game, more active participation is required.

Teddy's Fun Train is a vocabulary-building game. It teaches the child to match words to pictures and pictures to words.

Level one matches labeled pictures to labeled pictures. As the child advances through the levels of the program, the matching becomes more difficult, from matching words to labeled pictures, to eventually matching words to unlabeled pictures.

Chapter 7

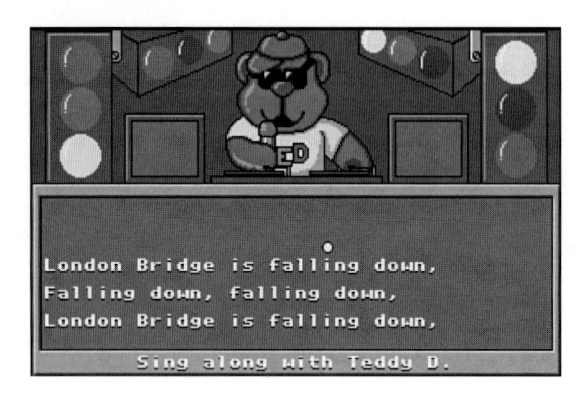

▲ *Karaoke with Fun School Learning Adventures with Teddy Bear.*

▲ *Matching words and pictures on Teddy's Fun Train.*

The remaining games in the package develop various other skills. The Addition game teaches addition skills, Teddy Paint is a creativity tool, Teddy's House teaches about colors and the different parts of a house, and Teddy's Books teaches counting and sequencing skills.

Required Equipment
- CGA, EGA, or VGA video
- DOS 3.3 or higher
- 80286 processor (or better)
- 640K of RAM
- Sound card

(*Note:* A mouse is recommended.)

Ping & Kooky's Cuckoo Zoo

Ping & Kooky's Cuckoo Zoo is a Windows edutainment product from the EA*Kids division of Electronic Arts and is designed for children ages 3 to 6. The child uses a train to travel through and play in five different areas of this zany zoo. Four of these areas are ecologically correct environments populated with the kinds of animals that would actually live there in the wild.

The animal inhabitants of this zoo sing, dance, and talk while teaching the child a variety of skills. In each of the environments, the child can learn the names and characteristics of the animals by playing Cuckoo Zoo Who's Who and Kooky's Animal Mix-Ups.

Restoring the animals to their proper conditions teaches the child about these animals. In Who's Who, the child can click an animal to make the program speak and display the animal's name. As a reward for choosing a particular animal, the program displays a fun animation involving that animal.

Mixed-up animals in Ping & Kooky's Cuckoo Zoo.

Each of the five areas has its own game or activity. On the Savannah, the child learns about colors by painting the animals. Fishing in the Polar Park teaches counting skills. Playing hide-and-seek with the animals on the Farm teaches recognition and matching skills. And the Rain Forest activity helps the child learn to recognize letters.

The fifth area is the Cuckoo Zoo Revue. Here, the child's creativity is encouraged. The child can create his own songs, with the animals doing the singing and dancing. In the following figure, the animals are singing a song I created.

Required Equipment
- DOS 3.3 or higher
- 25 MHz 80386 processor (or better)
- 256-color VGA video
- Sound card

(*Note:* Mouse and expanded memory recommended.)

Preschool Products 117

Creating a song with the zoo animals.

Dr. T's Sing-A-Long Kids' Classics (CD-ROM Edition)

Dr. T's Sing-A-Long Kids' Classics, from Dr. T's Music Software, is a music and reading skills program for children between the ages of 3 and 10. Running under Windows, this program combines music, animation, song lyrics, and musical notation into a singing experience for children and their parents.

The CD-ROM contains 26 children's songs. With classics such as "Twinkle, Twinkle, Little Star" and "Three Blind Mice," most children should find some songs they recognize. The child's reading skills are improved by seeing the words of the song displayed, and when used in Normal mode, the program also displays the song's musical notation.

The program can play just the music for the song, or both the music and the vocals. The music can be displayed either in standard notation or in chord grids for guitar. A Print option enables the child to print the music for the song in either format.

Two other modes are also available: Juke box mode and Little Kids mode. The Juke box mode lets the child select a series of songs to be played one after the other, through the entire list. The Little Kids mode is designed for young children to use without parental supervision. The user interface is simplified, and the program fills the screen. Because this mode has no Windows menus, the child can't switch to another program.

Little Kids mode contains a button for each song. Each button contains a picture that represents the song associated with that button. When the child clicks a button, the name of the song is pronounced, and the song begins to play. A Rabbit and a Turtle icon may also be visible. These icons control the tempo of the music when you are using the Computer Music (MIDI) mode (discussed shortly). Both the Normal and Little Kids modes contain animation that accompanies the song in progress.

Learning about music with Dr. T's Sing-A-Long Kids' Classics.

Dr. T's Sing-A-Long can provide music and singing in three different ways. First, it can generate Computer Music, which is in MIDI format and is generated by your sound card. The other two methods in which music is provided involve the two sets of 16-bit CD audio tracks included with Dr. T's Sing-A-Long. One set is music only; the second set consists of music plus vocals. The music-only set is ideal for karaoke. With a microphone plugged in to the mic jack on the sound card, a child can sing along and hear his own voice played through the speakers with the music.

Learning "This Old Man" in Little Kids mode.

Required Equipment
- CD-ROM drive
- Windows 3.1 or higher
- VGA display
- 80386 processor (or higher)
- At least 4M of RAM
- Windows-compatible sound card
- Mouse

Busytown

Busytown is a DOS CD-ROM published by Paramount Interactive. The program is based on Richard Scarry's popular Busytown books and is designed for children between the ages of 3 and 7. This program won a Parent's Choice Award in 1993.

Busytown is filled with interesting playgrounds, each of which mixes play with one or more educational concepts. The child can move between, and explore, each playground at will. The playgrounds themselves are inhabited by cartoon characters taken from the Busytown books.

Each character has a distinct personality, and they are always busy: playing, building, singing, and sometimes even getting into trouble. Even so, there is always something educational going on in each playground.

The Busytown manual adds additional value to the program. The Activities section of the manual contains non-computer activities that relate to the theme of each playground in the program. The CD-ROM version of the program contains a jukebox that can play music to accompany these activities. The manual also contains a certificate and two bookmarks that can be cut out and given to the child as rewards.

Required Equipment
- DOS 3.3 or higher
- CD-ROM drive
- 80286 processor (or better; 80386 or better recommended)
- 640K or more of RAM
- VGA video
- Sound card
- Mouse

Busytown is full of interesting and educational activities.

Children learn to identify body parts at Dr. Diane's Busytown office.

Summary

As this chapter pointed out, preschool products are one of the hottest categories in edutainment. Designed for children as young as three, they help develop skills and concepts that serve as a basis for all future learning. With bright colors, music, and sound effects to hold a child's attention, they provide interactivity and give youngsters some control over their own educations.

Products are available that teach letter and word recognition; others cover colors and shapes. Problem-solving and creativity are encouraged and stimulated. I believe that a child who has regular access to preschool edutainment products has a great advantage over those who don't.

Creativity is one of the skills that is crucial to a child growing up today. With the pace of change increasing almost daily, a person who can't think creatively about her career and her life will have trouble keeping up. Unfortunately, most Americans seem to have their creativity ground out of them long before they become adults.

If you want to see your child retain her innate creativity, or even increase it, you will want to read Chapter 8. Chapter 8 is all about creativity tools, which can encourage and stimulate a child's creative impulses. Read on to find out more.

Chapter 8

Creativity Tools

Creativity tools use the power of the computer to help the user indulge his or her creative urges. Children are creative. They endlessly paint, write, and build things. Creativity tools help them to express themselves.

The best creativity tools let the user control the action. Within the limits of the program, users can do anything they want. They can explore without worrying about getting the right answer or getting into trouble. At the end of it all, they have created something uniquely their own.

In this chapter, the following topics help you learn more about this exciting edutainment category:

- Common features of creativity tools
- Other interesting features
- A walk-through of Print Shop Deluxe
- A look at some of the products available

▲ *The Kid Works 2 interface.*

Common Features

Although creativity tools encompass a diverse group of products, the ones I looked at do have common features. Some of them apply to all products in this category, while others apply to a subset of the group as a whole. Let's start by looking at the features shared by all creativity tools.

The first common feature of these programs is that they are non-judgmental. They let you choose tools and do things without fear. There is no scoring, no right or wrong answer, no defined path to follow. You can't do anything wrong.

Because there is no right way to do things, you can feel free to do things your own way. These programs encourage experimentation, and there is always something new and different to try. Creativity tools not only assist in the act of creation, they encourage it.

After a child (or anyone, for that matter) creates something, he or she naturally wants to share it with others. Creativity tools make it possible for the child to print a copy of this creation. A product such as MECC's Storybook Weaver can create an illustrated storybook ready for binding. Some of the programs can even print in color if you have a color printer. Although a printed copy of a multimedia extravaganza pales beside the computerized original, a printed copy is much easier to store or to send to Grandma.

Fun and interesting interfaces set the tone for several of these products. Davidson's Kid Works 2 gives a child access to each of its four main parts through posters on the wall of a kid's room.

Creative Writer, from Microsoft, takes things one step further. Instead of a room, the child's environment is Imaginopolis, an entire four-story building! The following figure shows the lobby of this wild and crazy place.

Creativity Tools   123

▲ *The Imaginopolis lobby in Creative Writer.*

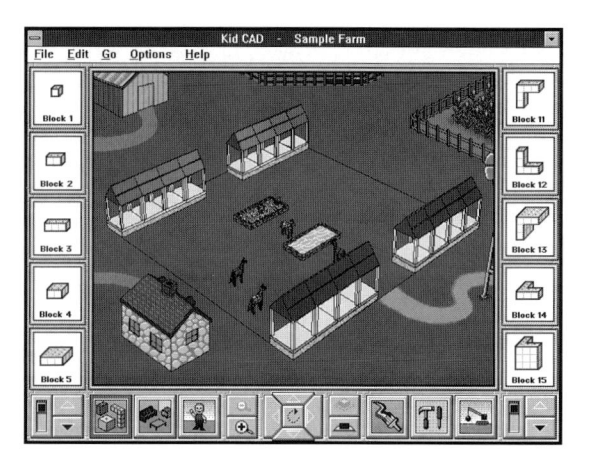

Computer-aided design for kids: Kid CAD.

Such interfaces make using the programs fun. They also make it easier for young children. No pull-down menus or cryptic icons here. Even products that don't have such unique interfaces take pains to be easy to use. Nothing stifles the flow of creative ideas like stopping to read the manual.

Many creativity tools are not only fun and easy to use, they make difficult subject matter fun and easy, too. Consider Kid CAD from Davidson & Associates. This program takes computer-aided architectural design (CAD) and turns it into something that is fun for seven year olds!

Computer-aided design work is normally done by architects and engineers. Kid CAD takes this technology, strips it down to the basics, and adds an interface and tools that children can appreciate. This results in a colorful and accessible program that teaches design and a variety of other skills.

Various products are available that make desktop publishing (DTP) accessible to youngsters (and to many of us adults). MECC's My Own Stories is a good example. It combines a simple word processor and a set of picture creation tools. With these, the user creates an illustrated story.

▲ *Creating a storybook page with My Own Stories.*

Actually publishing a project is as easy as creating it. With a few mouse clicks, the program prints a story ready for binding.

Other Features

Besides the common features found in all creativity tools, a number of other interesting features are unique to a particular product or shared by just a few. When you look at these features, you can see the amount of creativity applied by the developers.

The products from MECC (Storybook Weaver and My Own Stories) add a rudimentary multimedia capability to their stories. They provide various types of music that can be played at the beginning and end of each story. In addition, the child can assign sound effects to the objects that appear in the pictures.

Kid Works 2 shares an interesting feature with these MECC products: the child can add pre-created objects to the pictures he creates. To aid the child in writing about these objects, all three programs can automatically enter either the name of the object or the word for the object into the text of the story. This feature not only makes writing the story easier, but it helps the child associate objects and the words that go with them.

Kid Works 2 can read a child's stories using a text-to-speech converter. After the child creates a story, the program can read it out loud. If the PC has a microphone, a child can even record his own messages to be played back in the story.

Kid CAD, due to its original design concept, is full of unusual features. The 3-D virtual environment is unique. When the child creates a building, he views it from a particular perspective. All it takes is a click of a button to change the perspective, as the two figures illustrate. Here, a change of perspective shows different features of the same cottage.

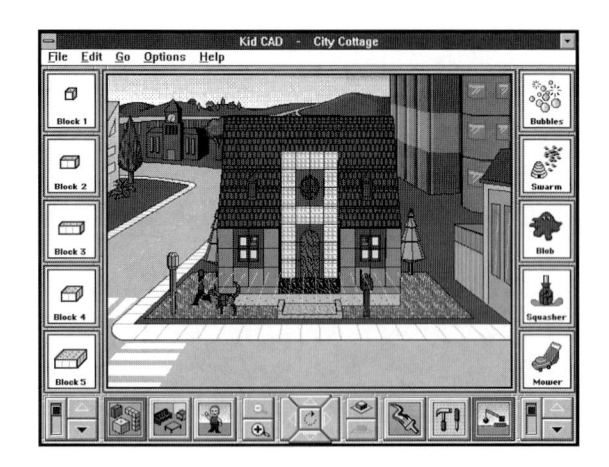

A perspective view in Kid CAD.

A new perspective on the same scene.

Using a Creativity Tool: Print Shop Deluxe

Creativity tools vary significantly in what they do and how they do it. Even so, the products I reviewed were well-designed and easy to use. To give you an idea of how easy it can be to create something with one of these packages, the next few paragraphs walk you through the creation of a sign using Print Shop Deluxe.

The first step in this project is to start Print Shop Deluxe; once the program is running, it displays the following screen.

This screen tells the program what type of project you want to create. To make a sign, for example, you click the Sign button. The program then asks you to choose between a tall orientation and a wide orientation, and let's assume that for this project you choose a wide one. In the next screen, you choose a backdrop. The program displays a drop-down list box of graphics libraries, and each graphics library contains a scrollable list with the names of the backdrops in that library. To display a particular backdrop, click a name from the list.

After you have selected a backdrop, you choose a layout for your sign. The layout determines where text and graphics are placed. Layouts are matched to backdrops to improve the appearance of the final result, and choosing a layout is actually very similar to choosing a backdrop.

After you have selected the layout, you begin adding text and graphics to the sign.

As you can see, I have already added a headline to the sign shown in the following figure. Clicking the *T* icon that appears in the gray area activates the text object. After you activate the text object, you can use the Edit command from the Object menu to enter and customize your text. When you are finished with the sign, you can use the File menu to save and print the final result. That's all there is to creating a basic sign with Print Shop Deluxe.

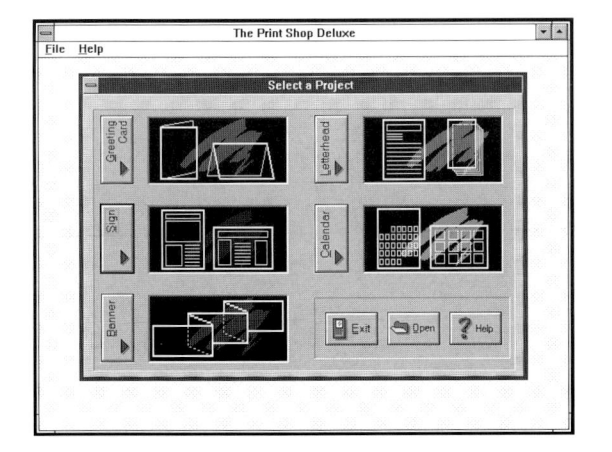

▲ *The screen where you select a Print Shop Deluxe project.*

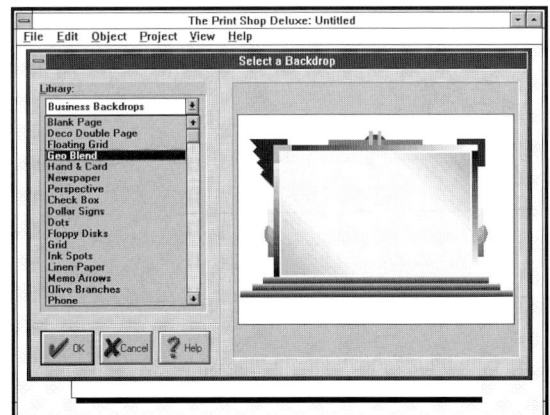

▲ *Selecting a backdrop.*

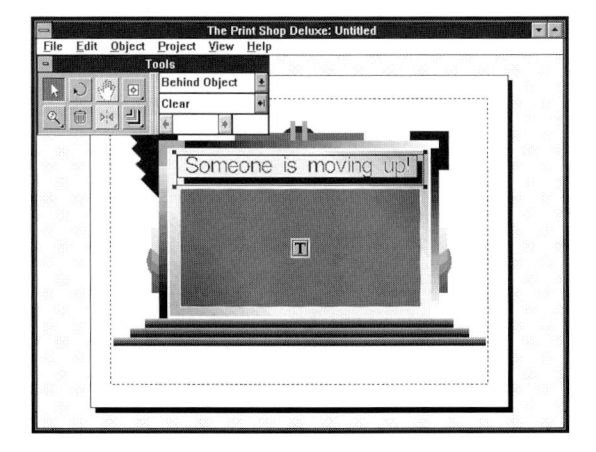

▲ *Filling in the blanks in the project.*

What's Available?

For a long time, it seemed that the only creativity tools around were the Print Shop family of programs. The situation has improved recently, with several publishers bringing out new products. The rest of this chapter discusses some of the creativity tools I was able to try out.

Kid CAD

Davidson's Kid CAD is exactly that—a CAD (computer-aided design) program for kids ages seven and up. Running under Windows, Kid CAD allows the child to design and build houses, castles, and other structures right there on the computer screen. Beyond the creation of the structures themselves, the child can decorate and furnish her creations, landscape the grounds, and populate the site with people and animals. Kid CAD was a Parent's Choice Award winner in 1993.

The farm: a panoramic setting that appears when you start Kid CAD.

After creating the structure and its surroundings, the child can explore the area using various perspective views. The scene can be observed from either a bird's-eye view or an eye-level view. The child's viewpoint can move around the structure to see the back or sides, and she can zoom in or out at will in order to explore small details or the entire scene.

Kid CAD incorporates computer-aided design concepts, such as texture mapping and object libraries, in a way that children can understand. The program also teaches visualization and measurement skills, while stimulating the child's creativity.

When the child first starts Kid CAD, she sees the panoramic view of a farm setting. Clicking a visible object (a horse, a silo, or anything else you can see) results in sound effects, music, or animation. When the child is ready to move on from the panoramic view, she can choose one of three settings—farm, town, or city—in which to build. Clicking the plot of land in the center of the screen activates the building options.

Kid CAD offers several categories of building options: architecture, interiors, living things, textures and colors, building tools, and demolition tools. In each category, the child can choose from a number of options, which enables her to create an endless variety of structures. To get the child off to a quick start, the program contains 10 pre-made structures and a dozen sample files.

After creating the structure, the child can customize it, add colors and textures, and landscape the area around it. Beyond that, she can furnish the rooms and add people and animals to the scene.

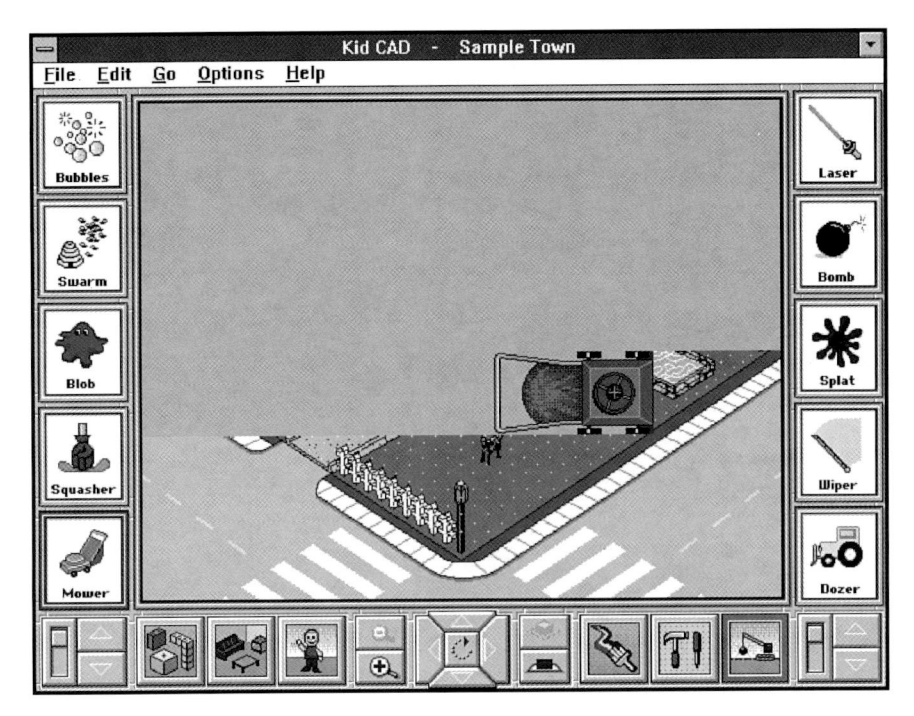

A mower in action in Kid Cad.

With plants ranging from Joshua trees to pine trees, and animals from turtles to a Tyrannosaurus Rex, the child can place her structures in a wide range of climates or historical periods.

The Demolition tools make it fun to clear away old structures and start on new ones, and the child can choose from a half-dozen different tools. The figure shows the mower tool in action.

Required Equipment

- Windows 3.1
- 80386 processor (or better)
- VGA or 256-color SVGA video card with Windows driver
- At least 4M of RAM
- Mouse

(*Note:* A Windows-compatible sound card is recommended.)

Note: You can find out more about the items in the equipment lists by looking in Chapter 2 for general information, Chapter 10 for SVGA video cards and sound cards, Chapter 11 for CD-ROM drives, and Chapter 12 for Windows information.

Kid Works 2

Kid Works 2, from Davidson, is a story-creation program for children ages 4 to 10. Both DOS and Windows versions are available. The Windows CD-ROM version includes extra coloring book pictures and picture icons. The program enables kids to write and illustrate their own stories, and when the story is complete, the program can even read it back to them.

The four sections of the program are accessible through the playful interface you saw in the first figure in this chapter. The Story Writer section is where the child creates the text of the story. As you can see in the following figure, the program allows picture icons to be included in the text.

Kid Works 2 knows the words associated with the picture icons and speaks them when it reads the story.

Story Writer has the capabilities of a basic word processor: the child can cut, copy, and paste text and icons, and an Undo feature undoes the most recent action. A smaller type style is available for older children to use.

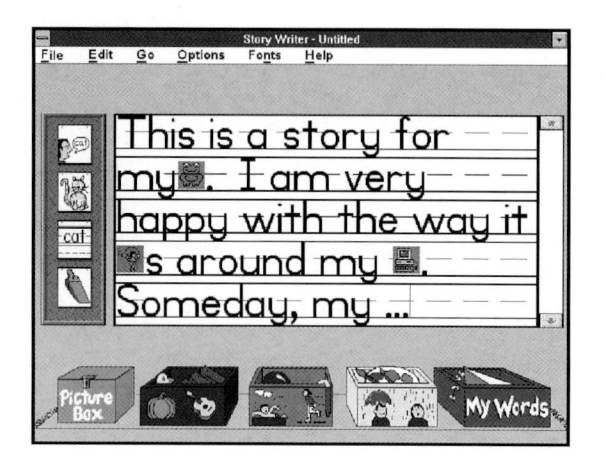

▲ *The Story Writer section of Kid Works 2.*

The Story Illustrator is a paint program with lively sound effects and a set of cool paint tools.

▲ *The Kid Works 2 Story Illustrator.*

All the standard paint tools (shapes, fills, text, and so on) are available. Not-so-standard tools include rubber stamps and crazy brushes. A set of predefined, uncolored pictures are available in the Coloring Book, and images can also be imported from other paint programs.

The program comes with two fonts, and the Windows version can use any of the fonts available to Windows. Lively sound effects make the Story Illustrator even more fun to use.

The other two sections of Kid Works 2 are the Icon Maker and the Story Reader. The Icon Maker lets the child assign words to existing picture icons or create his own. The Story Reader uses a text-to-speech conversion program to read the text of stories while displaying the illustration.

The program can print stories and illustrations. When it prints, the program miniaturizes the illustrations and embeds them in the body of the text to create picture icons.

Required Equipment

DOS version:

- At least 640K of RAM
- DOS 3.3 or higher
- 12 MHz 80286 processor (or better)
- Color VGA card and monitor
- Sound card
- Mouse

Windows version:

- Windows 3.1 or higher
- At least 4M of RAM
- VGA or SVGA video
- 16 MHz 80386 processor (or better)
- Windows-compatible sound card
- Mouse

Creative Writer

Microsoft's Creative Writer is a crazy Windows application that helps children between the ages of 8 and 14 publish illustrated stories and other projects. The program is full of sound effects, clip art, and tools. In addition to stories, it can create banners, cards, and newspapers.

Three characters live in Imaginopolis—the town in which all Creative Writer activities take place (although everything actually takes place inside one building). Max and Maggie help with suggestions on text and pictures. McZee provides a bag full of tools and instructs the child in their use.

A child spends most of his time in the Writing Studio. The studio is a fun and functional word processor with all the mundane features, as well as quite a few unusual ones. The program has access to all the fonts available to Windows, and beyond the usual styles, text can be colored, shadowed, or

▲ *The Writing Studio in Creative Writer.*

▲ *Creative Writer's Idea Workshop.*

bent. The program can insert illustrations that match individual words, and it can add clip art. A simple drawing program lets the child create custom clip art when he needs it. Both text and illustrations can be resized or otherwise manipulated. There is even a Secret Agent encoder that turns a story into a secret message—illustrations and all!

Other locations in the building can be reached through the lobby, which you saw in an earlier figure. The Idea Workshop provides inspiration for original stories and projects. The Splot Machine can generate over 8,000 original story ideas by combining random words, phrases, and pictures, and the Picture Window displays images that can inspire a story.

Required Equipment

- Windows 3.1 or later
- DOS 3.2 or later
- At least 2M of RAM
- 80386 processor (or better)
- VGA video (or better) with Windows driver
- Mouse

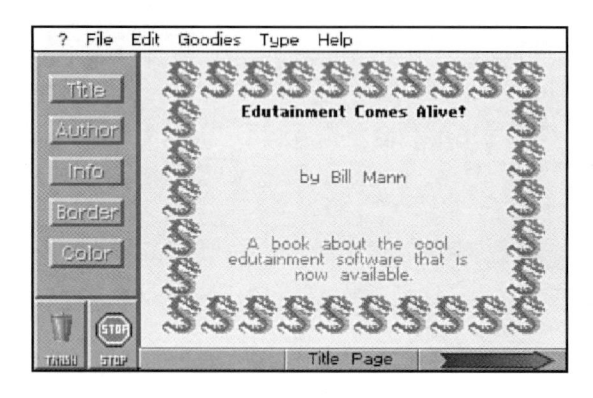

▲ *A title page in Storybook Weaver.*

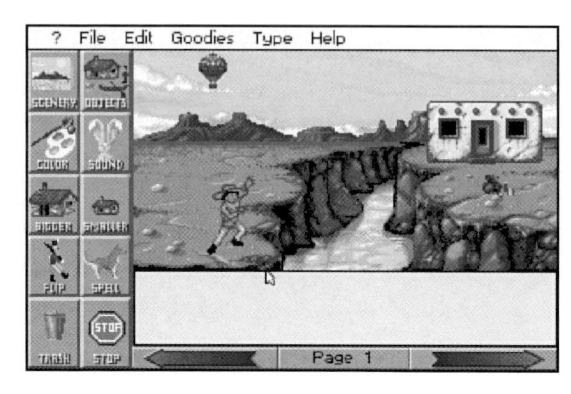

▲ *Creating a book page in Storybook Weaver.*

▲ *A page created with My Own Stories.*

Storybook Weaver and My Own Stories

Storybook Weaver and My Own Stories are sister products from MECC. Both give children the opportunity to write and illustrate their own storybooks. Storybook Weaver is designed for children between the ages of 5 and 10. It draws elements from the folklore of many cultures around the world. These elements are represented as images of people, places, and things, both real and imaginary.

Storybook Weaver contains hundreds of images and backgrounds, which can be combined with dozens of sound effects and songs to create a multimedia production. As the first two figures show, the child creates a custom title page for his book as well as each individual page.

Book pages can contain text, an illustration, or both, and the program makes it easy to add, change, or remove the elements on any page. Storybook Weaver can display the spelling for any object visible on-screen, which makes it easy to incorporate unfamiliar objects into the text of the story.

After completing his story, the child can save it to disk. He can also create a stand-alone copy of the story that he can distribute to friends or relatives. These stand-alone copies will run on other machines, even if the other computer does not have a copy of Storybook Weaver.

Storybook Weaver can also print all or part of the child's storybook. If a child is lucky enough to have a color printer, he can print the story in color. With a little extra effort to create a cover, a child can publish his own book.

My Own Stories is the follow-on to Storybook Weaver. Designed for an older audience (ages 8 to 14), My Own Stories replaces the exotic and imaginary elements of Storybook Weaver with elements drawn from contemporary life, such as those shown in the figure.

The program draws from the full range of cultures to represent the diversity of modern life. Functionally, both programs have the same capabilities.

Required Equipment
- 80386 processor (or better)
- DOS 5.0 or later
- At least 1M of RAM
- VGA color video
- Mouse

(*Note:* An AdLib or Sound Blaster-compatible sound card is recommended.)

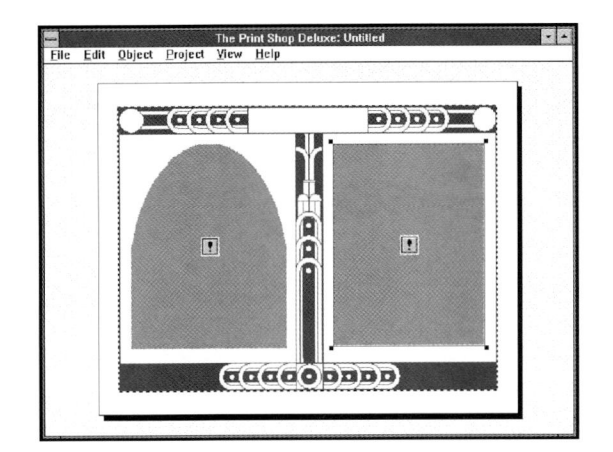

Creativity Tools | **131**

▲ *A design and layout combination in Print Shop Deluxe.*

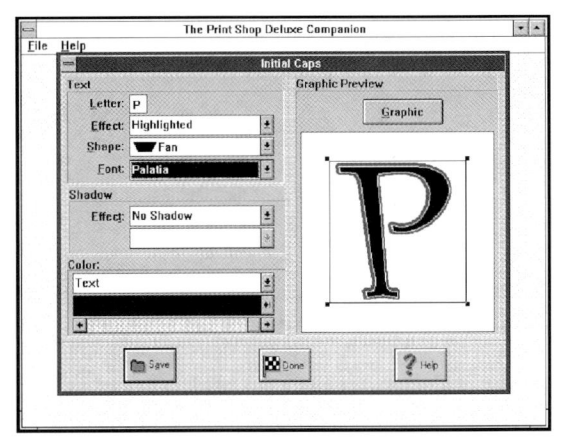

▲ *Creating an initial cap with The Print Shop Deluxe Companion.*

Print Shop Deluxe CD Ensemble

The Print Shop Deluxe CD Ensemble is a powerful Windows package from Broderbund. It helps users of any age create a wide variety of personalized printed material. It combines Print Shop Deluxe and four Print Shop Deluxe add-on products: The Print Shop Deluxe Companion, Sampler, Business Graphics Collection, and Amazing Animals Graphics Folio. Also included are 50 bonus graphics. Print Shop Deluxe was a 1993 Parent's Choice award winner.

Print Shop Deluxe can create five types of projects: greeting cards, signs, banners, calendars and letterhead. The Companion, which is a separate application, adds the ability to create certificates, envelopes, business cards, and post cards.

Each project has its own library of full-page designs and its own set of layouts. Layouts control the placement of graphics and text on the screen.

By coordinating the designs and layouts, the program helps ensure that the text and graphics take proper advantage of the background design.

Among the various products on the CD-ROM, over 1,000 graphics are available for use. Most of the graphics are square, but some consist of horizontal or vertical patterns that are perfect to use across the top or down the side of a page. Most of these graphics are in color, but all are designed to print satisfactorily on both black-and-white and color printers. The images cover a myriad of subjects, such as sports, animals, business, and holidays. Graphics can be resized or moved as necessary. The program can also import graphics from other sources and export its own.

The Print Shop Deluxe Companion adds Smart Graphics. A Smart Graphic is a custom-designed graphic that you can modify and save for use in future projects with Print Shop Deluxe and The Print Shop Deluxe Companion. Three types of Smart Graphics are possible: Initial Caps, Numbers, and Timepieces.

The CD-Ensemble disc contains 73 TrueType fonts that are added to those already on your system. Any TrueType font can be used in a project, and they can be scaled, stretched, or rotated as necessary. Colors, shading, and shadows can be applied character by character.

Required Equipment
- CD-ROM drive
- Windows 3.1
- 80386SX processor (or better)
- At least 4M of RAM
- VGA video (or better)
- Mouse

(*Note:* A printer, preferably color, is highly recommended.)

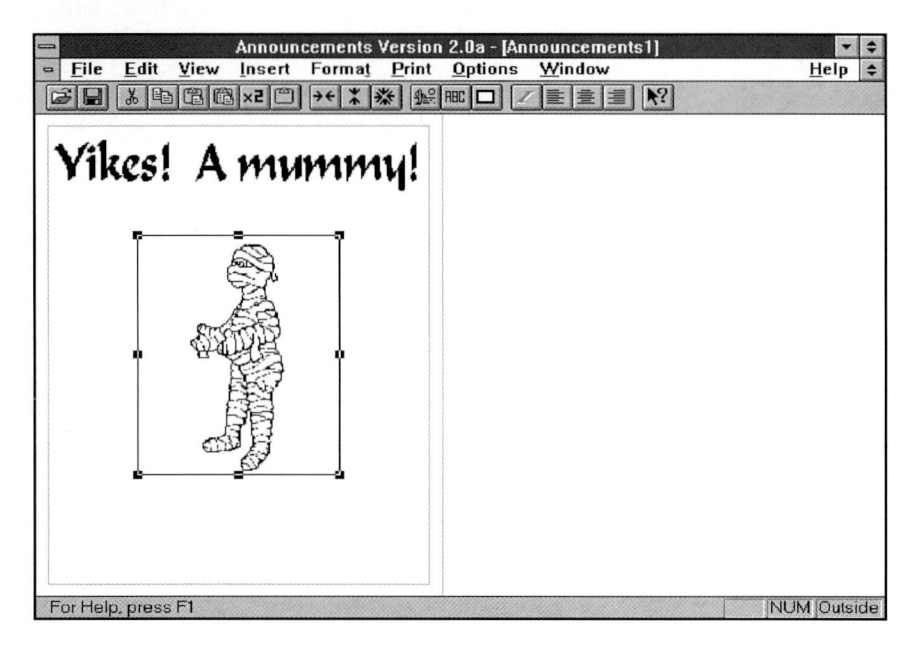

▲ *Creating a poster with Announcements 2.0.*

Announcements 2.0 for Windows

Announcements 2.0 for Windows, from Parsons Technology, lets you create announcements and other printed materials. You can use the program to create cards, posters, banners, envelopes, business cards, and gift certificates. The program enables you to move and rescale graphics, and you can enter text in a variety of typefaces and shapes. The program can use any Windows fonts on your system.

Announcements 2.0 comes with over 200 graphics, many of which are in color, and it also lets you import graphics from other sources. In addition, an Image Collection package is available that contains about 1,000 more graphics.

Required Equipment
- Windows 3.1 or higher
- At least 2M of RAM
- Printer
- Mouse

Summary

This chapter examined an exciting category of edutainment product: creativity tools. These products make it easy for users (in many cases, very young users) to create products such as posters, banners, and even illustrated storybooks. Their very designs encourage experimentation and exploration without the fear of doing the "wrong" thing.

One goal of this chapter was to introduce you to these innovative creativity products. It looked at the common features and characteristics, as well as those features that make individual creativity tools stand apart from the others. A walk-through of Print Shop Deluxe was provided so that you could see how easy it is to be creative when you have the right tools.

The last part of the chapter looked at some of the creativity tools currently available. As you would expect from products designed to foster creativity, they are a diverse lot. I hope that the information provided here encourages you to try at least one of these products.

The products covered in this chapter are quite different in many respects, but you can still see that they all belong in the creativity tools category. In the next chapter, however, you look at a very different set of products. Lumped together under the heading of "general edutainment," the products in Chapter 9 can't be squeezed into any of my other six categories. When you turn to the next chapter, you discover that their presence in the "general" category takes nothing away from their quality and usefulness.

Chapter 9

General Edutainment Products

The general edutainment category covers a wide variety of products. A significant percentage of all edutainment products falls into this category rather than into the other categories I have recommended. These programs cover the entire edutainment spectrum—from products that are primarily educational but have some entertainment value, to those that are primarily entertainment with some educational value. General edutainment products cover a full range of subjects from archaeology to zoology, and everything in between.

The material in this chapter does not lend itself to the same kind of structure found in the other product-related chapters (Chapters 3 through 8). In this chapter, I have simply grouped together products with similar themes or subject areas to make it easier for you to find what you are looking for. Information about similarities between products or unique features of products are found in the introduction to each major section. Read on and get a feel for the true variety of edutainment products available today.

In this chapter, general edutainment products in the following areas are discussed:

- Social studies
- Animals and ecology
- Language and music
- Brain teasers
- Math

What's Available

As I have already pointed out, a huge number of products fall into my "general edutainment" category. The following sections look at some of these products, grouped by subject.

Social Studies

Social studies courses cover a number of subjects, including geography, history, and sociology. Geography and history are two important subjects that our children don't seem to be learning. Studies have shown that many American students can't even find the United States on a world map! And unlike history, geography is not very controversial. The little bit of history American kids do learn has become embroiled in the "political correctness" ruckus. Whatever the merits of the arguments on either side, it seems unlikely that students will be getting a solid history education at school any time soon.

Four products are discussed in this social studies section: WHERE IN THE USA IS CARMEN SANDIEGO?, Eagle Eye Mysteries in London, Discovering America, and Normandy. All four programs deal with the history of their respective locations.

The phenomenal success of the Carmen Sandiego products has inspired companies to create look-alike programs, which is not necessarily bad. The Carmen Sandiego products are successful because they meet the needs of parents and teachers, while at the same time being popular with the kids. Following this successful formula will likely result in other successful edutainment products coming on the market.

Carmen Sandiego and the Eagle Eye Mysteries are very much alike. Both feature the player as a detective who is learning about his location to help solve a crime. Both give the player a special computer (simulated by your computer) that tracks clues and provides information. Finally, both use digitized speech, images of real scenes, and animated characters.

These two products are also different in several ways. Carmen Sandiego is a CD-ROM product, so it contains far more information, images, music, and sound effects. It also includes a book, *Fodor's USA* travel guide. The Eagle Eye Mysteries, on the other hand, includes a map and some information in the back of the manual.

WHERE IN THE USA IS CARMEN SANDIEGO? Deluxe Version

The Carmen Sandiego series from Broderbund is the best-known product line in this category. With officially licensed toys, books, and at least two television shows, Carmen Sandiego is probably the best-known edutainment product in the world. WHERE IN THE USA IS CARMEN SANDIEGO? Deluxe (Carmen USA Deluxe) is a DOS CD-ROM product for users age 9 to adult. The program teaches U.S. geography, history, and culture, while improving a child's research and problem-solving skills.

General Edutainment Products

In this installment of the series, Carmen and her gang are stealing our national treasures. As a member of the Acme Detective Agency, you (as the player/detective) must track the villains from coast to coast, accumulating the clues necessary to serve an arrest warrant. During your journeys, you visit all 50 states, and you enjoy digitized images and classic American music appropriate to whatever region you are in.

You have the latest crime-stopping equipment at your disposal. The Videophone provides an audio and video link to the Acme Detective Agency. The Dataminder serves as a personal digital assistant, storing clues and the dossier of each member of Carmen's gang. It also contains a notepad and maps and can automatically transmit clues to Wanda, who issues arrest warrants.

Digitized speech is used throughout the game. There are 10 talking characters, as well as a voice mail system for hot tips. The State-A-Base database provides a description of each state, spoken by a native of that state.

When you have gathered enough evidence, you can request an arrest warrant. If the evidence you have gathered enables Wanda to identify the villain, she will issue an arrest warrant. If you have a valid warrant (for the correct crook) when you reach the same city as Carmen's henchman, the arrest is made. As you continue to solve cases, you garner promotions and move up the ladder at the agency.

The Carmen USA Deluxe version contains more than 3,000 new clues involving the geography and culture of the USA. More than 300 of the clues are spoken in regional dialects. To help the player decipher all these clues, the package contains a special 800-plus page version of *Fodor's USA* travel guide. On-line topographical maps indicate the terrain and some man-made features of each state.

Required Equipment

- CD-ROM drive
- DOS 3.1 or later
- 16 MHz 80386 processor (or better)
- VGA video
- At least 640K of RAM
- Sound card
- Mouse

Note: You can find out more about the items in the equipment lists by looking in Chapter 2 for general information, Chapter 10 for SVGA video cards and sound cards, Chapter 11 for CD-ROM drives, and Chapter 12 for Windows information.

▲ *Carmen USA Deluxe combines digitized photographs with clever animation.*

▲ *Wanda is one of the many talking characters in Carmen USA Deluxe.*

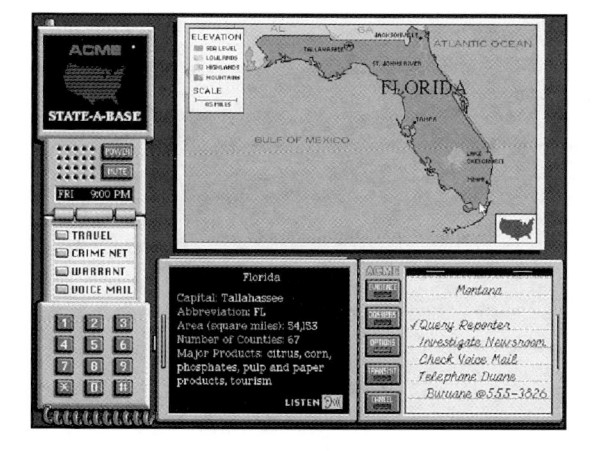

▲ *The State-A-Base is a database full of facts about the 50 states.*

Eagle Eye Mysteries in London

The Eagle Eye Mysteries series consists of DOS programs from EA*Kids, a division of Electronic Arts. Designed for users age 8 and up, the latest version takes place in London. The program teaches scientific and cultural facts, while improving a child's reading, reasoning, and interpretation skills.

Like Carmen Sandiego, Eagle Eye Mysteries combines digitized speech and photographs with animated graphics. As the player, you are a member of the Eagle Eye Detective Agency and are paired with either Jake or Jennifer Eagle. Cases come from the Eagles' Aunt Miranda and Uncle Basil, who have access to Scotland Yard and other useful sources of information.

The Eagles have their own high-tech crime-stopping tool. Known as T.R.A.V.I.S. (Text Retrieval And Visual Imaging System), this device is a portable computer that can store notes and photographic images. It also contains information about the many locations in London that you will visit. As you travel around the city, you are treated to digitized images of each location.

When you feel you have enough information to solve the case, you choose the clues in the T.R.A.V.I.S. that best support your suspicions. After you and your partner (Jake or Jennifer) agree on the best evidence, you can expose the mystery. If you have correctly solved it, you are rewarded with an entry in the Eagle Eye Detective Agency scrapbook.

The Eagle Eye detectives get a case from Aunt Miranda.

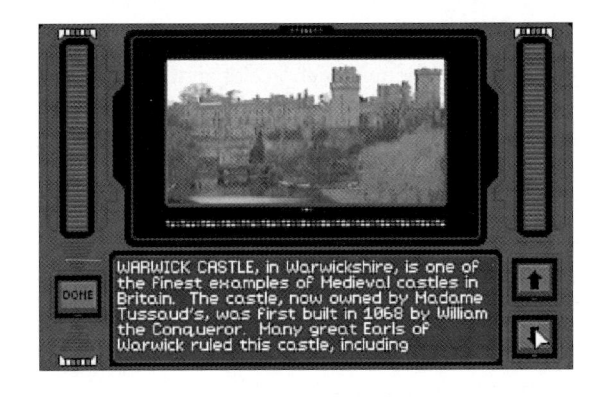

Warwick Castle, one of the many locations you visit as an Eagle Eye detective in London.

Eagle Eye Mysteries in London contains 50 mysteries. To further assist the player, the package contains a map of London, with the many possible destinations marked. The manual also contains playing aids such as a train schedule, hieroglyphs, semaphore, and other tables.

If you solve the case, you are immortalized in the Eagle Eye Detective Agency scrapbook.

Required Equipment
- DOS 5.0 or later
- 16 MHz 80386 processor (or better)
- 256-color VGA video
- 640K of RAM

(*Note:* Sound card and mouse recommended.)

Discovering America

Lawrence Productions' Discovering America is a DOS adventure for users age 8 and up. The game covers the Spanish exploration of North America in the 1500s, and colorful graphics and sound effects help to set the mood. The program is designed to teach early American history, reading, and thinking skills, and to expose the player to multicultural experiences.

In the game, you are the leader of a party of Spaniards. You have in your possession a piece of an amulet, given to you by Christopher Columbus himself. The amulet, when assembled, might lead the way to a great Aztec treasure. You have resolved to travel to America, explore the wilderness, and try to find the treasure.

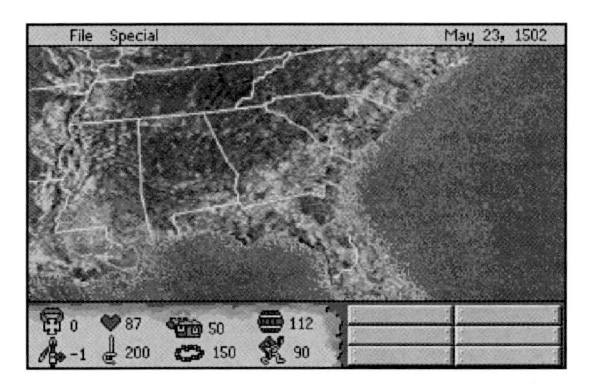

▲ *Discovering America is a game of the Spanish exploration of the New World.*

▲ *Many crucial decisions await you in Discovering America.*

Finding the Aztec treasure is only part of this game of exploration. While traveling through the uncharted wilderness that will one day be the Southeastern United States, your party encounters Indian tribes, ancient ruins, and other wonders. You may even run into historical European explorers.

As your party travels across America, its path is displayed on a topographical map. After the party arrives at a location, the display changes to show what you are seeing. There are many locations to explore and a variety of actions to pursue at each location. The program often presents you with situations that require a choice of actions. The action you choose affects the fate of your party as well as the friendliness of the natives.

While you are having adventures all across the New World, you are exposed to all sorts of facts and historical information. The program places particular emphasis on the Native American peoples, many of whom are now extinct. For the player to find all the pieces of Columbus's amulet without fighting, she must be able to answer questions about the information she has discovered during her travels.

Required Equipment
- DOS 3.3 or higher
- VGA video (or better)
- 500K of RAM free

(*Note:* A mouse is recommended.)

Normandy

Normandy, subtitled "The Great Crusade," is an interactive documentary from Discovery Communication. The subject is Operation Overlord, the Allied invasion of Normandy, France, on June 6, 1944. This unusual and dramatic product takes you back to D-Day and the crucial times before and after that fateful day. The program is a Windows program on CD-ROM.

Normandy is like a documentary, but a documentary in which you can take control at any time and explore any segment in more detail. The program contains more than 40 minutes of video. These video segments were created from actual archival footage recorded during the invasion. It is possible to view this video footage full-screen, instead of the usual quarter-screen view. Photographs, diaries, letters, and first-person accounts of those involved tell the story.

Radio was a prime source of information during the war. Normandy contains recordings of radio broadcasts heard during the invasion and the subsequent advance across France. These broadcasts chronicle, sometimes in a surprising fashion, the invasion and the advance.

You can play Normandy in two ways. It can be treated as a documentary (Auto Pilot mode) and viewed from beginning to end. It can also be treated as an interactive edutainment program and divided into chapters that can be studied in depth. Running the program in Auto Pilot mode first

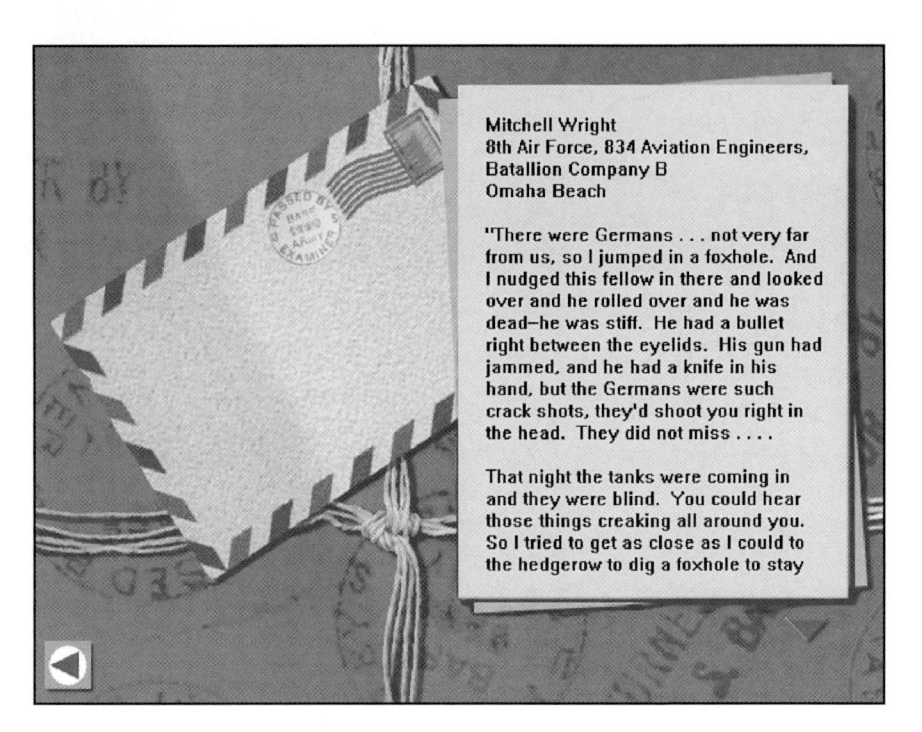

▲ *Letters from the troops involved at Normandy give us valuable historical insights.*

▲ *Radio broadcasts chronicle the Allied advance, sometimes in surprising ways.*

Required Equipment
- CD-ROM drive
- Windows 3.1
- DOS 3.1 or higher
- MSCDEX Version 2.2 or higher
- 80386SX processor
- SVGA video card with 640 x 480, 256-color Windows driver
- At least 4M of RAM
- Sound card with Windows driver
- Mouse

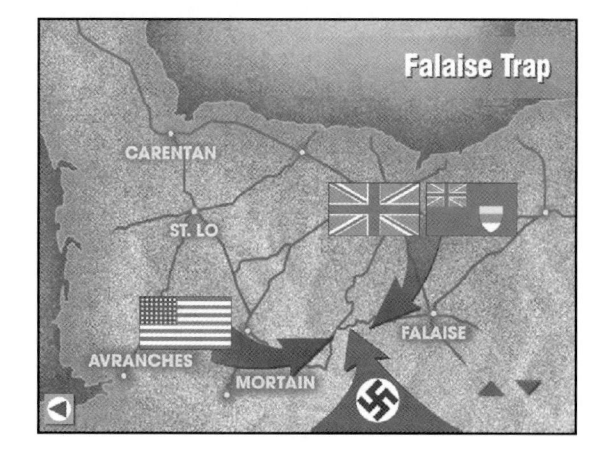

▲ *Maps of the action in Normandy provide a geographic context for the invasion.*

(select the Auto Pilot button on the Main Menu) enables you to get a feel for the overall product. You can then return to the segments that interest you and explore them in greater depth.

Normandy includes a generous amount of reference material that rounds out its coverage of the invasion. Articles provide detailed background information on historic events during the invasion. Profiles tell you about the lives and personalities of key figures. A set of four maps provides the geographic context for the operation.

Animals and Ecology

A number of products in this category deal with the animal world and ecological issues and offer programs for every age range. These products are similar because they deal with the animal world or

General Edutainment Products

ecology, but at the same time, they take a variety of approaches to the subject matter.

Products such as Ecology Treks focus on the science of ecology and increase the fun level with sound, graphics, and games. Others, such as Zoo Keeper, stress entertainment but embed educational aspects in the game.

Dinosaur Safari uses computer-generated animation to show prehistoric creatures engaging in lifelike activities. Oceans Below contains actual movies from dive sites around the world and is enhanced by narration and sound effects.

Ecology Treks

Ecology Treks is a DOS product from Magic Quest. It is designed for users age 9 and up and aims to be "the program that turns kids on to ecology." At the same time, the program helps the user develop critical thinking, recall/memory, research, and other skills.

Ecology Treks is divided into four sections: the Ecology Treks game, the EcoExplorer, the Rainforest, and the EcoSimulator. Each section takes a different approach to learning about ecology. The Ecology Treks game consists of a collection of different types of questions. You have to successfully answer more than 100 questions to complete this game.

The EcoExplorer lets you explore the cycles and relationships that sustain the major ecosystems of the earth. A graphical navigation screen helps you navigate among the various topics.

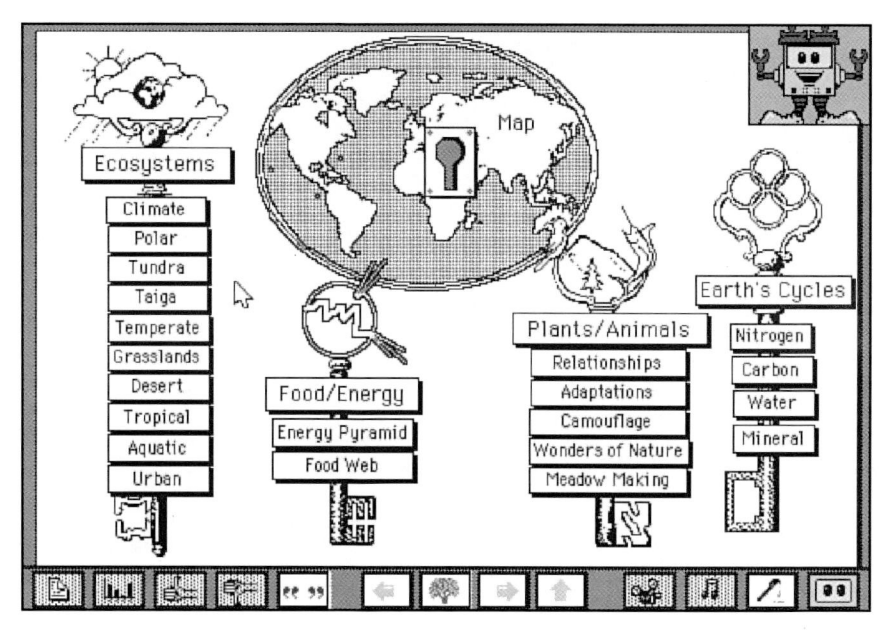

▲ *Ecology Treks' graphical design provides easy access to information.*

The Rainforest section lets you explore the flora and fauna of the Rainforest, as well as the structure of the forest itself. A bibliography and glossary of terms are also included in this section.

The EcoSimulator enables you to simulate populations and biomes, so you can experiment by changing things in the simulations and viewing the results. The results of these manipulations are displayed graphically. The EcoSimulator also includes a sound game and a sound lab.

Most screens in Ecology Treks display the Navigation Bar. The bar appears at the bottom of the

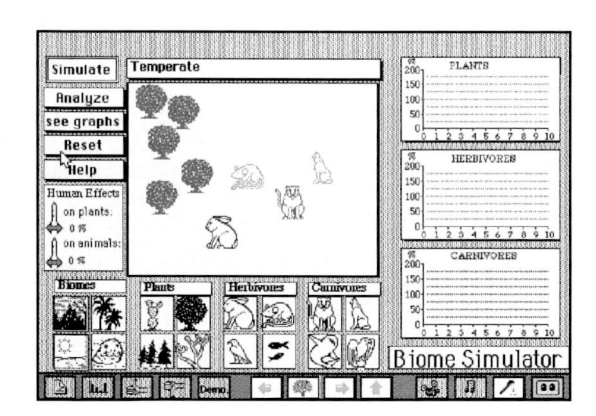

▲ *Preparing to simulate a balanced eco-system in the Ecology Treks EcoSimulator.*

screen and contains a set of buttons that lets you control the program. Two interesting features of this bar are the thumbs-up and thumbs-down buttons. The thumbs-up button displays positive programs and movements that are helping to save the environment. The thumbs-down button warns about environmental problems. Other buttons of interest include the color button, which resembles a dripping paintbrush and adds color to the current screen; the animation button, which resembles a movie camera and animates the current screen; and the quotes button, which resembles a set of quotation marks and displays an ecology-related quotation.

Required Equipment

- DOS 3.3 or later
- 80286 processor (or better)
- VGA video (or better)
- At least 640K of RAM
- Sound Blaster-compatible sound card
- Mouse

Zoo Keeper

Zoo Keeper, from Davidson, is a learning adventure that teaches about animals and the importance of protecting endangered species. It is a DOS product designed for users from age 6 to adult. Zoo Keeper was a 1993 Parent's Choice Award winner.

As the player, you must take care of World Zoo while the scientists and staff are off releasing an animal into the wild. More than 50 different animals inhabit World Zoo, and each needs to be kept happy and healthy. With the help of characters like Zoonie the Robot, you must ensure that the animals have the correct food to eat and the kinds of plants they like in their homes. The temperature and humidity also must be set correctly.

As if caring for all the animals isn't enough to keep you busy, trouble is afoot in the zoo. Four Troublemakers are on the loose, and they are stealing things, leaving litter about, and disturbing the animals' environments. An important part of your job is cleaning up the messes these villains leave behind and then capturing them so that they don't do any more harm.

You can use the Zoo Map and the Region Map to reach the home of every animal in the zoo. Finding your way around is important because the Troublemakers (cartoon characters that like to cause mischief at the zoo) will be causing trouble throughout the zoo. Before they head off to do mischief, the Troublemakers appear and give you a clue as to where they are off to next. These clues take the form of thought bubbles above the Troublemakers' heads. Early in the game, the thought bubbles contain a picture of one plant and one animal that can be found in the area to which the Troublemaker is heading. As you become more skilled, the clues become harder, they switch to words instead of pictures, and you begin getting only hints as to which animal will be bothered next.

If one of the Troublemakers has disrupted an animal's home, the animals will be in hiding and something is visibly wrong. You have to restore everything to its correct state; Zoonie can provide tips on animals and their habitats. After you have restored the animal's home to its proper state, the animals come out to play.

The animals are animated creatures. They play against a digitized background taken from the animal's environment in the real world. A pair of binoculars is available at each animal's home. When you click on these binoculars, you see a digitized photograph of the real animal.

> **Note:** The real-life photos and sounds used in this program were provided by the television show "ZooLife" and *ZooLife* magazine.

▲ *Authentic digitized scenery adds realism to Zoo Keeper.*

General Edutainment Products 141

▲ *Binoculars provide a close-up view in Zoo Keeper.*

Required Equipment

- DOS 3.3 or greater
- 12 MHz 80286 processor (or better)
- VGA video
- At least 640K of RAM (570K free)
- Mouse

(*Note:* A sound card is recommended.)

Oceans Below

Oceans Below is a Windows CD-ROM from The Software Toolworks. Billed as a "virtual underwater adventure," it turns the user into a scuba diver exploring undersea locations around the world. The program teaches the user about the life and environment at 17 dive sites scattered across the oceans. It also teaches about scuba diving.

As the player, you begin by choosing a dive site on the World Map. After you have selected a site, the program takes you there. You can look around on the surface to gather information about the location of the dive, and before actually beginning the dive, you can display the Sea Life Chart. This chart shows the types of creatures you may encounter at this particular site during your dive.

When you actually begin the dive, the program provides a video of the dive, along with some scuba tips. After these tips, the program provides a screen containing the objects the divers can see at this site. Clicking any of the objects causes the program to display a narrated video of the object.

▲ *This Sea Life Chart shows some of the inhabitants of the Sea of Cortez.*

▲ *After you get below the surface, you can select videos of the things you see.*

The ocean contains man-made items as well as sea creatures; consequently, the program's still photos and videos show the wreckage of planes and ships. Also hidden throughout the program are 68 sunken treasures. When you discover one of these treasures, you gain information about the past.

Required Equipment
- CD-ROM drive
- Windows 3.1
- DOS 5.0 or higher
- MSCDEX Version 2.21 or higher
- 25 MHz 80386SX processor (or better; 33 MHz 80486DX recommended)
- SVGA video card with 640 x 480, 256-color Windows driver
- At least 4M of RAM
- Sound card with Windows driver
- Mouse

The Animals!

The Animals! is a multimedia exploration of the plant and animal life in the San Diego Zoo. It is a CD-ROM product and is available for both DOS and Windows. The program is designed to help you learn about the hundreds of exotic creatures found at the zoo.

The Animals! is modeled on the long-range plans of the San Diego Zoo. These plans call for the creatures in the zoo to be grouped together in natural habitats called *biomes* or *bioclimatic zones*. By organizing the zoo in this manner, they hope to emphasize the interconnectedness of life. At the same time, the zoo shows how humans affect habitats and how many animal species are endangered.

The program is divided into many sections, and each section is accessible from the map that forms the Main Menu of the program. The zoo contains 10 biomes, each with its own plant and animal life. After you select a biome, information about the biome appears on the left side of the screen. The right side of the screen contains information and pictures of the exhibits within this biome. Some exhibits have only digitized photos, whereas others have full-motion videos with narration.

You can explore a number of other sections of the zoo besides the biomes. One section is the Storybook Theater, where narrators read stories that are illustrated with digitized photographs. Another is the Kid's Corner, where photos, facts, and activities geared for kids are available at the click of a mouse. Still other areas, such as the Center for Reproduction of Endangered Species and the Zoo Gardens, provide further depth and information.

The Media Library provides direct access to all the photos, videos, text, and sound effects in the program. With over 80 video clips, 1,300 color photos, 2,500 pages of text, 2.5 hours of audio, and information on hundreds of animals, the Media Library is a treasure trove.

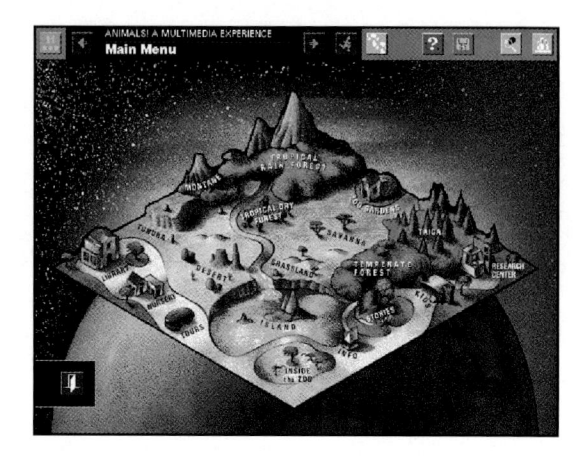

▲ *The Animals! is a multimedia preview of the future of the San Diego Zoo.*

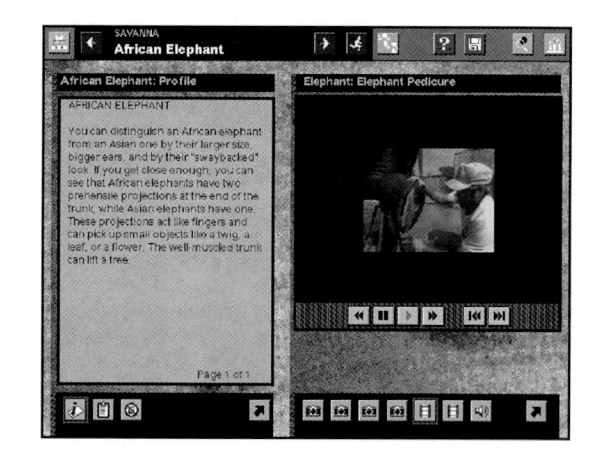

▲ *A video of an elephant pedicure from The Animals!*

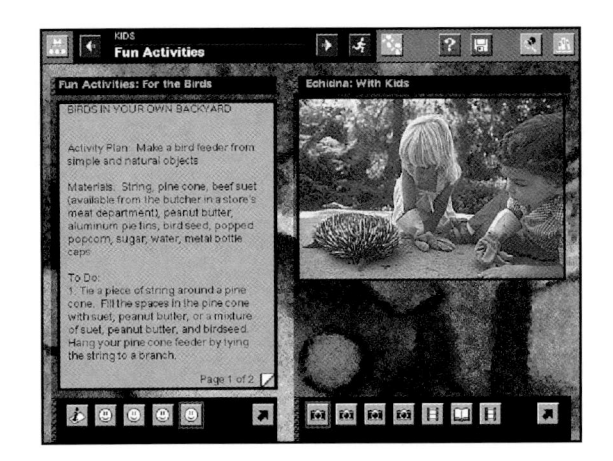

▲ *Photos, facts, and fun activities are just a mouse click away in the Kid's Corner of The Animals!*

Required Equipment

- CD-ROM drive
- Windows 3.1
- DOS 3.1 or higher
- MSCDEX Version 2.2 or higher
- 80386SX processor (or better)
- SVGA video card with 640 x 480, 256-color Windows driver
- At least 2M of RAM
- Sound card with Windows driver
- Mouse

Dinosaur Safari

Dinosaur Safari is a Windows time-travel game from Creative Multimedia. The program comes on CD-ROM and places you years ahead in the future, where you are preparing to travel back to the Mesozoic Era. Playing Dinosaur Safari teaches you about dinosaurs and the general methods of scientific classification of animals.

As the player, you are a photographer on special assignment for the National Chronographic Society. This organization employs time-travel to capture pictures, movies, and information from the past. The information is incorporated into the future version of a magazine, known as a *datazine*. Your assignment is to travel back to the Mesozoic era and take pictures of certain dinosaurs and other extinct reptiles.

Each journey to the past begins in the Cladogram Room. A *cladogram* is a term for the family tree that classifies the dinosaurs and other extinct reptiles found in Dinosaur Safari. *Clads* are families of related creatures. When you are ready to begin playing, you select target creatures by clicking the diamond shapes displayed on the cladogram. Doing so provides the name of the desired creature and a short description of it.

After you have selected your target creatures, you are ready to enter the Kronos Sphere and journey into the past. The Kronos Sphere is a time

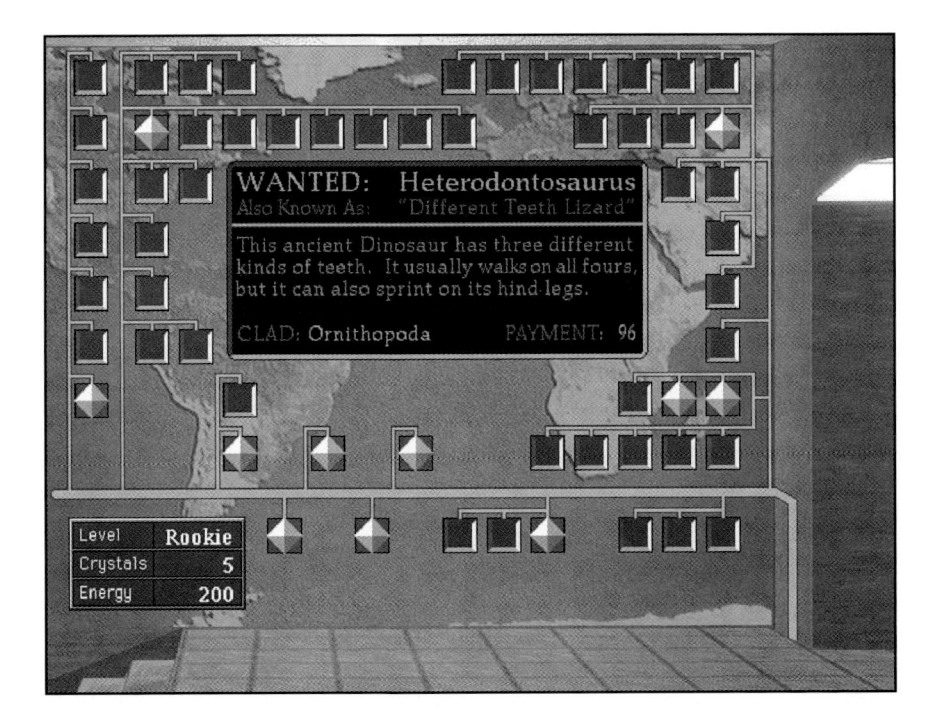

▲ *Going after a heterodontosaurus in Dinosaur Safari.*

machine that can travel to different locations—and different time periods—on the globe. When you activate the Sphere, it takes you to the time and location where the target creature is likely to be found. This can be anywhere on the surface of the earth or beneath the seas and oceans. When you arrive at your destination, your objective is to take high-quality photographs of the target creature. As you successfully complete missions to the past, you are rewarded with tougher assignments and more powerful tools.

The creatures are computer-generated, animated 3-D models. Each creature engages in lifelike activities while it is on-screen (hunting, flying, swimming, and so on). The action takes place in realistic computer-generated terrain.

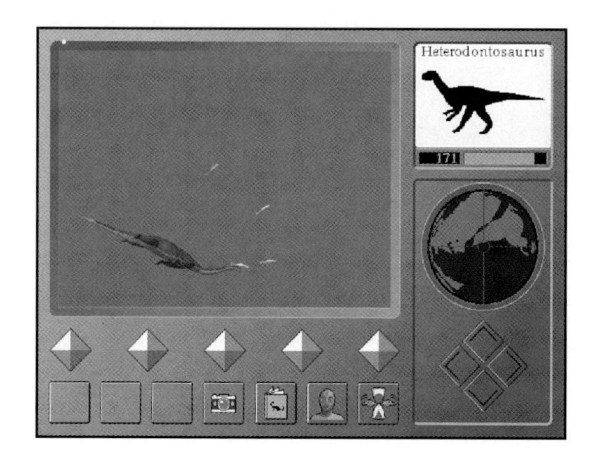

▲ *This safari can search for dinosaurs on land, in the air, and under the sea.*

Note: Dinosaur Safari was developed in collaboration with designers and scientists from the Oregon Museum of Science and Industry.

Required Equipment
- CD-ROM drive
- Windows 3.1
- 80386SX processor (or better)
- SVGA video card with 640 x 480, 256-color Windows driver
- At least 4M of RAM
- Sound card with Windows driver
- Mouse
- MSCDEX Version 2.2 or later

Language and Music
A full-blown edutainment machine, with a decent sound card and a CD-ROM drive, is absolutely essential to get the most out of sound and language products. Indeed, all three of the products discussed here *require* a sound card, CD-ROM drive, and Windows—in short, a machine that meets the MPC specifications.

Both of the language products described here shun the usual "memorize these 500 words" approach to learning a language. Instead, these products immerse you in the language to be learned and discourage translation between English and the target language. Both use the storage space on their CD-ROMs to hold words, phrases, and even dialogs—all pronounced by native speakers of the language. To provide feedback, these products enable you to record your voice and play it back for comparison to the native speakers.

All three products introduced here have unique features. Berlitz Think & Talk German is the largest product I have ever seen, with nine discs full of data! That equates to something like 5.7 billion bytes of data in the form of 50 lessons and hours of spoken German.

TriplePlay French not only eliminates the memorization of word lists, it completely does away with lessons. You are immersed in a multimedia French environment in which no English is used and all learning is in the form of games.

Multimedia Schubert explores the composer's work, using recordings, charts, and period artwork to illuminate the man and the music. It includes a game that trains the ear and enhances the user's appreciation for the music.

Berlitz Think & Talk German
Berlitz Think & Talk German is published by HyperGlot. It is a Windows package that comes on nine CD-ROMs! The program is designed to teach the user German through the Berlitz Method.

The Berlitz Method teaches a language without the translation and memorization required by most techniques. Instead, it exposes you to spoken German in everyday situations. You simply observe the situation, listen to what is said, and then repeat it. This method is very similar to how you learned your native language when you were a child. The Berlitz Think & Talk German software takes this method and turns it into a computerized self-study course.

The package contains 50 language lessons. Each lesson starts with a dialog, spoken exclusively in German. The dialog is accompanied by illustrations, music, and sound effects. These additional audio and visual cues help you to follow the dialog. The CD audio track contains pauses where you can repeat what you hear.

Step 2 of each lesson is a reading exercise. The dialog is repeated, but this time the text of the dialog appears on-screen as the words are spoken. This step calls for repeated reading of the text—at first with the sound track to provide support, and later with just the text. You can also request that the program pronounce the words on any individual line.

Step 3 asks you to write in German. The program vocalizes random lines from the dialog, and then you type what you hear. After you have written the line, you can click the image of the parrot on the right side of the screen to see the line written correctly in German. Performing this task again and again helps you develop your ability to write in German.

The final step in each lesson is Step 4: Think & Talk. In this step, you speak in German for five minutes or so. The program can provide prompts in the form of written or spoken sentences from the dialog, but the goal is for you to play with the words you know. If your PC is properly equipped, you can record your speech and play it back later to check your pronunciation.

Think & Talk German includes an English to German dictionary with more than 10,000 words. This dictionary is designed to meet your practical needs, so extraneous information is not included. Only the English word, its German equivalent, and what part of speech it is (noun, verb, masculine, feminine, and so on) are included. This dictionary is a stand-alone Windows application that can be used independently of the rest of the package.

▲ *Illustrations accompany the dialog in Think & Talk German.*

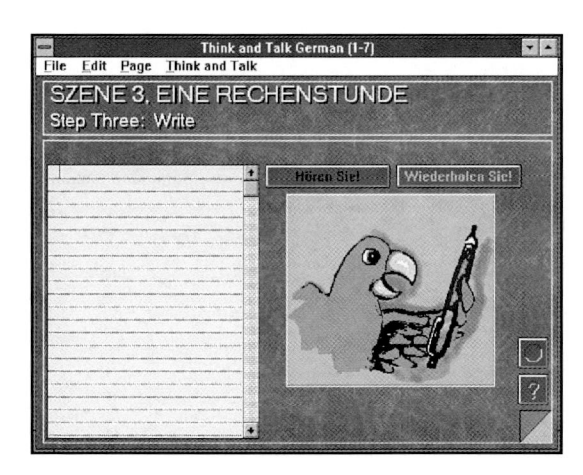

▲ *Think & Talk German reinforces learning through additional steps, such as writing.*

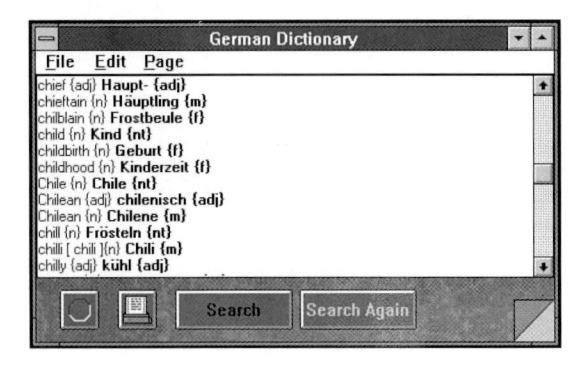

▲ *The English-German dictionary is available whether or not the Think & Talk German program is running.*

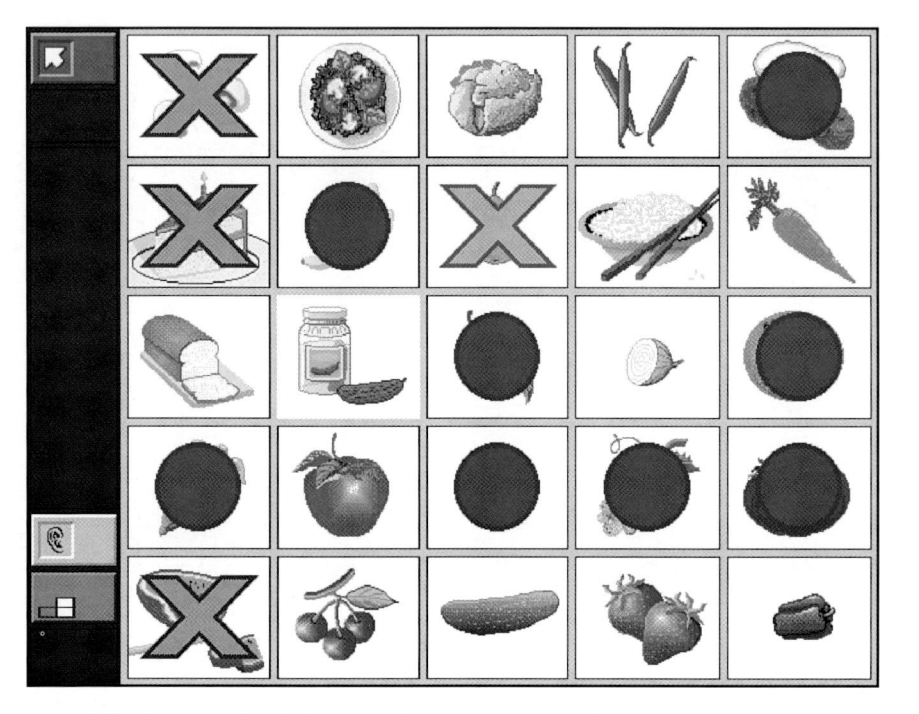

▲ *TriplePlay French teaches the language with multimedia games and stories.*

Required Equipment
- CD-ROM drive
- Windows 3.1
- 16 MHz 80386SX processor (or better)
- VGA video
- At least 2M of RAM
- Sound card with Windows driver
- Mouse

(*Note:* A microphone is optional.)

TriplePlay French

TriplePlay French is part of the Playing With Language series from Syracuse Language Systems. It is a Windows CD-ROM product for users age 9 and up. The program utilizes the *multimedia language immersion* method developed by researchers at Syracuse University, and the objective of this method is to teach French without lessons or vocabulary lists.

TriplePlay teaches the language through multimedia games. Each game has three levels of difficulty, and each level builds on the preceding level. You can choose between six topics: Food, People, Places & Transportation, Numbers, Activities, and Home & Office. Working in one category lets you focus on those things in which you are most interested.

Most of the games begin with a practice screen where you can experience the words and phrases that are used in the game. The games provide both audible and visible feedback. The audible feedback includes French comments spoken by natives. The program is 100 percent in French, with no English visible anywhere.

The games cover a wide range of skills and learning styles. Some rely on straight vocabulary skills and require you to match objects to their names. Other games call for more sophisticated skills, such as matching snippets of dialog to the scenes in which they belong. Some of the games provide clues if you get stuck.

General Edutainment Products   147

TriplePlay French teaches more than 1,000 words and phrases. Many of the games enable you to record your voice and compare your spoken French to that of a native speaker.

Required Equipment

- CD-ROM drive
- Windows 3.1
- DOS 3.1 or greater
- 80386SX processor (or better)
- SVGA video with 640 x 480, 256-color Windows driver
- At least 4M of RAM
- Sound card with Windows driver
- MSCDEX Version 2.2 or later
- Mouse

(*Note:* A microphone is optional.)

Multimedia Schubert

Microsoft's Multimedia Schubert is part of its CD-ROM-based multimedia composers series for Windows. It is an exploration of Schubert's "Quintet in A Major," also known as the "Trout Quintet." The product is designed to help the user understand this beautiful piece and the man who created it.

The "Trout Quintet" was inspired by a song that compared leaping young fish to the spirit of youth. The program explores the piece in several ways. The Close Reading section explores the music in detail, with commentary from Alan Rich, a music critic. Special charts show the "shape" of the music as it plays.

▲ *The multimedia language immersion method used in TriplePlay French helps you understand stories like this.*

The program contains a great deal of information and insight into the life and times of the composer. The Classical Background section contains the historical and social context for the Quintet. The Inside Schubert section enables you to learn about the composer himself. It delves into Schubert's life in Vienna and the experiences that shaped his music.

Other sections of the product provide additional ways to experience and understand the music. The Pocket Audio Guide lets you listen to any section of the music whenever you want. The Die Forelle (The Fish) section looks at the song that inspired Schubert in the first place.

The Trout Game is a musical challenge. You must match themes from the "Trout Quintet" by clicking stones in a riverbed. The game trains your ear and tries to induce a greater appreciation for Schubert's music.

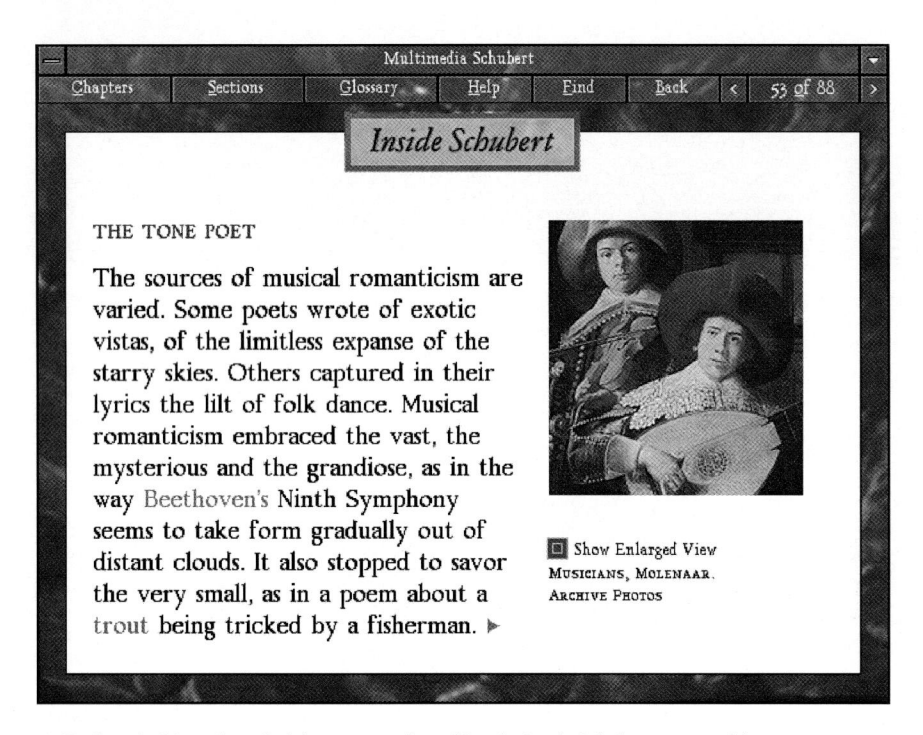

▲ *Explore the life and mind of the composer himself in the Inside Schubert section of the program.*

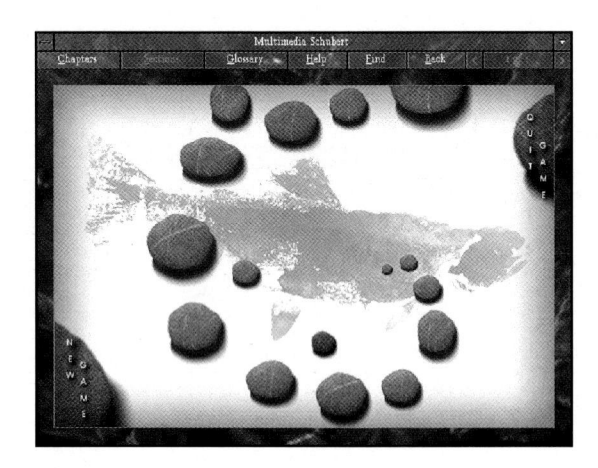

▲ *The Trout Game challenges you to match themes in Schubert's "Quintet in A Major."*

The disc contains full-color reproductions of artworks from Schubert's time. Some of these are provided simply to offer a sense of the era, whereas others deal directly with Schubert and those who influenced his life. A bibliography provides a list of readings for those who want to learn more.

Note: The CD-ROM *Edutainment Comes Alive!* contains a demonstration of Multimedia Mozart, a sister program to Multimedia Schubert.

Required Equipment

- CD-ROM drive
- Windows 3.1
- 80386SX processor (or better)
- VGA video (or better; SVGA with 640 x 480, 256-color Windows driver recommended)
- At least 4M of RAM
- Sound card with Windows driver
- Mouse

Brain Teasers

These products are for people who like puzzles. Each program contains piles of puzzles, all wrapped up inside a game. Although each product presented here deals with a different subject, they all help users to develop reading and thinking skills.

The Castle of Dr. Brain is a graphical adventure game in which you must solve problems and puzzles to become the doctor's assistant. The puzzles cover a range of subjects, including math, logic, and computer programming.

Super Solvers Gizmos & Gadgets is filled with arcade action, science puzzles, and simulations. Solving the puzzles is a primary part in the quest to defeat Morty, the Master of Mischief.

Mind Castle, The Spell of the Word Wizard, is a simple graphical adventure game. You must work your way through a five-story castle, solving puzzles and more, before you can achieve freedom.

Castle of Dr. Brain

The Castle of Dr. Brain is a DOS package from Sierra. Designed for users age 12 and up, it contains dozens of different types of problems and puzzles. The program develops problem-solving skills across a wide variety of subjects.

The program plays like a graphical adventure game. You must travel through the castle, examining everything you find and exploring every nook and cranny. Locations inside the castle are displayed graphically and contain all sorts of objects. Some of these objects help you to advance in the game, while others provide valuable clues. Appropriate sound effects help draw you into the game.

Some of the items in the castle behave as they would in the real world. Drawers and doors open, revealing new places to explore or new problems to solve. Successfully solving problems and puzzles yields useful items such as keys and special coins that let you buy hints. Some solutions reveal secret code words that you need later in the game.

In your journey through the castle, you must accumulate useful items—or at least know where you can find them if you need them. Players who expect to complete the game should draw a map of the castle. This map should contain information about each area, including the objects in the room and the danger spots.

Some of the subjects covered in this program are math, language, astronomy, and programming. Each subject has its own problems and puzzles to solve, and the game has three levels of difficulty.

The Castle of Dr. Brain comes with the *Fantastic Book of Logic Puzzles*, a 128-page book containing 70 logic puzzles. The puzzles are set in fantastic locales such as mythical kingdoms or alien worlds. Explanations of the logic required to solve the problems are included in the book, as is a set of clues.

Required Equipment

- 80286 processor (or better)
- VGA video
- 640K of RAM

(*Note:* Sound card and mouse recommended.)

▲ *Solving puzzles and problems earns the player various rewards, such as this secret code word. The setting is the entry hall in the Castle of Dr. Brain.*

Super Solvers Gizmos & Gadgets

Super Solvers Gizmos & Gadgets is part of the Super Solvers series from The Learning Company. Designed for users between the ages of 7 and 12, it is a DOS science program. Gizmos & Gadgets is designed to teach science and thinking skills, and it accomplishes that task with enjoyable sounds and graphics.

The game places the child in competition with Morty, the Master of Mischief. Morty has taken over the Shady Glen Technology Center and claims that he can build better automobiles, aircraft, and alternative energy vehicles than anyone else. As a Super Solver, it is up to the child to beat Morty at his own game by building the best vehicles.

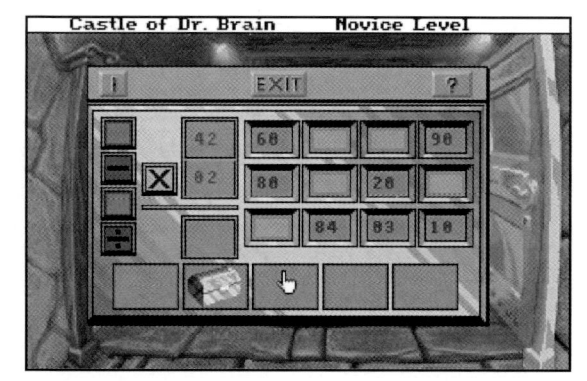

▲ *One of the dozens of puzzles created by Dr. Brain.*

To build the vehicles, the child must gather the appropriate parts. And before the child can get a part, he must first travel through the factory and solve a science puzzle. These puzzles feature everyday gadgets such as scissors and light bulbs, and develop the child's understanding of the scientific principles that make these gadgets work.

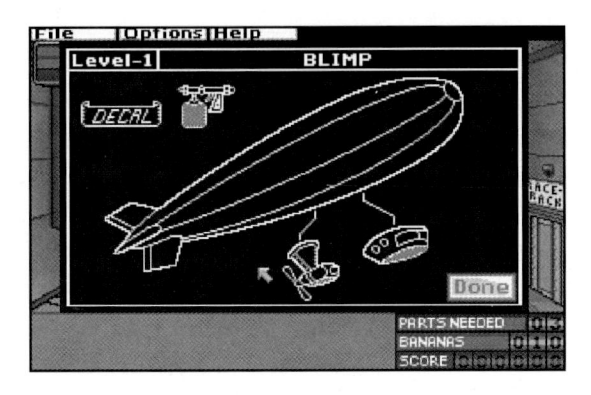

Creating a vehicle is complicated by the variety of parts available and by the presence of Morty's Cyber Chimps. The various types of a specific part have different qualities (some wheels or engines are better than others, for example). These qualities tell how useful a particular part is in creating a fast vehicle. The child can determine the qualities of a part by clicking the part and reading the description that appears. The child can hold two of each type of part. If he wishes to take a third, he must first recycle one of the other two. Cyber Chimps try to steal the child's parts; they must be avoided or distracted by bananas.

After the child builds his vehicle, the race is on! Win or lose, he can move on. If he loses, he can head back to the workshop, improve his vehicle, and challenge Morty again. If he wins 15 races (5 with each type of vehicle), he becomes the head scientist at Shady Glen, and Morty is driven away to commit mischief somewhere else.

The program contains over 200 science puzzles and simulations and includes 8 different types of puzzles. All the puzzles adjust themselves to the child's skill level, so he can work on the types he is having trouble with, while continuing to advance on the ones he has mastered.

▲ *A blimp is just one of the many vehicles the child must build in* Gizmos & Gadgets.

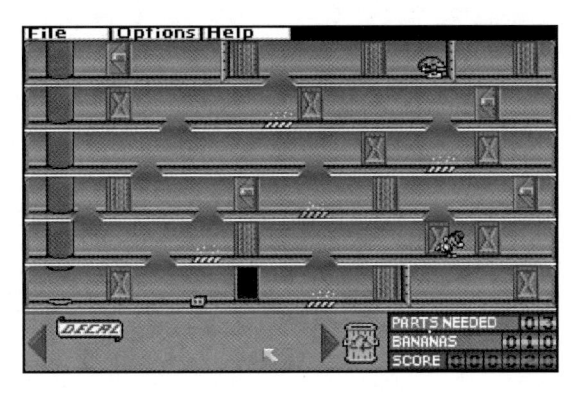

▲ *Traveling through the* Gizmos & Gadgets *factory calls for some rudimentary arcade-game skills.*

▲ Super Solvers Gizmos & Gadgets *contains hundreds of scientific puzzles like this one.*

General Edutainment Products

Required Equipment
- DOS 3.3 or greater
- 10 MHz 80286 processor (or better)
- At least 640K of RAM
- VGA video (or better)

(*Note:* A sound card is optional.)

Mind Castle

Mind Castle, subtitled "The Spell of the Word Wizard," is a word-puzzle game from Lawrence Productions. Designed for users age 8 and up, Mind Castle challenges the player to solve word puzzles and to find secret portals in a spooky old castle. Playing this game tests the child's vocabulary skills and knowledge while developing her critical thinking and reading skills. Mind Castle received a Parent's Choice Honors award in 1993.

The game begins shortly after the child, as the player, is turned into a frog by the Word Wizard! To regain her human form, she must work her way through the five floors of the castle. She must travel from room to room, solving puzzles and decoding passwords as she goes. Each room is displayed in 256 colors and contains numerous objects. Clicking an object may uncover one of the hidden puzzles, which the child must then solve.

As the child solves the puzzles and finds the secret portals, she moves down through the castle toward the ground floor—and freedom. As she descends, the puzzles become more numerous (and more

▲ *The player must solve the word puzzles in time to break the spell of the Word Wizard.*

difficult). What's more, if she doesn't escape within two hours (game time), she will never get away.

Mind Castle features 200 vocabulary-building puzzles and contains more than 600 words and definitions for use in these puzzles. The puzzles and portals are arranged randomly for every game so that each game is unique.

Required Equipment
- DOS 3.1 or higher
- VGA video
- At least 640K of RAM (with 400K free)

(*Note:* A mouse and sound card are optional.)

Math

Math was one of the first subjects to be taught by computer. Those early programs typically served as computerized versions of worksheets or flash cards;

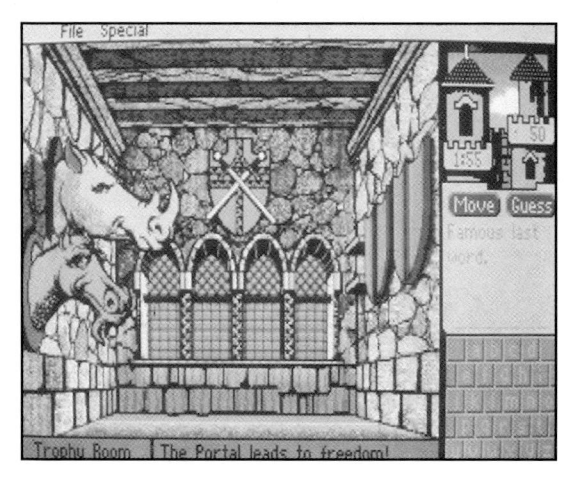

▲ *The path to freedom sometimes passes through the trophy room of the Mind Castle.*

they did little to improve the teaching of the subject beyond simplifying the teacher's record keeping. The three programs discussed here show that math programs have come a long way since then. All of these programs use arcade-style games to hold the user's attention while teaching them math. In each case, solving problems is a necessary part of winning the game. And as necessary, the player can customize the problems encountered during the game.

Math Ace consists of more than just a game. It contains the Smart Lab, a facility that explains and illustrates the concepts behind the math.

Operation Neptune does a fine job of integrating its pre-algebra training into the game. The problems deal directly with the player's mission and the tasks necessary to complete that mission.

Math Rescue stresses entertainment. Lots of arcade action (although no people, or even Gruzzles, get killed) keeps the player on his toes between the equations and word problems.

Math Ace

Math Ace is a "math adventure" from Magic Quest. Designed for children between the ages of 8 and 14, this DOS program takes a number of different approaches to teaching math. Math Ace is designed to develop critical-thinking, problem-solving, and reasoning skills, as well as to stimulate a child's curiosity and interest in math.

Math Ace asks the child to help defend the Global Math Archives against an insidious virus. The virus must be stopped before it eats the math microchips, which contain the world's entire store of mathematical knowledge.

Solving random math problems is the key to stopping the evil virus. Correctly solving the problems causes virus shields to appear; by solving problems correctly and choosing shield locations wisely, the child can trap the virus. After the virus is completely stopped, the child wins that level and moves to the next. Unfortunately for the child, the virus is constantly on the move, chewing its way through more memory chips and laying virus eggs. Speed, accuracy, and strategy are all required to save the Archives.

The child can control the difficulty level of the game in two ways. First, the game has two data levels that control the difficulty of the problems presented to the player. Second, the virus "hunger level" determines how fast the virus eats. The higher the hunger level, the faster the child must solve the problems to keep the virus in check.

Sometimes the program presents something other than a math problem for the child to solve. The Backdoor Code requires the child to guess a secret code. If he guesses it correctly, he immediately wins the level. The program also offers four "Math Duels," which are games that challenge the child's math skills. Winning a duel lets the child place more shields; losing a duel causes a virus egg to hatch, which leaves the child with more viruses to contend with.

Another big part of Math Ace is the Smart Lab. The Smart Lab is an area in which to learn, and practice, different math skills and types of problems. The Lab lets the child explore problems differently than he does in the game. The Smart Lab also provides animated tools for exploring concepts and buttons that teach key definitions. A Reference section contains all sorts of tables and definitions that the child might find useful.

Required Equipment
- DOS 3.1 or higher
- 80286 processor (or better)
- At least 640K of RAM
- VGA video (or better)
- Sound card
- Mouse

Operation Neptune

Operation Neptune is a DOS CD-ROM from The Learning Company. Designed for children between the ages of 9 and 14, it is an undersea math adventure. The program teaches pre-algebra

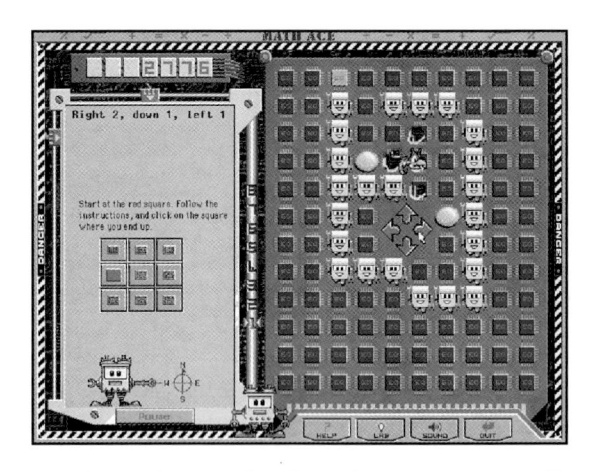

▲ *Only a Math Ace can keep the insidious virus from eating all the math microchips. (Courtesy of Magic Quest)*

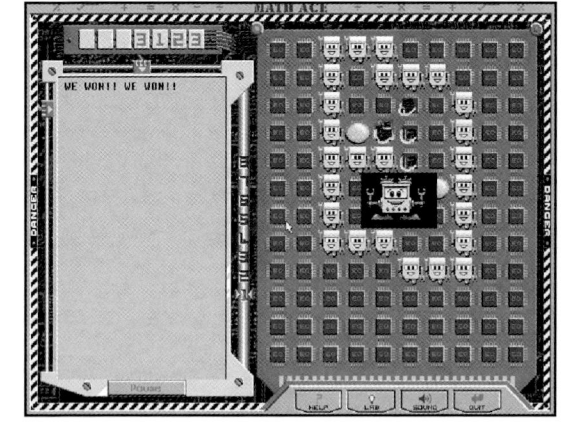

▲ *The Bubble Gum Machine is one of four Math Duels in Math Ace. (Courtesy of Magic Quest)*

and problem-solving skills, while the player tries to save the Earth's oceans and retrieve secret data canisters. Operation Neptune won a Parent's Choice Award in 1992.

The Neptune is a high-tech mini-sub equipped with sophisticated sensors and computers. The child, as the player, must search the ocean for the wreckage of the space capsule Galaxy. Filled with classified information, the capsule was sent back to Earth by scientists at a secret research station on the very edge of our solar system. An apparent malfunction caused the capsule to change course over the Pacific Ocean and break into pieces before disappearing beneath the waves. Toxic substances are leaking from the capsule and endangering the world's oceans.

Math skills are vitally important to completing the mission. The child has to solve word problems and use pre-algebra concepts to compute her position and supply levels, among other things. When not exercising her math skills, the child must maneuver the Neptune through undersea mazes and avoid colorful (and dangerous) sea creatures—all the while searching for supplies and wreckage from the Galaxy capsule.

Operation Neptune provides hours of learning and adventure. The game can be played at two different levels of difficulty, which increases its replay value. The math problems can be customized to cover the specific math skills a child needs to work on. If the child fails to get a problem right the first time, the program provides a hint for solving it. If she still gets the wrong answer, the program provides a step-by-step solution. Digitized speech and sound effects are combined throughout the adventure to make it even more realistic and absorbing.

Required Equipment
- Double-speed CD-ROM drive
- DOS 5.0 or higher
- 25 MHz 80386 processor (or better)
- VGA video (or better)
- Sound card

Math & Word Rescue

Math Rescue and Word Rescue are shareware products published by Apogee Games. Math Rescue is designed to teach basic math to children between the ages of 6 and 13. Word Rescue teaches basic reading to children between the ages of 5 and 9. Both products combine learning with arcade-style action.

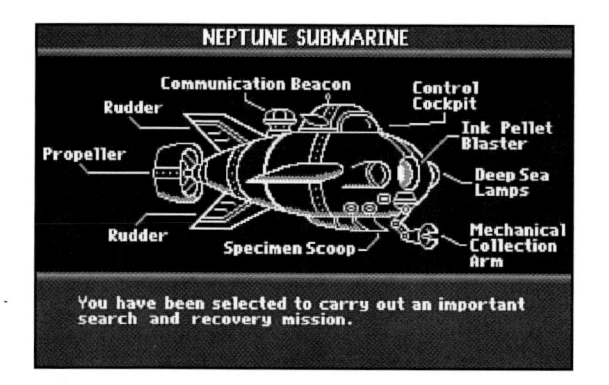

▲ *Using the Neptune submarine, players search for undersea wreckage during Operation Neptune.*

▲ *It's smooth sailing for the Neptune in this screen, but just wait!*

▲ *Solving word problems is necessary to keep Operation Neptune moving forward.*

Word Rescue pits the player against the evil Gruzzles. The Gruzzles are stealing the words out of all the books in the world, and only the player can stop them! As the player, the child must avoid Gruzzles while matching words to their meanings. The action takes place on a scrolling background, where the child's game character can run, jump, and climb. Word Rescue has three levels of difficulty, with higher levels increasing the number of Gruzzles on the level.

In Math Rescue, the Gruzzles are back, stealing all the numbers in the world. The child must stop them by solving math problems. Once again, the action takes place on a scrolling arcade-style background. Math Rescue can display problems involving addition, subtraction, multiplication, division, or a mixture. The percentage of problems presented as word problems can also be adjusted.

Although it is hard to track sales in the shareware world, the Rescue games are believed to be the best-selling educational shareware of all time. Enhanced versions of Math Rescue and Word Rescue are also available as retail products published by Good Times Software. Look for Math Rescue and Word Rescue Deluxe to appear very soon. These 256-color versions of the games contain new art, new levels, and new words and word problems.

Required Equipment

EGA or better video. A sound card and joystick are optional.

What Is Shareware?

Shareware is the name for the method in which some software products are marketed. Also known as "try-before-you-buy" software, products marketed as shareware are made available to the user for free or for a small fee (charged by the distributor who provides the disk). The user can evaluate the product for a certain amount of time (ranging from days to months) without any obligation. If the customer chooses to continue using the product beyond the evaluation period, he is ethically and legally obligated to pay a registration fee.

Many authors provide incentives to register. These incentives may include such things as an enhanced version of the original product, a printed manual, and technical support. The shareware concept enables end-users to evaluate products before paying for them. At the same time, this concept provides authors with an alternative way to get their products to market.

Colorful screens and lots of action make the Rescue games captivating.

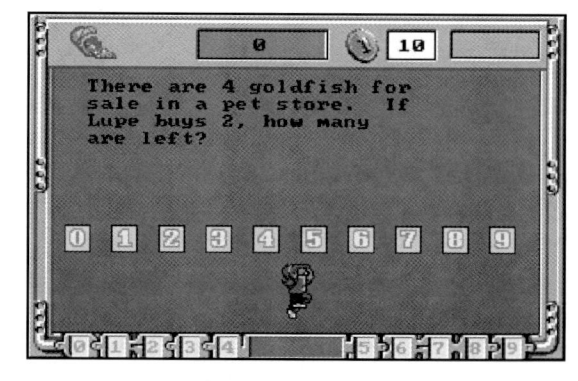

Solving a word problem in Math Rescue.

▲ *With this level successfully completed, Benny the Bookworm magically restores words to the world's books in Math Rescue.*

Summary

This chapter looked at some of the diverse offerings in the general edutainment category. Many products, including such big names as the Carmen Sandiego series, fall into this category. A major goal of the chapter was to give you a taste of the range and variety of the edutainment products available.

With this chapter, you have completed Part II of *Edutainment Comes Alive!* You should have a good feel for the kinds of products on the market and some idea of the products that are right for you or your child. You should also know the kind of equipment you need to run those products.

Part III of this book, "Upgrading Your System for Edutainment," returns you once again to your computer. In this third part, you find information on how to upgrade your system to meet the demands of modern edutainment software, as well as useful information about troubleshooting—what to do when it doesn't work right.

UPGRADING YOUR SYSTEM *for* EDUTAINMENT *Part III*

You are about to begin Part III of *Edutainment Comes Alive!* This portion of the book helps you upgrade your PC so that it can run all the exciting software you read about in Part II. Unfortunately, it's impossible to talk about upgrading your system without getting a bit technical; I've tried to explain things in English and minimize the jargon. If you want more technical information than is found in the main text, you can read the sidebars.

Part III is divided into six chapters. Each chapter looks at one or two specific aspects of upgrading your system. Chapters 10 and 11 discuss specific hardware you can add to improve your system's capabilities. Chapter 12 talks about Windows, the MPC specifications, and why they are important to you as an edutainment software user. Chapter 13 is dedicated to users with special computing needs. Chapters 14 and 15 give you advice on what to do when things go wrong. A short description of each chapter is provided below.

Chapter 10, "Sight and Sound"

Sight and sound are the means by which an edutainment system communicates with its users. Super VGA video and a sound card are necessities if you want to take full advantage of the edutainment products available today.

This chapter covers many subjects related to sight and sound on an edutainment system, including the types of SVGA video cards, the factors that affect video performance, the features of sound cards, and video and sound buying tips.

Chapter 11, "CD-ROM Drives"

A CD-ROM drive is almost a necessity for an edutainment system. With many edutainment products containing tens to hundreds of megabytes of sound and pictures, distributing products on floppy disk becomes totally impractical. Besides, how many users have a few hundred megabytes of free space on their hard disks!

The chapter begins with a general introduction to CD-ROM. Then the remainder of the chapter discusses important features of CD-ROM drives and gives you tips on what to look for when you buy a drive.

Chapter 12, "Edutainment and Windows"

This chapter has two objectives. The first is to convince you that Windows is the future of edutainment software. The second objective is to teach you enough about Windows that you can successfully run an edutainment program under Windows.

The chapter includes information on the Multimedia Personal Computer (MPC) specifications, which define minimum standards for hardware and software for multimedia PCs. These specifications are becoming increasingly important as more edutainment products become multimedia products.

Chapter 13, "Upgrades for Users with Special Needs"

I believe that the benefits of edutainment products should be made available to as many people as possible. This chapter discusses the things you can do to make an edutainment PC, and edutainment software, more accessible to users with special needs.

Edutainment software, with its multimedia approach, is not always easy to use for those with physical challenges. This chapter discusses some of the hardware and software available to help these users take advantage of the available software.

Chapter 14, "Troubleshooting DOS and Windows"

This chapter contains information about problems you may encounter when you use DOS or Windows. For each problem, the symptoms are described, an explanation is provided about why the problem occurs, and you are given some solutions. Because a mouse is virtually indispensable when you use Windows, common mouse problems are also discussed in the Windows portion of the chapter.

The chapter begins by explaining some of the more common DOS error messages. Considering that everything that runs on your PC uses DOS (even Windows), this is a sensible starting point. The rest of the chapter is dedicated to common Windows problems, including some obstacles you may stumble across while using the mouse.

Chapter 15, "Troubleshooting CD-ROM Drives and Sound Cards"

A sound card and CD-ROM drive are the two pieces of hardware that you must add to a basic PC to get it ready for edutainment use. Unfortunately, adding these devices to your PC is more complicated than simply dropping a card into a slot. Some sort of problem is almost inevitable when you add these devices to your system.

This chapter contains information about the problems you may run into when you add a sound card or CD-ROM drive to your system. It helps you in troubleshooting these devices, discusses what you should check first when you run into a snag, and presents some of the common error messages and problems that may arise.

Chapter 10

Sight and Sound

Your PC's video system (monitor and graphics card) is its primary means of providing you with information. Now that much of the information in edutainment products comes in the form of graphics, the power and quality of your video system are even more important. This chapter gives you the background to understand the workings of that video system.

In addition to graphics, sound has now become an indispensable part of edutainment software. If your PC does not have a sound card, you are missing out on some of the edutainment experience. In addition, many of the newer edutainment products provide music and voice as an integral part of the experience and *require* sound.

This chapter can provide you with a solid understanding of the basics of PC sound systems. The available hardware and software changes from week to week, but if you understand the basics, you can choose the appropriate equipment.

This chapter covers a variety of subjects, including the following topics:

- The types of Super VGA cards
- Factors that affect graphics performance
- Modes, resolution, and colors
- Image types
- File formats
- Monitor buying tips
- Important features of sound cards
- Speakers and microphones
- General buying tips

When you finish this chapter, you should have the information you need to ensure that your PC can provide the sights and sounds that make edutainment products so exciting.

Types of Video Cards

A wide variety of video cards is currently available for PCs. Chapter 2, "The Capabilities of the Basic PC," covered VGA and lesser cards (MDA, CGA, EGA, and Hercules); here you learn about Super VGA cards. Super VGA cards, usually just called *SVGA* cards, go beyond the VGA standard in the number of colors available, the maximum resolution, or both. Although most edutainment products will work with a normal VGA video card, products that can use—or even require—SVGA video modes are becoming more numerous all the time. A good SVGA card can take care of your edutainment video needs for the next several years.

Types of SVGA Cards

Super VGA graphics cards are available in three primary types: frame buffer cards, graphics accelerator cards, and coprocessor cards. Although each has advantages and disadvantages, you probably can get the best value from a graphics accelerator card.

Frame Buffers

Frame buffer cards are the oldest type of graphics card. These cards are little more than a buffer, or storage area, for images on their way from the microprocessor to the monitor. When working with a frame buffer card, the microprocessor must compute the location and color of everything drawn on the screen. This information is then passed, pixel-by-pixel, to the graphics card. Finally, the graphics card transfers the image to the monitor. Because the processor must do all the work itself, and pass the information along to the graphics card over the system bus, frame buffer cards provide the slowest video of the three types. These cards are best suited for low-resolution (VGA or less) DOS edutainment titles.

Graphics Accelerators

A graphics accelerator card is a video card that contains a special processor that can perform certain graphics operations. When Windows wants to draw things on the screen, it sends out graphics commands. These commands tell your computer to do such things as "fill this area with this pattern," or "move this image from this location on the screen to that location." (For more information, see the following sidebar, "Operations Performed by Graphics Accelerators.")

With a standard frame buffer card, the microprocessor receives these commands, figures out how to do the job, and does it. All the information must move back and forth over the system bus, which slows things down even more.

When your machine has a graphics accelerator card, however, the graphics card can interpret many of the graphics commands, and so it can do the work itself. The special processor is specifically designed to handle Windows graphics commands, so it does the work much faster than the PC's processor can. Any information that the graphics card can generate is information that does not have to go on the bus, which yields additional improvements in speed.

You can find a wide variety of graphics accelerator cards on the market. They are the most popular general-purpose graphics cards available, and they provide the best Windows price-performance ratio of the three types of graphics card.

You should watch out for one thing with this kind of card, however. Some graphics accelerator cards can actually slow down DOS applications. If you plan to stick with DOS edutainment products, you probably should stick with a frame buffer card. If, however, you see yourself moving to Windows someday (and I think most users eventually will), you should go with one of the graphics accelerator cards.

Programmable Graphics Coprocessors

Programmable graphics coprocessor cards (also known simply as coprocessor cards) define the high-end of the graphics performance spectrum. These cards contain their own high-powered processor that can be reprogrammed for the application in use. They often can perform more

Operations Performed by Graphics Accelerators

All Windows graphics accelerator cards handle two primary types of graphics commands. For most uses, the ones that provide the greatest speed improvement are the bit-block transfers. *Bit-block transfers*, commonly know as *BitBlts*, are commands that involve moving a rectangular area of the screen (a block of bits). BitBlts occur when you perform common Windows activities, such as moving windows, scrolling the screen, or displaying menus.

Accelerators also handle the set of commands for area fills. *Area fills* occur when Windows wants to fill the interior of a rectangle, or other polygon, with a solid color. Windows uses area fills when it draws items such as scroll bars, and lines on the screen are also drawn using area fills; the line is treated as a very thin rectangle. In addition, paint programs make frequent use of area fills.

Windows graphics commands than a graphics accelerator card can, theoretically making them faster.

Unfortunately for the makers of coprocessor cards, there are a couple of reasons why you probably won't buy one. The first is price. As of this writing, these cards are several times more expensive than decent graphics accelerator cards. For a typical edutainment user, a card that costs three times as much had better make a major difference in the quality and enjoyment of edutainment products. This usually isn't the case.

Although I can't give you specific numbers (they change weekly, as new cards come on the market), the performance of graphics accelerator cards seems to be closing in on that of coprocessor cards. In the day-to-day use of your machine, you probably wouldn't notice much of a performance difference between the two.

The graphics accelerators are the most popular type of card today, which draws more companies into the market and creates more competition. The increased competition causes manufacturers to develop more powerful cards, at lower prices, and to get them to market faster. It seems likely that graphics accelerator cards will remain the most cost-effective type and will continue to gain ground on coprocessor cards.

Features to Look For

Many factors affect the performance of a graphics card, and this is particularly true of frame buffers, in which the PC's processor does all the work. If your video system can't display images fast enough, the performance of your edutainment programs suffers; video clips and animation become jerky, and the overall responsiveness of the program can decline. The next several sections describe the primary factors that affect video performance.

Type of Bus

Beyond the design of the card itself, the bus that it connects to has the largest impact on video speed. The frame buffer cards communicate with the processor through the *system bus*, which is the standard path by which cards communicate between themselves and the processor. This bus moves data 16 bits at a time, and runs at a clock speed of 8 MHz (megahertz). Because the microprocessor in your system may be running at 33 MHz or more, the system bus is often a limiting factor for video speed.

Computer manufacturers have developed newer, faster buses, such as IBM's Micro Channel Architecture (MCA), but an even better solution is available: local-bus video.

Local-bus systems have a separate bus running from the processor to the graphics card. The most common type of local bus is the VESA local (VL) bus. This bus transfers data 32 bits at a time, and runs at the speed of your microprocessor. Any decent edutainment system should have a processor that runs at a minimum of 20 MHz, so an edutainment system with a VL bus can move data to the graphics card at least five times as fast as a traditional design!

The video card in your current machine already is matched to the bus it is on. If you are considering a new machine, look for one with a VL bus.

The Microprocessor

The microprocessor in your PC has a significant impact on the speed of your video display. The effect of the processor varies with the type of graphics card you use. As you know, frame buffer cards depend on the processor to compute the color of every pixel on the screen, making these cards the most dependent on the speed of the processor.

Graphics accelerator cards are less influenced by the speed of the processor. The graphics card itself does a significant part of the work—at least when you are running Windows. When you are running most DOS applications, the built-in graphics accelerator functions are of little or no use. Many of these cards do come with special drivers for the most popular DOS applications, but none of them help with any edutainment programs.

If you are buying a new machine, you want the fastest processor you can afford—not only for its effect on video speed, but for all other operations.

Type of Video Memory

Graphics cards come with two different types of video memory. The less expensive cards tend to use DRAM, which is short for dynamic random-access memory. DRAM is both less expensive and slower than VRAM. VRAM (video RAM) is specially designed to be used on graphics cards. It is dual-ported, which allows it to pass information to the display, while simultaneously accepting data from the bus.

VRAM versus DRAM is a classic tradeoff for graphics card designers. VRAM is faster, but more expensive. For the typical edutainment user, the type of memory on the graphics card doesn't really matter. Other considerations, such as the type of bus or the processor speed, are more important.

Size of Video Memory

The other thing to consider with video memory is how much of it you need. Although this doesn't directly affect the speed of your video, it does determine the maximum resolution and number of colors that a card can display.

Most SVGA cards come with 1M of video memory. This is enough memory for a display of 1024 pixels horizontally by 768 pixels vertically, with each pixel being one of 256 colors (1024 x 768, 256 colors). 1M of video memory is also enough for 640 x 480 with 16.8 million colors! Although this would certainly appear to be sufficient for most people, many of the newer graphics cards contain 2M of video RAM.

Cards with 2M of memory can display higher resolution images, with more colors, than the 1M cards. At the same time, they often use some of this extra memory for storing fonts or for creating a virtual screen. Unless you plan to do some heavy-duty image processing on your machine, either a 1M or 2M card should work just fine in your edutainment machine.

System Memory

Although you might not think that system memory would have an impact on your video performance, it can. Graphics cards are becoming so fast that the amount of time it takes to move information from your hard disk can slow things down. A disk cache (which uses system memory to store data from the hard disk) speeds up average disk access time. The more system memory you have, the bigger the cache you can have, and the lower your average access time.

On an edutainment system, images that are big enough and colorful enough to cause problems are likely to be coming from a CD-ROM, which is much slower than a hard disk. A large disk cache is a plus for any edutainment system.

DOS or Windows

Whether you use DOS or Windows products can make a big difference in your video performance. Graphics accelerator cards mainly speed up the video for Windows applications. The graphics processors on accelerator cards can't do anything for most DOS applications. In fact, some graphics accelerator cards reportedly slow down DOS video.

You can get by just fine with a frame buffer card if you want to stay with DOS edutainment products. Just buy an inexpensive frame buffer card that supports at least 640 x 480 in 256 colors. That way, when you do find yourself moving to Windows, you can replace your old card without taking much of a financial loss.

Driver Software

One of the most important, and most overlooked, features of graphics cards is the driver software that comes with them. Video drivers are programs that allow your system to take advantage of the special features of a card. In some ways, the video driver software that comes with a card is the most important feature of all.

Windows generates graphics commands through its graphics device interface (GDI). When the GDI determines that a BitBlt or area fill command is required, it checks with the video driver before sending the command to the processor. If the driver responds that the card can handle the command, the GDI tells the driver to send the command to the card and refrains from sending the command on to the processor.

From the previous description, you can see that the video device driver serves as the interface between the graphics card and the rest of the system. This example used a Windows driver, but the process is similar for any of the drivers supplied with a card.

Poorly designed drivers can significantly reduce the performance of an otherwise capable card. Bug-ridden drivers can give you strange results on-screen or even cause your system to crash.

When shopping for a card, you should first make sure that it has the drivers you want. For edutainment users, the only drivers that are really important are ones for Windows. Drivers for your favorite word processor or spreadsheet are a nice bonus if you can get them.

You can do a couple of things to ensure that you receive, or at least have access to, quality drivers. First, don't buy a graphics card that is new on the market. Brand new cards are the ones most likely to have driver problems. If you wait at least a few months, the manufacturer should have most of the problems corrected.

The next step should be to ensure that you have a source of updated drivers. Most card manufacturers make new or updated drivers available for free. Usually, a vendor has its own bulletin board or a forum on CompuServe. In either case, you can just log in and download the latest drivers.

Resolution

The resolution of a video mode is the number of pixels it contains horizontally and vertically. The highest resolution mode on a standard VGA card is 640 pixels horizontally and 480 pixels vertically, or 640 x 480. The higher the resolution, the more information you can get on the screen.

Super VGA card manufacturers quickly moved beyond 640 x 480. One of these new resolutions is 800 x 600. Although some manufacturers came up with unusual intermediate resolutions, the next most common one after 800 x 600 is 1024 x 768.

For an edutainment system, very high resolution is not necessary. Many edutainment products are designed for a 640 x 480 display or include video clips or animation. Due to the difficulties involved in displaying real-time videos, they are seldom displayed full-screen. A common size for video clips is *quarter-screen,* in which both the horizontal and vertical resolutions of the image are one-fourth that of the basic 640 x 480 Windows display. This results in an image that is 160 x 120 (actually 1/16 of the total area of the screen).

The size of your monitor doesn't change when you use a higher-resolution video mode, so the clip itself becomes physically smaller. Unless you buy a very large monitor (thereby increasing the physical size of the display and the video clip displayed on it), you probably won't be happy with video clips on backgrounds larger than 800 x 600. The following figures show you why.

▲ *A quarter-screen video clip on a 640 x 480 background.*

A quarter-screen video clip in 640 x 480 is small, but usable. The following figures show the same clip displayed against 800 x 600, 1024 x 768, and 1280 x 1024 backgrounds.

DOS edutainment products seldom use a resolution greater than 640 x 480. Many of them still work with 320 x 200, or its non-standard derivative mode, 320 x 240.

▲ *A quarter-screen video clip on an 800 x 600 background.*

▲ *A quarter-screen video clip on a 1024 x 768 background.*

▲ *A quarter-screen video clip on a 1280 x 1024 background.*

The upshot of all this is that you don't need a really high-resolution graphics card for edutainment work. Virtually all of the accelerated cards available can display 1280 x 1024, so you have high resolution available if you need it. Your main concern, however, should be with the lower resolutions.

Colors

The number of colors a graphics card can display simultaneously has a profound effect on the quality of images. When you are looking at a realistic image, the number of colors can be more important than the resolution.

The high-resolution mode of the VGA standard is 640 x 480 with 16 colors. While this is fine for text-mode programs or basic Windows use, it really is not adequate for edutainment products.

The VGA standard also supports one 256-color mode. The 256 colors come from a palette of 256K colors. Each pixel in the image consists of one byte (8 bits). This byte is a pointer to one of the 256 colors in the palette. If you are curious as to how this palette scheme works, check out the following sidebar ("Video Palettes").

Even though the 256-color VGA mode has a low 320 x 200 resolution, the relatively large number of colors makes it usable for displaying some real-world images. Many DOS edutainment products use this mode, or a derivative of it.

To display more realistic images, even more colors (and higher resolution) are necessary. As PCs evolved and memory became cheaper, it became practical to include large amounts of memory on graphics cards. This paved the way for more colorful video modes, eventually reaching 24-bit true color.

A true color image uses 24 bits to represent each and every pixel. By allocating 8 bits to each of the red, green, and blue components, true color cards can display 16.7 million colors simultaneously ($256 \times 256 \times 256 = 16,777,216$)!

This is truly a huge number of colors; the human eye can't distinguish that many. Images stored in 24-bit true color can appear to match the colors of the original photograph perfectly. Except for a few specialized applications that use additional pixels for other purposes, 24 bits is the ultimate.

Video Palettes

The palette itself consists of 256 colors, each containing a red, green, and blue component. All the colors on the screen are created by combining these red, green, and blue components. Although it may sound strange, this is also how your TV set creates colors.

Due to IBM's original design, the VGA palette uses 6 bits to represent each of the red, green, and blue components. These 6 bits permit 2^6 (2 to the sixth power), or 64 different intensities for each component. When you combine 64 reds, 64 greens, and 64 blues, you get $64 \times 64 \times 64 = 262,144$, or 256K possible colors.

Creating images with palettes has some distinct advantages. The biggest one is size. To represent a 256-color image you need 1 byte for each pixel, plus the space required for the palette (this turns out to be 768 bytes). A 256-color image with a resolution of 320 x 200, therefore, would require 64,000 bytes plus the space for the palette. If you didn't use a palette, you would need to store the red, green, and blue components for every pixel. Because PCs store information in 8-bit chunks, each component of each pixel would require 8 bits. Each pixel would require 24 bits, and the same 320 x 200 image would require 192,000 bytes. Of course, it would save the 768 bytes required for the palette, but the palette method still ends up much smaller.

Another advantage of palettes is that it is easy to change the colors that are displayed. Say you want to fade an image to black. If your image has a palette, you only have to dim the colors in the palette in order to dim the entire image. If you are directly storing the colors of each pixel, you must modify every pixel individually. My screen saver, Desert Frog Screen Scenes, takes advantage of this attribute of the palette to create some truly wild scenes.

Virtually all the new graphics cards have at least one true color mode. Make sure that your card does; sooner or later true color will appear in edutainment products.

Refresh Rate

The *refresh rate* is the rate at which a graphics card (or monitor) can redraw (refresh) an image. You also may see the refresh rate referred to as the *vertical scan rate*.

The image you see on your monitor is actually refreshed many times a second. Most graphics card and monitor combinations support a refresh rate of at least 70 Hz, or 70 times a second. This is the minimum you want for an acceptable display. Higher rates produce steadier displays with less flickering.

When considering refresh rates, you must also consider interlacing. An *interlaced* display is one that draws only half the lines each pass. By drawing the odd-numbered lines one pass and the even-numbered lines the next, interlaced displays refresh the complete image in two passes. An interlaced display with a 70 Hz refresh rate actually draws all the information on the screen only 35 times each second.

Because interlaced displays require two passes to draw all the information on the screen, they inherently have more flickering than non-interlaced displays. The graphics card you choose should support at least a resolution of 800 x 600, 256 colors, at a non-interlaced 70 Hz refresh rate. Ideally, you would like a refresh rate greater than 70 Hz (non-interlaced), with a resolution of 1024 x 768, and 256 colors.

It is important to check refresh rates carefully. A card that provides 72 Hz non-interlaced with a 640 x 480, 16-color display does not necessarily work as well with a 1024 x 768, 256-color display. In other words, just getting all the right numbers on the same card is not enough, you have to have all the right numbers simultaneously.

VESA Standards

When you get beyond the VGA video modes, no standards are universally accepted. The Video Electronics Standards Association (VESA) was formed to address this problem. VESA is a consortium of many of the top graphics card and monitor manufacturers who are working together to create standards for many video-related areas.

One of the standards created by VESA defines a set of video modes that VESA-compatible cards can support. Cards can be made VESA-compatible either through the design of the card itself or through the use of a TSR. In either case, VESA-compatibility is the closest thing there is to a standard in the SVGA world. If possible, make sure that your card is VESA-compatible.

Monitors

A quality monitor is very important to your enjoyment of edutainment products. Low-quality monitors may give you headaches (figuratively, and sometimes literally), so spending a little extra on a quality monitor is well worth the expense.

You should look for several things in a monitor. One of the most important elements is the dot pitch of the display. The smaller the dot pitch, the sharper the lines and characters on the screen. You want a dot pitch no larger than .28 mm (millimeters).

Another important feature of a monitor is the size of the display. A display that is too small leaves you squinting with your nose pressed up against it. For general edutainment work, you want a 15-inch or larger display. If you plan to do a great deal of work in the 1024 x 768 or 1280 x 1024 Windows modes, go for a 17-inch model.

> **Note:** The sizes quoted for monitors are diagonal measurements. Television screen sizes are measured the same way.

Whatever size or dot pitch monitor you buy, it won't do you any good if it can't support the resolution, number of colors, and refresh rate of your graphics card. Make sure that your monitor matches or exceeds the specs of your video card.

It's also a plus to have some way to reduce glare on your monitor. One thing that helps is a flat screen. These can reduce glare and are generally easier to look at than traditional curved screens. Other ways to reduce glare include coated or etched screens and separate glare filters. You can also reduce glare by adjusting the placement of your monitor and the lighting in your work area.

If you are willing to spend more money, you can get a monitor with controls that reduce distortion and other problems.

Finally, the quality of the picture is the most important factor in choosing a monitor. With the selection of monitors changing continually, a good strategy would be to start with reviews in the popular computer magazines. After you have narrowed down the choices, try to see the monitors in action, preferably displaying some of your edutainment software. Choose the one that looks best to you. After all, you are the one who will be using it.

Sound Cards

As you learned in Chapter 2, the sound-producing capability of a basic PC is very limited. Even with clever programming techniques, the quality of the sound is poor. As sound effects and music become a more important part of the edutainment experience, the deficiencies of the PC's built-in sound system become more obvious. The solution to PC sound problems is the addition of a sound card and speakers. A typical sound card provides amplified stereo output of digitally recorded or synthetically generated sound.

Although the sounds produced by a sound card may not be at the same quality level as an audio compact disc (CD), they beat the heck out of the buzzes and clicks an unaided PC can produce. The best sound cards actually *do* approach the quality of a CD, and any decent card gives you sound quality that is fine for edutainment work.

Features of Sound Cards

A large number of sound cards is currently available. Each one has features that differentiate it from others on the market. To choose the correct card for your edutainment system, you have to understand these features and what they mean to you. The next several sections describe the various sound card features. As you read about them, think about which features are important to you. I give my recommendations at the end of each section.

Sampling Rate

The *sampling rate* of a sound card is the number of times per second the card records or outputs the level of a sound. To accurately reproduce sounds across the full range of human hearing, a sound card must be capable of producing about 40,000 samples per second! A card that can sample 40,000 times per second is said to have a sampling rate of 40 kHz (kilohertz). This rate is similar to that for audio CDs, which sample at 44,100 samples per second. See the following sidebar ("Sampling Rate and Sound Reproduction") for more information.

Sound cards actually have two different sampling rates. One is the rate at which it can *play back* a sound sample; the other is the rate at which it can *record* a sound sample. They may or may not be the same.

Inexpensive sound cards typically provide a sampling rate that is better than that required for speech recognition (greater than 6 kHz) but that doesn't allow for accurate reproduction of the full range of human hearing.

For edutainment use, the playback sampling rate is the important number. You should choose a card that provides at least a 40 kHz playback sampling rate.

8-bit versus 16-bit Resolution

The first generally available PC sound cards provided 8 bits of resolution for each sample. Although this was a great improvement over the PC speaker (normally one bit of resolution!), it still left room for improvement. Although I don't understand all the math, each bit of resolution provides 6 dB (decibels) of *dynamic range*. Dynamic range is a measure of the difference between the loudest and softest sounds the card can generate.

The dynamic range of an 8-bit sound card is 48 dB (8×6 dB = 48 dB). A dynamic range of 48 dB is roughly comparable to that of an average cassette tape player.

As the technology advanced, 16-bit sound cards became available. Along with a slew of other advantages, 16-bit cards provide a dynamic range of 96 dB (16×6 dB = 96 dB). Ninety-six dB is equivalent to the dynamic range of an audio compact disc. If you have ever listened to a good audio CD, you understand the magnitude of the difference in sound quality.

Cards with 16-bit playback are the standard today. Some also record sound with a 16-bit resolution, while others use only 8 bits. The one you choose depends on your recording needs. If you don't intend to ever record any sounds, or you will be recording only voice, a card with 8-bit recording capability is fine. Using 8-bit resolution for recording also saves you disk space because 8-bit sound files are half the size of the equivalent 16-bit files.

If you plan to record music, or otherwise need the higher quality, go for the 16-bit recording capability.

Sampling Rate and Sound Reproduction

To accurately reproduce a sound, a digital recording device must sample twice as fast as the highest frequency to be recorded. This rule was determined by an engineer named Harry Nyquist. The highest frequency that can be reproduced for a given sampling rate is the Nyquist frequency. Similarly, the interval between the samples is known as the Nyquist interval.

Because a recorder must sample at twice the highest frequency, and human hearing ranges up to about 20 kHz, a recording system that can reproduce the full range of human hearing must be able to sample at 40 kHz. That is 40,000 samples per second of recorded sound!

For various technical reasons, audio compact discs actually sample at a higher rate than is necessary.

Systems that do not reproduce sounds across the full range of human hearing can still be useful. The telephone, for example, only reproduces from around 300 Hz (hertz) to 3 kHz. Because this is in the range of human speech, it is enough to allow you to talk on the phone. Recording this range of frequencies only requires about 6,000 samples per second, rather than the 40,000 required for the full hearing range.

MIDI

The Musical Instrument Digital Interface (MIDI) is a standard that enables electronic instruments to communicate with each other. MIDI is the standard non-waveform file format for Windows. (For an explanation of waveform and non-waveform file formats, see the sidebar "Sound File Formats".)

MIDI files contain detailed information on every action performed on a MIDI instrument. Keyboards are common MIDI instruments. A MIDI file of a keyboard performance contains information on which keys were pressed, how hard they were pressed, and how long they were held down. By recording this information, instead of the resulting waveform, MIDI files can be vastly smaller than the equivalent waveform file.

Because MIDI files contain instructions, instead of waveforms, the sound card must know what instructions correspond to which instruments. Typically, a MIDI file contains up to 16 sets of instructions, with each set controlling a different instrument. These sets of commands are called *channels*. It is up to the sound card to know which instrument each channel is supposed to be.

Sound File Formats

There are two categories of sound file formats and multiple formats in each category. The categories differ in the way they represent sounds—waveform formats record the amplitude of the sound thousands of times a second; non-waveform files contain instructions for generating the sounds.

The Windows .WAV file format is an example of a waveform file format. The file consists of some header information followed by thousands (or even millions) of sound samples. Each sample consists of the amplitude of the recorded sound at a particular instant in time. By recording thousands of samples a second, an accurate representation of the original sound can be stored. Because so many samples must be stored for each second of sound, waveform files quickly grow immense, often occupying several megabytes. On the other hand, a waveform file can represent any arbitrary sound, making waveform files ideal for unusual sound effects and speech.

A common example of a non-waveform file is a MIDI (.MID) file. Non-waveform files do not contain an exact representation of a sound. Instead, they contain instructions that a sound card or synthesizer can use to generate a new sound that resembles the old sound. A MIDI file contains instructions on which musical notes to play, how long to play them, and which instruments to use. Because non-waveform files contain only instructions for creating the sounds rather than an exact representation of the sound, they tend to be much smaller than waveform files. And because they rely on your sound card to recreate the sounds, they are very dependent on the quality and capabilities of the sound card. Because the sound card must know how to generate the sounds specified in a MIDI file, the range of sounds that can be stored this way is limited.

The parameters that generate the sound of a particular instrument are known as *patches*. A program number identifies each patch. Unfortunately, within the basic MIDI standard the relationship between program numbers and patches is not standardized. One sound card may assign program number 10 to a glockenspiel, while on another card that same number may refer to a harmonica! This chaotic situation inspired the creation of the General MIDI standard.

General MIDI

The General MIDI standard assigns specific program numbers to specific patches. Each of 128 program numbers is assigned to a specific sound. If a sound card complies with the General MIDI standard, it always equates program number 0 to an acoustic grand piano, the number 1 to a bright acoustic piano, and so on for the other 126 patches. Windows supports the General MIDI standard, so MPC-compatible sound cards support it as well.

The General MIDI standard eliminates the problem of incompatible program numbers. Cards that support the standard know that program number 72 is a piccolo, so they should use their piccolo patch to generate the sound. Table 10.1 lists just a fraction of the program numbers and their corresponding sounds as defined by General MIDI.

As you can see from this partial listing, the 128 different sounds provide a tremendous variety of instruments and sound effects. General MIDI meets the needs of the vast majority of applications.

The General MIDI standard ensures that a sound card knows what sounds correspond to which program numbers. But how does the card generate the sounds?

Table 10.1. A sampling of the instrument sounds covered by the General MIDI standard.

Program Number	Sound
0	Acoustic grand piano
1	Bright acoustic piano
2	Electric grand piano
3	Honky-tonk piano
4	Rhodes piano
...	
40	Violin
41	Viola
42	Cello
43	Contrabass
44	Tremolo strings
...	
80	Synthesizer lead 1 (square)
81	Synthesizer lead 2 (sawtooth)
...	
96	Sound FX 1 (rain)
...	
127	Gunshot

You can get MIDI playback from your system in a couple of ways. One way is to pass the MIDI commands right through the card, to a MIDI interface port. The interface port enables you to connect an electronic instrument, typically a keyboard, to your PC. The keyboard then generates the sound. Many cards include a MIDI connector, but having a keyboard hanging off your PC can be awkward. Most PC users let their sound card generate the sounds.

Sound cards generate MIDI sounds with a built-in synthesizer. A synthesizer creates a replica of the characteristic waveform of the instrument to be played. The method used to synthesize the waveforms determines the quality of the final sound.

Wave-Table versus FM Synthesis

There are two popular ways to synthesize the sounds required by MIDI. The most common (and least expensive) method is *FM synthesis*. This method generates sounds by changing (modulating) the frequencies of sound waves to emulate the sounds of instruments. FM synthesis does not provide high-quality instrument sounds.

The higher-quality (and more expensive) method of generating instrument sounds is through *wave-table synthesis*. Wave-table synthesis uses digitized samples of actual instruments to generate sounds. By varying the frequency of playback of the samples, the card can generate the different notes. The sound information then passes through various filters and amplifiers that complete the shaping of the waveform.

As more instrument samples are added to a card, the amount of memory required to store them increases, thereby driving up the cost of the card. Some cards offer a compromise: they use FM synthesis for some instruments and wave-table synthesis for others. This helps keep down the cost, while providing wave-table synthesis for those instruments that most need it. See the following sidebar ("Chipsets for Sound") if you are interested in the hardware that actually does the synthesis on the cards.

If you can afford it, buy a card that provides wave-table synthesis. Some cards come without it but provide a way to add it later. These cards could make a good second choice.

Compatibility

Compatibility with popular software is important. It doesn't matter how sophisticated, powerful, or affordable a card is if it won't work with your software. You should look for two types of compatibility.

Chipsets for Sound

Whether a sound card uses FM synthesis, wave-table synthesis, or a combination of the two, the actual work is done by one of a few different synthesizer chips. The chipset used determines the type of synthesis, as well as the number of voices that can play simultaneously.

The most commonly used sound chips are the Yamaha OPL series. The OPL2 and OPL3 are used in the two best-selling sound card families: Sound Blaster and Media Vision Pro Audio Spectrum. The OPL2 and OPL3 chipsets use FM synthesis to produce sounds. The OPL2 can produce 11 voices simultaneously, while the OPL3 can produce 20. The OPL3 also uses 4-operator synthesis, while the OPL2 uses only 2. The higher the number of operators used, the more realistic the sound can be.

The OPL3 is the most common chipset, but for technical and compatibility reasons, most of the available software still targets the OPL2.

The latest addition to this chipset family is the OPL4. This chipset combines FM and wave-table synthesis in one package. With a total of 20 FM and 24 wave-table voices, the OPL4 provides backward-compatibility with the OPL2 and OPL3, while still delivering the higher-quality output of wave-table synthesis.

Another popular sound chipset is Sierra Semiconductor's Aria. The Aria chipset provides 32 wave-table voices, as well as OPL2-compatible FM synthesis. This chipset also contains a Digital Signal Processor (DSP) produced by Texas Instruments. A DSP allows software to add such effects as reverberation and echoes to the basic audio capabilities.

Several manufacturers use the Aria chipset, although none of them have a market share near that of the Sound Blasters and Pro Audio Spectrums.

Some card manufacturers, such as Turtle Beach, use custom chipsets. Turtle Beach manufactures cards like the Monterey, which provide wave-table synthesis and DSPs. This card can contain up to 4M of RAM, which can be loaded with custom sounds needed by specific software. Specially written software is necessary to take advantage of this feature.

Turtle Beach cards provide premium sound at a premium price.

First, you should look for Sound Blaster compatibility. The Sound Blaster is the 8-bit sound standard. Virtually every DOS edutainment product supports Sound Blaster, and most of the cards on the market do, too.

The other thing to look for is MPC compatibility. The Multimedia PC (MPC) standard defines the capabilities of a multimedia computer. Cards that are MPC-compatible work with any

MPC-compatible Windows edutainment product. Virtually all the new products are MPC-compatible.

The MPC-2 standard is now gaining strength. MPC-2 is a tougher standard, with bigger, better, and faster equipment required to meet it. Sound boards that meet the MPC-2 standard must have 16-bit resolution at a 44.1 kHz sampling rate. Chapter 11, "CD-ROM Drives," contains detailed information on the MPC and MPC-2 standards.

Sound Blaster support is the industry standard for DOS edutainment programs; MPC-compatibility is the standard in Windows. Your best bet is to purchase a card that supports both standards. Such a card supports virtually every edutainment program on the market.

In most cases, your best choice is a card that is both Sound Blaster- and MPC-2-compatible. Such a card should meet your needs for the foreseeable future.

CD-ROM Interfaces

The sound card often provides the PC's CD-ROM interface. This arrangement saves space within your system, but requires the two devices to work together correctly. Some cards come with proprietary interfaces, while others employ a standard one. Because CD-ROM is becoming a necessity for edutainment users, it is important to choose an interface that can support your CD-ROM needs today, and can also support it tomorrow when you want to upgrade to a triple- or quad-speed CD-ROM drive.

Until recently, the Creative Labs Sound Blaster cards all came with a proprietary CD-ROM interface. Because Sound Blaster cards have a large share of the total market, the proprietary interface isn't a big problem. CD-ROM drives that support this interface should be around for several years. Just make sure that the drive you want is compatible with the interface.

The emerging standard for CD-ROM interfaces is SCSI-2. SCSI (pronounced *scuzzy*) stands for Small Computer System Interface, and SCSI-2 is the latest version of this standard. For more details, refer to the sidebar ("The SCSI Standard"). A sound card with a SCSI-2 CD-ROM interface gives you access to the largest variety of CD-ROM drives. This can be important if someday you decide to upgrade your CD-ROM drive. Buying a good sound card with a SCSI interface now may save you from replacing it later.

Even Creative Labs is joining the move to SCSI interfaces. Several of the newer Sound Blaster cards have either multiple interfaces or SCSI-2 interfaces. Some CD-ROM drives come with a separate interface card that can be plugged into your machine. Although this eliminates the need to worry about the sound card's interface, adding a separate CD card uses up space in the machine.

Look for a sound card that has a SCSI-2 CD-ROM interface. This gives you access to the widest range of CD-ROM drives—now and in the future. A Sound Blaster card with the proprietary interface is also a good choice if you know that the CD-ROM drive you want is compatible.

The SCSI Standard

The SCSI standard isn't specifically designed for sound cards or CD-ROM drives. It is a general-purpose computer interface standard. Any device that hooks up to your PC can have a SCSI interface. Besides CD-ROM drives, many large hard drives use it, as do many of the less common devices you can connect to a PC (writeable optical drives, scanners, tape back-up systems, and so on).

The SCSI standard enables you to connect up to eight SCSI devices to a single SCSI port. The devices are connected to the port via cables that act like the system bus in your PC. This method saves space inside your machine because the devices don't require their own controller cards plugged into the limited number of slots on the system bus.

SCSI also provides a speedy interface for those devices that can take advantage of it. Current CD-ROM drives are slow, but a SCSI interface can accommodate whatever speed increases are likely to occur.

In time, most peripherals probably will support the SCSI-2 standard.

Speakers and Microphones

Quality speakers are crucial to the performance of your PC sound system. Just as with your home stereo system, no matter how good the rest of the system is, low-quality speakers result in low-quality sound. The key to good performance lies in matching the speakers to the rest of the sound system.

Before looking at anything else about them, be sure that the speakers are self-powered or self-amplified and are designed for PC use. The signal coming from a sound card is low power; it has to be amplified to provide reasonable volume. You probably want at least 5 watts per channel.

Speakers designed for use with PCs are magnetically shielded so that they don't interfere with your monitor or hard disk. This is crucial because one of the most common places to mount speakers is on either side of the monitor.

When you are certain that you are looking at the right kind of speakers, you should focus on the sound quality. The frequency response should match the output range of your sound card. Remember that the sampling rate of a card is about two times the highest frequency. A card with a sampling rate of 22 kHz only reproduces sounds with a frequency of 11 kHz. A card with a sampling rate of 44.1 kHz, on the other hand, covers the highest frequencies (about 20 kHz) that humans can hear. The lowest frequency you need is 20 Hz. More expensive speaker systems may cover this range by including additional speaker cones (*woofers* and *tweeters*). Some even include optional *subwoofers* for really powerful bass.

Look for speakers that have built-in controls. Volume control is mandatory. Tone, or bass and treble controls, enable you to compensate for room acoustics, as well as adjust the sound to your taste. Some speakers enable you to connect multiple sound sources and provide controls that handle mixing and switching them. If you buy a sound card that is MPC- or MPC-2-compatible, (and I strongly suggest it) multiple sound-source capability is not necessary.

The physical size and form of the speakers can be very important. Small speakers reduce the clutter on your desktop. Separate speakers enable you to position them for the best listening. Some separate speakers even come with brackets that make mounting them on either side of your monitor easy. Integrated speaker packages sit beneath the monitor and take up no additional desk space, but they also don't allow individual positioning of the speakers. Ultimately, the choice is up to you.

There is an alternative approach to speakers. If you have a stereo system in your computer room, you can connect your sound card's output to the stereo. If you have a decent stereo, the advantages are obvious.

Using your stereo system, however, has one disadvantage. Some products, mostly games, rely on the position of the speakers. These games manipulate the sound coming from the speakers to provide audible cues to the player. If your stereo speakers are not positioned on either side of the monitor, these cues do not work.

I use a Sony CD boom box for sound output. Although it takes up some space on the desktop, it provides good quality sound and saved the cost of new speakers.

If you plan to record your own sounds, the quality of your microphone may be important. Once again, the key is matching the microphone to the sound card. It doesn't make sense to use a microphone that exceeds the capability of your card to store the information generated by the microphone.

For the few edutainment products that ask you to record sounds, an inexpensive microphone works just fine.

Summary

In trying to help you understand how images get on to your monitor, this chapter offered a great deal of information for you to digest. This chapter presented the kind of information an edutainment user requires.

When you look at the video system on your PC, you should be thinking Super VGA (SVGA). Although you can get by for a while with a VGA (and to a lesser extent EGA or CGA) video system, to really take advantage of the edutainment products coming out in the near future, you will need SVGA video.

Look for a graphics accelerator SVGA card that has been on the market for at least a few months, has at least 1M of RAM, and has at least one true-color (24-bit) video mode. Beyond that, you want VESA support and a non-interlaced refresh rate of 70 Hz or better.

The monitor you choose needs to match the characteristics of your video card. In addition, it should have at least a 15-inch screen, with a .28 or smaller dot pitch. If at all possible, get a look at the monitor and the video card together before you buy.

A sound card is a necessity for all but the most basic edutainment system. All the better edutainment products provide features such as musical soundtracks, voice recordings, and special effects that greatly enhance the product. Many edutainment products—language tutorials and music studies, for example—are useless without a quality way to play sound.

This chapter covered the basics of PC sound and provided lots of useful facts about the subject. The major features of sound cards were discussed, and I gave my opinion on which features were worthwhile and why. You should now be ready to purchase a sound card based on the features and capabilities that you require.

Here is a capsule summary of the sound card buying tips: Choose a card that provides Sound Blaster support, MPC-2 support, and wave-table synthesis. Purchase speakers that match the capabilities of the sound card.

Now turn to Chapter 11 where you learn how to choose a CD-ROM drive that can enhance your edutainment system.

Chapter 11

CD-ROM Drives

A CD-ROM (*compact disc–read-only memory*) drive is quickly becoming a necessary part of a true edutainment system. Many of the most exciting edutainment titles are available only on CD-ROM. Indeed, with the vast amounts of sound, images, and information included in these products, they simply won't fit on a manageable number of floppy disks. Consider just two samples that I pulled from the pile of CD-ROMs on my desk. The first is Arthur's Teacher Trouble, which contains about 68M of information on the CD-ROM. This translates into around 50 3 1/2-inch, high-density floppy disks! Aside from the hassle of installing the program (imagine how long it would take to install 50 floppy disks), can you spare 68M of hard disk space for *one* program?

The next disc I grabbed from the pile was the Software Toolworks Multimedia Encyclopedia. This product takes up about 360M of space on its CD-ROM, which is equivalent to more than 250 high-density floppy disks! This also is two to three times more information than an average hard disk can hold.

If you want your PC to be a fully functional edutainment system, you need to add a CD-ROM drive. Fortunately, doing so has become practical for most people. The price of a good, double-speed drive has finally dropped to an acceptable level. The confusion over standards is pretty much over, and the majority of drives support all the standards that an edutainment user is likely to encounter. Installing a drive is still difficult, but many computer shops and electronics superstores will now do the job for a reasonable fee. When you combine these factors with the number of CD-ROM titles (edutainment or otherwise) that have become available, it's no surprise that sales of CD-ROM drives are skyrocketing.

This chapter provides an introduction to CD-ROMs and to CD-ROM drives. Without delving into the really complex technicalities, you learn a little bit about how data gets on to a compact disc (the basic process is the same for audio CDs and CD-ROMs), how so much information is stored in such a little space, and how the drive gets the information off the disc and into your PC.

CD-ROM is a latecomer to the PC world. A basic machine doesn't know anything about CD-ROM and can't talk to a CD-ROM drive without a great deal of help. When you add a CD-ROM drive, you actually add a CD-ROM system. This system consists of hardware and software, all of which must be set up properly before the PC can get at all that information on those shiny little discs. Learning what all these parts are, and how they work together, is mighty handy if you ever have trouble getting your CD-ROM drive to work.

The remainder of this chapter discusses important features of CD-ROM drives and tells you what to look for when you buy one.

The following topics are covered in this chapter:

- Introduction to CD-ROM
- The elements of a CD-ROM system
- Important features to look for when you buy a CD-ROM drive

Introduction to CD-ROM

OK. You are ready to consider adding a CD-ROM drive to your edutainment system. Before you spend a few hundred dollars on one, you probably want to know a little more about them. The place to start is with CD-ROMs themselves.

A CD-ROM is a close relative to the audio CDs that have replaced LP records over the last few years. Both audio CDs and CD-ROMs are recorded on exactly the same object, a compact disc (CD). The CD itself is a little less than five inches in diameter and has a hole in the middle. The disc is made of polycarbonate, an extremely tough plastic that is also used for such things as motorcycle helmet visors and bulletproof glass.

The data to be stored on the CD is first etched on a metal pattern. More metal patterns are made from the first one, and these are used to stamp a pattern into the surface of the disc. This pattern of indentations (the indented areas are called *pits*, and the flat areas are called *lands*) is laid out in a continuous spiral. All the information stored on the CD is somewhere along that spiral path.

After the data has been pressed into the surface of the disc, a thin layer of aluminum is deposited over the pattern. The aluminum provides a reflective surface that is responsible for the CD's mirror-like finish. Finally, the aluminized surface of the disc is sealed with a protective layer of lacquer, and the disc is ready for labeling.

You can gather a few facts from the methods and materials with which CDs are made. Because the information stored on a CD is in the form of physical indentations coated with aluminum and sealed with lacquer, there is no way you are going to be able to change it. A CD-ROM drive can only read the information, which is where the *read-only memory* (ROM) part of the term CD-ROM comes from.

Another fact is that these things are tough. Although it is possible to scratch or even break a CD, they are much sturdier than floppy disks or magnetic tapes. A CD is an ideal place to permanently store information.

Audio CDs and CD-ROMs are both compact discs, so what is the difference between them? The thing that makes a particular compact disc into a CD-ROM is the way data is stored on it. Audio CDs store their information using one particular specification. This specification tells how the information must be encoded and includes methods for detecting and correcting errors.

CD-ROMs use a different specification. The information is encoded differently than on an audio CD, and error detection and correction are greatly enhanced. Audio CDs contain 44,100 samples of sound for every second you hear. An error in one of those samples is imperceptible. On a CD-ROM, a single error can be disastrous. The error-detection and error-correction methods used on CD-ROMs are so effective that fewer than one in a thousand CD-ROMs contains a single uncorrectable error. That is one byte of bad data in 1,000,000,000,000 (one trillion) bytes!

If you are really curious about how the data is encoded and decoded, and the differences between a floppy or hard disk and audio CD and CD-ROM, you can read the following sidebar ("Comparing Magnetic and Optical Media"). Let me warn you, though, this stuff is heavy going. I have tried to reduce it to laymen's terms as much as possible, but it is inherently complex material.

Comparing Magnetic and Optical Media

The differences between magnetic media (floppy or hard disks) and optical media (CDs and CD-ROMs) are profound. The first difference is that you can change information stored on magnetic media. Optical media are read-only. CD-ROMs that allow you to change the data (rewritable CD-ROMs) are becoming available, but they are not anything an edutainment user is likely to use in the near future.

Optical media also are much slower than magnetic media. This is due to an inherent difference in the way that they store information.

Magnetic disks are divided into concentric tracks. Each track is divided into an equal number of sectors, regardless of where it is located on the disk. Sectors on the outer edge of the disk are physically longer than those near the center.

If this doesn't make sense to you, envision a pie cut into four slices. The slices are wider near the outside then they are near the center. Each slice also occupies a certain portion of the whole circle of the pie. In a pie with four slices, each piece ideally covers 90 degrees of the 360 degrees in the full circle. No matter how far you are from the center of the slice, a sector would cover 90 degrees.

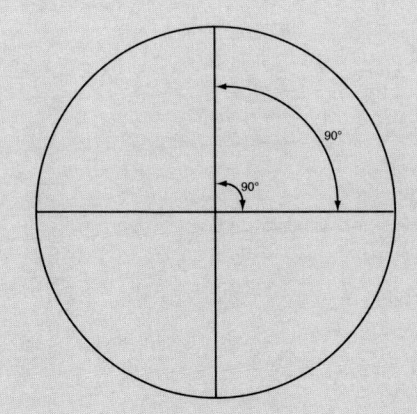

Files stored on such a magnetic disk might be located in any sector of any track on the disk. Files larger than one sector (virtually all of them) are stored in pieces, with each piece placed in an available sector. These sectors do not have to be adjacent to one other. A special file, called the File Allocation Table (FAT), keeps track of where all the pieces of every file are stored.

The amount of information a device stores is determined by the size of the storage area and the density of the information. Because the sectors of magnetic media are physically longer near the edges than they are near the center, and because each sector contains the same amount of information, the information in the outer sectors takes up more space than that in the inner ones. The information density of the disk decreases as you get closer to the edges.

Magnetic media spin at a constant speed at all times. Because of this fact, the information on the disk travels past a point (such as the disk drive read head) at a constant angular velocity (CAV). When the constant angular velocity of the drive is combined with the way the sectors are laid out, the data moves past the read head at the same speed all the time.

The task of reading information from the disk is improved because no time is lost waiting for the drive to adjust the speed of the disk.

Optical media, on the other hand, consist of one continuous spiral track. This track, which wraps around the disc like the groove on an LP record, is divided into sectors of equal size and information density. With all the information on the disc stored at maximum density, the disc can hold far more information. The trade-off for this density is speed and complexity.

Because the data is stored at a constant density, it must move past the read head at a constant linear velocity (CLV). This means that the optical disc must spin at various speeds, depending on where the information is located on the track. Furthermore, as the data is read off the track, the speed of the disc must continually change.

Optical drives require a highly accurate, precisely controlled turntable motor to maintain a constant linear velocity. This increases the complexity of the drive.

Information about the location of information on the disc is contained in the Path and Directory tables, two special areas near the beginning of the track.

After the drive looks up the location of the information in these two tables, it moves the read head to the approximate location of the information. It then locates the track and starts reading along it. While the head is moving to the correct position, the turntable motor adjusts its speed to ensure that the data passes the head at the correct velocity. When the head can read the data, it searches out the desired information and begins reading. During the read, the turntable motor varies its speed to maintain a CLV.

The search for information is slowed because the speed of the disc must physically change. The complexity of a CLV system reduces the speed at which the motor can spin, which in turn reduces the transfer rate.

Finding and reading the appropriate data is only half the battle. The other part of the job is decoding the information and converting it into a form that the PC can use.

Believe it or not, the way information is encoded on optical media is much more complicated than what you have just read. Terms such as PCM (Pulse Code Modulation), CIRC (Cross-Interleaved Reed-Solomon Code), and Layered EDC/ECC (Layered Error-Detecting Code/Error-Correcting Code) abound. Really! I'm not making this up! These techniques use such things as interleaved parity bits, polynomials, and complex Galois fields (!) to encode the information.

If you are really interested in the gory details, you should find yourself a copy of the Red, Yellow, and Green books, as well as ISO 9660. Good luck.

Here is what I really want you to take from this section: A CD-ROM is a relative of the audio compact disc. It uses special coding and error-correction schemes to store 680M of information on a single disc. This information is virtually certain to be *exactly* identical to the information the manufacturer attempted to put on the disc. This would be equivalent to more than 470 high-density, 3 1/2-inch floppy disks, all without a single error. The following sidebar ("The Numbers Behind That 680M") contains some of the amazing numbers involved in storing that much information, with that much accuracy, all in one place.

What Is a CD-ROM System?

A CD-ROM system consists of the CD-ROM drive, some sort of interface between the drive and the PC, and the software required to let the two work together. The same kinds of components are required for any peripheral device that you add to your PC. Even devices such as your disk drives and keyboard have interfaces and software that enable the operating system (DOS) to control them. The difference between these common devices and a CD-ROM is that the interfaces these common devices require are already included in every PC, and DOS includes the software to control them. With a CD-ROM drive, however, you (or whoever installs the drive) must install the hardware and software before the drive will work.

The next few sections look at each component of a CD-ROM system in more detail.

The Drive

To read the information on a CD-ROM, you must have a CD-ROM drive. These drives are more capable descendants of audio CD players. They have all the capabilities of audio CD players, as well as the capabilities required to be a practical computer data-storage medium. Most CD-ROM drives, when teamed with the appropriate software, can be used as audio CD players; the audio quality, however, is normally not nearly as good.

The drive itself consists of several major components. The optical head is responsible for actually reading the information on the disc. It contains a laser, a focusing system, and a set of light sensors. The laser shines on the disc, where the reflection varies with the pattern of pits and lands impressed into the disc. The light sensors receive these reflections and convert them into a signal containing a copy of the information recorded on the disc.

Accuracy is vital throughout the process of reading the data on a CD-ROM. The optical head focuses the laser light on the surface of the disc in such a way that small scratches and marks on the disc can be ignored. In addition to reading the information off the disc, the light sensors constantly monitor the focus and position of the beam. If the beam is out of focus or out of position, logic in the optical head corrects these problems.

The turntable motor spins the disc at precisely the right speed to enable data to be read. Because of the way drives are designed, the speed of the turntable motor varies. The disc speed at any given time depends on the part of the disc being read. This requires a precision motor that can quickly and accurately change speeds. It also requires precise commands to the motor.

The Numbers Behind That 680M

Number of single-spaced pages of text: 300,000

Number of pits (indentations) on a CD-ROM: approximately 2.8 billion

Width of a pit: about one half-micron

Size of one half-micron: about 500 hydrogen atoms laid end-to-end

Number of times the spiral track of indentations goes around the disc: 20,000

Number of tracks per inch: 16,000

Acceptable error rate: 1×10^{-12}, or one in one trillion

The speed of the turntable motor and everything else that goes on in the drive is controlled by a built-in microprocessor. This processor accepts requests for information from your computer and coordinates the actions of the components inside the drive to retrieve that information. The processor determines where the information is on the CD-ROM and then positions the optical head in the correct spot. At the same time, the processor adjusts the speed of the turntable motor to ensure that the information rotates past the optical head at the appropriate speed to be read. When the information has been read from the disc, the processor checks it for errors and corrects any that it finds. When the information is correct, the processor organizes it and sends it off to the interface, where it is passed on to the PC. At the same time, the microprocessor monitors the manual eject button and any other user controls on the drive itself.

The Interface

The interface is the means by which a CD-ROM drive connects electrically to a PC. The drive can physically connect to the system in two different ways. The most popular method is to connect the drive to the sound card. Although this method may seem odd, it actually does make sense. A sound card is another device that frequently is added to a basic PC, often taking up the last expansion slot inside the machine. Connecting the CD-ROM drive to the sound card prevents you from having to add another new card (the CD-ROM interface card) to the system.

The other method of physically connecting the drive to the system is through a separate interface card. Most CD-ROM drives come with an interface card that you can use. It is also possible to connect the drive to an interface card already in the PC, if the drive and the card use the same interface standards.

The number-one interface standard for CD-ROMs is the Small Computer System Interface. This standard, abbreviated SCSI and pronounced *scuzzy*, governs the way many types of peripheral devices communicate with a PC. If a drive uses the SCSI interface, it contains the necessary electronics to communicate with SCSI interface circuitry, which can be on a separate card (often called a SCSI controller) or the sound card.

Some drives use a proprietary interface. These interfaces are designed to work with hardware from a particular vendor. One big advantage to this approach is that you know that the drive and controller will work together properly. Another advantage is price. Drives that use a proprietary interface are usually less expensive than those that use a SCSI interface.

CD-ROM Device Driver

A device driver is a program that tells DOS how to control a peripheral device, such as a CD-ROM drive. Every piece of hardware attached to your computer requires a device driver. DOS has built-in device drivers for some devices, such as floppy disk drives and monitors. Other devices (CD-ROM drives, for example) require a separate device driver. This driver must be loaded from the hard drive whenever you start your machine, or the device will not work.

If you installed a mouse in your machine, you already have dealt with device drivers. Because there are many brands of mice, each with its own characteristics, DOS needs some information about your particular mouse. This information is normally found in a device driver with a name like MOUSE.SYS. Part of the mouse-installation process is adding this device driver to your system. The normal place for device drivers is in CONFIG.SYS, a file found in the root directory of the hard disk. DOS reads and executes the commands in this file every time you start up your computer.

At some point in the installation process, either you or the installation program added a line to your CONFIG.SYS. This line identifies the program MOUSE.SYS as a device driver and loads it into memory where DOS can get to it as needed.

Installing a CD-ROM device driver is just like installing a mouse device driver. Each CD-ROM drive comes with its own device driver that you add to your CONFIG.SYS file. If this file is not added, the CD-ROM drive will not work.

Microsoft CD-ROM Extensions

A device driver is not the only piece of software a PC needs before it can work with a CD-ROM drive. Certain characteristics of CD-ROMs require the capabilities of DOS itself to be extended.

Microsoft created a program named MSCDEX.EXE to enable DOS to access the data on a CD-ROM. This program is necessary because the data on a CD-ROM is not encoded in the format that DOS is used to. It is also necessary because a CD-ROM contains much more information than DOS was designed to handle.

You add MSCDEX.EXE to your AUTOEXEC.BAT file. AUTOEXEC.BAT is another file that the PC executes every time you start it. Both MSCDEX.EXE and the CD-ROM device driver must be run before DOS can successfully talk to your CD-ROM drive.

Types of CD-ROM Drives

CD-ROM drives are available from a variety of manufacturers. When CD-ROM drives first became available, no widely accepted standards existed for the discs or the drives. In a situation somewhat like that of VHS and Beta VCRs, certain discs only worked with certain players, and vice versa. Over the last few years, the industry has settled on a set of standards to which drives must adhere. Any CD-ROM drive you can find today will work just fine—at least with basic CD-ROMs (those without CD audio, PhotoCD, or other enhancements).

Even though all drives can now read basic CD-ROMs, each manufacturer equips its drives with slightly different features and capabilities. Earlier in this chapter, you learned that the interface between the drive and the PC can vary in several important ways. Other features that vary from drive to drive include the speed of the drive, the standards it complies with, the way the disc is loaded, and other physical characteristics.

With all the different features and capabilities available, shopping for a drive can get very confusing. The rest of this chapter is dedicated to giving you the information you need to shop knowledgeably for a CD-ROM drive.

Features to Look For

The next several sections cover the major features and capabilities of CD-ROM drives. The sections are arranged in order of importance, with speed—the most important feature—listed first. Where appropriate, I give my recommendations for the features or capabilities that are important in an edutainment system.

Speed

The speed of a CD-ROM drive is the most important feature to look for. Drives are commonly referred to by their speed, using the terms single-speed, double-speed, triple-speed, and quadruple-speed. These terms refer to the *sustained data transfer rate* of the drive, which measures how fast it can move information from the CD-ROM to the computer over a period of time. The rate is a function of the speed at which the drive spins the disc. The original drives ran at the same speed as audio CD players and could transfer data at a sustained rate of 150K per second (kilobytes per second). Although this rate is fine for audio CDs, it has proved inadequate for CD-ROM applications.

Double-speed drives spin the disc at twice the speed of the original drives, giving them a sustained data transfer rate of 300K per second. Triple- and quadruple-speed drives transfer data at three and four times, respectively, the rate of the original CD-ROM drives.

The sustained data transfer rate is particularly important for products that display video clips. A video clip requires large amounts of information—each frame of the video—to be moved to the PC rapidly (up to 30 frames per second). Drives with a low sustained transfer rate cannot supply the information fast enough, and the application compensates by skipping frames when necessary. This results in jerky videos. Because an increasing number of edutainment products include video clips, a drive with a high sustained data transfer rate is important.

Double-speed drives are the most popular right now, with single-speed drives being too slow, and triple- and quadruple-speed models too expensive for most users.

The other important speed measure is the average access time of a drive. This is a measure of the length of time it takes, on average, for the drive to find and retrieve a piece of data from the disc. Average access times of 200 to 400 milliseconds (ms) are typical, with the fastest drives closest to 200.

Average access time is most important when the drive must find random bits of information scattered here and there across the disc. Video clips and images can normally be read straight through from start to finish just by reading along the track. Looking up bits of information in a multimedia reference work, however, requires the optical head of the drive to jump from place to place as the user follows references and looks up new material.

Look for a drive with an average access time close to 200 ms, particularly if you plan to use a lot of multimedia reference works.

The apparent speed of a drive is affected by the size of the buffer in it. A buffer is an area of memory reserved for holding data recently read from the CD-ROM. When a request for information is made to the drive, it first checks the buffer to see if the information is there. Reading the buffer is immensely faster than reading the disc, so the more frequently the drive can take the data from the buffer, the faster the drive appears to be to the user.

Drives come with buffers ranging in size from 64K up to 256K. Although a bigger buffer is helpful, I'm not sure how much of a performance improvement you will see from one. When you consider that a double-speed drive can transfer 300K of data a second, even a 256K buffer isn't very big.

A disk cache does the same thing for disk drives that the buffer does for the CD-ROM drive. A disk-caching program sets aside a section of your PC's main memory to hold recently read data. The program intercepts disk-access requests and looks for the information in the cache. If the information is in the cache, it isn't necessary to access a disk drive.

Most of the newer disk-caching programs can cache data from the CD-ROM drive, as well as from the other disk drives in your system. Even the latest version of the DOS cache program, SMARTDrive, now supports CD-ROM drives. Because a disk cache in main memory is usually much larger than the buffer in a CD-ROM drive (my disk cache is 2M), much of the effect of the drive buffer probably will be swamped by that of the cache.

Remember that the CD-ROM drive is the slowest component in an edutainment system. Anything you can do to speed your access to the drive is advantageous. Few products currently available require a double-speed (or faster) drive, but even products that don't require one can benefit if you have one. And besides, in a year or two most products *will* require a double-speed drive.

Standards

At one point, it looked as if the CD-ROM market would be fragmented into a host of incompatible drives and the discs that played on those drives. It wasn't very long ago that companies like Microsoft, Phillips, Commodore, and Sony were all pushing their own standards. Fortunately for consumers, the industry settled on a common set of standards to which virtually all drives now adhere. There are just a few key words you have to look for to ensure that a drive meets the standards necessary for edutainment (and virtually all other PC) use.

The standards presented here are appropriate at this time, but the CD-ROM world is still evolving. The standards have changed as the demands on drives have increased and as people have discovered new uses for CD-ROM. A drive that meets the current standards should serve you well for the next few years. Beyond that, who knows?

MPC 1 and 2

For edutainment, the most important standards are MPC 1 and 2. The MPC standards are defined by the Multimedia PC Marketing Council. They define the minimum hardware configuration required to successfully run Multimedia PC (MPC) software. These standards are important to you because software developers know what kind of capabilities they will find on an MPC-compatible machine and can design their software to take advantage of these capabilities.

The CD-ROM portion of the original MPC standard required a single-speed CD-ROM drive. This drive had to occupy less than 40 percent of the host computer's microprocessing time while transferring data. The maximum seek time was limited to less than *one second!*

This original standard has proved to be inadequate for the demanding multimedia software that is now available. The Marketing Council went back to the drawing boards and defined a new standard, MPC-2, in 1993.

To comply with the MPC-2 standard, a CD-ROM drive must be at least double-speed. The drive should also use less than 60 percent of the microprocessor's (CPU's) time to transfer this data. The average seek time must be less than 400 ms.

Buy a CD-ROM drive that meets the MPC-2 requirements. Only a few products that require MPC-2 are available right now. It should be a few years before the industry outgrows this standard.

Photo CD

Photo CD (PCD) is a standard developed by Kodak. Not surprisingly, it is a standard for storing scanned photographs on a CD. The original idea was for consumers to have their photographs transferred to CD, and then view them on their television sets. Although this market hasn't been very hot, many PC users have adopted the standard.

PCD support is not a necessity for edutainment users. Even so, virtually all double-speed drives do support the standard, so there is no reason to buy a drive that does not support it.

You should ensure that the drive is multisession-capable. Photographs need not be stored on a Photo CD all at the same time. Each group of photographs that is added together is called a *session*. The first drives that supported the PCD standard could only find photographs stored in the first session on a disc.

Drives that are multisession-capable can find the photographs recorded in any session. Again, most double-speed or better drives are multisession-capable.

CD-ROM XA

CD-ROM XA (the XA stands for *extended architecture*) is a new standard that governs the way audio and video data are combined on a disc. At this time, some disagreement exists about whether full support of the XA standard is, or ever will be, necessary. MPC-2 requires partial support of this standard. It appears that few products, if any (edutainment or otherwise), are coming to market that go beyond this partial support.

With CD-ROM XA, the key again is to buy an MPC-2 drive. If you do, you will get all the XA support you are likely to need for quite some time.

System Interfaces

The primary interface between a CD-ROM drive and your PC is the one that carries control signals and data back and forth. This interface was discussed in some detail earlier in this chapter, during the description of a CD-ROM system. Refer to that section if you need a refresher.

SCSI interfaces are supported by hardware from a wide variety of vendors, so you have a broad choice of drives. A SCSI controller can handle up to eight devices simultaneously, so normally only one controller per PC is required. If you have a scanner or a large hard drive, your system may already contain a SCSI controller card. If so, you should be able to add a SCSI-capable drive to your PC without installing a new controller card.

Early SCSI devices had compatibility problems, which means that two SCSI devices might not be able to talk to each other. Newer devices, however, seem to have fewer problems. The original SCSI standard was recently updated. The new standard, SCSI-2, provides better performance than the original standard and is found on an increasing number of CD-ROM drives. SCSI-2 should also eliminate the compatibility problems of earlier SCSI devices.

Proprietary interfaces lock you into buying hardware from just one vendor (or at best a few vendors). With SCSI devices you can replace one without disturbing the rest of them. With a proprietary interface that connects the CD-ROM drive to the sound card, replacing one device may force you to replace the other.

I have a drive with a proprietary interface. The drive is a Creative Labs Omni CD. I felt comfortable buying it for two reasons. First, the Sound Blaster card that it connects to is a market leader, and Creative Labs is the biggest sound card manufacturer. It seems likely that Creative Labs will be around to support my equipment for a long time. Second, the drive comes with a stand-alone interface card. Even if I decide to buy a sound card that can't talk to my CD-ROM drive, I can always install the interface card and control the drive that way.

I recommend that you get a drive with a SCSI interface and connect it to the sound card. Even Creative Labs is adding SCSI interfaces to its new sound cards.

The other connection between your PC and the CD-ROM drive is the audio output of the drive. This one is easy. The audio output of any drive will plug into the audio input of any sound card. No options, no choices, no problems.

Physical Characteristics

CD-ROM drives come in different shapes and styles. Most fit into a standard half-height floppy disk bay, but some are external models that have their own case and sit on the desktop. Both types of drives give the same performance.

There are two different ways to get discs into and out of the drive. One way is to put the disc in a caddy, and then place the caddy into the drive. The other way is to place the disc on a motorized tray that carries the disc into the drive.

Because CD-ROM drives use a laser to read the information off the disc, they can be affected by dust. The caddy system may be better at keeping dust out of the drive than the tray system. Many drives also have a device that cleans the laser lens each time you insert or remove a disc.

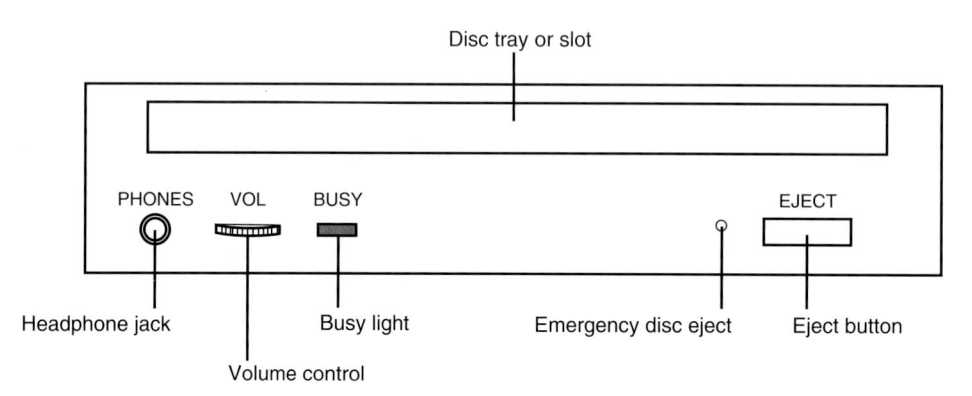

▲ *A typical CD-ROM drive.*

Most drives now come equipped with a headphone jack and volume control. These enable you to use your CD-ROM drive as an audio CD player. To accomplish this, you can use the Media Player application that comes with Windows. You can also do so with one of the myriad shareware and public domain player programs available.

Many CD-ROM drives have an emergency disc-eject mechanism. Drives are mechanical devices and can fail. If the drive fails with a disc in it, this is a valuable feature.

Multimedia Upgrade Kit

If you need to add both a sound card and a CD-ROM drive to your system, a multimedia upgrade kit may be the way to go. These kits combine a sound card and a drive and usually include a pile of software on CD-ROM. These kits can save you some money and eliminate any worry about whether the sound card and the CD-ROM drive will work together.

If you do decide to get a kit, just be sure to check the specifications of each component. Make sure that you don't get stuck with an inferior drive that some manufacturer is trying to clear out.

Summary

One of the best things you can do for your edutainment system is to add a CD-ROM drive. CD-ROM discs are inexpensive to manufacture, durable, and hold huge amounts of data. It is only a matter of time before all the best edutainment software will come out first on CD-ROM and only later, if at all, on floppy disk.

The first part of this chapter introduced you to CD-ROM discs and drives. You learned that adding a CD-ROM drive actually requires adding an entire system of hardware and software to your machine. As with every other peripheral device added to a PC, a CD-ROM drive requires an electrical interface through which commands and data can travel between the host computer and the drive. A CD-ROM drive also requires a device driver that can tell DOS how to control the drive. Unlike other devices, a CD-ROM drive requires a special program that extends the capabilities of DOS, enabling it to deal with the special file formats and immense capacity of a CD-ROM.

The rest of the chapter covered the features and capabilities you should look for when you buy a CD-ROM drive. To summarize this advice, buy a double-speed drive that is MPC-2 compatible. Such a drive should meet the needs of an edutainment user (for the next few years, anyway). I hope that this chapter increased your understanding of, and appreciation for, the hottest PC add-on today: the CD-ROM drive.

In this chapter, and in the preceding one (Chapter 10, "Sight and Sound"), the acronym MPC came up frequently. The MPC standard is intimately connected to Microsoft Windows. Chapter 12 focuses on how Windows and the Multimedia PC can work together to enhance your edutainment experience. You get the full story on the MPC standard, Windows, and why I think they are the keys to a powerful edutainment system.

Chapter 12

Edutainment and Windows

One of the premises of this book is that Windows is the future of edutainment. In this chapter, I show you why I believe this and attempt to convince you that I am correct on this point.

After I have convinced you that Windows is the way to go, you will want to put it to use. The final part of this chapter is a basic introduction to Windows for edutainment product users. It takes you through the steps for such tasks as installing Windows, running an application, and creating a program group for your edutainment products.

The following topics are discussed in this chapter:

- Why you should use Windows instead of DOS
- The MPC specifications, and why they are important
- Starting Windows
- Using Windows
- Running Windows applications
- Creating an Edutainment program group

When you finish this chapter, you will be ready to begin using Windows edutainment products.

Why Windows?

You are likely to select Windows edutainment products over DOS products for a number of reasons. Some of these reasons are discussed in the next several sections.

Ease of Use

Windows is easier to use than DOS because of several factors. The first factor is its graphical nature. For most people, pointing at something and clicking is a lot easier than typing a string of commands. Jennifer (my three-year-old) knows how to turn on our two PCs by herself. On the machine that comes up in Windows, she can double-click the icons that start her edutainment programs and be on her way. On the machine that comes up in DOS, she is stuck until I start the programs for her.

The second factor is consistency. All Windows programs work fundamentally the same. After you learn how a typical Windows application works (see the "Edutainment User's Guide to Windows" section later in this chapter), you should have a pretty good idea about how other Windows applications work.

Device Independence

Device independence means that applications don't have to know what kind of hardware is in your machine. Each hardware device that works with Windows has a software driver that provides a consistent interface to Windows programs. After you install the correct driver, all Windows applications can use your hardware. What happens if you change the hardware? Just change the software driver, and all your Windows applications can use it.

In the DOS world, each program must know how to deal with all the hardware it might encounter. The end result is that you must configure each new DOS program for your hardware. What happens if you change the hardware? You have to reconfigure each program that uses that hardware.

Memory Management

A typical PC sold today might have 4M of memory (RAM) installed. You would assume that your DOS programs would use all that memory to run fast and efficiently. Wrong! DOS only gives programs access to 640K of RAM, no matter how much you have installed. Even worse, your programs must share that 640K of RAM with DOS, device drivers, and TSRs. On a typical PC, only 550K or so of RAM may be available by the time you are ready to run your program. For most DOS programs, any memory beyond the first 640K is wasted.

Windows lets your programs take advantage of all the memory you have in your machine. There is no 640K memory limit for Windows programs. Furthermore, Windows uses a technique called *virtual memory* that effectively gives programs access to more RAM than your machine even has!

A virtual memory scheme uses part of your hard disk as a temporary storage area. My PC has 8M of RAM installed. Some of this memory is, of course, occupied by Windows. Even so, take a look at the `Memory:` line in the following figure.

Edutainment and Windows

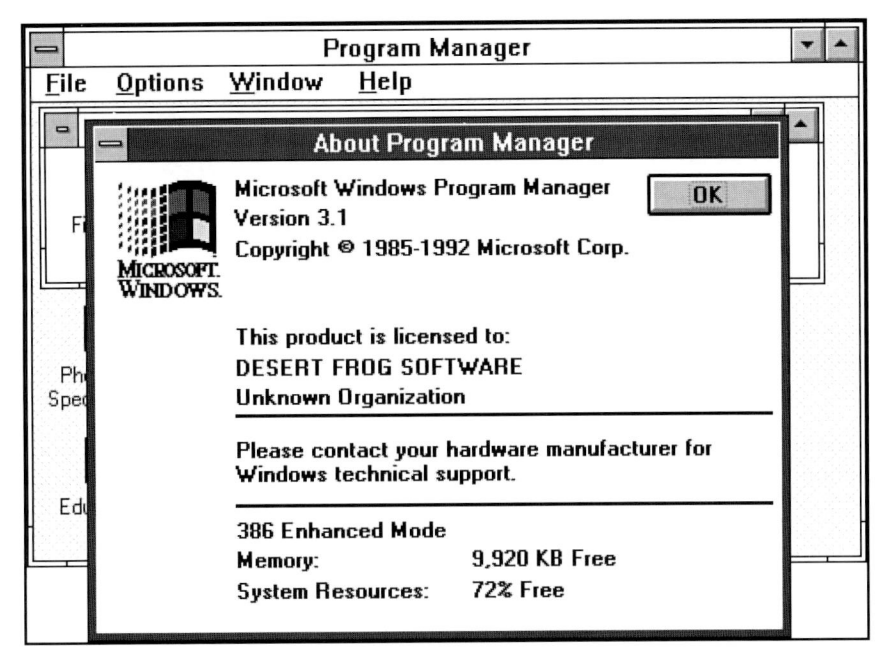

▲ *The "magic" of Windows memory management.*

According to the figure, my PC has 9,920K of RAM free. This is equivalent to almost 9.7M of free memory on a machine with 8M of RAM installed! And don't forget, Windows is using some of that memory, as is my word processor. Virtual memory makes this possible.

By making large amounts of memory available to programs, Windows enables developers to create powerful edutainment applications that would be impractical in DOS.

The MPC Specifications

The Multimedia PC (MPC) specifications were created by the Multimedia PC Marketing Council. The purpose of these specifications is to define a standard multimedia computer. They do not specify a particular computer. Instead, they define a minimum level of hardware and software. Windows is an important part of the MPC specifications.

The specifications let software publishers create MPC products with the confidence that the PC running the software will have the ability to run it effectively. For example, the MPC specifications require a CD-ROM drive, so publishers know that they can release their MPC product on CD-ROM. Being able to support a single standard simplifies the task of creating new products and should result in an increased number of higher-quality products.

There are two MPC specifications. The original one, now known as MPC-1, was created several years ago. This specification has proven inadequate for newer multimedia products, which prompted the Multimedia PC Marketing Council to create a follow-on specification. The sidebar, "Minimum MPC-1 Equipment," provides a summary of the required MPC-1 hardware and software.

The new specification created by the Council is known as MPC-2. Although few products require MPC-2 compatibility right now, any MPC software benefits from the greater power of an MPC-2 system. The sidebar, "Minimum MPC-2 Equipment," summarizes the MPC-2 requirements.

Note: Appendix C contains a full copy of the MPC-1 and MPC-2 specifications as posted in the CDROM forum on CompuServe.

Minimum MPC-1 Equipment

CPU	386SX or compatible microprocessor
RAM	2M
Magnetic storage	High-density, 3 1/2-inch floppy drive; hard drive (30M minimum)
Optical storage	CD-ROM with CD-DA outputs
Audio	DAC, ADC, music synthesizer, on-board analog audio mixing
Video	VGA graphics adapter
Input	101-key keyboard (or functional equivalent), two-button mouse
I/O	Serial port, parallel port, MIDI I/O port, joystick port
System software	Windows 3.0 with multimedia extensions

Minimum MPC-2 Equipment

CPU	25 MHz 486SX or compatible microprocessor
RAM	4M (8M recommended)
Magnetic storage	High-density, 3 1/2-inch floppy drive; hard drive (160M minimum)
Optical storage	Double-speed CD-ROM with CD-DA outputs, XA ready, multisession-capable
Audio	16-bit DAC, 16-bit ADC, music synthesizer, on-board analog audio mixing
Video	Display resolution of at least 640 x 480 with 65,536 (64K) colors
Input	101-key keyboard (or functional equivalent), two-button mouse
I/O	Serial port, parallel port, MIDI I/O port, joystick port
System software	Windows 3.0 with multimedia extensions or Windows 3.1

Popularity of Windows

Windows is an incredibly hot product. Millions of copies ship each year, and virtually every new PC comes with Windows ready to run. People are buying more Windows than DOS applications and have been doing so since sometime in 1993. It makes sense for developers and publishers to concentrate on the market that has the best sales.

With all the major (and many minor) companies concentrating on Windows, the competition is fierce. The competition forces publishers to bring out their best products for Windows first. It also causes them to keep pushing, constantly developing better products. Windows is where you will find the best edutainment products.

Installing Windows

Windows is easy to install. I recommend you perform the Express Setup so that the Setup program does all the work for you. The program checks out your hardware and software and configures Windows to run with them. You only have to insert disks when you are prompted and answer a few questions, such as "What is your name?," "What kind of printer do you have?," and "What port is it connected to?". You might want to grab a magazine, however. Windows comes on seven 3 1/2-inch, high-density disks, and takes about 30 minutes for a full installation. The following steps can help you to get started.

From the DOS prompt, perform these steps:

1. Insert Windows Disk 1 in the floppy drive.
2. Switch to the drive containing the Windows floppy disk. If you have inserted the disk in the A drive, enter **a:**, and you should see the drive light on the floppy disk drive come on. The DOS prompt should then change to something similar to A:>. (If you inserted the Windows disk in the B drive, substitute **b:** in the preceding instruction.)
3. Type **setup** and then press the Enter key to begin the Setup program.
4. Follow the on-screen directions.

Edutainment User's Guide to Windows

So you have decided to give Windows a try. This section assumes that you have never used Windows before, but you have an MPC-compatible PC and have just acquired an MPC edutainment product you want to use. This section tells you everything you need to know to give your new software a try.

Starting Windows

If Windows is properly installed on your system, starting it is a piece of cake. Just type **win** at any DOS prompt, and you are on your way.

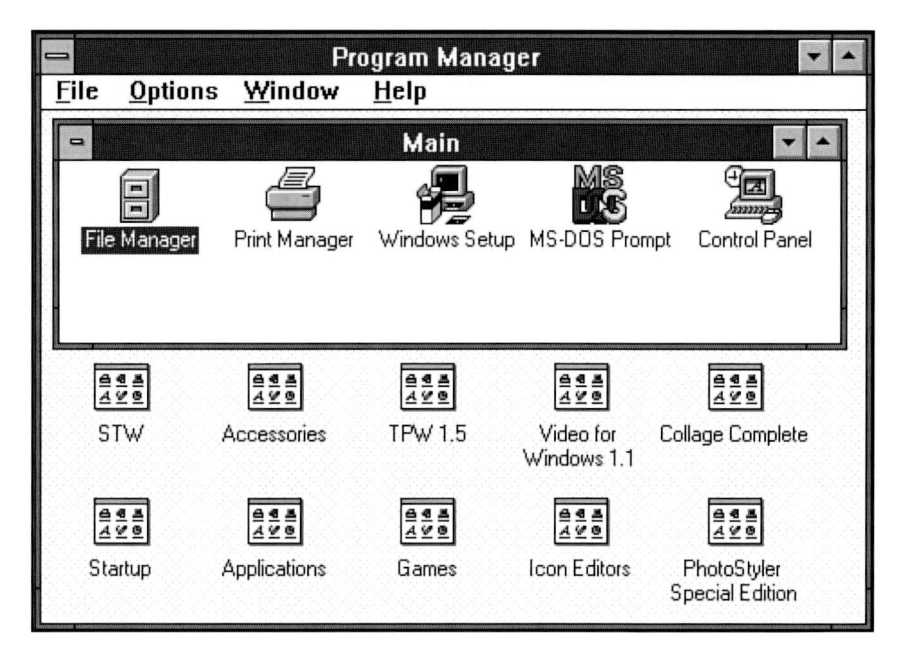

▲ *The Windows screen is often filled with windows and icons (here you can see the Main program group and its icons).*

Using Windows

After Windows is running, you should see a screen similar to the preceding figure. A rectangular box (a *window*) with the title Program Manager is displayed. Inside this box are other boxes (more windows) and little pictures with captions (*icons*). The actual layout you see will be different, but this is the kind of view you see often when you use Windows.

Windows is an aptly named product. Just about everything occurs in those rectangular windows you see in the figure. Even when a program occupies the full screen, it is in a window; you just can't see its borders.

Almost everything you do in Windows involves windows, so the remainder of this section is much easier to understand if you learn the names of the different parts of a window. The following figure shows the parts of a typical window.

[Figure: The parts of a window — labeled diagram of a "Write - (Untitled)" window showing Control menu box, Menu bar, Title bar, Minimize button, Maximize button, Scroll box, Window corner, Window border, Scroll bar, and Scroll arrow.]

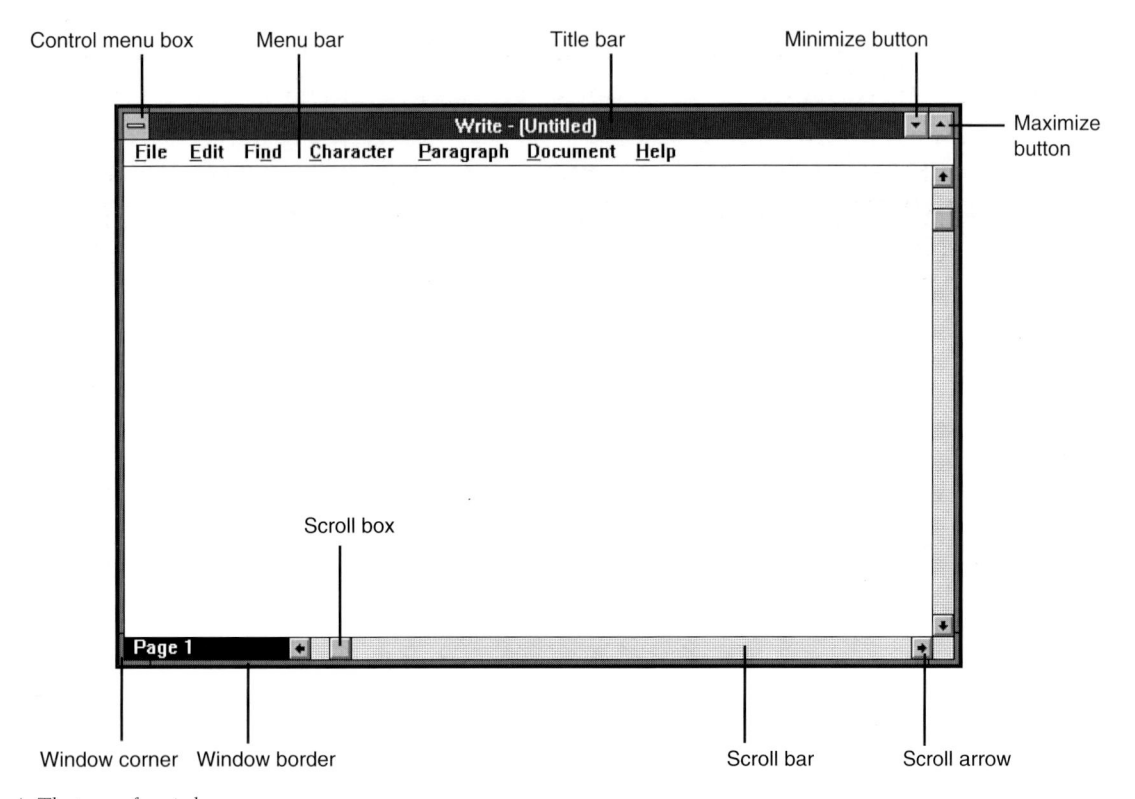

▲ *The parts of a window.*

Here is a short description of each of the parts shown in the figure.

- *Control menu box*—Displays a menu of window control options when you click it.
- *Menu bar*—Displays the names of the menus, which in turn contain the various commands that apply to the application currently open in the window.
- *Title bar*—Displays the name of the application or document contained in the window. If more than one window is open, the title bar for the window in which you are currently working is a different color than the title bars of the other windows in Program Manager.
- *Minimize and Maximize buttons*—Used to change the size of the window.
- *Window borders and Window corners*—Form the boundaries of the window. You can drag them to change the size of the window.
- *Scroll bars*—Used to view portions of a document that are not currently visible in the window. The *scroll arrows* and *scroll boxes* are also part of the scroll bars.

The primary way to control things in Windows is with a mouse. If you don't have a mouse, you can still use Windows; it just is more difficult.

> **Note:** Considering that a mouse is required for a PC to meet the MPC specifications, and considering that most edutainment programs require a mouse, your first edutainment purchase should be a mouse if you don't have one.

Assuming that you do have a mouse, how do you use it? Try moving the mouse around a little while you look at the screen. As you move the mouse, you should see a little arrow move around on the screen. That arrow is the *mouse pointer*. To use the mouse, you move the pointer over the item you want to manipulate and then press the left button on the mouse.

Actually, you can press the mouse buttons in several different ways! (I know I said Windows was

Edutainment and Windows

easy to use. It is. You just have to master a few basic skills, and mouse-button pressing is one of them.) The first way to press the button is to click it. When you click the mouse button, you press it until it clicks, and then quickly release it. A single click of the left button selects (highlights) an item, but does not activate it. If you click an icon, for example, the caption is highlighted to signify that the icon is selected, but nothing else happens.

Another way to press the mouse button is to double-click it. You double-click by pressing and releasing the button two times in rapid succession. Double-clicking something with the left button activates it. If you double-click an icon that represents a program, for example, the program begins running.

The third way to press a mouse button is to drag with it. In this case, you press and hold down the left mouse button while you move the mouse. You can then move things around the screen by dragging them.

Now that you know the names of the parts of a window, and you know the basics of using a mouse, you are ready to run your new edutainment program.

Running a Program

For this example, let's say you have purchased Arthur's Teacher Trouble, by Broderbund. This CD-ROM storybook is easy to use and doesn't require any special installation. The first step in running this program is to find the File menu option in the Program Manager's menu bar. If you have just started Windows, the Program Manager should be the largest window visible.

Select the File menu option by moving the mouse pointer on top of the word *File* in the menu bar and clicking the left mouse button. When you do this, the File menu appears. It should resemble the menu shown in the figure.

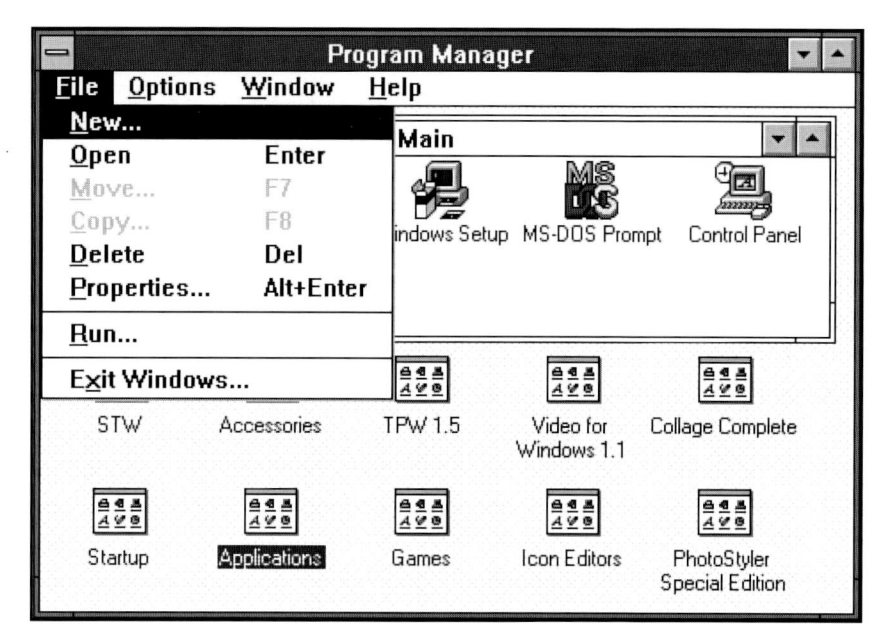

▲ *The Program Manager File menu.*

Notice that the File menu contains several options that have an ellipsis (...) following the name of the option. The ellipsis indicates that those options lead to other options. Click the Run option to select it. When you do, the Run dialog box appears.

If you know the name and path to the executable program for Arthur's Teacher Trouble, you can type it in the box labeled Command Line. The

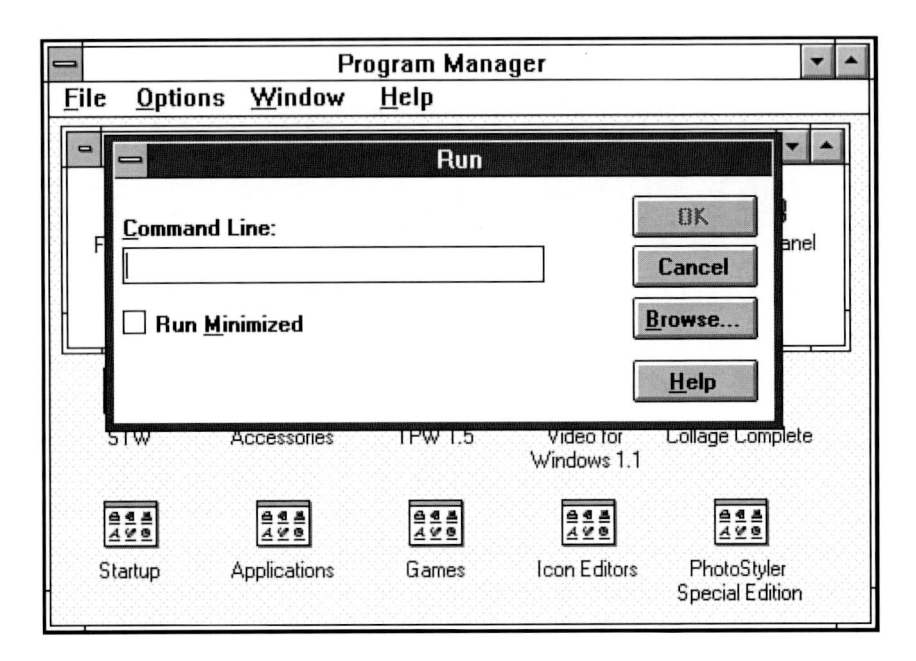

▲ *The Run dialog box.*

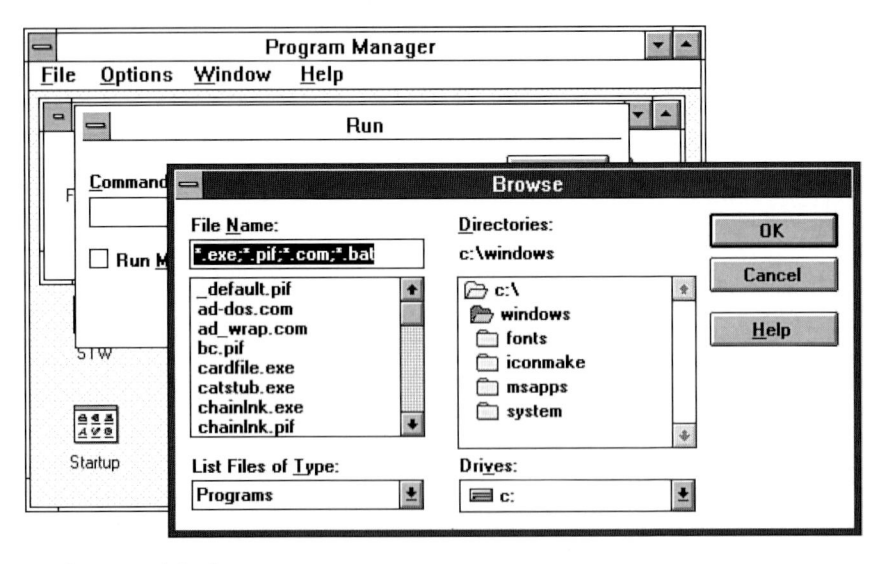

▲ *The Browse dialog box.*

blinking vertical line on the left side of the box is the cursor and shows you where any text you type will appear. Entering the information in the Command Line box is a shortcut to get the program running, but the drawback is that you have to remember the appropriate information. Instead of memorizing strings of text, such as C:\TP\XYZ\FRED.EXE, you can use the Browse dialog box.

> **Note:** When you are asked to *enter* information in a box, you actually are being requested to perform a two-step operation. You first type the information, and then you either press the Enter key or click the OK button.

To open the Browse dialog box, click the button labeled Browse.

The Browse dialog box is easy to use. On the left side of the window, the large box under the File Name box shows a list of all the programs in the current directory. In the middle of the window, the large box under the Directories heading shows the current directory and its subdirectories. The current directory is portrayed as a highlighted, open file folder. In the figure, the current directory is C:\WINDOWS, and the subdirectories of that directory are Fonts, Iconmake, Msapps, and System. The Drives box gives you access to all the disk drives on your system, including the CD-ROM drive.

Since Arthur's Teacher Trouble is a CD-ROM, the executable file for it must be on the CD-ROM drive. To switch drives, click the little down arrow on the right side of the Drives box, and a list of available drives appears. On my system, the Drives menu looks like the one in the top figure.

The symbols for each type of drive are meant to resemble the physical appearance of that particular type of drive. In my drop-down list, the symbols next to drives A and B signify floppy disk drives, the symbols next to drives C and H represent hard drives, and the symbol next to drive D represents a CD-ROM drive. If you click a drive symbol, the Browse box displays information about that drive.

To switch to the drive that contains Arthur's Teacher Trouble, select the CD-ROM drive symbol. The bottom figure shows the Browse dialog box after I selected my D: drive.

Notice that the large File Name box contains only one file, ARTHUR.EXE. This must be the file to choose to make the program run. If there were more filenames in this box, you would have to refer to the instructions that came with the program.

Double-click the text ARTHUR.EXE. The Browse dialog box closes, leaving you back at the Run dialog box. This time the Command Line box contains the information required to activate the program. Click the OK button to start Arthur's Teacher Trouble.

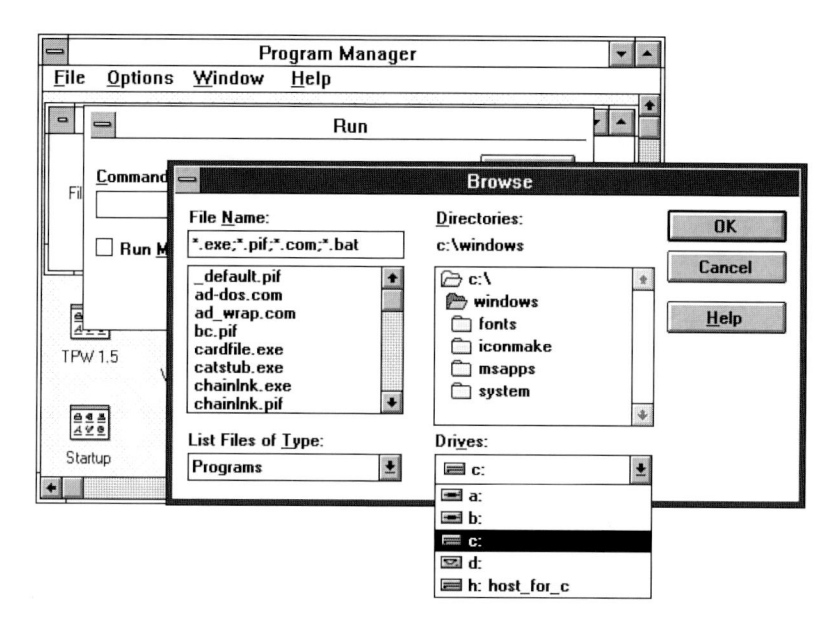

▲ *The Drives drop-down list.*

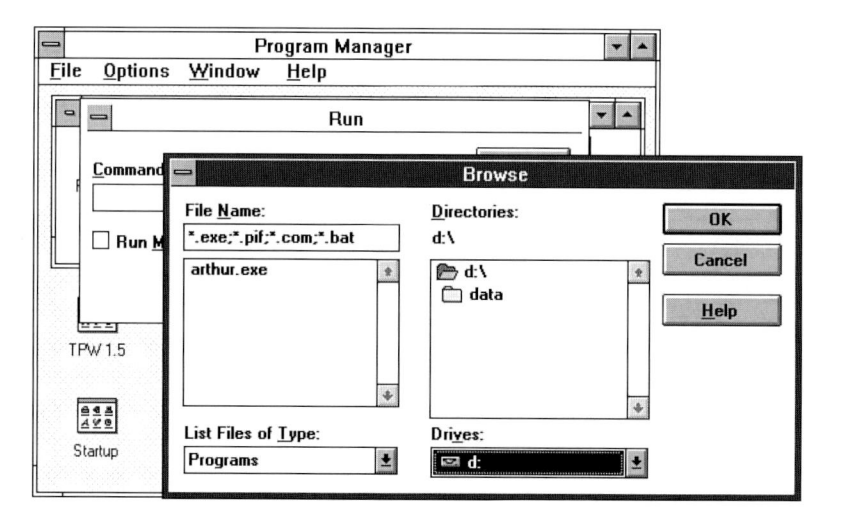

▲ *Browsing the Arthur's Teacher Trouble CD-ROM.*

Creating an Edutainment Program Group

One nice thing about Windows is the way you can organize your programs. Each program group consists of a window containing icons. In a program group, each icon represents a different program (application). Every program group has a title, which usually describes the kind of applications in the group. When a program group is minimized (see "Resizing Windows" later in this chapter), the title becomes the caption of the icon that represents the program group. The Main program group is a perfect example.

If you refer back to the earlier figure that showed the Main program group, you can see that my Main program group contains five icons: File Manager, Print Manager, Windows Setup, MS-DOS Prompt, and Control Panel. Each one of these icons represents an application. Double-click any one of those icons and you activate the application that the icon represents.

To create an Edutainment program group and then add programs to that group, you first must activate the Program Manager's File menu. You encountered this menu earlier in the chapter. From the File menu, select the New option, and the New Program Object dialog box appears.

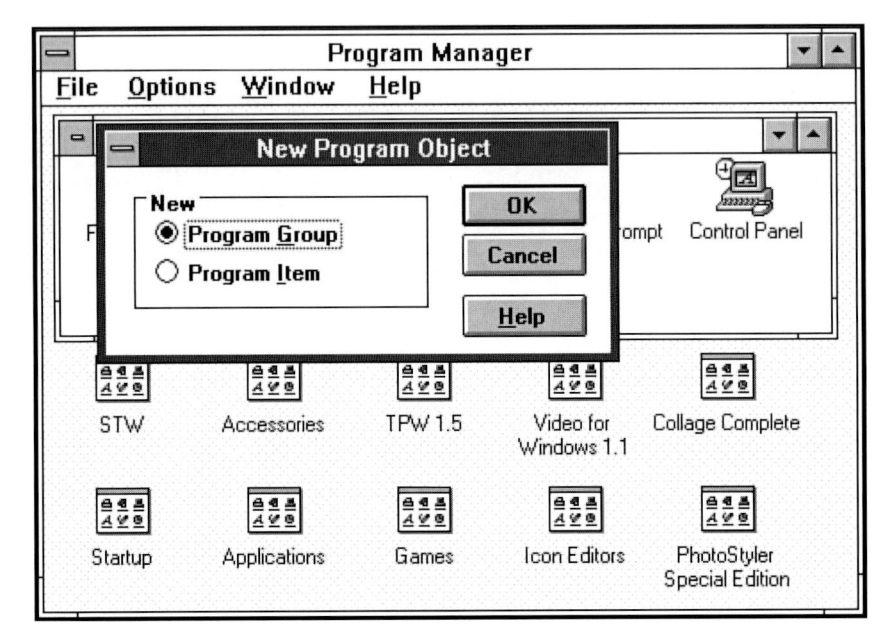

▲ *The New Program Object dialog box.*

In this dialog box, you can create both new program groups and the icons (program items) that go in the groups. Make sure that the little circle next to the Program Group option is filled with a black dot, as it is in the figure. These little circles are called *radio buttons*. When you select one of the buttons in the New box, it fills with a black dot, and the black dot is removed from the other circle. If the button next to Program Group is not selected, click it. The button should now resemble the one in the figure.

After you have selected Program Group, click the OK button. This closes the New Program Object dialog box and activates the Program Group Properties dialog box.

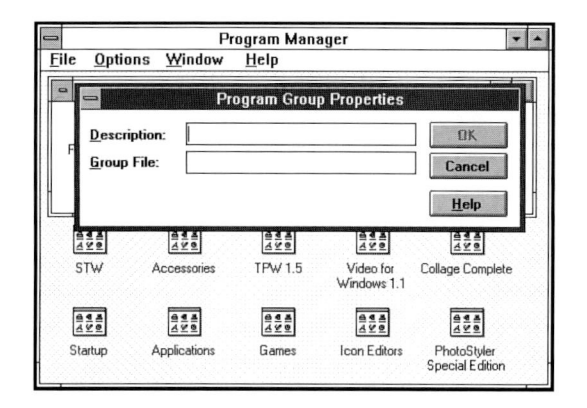

Edutainment and Windows   199

▲ *The Program Group Properties dialog box.*

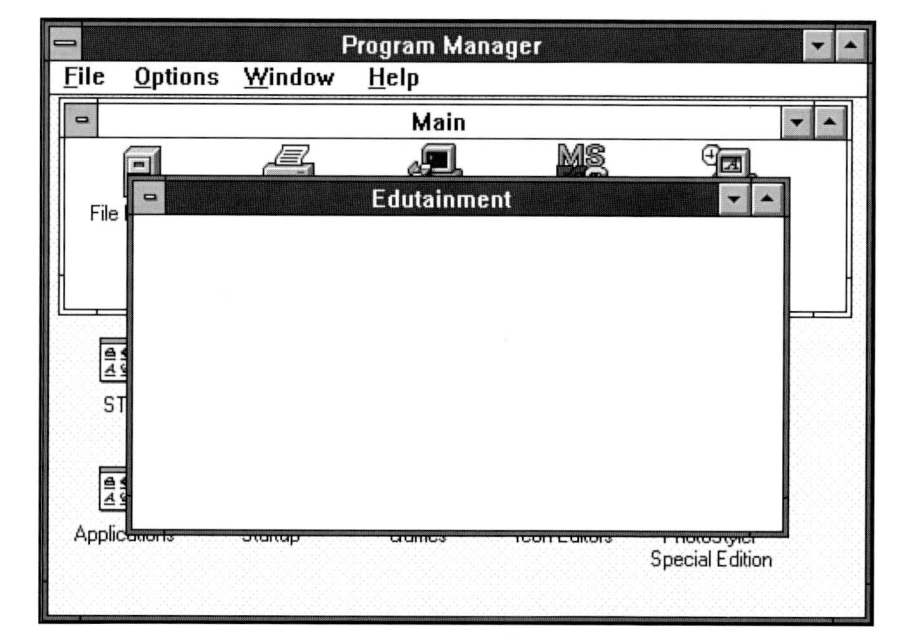

▲ *The empty Edutainment program group.*

In the Description box, enter the title you want to use for this program group, such as **Edutainment**. Notice that the blinking cursor is already in this box, so all you have to do is start typing. You can ignore the Group File box in normal circumstances. When you finish entering the description, click the OK button. The Program Manager then creates an empty program group with the description you specified.

After you have a program group created, you can add an icon for Arthur's Teacher Trouble to it. Open the Program Manager File menu and select New. In the New Program Object dialog box, click the button next to Program Item to select it. When the Program Item button is highlighted, click the OK button. This action closes the New Program Object dialog box and opens the Program Item Properties dialog box.

This dialog box is more complicated than the Program Group Properties box. Windows requires more information to create an icon representing an application than it does to create an empty group.

In this dialog box, first enter the description for the icon. The blinking cursor is in the Description box, so the box is set up to receive this information. After you have entered the description you

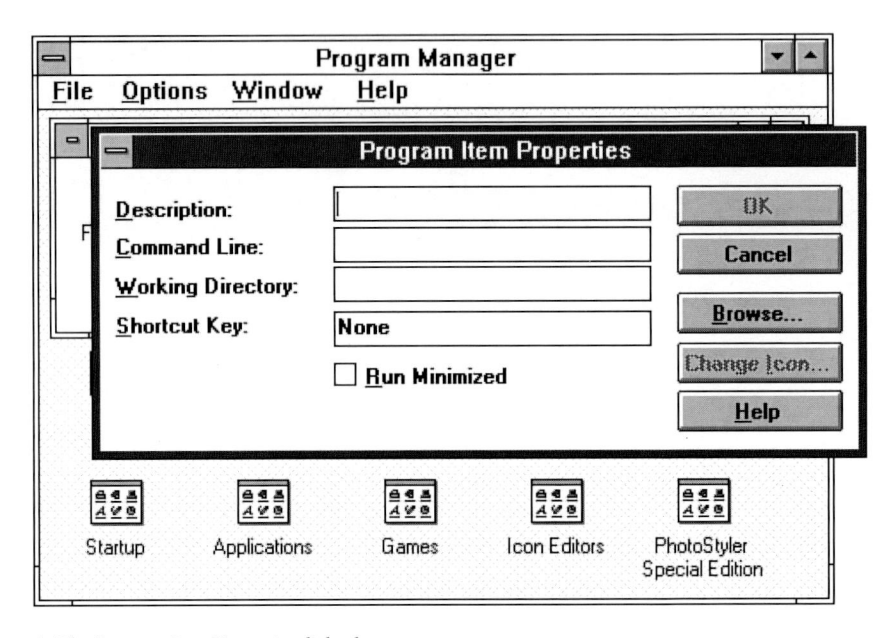

▲ *The Program Item Properties dialog box.*

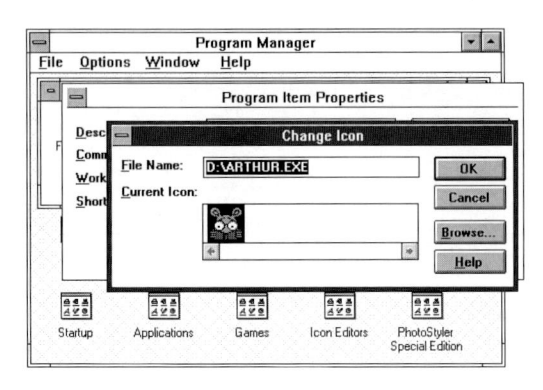

▲ *The Change Icon dialog box.*

want to use, press the Tab key on your keyboard. The Tab key moves the cursor down to the box labeled Command Line. At this point, you can fill in this box and the Working Directory box manually, or you can click the Browse button. Clicking the Browse button brings up the Browse dialog box you encountered earlier. (Refer back to that figure, if you want to refresh your memory.)

When you use the Browse dialog box to find the executable file (ARTHUR.EXE in this example), Windows fills in the Command Line and Working Directory boxes for you. The Shortcut Key box enables you to enter a quick key combination that you can use to activate this program. (To learn more about shortcut keys, click the Help button in the Program Item Properties dialog box.)

You can click the OK button at this point, and an icon for Arthur's Teacher Trouble is added to the Edutainment program group. Unfortunately, the icon itself is just a generic one. You have to do a little more work to get an icon specific to Arthur's Teacher Trouble.

All Windows applications come with their own icons. Windows just needs to know how to find them. To tell Windows where the icon you want to use is located, click the Change Icon button. This activates the Change icon dialog box, shown in the preceding figure.

The contents of the File Name and Current Icon boxes reflects the information for the program shown in the Program Item Properties dialog box. The Current Icon box shows the icon (or icons) that are included in the program on which you are

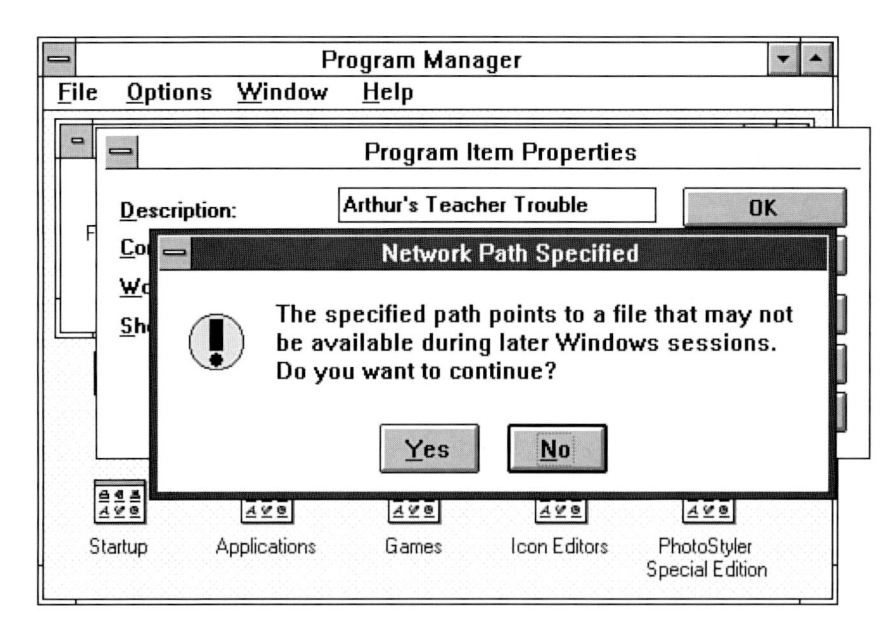

Edutainment and Windows

▲ *A path warning.*

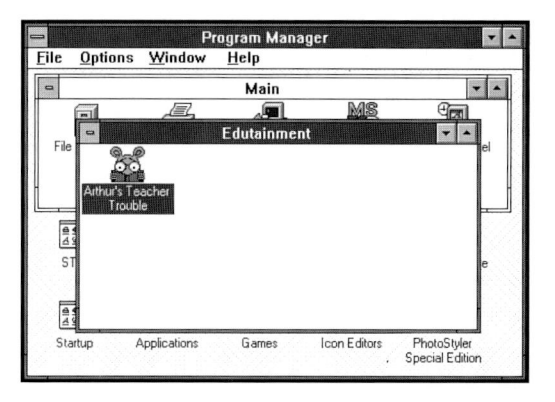

▲ *The Edutainment program group with its icon.*

If you forget to load the appropriate CD-ROM before you try to start an application, Windows displays an Invalid Path message box.

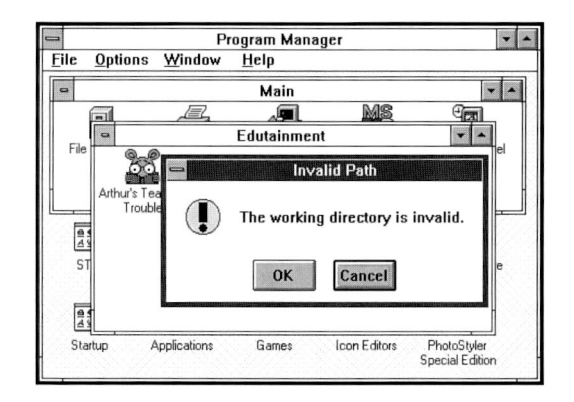

▲ *An Invalid Path warning.*

working. Click the icon you want to use, and then click the OK button. This closes the Change Icon dialog box and puts the chosen icon into the lower-left corner of the Program Item Properties dialog box. Select the OK button to tell Windows that you are finished creating the icon.

Windows knows that an application found on a CD-ROM may not always be accessible. Change the CD-ROM and a different set of applications becomes available. To warn you about this, Windows displays a path warning. The preceding figure shows the Network Path Specified message box, which Windows uses for this kind of message.

Because, as you will see in a moment, nothing disastrous happens if you do try to activate an application that "isn't there," click the Yes button to finish adding the icon to the program group. After you do, the box closes and you can see your Edutainment group with the application icon in it.

If you see this message, you have two choices. Your first option is to click the Cancel button. This aborts your attempt to run the application. Your second option is to insert the appropriate CD-ROM and then click the OK button. The application should then start normally.

Resizing Windows

Whenever an application appears in a window, you can resize that window. You normally want an edutainment application to occupy the full screen because this shows you the most information and also eliminates the distraction of other windows that might be visible in the background.

Notice how cluttered and distracting the screen on the left is because the edutainment program is not running full-screen. Because the edutainment application window occupies less than the full screen, less information is visible.

Making a window occupy the full screen is called *maximizing* it. Maximizing a window is easy. Double-click the title bar of the window. If the window is not currently maximized it then maximizes itself. If the window is currently maximized, double-clicking the title bar causes it to return to the size and position it occupied before it was maximized.

Exiting a Program

When you are finished using an application, you want to exit it. Most Windows edutainment programs display their menu bars while they are active. With any applications that do this, it is easy to exit, or close, the application.

Open the File menu on the application's menu bar. The following figure shows the File menu of The People's Chronology in Microsoft Bookshelf '94. (By the way, notice that you can see much more of your edutainment application when the screen is maximized. And closing all other windows is much less distracting to your eye.)

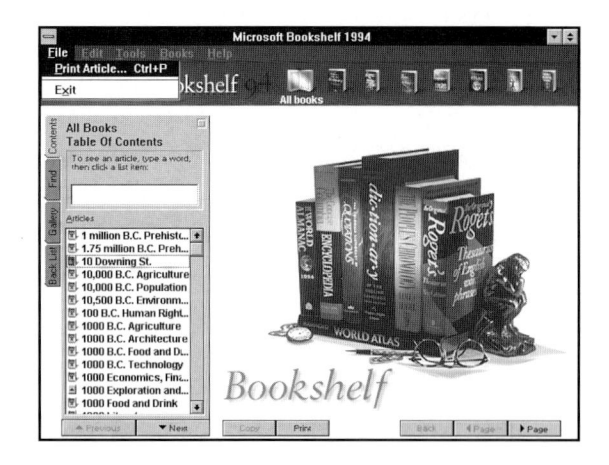

▲ *Windows, windows, everywhere.*

▲ *An application's File menu.*

The last option on the File menu is Exit. Select this option, and Windows closes the window and exits the application.

Some edutainment applications do not display their menu bars while they are in use. For those applications, you must refer to the documentation that came with the program to find out how to exit.

Summary

In this chapter, you learned why I think Windows is the future of edutainment. Its power, ease of use, and popularity make it the first choice for software developers. This means that the newest, most-powerful, and most innovative edutainment titles will be available first for Windows. DOS versions will come later, if at all.

The MPC specifications (which require Windows) give software developers a standard system for which to design. They know that all MPC-compatible PCs have certain hardware and particular capabilities, and they can design their software to take advantage of those capabilities. By the same token, developers are less likely to require hardware and capabilities that are not part of the specifications, which means that you can feel quite safe buying MPC software for an MPC-compatible PC.

The remainder of this chapter showed you how to put Windows to use. You learned how to start Windows and how to use the mouse to run an application. You learned how to create a program group and how to add to that group icons representing your edutainment applications. Finally, you learned how to exit an application when you are finished using it. These basic skills should give you the confidence you need to begin using Windows edutainment products.

The last several chapters prepared a typical user to upgrade his or her PC into a powerful edutainment system. The next chapter is a little different. It focuses on upgrades for users with special needs. If you or someone you know has special computing needs, this chapter may have just the information you are looking for.

Chapter 13

Upgrades for Users with Special Needs

I believe that edutainment products can give kids a real head start on a lifetime of learning. That being the case, it is important to make the advantages of edutainment products available to as many users as possible—including users with special needs.

Few edutainment products are designed with the needs of physically challenged users in mind. Fortunately, a wide range of adaptive hardware and software is available that can make the computer easier to use. This chapter is designed to give you some information on adaptive access. The information included here should be enough to get you started and should give you some ideas about where to go next.

The following topics are discussed in this chapter:

- The basics of adaptive access
- Possible solutions for users with low vision
- Possible solutions for blind users
- Possible solutions for users with hearing impairments
- Possible solutions for users with mobility impairments
- A representative list of manufacturers of access products
- Suggestions on where to go for more information

The Basics of Adaptive Access

When looked at from a fundamental level, computers accept commands from the user (input), perform calculations (process), and provide the results to the user (output). While few of the new edutainment programs make accommodations for users with special needs, products are available that adapt the input, processing, and output of the computer in order to provide access to these users.

Most of the available adaptive products for the PC have been designed to work with programs running under DOS, in text mode. A program that runs in text mode displays alphanumeric characters (including some simple shapes that are part of the extended character set found on PCs). Text-mode programs have no real graphics, digitized images, animation, or video clips. Such programs usually have limited or no sound effects or music. The user interacts with these programs through the keyboard, so it is relatively easy for adaptive hardware and software to interact with text-mode programs.

Modern edutainment programs, however, run in graphics mode. The displays are colorful and visually stimulating, filled with cartoon characters, animation, and sometimes even digitized images and video clips. Sound effects, music, and digitized speech play an important part in these products, providing helpful feedback or even being essential to the successful use of the product. The user usually interacts with these products using a combination of the keyboard and the mouse. It is much harder for adaptive hardware and software to interact with these products.

Researchers and manufacturers have looked at these problems and have come up with a number of possible solutions. The next few sections cover some of the possible solutions listed in the Managing Information Resources for Accessibility handbook published by the Clearinghouse on Computer Accommodation (COCA) of the Information Resources Management Service (IRMS), General Services Administration (GSA).

Possible Solutions for Users with Low Vision

The term *low vision* covers a range of conditions and types of visual impairment. The following list contains solutions that may be appropriate for low-vision users of edutainment products. Which of these solutions, if any, is appropriate for an individual user must be determined by that user.

- *Glare protection screen*—Reduces eyestrain associated with glare on the monitor.
- *Large monitor*—The larger display area of a 19-inch or larger monitor proportionally increases the size of text and images on the screen. The selection criteria found in Chapter 10, "Sight and Sound," are still appropriate; only the size of the monitor itself is different. When appropriate, this solution is a good one for edutainment users

because it does not depend on any support from the edutainment program itself.

- *Screen magnification software*—Products are available that enlarge the items on the screen. Most of these products are designed to work with text-mode applications, but some are available that work in graphics mode. At least one program is available that enlarges the display while a user is running Microsoft Windows.
- *Screen magnification hardware*—Some sort of magnifying lens is attached to the monitor to enlarge items on the screen. When appropriate, this solution is a good one for edutainment users because it does not depend on any support from the edutainment program itself.
- *Color and contrast selection*—The colors used by both DOS and Windows can be adjusted. Unfortunately, most edutainment products control the display colors used when the program is active and don't provide any provisions for varying them.
- *Keyboard orientation aids*—Adding a raised dot or bleb to certain keys can help a user orient and place his or her fingers with little or no visual feedback. The number five key on the numeric keypad and the home row keys are frequently the ones marked in this way.
- *Other keyboard aids*—Keycap labels with large, bold letters can be applied to the keys on a standard keyboard. These keycaps are available in a variety of colors and styles from a number of manufacturers.

Possible Solutions for Blind Users

A few solutions are available that make edutainment products accessible to users who are blind. Most edutainment products, however, are highly visual and would be ineffective or even useless to users who cannot see the display at all. The following list contains a selection of devices that may be useful in certain cases.

- *Speech synthesizer*—A hardware device that converts the screen contents into spoken form, a screen synthesizer ordinarily is used with a screen reader. Some edutainment products make extensive use of digitized speech. In those cases, the speech is generated by the sound card installed in the computer and does not require a separate synthesizer.
- *Screen reader software*—These programs capture the contents of the screen and direct them to a speech synthesizer. Often, a user can choose the way in which the reader passes the information to the synthesizer (sending it to the synthesizer by the letter, word, line, or screen).
- *Refreshable Braille*—Hardware that contains a row of Braille cells that change to reflect what is shown on the display. As the cells change, a user can read what is on the screen.
- *Braille input software*—Utilities that enable a user to reconfigure the keyboard as a Braille input device.
- *Braille input hardware*—The standard PC keyboard can be replaced by a special Braille input device.
- *Keyboard enhancements*—Adding a raised dot or a Braille marker to certain keys enables a user to orient and place his or her hands on the keys properly. Another type of enhancement provides audible feedback on the state of the Caps Lock and other toggle keys.
- *Speech recognition hardware*—Some devices are available that enable a user to replace keystrokes and mouse movements with spoken commands.

Possible Solutions for Users with Hearing Impairments

The term *hearing impaired* is used both for individuals who are hard of hearing and those who are deaf. The needs of these two groups obviously vary. The edutainment situation is somewhat better for individuals who are hard of hearing. A number of products can help these users utilize the sounds generated by edutainment programs.

For now, at least, not much can be done to enhance edutainment products for deaf users. Fortunately, however, sound effects, music, and even digitized speech are secondary sources of information in most edutainment products. They may provide helpful cues or additional information, but normally they are not crucial to the use of a product.

The following list describes a couple of possible solutions for users with hearing impairments.

- *Amplified speakers*—Most edutainment products provide their audio output through a sound card. Connecting the card to a set of amplified speakers may provide enough amplification to make the sounds usable.
- *Stereo with headphones*—An alternative to amplified speakers is a stereo system with headphones. The sound card provides the input to the stereo, which drives the headphones. The stereo enables a user to adjust the amplification without disturbing others nearby.

Possible Solutions for Users with Mobility Impairments

Users with mobility impairments can be accommodated in a number of ways. The physical setting of the computer work area must be considered, as well as the actual interfaces to the computer. Here are some possible solutions:

- *Sequential keystroke input*—Utility programs that enable a user to enter certain keystrokes sequentially. Many commands require a user to press two or more keys simultaneously, such as the Ctrl+Alt+Del combination used to reboot the computer. These special utility programs enable a user to press the keys sequentially and still achieve the same effect. AccessDOS and the Access Pack for Microsoft Windows both provide this capability.

> **Note:** Both AccessDOS and the Access Pack for Microsoft Windows are available electronically from the Microsoft Download Service at (206) 936-6735. To obtain the Access Pack for Microsoft Windows, download the file ACCP.EXE. The AccessDOS utility programs, on the other hand, are part of the DOS Supplemental disks and are stored on the Microsoft Download Service under filenames that relate to specific DOS versions. Download the file that is appropriate for your version of DOS.

- *Key repeat rate control*—Some utilities are available that enable a user to control the keystroke repeat function. This is another feature available in AccessDOS and the Access Pack for Microsoft Windows.
- *Alternative keyboards*—Several alternative keyboard styles are available that are designed to be used by mobility-impaired individuals. Some are smaller versions of keyboards, while others are large, expanded keyboards. Another style includes keyboards that are connected to the PC by infrared or other wireless links. Finally, some keyboards are designed for users who type with a single hand (both left- and right-handed models are available).
- *Non-keyboard input devices*—A number of alternative input devices are available with which keystrokes can be generated by various mechanisms and then transmitted as if generated by the keyboard. These devices include sip-and-puff systems, muscle switches, optical pointer devices, Morse code input systems, and eye-scanning systems.
- *Speech-recognition hardware*—Hardware is available that enables a user to replace keystrokes and mouse movements with spoken commands. This equipment can either supplement or replace the keyboard.
- *Mouse alternatives*—Some programs, such as Microsoft Windows, provide keystrokes that replace mouse functions, and some manufacturers produce devices that enable mouthstick users to manipulate a mouse. A trackball may also be an appropriate alternative.
- *Keyguard*—A keyguard is a smooth template with holes corresponding to key locations. You can place it over a standard keyboard to stabilize the user's hand movements and prevent inadvertent multiple keystrokes.

Manufacturers of Access Products

The companies and products listed here are by no means the only ones that offer these products. They are simply a sampling selected from a list provided by the Clearinghouse on Computer Accommodation (COCA).

Input Hardware and Software

Ability Systems Corporation
1422 Arnold Avenue
Roslyn, PA 19001
215-657-4338
Key scanner with sip-and-puff or joystick control

Brown & Co., Inc.
Box 2443
South Hamilton, MA 01982
508-468-7464
A foot pedal to allow one-finger input of combined keystrokes

Computability Corporation
40000 Grand River
Suite 109
Novi, MI 48375
313-477-6720
800-433-8872
A collection of keyboard alternatives and enhancements

Data-Cal Corporation
531 E. Elliot Road
Suite 145
Chandler, AZ 85225
800-223-0123
602-545-1234
Fax 602-545-8090
Large print and Braille keycap overlays

Extensions for Independence
555 Saturn Boulevard
Suite B-368
San Diego, CA 92154
619-423-7709
619-423-1748
Mouthsticks, and a device that lets a mouthstick user control a mouse

IBM National Support Center for Persons with Disabilities
P.O. Box 2150
Atlanta, GA 30055
800-426-2133 voice
800-284-9482 TDD
AccessDOS and other utilities; VoiceType speech recognition package

Kinetic Designs, Inc.
14231 Anatevka Lane SE
Olalla, WA 98466
206-857-7943
Filch keyboard configuration utility and Morsek Morse code input system

MicroTouch Systems, Inc.
55 Jonspin Road
Wilmington, MA 01887
508-694-9900
800-866-6873
Fax 508-694-9980
UnMouse touch-sensitive mouse-replacement tablet

nView
11835 Canon Boulevard
Newport News, VA 23606
804-873-1354
800-736-8439
Fax 804-873-2153
Toteboard small-footprint, wireless keyboard with single-key operation

RoseSoft, Inc.
P.O. Box 70337
Bellevue, WA 98007
206-562-0225
Fax 206-562-9846
ProKey keyboard macro utility

Trace R&D Center
S-151 Waisman Center
1500 Highland Avenue
Madison, WI 53705
608-262-6966 voice
608-263-5408 TDD
One-finger sequential keyboard input utility; Access Pack for Windows

Typewriting Institute for the Handicapped
3102 West Augusta Avenue
Phoenix, AZ 85051
602-939-5344
One-handed keyboards for either hand

WesTest Engineering Corporation
1470 North Main Street
Bountiful, Utah 84010
801-298-7100
Fax 801-292-7379
DARCI joystick, single- or multiple-switch keyboard replacement

St. West
Suite 202
P.O. Box 1229
Lancaster, CA 93534
805-949-8331
Long-range optical pointers and other input devices

Votan PC
210 Hammond Avenue
Fremont, CA 94539
415-490-7600
800-877-4756
Fax 415-490-1648
Votan Voice Card speech recognition systems

Output Hardware and Software

AI Squared
1463 Hearst Drive, NE
Atlanta, GA 30319
404-233-7065
Large-print display software for text and graphics

Artic Technologies
55 Park Street
Suite #2
Troy, MI 48083
313-588-7370
Fax 313-588-2650
Screen reading and large-print systems

Florida New Concepts Marketing, Inc.
P.O. Box 261
Port Richey, FL 34673-0261
813-842-3231
800-456-7097
Beamscope II Fresnel lens screen magnifier

Interface Systems International
P.O. Box 20415
Portland, OR 97220
503-665-0965 voice or fax
ProSpeech user interface for Prodigy; ISOS screen-reading utility

Microsystems Software Inc.
600 Worcester Road
Suite B2
Framingham, MA 01701
508-626-8511
Fax: 508-626-8515
MAGIC and MAGIC Deluxe large-character displays for DOS and Windows

SkiSoft Publishing Corp.
1644 Massachusetts Avenue
Suite 79
Lexington, MA 02173
617-863-1876
800-662-3622
No-Squint II cursor-attribute controller

Furniture

Modular Turntable Desks
Vari-Hi Modular Compu-Desk
Extensions for Independence
555 Saturn Boulevard
Suite B-368
San Diego, CA 92154
619-423-7709
619-423-1748

Several styles of turntable desks are available, each with large, easily-rotated turntables built in. The turntables give the user easy access to items on any portion of the desk. The Vari-Hi desks can have the height of their surfaces adjusted to accommodate wheelchair users.

Where You Can Go for Further Information

The material in this chapter is meant to introduce you to some of the possibilities in adaptive access devices. It is not meant to be a guide to choosing products. A number of sources are available that you can refer to for specific details.

The first source of information is the professionals that currently provide services to the user with special needs. They should be able to provide much valuable assistance, particularly with respect to seating and equipment placement.

Other useful sources of information include the nearest Alliance for Technology Access (ATA) center or organizations such as the Easter Seal Society. Users who want to do their own research may want to check out the ABLEDATA Database of Assistive Technology (see Appendix D for more information). The database includes information on over 19,000 products!

Summary

Edutainment products provide a head start on a lifetime of learning for the children who use these products. Users shouldn't be denied this head start because they have some special needs when it comes to using a PC. This chapter provided an overview to adaptive access technologies. These technologies assist users with special needs in using computers. The focus throughout this chapter was on products and solutions that are appropriate for edutainment users.

The chapter began with a discussion of the basics of adaptive access. The bulk of the chapter covered possible solutions to access problems and a list of providers. Solutions were discussed for users with low vision, or those who are blind, hearing impaired, or mobility impaired. The list of providers offered here is just a small sample taken from the hundreds listed in the COCA handbook.

Chapter 14

Troubleshooting DOS and Windows

PCs are complex devices. No matter how much effort goes into making them foolproof, you can still get into trouble. Some problems are easy to spot: DOS or Windows displays a message telling you that a problem exists. Other problems are more subtle: the machine just seems more sluggish than it did when you bought it. And some problems are catastrophic, halting or crashing the system.

This chapter discusses some of the problems you may encounter while you are using DOS or Windows. For each problem, some of the symptoms are described, along with an explanation of why the problem occurs and what you can do about it. Because a mouse is virtually indispensable when you use Windows, common mouse problems are covered in the Windows part of the chapter.

Because edutainment products demand so much from your system, you are more likely to encounter problems when you run them than you do with most other types of software. I have run into disk space problems, out-of-memory warnings, and low-system resources while running some of the programs mentioned in this book.

The following topics are discussed in this chapter:

- DOS error messages
- General DOS problems
- Mouse problems
- General Windows problems

Common DOS Errors and Problems

Even though DOS has been around for a long time (or perhaps because it has), there are still any number of ways that you can get into trouble when you use it. Because everything that happens on your machine involves DOS (even Windows runs "on top of" DOS), it is important for you to know how to handle common DOS problems.

DOS Error Messages

DOS provides error messages to let you know when a problem occurs. Unfortunately, many of these error messages are hard to figure out. Here, in plain English, are explanations of common DOS error messages and tips on what to do when they occur. The error messages are listed in alphabetical order.

Bad command or filename

This message appears after you enter something at the command prompt. It means that DOS can't find the command or program you are trying to run. Some DOS commands, such as DIR and CD, reside in memory, while others are on the hard disk. The commands that reside on the disk are regular programs that come with DOS. When you enter something at the command prompt, DOS first looks at its resident commands to see if what you typed matches one of them. If not, it starts looking for a file that matches what you entered.

DOS first searches the current directory for a filename that matches what you typed. It only looks at files with .COM, .EXE, and .BAT extensions because these are executable files (programs or batch files that you can run). If DOS cannot find a matching file in the current directory, it searches all the directories in the path. If it finds a matching file, it runs it. If DOS does not find the file, it displays the `Bad command or filename` message.

You have several options to resolve this problem. First, check your typing. If you misspelled something, DOS certainly won't be able to find a file to match. Retype the command correctly, and you should be on your way.

Assuming that you spelled everything correctly, check to see whether you are in the correct directory. As explained before, DOS only looks in certain places when it is trying to execute your commands. If you are in the wrong directory, change to the correct directory and retype the command.

If you are in the right directory, are typing everything correctly, and the command still doesn't work, you may have to modify your PATH statement. DOS looks at the PATH statement to know where to find files or programs, including the non-resident DOS commands. At this point, you should take a look at the documentation that came with your version of DOS. If you have to modify the PATH statement, the installation section of the documentation tells you how to do so. If you have DOS 5.0 or later on your system, it's easy to modify the PATH statement.

Suppose that you want to add C:\EDUTAIN to your PATH statement, and you are running DOS 6.2. The first step is to run EDIT, a basic editor that comes with DOS 5.0 and later versions. At the DOS prompt enter the following:

`C:\DOS\EDIT C:\AUTOEXEC.BAT`

This statement activates EDIT and loads your AUTOEXEC.BAT file so that it is ready to modify. The first figure shows my AUTOEXEC.BAT loaded into EDIT.

Look through this file until you find the line that begins with PATH. This line is the PATH statement. The statement consists of several individual paths separated from each other with semicolons (;). Using the arrow keys, move the cursor (the blinking rectangular block in the upper-left corner of the screen) to the end of the line containing the PATH statement. If the last path is not followed by a semicolon, add one. Type the path you want to add—in this case, type

`C:\EDUTAIN`

After you add the new path, you must save this change. Press the Alt+F key combination to display the File menu, as shown in the middle figure.

Choose the Save option. EDIT saves the revised AUTOEXEC.BAT file and writes it over the old version. To exit EDIT, activate the File menu again (press Alt+F) and choose the Exit option. Finally, for your changed PATH statement to take effect, you must restart your computer (press Ctrl+Alt+Delete, or turn the power off and then back on).

Cannot load COMMAND, system halted

DOS provides applications with more memory by letting them overwrite part of the command interpreter, COMMAND.COM. When DOS needs the part of COMMAND.COM that was overwritten, it reloads it from your hard disk. This error message is displayed when DOS cannot find COMMAND.COM to reload it.

Part of the SHELL command in the CONFIG.SYS file specifies the path to COMMAND.COM. An environment variable named COMSPEC is created from this path. Normally, the path to COMMAND.COM is C:\DOS\, as you can see on the SHELL line in the CONFIG.SYS file shown in the bottom figure.

To resolve this error, you first must restart your system. If it does not restart normally, turn off the power, wait 30 seconds, and turn the machine on again. When you see the message `Starting MS-DOS...`, press and release the F5 key. If you are using DOS 6.0 or later, this starts the machine without executing all the commands in your AUTOEXEC.BAT and CONFIG.SYS files and, with any luck, takes you to a DOS prompt. If this doesn't work, you need to pull out your emergency boot disk (the one you created when you originally installed DOS; sometimes called a *system* disk) and restart the machine with that disk in drive A.

▲ *My AUTOEXEC.BAT file ready to be edited.*

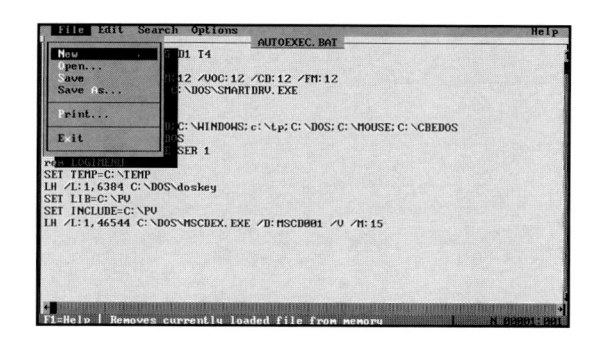

▲ *Activating the File menu in EDIT.*

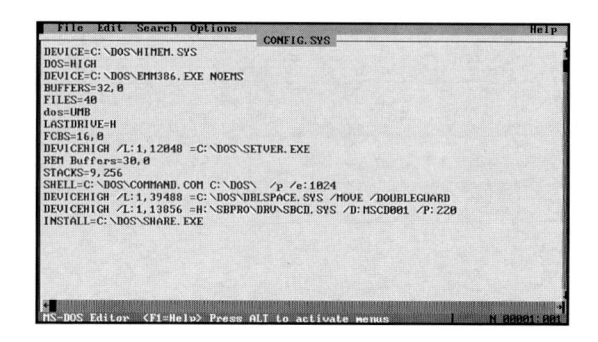

▲ *Examining the CONFIG.SYS file.*

After you have the system restarted, you must check your CONFIG.SYS file. The easiest way to do this is to enter the following command at the DOS prompt:

`TYPE \CONFIG.SYS`

This displays the contents of your CONFIG.SYS file on-screen. Take a look at the SHELL command. If the first part of the command is not

`SHELL=C:\DOS\COMMAND.COM C:\DOS\`

you probably have found the problem.

To activate EDIT and load your CONFIG.SYS file into it so that you can modify the file, enter the following command:

`C:\DOS\EDIT C:\CONFIG.SYS`

Unless you have a good reason not to do so, change the SHELL command to the following:

`SHELL=C:\DOS\COMMAND.COM C:\DOS\`

Save the file and restart the system. If you used the emergency boot disk, remove it from the drive first. If changing the SHELL command fixed the problem, your machine should start up and run normally. If you still get the error message, COMMAND.COM has probably become corrupted.

When you install DOS, a copy of the file COMMAND.COM is placed in your root directory. This copy is placed there specifically to speed recovery from the very type of problem we're trying to correct here. Restart the system using whichever method last got things running. Get to a DOS prompt and type the following command:

`COPY C:\COMMAND.COM C:\DOS\COMMAND.COM`

This command copies COMMAND.COM from the root directory into the DOS directory, thereby replacing the bad copy with a good one.

Data error reading drive x: Abort, Retry, Fail?

This error indicates that DOS cannot read information from drive *x:*. Press A (Abort) to stop reading the disk. Press R (Retry) to try rereading the data that caused the error. Press F (Fail) to skip the bad data and read the rest of the disk.

If the drive that gave you the error is a floppy drive, you can try to remedy the problem with a disk-cleaning kit. These kits contain a special disk and a cleaning fluid. Just apply some fluid to the opening in the cleaning disk and insert it in the drive. To actually clean the drive, you must make it spin, so enter the command

`DIR x:`

in which *x:* is the drive to be cleaned. The disk will spin, and DOS will report a `General failure reading drive x:` message, followed by the familiar `Abort, Retry, Fail?` prompt. Press R to retry a few more times. Then remove the cleaning disk, mark off one of the available uses of the disk (cleaning disks can usually be used about a dozen times), and store the disk and cleaning fluid in a safe place. The cleaning fluid is toxic, so make sure that the kids can't get to it.

Reinsert the disk that originally gave you problems, and try to read it again. If DOS still cannot read the disk, and if you have access to another computer with the same-size disk drive, you have another option you can try. Create a temporary directory on the other PC's hard drive. Copy the contents of the disk that gave you the problems into this temporary directory. If everything copies correctly, remove the problem disk; insert a blank, formatted disk of the same size; and copy the contents of the temporary directory onto the new disk. Try the new disk in your PC. If your PC reads the new disk correctly, you are all set. (This may seem like a silly idea, but it has worked for me; it's definitely worth a shot.)

Exception error #12 — press Enter to reboot

This message and its cousin `Stack overflow, system halted` occur when your PC can't handle the number of hardware interrupts occurring. It is more likely to occur as you add hardware devices such as CD-ROM drives to your system.

DOS allocates a data stack each time there is a hardware interrupt. Data stacks are just sections of memory set aside to hold information related to the hardware interrupts. The hardware interrupts are requests for attention generated by hardware devices (CD-ROM drive, mouse, printer, and so on). DOS provides these stacks to prevent the system from crashing when many hardware devices are clamoring for attention simultaneously.

To solve this exception error, you must increase the number and, possibly, the size of the stacks reserved by DOS. You assign stacks with the STACKS command in your CONFIG.SYS file. You can see the STACKS command in the earlier figure that shows the CONFIG.SYS file. The STACKS command is located just above the SHELL command. My stacks are set at 9,256, which means that DOS is to set aside 9 stacks, each 256 bytes long. The number of stacks, and the size of them, is something you must determine by trial and error. If your CONFIG.SYS has no STACKS command, start with a setting of 9,128, which is the default value for many machines.

If you still receive the error message, try increasing the size of the stacks to 256 bytes by using the command

STACKS=9,256

This setting works well on my machine. If you still have problems, increase the number of stacks to 18 with the command

STACKS=18,256

The number of stacks can be 0, or anywhere from 8 to 64. The size of the stacks can be 0, or anywhere from 32 to 512 bytes.

Stacks occupy some of your conventional memory. You want to minimize the number and size of the stacks to leave as much memory as possible for your programs. With my stacks set at 9,256, 2304 bytes of memory are allocated to stacks and are unavailable for use by my regular programs. Setting STACKS=64,512, the maximum setting, would use up 32,768 bytes (32K) of your conventional memory.

General failure reading (writing) drive x: Abort, Retry, Fail?

This error indicates that DOS cannot do anything with the disk in drive x:, Normally this message indicates that the disk in the drive is not formatted. Use the A (Abort) option to get out of this. Format the disk or use a previously formatted one.

Incorrect DOS version

You may see this error message (or one similar to it) if you followed my advice and upgraded to DOS 6.2. Many programs, including most of the DOS commands that reside on the hard disk, check the DOS version number before they run. If the version number is higher than the program likes, it displays a message and refuses to run.

Starting with version 5.0, DOS includes a command called SETVER. SETVER lets you trick programs into thinking that they are running under a different version of DOS than they actually are. SETVER comes configured with a version table that changes the version number for many applications that need it. You can also add applications to, and delete them from, the list.

The DOS installation program automatically adds SETVER to your CONFIG.SYS file when you install DOS 5.0 or greater. Assuming you haven't removed it, that part of the job is already done. Here is what you need to do to add a program to the version table.

Suppose that you have a program named MYTESTER that is designed to run with DOS versions 3.0 to 4.0. At the DOS prompt, enter the following command:

SETVER MYTESTER 4.0

Even though Microsoft supplies SETVER to resolve version number problems, it is not a guaranteed fix. When you add a program to the version table, DOS displays the message shown in the following figure.

```
C:\>SETVER MYTESTER 4.0

WARNING - Contact your software vendor for information about whether a
specific program works with MS-DOS version 6.2. It is possible that
Microsoft has not verified whether the program will successfully run if
you use the SETVER command to change the program version number and
version table. If you run the program after changing the version table
in MS-DOS version 6.2, you may lose or corrupt data or introduce system
instabilities. Microsoft is not responsible for any loss or damage, or
for lost or corrupted data.

Version table successfully updated
The version change will take effect the next time you restart your system

C:\>
```

▲ *Message displayed when you add a program to the version table.*

This message protects Microsoft and warns you that changing the version table may make a program run, but it doesn't guarantee that the program will run correctly. If you want to be safe, contact the publisher of the program in question. Ask if the program has been tested with DOS 6.2 or if they have a version that works with your version of DOS.

Internal stack overflow, system halted

This message and its cousin, `Exception error #12 — press Enter to reboot`, occur when your PC can't handle the number of hardware interrupts occurring. It is more likely to occur as you add hardware devices such as CD-ROM drives to your system.

DOS allocates a data stack each time there is a hardware interrupt. Data stacks are just sections of memory set aside to hold information related to the hardware interrupts. The hardware interrupts are requests for attention generated by hardware devices (CD-ROM drive, mouse, printer, and so on). DOS provides these stacks to prevent the system from crashing when many hardware devices are clamoring for attention simultaneously.

To resolve this error, you must increase the number and, possibly, the size of the stacks reserved by DOS. You assign stacks with the STACKS command in your CONFIG.SYS file. (You can see the STACKS command in the earlier figure that showed the CONFIG.SYS file. The STACKS command is located just above the SHELL command.) My stacks are set at 9,256, which means that DOS is to set aside 9 stacks,

each 256 bytes long. The number of stacks, and the size of them, is something you must determine by trial and error. If your CONFIG.SYS has no STACKS command, start with a setting of 9,128, which is the default value for many machines.

If you still receive the error message, try increasing the size of the stacks to 256 bytes by using the following command:

STACKS=9,256

This setting works well on my machine. If you still have problems, increase the number of stacks to 18 with the following command:

STACKS=18,256

The number of stacks can be 0, or anywhere from 8 to 64. The size of the stacks can be 0, or anywhere from 32 to 512 bytes.

Stacks occupy some of your conventional memory. You want to minimize the number and size of the stacks to leave as much memory as possible for your programs. With my stacks set at 9,256, 2304 bytes of memory are allocated to stacks and are unavailable for use by my regular programs. Setting STACKS=64,512—the maximum setting—would use up 32,768 bytes (32K) of your conventional memory.

Non-system disk or disk error
Replace and strike any key when ready

When you turn on your machine, it must do many things before it is ready for use. A small program in the machine's ROM is responsible for starting DOS. The machine lifts itself up by its own bootstraps by running this code, which in turn finds and runs DOS. This process is known as *booting up*, and the little program that starts it all is the *bootstrap loader*.

The bootstrap loader begins its search for DOS by checking the A: drive. If it finds a disk in the A: drive, it assumes that the disk is a system disk. System disks contain a copy of DOS and the other files required to make your machine fully operational. If the bootstrap loader doesn't find a disk in drive A, it looks for a hard drive and gets the system information from that. If a disk is in drive A, and it doesn't contain the system information, you receive this error message.

Normally, this message indicates that you left a disk in drive A when you last turned off the machine. Remove the disk from the drive and press any key. Your machine will then finish booting up.

Not ready reading (writing) drive x: Abort, Retry, Fail?

Drive *x*: is not ready to read or write information. Either you don't have a disk in the drive, or the drive latch is not properly closed. Enter A (Abort) to terminate the operation, or insert a disk, check the drive latch, and press R to retry the operation.

Out of environment space

Some programs use the DOS SET command to create environment variables. Environment variables are names for information that resides in memory and is accessible to any program. Environmental variables control the behavior of some programs and batch files, and they also control some aspects of how DOS works. Programs typically modify your AUTOEXEC.BAT file to ensure that their environment variables are set each time you turn on the computer.

DOS provides a limited amount of space for environment variables. You usually see an `Out of environment space` message when you restart your computer after you install a new program. This problem has two solutions. The first solution is to remove some of the SET commands from your AUTOEXEC.BAT file. Obviously, this solution is feasible only if some of the variables are no longer required.

The other solution is to increase the amount of environment space available. This requires a modification of the SHELL command in your CONFIG.SYS file. The first step is to load CONFIG.SYS into EDIT.

From the DOS prompt, enter the following command:

`C:\DOS\EDIT C:\CONFIG.SYS`

Refer back to the earlier figure that shows the CONFIG.SYS file. Towards the bottom of the screen you can see the SHELL command. SHELL specifies the name of the command interpreter that DOS uses. In most cases, that is COMMAND.COM, the interpreter that comes with DOS.

To increase the environment space, you must add or modify the /E parameter of COMMAND.COM. If a /E parameter already exists, move the cursor over to it and increase the number to the right of the colon. The default environment size is 256 bytes, so change it to 512. If you refer back to the figure showing my CONFIG.SYS file, you can see that I have already fiddled with the environment parameter and changed the amount of space to 1024 bytes. That is certainly more than enough, but I have never taken the time to find out the exact amount I need. Remember to save the changed CONFIG.SYS file. (Press the Alt+F key combination to display the File menu and then choose the Save option.)

The environment size changes take effect the next time you start your machine.

General DOS Problems

Besides specific errors, several general classes of problems affect the performance of DOS. The next few entries talk about the most common problems. Each section contains suggestions and recommendations that can help you resolve the problem.

Slow Hard Drive

One of the key determinants of the speed of your PC is the speed of your hard drive. A slow drive can cripple even the fastest system. Aside from buying a faster drive, you can do a few things to speed up disk access.

You can speed up disk access (and, consequently, overall system speed) by defragmenting your hard disk. A hard disk becomes fragmented when files are added to and deleted from the disk. Although the phrase "defragmenting your hard disk" seems to indicate that something has happened to the disk itself, in reality, it is the files on the disk that become fragmented.

In order to ensure efficient use of the hard disk, DOS breaks up files into smaller chunks and puts these chunks into open spaces on the disk. As you delete files from the disk, they leave various-sized areas where DOS can stick a portion of a file. Files end up in pieces, scattered around the disk. It is much faster to read adjacent sectors of a disk than it is to read pieces of files scattered all over the disk. A defragmenting utility rearranges the files on the disk so that they are contiguous.

The following instructions assume that you have DOS 6.2, which comes with all the utilities necessary for you to defragment your hard disk.

At the DOS prompt, execute the ScanDisk utility by entering the following command:

`C:\DOS\SCANDISK`

ScanDisk checks your hard disk for all sorts of errors. It displays instructions as you go, so you should have no trouble with it. If ScanDisk does turn up any bad sectors on the disk, it gives you the option of saving these bad sectors as files. Don't bother. There is virtually no chance that you will find anything valuable in these files.

After ScanDisk is finished cleaning up your hard disk, it is time to defragment it. DOS 6.2 provides DEFRAG to do this job. At the DOS prompt, enter the following command to activate the program:

`C:\DOS\DEFRAG`

Like the SCANDISK command, DEFRAG is pretty straightforward to use. Simply follow the on-screen prompts and you will get the job done. The only problem with DEFRAG is that it takes a long time to do what it has to do. Defragmenting your hard disk can take anywhere from ten minutes to an hour or more, particularly if you use DoubleSpace (see the "Disk Space Problems" section for more information about DoubleSpace).

DOS 6.2 provides two other utilities that can effectively speed up your hard drive. Which one you use depends on whether your PC has expanded memory (EMS) or extended memory (XMS).

If your PC has EMS but not XMS, you can use Fastopen to speed your disk access. Fastopen is a memory-resident program that decreases the amount of time it takes DOS to open frequently used files. Fastopen can track as many as 99 files, keeping their locations in memory so that DOS can find them faster.

Using Fastopen has the following disadvantages: it uses some of your memory to hold the program and the information for the files; you should not use Fastopen if you use Windows; and you should not run DEFRAG, or any other disk defragmentation program, while Fastopen is loaded. Additionally, if your PC has extended memory, forget Fastopen; SMARTDrive is the program you want.

SMARTDrive is a disk-cache program. It creates a temporary storage area (a cache) in extended memory, which stores data read from the hard disk. It is much faster to get data from the cache than from the hard disk, so using a cache reduces the amount of time your system spends waiting for information from the hard drive.

DOS normally installs SMARTDrive for you. You can see if it is running by entering the following command at the DOS prompt:

`SMARTDRV`

If SMARTDrive is installed, a screen appears similar to the one shown in the following figure.

If SMARTDrive is not installed, you can add it manually to your AUTOEXEC.BAT file. SMARTDrive has a number of options associated with it, so your best bet is to consult your DOS manual and the DOS on-line help system. To get on-line help with SMARTDrive, enter the following command at the DOS prompt:

`HELP SMARTDRIVE`

Out-of-Memory Problems

Out-of-Memory problems are becoming more common all the time. Programs keep getting larger, demanding more and more memory. At the same time, new hardware (such as CD-ROM drives) requires new device drivers, which leaves even less room for your programs. The result: out-of-memory messages and programs that won't run.

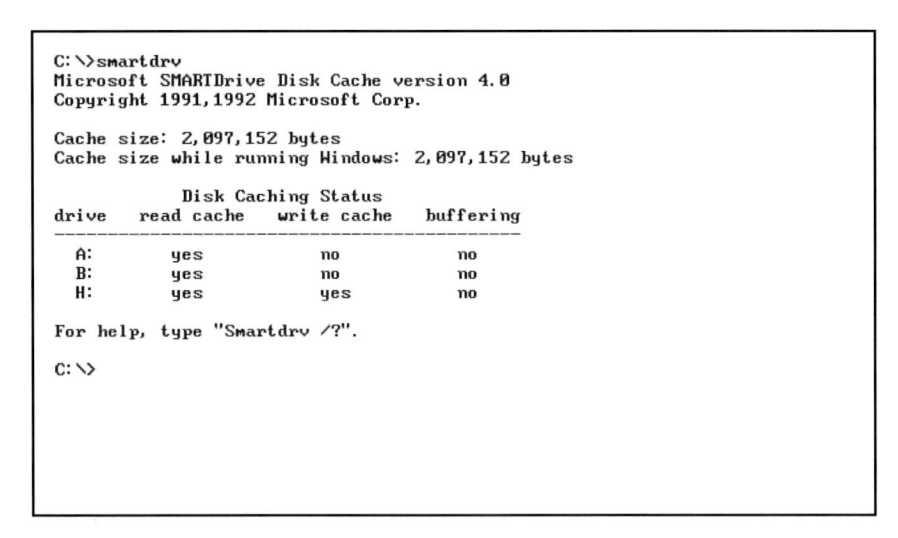

```
C:\>smartdrv
Microsoft SMARTDrive Disk Cache version 4.0
Copyright 1991,1992 Microsoft Corp.

Cache size: 2,097,152 bytes
Cache size while running Windows: 2,097,152 bytes

            Disk Caching Status
drive    read cache    write cache    buffering
---------------------------------------------------
  A:         yes            no            no
  B:         yes            no            no
  H:         yes            yes           no

For help, type "Smartdrv /?".

C:\>
```

▲ *A SMARTDrive status report.*

If your PC has at least an 80286 processor, extended memory, and DOS version 6.0 or greater, you may be able to solve this problem by running DOS in the high-memory area.

The first thing you can do is see if DOS is already running in the high-memory area. At a DOS prompt, enter the following command:

MEM

This command provides all sorts of information about memory usage in your machine. The resulting display looks something like the following figure.

Look at the last line of the report. It says MS-DOS is resident in the high-memory area. If you do not see that line when you execute the MEM command, DOS is not loaded high, and you should be able to free a significant amount of memory by loading it high.

> **Note:** If you want an explanation of terms such as *extended memory* and *high-memory area*, refer back to the "Memory" section of Chapter 2.

To load DOS high, you must modify your CONFIG.SYS file. The first step is to run EDIT, a basic editor that comes with DOS 5.0 and later versions. At the DOS prompt enter the following:

`C:\DOS\EDIT C:\CONFIG.SYS`

This statement activates EDIT and loads your AUTOEXEC.BAT file so that it is ready to modify.

After you load CONFIG.SYS into EDIT, look for a line that says DEVICE=C:\DOS\HIMEM.SYS. This line should be near the top of your CONFIG.SYS file. (In my CONFIG.SYS file presented in an earlier figure, you can see that this is the first line of the file.)

HIMEM.SYS is a program that coordinates the use of extended memory. It prevents two programs from using the same section of memory at the same time. HIMEM.SYS must be activated before DOS or any other program can use extended memory, and it should be on the first line of your CONFIG.SYS file.

If you did not find the line containing HIMEM.SYS, you must add it. Place the cursor on the first character of the first line in your CONFIG.SYS and enter the following command:

`DEVICE=C:\DOS\HIMEM.SYS`

The text previously occupying the first line is pushed to the right as you type, and it is moved to the second line when you press Enter. Do not save or exit yet; you first must add another line.

Now look for a line that says DOS=HIGH. This command loads DOS into the high-memory area. If this command is not in the file, place the cursor on the first character of the line *after* the line that

```
C:\>mem

Memory Type        Total   =   Used   +   Free
-----------------  -------     -------    -------
Conventional        640K        159K       481K
Upper               155K        155K         0K
Reserved            128K        128K         0K
Extended (XMS)    7,269K      6,245K     1,024K
-----------------  -------     -------    -------
Total memory      8,192K      6,687K     1,505K

Total under 1 MB    795K        314K       481K

Largest executable program size        481K  (492,640 bytes)
Largest free upper memory block          0K        (0 bytes)
MS-DOS is resident in the high memory area.

C:\>
```

▲ *A report generated by the MEM command.*

says DEVICE=C:\DOS\HIMEM.SYS and enter the following command:

DOS=HIGH

The text that was on this line moved to the right as you typed and down to the next line when you pressed Enter.

The necessary changes are now complete. Exit EDIT (don't forget to first save the modified CONFIG.SYS) and restart your computer so that the changes go into effect. Use the MEM command to confirm that DOS is now loaded into the high-memory area. You should now be able to run the program or programs that gave you the out-of-memory message.

If you still get out-of-memory messages, you need to run MEMMAKER. MEMMAKER is a program that comes with DOS 6.0 or later. It is designed to increase the amount of conventional memory you have available for running programs. It works by moving device drivers and TSRs out of conventional memory and into the upper-memory area.

I strongly urge you to read the part of the DOS manual that discusses MEMMAKER before you run it. Although the program is not difficult to use, it does a number of things and gives you several options.

After you run MEMMAKER, you should be able to run the programs that gave you the out-of-memory messages.

Disk Space Problems

Running out of disk space is a fact of life. It seems that no matter how large a hard disk you have, it fills up in a matter of months. Software provided on CD-ROM should help lessen the problem because most of the program's files remain on the CD-ROM. Even so, you certainly will fill your hard disk sooner or later.

The obvious solution to this problem is to increase the amount of disk space you have by adding another hard drive to the system. With drive prices down below one dollar per megabyte of storage, adding a larger hard drive to your system is certainly a viable option. As an added bonus, larger hard drives are usually significantly faster than smaller ones.

The next most obvious solution is to delete unnecessary files from your current hard disk. Hard disks tend to fill up with all sorts of odd files that you no longer use. Spending a little time going through the files on your system can pay big dividends in terms of reclaimed disk space. The problem with this approach is that it is often hard to figure out which files you don't need; if you delete the wrong ones, you can disable an application you do use.

You also have a third option to consider when you are running low on disk space. Thanks to some sophisticated software, you can actually increase the apparent size of your existing hard disk. Several companies sell programs that compress and decompress files as you read them from, or write them to, the disk. These disk-compression programs work in the background, totally transparent to the user. The only visible difference is that the hard drive seems to have grown. The exact results depend on the particular files on the disk, but most people seem to get about twice as much storage space as before. Best of all, DOS 6.0 and 6.2 include a disk-compression program—DoubleSpace.

> **Note:** Due to legal problems, Microsoft no longer sells DOS 6.0. Instead, they sell DOS 6.2.1, which does *not* include DoubleSpace or any other disk compression utility. Fortunately, third-party disk compression utilities are available. Stacker, from STAC Electronics, is a superior product. It was STAC that won the patent infringement lawsuit that stopped Microsoft from shipping DoubleSpace.

All you have to do to set up DoubleSpace is get to a DOS prompt (exit DOS Shell or Windows if you are running either of them), and enter the following command:

DBLSPACE

The DoubleSpace Setup routine gives you step-by-step instructions as it runs. You really don't have to do much; DoubleSpace can handle almost everything by itself.

You should realize, however, that DoubleSpace takes quite a long time to reorganize and compress all the files on your hard disk. With a large drive, it can take hours!

DoubleSpace first appeared on the scene with DOS 6.0. Although Microsoft conducted a huge test program, users started reporting problems as soon as the product was released. Microsoft responded by releasing DOS 6.2, which includes an enhanced version of DoubleSpace, as well as ScanDisk, a disk-repair utility.

The new version of DoubleSpace adds a feature called DoubleGuard. DoubleGuard protects the memory that DoubleSpace uses. If another program were to write information into the memory that DoubleSpace was using, you could end up with bad data on your hard disk. DoubleGuard prevents this by halting the computer if a program tries to use the memory used by DoubleSpace.

DOS 6.2 resolved the problems people had with DoubleSpace. You can now safely and easily increase the capacity of your hard disk for the cost of an upgrade to DOS 6.2. The adjacent figure shows the tail end of a directory listing of my root directory, after I ran DoubleSpace.

I created this directory listing by typing the command DIR /C, which lists the compression achieved for each file in the directory, as well as the overall compression ratio for the entire directory. Notice that the compression ratios ranged from 1.0 to 1.0, all the way up to 16.0 to 1.0, with an overall compression ratio for this directory of 2.2 to 1.0. I now have more than double the disk space I had previously!

Common Windows Errors and Problems

Many of the same errors that occur in DOS can also occur in Windows. The advantage when you run Windows is that the error messages are usually easier to understand. For example, when you try to read or write an unformatted disk in DOS, you get a `General failure` message. When you do the same thing in Windows, you get the error message box shown in the figure.

As a result, it's usually easier to recover from common errors in Windows than in DOS. If you see an error message that doesn't make it immediately obvious how to resolve the problem, you should read through the DOS error message section and look for a corresponding error. Follow the directions provided there to resolve the problem.

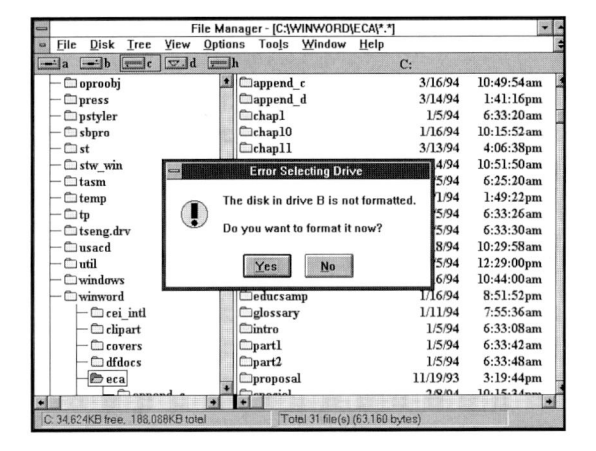

▲ *An error-message box.*

▲ *The reward for using DoubleSpace.*

Mouse Problems

A mouse is virtually indispensable for a Windows user. You can accomplish anything you need to do in Windows using only the keyboard, but even simple tasks are more difficult without the mouse. Anything that interferes with efficient mouse use is therefore a big problem in Windows.

You wouldn't know it from looking at one, but a mouse is a complex device. It contains sensors that detect when you move the mouse or press the buttons. It also contains a processor that translates the signals from the sensors into ones that your PC can understand. Although the processor seldom causes any problems, the mechanical or optical sensors that detect button pushes and mouse movement are sensitive to dust and dirt and can just plain fail. The next section describes various mouse-related problems and provides directions for resolving them.

No Mouse Pointer Appears

This problem most likely is caused by the use of the wrong serial port or an interrupt conflict. Either one of these problems is beyond the scope of this chapter. Check the documentation that came with the mouse and your other hardware, or contact the person who set up your system for you.

Mouse Pointer Won't Move

If the mouse pointer appears on the screen, but won't move when you move the mouse, Windows is probably not configured properly for your mouse. You can resolve this problem by using Windows Setup.

Find the Setup icon. Normally, it is located in the Main program group. The icon is labeled Windows Setup and looks like a PC with a box of disks beside it. Double-click the Windows Setup icon to display the Windows Setup dialog box.

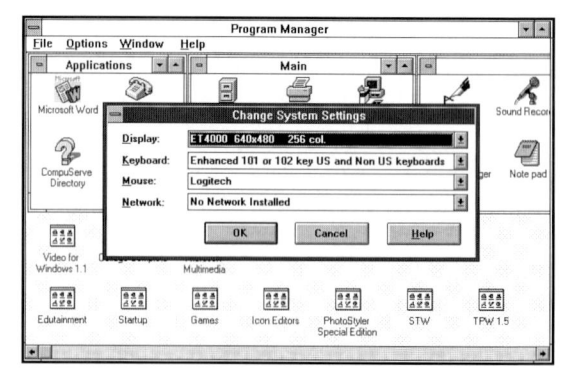

Click Options in the menu bar of the dialog box to open the Options menu. Choose the Change System Settings command and the Change System Settings dialog box appears.

Click the button on the right side of the Mouse text box to open a drop-down list containing the names of a variety of mouse drivers. Click the name that best describes your mouse. The menu closes and you are back to the Change System Settings dialog box. Click the OK button to make the change permanent. Restart Windows so that the change takes effect.

If the mouse pointer still doesn't move, there may be an interrupt conflict between the mouse and another piece of hardware in the system. Consult the documentation that came with the mouse for more information.

Erratic Pointer Movement

Most mice contain a "rubber" ball that rolls around as you move the mouse across the desktop or mouse pad. Sensors within the mouse detect this motion and signal the processor. As with any mechanical device, dirt, dust, animal hair, or just plain wear and tear can prevent proper operation. If the mouse pointer doesn't move smoothly or won't go to certain parts of the screen, it's a good bet that the mouse needs to be cleaned. Consult the mouse manual for instructions on cleaning it. The following instructions came with my Logitech mouse.

To clean the motion detection system, you should first turn off your computer. Next, turn the mouse upside-down. In the center of the mouse, you

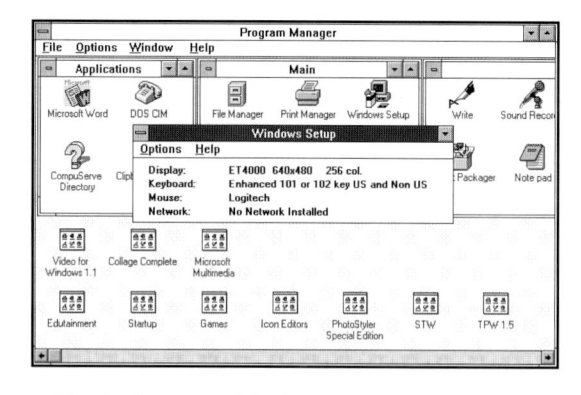

▲ *The Windows Setup dialog box.*

▲ *The Change System Settings dialog box.*

should see a circular cover with a hole in the middle. In that hole, you should see a black "rubber" ball.

Place your fingers in the slots in the cover and rotate it in the direction indicated by the arrows. Remove the cover to expose the ball.

Remove the ball from the housing and then blow any dust out of the housing. Clean the ball with tap water. Dry it with a lint-free cloth and put it back into the housing. Replace the cover and rotate it in the opposite direction of the arrows until it clicks into place.

Mouse Buttons Won't Work

If one or more of the buttons on your mouse stop working, you are out of luck. It is cheaper to replace a mouse than it is to repair it (if you can even find someone who will work on it for you).

Out-of-Memory Problems

Windows is a lot better at taking advantage of your PC's memory than DOS. Most DOS programs are limited to using the base 640K of memory in your machine. They must also share that memory with TSRs, device drivers, and DOS itself. Windows lets programs use virtually all the memory in the machine. If you have 16M of memory in your machine, Windows applications can use it. DOS applications, however, are still stuck with the base 640K.

With its capability to use so much more memory than DOS, you might think that out-of-memory problems would be unheard of in Windows. Wrong! There are two main reasons why it is quite possible to run out of memory in Windows. One reason is that Windows applications tend to be far larger than their DOS counterparts. The other is the nature of Windows.

As you know, the world of Windows is a highly graphical place. Icons, windows, and even text are all graphical images. This fact is what gives Windows much of its power, but it also exacts a heavy price in required computing power and memory usage.

Windows is a multitasking environment, which means that more than one program can run at a time. Having multiple applications active simultaneously, however, requires a great deal of memory.

Windows also does a lot more for programs than DOS does. It serves as the middleman between applications and the computer hardware. It provides many of the interface elements that programs use, such as common dialog boxes. Because it does so much more, Windows uses far more memory than DOS does. Windows will barely run on machines with less than 2M of RAM.

You should now understand why out-of-memory problems can occur in Windows. If you run into one, you have several options to resolve the problem. The most obvious solution is to buy and install more memory. Assuming you are unwilling, or unable, to buy more memory, you can try one or more of the following suggestions:

- Close applications you aren't using. To close an application, click its Control menu box (the box in the upper-left corner of the window) to display the Control menu and then click the Close menu option. For many applications, you can close by simply double-clicking the Control menu box.

- Reduce applications to icons when you don't want to close them but aren't actively using them. Applications often use less memory when they are iconized than when they are windowed. To iconize an application, click its minimize button in the upper-right corner of the window. Alternatively, you can click the control menu box and then click the Minimize menu option.

- If you are using wallpaper on your Windows Desktop, change the wallpaper type to None. Wallpaper uses up memory even though it isn't an application and doesn't actually do anything. If you don't want a blank Desktop, you can use one of the Desktop patterns instead. Patterns use a little more memory than a blank Desktop, but far less than most wallpaper. To change the wallpaper or Desktop pattern, first click the Control Panel program group icon and then click the Desktop icon. The Desktop dialog box appears and enables you to adjust the wallpaper or pattern.

- Make sure that there is enough free space on your hard drive for Windows to create swap files. Swap files are files that Windows uses to temporarily store data and parts of applications it is not using at the moment. You can create more space on your hard disk by deleting unused files. You may be able to delete some of the files that came with Windows. See the "Optimizing Windows" chapter in your Windows manual for a list of files that you can delete.

- Delete TSRs and other memory-resident programs from your AUTOEXEC.BAT and CONFIG.SYS files. All of these programs occupy some memory that could be used by your Windows applications. Most TSRs won't even run while Windows is running, so get rid of them if at all possible.

By using one or more of these techniques, you should be able to free enough memory for your application to run. If it still doesn't have enough memory, and you are running DOS applications from within Windows, you have a few more tricks to try. These tricks involve modifying the PIF files that control your DOS applications under Windows. Consult the "Optimizing Windows" chapter in your Windows manual for more information.

Low System Resources

You can run into memory-related problems even if you have tons of unused memory. Windows keeps track of everything that appears on the screen: every icon, window, bitmap, menu, and font. Regardless of how much memory you have available on your system, Windows allocates two 64K areas of memory (known as *heaps*) to keep track of these system resources.

When too many system resources are in use, one or the other of these heaps gets filled up, and things can get ugly. Windows may prevent you from starting any more applications. The system may slow down drastically. You may see random error messages. As I said, it can get ugly.

If you suspect that you are experiencing a low system resources problem, you can easily confirm your diagnosis. At the Program Manager, click the Help option in the menu bar. When the Help menu opens, click the About command. You should see a dialog box similar to the one shown in the figure.

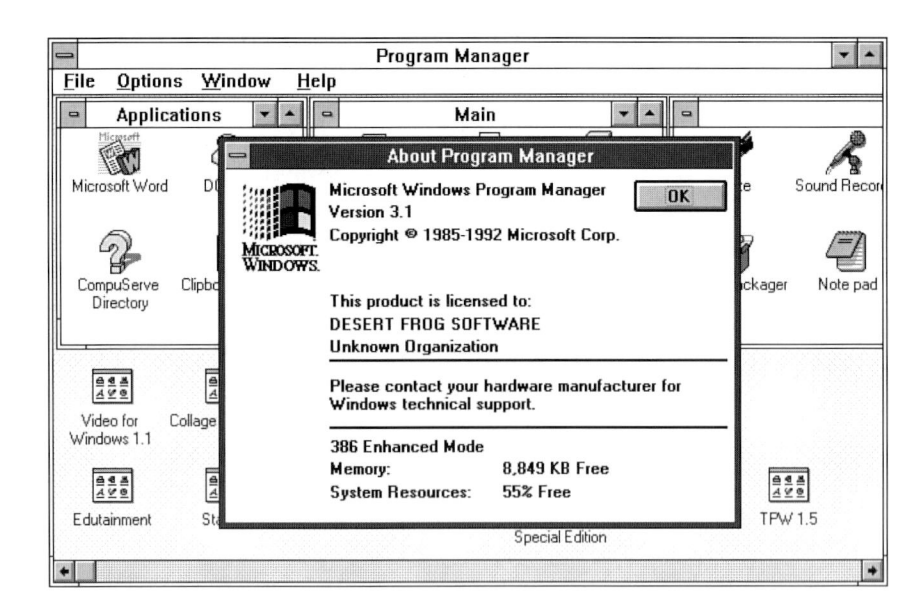

▲ *Use the About box to check system resources.*

The last line in the About Program Manager dialog box shows the percentage of System Resources that are free. Windows determines this number by computing the amount of free space in each of the stacks and then displays the smaller value. If you see a free value of less than 20 percent or so, you are in trouble.

There are a few easy ways to improve your system resource situation. The first method is to remove excess fonts from your font list. Some people end up with hundreds of different fonts on their system, the majority of which they never use. As an experiment, I went through my font list and deleted 15 fonts that I never use. Without doing anything else, I increased my free system resources by 2 percent. The font list is reached from the Fonts icon in the Control Panel program group.

Another way to free up resources is to eliminate your wallpaper. Although it is just a passive backdrop, Windows must keep track of wallpaper so that it can redraw it when necessary.

If you have more than one application running, close all but the one that you are working with. Unfortunately, some applications don't give back all the resources that they take. Others fail to recycle the resources they use and keep grabbing more. This results in a slow decrease in free system resources over time. In some cases, the only solution is to exit Windows and start over. While writing this passage, I was able to increase my free system resources by 2 percent and my free memory by 47K simply by exiting Windows and then restarting it.

Programs Are Very Slow

Very slow is a relative term. Windows applications generally run slower than comparable DOS applications. The overhead of a graphically oriented, multitasking environment makes this inevitable. When I say very slow, I mean unusual slowness or a noticeable decrease in speed from the way the system ran last week or last month.

The primary reason Windows becomes slow is lack of memory. If your hard drive light is on much of the time, you can be sure that this is the case. The solutions to this problem are the same as those in the "Out-of-Memory Problems" section. If you follow the advice in that section, you should see your system speed up again.

You can speed up disk access (and therefore overall Windows speed) by defragmenting your hard disk. See the "Slow Hard Disk" section under "General DOS Problems" earlier in this chapter for instructions on defragmenting your hard disk. Make sure that you exit Windows before starting the process.

Another way to speed up Windows is to use a permanent swap file. Windows uses a swap file as a temporary storage area. It treats this space on the hard disk as if it were normal memory, moving information to and from it as necessary. When Windows treats part of the disk as if it were normal memory, it is said to be using virtual memory.

When you install Windows, it normally creates a temporary swap file. This file exists only when Windows is running and varies in size as necessary. A permanent swap file remains on the hard disk even when Windows is not active.

Right after you finish defragmenting your hard disk is an ideal time to create a permanent swap file. This is the perfect time because a permanent swap file requires contiguous sectors on the disk, and DEFRAG reorganizes the disk to create contiguous files and to free contiguous space.

To create a permanent swap file, start Windows. Double-click the Control Panel icon in the Main program group. Look for an icon labeled 386 Enhanced. The icon itself looks like an integrated circuit chip with the number 386 on it. If this icon is not present, Windows is not running in 386 Enhanced mode, and you cannot create a permanent swap file. If the icon is present, double-click it to display the 386 Enhanced dialog box.

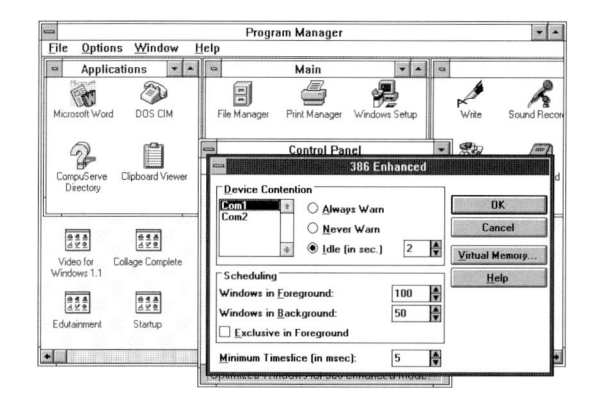

▲ *The 386 Enhanced dialog box.*

You control the swap file through the Virtual Memory dialog box. Click the Virtual Memory... button to display this dialog box.

My system is using a permanent swap file of 5,652K (about 5M). This file is located on the H: drive and Windows can access it 32 bits at a time. If you click the Change button, the dialog box expands and allows you to modify the current settings. The newly expanded box contains a recommendation for new settings and resembles the bottom figure on the next page.

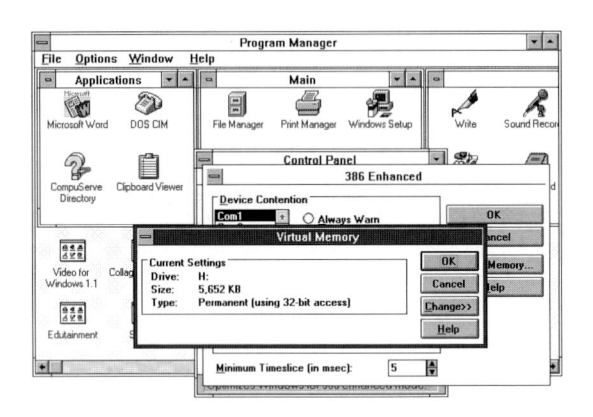

▲ *Current swap file settings in the Virtual Memory dialog box.*

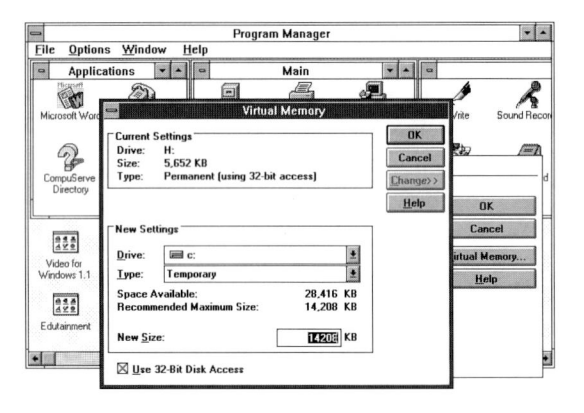

▲ *Changing swap file settings.*

Note: On battery-powered portable computers, 32-bit disk access may be unreliable.

You can click the arrows to the right of the Drive and Type boxes to change those settings. In the Type box, select a Permanent swap file. Windows recommends an optimum size for the file. Normally, you are smart to accept the recommended values.

Look at the Use 32-Bit Disk Access check box near the bottom of this dialog box. If the box and text are dimmed, you cannot use this feature. If they are not dimmed, Windows believes that you can successfully use 32-bit disk access, which is faster than the 16-bit access normally used by hard disk controllers. Click the box to take advantage of the faster disk access.

Click OK when you are satisfied with the changes you have made. Windows gives you a chance to confirm that you want to change the virtual memory settings. If you click the Yes button, you get the opportunity to restart Windows immediately. Any changes you make to the virtual memory settings won't take effect until the next time you start Windows.

If you want Windows to run even faster, there are some more tricks you can try. If you have a lot of memory (say 8M or more), and you only run one or two programs at a time, you can speed Windows up by eliminating the swap file completely.

To eliminate the swap file, follow the instructions in the preceding paragraphs until you reach the expanded Virtual Memory dialog box shown in the figure. Click the button next to the Type drop-down list box and select None. Click the

OK button and follow the directions to restart Windows. You should notice that the system responds somewhat faster.

If you don't run multiple programs simultaneously, you can run Windows in Standard mode instead of 386 Enhanced mode. Standard mode doesn't support multitasking (running two programs simultaneously), so it can do without the overhead required to support multitasking. This makes it run faster.

To run Windows in Standard mode, start the program with a /S command-line switch. So instead of starting Windows by entering **win**, you enter

```
WIN /S
```

You should see a noticeable increase in speed.

If none of these tricks makes Windows run fast enough for you, your choices are buying more memory, which may help somewhat, or buying a faster machine.

Disk Space Problems

Many of the solutions to disk space problems are independent of whether you are running Windows or DOS. A few tricks, however, are Windows-specific. One such trick involves unused Windows files, and the other trick involves Windows swap files.

You may be able to delete some of the files that come with Windows. If you look in the "Optimizing Windows" chapter of your Windows manual, you will find a section on deleting unnecessary files. The specific files you delete depend on how you use Windows, but the manual has a list of all the files you might want to delete.

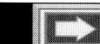

If you really need disk space, you should consider running Windows without any swap files—temporary or permanent. This trick works best if you have 8M or more of memory, and you work with only one program at a time. You can find instructions on how to configure Windows with no swap file in the "Programs Are Very Slow" section of this chapter.

A Program Stops Responding

Sometimes applications just stop responding to keystrokes and mouse clicks. When this happens, you can regain control of your system by pressing the Control, Alt, and Delete keys simultaneously (Ctrl+Alt+Delete). Windows displays a screen that gives you the option of terminating the program that is not responding. Follow the directions in the message.

Summary

With any system as complicated as a PC and its software, it is inevitable that problems will occur. This chapter covered the kinds of problems you may encounter when you are running DOS or Windows. Beyond specific problems that generate obvious errors (usually with their own error messages prominently displayed), it addressed some of the more subtle problems, such as low system resources and insufficient disk space. These problems usually manifest themselves as reduced system performance rather than as an error message. For each problem discussed, specific suggestions were provided for resolving them.

The next chapter also covers troubleshooting. Instead of focusing on the operating system, however, Chapter 15 deals with sound card and CD-ROM problems. These devices bring new capabilities to your PC, while simultaneously creating a new set of problems.

Chapter 15

Troubleshooting CD-ROM Drives and Sound Cards

A sound card and CD-ROM drive are the two pieces of hardware you have to add to a basic PC to get it ready for edutainment use. It would be nice if you could just drop them into your system and be ready to go. Unfortunately, it doesn't usually work that way.

PCs have an "open" design. This open design makes them expandable and enables them to accept new peripheral devices. This expandability is crucial, because sound cards and CD-ROM drives hadn't been invented when the PC was originally introduced.

With hundreds of companies producing PCs, there is no such thing as a standard PC configuration. Every manufacturer does things a little differently. The result is a number of conflicts and problems.

This chapter contains descriptions of, and possible solutions for, problems that arise when you add a sound card or CD-ROM drive to your system. The following topics are discussed in this chapter:

- Troubleshooting a CD-ROM drive
- Troubleshooting a sound card
- Things to check first
- Common error messages
- Other problems

Troubleshooting a CD-ROM Drive

If you install your new CD-ROM drive, and it doesn't work, it is quite natural to get upset. Luckily, however, you can try several things to correct the problem.

Things to Check First

Lots of things can go wrong when you (or the technician) install a CD-ROM drive. Although most manufacturers do their best to ensure that their directions are easy to follow, adding a drive is not a trivial task. Consider that I chose a drive that is known to work well with my sound card (a Creative Labs Omni CD drive with a Creative Labs Sound Blaster Pro sound card), and it still took me a couple of hours to get everything working right. The scary part is that I have a degree in electrical engineering! If you install a CD-ROM drive yourself, expect some sort of problem before everything works right.

If the entire PC locked up when you turned it on, you probably have a hardware conflict. This means that something in your machine is using the same base address, interrupts, or DMA channel as the CD-ROM interface card. Consult the CD-ROM drive manual for instructions on resolving this problem.

From this point on, I assume that you have the drive installed in your machine or connected to it (if it's an external drive). I also assume that you (or the technician) have already installed the software that came with the drive. Presumably, you have done these things and the drive doesn't work.

The first thing to do is to run any diagnostic software or self tests that came with the drive. Check your documentation to see if yours came with any, and run it. Follow any instructions or advice that this generates.

If the self-test doesn't reveal anything, but the CD-ROM drive still doesn't work properly, you can start looking for problems in a systematic manner. The first thing to do is to turn off the power to your PC. Then turn the power back on. Observe the messages that scroll by as the machine powers up. Look for one that is similar to what is shown in the top figure on the following page.

The Microsoft CD-ROM Extensions (MSCDEX) must be loaded in order for your CD-ROM drive to work at all. If you don't see a message containing the text

MSCDEX

when you start your system, you need to check your AUTOEXEC.BAT file.

At the DOS prompt, enter the following command:

TYPE \AUTOEXEC.BAT

```
MSCDEX Version 2.23
Copyright (C) Microsoft Corp. 1986-1993. All rights reserved.
        Drive F: = Driver MSCD001 unit 0
399520 bytes free memory
0      bytes expanded memory
12948  bytes CODE
2112   bytes static DATA
31212  bytes dynamic DATA
46528  bytes used
```

▲ *A typical MSCDEX message.*

```
SET BLASTER=A220 I5 D1 T4
SET SOUND=C:\SBPRO
C:\SBPRO\SBP-SET /M:12 /VOC:12 /CD:12 /FM:12
LH /L:0;1,45504 /S C:\DOS\SMARTDRV.EXE
@ECHO OFF
PROMPT $p$g
PATH C:\VIEWER;c:\;C:\WINWORD;C:\WINDOWS;c:\tp;C:\DOS;C:\MOUSE;C:\CBEDOS;c:\QTW\
bin
SET CBACKUP=C:\CBEDOS
LH /L:1,40064 MOUSE SER 1
rem LOGIMENU
SET TEMP=C:\TEMP
LH /L:1,6384 C:\DOS\doskey
SET LIB=C:\PV
SET INCLUDE=C:\PV
LH /L:1,46544 C:\DOS\MSCDEX.EXE /D:MSCD001 /V /M:15
```

▲ *My AUTOEXEC.BAT file.*

This command displays on-screen the contents of your AUTOEXEC.BAT. My AUTOEXEC.BAT is shown in the bottom figure.

The key here is to look for a line that contains the text MSCDEX.EXE. In my AUTOEXEC.BAT file, this text is in the last line of the file. If this file is not anywhere in your AUTOEXEC.BAT, the Microsoft CD-ROM Extensions are not getting loaded.

If the CD-ROM extensions are not loading, you should consult your CD-ROM drive manual. Follow the instructions for installing the software that came with the drive. Microsoft lets CD-ROM drive manufacturers include the CD-ROM extensions with their products, so your drive's setup software should automatically install it.

If the CD-ROM extensions are loading, you should check your CONFIG.SYS file for the other piece of software required for the CD-ROM drive to function: the CD-ROM device driver. The card manufacturer supplies this piece of software, and it communicates with the actual hardware of your drive.

The device driver is more difficult to check than the CD-ROM extensions. Begin by entering the following command at the DOS prompt:

TYPE \CONFIG.SYS

The next figure shows my CONFIG.SYS file, and your screen should look something like this figure.

```
DEVICE=C:\DOS\HIMEM.SYS
DEVICE=C:\DOS\EMM386.EXE NOEMS
BUFFERS=32,0
FILES=40
dos=UMB
LASTDRIVE=H
FCBS=16,0
DOS=HIGH
DEVICEHIGH /L:1,12048 =C:\DOS\SETVER.EXE
REM Buffers=30,0
STACKS=9,256
SHELL=C:\DOS\COMMAND.COM C:\DOS\ /p /e:1024
DEVICEHIGH /L:1,39488 =C:\DOS\DBLSPACE.SYS /MOVE /DOUBLEGUARD
DEVICEHIGH /L:1,13856 =H:\SBPRO\DRV\SBCD.SYS /D:MSCD001 /P:220
INSTALL=C:\DOS\SHARE.EXE
```

▲ My CONFIG.SYS file.

Look for a line near the end of the file that contains text that reads something like

D:MSCD0001

or otherwise indicates that it is doing something with drive D. In most cases, your CD-ROM drive is drive D.

If you can't tell about the device driver from what you see in your CONFIG.SYS, you can find out if it is loaded by restarting your machine. As the machine powers up, look for a message that mentions a CD-ROM device driver or the name of the manufacturer of your drive. If you don't see it, rerun the setup software that came with the drive; pay particular attention to any instructions on device drivers.

If you have the software installed and the drive still doesn't work, you can try several more things. When you turn on your machine, do the lights on the drive come on? Press the eject button (if the drive has one). Does the drive bay open? If not, the drive may not be getting power. You should then follow the instructions that came with the drive to recheck all the connections. If you have an external CD-ROM drive, make sure that it is plugged in and turned on.

When you are sure that the software is installed and you have power to the drive, you should make sure that the drive itself works. Insert a disc in the drive. Listen. Does it spin the disc when the drive door first closes? Does the Busy light come on? If not, the drive is probably dead. Work through all the hardware installation instructions one more time and confirm that all the connections are made and everything is seated properly. If the drive still fails to respond, package it up and return it to where you bought it.

If the drive seems OK, but you can't access it, make sure that you have inserted a CD-ROM in the drive. They should be inserted so that the mirrored side is facing down. If your drive uses disc caddies, make sure that the disc is inserted properly in the caddy.

Error Messages and What to Do about Them

Some of the problems you encounter with CD-ROM drives generate an error message. If you are reading this section, you probably have one on your screen right now. The following sections list several of the most common error messages and some advice on what to do about them. The exact wording of the error messages may vary.

A *CDR101* Error

This is a general CD-ROM error message. It indicates that something is wrong with your CD-ROM drive, its connections, its interface, or the disc in the drive. You should first remove the disc and take a look at it. Is it an audio CD? An audio CD can cause this message even if your drive can play audio CDs.

If you did not accidentally insert an audio CD, try inserting another CD-ROM. If the drive can read this disc, reinsert the original one and try again.

If the drive still can't read the original disc, try cleaning it. Remove the disc and use a clean, dry cloth to wipe the side without the label. Wipe from the center of the disc to the outer edge. Try inserting it again. If it *still* won't work, you may have received a bad disc. This is extremely rare, but it can happen.

If the drive can't read either disc, you probably have a hardware problem. Check the CD-ROM drive manual for instructions. If no specific instructions are given, go back through the hardware installation. Check each connection, and then make sure that everything is seated properly.

A *CDR103* Error

This message indicates that you have the wrong kind of CD-ROM in the drive. Usually, it means you have a Macintosh CD-ROM rather than one for a PC. Pop out the disc and return it if it isn't a PC CD-ROM.

If the disc is the right format, it may be damaged, or there could be a conflict between the CD-ROM interface card and other cards in your system. Try another disc. If it works, clean the original disc and try it again. If it still doesn't work, return it.

If none of your CD-ROMs work, you most likely have a hardware conflict. Consult the manual that came with the drive.

A *Device not responding* Error

This error indicates that the interface card cannot talk to the CD-ROM drive. The likely cause of this problem is a bad connection between the drive and the interface card. Using the hardware installation instructions as a guide, check the connection, making sure that all the cables are plugged in and the connectors are fully plugged in. If the problem persists, consult your manual for further instructions or call the technical support line for your drive.

An *Incorrect version* Error

This error tells you that you are not using the correct version of the Microsoft CD-ROM Extensions (MSCDEX). The probable cause is the software that came with the CD-ROM drive. The version of MSCDEX that came with the drive is probably too old to work with your version of DOS. The solution is to modify the MSCDEX line in your AUTOEXEC.BAT so that it uses the correct version.

Each new version of DOS comes with a compatible version of MSCDEX. This version is stored in the DOS directory. You must change your AUTOEXEC.BAT to use the correct version of MSCDEX. It is easy to make this change with the EDIT text editor that comes with DOS version 5.0 or later.

At any DOS prompt, change to the root directory by entering the following command:

`CD \`

Then enter

`EDIT AUTOEXEC.BAT`

The next figure shows my AUTOEXEC.BAT loaded into EDIT. Your screen should look something like this figure.

Find the line containing the filename MSCDEX.EXE. Then look at the text just before this filename and see if it says something other than

`C:\DOS\`

If it does, the CD-ROM drive setup program used the wrong version of MSCDEX, and you need to change it.

Place the cursor on the first character of the text that precedes MSCDEX.EXE. If the line contains something like

`C:\DRIVERS\MSCDEX.EXE`

place the cursor on the first C in the string of characters. Tap the delete key to delete the C. The text after the cursor moves to the left and the next character is then under the cursor. Keep deleting until the cursor is over the M in MSCDEX.EXE. Type the following, but do *not* press the Enter key:

`C:\DOS\`

Chapter 15

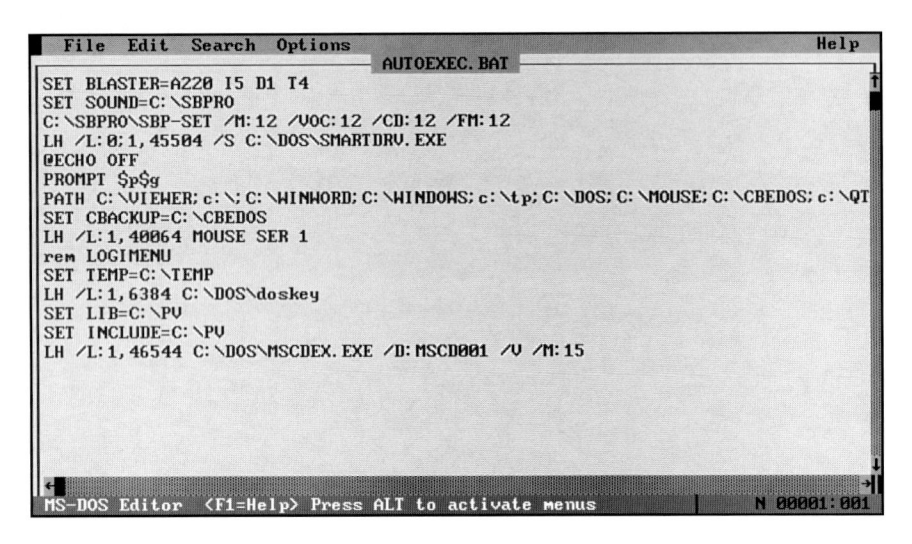

```
 File  Edit  Search  Options                              Help
                         AUTOEXEC.BAT
SET BLASTER=A220 I5 D1 T4
SET SOUND=C:\SBPRO
C:\SBPRO\SBP-SET /M:12 /VOC:12 /CD:12 /FM:12
LH /L:0;1,45504 /S C:\DOS\SMARTDRV.EXE
@ECHO OFF
PROMPT $p$g
PATH C:\VIEWER; c:\; C:\WINWORD; C:\WINDOWS; c:\tp; C:\DOS; C:\MOUSE; C:\CBEDOS; c:\QT
SET CBACKUP=C:\CBEDOS
LH /L:1,40064 MOUSE SER 1
rem LOGIMENU
SET TEMP=C:\TEMP
LH /L:1,6384 C:\DOS\doskey
SET LIB=C:\PV
SET INCLUDE=C:\PV
LH /L:1,46544 C:\DOS\MSCDEX.EXE /D:MSCD001 /V /M:15




MS-DOS Editor  <F1=Help> Press ALT to activate menus      N 00001:001
```

▲ *My AUTOEXEC.BAT file loaded into EDIT.*

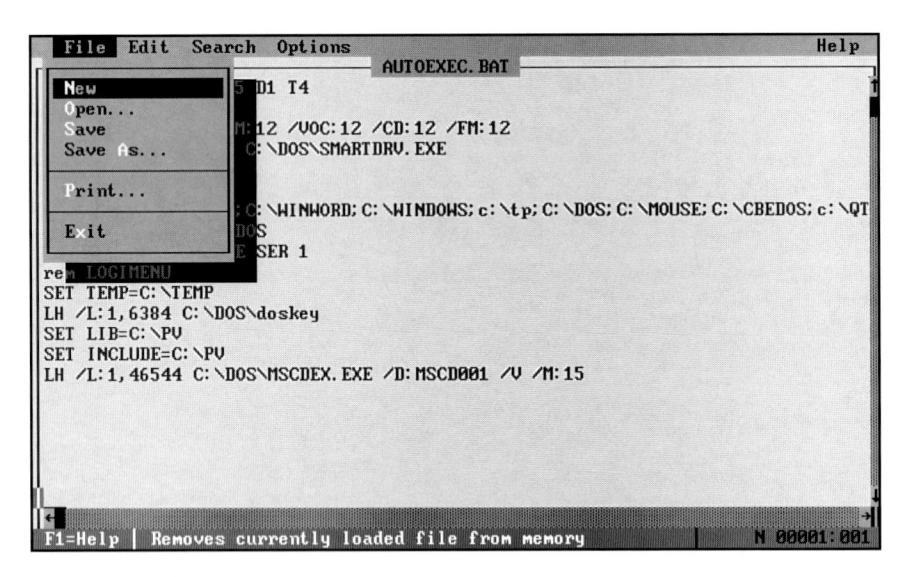

```
 File  Edit  Search  Options                              Help
                         AUTOEXEC.BAT
┌─────────────┐
│ New         │ D1 T4
│ Open...     │
│ Save        │ M:12 /VOC:12 /CD:12 /FM:12
│ Save As...  │ C:\DOS\SMARTDRV.EXE
│             │
│ Print...    │
│             │ C:\WINWORD; C:\WINDOWS; c:\tp; C:\DOS; C:\MOUSE; C:\CBEDOS; c:\QT
│ Exit        │ DOS
│             │ SER 1
└─────────────┘
re  LOGIMENU
SET TEMP=C:\TEMP
LH /L:1,6384 C:\DOS\doskey
SET LIB=C:\PV
SET INCLUDE=C:\PV
LH /L:1,46544 C:\DOS\MSCDEX.EXE /D:MSCD001 /V /M:15



F1=Help │ Removes currently loaded file from memory       N 00001:001
```

▲ *The EDIT File menu.*

The line should now read

`C:\DOS\MSCDEX.EXE`

Other text may appear before and after this string of characters, but you can ignore it.

Now press the Alt key. While holding down the Alt key, press the *F* key. Pressing these two keys together is known as pressing Alt+F. Now release both keys. If you did this correctly, you should now see the EDIT File menu.

When the File menu appears, press the *x* key, which is the hot key (shortcut) for the Exit command. EDIT automatically offers you the chance to save your work if you have made any changes to your AUTOEXEC.BAT file. Restart your computer to make this change take effect and to eliminate the error message.

An *Invalid drive specification* Error

This message appears when MSCDEX doesn't load properly. This message appears for three possible reasons. The first possibility is that MSCDEX didn't get loaded at all. This can happen if you use a menu (shell) program, or if you load Windows through your AUTOEXEC.BAT file. You can check for this by listing your AUTOEXEC.BAT file with the following command:

`TYPE \AUTOEXEC.BAT`

Make sure that the line containing MSCDEX.EXE comes *before* the command that starts your menu program or Windows. If it doesn't, the following instructions tell you how to edit your AUTOEXEC.BAT file.

At any DOS prompt, change to the root directory by entering the following command:

CD \

Then enter

EDIT AUTOEXEC.BAT

Find the line containing MSCDEX.EXE. If it does not come before the command that starts Windows or your menu program, you must move it.

To move the line, place the cursor on the first character of the line that activates Windows or your menu program (this should be very near the end of the AUTOEXEC.BAT file). Type the line that contains MSCDEX.EXE. Type it exactly as it appears and then press Enter. You now have two copies of the line containing MSCDEX.EXE: one before the line that starts Windows or your menu program and one after.

When you are sure that the lines are identical, move the cursor to the beginning of the original line containing MSCDEX.EXE. Tap the Delete key repeatedly until the line is entirely deleted. You should now have only one line that mentions MSCDEX.EXE, and it should be right before the line that activates Windows or your menu program.

Now press Alt+F to access the EDIT File menu. When the File menu appears, press x to select the Exit command. EDIT automatically offers you the chance to save your work if you have made any changes to your AUTOEXEC.BAT file. Restart your computer to make this change take effect and to eliminate the error message.

Another reason for the Invalid drive specification error may be that the CD-ROM device driver did not load properly. If the device driver didn't load, it can't define the drive name that the MSCDEX uses to talk to the drive. You can check for this problem by watching for the messages that appear when you start your system. If you don't see a message that talks about a CD-ROM device driver, this is probably the problem. Rerunning the setup program that came with your drive should resolve this problem. If you still don't see the message, display your CONFIG.SYS file on the screen by entering the following command

TYPE \CONFIG.SYS

and then call the technical support line for your CD-ROM drive.

A final possibility is that something is wrong with the MSCDEX command in your AUTOEXEC.BAT file. If the preceding two possibilities don't account for the problem, this may be the culprit. I can't give you much advice here; the setup program that came with your drive should be able to add this line correctly. The best you can do at this point is pull out the drive manual and check the DOS HELP for MSCDEX. To display the DOS HELP, enter the following command at the DOS prompt:

HELP MSCDEX

The figure shows the first screen of help for MSCDEX.

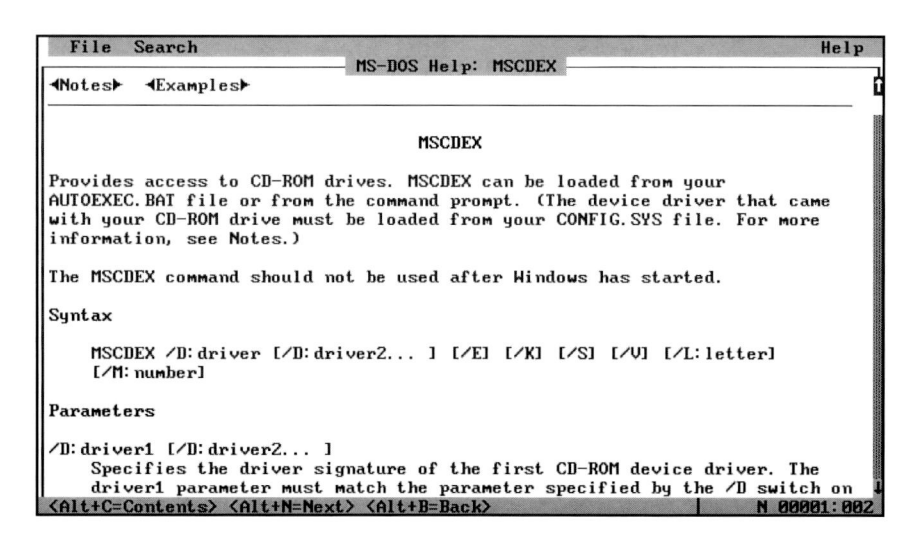

▲ *DOS HELP for MSCDEX.*

Between these two references, and with any luck, you will be able to figure out the problem. If not, it is time to call the technical support line for your drive.

An *Out of environment space* Error

This kind of error may appear the first time you turn on your system *after* you install the CD-ROM drive. The environment is an area of memory that is available to all programs. Information can be stored there when the system starts. The setup program may modify your system to add some more information to this area. If it adds too much, you will see this message.

You have to modify your CONFIG.SYS file to resolve this problem. The CONFIG.SYS file should contain a line with some text similar to

```
SHELL=C:\DOS\COMMAND.COM
```

The SHELL command tells DOS what command interpreter to use, and it sets various parameters for that command interpreter.

The first part of the SHELL line usually is followed by some additional hieroglyphics. Look for some text that begins with /e: or /E:. This sets the size of the environment area. If you look at the twelfth line in my CONFIG.SYS file (refer back to the earlier figure in this chapter), you can see that my system uses /e:1024. This text indicates that my system has 1024 bytes set aside for the environment space. If your CONFIG.SYS shows /e:256, change it to /e:512. If it already has /e:512, change it to /e:1024. You shouldn't have to go beyond 1024.

If your SHELL line doesn't include any /e or /E option, add **/E:512** to the end of the line. You can use the EDIT text editor to do this. To load your CONFIG.SYS file into the editor, enter the following command:

```
EDIT \CONFIG.SYS
```

Then modify the line and save it using the following instructions. Remember, you must restart your computer for the changes to take effect.

Find the line containing the text SHELL. Place the cursor at the end of the line and then type

```
/E:512
```

Now press Alt+F to access the EDIT File menu. When the File menu appears, press x to select the Exit command. EDIT automatically offers you the chance to save your work. Save the file and then restart your machine.

Other Problems

This is where you should turn if your drive "sort of" works. Perhaps your system reads the disc, but you don't hear any sound when you should. Or maybe Windows refuses to acknowledge your drive. Whatever the problem, if it doesn't fit anywhere else, look here before you call the tech support line.

No Sound

If your drive can read the CD-ROM, but you don't hear any sound when you think you should, you can check a couple of things. First, try another disc to ensure that there really is a problem with the sound. Next, make sure that your speakers are plugged in and turned on and the volume is turned up. If the sound card has a volume control, turn that up as well. If you still don't hear any sound, try the following suggestions.

If your drive has a headphone jack, plug a set of headphones into the jack and listen. Don't forget to turn up the volume control on the drive (assuming that there is one). If you still don't hear anything, the audio connection between the drive and the interface card may be disconnected or improperly connected. Check the connection, using the hardware installation instructions as a guide.

If you do hear something when the headphones are plugged in to the drive, the connection between the CD-ROM system and the sound card is probably at fault. Check the connection, using the hardware installation instructions as a guide.

No Sound in Windows

If your drive plays sounds fine when you are in DOS but is silent in Windows, you probably need to install the MCI (Multimedia Control Interface) CD audio driver. The following instructions can guide you through the process.

Open the Drivers dialog box by choosing the Drivers icon in the Control Panel window. Choose the Add button to open the Add dialog box.

Troubleshooting CD-ROM Drives and Sound Cards

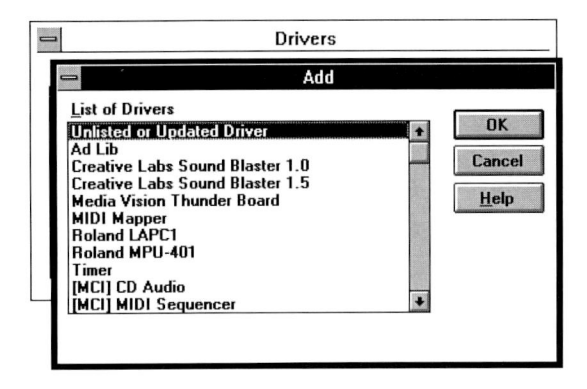

▲ *The Add dialog box.*

Look for the [MCI] CD Audio driver in the list. Select it and click the OK button. The Install Driver dialog box appears.

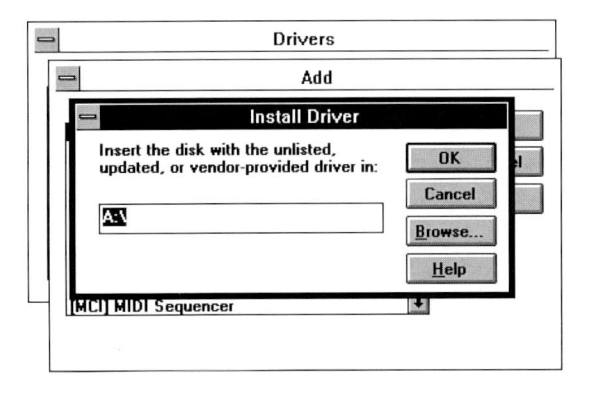

▲ *The Install Driver dialog box.*

Normally, this driver is found in the WINDOWS\SYSTEM directory, so in the text box enter

`C:\WINDOWS\SYSTEM`

When you press the Enter key, you are returned to the Add dialog box.

You must restart Windows to activate the new driver. A dialog box may appear, asking if you want to restart now. If it does not, exit Windows and restart it.

Troubleshooting a Sound Card

Installing a sound card, or any other peripheral, in a PC can lead to all sorts of problems. The following sections give you some options to try.

Things to Check First

This section assumes that you have installed the sound card and have run any setup software that came with the card. If you installed the card, and the system locks up when you turn it back on, you have a hardware conflict. Consult the documentation that came with the card to find the solution to this problem.

Now you have installed the sound card and run the setup program, but no sound comes out. The first thing to check is the speakers. Make sure that the speakers are plugged in (if self-powered), turned on, and connected to the sound card's audio output. If the speakers have a volume control, turn that up to mid-range. If the sound card has a volume control, turn that up to mid-range as well. Try running the test program that came with the card.

If you still have no sound, you need to open your machine and check the installation of the sound card. (Make sure that you turn off your PC and unplug it before you open the case or disconnect any cables!) Using the hardware installation instructions as a guide, make sure that the card is installed properly. Then restart the machine, rerun all the setup software, and try the test program again.

Other Problems

The steps just outlined won't resolve every problem. This section covers several irritating problems that can occur after you have the card essentially working. Check here before you call the manufacturer's technical support line.

An *Out of environment space* Error

This kind of error sometimes appears after you install the sound card. The environment is an area of memory that is available to all programs. Information can be stored there when the system starts. The setup program may modify your system to add some more information to this area. If it adds too much, you will see this message.

You have to modify your CONFIG.SYS file to resolve this problem. The CONFIG.SYS file should contain a line with some text similar to the following:

`SHELL=C:\DOS\COMMAND.COM`

The SHELL command tells DOS what command interpreter to use, and it sets various parameters for that command interpreter.

The first part of the SHELL line usually is followed by some additional hieroglyphics. Look for some text that begins with /e: or /E:. This sets the size of the environment area. If your CONFIG.SYS shows /e:256, change it to /e:512. If it already has /e:512, change it to /e:1024. You shouldn't have to go beyond 1024.

If your SHELL line doesn't include any /e or /E option, add /E:512 to the end of the line. You can use the EDIT text editor to do this. To load your CONFIG.SYS file into the editor, enter the following command:

`EDIT \CONFIG.SYS`

Then modify the line and save it using the following instructions. Remember, you must restart your computer for the changes to take effect.

Find the line containing the text SHELL. Place the cursor at the end of the line and then type

`/E:512`

Now press Alt+F to access the EDIT File menu. When the File menu appears, press x to select the Exit command. EDIT automatically offers you the chance to save your work. Save the file and then restart your machine.

Background Noise

Computers are full of electrical interference. This interference (noise) can affect the quality of sound from your sound card. The biggest noisemaker inside your PC is probably the power supply. Power supply noise adds a low-frequency hum or buzz to your sound card's output.

There isn't much you can do to reduce power supply noise, but you can try one thing if you use powered speakers. Turn down the volume control on the sound card, and turn up the volume on the speakers. This sometimes reduces the level of the noise.

No Sound in Windows

If your sound card works fine in DOS, but you don't hear any sounds with Windows applications, the Windows sound driver (or drivers) are probably not installed. Rerun the sound card setup program.

If you still don't hear any sounds in Windows, you can install the appropriate sound drivers yourself. The following instructions guide you through making this change.

Open the Drivers dialog box by choosing the Drivers icon in the Control Panel window. Choose the Add button to open the Add dialog box.

Look for one or more drivers in the list that contain the name of your sound card. Select the first one and click the OK button. The Install Driver dialog box appears.

Refer to the manual that came with your sound card to find out where the drivers were installed on your hard disk.

In the text box of the Install Driver dialog box, enter the name of the directory that was specified in your sound card manual. When you press Enter, you are returned to the Add dialog box.

Repeat these steps until you have installed all the drivers that have the name of your sound card; then restart Windows to activate the drivers. A dialog box may appear, asking if you want to restart now. If it does not, exit Windows and restart it.

Note: Rather than looking in the manual to find out where the drivers were installed on your hard disk, you can use the Browse dialog box to find them yourself.

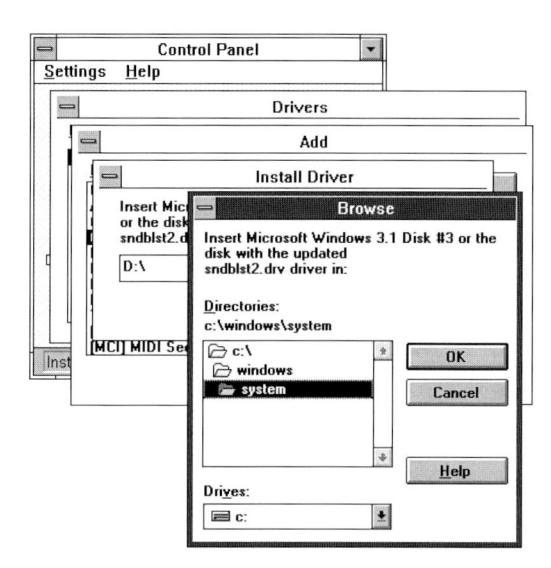

▲ *The Browse dialog box for adding drivers.*

This Browse dialog box has two interesting features. One is the lack of files to choose from. Windows knows what program it is looking for; it just doesn't know where to find it. The dialog box lets you specify the directory that the file is in.

The other interesting thing about this dialog box is that it suggests using one of the Windows installation disks as the source for the file. Windows comes with drivers for many popular sound cards. Normally, you want to use the driver that came with the sound card rather than the one that came with Windows. The one exception is if you have problems with the driver that came with the card. If the driver that came with your card gives you problems, try using the driver that came with Windows. It just might work.

Summary

A sound card and a CD-ROM drive are necessary if you want to get the most out of edutainment software. Unfortunately, adding either of these devices invites problems. This chapter covered many of the problems you are likely to encounter and suggested possible solutions for them.

This chapter ends Part III of this book. The goal of this part was to help you to upgrade your PC to make it a powerful edutainment system. I hope you found this information useful, if not exactly fun and exciting.

Now turn to Part IV to find out some of the exciting possibilities for the future of edutainment.

EDUTAINMENT *in the* FUTURE

Part IV

Part IV is the final part of this book, and it differs significantly from the previous three parts. Part I helped you to get ready to explore edutainment. It provided background information on the subject of edutainment and helped you understand the fundamental components of your PC. This information was beneficial when you moved on to Part II, where you learned about the edutainment products currently available. You were also able to carry this basic information along as you turned to Part III, where you learned about upgrading your system so that you could run all those exciting edutainment programs.

Part IV looks to the future of edutainment. The computer industry as a whole is marked by rapid, often chaotic change and growth, and the edutainment portion of the industry is not much different. Rapid change is certain, and it is driven primarily by the development and adoption of new technology.

This part of the book is divided into two chapters and is designed to give you an idea of what lies ahead for edutainment. Chapter 16 describes the current trends and where they are taking us. Chapter 17 lets the people who create, publish, and distribute the products tell us where they think things are headed and how their companies fit into the big picture.

Chapter 16, "Trends"

One of the things you can say about the edutainment industry is that it is changing rapidly. This change involves more than just new products and increasing sales. The very technologies are changing and evolving. Whole new technologies are becoming part of the mainstream, with once-exotic features such as sound cards and CD-ROM drives now viewed as necessities.

This chapter takes a look at the future of the edutainment industry. I describe some of the trends that are in place, and I try to predict where they are leading and what their impact will be on the future of edutainment.

Chapter 17, "Interviews"

In this chapter, industry insiders (executives, company founders, and authors) give their views on the future of edutainment. These industry leaders will be the ones creating the new edutainment products, so their comments give us valuable insights into the future of this important industry.

Chapter 16

Trends *in the* Future

The computer industry is characterized by rapid, often unpredictable change. Such changes have a direct impact on the edutainment portion of the industry, suddenly making new features available or driving everything in a new direction. Nevertheless, some things are fairly predictable, and trends are visible.

Some trends, such as the acceptance of sound cards and CD-ROM drives, or the transition to Windows, are virtually irreversible. Others, such as the ever-increasing power of new generations of microprocessors, depend on continuing technological advances.

This chapter examines the trends that will shape the future of the edutainment industry. It describes the trends that I believe will have the most impact and contains my predictions of where these trends are leading. The following three principal types of trends are discussed in this chapter:

- Hardware trends
- Software trends
- Other trends

Hardware

Advancing hardware capabilities are the primary driver for the PC edutainment market. Graphically oriented software was impractical until video cards with graphics capabilities became available. Programs with quality sound effects and music couldn't arrive until sound cards did. Huge audio, video, and data files were impractical until CD-ROMs became available to store these files. Finally, modern edutainment products that take advantage of all these capabilities couldn't be developed until PCs were smart enough, fast enough, and equipped with enough storage capacity to handle all of these elements.

Because available PC hardware is the base on which edutainment products are built, looking at the trends in hardware can give you an idea of what will be possible in software. Fortunately, all the trends in computer hardware are positive. The technology is advancing at an incredible rate. Processing power, memory capacity, and hard disk capacity are all increasing rapidly and, in general, are doubling every few years. Even as their power, speed, and capacities skyrocket, the devices have become less expensive. Innovations, such as graphics accelerators and local-bus architectures, have elevated memory and video systems to entirely new levels of performance. In short, the future of PC hardware looks bright. The next few pages look at the various elements of PC hardware and try to show where the trends are leading.

Keeping Up with the Trends

The information gathered here comes from a wide variety of sources. The best way to keep up with trends in PC hardware, and in edutainment in general, is to read one or more of the general-interest computer magazines. Although it is focused mainly on business applications for computers, I find *PC Magazine* to be useful for tracking the latest hardware trends. *HomePC*, which premiered in June, and *FamilyPC*, which had a sneak preview in the June/July issue of *FamilyFun* magazine, both look like good sources of information on home PCs and edutainment.

Processing Power

The power of a microprocessor is determined by a number of characteristics. One such characteristic is the speed of the processor. All other things being equal, a faster processor gets more work done in a given amount of time than a slower processor.

If speed were the only variable, it would be easy to determine which microprocessor is the most powerful. But speed is only one element in the equation. Even more important than raw speed is the amount of data the processor works with at one time. This amount has been increasing steadily, which has had the effect of amplifying speed increases.

Finally, a significant amount of the power of newer microprocessors comes from new capabilities. With the addition of new ways to access memory and new modes of operation, newer processors have become more powerful in fundamentally different ways. In the following sections, you find out more about each of the characteristics that determines the power of a microprocessor.

Processor Speed

The speed of microprocessors has increased dramatically over the years. One commonly mentioned number is the *clock speed*, which is the fundamental unit of time in a microprocessor. Early microprocessors took multiple clock cycles to execute each operation. State-of-the-art processors, such as the Pentium, have sophisticated designs that enable them to complete more than one instruction per clock cycle.

The first IBM PCs used an Intel 8088 microprocessor, which had a clock speed of 4.77 MHz. Because an 8088 takes an average of 12 clock cycles per instruction, a PC using this processor could execute something under 400,000 instructions per second. The Pentium, Intel's latest PC microprocessor, has a clock speed of 60 MHz (or more) and averages almost two instructions per clock cycle, for a total of more than 110 million instructions per second (MIPS).

Intel's next-generation processor, code-named P6, is due to arrive in 1995 and will execute at about 250 MIPS! The P7 is already in the works, with a planned release date of 1997. It's hard to imagine the MIPS level at which the P7 will run.

If you study the preceding graph, the trend in microprocessor speed is clear: each new generation is more than twice as fast as its predecessor. The design cycle has gotten shorter, too. The Pentium arrived four years after the 486, the P6 will arrive two years after the Pentium, and the P7 two years after that.

Bus Width

At the same time microprocessors have increased the number of instructions per second they can execute, they have also increased the amount of data they can handle in each of those instructions. The amount of data that a processor can handle at one time is determined by the width of the microprocessor's data bus. The 8088 processor in the first IBM PCs handled 8 bits of data at a time. The Pentium and P6 processors handle 64 bits of data at a time—an eight-fold increase in power for any given speed.

The width of the microprocessor's address bus determines how much memory it can address. Since the 386, new processors have had 32-bit address buses, enabling them to address a few gigabytes (billions of bytes) of memory. Because this is hundreds of times more memory than PCs currently use, and because it would cost several tens of thousands of dollars to add that much memory to a machine, it is unlikely that the address bus width will change from 32 bits anytime soon. Table 16.1 provides an overview of the bus widths for the various processors.

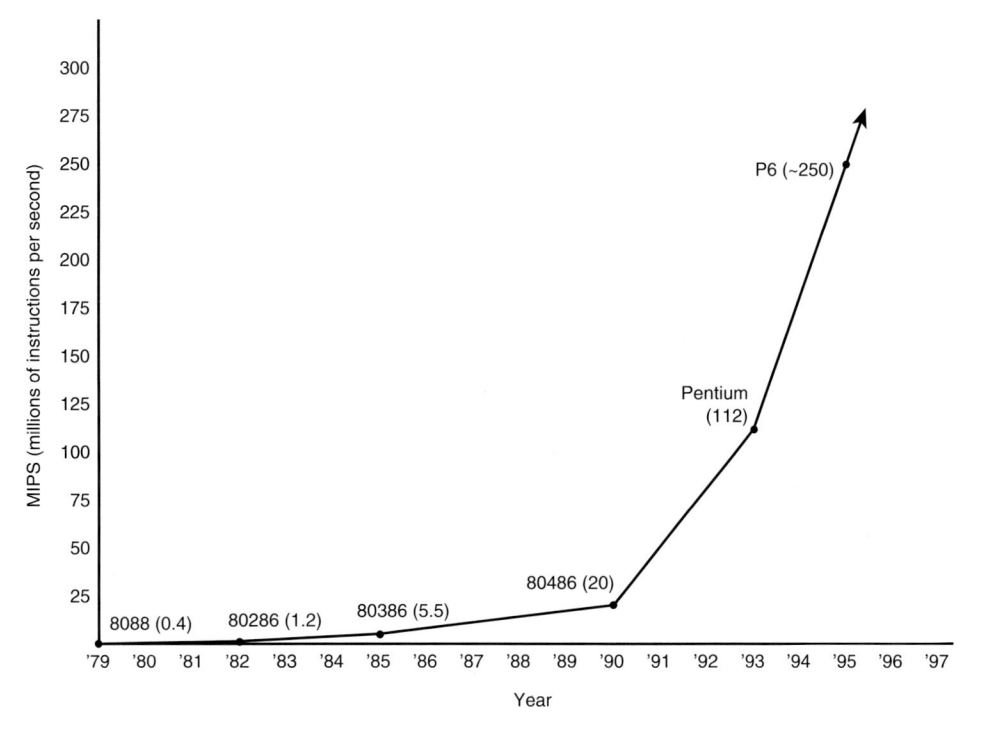

▲ *Number of MIPS for successive generations of PC microprocessors.*

Table 16.1. Microprocessor bus widths.

Processor	Data Bus Width	Address Bus Width
8088	8-bit	16-bit
80286	16-bit	24-bit
80386	32-bit	32-bit
80486	32-bit	32-bit
Pentium	64-bit	32-bit
P6	64-bit?	32-bit?
P7	64-bit?	32-bit?

It appears that data buses will remain at a width of 64 bits for at least the next five or six years.

New Capabilities

Besides becoming faster and capable of handling more data at once, successive generations of Intel microprocessors have gained entirely new capabilities. These capabilities increase the power of the new chips in fundamental ways. Some of these improvements include the development of protected mode in the 80286, multitasking in the 80386, and the built-in floating-point math unit (math coprocessor) of the 80486. The Pentium and P6 don't introduce any new capabilities; they are "merely" much faster and more capable than earlier processors.

Although not much is known about the P7 at this point, I understand that it may have some new capabilities. Foremost of those will be hardware support for digital video playback. If this is true, it could make PCs equipped with P7 processors the ideal edutainment machines.

Processing Power Summary

In the short term (prior to 1997 when the P7 arrives), the trend is speed. Although processor speeds can't keep increasing indefinitely, they don't show any signs of being near their limits yet. Already some 486s and Pentiums are running at around 100 MHz. Expect these numbers to climb somewhat more between now and when the P6 arrives in 1995.

The other components of increasing processor power—bus widths—are likely to remain where they are (64 bits for data, 32 bits for addresses) for a while. Any major new capabilities will probably appear in the P7.

Memory

Until recently, each new generation of microprocessor could address more memory than the previous generation. An 8088 could address 1M of memory. By the 486, the maximum amount of memory had reached 4G (or 4 billion bytes). The Pentium is also limited to 4G, and it seems likely that the P6 and P7 will be, as well. At the risk of sounding naive 10 or 20 years from now, I believe that 4G of memory will be more than enough for quite a long time.

Another issue concerning memory, however, is the amount of memory a PC comes equipped with. This number has been increasing and will likely continue to do so with each new processor. As each generation of processor comes along, its increased power enables developers to create more sophisticated applications.

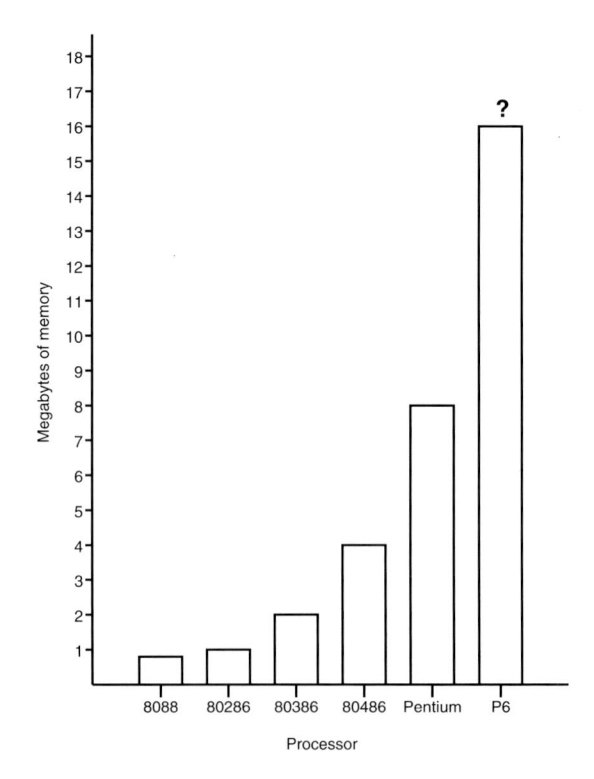

▲ *Typical installed memory for successive generations of PCs.*

Think about the kinds of programs that run on a machine with an 8088. Usually, they are relatively simple, text-based applications. Now think about the kinds of applications that require a 386 or 486 processor. Usually, they are graphical, with tons of features and capabilities far beyond those of earlier programs. All of this requires more memory.

The preceding graph shows the amount of memory typically installed on systems using each generation of Intel processor. As you can see, since the 286, each new generation of PC has about twice as much memory as the generation before. With the advances in memory chip design and the appearance of memory-intensive applications and operating systems, it is likely that this trend will continue.

Hard Disk Drives

Hard drive technology is another element of PCs that is advancing rapidly. The drives continue to get smaller and faster, while costing less and holding more information. Disk drive storage capacity has doubled in less than two years, and manufacturers are working on sophisticated new techniques to keep the growth trend alive.

Drive access time will continue to decline, and more drives will come with built-in caches that speed the average access time even more. Competition between the IDS and SCSI interfaces will continue, which will result in improved features. All in all, expect to be able to get more drive for less money every year.

Video Cards

It's easy to see the trend in video cards: Display more pixels, with more colors, in less time. More pixels are necessary because users are moving towards 1024 x 768 displays. More colors are required because users want to be able to use high-color (16 bits of color per pixel) and true-color (24 bits of color per pixel) modes. All of this has to happen in less time because the new standard for refresh rates is 72 Hz, which produces flicker-free displays.

To meet these goals, manufacturers are adding more memory to their video cards and implementing new ways to achieve higher speeds. Local bus video is one such method. By creating a wide, high-speed path to the video card, the processor can transfer information to the card at much higher speeds than it can over the standard system bus. A local bus typically runs at around 33 MHz, which is about four times the speed of the system bus. While the system bus transfers data across the bus 16 bits at a time, local bus designs can transfer 32, or even 64 bits at a time. A local bus system can move data at a maximum rate of 100M to 300M per second, while an old-style (Industry Standard Architecture, or ISA) bus can do so at a maximum rate of 8M per second.

Graphics accelerator cards speed up your computer system by performing some of the work that the processor would otherwise have to do. When installed with the appropriate video driver, an accelerator card can directly respond to many of the video commands that Windows issues. Because a graphics accelerator card is designed specifically and exclusively for performing certain Windows video operations, it is much faster at performing these operations than the main microprocessor in the PC.

The newest trend in graphics accelerator cards is a 64-bit architecture. Most current cards operate on 32 bits of data at a time. Manufacturers have just begun shipping cards that can operate on 64 bits of data at once. All else being equal, this architecture should nearly double the speed of the newer cards.

Video Card Summary

The trend in video cards is towards a 64-bit graphics accelerator with at least 2M of RAM. This card will be able to display at least 1024 x 768 pixels, in full 24-bit color, while maintaining a 72 Hz refresh rate. Such a card will meet the needs of even hard-core users—and they may be the only ones willing to pay the high price for such a card.

If the primary use for your PC is edutainment, or if you don't run the kinds of applications that require super graphics performance, you can ignore the high-end video cards. Their only impact on you will be the way they drive down the price of lesser cards. A local bus card (if your machine supports it) that can display at least one 24-bit mode and supports 640 x 480 at 256 colors should adequately meet your needs for the next several years. Edutainment products are unlikely to require more than a 640 x 480, 256-color display any time soon.

Sound Capabilities

A sound card is another device that is quickly becoming a necessity, particularly for edutainment systems. The industry is rapidly moving from 8-bit to 16-bit hardware, which theoretically is capable of producing sounds with the quality of an audio CD player.

For 8-bit cards, the standard is Sound Blaster compatibility. For 16-bit cards, no such standard exists. Creative Labs, the creator of the Sound Blaster, is pushing for its Sound Blaster 16 card to become the new standard. At the same time, companies such as Roland and Media Vision are pushing their own standards. Consequently, no clear leader has emerged, and no real trend has developed. Indeed, many, if not most, developers are still designing their products for Sound Blaster compatibility and ignoring 16-bit sound altogether.

CD-ROM

CD-ROM drives are quickly moving from the status of a neat toy, through that of a useful addition, and into the status of a necessity. Soon, virtually all PCs will come with a CD-ROM drive as standard equipment. These drives will be at least double-speed, with triple- and quad-speed models available for those willing to pay for them.

As the technology advances, expect the speed to increase but not the storage capacity. Because CD-ROMs are distribution media and must run in drives from a variety of manufacturers, you are unlikely to see the kind of incremental storage capacity increases that you see in hard drives. The successor to the CD-ROM probably will have to accommodate three to four times the storage capacity of a CD-ROM before people will spend the money to switch over. That most likely won't happen in the next several years, but the way technology is advancing, you never know.

The future interface between the PC and the CD-ROM drive is still somewhat unsettled. SCSI-2 looks like the interface of choice right now, but a new design, similar to the IDE interfaces used on many hard drives, has just come on the scene. The only clear trend here is that proprietary interfaces are on the way out.

Edutainment-Ready Machines

Computer system manufacturers and distributors have begun to ship systems that are MPC-compatible right out of the box. Although not billed as such, any MPC-compatible system is basically an edutainment-ready machine. Expect to see more and more machines configured this way, particularly in consumer retail channels.

Software

Although hardware is the base upon which edutainment software is built, the software is what makes the hardware more than an expensive paperweight. To get the most out of a computer system, the hardware and software must advance together. The best edutainment programs take advantage of the multimedia capabilities of today's hardware to provide engaging, stimulating learning experiences.

The following sections look at the major trends in edutainment software. Taken together, they indicate that the future will bring a variety of ever-more-powerful and engaging products. You just have to make sure that your hardware has enough horsepower to run them.

The Move to Windows

As you learned in Chapter 12, "Edutainment and Windows," the entire software industry is moving to Windows for a number of reasons. These reasons are as valid for edutainment as for any other type of software. Well before the turn of the century, I expect that nearly all new PC edutainment products will be designed to run under Windows. If you intend to keep up with new developments in edutainment, be sure that your next PC is at least MPC-2 compatible, and plan to learn how to use Windows.

Larger, More Power-Hungry Products

The introduction of larger and more power-hungry products is one of the strongest trends in software today, and edutainment software is not immune. As developers add features to programs, they naturally grow larger. Now that products are multimedia extravaganzas, this growth has surged. Color graphics images take up a great deal of space. Digitized sound and video clips take up

▲ *Think & Talk German comes on nine CD-ROMs and contains more than 5G of data!*

vastly more. The largest product I have ever seen is Berlitz Think & Talk German from HyperGlot. It occupies nine CD-ROMs and includes over 5G of data, mostly in the form of digitized voices. Even typical edutainment applications now occupy multiple megabytes of hard disk space.

As the programs grow larger, they also become more demanding of system resources. Many, if not most, of the edutainment products I reviewed for this book will not run on my wife's PC, a decrepit 20 MHz 386 with 2M of RAM. That machine was considered a mid-range business machine when we bought it a few years ago. Now it can't even run my daughter's favorite games!

The trend towards bigger, hungrier applications shows no sign of abating. About all you can do is buy a machine with a 486 or better processor and a large hard drive. A system like that, when outfitted the way I recommend in Part III of this book, should last you at least a few years.

Many Different Approaches

Publishers have their own ideas on the best ways to create edutainment products. Besides the obvious differences between preschool programs and multimedia reference works, or CD-ROM storybooks and simulation programs, significant differences exist even within categories. Some publishers strive to make their software more like Hollywood productions (linear narratives with strong story lines, characters, and visual production values), while others emphasize interactivity and intelligent, lifelike characters. Still other publishers focus on the machine's capability to organize and present information.

The trend is for publishers to keep taking different approaches to edutainment. Users have different learning styles, and publishers will continue to cater to those various styles. At the same time, publishers will continue to strive to maintain unique identities that set them apart from each other.

Lifelike Characters

Edutainment publishers are striving to make their characters more lifelike. Users can more easily identify with characters that have their own personalities and mannerisms. Presumably, more lifelike characters make the user more comfortable with the program and more receptive to learning.

The people at Sierra On-Line are particularly good at endowing their characters with human characteristics. Take Spooky, the friendly ghost in Kid's Typing. He has his own personality, which includes favorite expressions and habits, such as the way he moves his hands when he talks. His lips are even synchronized with his speech. By attending to all the little details, the developers have created a character that seems almost alive.

▲ *Spooky has lifelike characteristics and mannerisms.*

Although Sierra On-Line may be in the forefront of this trend, other companies are also making their characters ever more lifelike. Expect to see more realistic, more human characters in the edutainment products of the future.

Speech Recognition

Speech recognition has proved to be one of the more elusive goals of computer scientists. For years, we have heard of the wonders that will occur when computers can understand spoken English. The problem has always been to develop a reliable and accurate speech-recognition system. Practical speech recognition has finally come to the PC, and Syracuse Language Systems (SLS) is applying it to an edutainment product.

By the time you read this, SLS should have released its first foreign language product to incorporate speech recognition technology. Running on any MPC-compliant PC, the software will teach the language by listening to, understanding, and replying to the user's voice. The result will be conversations between the user and the computer, conducted entirely in the foreign language being studied.

While this is probably the first use of speech recognition technology in general edutainment, it certainly won't be the last. Look for other publishers to follow SLS's lead and add speech recognition to their products.

Other Trends

Two important edutainment trends do not deal directly with the hardware or software. Instead, they deal with how the end user acquires and uses edutainment products.

Other Distribution Channels

Edutainment products sometimes have problems when it comes to finding shelf space in stores. In general, edutainment products sell far fewer copies each month than games. A hit game, for example, might sell a few hundred thousand copies, with maybe 80 percent of those sales in a period of two or three months. Edutainment products, on the other hand, tend to sell at a much slower pace but over a much longer time period. The end result is that the hot-selling products—such as games—get most of the shelf space in stores.

Fortunately, there are other distribution channels available for edutainment products. Given the increasing number of edutainment products on the market, and the increased interest in the genre, it is likely that these non-traditional distribution channels will grow. The following paragraphs provide short descriptions of the distribution channels that I think will grow the most in the future.

Multiple-Product CD-ROMs

Most software products, edutainment or otherwise, can fill only a tiny portion of the 660M of storage space on a CD-ROM. A number of companies have taken advantage of this fact and have developed a new software distribution method. This method involves offering multiple applications on one CD-ROM and selling (or giving) it to potential customers.

For this method to work with retail products (see the next section "Shareware Distribution"), manufacturers must be able to prevent users from keeping the software without paying for it. The full, unrestricted retail versions of the products are inaccessible without some sort of password or special code. The user can try the products for a limited time, or try limited versions of the products. To get permanent use of the full, unrestricted product, a user must call a certain phone number and use a credit card to pay for the particular products he or she wants. In exchange, the user receives the proper codes to unlock the applications and make them fully accessible.

These CD-ROMs enable the user to evaluate individual applications before purchasing them (sounds like shareware, doesn't it?). The advantage to users is that they get to try multiple products before paying for them. The advantage to publishers is that they can put their products into the hands of many users—cheaply, and without fear of piracy. After a user pays for a product, he or she receives the documentation by mail.

As more users add CD-ROM drives to their systems, the distribution of multiple-product CD-ROMs is likely to increase.

Shareware Distribution

Shareware distribution is based on giving the user the opportunity to try a product before paying anything more than a nominal distribution fee. Users can get shareware from on-line bulletin board systems, on-line services such as CompuServe and America Online, racks in stores, shareware CD-ROMs, and from any number of shareware catalogs. When shareware is downloaded from a BBS or on-line service, the usual fees associated with the BBS or service apply. When ordering from a catalog or purchasing a shareware CD-ROM, the user pays a small fee to cover the catalog's costs.

The user can evaluate shareware products without paying further for them. If the user decides to continue using the product beyond a limited evaluation period, he or she must register it. Normally, the developers of shareware products only receive money when the customer registers the product.

For the end user, one advantage of shareware is that you get to try the product—at home, on your own system—before you pay for it. Another advantage is that shareware prices are usually much lower than the price of comparable retail products. By using shareware distribution methods, the developers can avoid many of the expenses incurred with retail products and can offer the product at a reduced cost to the customer.

Public awareness and acceptance of shareware seems to be growing. Even mass-audience publications such as *U.S. News and World Report* have run stories on shareware. When you combine the increased awareness with the growth of telecommunications and the impending information superhighway, it seems certain that the shareware distribution method will continue to expand.

Electronic Distribution

Electronic distribution refers to systems that enable the consumer to preview, pay for, and download software. These systems would reside on Vice President Gore's information superhighway, which eventually will link every home and business in the country. Beyond this, little is known about the details. The information superhighway is still under construction, and none of the electronic distribution systems are in operation yet. What we do know is that cable companies and their competitors are pouring money and manpower into creating the highway, and companies like Electronic Arts are working on providing the applications.

Edutainment products probably will not be the first ones to become available on the information superhighway, but eventually they will appear. When they do, you will be able to access new edutainment products at will, any time of the day or night. With a little luck, we may see results by the end of the decade.

Summary of Non-Traditional Distribution Channels

I believe that three non-traditional distribution channels for edutainment products will grow rapidly in the future: multiple-product CD-ROMs, shareware, and electronic distribution. The first two are here today and growing in awareness and acceptance. They will continue to do so.

The third channel, electronic distribution, is the wave of the future. Although downloading products may never replace physically carrying them home from the store, downloading is likely to become the method of choice for acquiring hard-to-find edutainment products.

On-Line Edutainment

You have already seen how telecommunications, with electronic bulletin board systems and on-line services, serve as a primary distribution channel for shareware products. You have also learned that retail products will one day be distributed electronically. In both of these cases, the on-line environment is more of a delivery channel than anything else and provides a different way to move the products from the publisher to the consumer.

Telecommunications can also be an integral part of the edutainment experience with the development of on-line edutainment systems. On-line edutainment enables a user to participate in edutainment, while interacting with an on-line service. Such systems are still in their infancy, but two facts point toward their future growth:

1. Sierra On-Line is hard at work creating an edutainment environment on the ImagiNATION Network (INN). Few details are available publicly, but here is the gist of what Elon Gaspar, vice president of research and development at Sierra, told me.

    A little red school house resides in the simulated world of the ImagiNATION Network. At present, the school house is empty. It will not remain so. Some time in the not-too-distant future, the school house will be populated by Sierra's lifelike edutainment characters. Information is not yet available on what subjects these characters will teach and how everything will work.

    Eventually, some sort of link will be established between the activities and characters on INN and Sierra's retail product lines. Presumably, this system will eventually spread into schools, as well as homes, to provide a seamless edutainment environment wherever the child may be.

2. Researchers are creating simulated environments in which people from around the world can interact and learn together. Current systems are text-based and far less structured than edutainment products. As systems become more powerful, and as the information infrastructure increases its carrying capacity, such systems will be able to provide environments more like those we see on PCs today. The combination of a graphical learning environment and the opportunity to interact with people from around the world may make such systems irresistible.

The trend here is for new and exciting developments that link edutainment to the on-line world. Apart from Sierra On-line's activities on the ImagiNATION Network, it's hard to predict exactly what will happen. Keep your eyes open.

Summary

Quite a number of trends affect the edutainment industry. Fortunately, if you can afford to upgrade your hardware and software every few years, all the trends are positive. They indicate a future with a wide variety of powerful, engaging, effective edutainment programs running on incredibly powerful PCs. The following list summarizes these trends:

Hardware Trends

- Processing power is increasing rapidly.
- New PCs will require, and will come with, much more memory.
- Hard drives will continue to increase in speed and in storage capacity.
- Video card capabilities continue to grow far beyond the needs of edutainment users, which translates into lower prices on the cards you will want.
- Sound cards will quickly move to 16-bit hardware, but the software will lag behind. They will become standard equipment on new PCs.
- The demand for CD-ROM drives will continue to grow and they will become standard equipment on new PCs.
- Manufacturers will supply more MPC-compatible PCs. Such machines can be considered edutainment-ready.

Software Trends

- Within a few years, nearly all new edutainment products will run under Windows.
- Edutainment applications will grow ever larger and demand ever more from your hardware.
- Publishers will continue to take different approaches to edutainment and provide choices for the consumer.
- Characters in edutainment products will become more and more lifelike and will assume human traits.
- Speech recognition will finally become practical, enabling users to talk to their machines (with a reasonable expectation that it will understand)!
- Non-traditional distribution channels will become important sources of edutainment products.
- Edutainment will move on-line, with the potential for users to learn while they interact with people from around the world.

This chapter examined the trends that I believe will affect the future of edutainment. The final chapter of this book, Chapter 17, lets you see what the movers and shakers in the edutainment industry think the future will be like. It contains interviews with edutainment company founders and executives and includes their views on where the industry is going. Because these people will be creating the products that will shape that future, I think you will find their views fascinating.

Chapter 17

Interviews

This chapter is designed to be a forum for the publishers of edutainment software. It consists of interviews with representatives of many of the companies whose products are examined throughout this book. These interviews were conducted by e-mail, fax, and telephone. The participants were asked for their views on the future of edutainment.

Each company has its own personality and its own views on the subject of edutainment. The wide variety of views and approaches seems to bode well for the future of edutainment. Different approaches appeal to different users, and only by trying various approaches will the industry as a whole be able to improve the effectiveness with which its products teach our children.

I think you will find these interviews enlightening, and I hope that they give you a better idea of what to expect in the future of edutainment.

The Interviews

The interviews are presented here in alphabetical order, by last name of the interviewees. Some of the participants chose to respond directly to a set of questions I posed, while others addressed the subject in a more free-form manner. Where the participants responded to specific questions, those questions are listed.

Greg Bestick, VP and General Manager Infotainment, Creativity, and EA*Kids Electronic Arts

Q: What do you see as the future of edutainment software, and where does EA*Kids fit into that future?

A: Edutainment will increasingly become the blend of high-quality production values (indistinguishable from entertainment products) and age-appropriate content. Distribution will change from off-the-shelf packaged goods software, to on-line delivery to the computer or television in the home. On-line delivery will also allow for group collaboration on problem solving within products and for peer-to-peer communication. What we can safely predict is that the platforms will become more powerful, the quality will get better, and the interactions will become richer. What is still unknown is the correct business model for [the] new publishing environment.

Electronic Arts and EA*Kids will be major players in this environment because of our extensive experience in creating engaging software used by consumers in the home and our strong distribution capabilities.

Q: How will your products evolve over the next few years?

A: Increasingly, the software and entertainment worlds will converge into a single production process. Our products will combine the engagement of linear narrative—strong story lines, characters, and visual production values—with the navigational efficiencies of the computer. We'll create rich content and story-based worlds that can be accessed and rearranged by the user in ways that make personal sense. These products increasingly will be delivered into group settings, such as the living room, instead of being used in solitary settings on the computer. The ability to create multiple levels of content and interaction will become important as family members of various ages gather together to play a single software product.

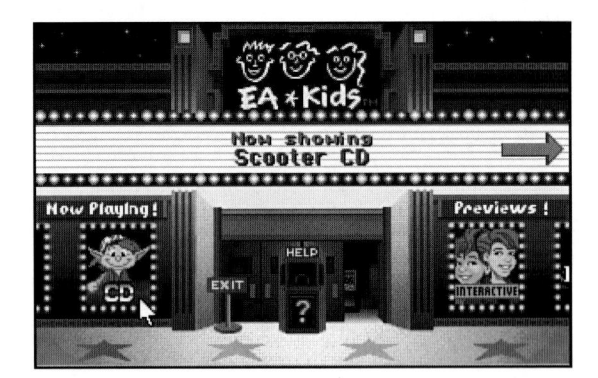

▲ *EA*Kids products look to the entertainment industry for inspiration.*

Q: American students score near the bottom on most standardized international tests. Do you feel that edutainment products in general, and EA*Kids products in particular, can help to improve this situation?

A: Two things that we know have a positive influence on student performance are increased time on task and parental involvement. Software with educational content that is used in the home, effectively increases the amount of schooling a child has in a day. To the extent that parents purchase, install, and play this software with their children, it sends a message that this sort of intellectual activity is valued. Parental involvement in the educational process is enhanced by software that can be used in the home, and it can be used to complement what goes on in the classroom.

Douglas M. Brannan
Vice President of Sales
Software Marketing Corporation

Q: What do you see as the future of edutainment software, and where does SMC fit into that future?

A: *Edutainment* is a word used in the software community to describe all kinds of software that entertains the user while they are learning about one or more subjects. More and more titles are being developed with an in-depth value in using and learning the program. Many parents and families do not

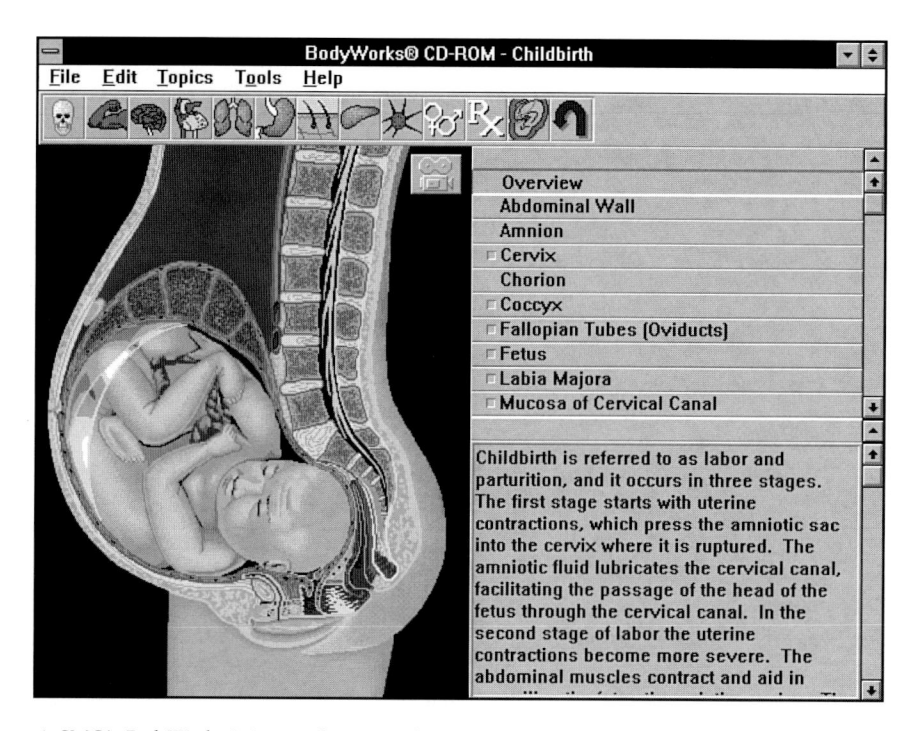

▲ *SMC's BodyWorks 3.0 is an edutainment hit.*

want their children playing games that only have as a goal to kill the enemy, or games in which they fly around without any meaningful goals. Therefore, the home user is looking for more sophisticated titles that will enhance learning and also not bore the user to death!

As a software manufacturer and publisher, Software Marketing Corporation strives to be on the cutting edge of both technology and program content. We were the first company to bring a human anatomy program to the consumer marketplace. BodyWorks 3.0 proved to be a smash hit because of its edutainment qualities and the uniqueness of the program. The name BodyWorks is synonymous today with quality learning, while users are dazzled and amazed at the graphical interface and program content. Our plans are to continue bringing quality, valuable products to the marketplace. Our track record has proven our reputation within the software industry, and even more so within the educational/entertainment community.

Q: How will your products evolve over the next few years?

A: Obviously any good software manufacturer will need to keep up with the current technology and also foresee what technology is coming down the road. For instance, everybody is now fighting to get their products onto CD-ROM. We at Software Marketing Corporation have had products on CD-ROM for several months. It is very important for any manufacturer to stay on top of what the consumer wants, needs, and likes.

Q: American students score near the bottom on most general standardized international tests. Do you feel that edutainment products in general, and your products in particular, can help to improve the situation?

A: Absolutely! It is a well-known fact within the educational arena that students learn more when they are interested and can interact with what they are learning. A computer offers hands-on learning while the student interacts with the subject matter. There is also the element of students remembering and retaining information through graphical interfaces, animation, and illustrations. What better medium than a computer? Computers are currently being used to educate patients of physicians, dentists, orthodontists, and even psychotherapists. The medical community realizes the potential that computers have to convey certain messages and to ensure that their patients understand what is being explained to them. The same thing happens in an educational setting. A teacher is capable of communicating more information in a shorter period of time with the help of a computer.

Our products are perfect for the educational community; in fact, they are already being used in many school systems and private institutions. We have geared all of our educational packages to cater to the school systems by providing lab packages, educational workbooks, and site licenses. These are additional tools to help the teacher implement our products as part of the overall curriculum. Again, relying on the edutainment aspect of our products, the students learn much more from a colorful, graphically oriented software program than they would from a dry textbook.

Jeff Braun, CEO
Maxis

Q: What do you see as the future of edutainment software?

A: We see all entertainment products as educational, so the term *edutainment* becomes meaningless. Mortal Kombat is an educational product in that it teaches you how to kick box. Super Mario is educational in that you learn how to navigate Mario through the maze. The issue isn't whether Mortal Kombat or Mario is educational, but whether they are teaching valuable things.

Maxis looks at play and learning as the same thing. When people play, they are always learning about something. We see the biggest area of growth for the educational software side to be parents buying software to supplement what their child is learning in school and to make up for those things the child is not getting. For example, schools have been cutting back in fine arts studies, so parents may wish to supplement their kids' education with fine arts-related software.

Q: What do you see as the future of simulation software?

A: The role of simulation is to mimic the real world as closely as possible. People love models and simulations of the real world, so we don't think this will go away any time soon. We foresee the object-oriented software development paradigms being brought into the simulation world so that different simulations can be "connected." Maxis is currently working on a new version of SimCity that will allow you to fly, drive, and walk through the city you built. You will be able to furnish your own home and start your own business in SimCity.

▲ *Today you can create your own SimCity; someday you will be able to live in it! (Courtesy of Maxis)*

Q: Where does Maxis fit into this future (edutainment and simulation)?

A: We will build it. Maxis has always created its own market. And we will continue to do so by developing our own unique education/entertainment and simulation titles.

Q: American students score near the bottom on most standardized international tests. Do you feel that edutainment products in general, and Maxis products in particular, can help to improve this situation?

A: You can tell a child, "Don't put your hand in the fire, it's hot!" but this is not learning. If a kid puts his hand in the fire, that's learning for life. Learning by doing is the way of the future for learning. Simulation models allow a student to learn by doing on the computer. We see this as a new, powerful technique for learning about complex subjects, such as finance, math, and the sciences.

Karen Crowther
President, Redwood Games
Director, Alliance Interactive Software

Along with her other titles and responsibilities, Karen is the author of Math Rescue *and* Word Rescue. *These products are the most successful shareware edutainment products ever written.*

Q: Where are the Rescue games going now?

A: I am negotiating a contract now that will combine all four games (Episodes 1, 2, 3, and Plus) of each Rescue game into an anthology.

I am working on writing the sequels, which will be in full 256-color and will have some new characters, new art, levels, words, and so on. We will release a bilingual CD-ROM with both the Spanish and English versions.

I am working on Rescue the Scientists, which will be published through Compton's New Media this Christmas. It is a high-end CD-ROM product.

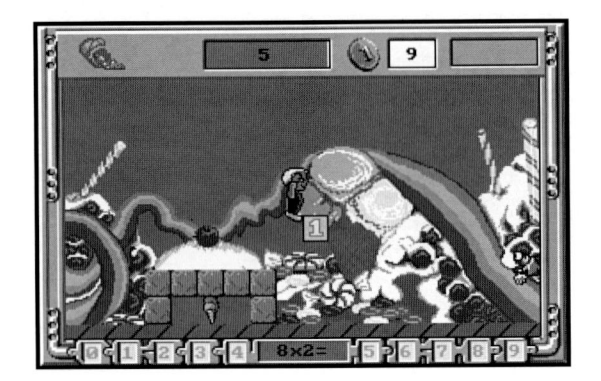

▲ *The future will bring more Rescue games, including 256-color versions and bilingual (English and Spanish) versions!*

▲ *The Reader Rabbit series, like other Learning Company products, offers appealing characters in an engaging environment.*

Q: Will we be seeing any more edutainment products from you? Can you tell us anything about them?

A: In the line-up (but not yet started) are more Rescue games on different educational subjects and Gruzzle Puzzles that will be a puzzle game.

Q: What thoughts do you have on the future of edutainment software?

A: Edutainment software is moving away from rote learning and stressing exploration. I've seen the tools that Gecko Games (one of our retail publishers) has for the next generation of games, and we will be seeing realistic sound and video used to immerse the child in experiences. I predict an upsurge in history titles that take advantage of this.

Bill Dinsmore, President and CEO
The Learning Company

The outlook for the future [of edutainment] is very bright because for the first time, the microcomputer gives us the ability to create and deliver an experience in ways that are highly educational and entertaining, and are unlike any other educational toys, products, or games. The microcomputer has the power and capacity to engage kids and young people for hours on end, while also delivering educational content that will really make a difference in their educational development.

The promise of technology opens up a whole new world for edutainment. We now have the ability to bring life to the characters that teach our children. They are engaged by lively animation, lifelike speech, appealing characters, and enticing sounds and music that only technology could have brought to edutainment. But edutainment still has a single focus that is the same today as it will be in the future—and that is to educate our children. Education will shape our children's futures, and technology is just the delivery mechanism.

Elon Gaspar
Founder, Bright Star Technology, Inc.
VP of Research and Development
Sierra On-Line.

The following comments were generated from a wide-ranging telephone conversation between Mr. Gaspar and the author. Although the following interview is not an exact quotation, it does fairly represent the substance of the conversation and has been approved by Mr. Gaspar.

Q: What are your thoughts on the future of edutainment?

A: The next few years will be a very exciting time for edutainment. There is now enough of a market for products that companies can make some money selling edutainment products. At the best edutainment companies, this money will be reinvested in better products, while at other companies it will not. The growth and popularity of this category will result in an incredible number of new products, and in many new companies creating them.

All the action will make this a very confusing time for consumers. It will be hard to know which products are worthwhile and which are junk. A tremendous number of products will be fighting for shelf space and mind share. Some publishers will rely more on packaging and licensed characters to sell their products, while others will try to create superior educational environments.

From this confusion come responsibilities. It is the publishers' responsibility to ensure that they publish high-quality products. It is the responsibility of the media to inform and educate users about the products. And it is the responsibility of parents to choose quality products.

Mr. Gaspar offers several suggestions that can help parents choose wisely. His first suggestion is for parents to read product reviews. Virtually every computer publication includes reviews, and most publications include edutainment products in those reviews.

Another suggestion is to look for established companies. Mr. Gaspar believes that companies that have been producing edutainment products for years are more idealistic and dedicated to teaching our children. He worries that companies that are just entering the field may be doing so more to make a quick buck in a hot product category than to educate children.

His final suggestion for choosing products is to look for those products with money-back guarantees. Sierra products offer such a guarantee. If a product does not offer such a guarantee, you should ask yourself, "why not?"

▲ *Sierra On-Line's intelligent, animated characters (like Loid) are designed to simulate human behavior.*

When talking about the act of education itself, Mr. Gaspar has definite opinions. He states that we know how to educate children successfully; we just lack the will and the resources to do it. The key is in the personal interaction of a skilled teacher and a child. Unfortunately, society does not provide individual full-time tutors for each child. This is where edutainment products come into the picture.

The goal at Sierra On-Line is to create products that simulate human behavior. These products can then be used to provide the individual tutoring that children need. Mr. Gaspar feels that humans are designed to learn best from other people. When a child is in the presence of a caring, attentive adult, the child feels safe and is ready to learn. By designing the characters in their products to simulate human behavior, Sierra hopes to cause children to respond to the programs as they do to that hypothetical caring adult.

The characters in Sierra programs are animated. They talk to the child (with perfect lip synch) and provide encouragement, feedback, and support. They are fun to play with. They are also intelligent, and they adapt their lesson plans to the performance of the child.

The lesson plans used in these products are not radical new schemes—they are standard curriculum elements accepted by professional educators. An example is the Alphabet Blocks program. Two characters, Bananas the chimp and Jack the jack-in-the-box, teach the alphabet using a technique developed by Maria Montessori decades ago. What makes the products effective is the one-to-one relationship of the child to the characters in the program.

Mr. Gaspar has a vision of technology's place in the future of education for all of mankind. He cites the fact that computing power continues to become cheaper, virtually by the day, and he sees us applying that computing power to teaching all the people. He sees a future in which technology will provide tools that teach all the "mechanical" skills that people need, leaving human teachers to deal with creativity and imagination. As the price of such power drops, he would like to see that all the citizens of the Earth have access to this power. The billions of people alive in the world today can contribute to our future. They need the basic skills and the ability to communicate. Elon Gaspar's dream is to help give them that power.

Sierra On-Line is involved in creating an edutainment environment on the ImagiNATION Network (INN). Although details are not publicly available at this time, the little red schoolhouse in INN, now empty, will one day be populated by Sierra's intelligent characters. Sometime after that, a link will be established between INN and Sierra's edutainment product line.

▲ Kid's Zoo, like other Knowledge Adventure products, emphasizes learning through exploration.

Bill Gross, Chairman and Founder Knowledge Adventure

Q: What do you see as the future of edutainment software, and where does Knowledge Adventure fit into that future?

A: Computers are imagination machines for children. The children can have control, and with the best software, they can direct their own exploration voyages. In the future, edutainment software must continue to meet this challenge.

The Knowledge Adventure mission is to create the most compelling software that encourages learning through exploration, rather than through highly structured exercises or games. Through our research, we have found that children learn better in situations in which they can make their own discoveries.

I feel that the way to ignite a child's intellect is to introduce him or her to the fun of learning. If we can truly achieve this, we no longer have to come up with sneaky ways to get kids to learn; once they recognize the inherent joy of learning, nothing will stop them from finding out everything they want to know. In the design of our future products, we plan to provide avenues with many possible directions from which children can explore and learn according to their own interests.

Q: How will your products evolve over the next few years?

A: Over the next few years, we will (continue) to develop interactive multimedia products that combine rich content and unmatched technology, in innovative and compelling exploratory formats. Our goal will be to develop products that are both fun and educational—products that achieve their "fun-ness" not with buzzers or timers, but by energizing your imagination and curiosity.

Q: American students score near the bottom on most general standardized international tests. Do you feel that edutainment products in general, and your products in particular, can help improve the situation?

A: Improvement of students' scores on standardized tests requires a stronger commitment to improving our overall focus on education—at school as well as in the home environment. Edutainment products alone cannot improve students' scores; however, when quality edutainment products are used in concert with a focused curriculum and a supportive home environment, results will be evident. It will continue to be our mission to challenge the boundaries of electronic exploration by developing and constructing vivid digital environments that foster a participatory, multisensory learning experience.

Dale LaFrenz, President and CEO
MECC

Q: What is MECC's vision of the future of edutainment?

A: There will be a split in the market between the companies that sprinkle education into their products to add value to entertainment titles, and companies whose primary experience and commitment is to education—creating learning environments in the most engaging way possible. Companies that are committed to children and their learning will best serve the demands for edutainment. Because MECC's focus is the child, and we have a twenty-two year history of serving education in schools, we are aptly positioned to lead in the edutainment market.

Technology advances provide opportunities for greater realism, greater access to more information, greater communication, greater opportunities to address diverse learning needs, and more choices for people in terms of how they want to teach and learn. MECC has the expertise to seize these new opportunities to provide creative solutions based on the most appropriate use of the new technologies.

Telecommunications will provide new channels for edutainment promotion, delivery, and support. This will impact edutainment access, design, and the kinds of experiences that are possible. MECC is exploring new avenues for linking its products with telecommunications.

MECC always strives to improve the quality of children's education by providing sound instructional design through engaging computer environments. We believe if children are active participants in their own learning, they will naturally benefit in all areas of their lives, including the capacity to compete in a global economy. Technology can positively impact children's motivation, which in turn affects achievement.

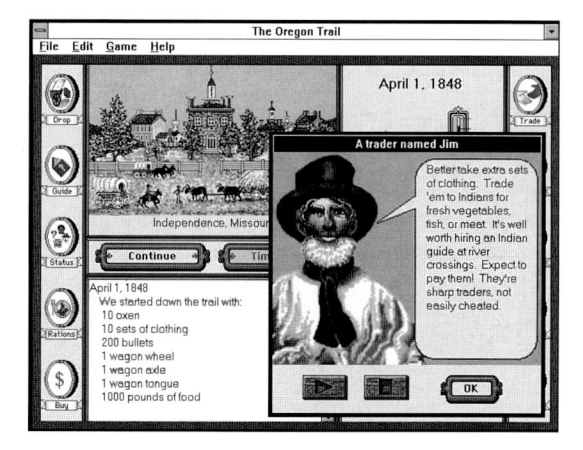

▲ *Oregon Trail and other MECC products provide engaging computer environments for learning.*

Scott Miller, President and Founder Apogee Software, Ltd.

Q: As the publisher of some of the most successful edutainment products of all time (the Rescue games), how important are edutainment products to Apogee?

A: Educational games are important to Apogee because we know the strong influence our games have on kids, so it made sense for us to design games that would help younger players learn basic reading, matching, and math skills.

Most educational programs I've seen do not hold a child's attention, because they're not designed to be fun. Our approach was to disguise an educational program as a game. This seems like the obvious way to design educational products, but many publishers fail to do it this way.

Q: Will shareware channels (for edutainment in particular, but for other product types as well) continue to be a viable distribution method?

A: Apogee will continue to use shareware channels as our primary method of distribution. With the growth of on-line services, the Internet, bulletin boards, and talk of the "information superhighway," I see electronic distribution channels for shareware continuing to grow at an astounding rate.

Q: What part do edutainment products play in Apogee's current and future success?

A: Apogee has just two edutainment products now: Word Rescue and Math Rescue. We have plans to release more edutainment software. Our Rescue games have always been good sellers for us, while games show a steady decline over the years. Edutainment seems to have staying power, so Apogee sees this as an important market to support.

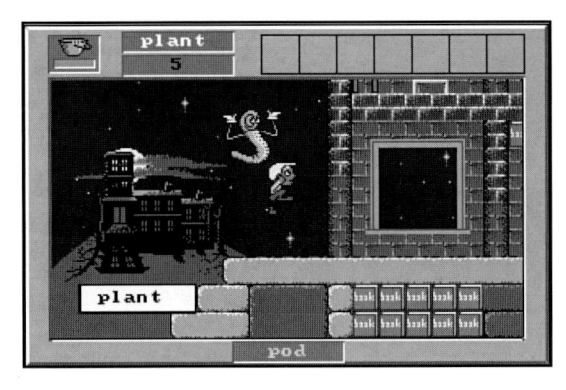

▲ *Look for more edutainment products, like Word Rescue, from Apogee.*

Q: Do you have any thoughts on the future of edutainment—shareware or otherwise?

A: Games receive all of the attention, so I'm not sure if other companies will want to produce edutainment to the same degree. However, there's no doubt that shareware channels will grow, following the increasing sales of modems and competition in the telecommunications industry, which will force cheaper rates.

Ian R. Wade, Director of Marketing Waterford Institute

Contacted by fax, and later by telephone, Mr. Wade offered the following comments on edutainment products and their future. Although the following interview is not an exact quotation, it does fairly represent the substance of the conversation and has been approved by Mr. Wade.

Here are Mr. Wade's four key points about edutainment and its future:

1. Parents will continue to demand edutainment products for home use as an alternative to Nintendo/Sega type games, which kids will prefer.

2. If research is done on edutainment software's impact on learning, it will show no results with current products.

   Mr. Wade feels that current edutainment products are not used long enough to have a large positive effect. He states that some studies have shown mild positive effects from integrated learning systems. (An integrated learning system is a networked, centrally managed system that is installed in a classroom or computer lab at a school and is directly controlled by the teacher.)

3. Teachers will use edutainment products as a diversion for students but will not make them part of their core curriculum.

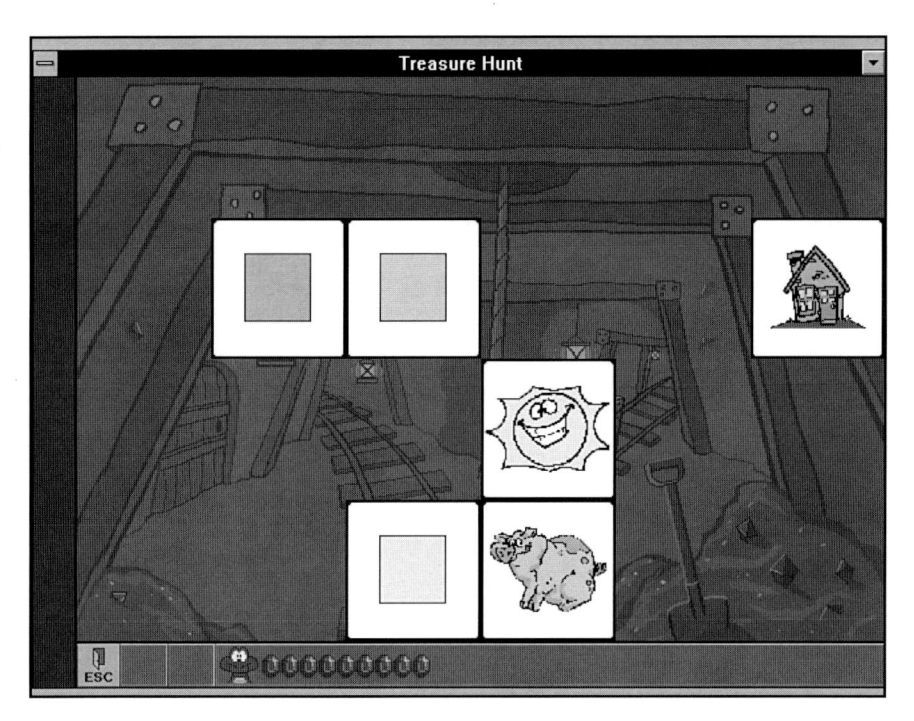

▲ *Edutainment products, like Treasure Hunt from the Waterford Institute, provide a healthy alternative to the many violent games available.*

4. Vendors who develop entertaining products that they can then demonstrate are educationally effective will win loyal customers in schools and in homes. This may be a new category, since edutainment will have little credibility as educationally helpful.

Mr. Wade is convinced that today's edutainment products are merely stepping stones on the path to creating really useful educational computer products. He feels that such products will probably have to be integrated into a formal program that provides structure and that guarantees a sufficient amount of time is spent on the task.

Summary

As you can see from the interviews in this chapter, it is an exciting time for edutainment providers and consumers. Almost all of the interviewees feel that edutainment products are effective educational tools today. Their enthusiasm is obvious, as is their commitment to bringing you an ever-growing number of new-and-improved products.

Appendix A

The Companion CD-ROM

Adventures with OSLO, Tools and Gadgets, Page 282
Adventure Math, Page 274
Aesop's Multimedia Fables, Page 279
Amy's Fun-2-3 Adventure, Page 272
Beat the Bomb, Page 275
Beyond Planet Earth, Page 278
Busytown, Page 274
Christmas Carol, A, Page 279
Color Wizard, Page 276
Detroit, Page 273
Don Quixote, Page 279
Dr T's Sing-Along Kids Classics, Page 279
Fatty Bear's Birthday Surprise, Page 273
Goferwinkel's Adventures—The Lavender Land, Page 279
Impressionism and Its Sources, Page 280
In the Company of Whales, Page 278
Jeopardy, Page 272
Kid CAD, Page 277
Lenny's Music Toons, Page 282
Mario Teaches Typing, Page 273
Math Rescue, Page 275
Math Sampler, Page 276
Mental Math Games, Page 282

Movie Select, Page 281
Mowgli's Brothers, Page 279
My First World Atlas, Page 273
Normandy, the Great Crusade, Page 278
Professor Iris, Page 278
Putt Putt Goes to the Moon, Page 272
Putt Putt Joins the Parade, Page 273
Renaissance Masters #1, Page 280
Renaissance Masters #2, Page 280
Rock, Rap, and Roll, Page 281
Rusty and Rosy Read with Me, Page 283
Sea School: Math Waves, Page 274
Sharks!, Page 278
Sound It Out Land 2, Page 277
The Star Child, Page 280
The Ugly Duckling, Page 281
The White Horse Child, Page 280
Trivia Shell, Page 276
TuneLand, Page 277
Wings Over Europe: W.W.II, Page 278
Word Puzzle, Page 274
Word Rescue, Page 275
Word Search , Page 281

Overview of the CD-ROM

The CD-ROM included with *Edutainment Comes Alive!* serves many purposes. First and foremost, it's there for you to enjoy. The CD-ROM contains many DOS and Windows demos of top edutainment programs: special limited versions, test-drives, slideshow demos, and shareware. Using this software, you can interactively experience many edutainment programs first hand. Whether you use Windows or DOS, you'll have hours of fun exploring the software on the companion CD-ROM.

This appendix provides you with all the information you need to take full advantage of the software on the CD-ROM. The topics covered are

- How to install and run the DOS software
- How to install and run the Windows software
- Information about the Windows and DOS software, including company contact information, special system requirements, limitations of the software, and short descriptions of each product

Installing and Running the DOS Software

To help you navigate through the DOS software titles on the CD-ROM, Sams Publishing has provided a graphical menu program. Using this menu, you can explore software in the seven categories of edutainment. Many of the programs and demos can be installed and run directly from the menu, while some are installed only, or require special setups. The menu provides you with all the information you need.

To begin the DOS menu program, perform the following steps:

1. Carefully open the packaging on the inside back cover of the book and remove the CD-ROM.
2. Place the disc label up into CD-ROM drive.
3. From the DOS prompt, switch to the drive holding the CD-ROM. For example, if your CD-ROM drive is E:, type **E:** and press the Enter key.
4. Type **DOSMENU** and press the Enter Key. This will start the menu program.

`C:\>E:` ← *Type the letter of your CD-ROM drive, followed by a colon, and press Enter.*
`E:\>DOSMENU` ← *From the CD-ROM drive prompt, type* **DOSMENU** *and press Enter.*

Your screen clears and you see a small clock icon in the middle of the screen; this icon remains on-screen until the program finishes loading. On some systems, loading may take a few moments. Once the program is loaded, you will be greeted with the welcome page of the DOS menu system.

The Opening Page

Along the top and bottom of the screen, you'll see series of icons and buttons. If you click the button in the upper left corner—the one labeled Software Index—you see a list of all the DOS software accessible from the menu, along with each product's category and page number for easy reference. The two rows of buttons along the top—the ones labeled with the names of the seven categories of edutainment software (the first row) and with page numbers (the second row)—provide quick access to the category or page to which you want to go. If you look at the software index, for example, you'll see that Busytown is a preschool product and is on page 3 of the menu. To go to the screen where you can play the Busytown demo, you can either press the Preschool button or the Page 3 button to go directly to the page that contains Busytown.

In the middle of the screen is a short text file that you can read using your mouse to click the down and up arrows on the right of the text.

At the bottom of the screen are more navigation and help buttons and icons. In the lower left and the lower right corner, you see icons labeled Page Up and Page Down that resemble upturned corners of a book page. If you click one of these icons or press the Page Up or Page Down key on your computer, you can move backward or forward through the menu one page at a time. On the welcome screen, however, you'll notice that the Page Down icon is dimmed. This is because you are currently on page 1 and can't go back any further.

> **Note:** Whenever you see a button or icon that appears dimmed, that button or icon performs no function on the current page of the menu.

In the middle center of the bottom of the screen, there is a door icon labeled EXIT. If you click the door, you will be asked whether or not you want to quit the menu.

To the left of the door icon is the Help button, which is labeled with a question mark. Clicking this icon brings up help screens that explain the use of the buttons and icons and provide additional help navigating the menu.

To the right of the door icon is the Find button, which is labeled with a magnifying glass. Clicking this icon enables you to search for text throughout the menus.

> **Note:** The Find utility will not find text on the face of buttons. To locate a specific program, click the Software Index button, find the program's name, and go to the category or page given.

To the right of the Find icon is the Title Page button. Click this button to return to the welcome screen.

The Category Pages

Whether you've located a program you want to check out or you're just browsing, you'll soon see one of the edutainment category pages, which are on pages 2 through 8. You'll notice that all the applicable buttons from the top and bottom of the welcome screen are on the category pages as well.

The category pages consist of the category name, a short description of the category, and series of buttons for installing, setting up, and running the various programs.

Each button face contains text that explains its function. Pressing a button does one or more of the following:

1. *Installs the software to your hard drive.* Some software cannot be run directly from the CD-ROM. If it cannot, it will be installed to a directory on your hard drive and run from there. If the software must be installed to your hard drive, the menu program notifies you and gives you the option to abort the installation. If the software is installed to your hard drive, make note of the name of the directory to which it was installed. You'll need to know this information to be able to run the software without using the DOS menu program.

2. *Runs an interactive setup program.* Some programs require you to enter information such as whether or not you have a sound card and its type. Again, if the software is installed to your hard drive, make note of the name of the directory to which it was installed. You'll need to know this information to be able to run the software without using the DOS menu program.

> **Warning:** If a setup program gives you the option of installing the software to a specific directory, accept the default directory. Failure to install the software to the default directory will not harm the software or your computer, but it will prohibit the DOS menu program from running the software. If you find it necessary to change the name of the install directory, exit the DOS menu program and run the software from the directory to which it was installed.

3. *Runs the software.* Many of the programs can be run directly from the CD-ROM. If so, you can run the program from the CD-ROM by clicking the button.

You can use the DOS menu program to run the programs as many times as you want, but you may want to run some of the programs—the ones installed to your hard drive—directly from the DOS directory to which it was installed. To do so, take note of the name of the directory in which the software was installed and the name of the file that starts the program. (The install or setup program provides you with this information.) Then you need only change to that directory, type the name of the file, and press the Enter key.

For example, on page 2, Drill-and-Practice, the first button enables you to install and run Adventure Math, a shareware program by Epic Megagames. When you click this button, the menu copies the files to your hard drive and runs the program for you. If you later want to run the program from DOS rather than from the menu, change to the \AMATH directory, type **AMATH**, and press Enter.

> C:\>CD \AMATH ← *Change to the Adventure Math subdirectory.*
>
> C:\AMATH\>AMATH ← *Type AMATH, and press Enter.*

If the software has any special information you need to know before you run it, such as special system requirements, there will be an additional button, labeled Click Me, that will provide the information you need to know. Be sure to read this information; it may affect whether or not you can run the software. You can navigate through the text that is displayed by clicking the scroll bar to the right of the text.

Special thanks go to NeoSoft Corporation, publishers of the NeoBook Professional software used to create the DOS menu system. You'll find shareware versions of NeoBook Professional and NeoPaint (a full-featured DOS paint program) in the \DOS\MISC\NEOBOOK and \DOS\MISC\NEOPAINT directories of the CD-ROM. For more information, you can contact NeoSoft at

NeoSoft Corporation
354 NE Greenwood Avenue, Suite 108
Bend, OR 97701-4631
(503) 389-5489
(503) 383-7195, BBS

Installing and Running the Windows Software

In addition to the DOS software on the CD-ROM, there are also many interesting and fun Windows programs.

Before you can run the Windows demos on the CD-ROM, you need to run a Windows setup program. This will create a Program Manager group named Edutainment. Follow these steps to run the setup program:

1. Start Windows if it isn't already running.
2. Click the **F**ile menu in Program Manager.
3. Choose **R**un from the **F**ile menu.
4. In the Command Line: box, type **D:\SETUP** and click OK. If your CD-ROM drive is not drive D, substitute the proper drive letter in this entry. For example, if your CD-ROM drive is F:, type **F:\SETUP**.
5. The setup program starts. Click the **C**ontinue button.
6. The program now creates a Program Manager group named Edutainment. Click the **C**reate button to continue.
7. The setup program informs you when the icons have been created. Click the OK button to exit.

This setup program doesn't copy any files to your hard drive; it simply creates icons for all the Windows demos on the CD-ROM. You can now double-click an icon in the Edutainment group to run or install any of the Windows demos. Icons are also created for any text files that need to be read. If a program needs to be installed to your hard drive, the title of the icon will tell you.

Company and Software Information for DOS Products

In the following sections, you will find information about the DOS software products on the CD-ROM and the companies that produced them.

Devasoft

Contact Information

P.O. Box 41250
San Jose, CA 95160
(408) 927-9645

Software Title Represented on the CD-ROM

Devasoft has generously provided the software in the following section for the *Edutainment Comes Alive!* companion CD-ROM.

Amy's Fun-2-3 Adventure
- *Location:* \DOS\PSCHOOL\FUN23
- *Category:* Preschool
- *Special System Requirements:* None
- *Limitations of the version of the companion CD-ROM:* None. Amy's Fun-2-3 Adventure is shareware. If you decide to use the software, you must register it. When you register the software ($21.95 plus s&h), you will receive the registered version of Amy's Fun-2-3 Adventure that includes a manual, as well as three additional edutainment titles: Amy's Shapes, Retrosprectro, and Amy's Play-B-C Time.
- *Product Description:* An entertaining educational game for 2- to 5-year-old children, previously only available commercially. Amy is a cute puppy who will lead your child on a number-learning journey.

Please register your copy Amy's Fun-2-3 Adventure.

Electronic Arts
Contact Information
1450 Fashion Island Blvd.
San Mateo, CA 94404

Software Title Represented on the CD-ROM
Electronic Arts has generously provided the software in the following sections for the *Edutainment Comes Alive!* companion CD-ROM.

EA*Kids Theater Collection
- *Location:* \EADEMO
- *Category:* General Edutainment
- *Special System Requirements:* None
- *Limitations of the version of the companion CD-ROM:* Each demo shows only a few of the many screens and activities available in the full products.
- *Product Description:* The EA*Kids Theatre sampler includes demos of Eagle Eye Mysteries, Peter Pan's Picture Painting Adventure, Ping & Kooky's Cuckoo Zoo (show only), Scooter's Magic Castle, and Video Jam.

Please purchase complete copies of EA*Kids software from your local retailer.

GameTek
Contact Information
2999 Northeast 191st St.
Suite 800
North Miami Beach, FL 33180

Software Title Represented on the CD-ROM
Electronic Arts has generously provided the software in the following sections for the *Edutainment Comes Alive!* companion CD-ROM.

Jeopardy
- *Location:* \DOS\GENERAL\JEOPARDY
- *Category:* General Edutainment
- *Special System Requirements:* None
- *Limitations of the version of the companion CD-ROM:* The demo contains fewer questions than the complete version.
- *Product Description:* Jeopardy is a drill-based trivia game based on the popular television game show.

Please purchase a complete copy of Jeopardy from your local retailer.

Humongous Entertainment
Contact Information
13110 NE 177th Place #180
Woodinville, WA 98072-9965
(206) 485-1212

Software Titles Represented on the CD-ROM
Humoungous Entertainment has generously provided the software in the following sections for the *Edutainment Comes Alive!* companion CD-ROM.

Putt Putt Goes to the Moon
- *Location:* \DOS\GENERAL\PUTTMOON
- *Category:* General Edutainment
- *Special System Requirements:* None
- *Limitations of the version of the companion CD-ROM:* The demo contains only a few of the many scenes in the complete version.

- *Product Description:* Putt Putt is a lovable little car that is your companion while you explore a zany moon.

Putt Putt Joins the Parade
- *Location:* \DOS\GENERAL\PUTTPUTT
- *Category:* General Edutainment
- *Special System Requirements:* None
- *Limitations of the version of the companion CD-ROM:* The demo contains only a few of the many scenes in the complete version.
- *Product Description:* Grab your car wax and buff your bumpers—it's time for the annual Cartown Pet Parade.

Fatty Bear's Birthday Surprise
- *Location:* \DOS\CDBOOKS\FBEAR
- *Category:* Storybooks
- *Special System Requirements:* Sound card recommended.
- *Limitations of the version of the companion CD-ROM:* The demo contains only a few of the many scenes available in the complete version.
- *Product Description:* Tomorrow is Kayla's birthday and Fatty Bear is planning a surprise party for her. By organizing the other toys (which come to life only at night), Fatty Bear sets off to decorate Kayla's room, bake cakes, and much more.

Please purchase complete copies of these titles from your local retailer.

Impressions Software
Contact Information
222 Third Street, Suite 0234
Cambridge, MA 02142

Software Titles Represented on the CD-ROM
Impression Software has generously provided the software in the following sections for the *Edutainment Comes Alive!* companion CD-ROM.

Detroit
- *Location:* \DOS\SIMS\DETROIT
- *Category:* Simulations
- *Special System Requirements:* None
- *Limitations of the version of the companion CD-ROM:* The demo contains only a few of the many scenes in the complete version.
- *Product Description:* Detroit is a simulation in which you challenge other players to run the best car production facility.

My First World Atlas
- *Location:* \DOS\MMREF\ATLAS
- *Category:* Reference
- *Special System Requirements:* None
- *Limitations of the version of the companion CD-ROM:* The demo contains only a few of the many scenes and areas available in the complete version.
- *Product Description:* An interesting adventure into the world of geography.

Please purchase complete copies of Impression Software's titles from your local retailer.

Interplay Productions
Contact Information
222 Third Street, Suite 0234
Cambridge, MA 02142

17922 Fitch Ave.
Irvine, CA 92714

Software Titles Represented on the CD-ROM
Interplay Productions has generously provided the software in the following sections for the *Edutainment Comes Alive!* companion CD-ROM.

Mario Teaches Typing
- *Location:* \DOS\DRILL\MARIO
- *Category:* Drill and Practice
- *Special System Requirements:* Sound card recommended.
- *Limitations of the version of the companion CD-ROM:* The demo contains only a few of the many screens and features in the complete version.
- *Product Description:* A fun, arcade-style typing tutor.

Please purchase a complete copy of Mario Teaches Typing Software's titles from your local retailer.

MVP Software

Contact Information

1035 Dallas S.E.
Grand Rapids, MI 49507-1407
800-968-9684 (Orders)

Software Titles Represented on the CD-ROM

MVP Software has generously provided the software in the following sections for the *Edutainment Comes Alive!* companion CD-ROM.

Word Puzzle

- *Location:* \DOS\GENERAL\WORDPUZ
- *Category:* General Edutainment
- *Special System Requirements:* Sound card recommended.
- *Limitations of the version of the companion CD-ROM:* None. Word Puzzle is shareware. If you decide to use the software, you must register (pay for) it.
- *Product Description:* Game Magazine Presents Word Puzzles, a graphical potpourri of word games for players too smart or bored with the shareware shoot-em-up scene. Includes 20 puzzles—Crosswords, Cryptograms, Double Crosses, Word Scrambles, and Quote Boxes. Features very nice graphics and an original musical score for most sound cards.

Sea School: Math Waves

- *Location:* \DOS\DRILL\SEA
- *Category:* Drill and Practice
- *Special System Requirements:* None
- *Limitations of the version of the companion CD-ROM:* None. Sea School is shareware. If you decide to use the software, you must register it. When you register the software ($32.95), you will receive the complete three episodes of Sea School.
- *Product Description:* Sea School is the first in a new learning game series. Bright, colorful graphics, delightful music, digitized sound effects, and speech will keep your young learner playing for hours.

Please register your copy of MVP's software.

Paramount Interactive

Contact Information

700 Hansen Way
Palo Alto, CA 94304

Software Title Represented on the CD-ROM

Paramount Interactive has generously provided the software in the following section for the *Edutainment Comes Alive!* companion CD-ROM.

Busytown

- *Location:* \DOS\PSCHOOL\BUSYTOWN
- *Category:* Preschool
- *Special System Requirements:* 486 33Mhz (recommended minimum), super VGA with 256 colors (640x480), Sound Blaster or Sound Blaster Pro, external speakers, 8Mb RAM (recommended minimum), 540Kb of free conventional memory minimum, and optional microphone.
- *Limitations of the version of the companion CD-ROM:* Only one of the many special areas you can visit is available in this demo.
- *Product Description:* A lively town full of adventure for a young child. In Busytown you can become a doctor, fight a fire, build a house, and more. (In the demo, you build a ship.)

Please purchase the complete Busytown from your local retailer.

Epic Megagames

Contact Information

354 NE Greenwood Avenue
Suite 108
Bend, OR 97701-4631
800-972-7434 (Orders)

Software Title Represented on the CD-ROM

Epic Megagames has generously provided the software in the following section for the *Edutainment Comes Alive!* companion CD-ROM.

Adventure Math

- *Location:* \DOS\DRILL\ADVMATH
- *Category:* Drill and Practice
- *Special System Requirements:* None

- *Limitations of the version of the companion CD-ROM:* None. Adventure Math is shareware. If you like Adventure Math, consider purchasing Adventure Math Deluxe for only $27.00. The deluxe version has more graphics, sound and music, as well as timed multiplication and division drills.
- *Product Description:* An educational game that teaches kids in grades 1-5 about addition and subtraction, while keeping them entertained with fun graphics, sound, and a bonus arcade sequence!

Please consider purchasing Adventure Math Deluxe from Epic Megagame's products.

Apogee Software Productions

3960 Broadway
Suite 235
Garland, TX 75043
800-426-3123 (Orders)

Software Titles Represented on the CD-ROM

Apogee has generously provided the software in the following sections for the *Edutainment Comes Alive!* companion CD-ROM.

Math Rescue

- *Location:* \DOS\GENERAL\MATHRESC
- *Category:* General Edutainment, Drill and Practice
- *Special System Requirements:* None
- *Limitations of the version of the companion CD-ROM:* None. Math Rescue is shareware. If you decide to use the software, you must register it. When you register the software ($19.00), you will receive the registered version, which includes two more complete episodes.
- *Product Description:* The Gruzzles are back and stealing all the numbers in this funny, adventure-filled, Nintendo-style EGA/VGA multi-scrolling learning game. Includes puzzling word-math problems and arithmetic.

Word Rescue

- *Location:* \DOS\GENERAL\WORDRESC
- *Category:* General Edutainment, Drill and Practice
- *Special System Requirements:* None
- *Limitations of the version of the companion CD-ROM:* None. Word Rescue is shareware. If you decide to use the software, you must register it. When you register the software ($19.00), you will receive the registered version, which includes two more complete episodes.
- *Product Description:* Word Rescue is Apogee's first educational game, yet is a great challenge for adults, too. Play as a male or a female character and explore many fascinating locations as you search for all the stolen words. Three difficulty levels, auto-save, unlimited lives, ADlib Music, Joystick and much more.

Please register your copies of Apogee's products.

First Magnitude

Contact Information

1249 Cedar Creek Circle
Dayton OH 45459-3223
1-800-2424-PsL (Public Software Library; orders only)

Software Titles Represented on the CD-ROM

First Magnitude has generously provided the software in the following sections for the *Edutainment Comes Alive!* companion CD-ROM.

Beat the Bomb

- *Location:* \DOS\DRILL\BTB
- *Category:* Drill and Practice
- *Special System Requirements:* None
- *Limitations of the version of the companion CD-ROM:* None. Beat the Bomb is shareware. If you decide to use the software, you must register it. When you register the software ($18.00), you will receive the enhanced version, which includes subtraction, multiplication, division, and combinations games.

- *Product Description:* Beat the Bomb is a timed addition game in which you race against a clock, a bomb, or a snail or build castles with correct answers.

Math Sampler

- *Location:* \DOS\DRILL\MSAMP
- *Category:* Drill and Practice
- *Special System Requirements:* None
- *Limitations of the version of the companion CD-ROM:* None. Math Sampler is shareware. If you decide to use the software, you can purchase Math Explore 1, 2, and 3 for $23.00.
- *Product Description:* Math Sampler, a working sample of Math Explorer, is a collection of six fully functional math lessons and games. Improves on other math games by providing animated math lessons and arcade-action games.

Please register your version of Beat the Bomb and Math Sampler.

ImagiSOFT, Inc.

Contact Information

Computer Games Division
P.O. Box 13208
Albuquerque, NM 87192

Software Title Represented on the CD-ROM

ImagiSOFT has generously provided the software in the following section for the *Edutainment Comes Alive!* companion CD-ROM.

Color Wizard

- *Location:* \DOS\CREATE\CWIZARD
- *Category:* Creativity Tools
- *Special System Requirements:* Sound card recommended
- *Limitations of the version of the companion CD-ROM:* None. Color Wizard is shareware. If you decide to use the software, you must register it. When you register the software ($33.95), you will receive the registered version of Color Wizard that includes ten screens to color in each coloring book instead of the two in this shareware version.
- *Product Description:* More than just another coloring book, Color Wizard tells stories and teaches art lessons! Choose from over 700 different colors. Learn about perspective, color, value, light, reflections, and shadows. Includes four books to color: Dinosaurs, Sharks, Aesop's Fables, and Rapunzel.

Please register your copy of Color Wizard.

Software Creations

Contact Information

26 Harris St.
Clinton, MA. 01510

Software Title Represented on the CD-ROM

Software Creations has generously provided the software in the following section for the *Edutainment Comes Alive!* companion CD-ROM.

Trivia Shell

- *Location:* \DOS\GENERAL\TRIVIA (Each Trivia Shell program is stored in its own subdirectory)
- *Category:* General Edutainment
- *Special System Requirements:* None
- *Limitations of the version of the companion CD-ROM:* Trivia Shell is shareware. If you decide to use the software, you must register (pay for) it.

Please register your copy of Trivia Shell.

Company and Software Information for Windows

In the following sections, you will find information about the DOS software products on the CD-ROM and the companies that produced them.

7th Level

Contact Information

1771 International Parkway
Suite 101
Richardson, Texas 75081
214-437-4858 (product information only)

Software Title Represented on the CD-ROM

7th Level has generously provided the software in the following section for the Edutainment Comes Alive! companion CD-ROM.

TuneLand

- *Location:* \WIN\PSCHOOL\TUNELAND
- *Category:* Preschool\General Edutainment
- *Special System Requirements:* 386/25MHz or better CPU, 4Mb RAM, SVGA Display, CD-ROM with audio connector, MPC compatible sound card, amplified speakers (optional) and headphones (optional).

> **Note:** Although the full retail version of TuneLand requires a CD Audio connection, the special limited edition on the companion CD-ROM does not.

- *Limitations of the version of the companion CD-ROM:* Contains one scene of the eight available in the complete product.
- *Product Description:* TuneLand, starring Howie Mandel, is the world's first fully interactive musical cartoon CD-ROM for MPCs. Lil' Howie, a friendly comic host, plays hide n' seek, tells jokes, and preforms hilarious gags as you meet many interesting characters in an interactive journey of fun and learning for children of all ages.

Please purchase the complete version of TuneLand through your local software distributor.

Conexus
Contact Information

5252 Balboa Ave
Suite 605
San Diego, CA 92117

Software Title Represented on the CD-ROM

Conexus has generously provided the software in the following section for the *Edutainment Comes Alive!* companion CD-ROM.

Sound It Out Land 2

- *Location:* \WIN\DRILL\SOUND2
- *Category:* Drill and Practice
- *Special System Requirements:* MPC Level 1 and 4Mb RAM
- *Limitations of the version of the companion CD-ROM:* Contains only a portion of the many sounds and scenes available in the complete product.
- *Product Description:* A musical adventure in phonics, Sound It Out Land uses catchy sing-along songs and games to teach children how to read phonetically.

Please purchase the complete version of Sound It Out Land 2 (and the original Sound It Out Land) through your local software distributor.

Davidson & Associates
Contact Information

19840 Pioneer Ave
Torrence, CA 90503

Software Title Represented on the CD-ROM

Davidson & Associates has generously provided the software in the following section for the *Edutainment Comes Alive!* companion CD-ROM.

Kid CAD

- *Location:* \WIN\CREATE\KIDCAD
- *Category:* Creativity Tools
- *Special System Requirements:* Sound card recommended
- *Limitations of the version of the companion CD-ROM:* Contains only a few of the many tools available in the complete product.
- *Product Description:* An amazing 3-D building and design studio lets you create houses, forts, gazebos, and all sorts of structures with electronic building blocks that click into place. Building, however, is only the beginning. You can paint and decorate everything in sight—including the kitchen sink. Then fill your customized creation with a huge assortment of people and pets, furniture and ferns—even a dinosaur!

Please purchase the complete version of Kid CAD through your local software distributor.

Discovery Channel, The
Contact Information

7700 Wisconsin Avenue
Bethesda, Maryland 20814
301-986-0444 x5880

Software Titles Represented on the CD-ROM

The Discovery Channel has generously provided the software in the following sections for the *Edutainment Comes Alive!* companion CD-ROM.

Normandy: The Great Crusade
- *Location:* \WIN\GENERAL\DISCOVER
- *Category:* General Edutainment
- *Special System Requirements:* 386 or greater CPU, Sound card, 4Mb of RAM.
- *Limitations of the version of the companion CD-ROM:* In this interactive demo, many of the functions in the complete product are not available.
- *Product Description:* The story of the greatest military invasion in history, told in the words, sights, and sounds of the era.

Beyond Planet Earth
- *Location:* \WIN\GENERAL\DISCOVER
- *Category:* General Edutainment
- *Special System Requirements:* 386 or greater CPU, Sound card, 4Mb of RAM
- *Limitations of the version of the companion CD-ROM:* In this interactive demo, many of the functions and screens in the complete product are not available.
- *Product Description:* An exploration of the mysteries of the solar system, including, video, graphics, and text.

Professor Iris
- *Location:* \WIN\GENERAL\DISCOVER
- *Category:* General Edutainment
- *Special System Requirements:* 386 or greater CPU, Sound card, 4Mb of RAM
- *Limitations of the version of the companion CD-ROM:* The demo is a view-only demo, and highlights only some of the many aspects of the complete product.
- *Product Description:* An interactive book in which Professor Iris leads children ages 3 and up on a wild African safari.

In the Company of Whales
- *Location:* \WIN\GENERAL\DISCOVER
- *Category:* General Edutainment
- *Special System Requirements:* 386 or greater CPU, Sound card, 4Mb of RAM
- *Limitations of the version of the companion CD-ROM:* In this interactive demo, many of the functions in the complete product are not available.
- *Product Description:* A journey of exploration into the fascinating world of whales.

Sharks!
- *Location:* \WIN\GENERAL\DISCOVER
- *Category:* General Edutainment
- *Special System Requirements:* 386 or greater CPU, Sound card, 4Mb of RAM
- *Limitations of the version of the companion CD-ROM:* The demo is a view-only demo, and highlights only some of the many aspects of the complete product.
- *Product Description:* A journey into the world of nature's most misunderstood predators, the sharks.

Wings Over Europe, W.W. II
- *Location:* \WIN\GENERAL\DISCOVER
- *Category:* General Edutainment
- *Special System Requirements:* 386 or greater CPU, Sound card, 4Mb or RAM
- *Limitations of the version of the companion CD-ROM:* The demo is a view-only demo, and highlights only some of the many aspects of the complete product.
- *Product Description:* A story of the planes flow in the European theatre of World War II, the pilots who flew them, and their battles and missions.

Please purchase the complete versions of the Discovery Channel's software through your local software distributor or call the number listed for more information.

Dr. T's Music Software
Contact Information
124 Crescent Road
Needham, MA 02194
617-455-1454/800-989-6434

Software Title Represented on the CD-ROM

Dr T's Music Software has generously provided the software in the following section for the *Edutainment Comes Alive!* companion CD-ROM.

Dr. T's Sing-A-Long Kids Classics

- *Location:* \WIN\PSCHOOL\DTSING
- *Category:* Preschool
- *Special System Requirements:* Sound card
- *Limitations of the version of the companion CD-ROM:* Contains 5 of the 26 songs available in the complete product.
- *Product Description:* A children's musical theatre.

Please purchase the complete version of Dr. T's Sing-A-Long Kids Classics through your local software distributor or call the number listed for more information.

EBook, Inc.

Contact Information

32970 Alvarado-Niles Rd.
Suite 704
Union City, CA 94587
(510) 429-1331
Fax: (510) 429-1394
1-800-245-4525 (Orders)

Software Titles Represented on the CD-ROM

EBook has generously provided the software in the following sections for the *Edutainment Comes Alive!* companion CD-ROM.

Aesop's Multimedia Fables

- *Location:* \WIN\CDSTORY\AESOP
- *Category:* CD-ROM Storybooks
- *Special System Requirements:* None
- *Limitations of the version of the companion CD-ROM:* Show only; contains only a few of the many pages available in the complete product.
- *Product Description:* A multimedia version of a classic edition of Aesop's Fables illustrated by Sir Arthur Rackham.

A Christmas Carol

- *Location:* \WIN\CDSTORY\CCAROL
- *Category:* CD-ROM Storybooks
- *Special System Requirements:* None
- *Limitations of the version of the companion CD-ROM:* Show only; contains only a few of the many pages available in the complete product.
- *Product Description:* From the bustling snowy streets of 19th century London to the ghastly apparition of Scrooge's Christmas future, the classic illustrations of Arthur Rackham visually render the full emotional impact of Charles Dickens' classic Christmas tale.

Don Quixote

- *Location:* \WIN\CDSTORY\QUIXOTE
- *Category:* CD-ROM Storybooks
- *Special System Requirements:* None
- *Limitations of the version of the companion CD-ROM:* Show only; contains only a few of the many pages available in the complete product.
- *Product Description:* Translator Magda Bogin joins Spanish artist Manuel Boix to faithfully present Miguel Cervante's masterpiece.

Goferwinkel's Adventures— The Lavender Land

- *Location:* \WIN\CDSTORY\GOFER
- *Category:* CD-ROM Storybooks
- *Special System Requirements:* None
- *Limitations of the version of the companion CD-ROM:* Show only; contains only a few of the many pages available in the complete product.
- *Product Description:* What happens when an ambitious ten-year old boy called William plays a virtual reality game on his computer? He becomes Goferwinkel, the first brave and lovable multimedia comic book hero of his kind.

Mowgli's Brothers

- *Location:* \WIN\CDSTORY\MOWGLI
- *Category:* CD-ROM Storybooks
- *Special System Requirements:* None

- *Limitations of the version of the companion CD-ROM:* Show only; contains only a few of the many pages available in the complete product.
- *Product Description:* The Jungle Book is a collection of stories for children by Rudyard Kipling. These timeless classics have been captivating imaginations since they were first published in the late 1800s. Mowgli's Brothers, the first in the Ebook Jungle Book series, tells the tale of Mowgli, a little boy who is found and raised by wolves.

Impressionism and its Sources
- *Location:* \WIN\MMREF\IMPRESS
- *Category:* CD-ROM Storybooks
- *Special System Requirements:* None
- *Limitations of the version of the companion CD-ROM:* Show only; contains only a few of the many pages available in the complete product.
- *Product Description:* An electronic slide library with accompanying data cards that serve as an introduction to Impressionist painting and its sources and successors in Classicism to Post-Impressionism.

Renaissance Masters #1
- *Location:* \WIN\MMREF\RENAISS1
- *Category:* CD-ROM Storybooks
- *Special System Requirements:* None
- *Limitations of the version of the companion CD-ROM:* Show only; contains only a few of the many pages available in the complete product.
- *Product Description:* The old masters come to life in this Electronic Library of Art volume, which covers painting, sculpture, and architecture from the early Italian Renaissance.

Renaissance Masters #2
- *Location:* \WIN\MMREF\RENAISS2
- *Category:* CD-ROM Storybooks
- *Special System Requirements:* None
- *Limitations of the version of the companion CD-ROM:* Show only; contains only a few of the many pages available in the complete product.

Star Child
- *Location:* \WIN\CDSTORY\SCHILD
- *Category:* CD-ROM Storybooks
- *Special System Requirements:* None
- *Limitations of the version of the companion CD-ROM:* Contains only a few of the many pages available in the complete product.
- *Product Description:* Written by Oscar Wilde, this story takes you on a journey through imagination and fantasy.

The White Horse Child
- *Location:* \WIN\CDSTORY\WHCHILD
- *Category:* CD-ROM Storybooks
- *Special System Requirements:* None
- *Limitations of the version of the companion CD-ROM:* Show only; contains only a few of the many pages available in the complete product.
- *Product Description:* A creative and imaginative story is that explores a young boy's encounter with his imagination and censorship in school, home, and society.

Please purchase the complete version of EBook's software through your local software distributor or call the 800 number listed.

The Companion CD-ROM   281

Morgan Interactive

Contact Information

32970 Alvarado-Niles Rd.
Suite 704
Union City, CA 94587

Software Title Represented on the CD-ROM

Morgan Interactive has generously provided the software in the following section for the *Edutainment Comes Alive!* companion CD-ROM.

The Ugly Duckling

- *Location:* \WIN\CDSTORY\UGLYDUCK
- *Category:* CD-ROM Storybooks
- *Special System Requirements:* Sound card
- *Limitations of the version of the companion CD-ROM:* Contains only a few of the many pages available in the complete product.
- *Product Description:* Hans Christian Andersen's classic fairy tale, "The Ugly Duckling," is brought to life in a highly animated and musical fashion.

Please purchase the complete version of Morgan Interactive's software through your local software distributor.

MVP Software

Contact Information

1035 Dallas S.E.
Grand Rapids, MI 49507-1407
800-968-9684 (Orders)

Software Title Represented on the CD-ROM

MVP Software has generously provided the software in the following section for the *Edutainment Comes Alive!* companion CD-ROM.

Word Search

- *Location:* \DOS\GENERAL\WORDSRCH
- *Category:* General Edutainment
- *Special System Requirements:* None
- *Limitations of the version of the companion CD-ROM:* None. Word Search is shareware. If you decide to use the software, you must register it.
- *Product Description:* Solve any of the many included puzzles, or let the computer create one using your word list. Easy listening original sound track for your sound card, nice Windows interface, and lots of fun.

Please register your copy of Word Search for Windows.

Paramount Interactive

Contact Information

700 Hansen Way
Palo Alto, CA 94304

Software Titles Represented on the CD-ROM

Paramount Interactive has generously provided the software in the following sections for the *Edutainment Comes Alive!* companion CD-ROM.

Rock, Rap 'n Roll

- *Location:* \WIN\CREATE\ROCKRAP
- *Category:* Creativity Tools
- *Special System Requirements:* 486 33Mhz (recommended minimum), super VGA with 256 colors (640x480), Sound Blaster or Sound Blaster Pro, external speakers, 8Mb RAM (recommended minimum), 540Kb of free conventional memory minimum, and optional microphone
- *Limitations of the version of the companion CD-ROM:*
- *Product Description:*

Movie Select

- *Location:* \WIN\MISC\MOVIESEL
- *Category:* Miscellaneous
- *Special System Requirements:* 486 33Mhz (recommended minimum), super VGA with 256 colors (640x480), Sound Blaster or Sound Blaster Pro, external speakers, 8Mb

RAM (recommended minimum), 540Kb of free conventional memory minimum, and optional microphone

- *Limitations of the version of the companion CD-ROM:* Contains only a few of the many movies contained in the full version.
- *Product Description:* Based on your selections from this extensive database, Movie Select helps you choose other movies that may be of interest to you.

Lenny's Music Toons

- *Location:* \WIN\CREATE\LENNY
- *Category:* CD-ROM Storybooks
- *Special System Requirements:* 486 33Mhz (recommended minimum), super VGA with 256 colors (640x480), Sound Blaster or Sound Blaster Pro, external speakers, 8Mb RAM (recommended minimum), 540Kb of free conventional memory minimum, and optional microphone
- *Limitations of the version of the companion CD-ROM:* Contains only of few of the screens and functions available in the complete product.
- *Product Description:* Join PTV and make your own music video!

Please purchase the complete version of Paramount's programs through your local software distributor.

Science for Kids, Inc.
Contact Information

OSLO
c/o Science for Kids
9950 Concord Church Road
Lewisville, North Carolina 27023
1-800-KSCIENCE (572-4362)

Software Title Represented on the CD-ROM

Science for Kids has generously provided the software in the following section for the *Edutainment Comes Alive!* companion CD-ROM.

Adventures with OSLO, Tools and Gadgets

- *Location:* \WIN\GENERAL\OSLO
- *Category:* General Edutainment
- *Special System Requirements:* PC or compatible with 80386SX/25MHz minimum, MPC Compatible CD-ROM drive, MPC compatible Sound Card, 4Mb of RAM (8 recommended), Microsoft extension for CD-ROM 2.2 or higher

> **Warning:** Your display adapter must be configured to display 265 colors at 640 X 480 resolution. Otherwise, errors may result.

- *Limitations of the version of the companion CD-ROM:* Contains only a few of the many places and things to do that are available in the full product.

- *Product Description:* Adventures with OSLO, Tools and Gadgets is an engaging physical science program for children over 5 years of age. The package is comprised of five unified features that use animation, sound, graphics and video: an animated storybook, an interactive database, and adventure game, a series of maze puzzles, and a color gallery complete with musical markers.

Please purchase the complete version of Adventures with OSLO through your local software distributor or contact Science for Kids at the 800 number listed for more information.

Waterford Institute
Contact Information

1590 East 9400 South
Sandy, UT 84092

Software Titles Represented on the CD-ROM

The Waterford Institute has generously provided the software in the following sections for the *Edutainment Comes Alive!* companion CD-ROM.

Mental Math Games

- *Location:* \DOS\DRILL\MMATH
- *Category:* Drill-and-Practice
- *Special System Requirements:* None
- *Limitations of the version of the companion CD-ROM:* Show only demo; highlight the features of the software.

- *Product Description:* Seven entertaining and educationally effective games that teach math skills.

Rusty and Rosy Read with Me
- *Location:* \DOS\PSCHOOL\R&R_READ
- *Category:* Preschool
- *Special System Requirements:* None
- *Limitations of the version of the companion CD-ROM:* Show only, except Word Traveler, which is partially interactive.
- *Product Description:* Entertaining and educationally effective games that teach reading skills.

Please purchase the complete versions of Waterford Institute's products through your local software distributor.

Appendix B

The Basics of Telecommunication

This appendix introduces you to the world of telecommunication. Telecommunication is the electronic transfer of information, and with respect to personal computer users, telecommunication involves sending and receiving information through the phone lines. When you connect your PC to your phone lines, you gain access to vast amounts of information and huge numbers of people. All you have to do is add some inexpensive hardware and software.

The field of telecommunication has its own buzzwords and assumptions. The information in this appendix should help you understand enough to get started.

The following topics are discussed in this appendix:

- What telecommunication has to do with edutainment
- Modems
- Communication software
- The kinds of systems with which you can communicate
- An example of downloading an edutainment program

The sea of information on the other end of your phone line holds some valuable treasures for the edutainment user. Read on and find out more about these treasures.

Note: People commonly drop the *tele-* prefix from the word *telecommunication*. Throughout the rest of this appendix, I use *communication* and *telecommunication* interchangeably.

Telecommunication and Edutainment

Telecommunication is going to be an important part of edutainment in the future. It is already changing the way traditional educational material is prepared and delivered. Educators and software developers use systems such as the Internet (more on the Internet later in this appendix) to communicate with their colleagues, to gather information, and to collaborate on projects. An immense amount of information is available on computer systems around the world, and every day, more of that information becomes available to anyone with a modem. Children in the wide open spaces of the western United States take classes electronically, corresponding with classmates and the instructor through a modem. Educational software is available for downloading from huge information services and from tiny local bulletin boards.

Right now, the primary way that telecommunication affects edutainment is in the availability of software. A large body of edutainment software is distributed by a method known as *shareware*.

Shareware is basically a try-before-you-buy distribution scheme. Users are encouraged to try the program for some period of time before paying for it. Only when the user decides to keep and to continue using the product must he or she register and pay for it. Registration normally earns the user a more powerful version of the software, printed manuals, or other benefits.

Although this may sound like an odd way to market software, the system can and does work for many edutainment authors. Several of the edutainment products discussed in this book are shareware. A number of shareware products are also included on the *Edutainment Comes Alive!* CD-ROM that you'll find attached to the inside back cover of this book.

At this point, you may wonder what all this has to do with telecommunication. Unlike regular retail publishers, who actively discourage you from sharing software with others, shareware authors encourage you to pass along unregistered copies of their products. One of the primary distribution channels for shareware is through electronic bulletin boards (BBSs) and information services. Individuals use their PC telecommunication equipment to transfer copies of these products from BBSs and information services into their home computer. This process is known as *downloading* a program.

Using shareware edutainment products has some of the following advantages:

- You can download shareware any time of the day or night, without leaving your home.
- You can give a product a reasonable trial before you pay for it. If you don't like the product, just delete it from your hard disk.
- You can try many products at little or no cost.
- Shareware products must give you your money's worth, or you won't register.
- Because shareware doesn't have the marketing and packaging expenses that retail software does, shareware products normally cost less than their retail counterparts.
- When you contact a shareware company, you can usually deal directly with the author of a program.

Over the next decade or so, telecommunication systems will become much more powerful and accessible to the general public. As you know, the United States is developing an *information superhighway* that eventually will link every home, school, and business into one giant telecommunications network. The potential of such a network is incalculable. As the information superhighway becomes more accessible, more of our day-to-day activities, including education and entertainment, will involve telecommunication. Some of the following activities will merge edutainment and telecommunication:

- Software publishing giants such as Electronic Arts are looking at the information superhighway as a way to deliver their retail products and other interactive edutainment products.
- Researchers are creating simulated environments in which people from around the world can interact and learn together. Although current systems are text-based, more powerful PCs and communications equipment will eventually make these into virtual realities.
- The information-handling capabilities of the existing parts of the superhighway are being drastically increased.
- More efficient methods of data compression are being developed. Eventually it will be possible to transmit high-quality video and audio information across the superhighway.

To take advantage of current telecommunication technology, you have to understand the basics. The rest of this appendix introduces you to the hardware and software you will need to get started.

Modems

You need two pieces of hardware to get started in telecommunication. The first item you need is an active phone line, and the second item is a modem. Virtually all PC communication involves a modem connected to your phone line and PC. A modem is the device that enables a computer to communicate over phone lines. The modem converts the digital signals from the computer into analog signals for the telephone system. It also converts the analog signals from the phone system into digital signals that the computer can understand. The name modem is derived from the fundamental functions of the device: *mo*dulating and *dem*odulating the digital data.

Buying a modem can be complicated, and the rest of this section is designed to give you the information you need to do so successfully.

Types of Modems

There are two types of modems: acoustic and direct connect. The direct connect type is far and away the most popular. Acoustic modems are seldom seen anymore and are suitable only for special circumstances (for example, some foreign countries do not allow direct-connect modems to be attached to their phone systems). The rest of this chapter concentrates exclusively on direct-connect modems.

Direct-Connect Modems

Direct-connect modems are so named because they connect directly into the phone line, bypassing the telephone handset (indeed, the entire telephone) completely.

A direct-connect modem plugs into the telephone line through a standard RJ-11 phone jack. These little rectangular receptacles accept the RJ-11 plug found on virtually all telephone lines today. Most direct-connect modems include a cable that goes from the modem to your telephone, so both can reside on the phone line simultaneously. This setup enables you to use either the phone or the modem without constantly disconnecting and reconnecting things.

Because direct-connect modems bypass the telephone, it doesn't matter what kind of phone you have. You don't even need a telephone to use your modem (although you *do* need your phone service to be active).

Almost all direct-connect modems have auto-dial and auto-answer capacity. These features enable your communication software (see the Communication Software section later in the chapter) to dial or answer for you.

Because direct-connect modems are the most popular type of modem, the competition is fierce among direct-connect modem manufacturers. The latest features appear on direct-connect modems first, later (if at all) showing up on acoustic ones.

Modem Features

There are many different features to consider when you are shopping for a modem. Speed is vital, but there is more to the equation than just speed. A fast modem that cannot communicate with the systems you are interested in is of no use. Likewise, a modem that stays in the closet because you have no room on your desktop for it is not of much benefit. The next several sections cover the most important features of modems. In addition, I offer my own suggestions about what is appropriate.

Speed

The speed of a modem refers to the rate at which it transfers information. The unit of measure for modem speed is *bits per second*, or *bps*. For early modems, the number of bits per second corresponded to something called the *baud rate*. As modems became faster, the equivalence between the baud rate and the number of bits per second broke down. Many people still use the term baud in place of bits per second or bps. Although this term is now technically incorrect, it is a common usage. Expect to hear modems described either way.

As you can imagine, increasing the speed of a modem is one of the primary goals of modem manufacturers. My first modem ran at 300 bps. My current one runs at 2400 bps and is considered just about obsolete (I'll be replacing it soon). Right now, the most popular modems run at 14,400 bps.

The primary use for a modem in edutainment is to download files, so it is important to have a fast modem. There is a catch here, though. Because your modem must communicate with the modem on the other end of the line, the information transfer can only go as fast as the highest speed *both* modems can support. If you have a 14,400 bps modem and the BBS you are using only supports 9600 bps, then 9600 bps is as fast as you can go.

Although I believe that telecommunication (along with CD-ROM) will be the biggest growth area in edutainment, not everyone will be a big modem user in the near future. If you just want to try out the world of telecommunication, get a 2400 bps modem. Although considered slow, these modems are dirt cheap (you can find them for under $40 today) and acceptable for the occasional download from a local BBS. With the low prices, you can easily afford to replace it if you decide to get more involved in telecommunication.

If you are serious about telecommunication, go for a 14,400 bps modem. Although faster modems are available, 14,400 bps should be fast enough for any edutainment system (at least for the next few years). Make sure that you read the remainder of this section before you purchase a 14,400 bps modem. At this level, there is more to modem speed than just the number of bits per second.

Internal versus External

Just as there are two types of modems, acoustic and direct connect, there are also two styles, external and internal. An external modem is one that has its own case and resides outside your computer. An internal modem, not surprisingly, resides inside your PC. Each type has advantages and disadvantages.

An external modem has its own power supply and connects to one of your machine's serial ports. Assuming that you have a spare serial port for it to use, an external modem does not use up any of the slots inside your computer. Some machines have just one serial port built in, however, so using it for the modem makes it unavailable for your mouse or any other serial port device.

Finding an electrical outlet to plug the modem into also may be difficult, and the power cord makes one more wire dangling around behind your desk. By the same token, because the modem has its own power supply, it doesn't load down the power supply in your PC.

Still, the biggest problem with an external modem is finding a place for it. I can't imagine how I could fit another little box in my workspace.

An internal modem, on the other hand, is simply a card that installs in one of the slots inside your machine. It has a built-in serial port and draws its power from your computer's power supply. Because it has its own serial port, an internal modem doesn't steal the port from whatever else you may already have connected to it (the mouse, for example).

Many PC serial ports have trouble working efficiently with high-speed modems. This is not a problem with an internal modem because the serial port built into the modem will certainly work with the rest of the device.

Because an internal modem mounts inside your PC and draws its power from there, it has no power cord dangling from it. It also doesn't take up any desk space. It does, however, use up a slot inside the machine and draws some power from your PC.

Unless you want to be able to carry your modem back and forth between PCs, or if your system is just so filled up or loaded down that it can't accept one, an internal modem is by far the best choice.

Command Set

In order for the computer to tell a modem what to do, it must be able to issue commands to the modem through the serial port. Early in the history of PC telecommunication, many different command sets existed, each created by a modem manufacturer for its own modem. This situation made it difficult to develop communication software that worked with a wide range of modems. Eventually, common sense prevailed, and the industry settled on a modem command-set standard.

The command set that has become the standard is the Hayes, or AT, command set. The name Hayes comes from the modem manufacturer who created the standard (for its own very popular modems). The AT comes from the fact that most of the commands in the set start with the characters AT (which stand for *attention*).

Most of the time, you don't have to know anything about the Hayes command set. All you really need to know is that virtually all communication software supports it, so you want a modem that does too.

Some manufacturers advertise an extended AT command set or something similar. This just means that their modems have special features that are controlled by a superset of the AT (Hayes) command set. These modems can run the basic command set just fine.

I strongly advise you not to purchase a modem that does not claim to be Hayes-compatible or AT-compatible. If you do, you severely limit your choices of communication software. Fortunately, the vast majority of modems manufactured today are Hayes-compatible.

Standards

Standards are vitally important to telecommunication. The parties (modems) at either end of the line must speak the same language or nothing happens. Although the Hayes command set became the standard through its widespread popularity, other telecommunication standards are determined by committees.

An international set of standards determines the modulation techniques, along with the error-correcting and data-compression protocols used by modems of different speeds. For modems with speeds less than 2400 bps, both US and international standards exist. From 2400 bps up, the international standards are used.

The standards are set by an organization known as the ITU–TSS (International Telecommunications Union–Telecommunications Standard Section). You may know them by their much more descriptive former name: CCITT (Consultive Committee on International Telephony and Telegraphy)! This organization hammers out standards that are adopted by the majority of modem manufacturers so that most modems can talk to most other modems.

Unfortunately, the standard names are no more transparent than the name of the organization that creates them. For example, the standards that apply to 2400 bps modems are V.22bis, V.42, and V.42bis! Modem standards are one of those subjects in which a good memory comes in very handy. Table B.1 contains a list of the standards for modems of various speeds.

Table B.1. Modem standards.

Modem Speed	ITU-TSS (CCITT) Standard
2400 bps	V.22bis
	V.42
	V.42bis
9600 bps	V.29
	V.32
	V.32bis
	V.42
	V.42bis
14,400 bps	V.32bis

The important thing to remember here is that you want a modem that supports one or more of the standards listed for the speed of the modem you are considering. If you would like to know what some of these standards mean, read the following sidebar (see "V. What?: The ITU-TSS (CCITT) Modem Standards").

Almost all modems are compatible with the standards for speeds less than their full speed. This is an important fact because you want your modem to be able to talk to modems that can run at your modem's speed or slower, and you want modems that can run faster than yours to be able to talk to it.

At the present time, the ITU-TSS appears to be bogged down in the creation of the latest standard, V.34. This standard, commonly known as V.fast, will eventually be one of the standards that governs modems with speeds of 19,200 bps.

V. What?: The ITU-TSS (CCITT) Modem Standards

As you have probably surmised, just knowing the name of a standard doesn't tell you much. As you will discover, there really isn't much rhyme or reason to the names, anyway. If you really want to know what a particular standard means, read on.

V.22bis—This standard specifies a full-duplex transmission method that allows a 600-baud modem to transfer data at 2400 bps.

V.32—This standard specifies two modulation techniques: quadrature amplitude modulation and trellis coded modulation (don't ask) that enable a modem to transmit up to 9600 bps.

V.32bis—Adds another modulation technique to the two that are part of V.32. This enables a modem to transmit up to 14,400 bps.

V.42—This standard specifies support for LAPM and MNP 1 through four error-correction protocols. Modems that comply with V.42 (V.42-compliant) support LAPM error correction. Modems that are V.42-compatible can communicate with other V.42 modems but may or may not use LAPM error correction. They may use one of the MNP protocols instead.

V.42bis—This standard adds data-compression to the V.42 standard and allows up to four times the throughput when it is connected to another V.42bis modem. Unfortunately, a modem that meets V.42bis isn't necessarily faster than one that meets the V.32 standard. A 2400 bps modem can actually comply with V.42bis!

The situation is even more complex than this, with the various levels and types of error-correction dependent on what other types of error correction are active, and so on.

In the meantime, manufacturers have created an unofficial standard, V.32terbo. Modems that comply with V.32terbo run at 19,200 bps and are becoming accepted in the absence of V.34.

While all this is going on, Rockwell International has introduced its own new standard, V.32fast Class, which can take modems up to 28,800 bps!

To further add to the confusion, some manufacturers out there still have proprietary standards. A modem from one of these manufacturers normally can only use that standard with other modems by the same manufacturer, so stay away from these modems.

With all the ferment going on, it is impossible to tell you what standards to look for in high-speed modems. The best thing to do is to scour the magazine advertisements and look for the standard that seems to be most widely supported by the various manufacturers. Good luck.

If you buy a 2400 bps modem, just make sure you get V.22bis support.

Other Features

A variety of modem features do not directly affect the movement of data across the phone lines. This section discusses a number of the more popular features.

Auto-dial and auto-answer are standard features today. Auto-dial lets your modem call another modem without you dialing the number on a telephone. Combined with the appropriate communication software, auto-dial capability enables you to maintain a phone list on your PC. A call to your favorite BBS is then only a few mouse clicks away.

Auto-answer is the partner to auto-dial. This capability lets your friend's PC call your PC to initiate a direct connection. Many BBSs use a callback scheme to confirm your identity when you first join them; auto-answer is also useful in this case.

Your modem should be able to auto-dial using both touch-tone and pulse dialing. Although you probably won't need this feature, most modems come with the capability built in.

A built-in speaker can be nice when you have problems making a connection to another modem. If you hear a busy signal or a voice, you know that something is wrong. The problem with a speaker is that you have to listen to the annoying noises that modems make when they are getting ready to talk to each other. If you do buy a modem with a speaker, make sure that it can be turned down or off, whether manually or under software control.

Dual phone jacks enable you to have both the modem and the telephone on the same line. A modem with this feature comes with a short phone cord that plugs into the modem and into your telephone. When the other jack is connected to the regular phone line, both the modem and the phone can use it. Of course, you still can't make a phone call while the modem is active, and vice versa.

Many modems now have built-in fax capability. Usually, they can both originate and receive faxes. Fax software is necessary to use this feature, but fax/modems normally come with their own fax software.

Even if you add a fax/modem to your system, you should remember that it doesn't have all the capabilities of a stand-alone fax machine. The biggest limitation of fax/modems is that the information you want to fax must reside in the PC. You can't feed a piece of paper into a PC like you can with a stand-alone fax machine!

Although not a feature of the modem itself, it helps if you buy a modem that has been tested with the popular communication programs. Many of these programs provide a list of modems that the programs are known to work with. You can save yourself possible problems if you choose a modem that shows up on one or more of these lists.

Sending Information over Phone Lines

The preceding sections provided what you need to know about modems to get on-line. However, they still didn't explain how data actually travels along the phone lines. If you are interested in that information, read on. If not, skip ahead to the section "Special Considerations."

Data in your computer consists of groups of bits. Depending on the type of microprocessor your machine has, these bits are grouped into varioussized units for use inside the machine. For telecommunication, the most important grouping is a *byte*, which consists of 8 bits.

A byte can represent a number from 0 to 255 (see the following sidebar, "Binary Basics," for more information). These 256 different numbers can also be interpreted as codes identifying characters. A standard coding scheme for storing characters is called ASCII.

Binary Basics

Computers use the binary number system, in which each bit can represent one of two numbers, 0 or 1. By stringing bits together into larger groups, larger numbers can be represented. Two bits enable you to represent the numbers 0 through 3. To see how, think about the way we handle numbers.

Although computers use the binary number system (base 2), humans use the decimal system (base 10). Each digit in a number can range from 0 to 9. To create a larger number, we use more digits. Although we seldom think of it this way, the number 10 in decimal actually stands for 0 × (10 raised to the 0 power) + 1 × (10 raised to the first power). The number 111 is 1 × (10 raised to the 0 power) + 1 × (10 raised to the first power) + 1 × (10 raised to the second power). And on it goes, allowing us to create any size number we need.

Binary works the same way, except that each digit represents another power of 2 rather than a power of 10. The number 111 in binary is 1 × (2 raised to the 0 power) + 1 × (2 raised to the first power) + 1 × (2 raised to the second power). This is equivalent to the number 7 in our decimal system. Notice that the 3 bits in the binary number can hold from 0 (000 in binary) to 7 (111 in binary). This is a total of 8 different numbers, which is also 2 raised to the third power.

If you follow the analogy along, a byte (8 bits) can represent 2 raised to the 8 (eighth) power, or 256 different numbers. The numbers in a byte range from 0 to 255.

The ASCII (American Standard Code for Information Interchange) code uses the first 7 bits of a byte (the numbers 0 through 127) to represent text and some special characters. Because your PC uses 8-bit bytes and ASCII only requires 7 bits, the highest bit in each byte is set to 0 (zero). Virtually any computer system can understand ASCII, so it is *the* basic language of telecommunication.

Data moves around inside your machine in *parallel*. All 8 bits of a byte (and frequently larger 16- and 32-bit chunks) move along multiple (parallel) paths simultaneously. Moving all the data in parallel is a fast and efficient way to do things. Unfortunately, phone lines consist of a single pair of wires in a sort of loop, providing just one path on which data can move.

With only one path, data must move down a phone line bit-by-bit. Converting data from its internal parallel form into the bit-by-bit serial form is the first task in sending data by way of modem. Likewise, converting data from serial form back into parallel form is necessary at the other end. Compared to parallel, serial communication is slow and cumbersome, but it is the only way to send data using the phone system.

The device that converts data from parallel to serial form and back again is your serial port. A PC typically comes equipped with one serial port. An internal modem has its own serial port, which leaves any other serial ports available for other uses. Serial ports and modems know how to talk to each other and how to handle moving the data into and out of the computer. The other part of the process is getting the data into and out of the phone lines.

As you now know, the word modem is short for modulator/demodulator. A modulator varies the characteristics of the carrier wave to transfer information. A demodulator extracts the information from a carrier wave. For a modem, the carrier wave is an analog signal with a frequency that can be transmitted through the phone system.

An analog signal is one that varies continuously. Sound waves are analog in nature, as are the electrical representations of them that move through the phone system. The simplest wave is a sine wave. Notice how the sine wave in the first figure on the following page changes continuously from point to point.

The serial port works with digital signals. A digital signal is one that does *not* vary continuously. Instead, a digital signal is either in one state or the other. The second figure shows a square wave, which is a typical digital signal. Notice how the signal jumps from one level to another, spending no time in between levels.

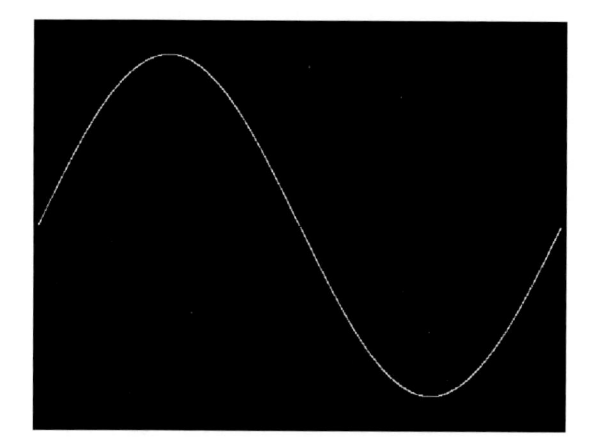

▲ *A sine wave.*

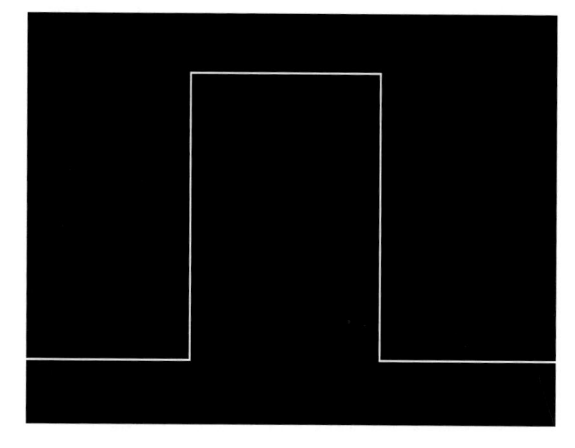

▲ *A square wave.*

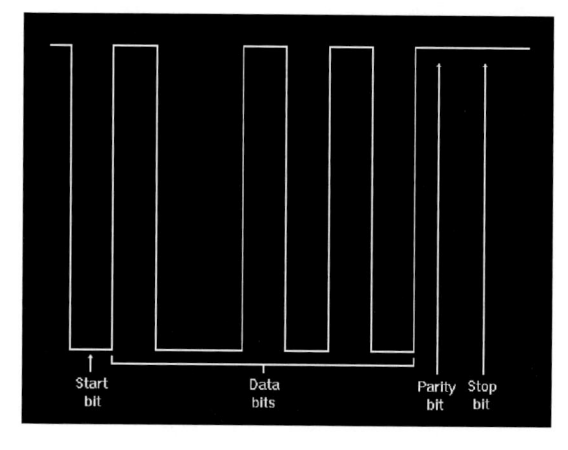

▲ *The letter J transmitted asynchronously.*

A modem uses various schemes to modulate the carrier wave with the digital data. The schemes range from changing the frequency of the carrier wave to using multiple carrier waves, and on to such things as *quadrature amplitude modulation* and other exotic techniques. Whatever the technique used, the modem eventually modulates the carrier wave to carry the data.

Just getting raw data into and out of the phone system isn't enough. The modem must also be able to determine which bits go together into a byte. Sometimes a bit of data is lost, or a spurious one is added along the way. Without some way of knowing where bytes of data start and end, the first mistake would corrupt all the rest of the data. Modems add additional bits to the data stream that identify the start and end of bytes. When the modem frames the data byte-by-byte, it is called *asynchronous* communication.

Besides the start and stop bits, the modem may add a parity bit. This bit can be used in error-correcting schemes, although it typically is ignored and removed by the serial port. The following sidebar (see "Parity") tells you how it works.

When you add start, stop, and parity bits (collectively known as *overhead*) to the data, you end up sending significantly more bits than your raw data includes. The next figure shows the bits a modem might actually send to transmit the letter J.

I hope this section has satisfied your curiosity about how modems communicate across phone lines. For even more information, you should purchase one of the many telecommunication-specific books now available.

Parity

Parity checking is a simple error-detection method. The most common type of parity checking is odd/even checking. To use parity checking, the transmitting computer first counts the number of bits that are set to 1 in the byte. It then sets the parity bit according to the type of checking used. If your system is set for even parity, it sets the parity bit either to 1 or 0 so that the number of bits set to 1 in the data byte, including the parity bit, is even. A similar process is used for odd parity.

When the other machine receives the data, it checks to see whether the data byte, plus the parity bit, still has the correct parity. If not, the PC requests that the data be sent again.

For parity checking to be effective, both machines must be using parity checking, and both must be set for the same kind of checking (odd or even).

Special Considerations

There are a few things to consider when you telecommunicate through the phone system. The principal concerns and various solutions are described next.

Line noise is a problem that you can't do much about. The same kinds of static and cross-talk (sounds from other lines) that can make voice communication difficult play havoc with modem communication. You can do a few things to work around it, such as call back, with the hope of getting a better connection, or you can run your modem at a lower speed. Generally, the faster the modem runs, the more sensitive it is to noise.

Luckily, the problem of line noise is receding as phone companies upgrade their systems to fiber optics.

For the fastest auto-dialing, you want a touch-tone phone. Most modems can talk to a rotary-dial phone using pulse dialing, but it's a far slower proposition than tone dialing. Pulse dialing works by sending a series of clicks for each digit of the phone number, so the speed difference between tone and pulse dialing is apparent. If you are concerned with the fastest, most efficient dialing (by both your computer and yourself), switch to touch-tone service.

Call-waiting can cause problems when you use your modem. The beep that signifies another call can cause the modem to think the carrier signal has been lost, which may cause it to disconnect and terminate the transmission. Even if the modem doesn't disconnect, it is possible for your communication software to become confused and lock up. To resolve this problem, you should contact the phone company to see if they can offer some simple procedure that disables call waiting for the duration of the call (prefixing the phone number you dial with a *70 works in many areas).

With the way phone systems currently work, using the modem means that your phone line is busy and that an urgent call from Uncle Charlie can't get through. Until the phone companies upgrade their systems to allow simultaneous voice and data communications on one line, you have two possible solutions to this problem. You can either subscribe to a voice mail service (available in many areas), or you can install a separate phone line for your computer room.

Communication Software

A modem without communication software is useless. Although the modem knows how to move information back and forth across the phone lines, something has to tell it what to do. Communication software (often called *comm* software for short) controls the modem, based on your commands. It also takes the raw data from the modem and puts it in a form that humans can understand.

Sophisticated comm programs can dial the phone for you, give your name and password when required, gather information in which you are interested, and disconnect from the BBS or information service it just called. The rest of this section discusses particular comm programs and presents the features and capabilities you should look for when you buy one.

Types of Communication Programs

Communication programs come in two basic types: front-end and terminal programs. *Front-end* programs are designed to work specifically with a particular on-line information service. These programs include various features and advantages that make them useful for the particular services for which they were intended.

The most common communication programs, however, are *terminal* programs (often simply called *communication* programs). These programs act as if they were terminals attached to the computer system on the other end of the phone line. They can talk to just about any of the bulletin board systems and on-line information services out there.

Features of Communication Programs

Beyond masquerading as a remote terminal, communication programs provide a range of capabilities. The most powerful programs provide built-in phone directories, let you automate common tasks, and have a host of other features. Because all communication programs perform the same basic tasks, their specific features are what distinguishes them from one another. The following sections describe features to look for when you are shopping for a communication program.

Supported Modems

Virtually all modems support the Hayes (AT) command set, so you might think that a list of supported modems is of little use. As it turns out, even modems that claim to be 100-percent Hayes-compatible have some slight incompatibilities. Major communication programs address this problem with a list of supported modems.

Any program is likely to support the brand name modems. Where you can run into problems is with a less expensive or less well-known modem. If you have one of these, check the supported modems lists of several of the major communication programs. Some programs list over 100 different modems with which their product is known to work!

If your modem isn't listed for the program you decide to use, make sure that the program lets you change command strings and initialization codes. Although this can be a pain to fool with, you usually can enter the correct codes for your modem and make the two work together.

Dialing Directory

This feature is a must. A dialing directory contains the names, phone numbers, and other parameters of the BBSs and information services you use. Look for a directory that can hold a large number of entries and can associate a script with each. Using software with a dialing directory and scripts—together with your modem's auto-dial capability—lets you get on-line at your favorite services with only a few keystrokes.

File Transfer Protocols

Sending ASCII characters back and forth works fine when all you are doing is chatting or reading messages on a bulletin board. But ASCII doesn't work for tasks such as uploading and downloading files. For that, you have to use file transfer protocols.

Remember that ASCII uses 7 bits to represent characters. The eighth bit in a byte is ignored (or sometimes used as a parity bit). Files such as executable programs or graphics images use all eight bits in every byte, rendering ASCII useless for transferring these files.

Although the name sounds intimidating, a file transfer protocol is nothing more than a set of rules that defines how data is sent between systems. These rules usually define, among other things, how the data is divided.

Most file transfer protocols send data in chunks (called *blocks* or *frames*) rather than byte by byte. A data frame may consist of 128 or 1024 bytes of data, preceded and followed by blocks of control information.

The control blocks often contain information about the block of data being sent, such as the number of bytes in the block, and perhaps a *checksum* that can be used for error-detection. A checksum is the sum of all the data bytes. The odds of an erroneous transmission having the identical checksum as the original are small, so the checksum can be used to indicate errors.

Many protocols also include error-correction schemes. These schemes use checksums or some other method to determine if the data in a block is corrupted. If it is, they can tell the transmitting machine to resend the data block.

Because file transfer protocols eliminate the start, stop, and parity bits that are added to each byte during ASCII telecommunications, they result in faster transfers than ASCII. This is true even with the additional overhead of error-detection and error-correction.

To further speed things up, some protocols include data compression. The data is compressed before going to the modem and decompressed when it comes out at the receiving machine.

It is important to choose communication software that supports a wide variety of file transfer protocols. Not every on-line system supports every protocol, so having an assortment of the most popular ones virtually guarantees that you will be able to talk to whatever systems you choose. The following sidebar (see "File Transfer Protocols") describes several of the most popular protocols.

File Transfer Protocols

Xmodem—Also known as Xmodem/Checksum, this protocol is about as close to universal as you get. It is in the public domain and is available in any general purpose communication software. Xmodem also works with any information service or BBS (except those that run only a proprietary protocol).

Xmodem is an error-checking protocol. Data is sent in 128-byte blocks, followed by a checksum byte. The transmitting machine calculates this checksum based on the data in the block. The receiving machine uses the same algorithm to calculate the checksum based on the data it received. The receiving machine then compares the calculated checksum to the received one.

After the transmitting machine sends the block and the checksum, it waits for a message from the receiving machine. If the calculated checksum agrees with the transmitted checksum, the receiving machine sends an acknowledgment message to the transmitting machine, which then sends the next block of data.

If the checksums do not agree, the receiving machine sends a message to the transmitting machine telling it to resend the current data block.

Xmodem/CRC—This is an improved version of Xmodem that adds an additional byte of error-detection information to each block. This additional byte significantly increases the chances that any error in a data block will be detected.

1K-Xmodem—This Xmodem variant transmits 1024-byte blocks (1024 is known as 1K in computer circles) rather than the 256-byte blocks of standard Xmodem, which makes it somewhat faster for sending large files. Where the connection is poor, the need to frequently retransmit larger blocks may make this protocol slower than regular Xmodem.

Ymodem—Ymodem uses larger (1024-byte) blocks and less error checking than Xmodem, for more speed when transferring large files. This works well as long as there is a good connection with little noise. In situations with many transmission errors, the larger block size can be a disadvantage.

Ymodem also permits *batch processing*. With Xmodem you must specify a file to be sent, send it, and then specify the next file. Ymodem lets you specify groups of files to be sent, and then sends them all, one after another.

Zmodem—This protocol uses blocks of 512 or 1024 bytes and doesn't wait for a message from the receiving system before sending the next block. If the receiving machine does report a problem, Zmodem goes back and retransmits the bad data.

Zmodem can resume interrupted file transfers. It can also check the date of a file against that of a file with the same name that resides on your hard disk. This enables Zmodem to avoid overwriting newer files with older ones. Zmodem is fast and efficient and is becoming very popular.

Kermit—Kermit is a very flexible protocol. It can transmit 7-bit or 8-bit data and change the size of its data blocks (known as *packets* to Kermit users). Other features include automatic resynchronization if the file transfer is disrupted. Kermit can also change the size of packets depending on line conditions.

Like Ymodem, Kermit allows batch file processing, and like Xmodem, Kermit provides error-checking.

Kermit even has a simple data-compression scheme. When Kermit finds that one byte is repeated several times, it can send the byte, followed by a key that tells how many times to repeat the byte. For certain types of files, this can save a lot of transfer time.

Besides these widely used protocols, you may come across proprietary ones. Proprietary protocols usually are associated with information services, such as CompuServe and America Online.

CompuServe's B protocol is included with its communication software and is also supported by many standard communication packages.

Some communication software also comes with its own proprietary protocol. These protocols are usually faster than, or have some other advantage over, the standard protocols. Unfortunately, because these protocols are not standard, few communication packages support them, so you can usually only communicate with people using the same software as you.

Some proprietary protocols are designed to work particularly well with the information service with which they are associated. Others are designed to be better than the standard protocols by offering faster transfers, better error-correction, or improved data compression.

Look for communication software that supports Xmodem and Zmodem (almost all packages do). Beyond that, B protocol is good if you will be logging on to CompuServe without the benefit of a CompuServe-specific package, such as WinCIM. Beyond these three protocols, whatever you can get is great.

Macros

A *macro* is a set of keystrokes or commands. These commands are assigned a one- or two-key name that represents the macro. By typing the appropriate key, or keys, you can execute the entire macro.

The capability to create macros is important for a communication program. After you use a BBS or other on-line system for a while, you find that you repeatedly enter the same keystrokes. Commands such as the ones you use to reach a favorite area of a bulletin board or to disconnect from an on-line service are ideal candidates for macros.

Most communication programs let you create macros, although the number of possible macros, and the ease with which you can create them, varies from program to program. Think hard before purchasing a communication program that does not allow you to create macros.

Scripts

Many communication programs enable you to create *scripts*. A script is a set of commands that the software executes. Although this sounds a whole lot like a macro, scripts are far more powerful. Whereas a macro just blindly transmits a set of keystrokes or commands, a script can do much more.

Although the power of the script language included with communication programs varies, they all provide some capability to interact with the system on the other end of the line. A simple script enables you to automate such common activities as logging on to a favorite BBS. The script may call the BBS, wait until a connection is established, and then enter your name and password at appropriate times. Many communication programs come with predefined scripts for connecting to popular services such as CompuServe.

The easiest way to create a script is to use a program that has a script recording capability. Such programs record your keystrokes as you perform a task and save that information as a script. This capability enables you to create most or all of the scripts you are likely to need.

To create really fancy scripts, you need a communication program with a powerful scripting language. These languages let you create scripts that can make decisions and perform other sophisticated activities. Creating such a script is comparable to writing a program and, therefore, can provide all the same joys and headaches.

Choose a communication program that lets you record your own scripts. If it has a powerful scripting language as well, consider that an added bonus.

Data Capture

Most communication programs let you capture whatever appears on the screen. Data capture comes in many forms; depending on the particular program, you may be able to capture data to your hard disk, the printer, or to a capture buffer.

A *capture buffer* is an area of memory set aside to hold the incoming data. You usually can save the buffer to disk and print all or part of its contents. The buffer also lets you scroll backwards through the session to see data that has already disappeared.

Look for a program with a capture buffer that you can resize as necessary.

Terminal Emulations

Although all non-proprietary communication programs behave like a generic terminal, most also offer the capability to act like, or emulate, specific terminals. Specific terminal emulations are useful if you want to connect to minicomputers or mainframes.

You should ensure that your communication program can emulate at least a VT-100 and one or two other terminals.

Other Features

All sorts of other features are available that can make your life easier when you use a communication program. A good user interface is important but difficult to quantify. The program you choose should have menus for most commands. Mouse support for any pull-down menus is also nice. Are the colors used pleasant? Can you change them? In general, is the display pleasing to look at? Try to spend some time using a communication program before you buy.

The capability to run DOS commands from within the program can come in handy. Look for a program that provides a DOS shell or gateway.

A *chat mode* provides a separate area on the screen for you to work on messages before you send them. Without a chat mode, whatever you type goes out as you type it, so you don't have an opportunity to edit.

A *snapshot feature* enables you to grab a single screen of data quickly and easily.

Most of the better communication programs offer all of these features, so there really is no reason to do without them.

If you buy a modem with fax capabilities, make sure that you check out the fax software that comes with it. It is possible that the software packaged with the modem will meet your needs. If that's the case, don't worry about the fax support in a communication program. The fax support in many communication programs is either limited or nonexistent.

Who Do You Talk To?

After you have a modem and a communication program, you need someone to communicate with. Literally millions of computers are equipped with modems, ranging from Commodore 64s up to the largest supercomputer. Theoretically, you can communicate directly with any one of them.

More commonly, you may want to communicate with machines that are specifically set up for you to dial into. These machines range from local bulletin board systems and commercial information services to the globe-circling Internet. Another growing target for communication is a community network, or *freenet* (discussed shortly).

Bulletin Board Systems

A computer bulletin board system (BBS) is a computer running special bulletin board software. The system has one or more phone lines connected to it, which permits access by other computers. The BBS software answers the phone and provides a menu of options to the caller.

Bulletin boards provide options such as electronic mail (e-mail), message databases, on-line games, and the capability to upload and download files.

Bulletin boards are normally active most or all of the time, allowing users to connect at any time of the day or night.

No one knows how many BBSs (also known as *boards*) are in service around the world. It takes only a modest investment of time and money to start one, and no special licenses or permissions are required. Many boards last only a short time, while others grow huge and continue for years.

Some boards are free of charge and open to anyone, others require membership fees, and still others are private and serve a specific clientele. Your phone book probably has a listing of local BBSs. Try looking in the Yellow Pages under *Computers–Bulletin Boards*.

Calling local public bulletin boards is a great way to get started in telecommunication.

Community Networks (Freenets)

Several freenets are active in the United States. These systems are designed to provide community information, and various other resources, to a community free of charge. Many of these systems also provide access to the Internet (see "The Internet" section that follows). A freenet is under development here in Phoenix but is not yet operational. If you are lucky enough to live in a town with a freenet, you should give it a try.

On-Line Information Services

On-line information services are the next step up in size and power from local bulletin boards and freenets. These services provide all the facilities of local bulletin boards. They also include a range of additional services, such as forums that cover a wide range of topics.

These forums are almost miniature bulletin board systems. Each one is organized around a particular subject. Many computer hardware and software vendors sponsor forums on one or more of the services. These forums give you access to the technical support staff of the manufacturer, as well as a community of users of the vendor's products. I find that other users can frequently answer your questions even before the tech support staff can get around to it.

Far beyond the capabilities of most BBSs are the information sources that these on-line services offer. The offerings include news services (such as Associated Press), the contents of major publications (such as *Newsweek* and *U.S. News and World Report*), and stock market data—and these are just the tip of the iceberg. All the major services have on-line encyclopedias that are updated as often as quarterly.

The amount of software available on these systems is hard to believe. Bulletin boards and information services are the main distribution points for shareware, so authors ensure that the major services all have copies of their products. For the same reason, the software on these systems is usually the latest version, and new products are usually available here first. In addition, the major services all scan software for viruses before making it available to the general public. Downloading edutainment products from one of the big information services is safer than getting a copy from a friend.

The drawback of these systems is cost. The price structures for the major services are in flux right now, but you can expect to pay a monthly fee of around $10, plus various fees and surcharges. These fees normally cover a certain number of hours of use per month and/or access to certain parts of the system. You also may have to pay hourly fees of between $3 and $20 depending on the particular services you are using.

For the average edutainment user, Prodigy and America Online (AOL) are probably the best bets. Both services offer access to a large variety of shareware edutainment files and have user-friendly interfaces. Prodigy's interface can be slow, and advertising is displayed across the bottom of the screen. The America Online interface is excellent, but the system has less information than Prodigy. AOL, however, provides direct Internet access.

The Internet

The Internet (or the *Net*) is a huge network of millions of computers around the world. It links computers and networks at thousands of schools, government facilities, and research labs. Tens of millions of people have access to the Internet, and its use is expanding at greater than 10 percent *per month!* The amount of information available on the Internet is staggering: not megabytes, not gigabytes (billions of bytes) but terabytes (trillions of bytes)!

Researchers use the Net to share data and to collaborate with colleagues anywhere in the world. Libraries around the world make their card catalogs available on the Net. Teachers tutor students living in isolated towns. People keep in touch with electronic mail (e-mail). And universities maintain huge libraries of public domain and shareware files.

The Internet is not like any of the on-line systems. It has no central control, only a common language that all the systems on the network can use to transfer files. There is a group called the Internet Society, but it is a volunteer organization that provides suggestions and guidance rather than any kind of actual control.

Acquiring access to the Internet is not difficult, but like everything associated with the Internet, it is an ad hoc process. Many users have access through their schools or employers. Others obtain access through commercial Internet service providers or on-line information services such as GEnie and America Online. What you pay, and even the services to which you have access, depends on how you connect to the system.

Finding information on the Internet can be extremely difficult. Tools such as Archie, Gopher, and WAIS are available to do the work for you, but using the Internet is not for the faint of heart. If you really want to try it out, I recommend that you first purchase one of the many Internet guide books now available. A good one is *Navigating the Internet* (Sams Publishing).

Downloading an Edutainment Product

Suppose that you decide to download a shareware edutainment program. How do you go about it? In this section, I walk you through the complete process. For this example, we use a piece of communication software that every Windows owner already has—Windows Terminal. Windows Terminal is one of the accessory programs that comes with Windows. Although Terminal is an extremely low-powered program, it is ideal for this demonstration.

Terminal is a bare-bones product. It lacks many of the features and capabilities you want in a communication program that you use every day. Without all the bells and whistles, you can concentrate on the downloading task instead of getting distracted by a lot of fancy features. The steps to downloading a program are the same, regardless of the communication program you use. More powerful programs just make the task faster and easier.

If you have a modem, and you don't mind spending a few dollars in long-distance charges, you can follow along with this example. The bulletin board used in this example is the Software Creations BBS. Software Creations is a huge system with the capacity to communicate with dozens of users simultaneously. In a 1993 survey conducted by Board Watch magazine, Software Creations was voted the best BBS in the country.

Not only is Software Creations the number one BBS in the country, it is also the home board for many of the top shareware companies.

Setting Up Windows Terminal

Before you can use Terminal, you have to configure it to work with your modem. Terminal is found in the Accessories program group. The icon for Terminal resembles a telephone sitting in front of a monitor. Double-click the icon to activate Terminal. The main window for Terminal looks like the following figure.

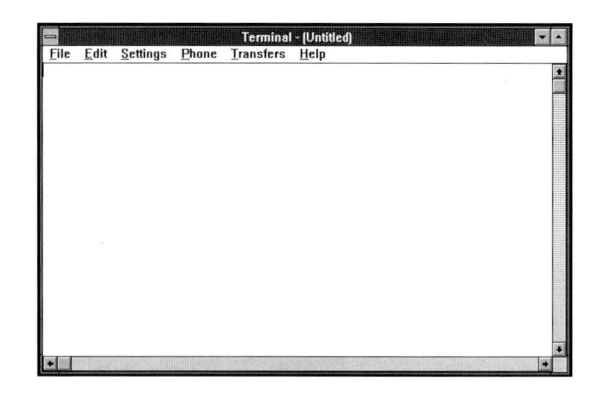

▲ *The Terminal main menu.*

Now that Terminal is active, you can begin configuring it. Click the Settings option in the Terminal menu bar to open the Settings menu.

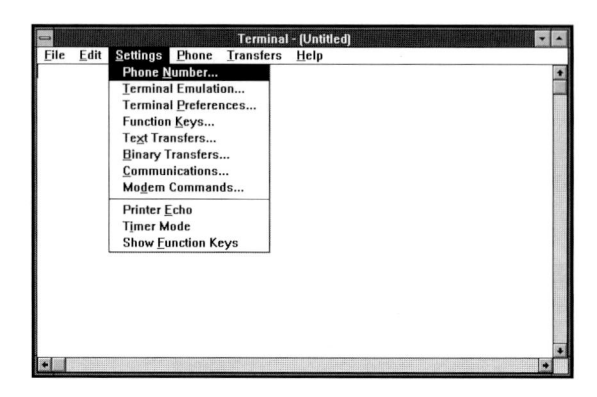

▲ *The Settings menu.*

First, let's set the communication parameters. Click the Communications menu option and the Communications dialog box appears.

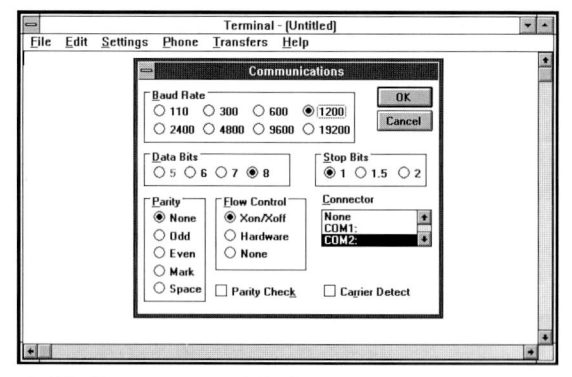

▲ *The Communications dialog box.*

Although the Communications dialog box isn't particularly pretty, it also isn't hard to work with. First, you have to set the Baud Rate. Terminal uses the term baud rate where, more properly, it should use bits per second. The figure shows that the default baud rate of 1200 is selected. Click the button next to the speed of your modem. If you have a 14,400 bps modem, select 9600.

Next, set the Parity, Data Bits, and Stop Bits. With the error-detecting protocols available, systems seldom use any parity bits, so click the button next to the word None in the Parity box. Most BBSs and information services use eight data bits, so click the button next to 8. Finally, most systems use one stop bit, so click the button next to 1.

After you have set these values, you have to check the Connector scroll box. The highlighted item should be the communications port to which your modem is attached. If you don't know which one is correct, choose COM2, which is the best guess for most modem installations. You can ignore the other parameters. Click the OK button.

You also must determine the modem command set that Terminal will use. Display the Settings menu again, and then select the Modem Commands menu option. The Modem Commands dialog box appears.

If you followed my advice and purchased a Hayes-compatible modem, you can simply select the Hayes option under Modem Defaults in the Modem Commands dialog box. Click the OK button when you are finished.

I like to do two additional things before I call a BBS: turn off the scroll bars and enlarge the

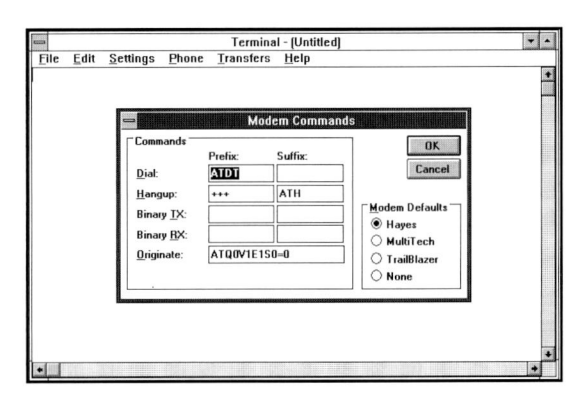

▲ *The Modem Commands dialog box.*

Terminal window. The goal in both cases is the same: ensure that a full screen of text from the BBS fits into the window. Resize the window by dragging the corners until you are satisfied. To turn off the scroll bars, open the Settings menu again and select Terminal Preferences. The Terminal Preferences dialog box appears.

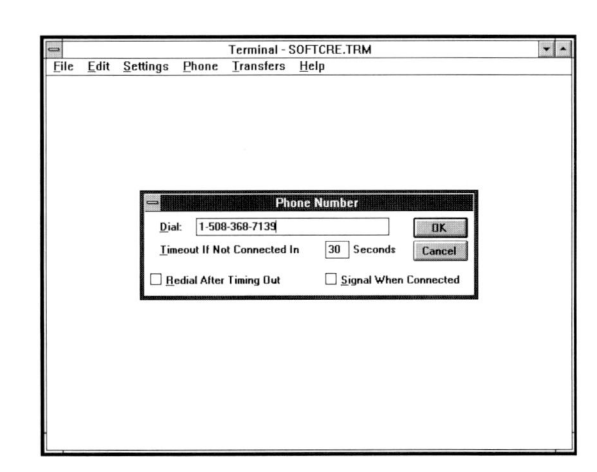

Click the check box entitled Show Scroll Bars until the box is cleared. Click OK when you are finished.

Finally, you have to set the phone number of the BBS you want to call. Again, open the Settings menu (not, as you might expect, the Phone menu), and this time select the Phone Number option. The Phone Number dialog box appears.

In the Dial text box, enter the phone number of the BBS you want to call. The number for the Software Creations BBS is 508-368-7139. The people at Software Creations welcome new users,

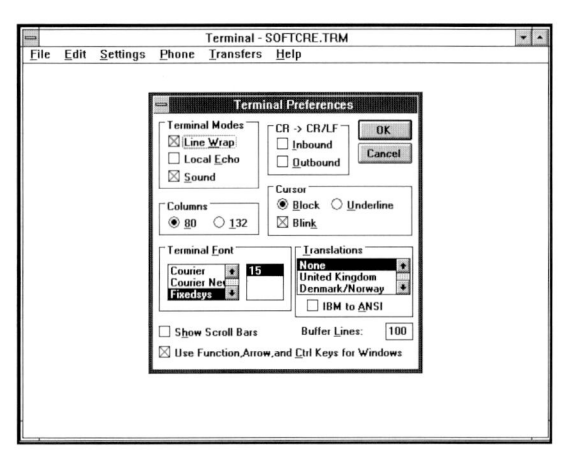

▲ *The Terminal Preferences dialog box.*

▲ *The Phone Number dialog box.*

so feel free to use this number. Use hyphens between each group of numbers as shown here, and don't forget to add any long distance prefix your long distance service requires. As always, click the OK button when you are finished.

> **Note:** Please note that to a certain extent each BBS is unique. The screens shown in this example are not identical to those you will find on other boards and, over time, are likely to change even on this board. This example is intended only to give you an idea of how this all works, not to give you step-by-step instructions that will work on any BBS.

Calling and Logging On

Now it is time to actually call the board. Select the Phone option from the menu bar to open the Phone menu and then choose the Dial option. If the Dial option is dimmed, click the Hangup option and wait for an OK to appear on the screen. Then reopen the Phone menu and again choose Dial. At this point, the modem dials the BBS and displays the dialing message box shown in the following figure.

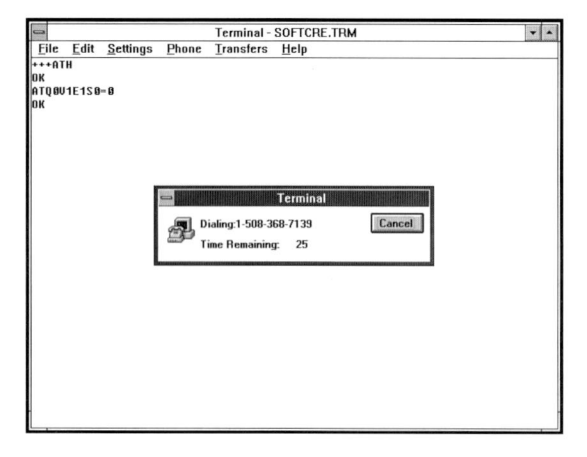

▲ *The dialing message box.*

Ignore the gibberish that appears on the left side of the Terminal window. Those strings of characters are the commands that Terminal sends to your modem. If you followed the suggestions about buying a modem that were provided earlier in this chapter, the strings you see on your screen should be similar or identical to the ones in the preceding figure.

If you get through to the BBS, a screen appears that resembles the one in the following figure. This is the first screen you see when you connect to the Software Creations BBS.

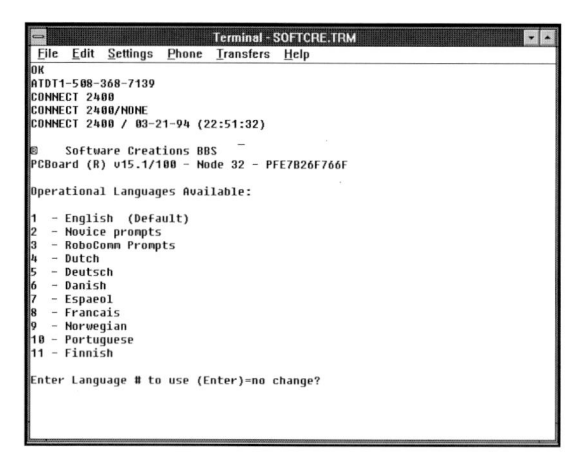

▲ *The initial screen for the Software Creations BBS.*

It may take 10 seconds or more for the entire screen to appear, so be patient. The last line of the screen says

`Enter language # to use (Enter)=no change?`

Bulletin board messages tend to be a little cryptic until you get used to them. This line means that you should select one of the languages from the list directly above this line and then enter the number corresponding to that language. Just type it; the program knows where it should go. Press Enter when you have typed the appropriate language number. The last part of the message means you can just press the Enter key, without typing any number, if you want to keep using the current (default) language (in this case, English).

After you select a language, additional information appears, and you end up at the actual opening screen for the board (refer to the following figure). Notice the odd characters on the screen? They represent codes that would be ASCII graphics if Terminal was capable of displaying them. They are only a decoration.

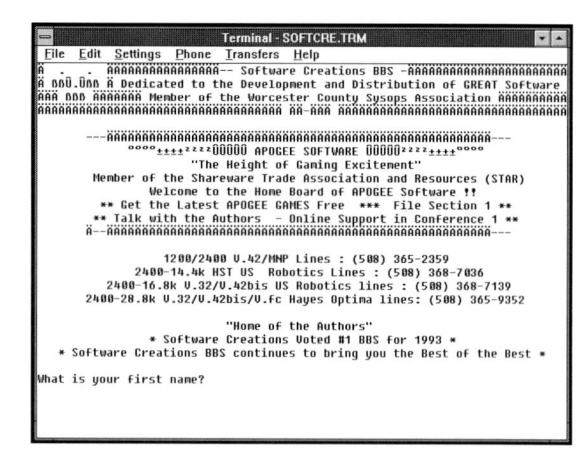

▲ *The opening screen and beginning of user identification.*

The last line on the screen requests that you enter your first name. Almost all bulletin boards require you to give a name and address when you log on. If

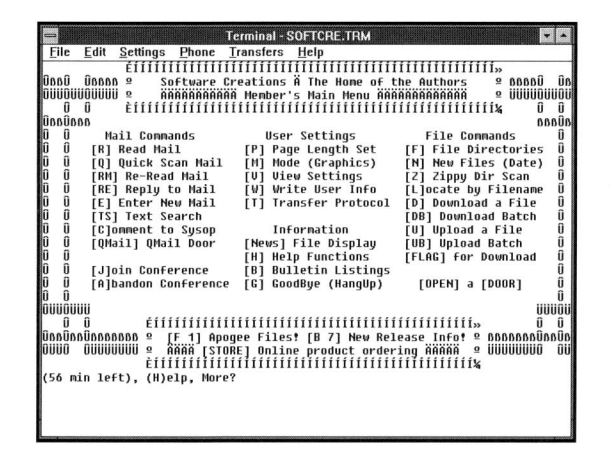

▲ *The member's main menu.*

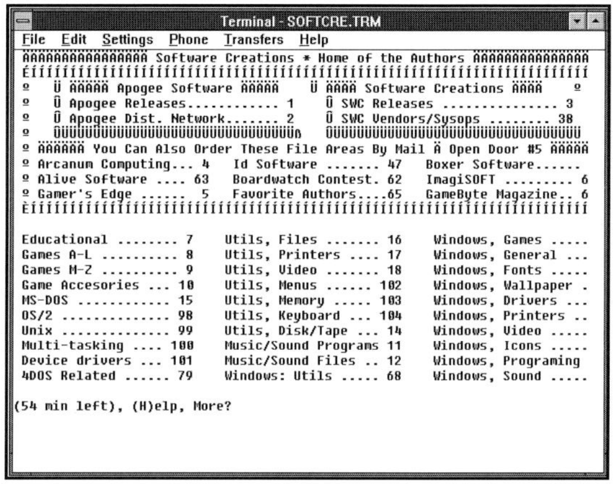

▲ *The beginning of the file area list.*

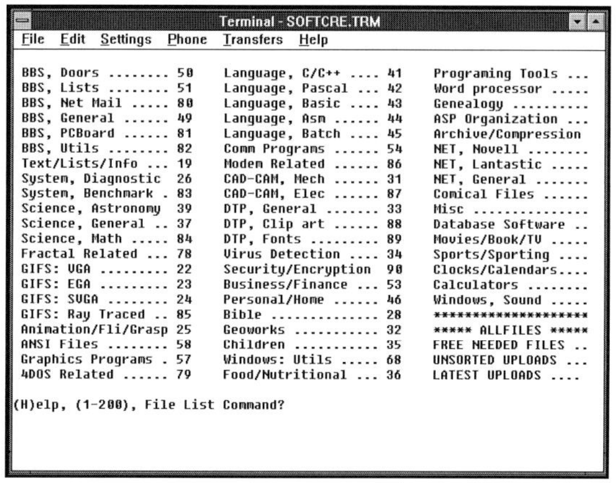

▲ *The end of the file area list.*

the system does not recognize your name, it then requires you to follow various procedures to confirm your identity. Because I am already a member of this board, I don't have to fill out the full questionnaire. When you first call the board, however, you have to go through the questionnaire procedure; just follow the directions, and you shouldn't have any trouble.

After you get through the user identification process, a screen appears that resembles the preceding figure. This is the member's main menu for the board. The one you see may differ slightly.

To search for edutainment products, press the letter *F* when the system asks for a main menu command. A message is then displayed that asks you for the number of the file area you want to view. If you press Enter instead of a number, the BBS lists all the file areas. You can get some idea of the number of files available on this particular board when you realize that *two* figures at the top of this page show the list of the file areas. And any number of files may be contained within each area.

Searching for Files

You can see from the figure showing the beginning of the file area list that educational products are in file area 7. When the `File List Command?` line is displayed, enter a 7 to view the Educational area.

When you enter the Educational file area, the screen fills with filenames, sizes, dates, and descriptions. To continue to view these file descriptions, press the Enter key (for More) whenever a line appears like the one shown at the bottom of the final figure on this page.

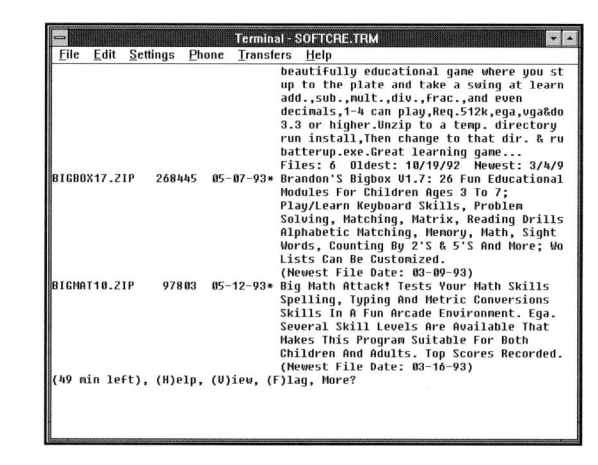

▲ *The file list provides descriptions of the various files.*

When you see a file you want to download, you can "flag" it. Instead of pressing Enter to display another screen of files, you press *F* to flag a file. The BBS then asks you to type the name of the file you intend to download. Spell the name exactly as it is shown in the File List, but you don't have to worry about the case of the letters. If you wanted to download Brandon's Bigbox V1.7, for example, you would type the filename **bigbox17.zip** (as shown in the following figure). Press Enter when you have correctly typed the name.

After you flag the file, the board checks your request. It confirms that you have the right to download the file, and then it determines how long the download will take, based on the file transfer protocol you chose when you filled out the initial questionnaire. Many BBSs require you to maintain a certain ratio of files that you contribute to the board versus the files you download from the board. You find out more about this when you read the introductory material that all boards provide as part of the initial sign-on process.

When you have finished flagging files, press the letter H to go to a Help screen. The Help screen can tell you how to stop viewing files and return to the main menu.

Downloading a File and Exiting the System

Now that you have flagged the files you want to retrieve and have returned to the main menu, it is time to download these files. At the `Main Board Command?` prompt, press *D* to tell the board you want to download your flagged files. Press *Y* at the `Download Flagged Files? (Y)` prompt. The board displays a set of statistics and readies itself to transfer files. Select the Transfers option from Terminal's menu bar, and the Transfers menu opens. Then choose the Receive Binary File menu option. Terminal displays the Receive Binary File dialog box. Choose a filename and directory for the file you are about to download. Click the OK button when you are finished, and the transfer begins. The following figure shows a download in progress.

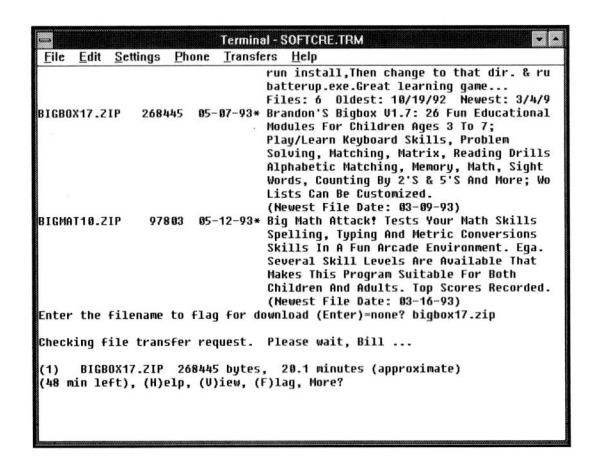

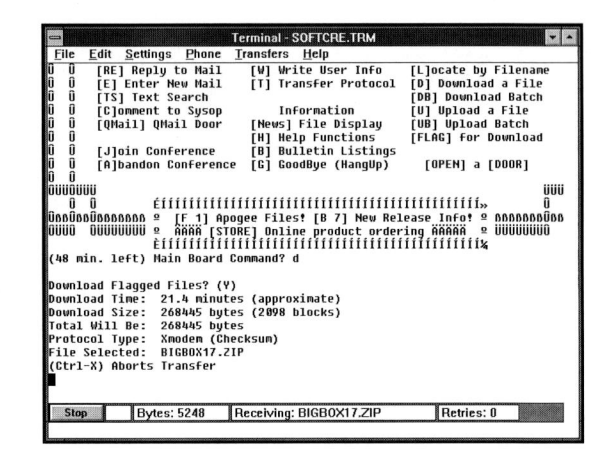

▲ *Flagging a file for download.*

▲ *A download in progress.*

After all the file transfers are complete, the board returns you to the main menu. Press the letter G to say goodbye to the board. Open the Phone menu and choose Hangup to disconnect the modem from the phone line. You have just downloaded your first file!

Appendix C

The MPC Specifications

This appendix contains the contents of the MPC-1 and MPC-2 specifications, as downloaded from the CDROM forum on CompuServe.

Multimedia PC Specification 1.0

The Multimedia PC Marketing Council, Inc., has developed a multimedia computer specification to encourage the adoption of a standard multimedia computing platform as an extension of the desktop PC already used by millions. When you see the distinctive Multimedia PC logo on computer systems or upgrade kits, you know that it guarantees that the hardware meets the Multimedia PC specification. End users can be assured that software bearing the Multimedia PC mark has been designed to work on Multimedia PC licensed hardware. By establishing a standard platform, and by guaranteeing plug-and-play simplicity for the consumer, the Council hopes to encourage widespread use of multimedia applications and hardware.

Hardware Specifications

CPU
: Minimum requirement: 386SX (or compatible) microprocessor

RAM
: Minimum requirement: 2M of RAM

Magnetic storage
: Requirement: 3 1/2 inch, high-density (1.44M) floppy disk drive

: Minimum requirement: 30M hard drive

Optical
: Requirement: CD-ROM drive storage with sustained 150KB/sec transfer rate; average seek time of 1 second or less; 10,000 hours MTBF; mode 1 capability (mode 2 and form 1 and 2 optional); MSCDEX 2.2 driver that implements the extended audio APIs; subchannel Q (subchannels P and R-W optional—if R-W subchannel support is provided, additional APIs must be implemented in MSCDEX driver; specifications for these additional APIs are available from Microsoft)

The drive must be capable of maintaining a sustained transfer rate of 150 KB/sec, without consuming more than 40 percent of the CPU bandwidth in the process. This requirement is for read block sizes no less than 16K and lead time of no more than is required to load the CD-ROM buffer with 1 read block of data. We recommend that the drive have on-board buffers of 64K and implement read-ahead buffering (read-ahead buffering is described in a specification available from Microsoft).

Audio
: Requirement: CD-ROM drive with CD-DA (Red Book) outputs and a front panel volume control. As an option, CD-ROM XA audio may be provided.

: Requirement: 8-bit (16-bit recommended) Digital-to-Analog Converter (DAC) with: Linear PCM sampling; DMA or FIFO buffered transfer capability with interrupt on buffer empty; 22.05 and 11.025 kHz sample rate mandatory; 44.1 kHz sampling rate desirable; optional stereo channels; no more than 10 percent of the CPU bandwidth required to output 11.025 or 22.05 kHz; no more than 15 percent for 44.1 kHz

: Requirement: 8-bit (16-bit recommended) Analog-to-Digital Converter (ADC) with: Linear PCM sampling; 11.025 kHz mandatory, (22.01 kHz, or 44.1 kHz sampling rate optional); DMA or FIFO buffered transfer capability with interrupt on buffer full; microphone input

Requirement: Internal synthesizer hardware with multi-voice, multi-timbral capabilities, 6 simultaneous melody notes, plus 2 simultaneous percussive notes

Requirement: Internal mixing capabilities to combine input from three (four recommended) sources and present the output as a stereo, line-level audio signal at the back panel. The four sources are: CD Red Book, synthesizer, DAC (waveform), and (recommended but not required) an auxiliary input source. Each input must have at least a 3-bit volume control (8 steps) with a logarithmic taper. (4-bit or greater volume control is strongly recommended.) If all sources are sourced with –10 dB (consumer line level: 1 milliwatt into 600 ohms=0 dB) without attenuation, the mixer will not clip and will output between 0 dB and +3 dB. Individual audio source and master digital volume control registers and extra line-level audio sources are highly recommended.

(Guidelines for synthesizer implementation available on request.)

Video

Requirement: VGA-compatible display adapter and a color VGA-compatible monitor. A basic Multimedia PC uses mode 12h (640x480, 16 colors). An enhanced configuration referred to as VGA+ is recommended with 640 x 480, 256 colors. The recommended performance goal for VGA+ adapters is to be able to blit 1, 4, and 8-bit-per-pixel DIBs (device independent bitmaps) at 350K pixels/second given 100 percent of the CPU, and at 140K pixels/second given 40 percent of the CPU. This recommendation applies to run-length encoded images and non-encoded images. The recommended performance is needed to fully support high-performance applications such as synchronized audio-visual presentations.

User input

Requirement: Standard 101-key IBM-style keyboard with standard DIN connector, or keyboard which delivers identical functionality utilizing key combinations.

Requirement: Two-button mouse with bus or serial connector, with at least one additional communication port remaining free

I/O

Requirement: Standard 9-pin or 25-pin asynchronous serial port, programmable up to 9600 baud, switchable interrupt channel

Requirement: Standard 25-pin bi-directional parallel port with interrupt capability

Requirement: 1 MIDI port with In, Out, and Thru, must have interrupt support for input and FIFO transfer

Requirement: IBM style analog or digital joystick port

System Software

The Multimedia PC system software shall conform to the APIs, function and performance described in the Microsoft Windows Software Development Kit Programmer's Reference, Volumes I and II (Version 3.0) and the Microsoft Multimedia Development Kit Programmer's Reference (Beta version, published November 15, 1991, and due to be updated at the final release of the Multimedia Development Kit).

Minimum Full-System Configuration

A full Multimedia PC system requires the following elements and components, all of which must meet the full functional specifications just outlined. Please note that this is a minimum system requirement and not a recommendation for a particular system configuration:

CPU	386SX or compatible microprocessor
RAM	2M of RAM
Magnetic storage	Floppy drive, hard drive
Optical storage	CD-ROM with CD-DA outputs
Audio	DAC, ADC, music synthesizer, on board analog audio mixing
Video	VGA graphics adapter 101-key keyboard (or functional equivalent), two-button mouse
I/O	Serial port, parallel port, MIDI I/O port, joystick port

Minimum Upgrade Kit Configuration

A Multimedia PC Upgrade Kit requires the following elements and components, all of which must meet the full functional specifications just outlined:

Optical storage	CD-ROM with CD-DA outputs
Audio	DAC, ADC, music synthesizer, on-board analog audio mixing
I/O	Serial port, parallel port, MIDI I/O port, joystick port

(Providing system software with upgrade kits is optional.)

Multimedia PC Specification 2.0

The Multimedia PC Marketing Council, Inc., has developed a second-level multimedia computer specification to encourage the adoption of enhanced multimedia capabilities. This specification is a backwardly compatible superset of the MPC Level 1 Specification, which continues in full effect. This specification defines the minimum system functionality for Level 2 compliance, but it is not intended as a recommendation for a particular system configuration.

Hardware Specifications

CPU	Minimum requirement: 25 MHz 486SX (or compatible) microprocessor
RAM	Minimum requirement: 4M of RAM (8M recommended)
Magnetic storage	Requirement: 3 1/2-inch, high-density (1.44M) floppy disk drive
	Requirement: 160M or larger hard drive
Optical storage	Requirements: CD-ROM drive capable of sustained 300KB/sec transfer rate

No more than 40 percent of the CPU bandwidth may be consumed when maintaining a sustained transfer rate of 150 KB/sec; average seek time of 400 milliseconds or less.

10,000 hours MTBF

CD-ROM XA ready (mode 1 capable, mode 2 form 1 capable, mode 2 form 2 capable)

Multisession capable

MSCDEX 2.2 driver or equivalent that implements the extended audio APIs

Subchannel Q support (P, R-W optional)

At 300 KB/sec sustained transfer rate it is recommended that no more than 60 percent of the CPU bandwidth be consumed. It is recommended that the CPU utilization requirement and recommendation be achieved for read block sizes no less than 16K

Audio	and lead time of no more than is required to load the CD-ROM buffer with 1 read block of data. It is recommended that the drive have on-board buffers of 64K and implement read-ahead buffering. Requirements: CD-ROM drive with CD-DA (Red Book) outputs and volume control. 16-bit Digital-to-Analog Converter (DAC) with: Linear PCM sampling; DMA or FIFO buffered transfer capability with interrupt on buffer empty; 44.1, 22.05, and 11.025 kHz sample rate mandatory; stereo channels; no more than 10 percent of the CPU bandwidth required to output 22.05 and 11.025 kHz; it is recommended that no more than 15 percent of the CPU bandwidth be required to output 44.1 kHz. 16-bit Analog-to-Digital Converter (ADC) with: Linear PCM sampling; 44.1, 22.05, and 11.025 kHz sample rate mandatory; DMA or FIFO buffered transfer capability with interrupt on buffer full; microphone input	Internal synthesizer capabilities with multi-voice, multi-timbral capacity, 6 simultaneous melody notes, plus 2 simultaneous percussive notes. Internal mixing capabilities to combine input from three (four recommended) sources and present the output as a stereo, line-level audio signal at the back panel. The four sources are: CD Red Book, synthesizer, DAC (waveform), and (recommended but not required) an auxiliary input source. Each input must have at least a 3-bit volume control (8 steps) with a logarithmic taper. (4-bit or greater volume control is strongly recommended.) If all sources are sourced with –10 dB (consumer line level: 1 milliwatt into 600 ohms=0 dB) without attenuation, the mixer will not clip and will output between 0 dB and +3 dB. Individual audio source and master digital volume control registers and extra line-level audio sources are highly recommended. CD-ROM XA audio capability is recommended.	Video User input	Support for the IMA adopted ADPCM software algorithm is recommended. (Guidelines for synthesizer implementation available on request.) Requirement: Color monitor with display resolution of 640 x 480 with 65,536 (64K) colors. The recommended performance goal for VGA+ adapters is to be able to blit 1, 4, and 8-bit-per-pixel DIBs (device independent bitmaps) at 1.2 megapixels/second given 40 percent of the CPU. This recommendation applies to run-length encoded images and non-encoded images. The recommended performance is needed to fully support demanding multimedia applications including the delivery of video with 320 x 240 resolution at 15 frames/second and 256 colors. Requirement: Standard 101-key IBM-style keyboard with standard DIN connector, or keyboard which delivers identical functionality utilizing key combinations. Requirement: Two-button mouse with bus or serial

I/O connector, with at least one additional communication port remaining free.

Requirement: Standard 9-pin or 25-pin asynchronous serial port, programmable up to 9600 baud, switchable interrupt channel.

Requirement: Standard 25-pin bi-directional parallel port with interrupt capability.

Requirement: 1 MIDI port with In, Out, and Thru, must have interrupt support for input and FIFO transfer.

Requirement: IBM-style analog or digital joystick port.

System Software

Multimedia PC system software must offer binary compatibility with Windows 3.0 plus multimedia extensions or Windows 3.1

Minimum Full-System Configuration

A full Multimedia PC Level 2 system requires the following elements and components, all of which must meet the full functional specifications just outlined:

CPU	25 MHz 486SX or compatible microprocessor
RAM	4M of RAM (8M recommended)
Magnetic storage	Floppy drive, hard drive (160M minimum)
Optical storage	CD-ROM double-speed with CD-DA outputs, XA ready, multisession capable.
Audio	16-bit DAC, 16-bit ADC, music synthesizer, on-board analog audio mixing
Video	Display resolution of at least 640 x 480 with 65,536 (64K) colors
Input	101-key keyboard (or functional equivalent), two-button mouse
I/O	Serial port, parallel port, MIDI I/O port, joystick port
System software	Binary compatibility with Windows 3.0 plus multimedia extensions or Windows 3.1

Minimum Upgrade Kit Configuration

A Multimedia PC Level 2 Upgrade Kit requires the following elements and components, all of which must meet the full functional specifications just outlined:

Optical storage	CD-ROM double-speed with CD-DA outputs, XA ready, multisession capable
Audio	16-bit DAC, 16-bit ADC, music synthesizer, on-board analog audio mixing
I/O	MIDI I/O port, joystick port

(Providing system software with upgrade kits is optional.)

Appendix D

Resources

This appendix contains a list of useful resources. Included here is only a small selection of the total resources available, but they should serve as a solid starting point for you to find out more about edutainment and to help you upgrade your PC to run edutainment software.

Books

The following books proved to be valuable resources during the creation of this book.

Berliss, Jane R. *Trace Resourcebook*. Minneapolis: Trace Research and Development Center, 1992.

Morrison, Mike. *The Magic of Interactive Entertainment*. Indianapolis: Sams Publishing, 1994.

Pivovarnick, John. *The Complete Idiot's Guide to CD-ROM*. Indianapolis: Alpha Books, 1994.

Magazines and Newsletters

The following magazines and newsletters provide information about edutainment products or about hardware and software upgrades.

CD-ROM Professional
Pemberton Press, Inc.
462 Danbury Road
Wilton, CT 06897-2126
(203) 761-1466
Fax (203) 761-1444

CD-ROM TODAY
GP Publications, Inc.
300-A S. Westgate Drive
Greensboro, NC 27407
(910) 852-6711
Fax (910) 632-1165

CD-ROM WORLD
Meckler Corporation
11 Ferry Lane West
Westport, CT 06880
(203) 226-6967

Club KidSoft
718 University Avenue, Suite 112
Los Gatos, CA 95030-9958
(800) 354-6150
Fax (408) 354-1033

COMPUTE
COMPUTE Publications International Ltd.
1965 Broadway
New York, NY 10023-5965

Computer Entertainment News
GP Publications, Inc.
300-A S. Westgate Drive
Greensboro, NC 27407
(910) 852-6711
Fax (910) 632-1165

Educational Technology
Educational Technology Publications
720 Palisade Avenue
Englewood Cliffs, NJ 07632

Electronic Entertainment
Infotainment World, Inc.
951 Mariner's Island Boulevard, Suite 700
San Mateo, CA 94404

HomePC
CMP Publications, Inc.
600 Community Drive
Manhasset, NY 11030
(516) 562-7124
Fax (516) 562-5482

InterAction
Sierra On-Line, Inc.
P.O. Box 485
Coarsegold, CA 93614
(209) 683-4468

MULTIMEDIA WORLD
501 Second Street
San Francisco, CA 94107
(415) 281-8650
Fax (415) 281-3915

NEW MEDIA
Hypermedia Communications Inc.
901 Mariner's Island Boulevard, Suite 365
San Mateo, CA 94404
(415) 573-5170
Fax (415) 573-5131

PC Magazine
Ziff-Davis Publishing Company, L.P.
One Park Avenue
New York, NY 10016-5802
(212) 503-5255

Resources

PC/Computing
Ziff-Davis Publishing Company, L.P.
One Park Avenue
New York, NY 10016-5802
(212) 503-5255

The ESC Newsletter
Educational Software Cooperative
P.O. Box 575
Siloam Springs, AR 72761

The Exceptional Parent
Psy Ed Corporation
170 Commonwealth Avenue
Boston, MA 02134

WINDOWS Magazine
CMP Publications, Inc.
600 Community Drive
Manhasset, NY 11030
(516) 562-7124
Fax (516) 562-5482

Windows Sources
Ziff-Davis Publishing Company, L.P.
One Park Avenue
New York, NY 10016-5802
(212) 503-5255

On-Line Services and BBSs

On-line services and BBSs are excellent sources of shareware edutainment products. The latest versions of products are often available on these systems weeks, or even months, before they show up in catalogs or on shelves. On-line services are also excellent sources of information and technical support for products.

ABLEDATA
8455 Colesville Road, Suite 935
Silver Spring, MD 20910
301-589-3563 (1200 to 9600 bps, N-8-1)

America Online
8619 Westwood Center Drive
Vienna, VA 22182-2285
(703) 448-8700

CompuServe
5000 Arlington Centre Boulevard
P.O. Box 20212
Columbus, OH 43220
(800) 848-8199

Delphi
General Videotex Corporation
3 Blackstone Street
Cambridge, MA 02139
(800) 544-4005

GEnie
GE Company Information Services Division
401 N. Washington Street
Rockville, MD 20850
(800) 638-9636

The ImagiNATION Network (INN)
41486 Old Barn Way
Oakhurst, CA 93644
(209) 642-0700
Fax (209) 683-3633

Prodigy Services Co.
445 Hamilton Avenue
White Plains, NY 10601
(800) 776-0845
Fax (914) 684-0278

Mail-Order Catalogs

These catalogs provide alternative sources for edutainment products. In general, their selection is much greater than the selection in retail stores. The shareware catalogs provide access to shareware edutainment for users who do not have a modem.

Educational Resources
1550 Executive Drive
Elgin, IL 60123
(708) 888-8300
Fax (708) 888-8499

EDUCORP
7434 Trade Street
San Diego, CA 92121-2410
(619) 536-9999
Fax (619) 536-2345

The Edutainment Company
932 Walnut Street
Louisville, CO 80027
(800) 338-3844

PsL News
P.O. Box 35705
Houston, TX 77235-5705
(713) 524-6394

Public Brand Software
P.O. Box 51315
Indianapolis, IN 46251
(317) 856-7571
Fax (317) 856-2086

Reasonable Solutions
1221 Disk Drive
Medford, OR 97501-6639
(503) 776-5777
Fax (503) 773-7803

The Software Labs
8700 148th Avenue, NE
Redmond, WA 98052
(800) 569-7900
Fax (206) 869-1503

Edutainment Product Providers

The companies listed here are known to publish edutainment products. This list is certainly incomplete because new companies are joining the fray virtually every week.

Applied Optical Media Corporation
1450 Boot Road, Building 400
Westchester, PA 19380
(800) 321-7259
Fax (215) 429-3810

Arnowitz Studio
650 E. Blithedale Avenue, #A
Mill Valley, CA 94941
(415) 383-2878

Avalon Hill Game Company
4517 Harford Road
Baltimore, MD 21214
(800) 999-3222
Fax (410) 254-0991

Baker & Taylor, Inc.
3850 Royal Avenue
Simi Valley, CA 93065
(800) 775-4100
Fax (805) 522-7300

Broderbund Software Inc.
17 Paul Drive
San Rafael, CA 94903-2101
(415) 492-3299
Fax (415) 492-3154

Bureau of Electronic Publishing, Inc.
141 New Road
Parsippany, NJ 07054
(201) 808-2700
Fax (201) 808-2676

Cambrix Publishing
6269 Variel Avenue, Suite B
Woodland Hills, CA 91367
(800) 992-8781
Fax (818) 992-8781

Compact Publishing Inc.
5141 MacArthur Boulevard, NW
Washington, DC 20016
(206) 244-4770

Compton's New Media
2320 Camino Vida Roble
Carlsbad, CA 92009
(619) 929-2500
Fax (619) 929-2555

Compu-Teach
16451 Redmond Way, Suite 137-C
Redmond, WA 98502-4482
(206) 885-0517 x13
Fax (206) 883-9169

Comtrad Industries
2820 Waterford Lakes Drive, Suite 106
Midlothian, VA 23113
(800) 992-2966

Context Systems, Inc.
The Technology Center
2935 Byberry Road
Hatboro, PA 19040
(215) 675-5000

Creative Multimedia Corporation
514 NW 11th Avenue, Suite 203
Portland, OR 97209
(503) 241-4351

Davidson & Associates, Inc.
19840 Pioneer Avenue
Torrance, CA 90503
(800) 545-7677
Fax (310) 793-0601

Delorme Mapping
Lower Main Street
Freeport, ME 04032
(800) 452-5931
Fax (207) 865-9291

Dinosoft, Inc.
9801 Dupont Avenue South
Bloomington, MN 55431
(612) 884-7935
Fax (612) 881-3882

Discis Knowledge Research, Inc.
P.O. Box 66
Buffalo, NY 14223-0066
(416) 250-6537

The Discovery Channel
7700 Wisconson Avenue
Bethesda, MD 20814
(301) 986-0444
Fax (301) 986-9537

Dr. T's Music Software, Inc.
124 Crescent Road
Needham, MA 02194
(800) 989-6434
Fax (617) 455-1460

Ebook Inc.
32970 Alvarado Niles Road, Suite 704
Union City, CA 94587
(510) 429-1331
Fax (510) 429-1394

Edmark
P.O. Box 3218
Redmond, WA 98073
(206) 556-8486
Fax (206) 556-8998

EduQuest/IBM
411 Northside Parkway
Atlanta, GA 30327
(404) 238-1233
Fax (404) 238-4301

Electronic Arts
1450 Fashion Island Boulevard
San Mateo, CA 94404
(800) 245-4525
Fax (415) 571-7995

Europress Software
P.O. Box 2961
Torrance, CA 90509
(800) 545-7677

Gazelle Technologies/EDUCORP
7434 Trade Street
San Diego, CA 92121
(619) 636-9999

Great Bear Technology Inc.
1100 Moraga Way
Moraga, CA 94556
(510) 631-1600
Fax (510) 631-6735

Grolier Electronic Publishing, Inc.
Sherman Turnpike
Danbury, CT 06816
(203) 797-3500
Fax (203) 797-3197

Humongous Entertainment, Inc.
12930 NE 178th Street
Woodinville, WA 98072
(206) 487-0505
Fax (206) 486-9494

HyperGlot Software Co., Inc.
P.O. Box 10746, 5108-D Kingston Pike
Knoxville, TN 37919-0746
(800) 800-8270
Fax (615) 588-6569

IBM Multimedia Publishing Studio
1374 W. Peachtree Street, Suite 200
Atlanta, GA 30309
(404) 877-1313

InterActive Publishing Corp.
300 Airport Executive Park
Spring Valley, NY 10977
(914) 426-0400
Fax (914) 426-2606

IVI Publishing
1380 Corporate Center Curve
Eagan, MN 55121
(612) 686-2600
Fax (612) 686-2601

Knowledge Adventure, Inc.
4502 Dyer Street
La Crescenta, CA 91214
(818) 542-4200
Fax (818) 542-4205

Labtec Enterprises, Inc.
11010 N.E. 37th Circle, Unit #110
Vancouver, WA 98682
(206) 896-2000
Fax (206) 896-2020

Lawrence Productions, Inc.
1800 S. 35th Street
Galesburg, MI 49053
(800) 421-4157
Fax (616) 665-7060

The Learning Company
6493 Kaiser Boulevard
Fremont, CA 94555
(510) 792-2101

Macmillan New Media
124 Mt. Auburn Street
Cambridge, MA 02138
(800) 342-1338

Magic Quest, Inc.
125 University Avenue
Palo Alto, CA 94301
(415) 321-5838
Fax (415) 321-8560

Maxis
2 Theatre Square, Suite 230
Orinda, CA 94563-3346
(510) 254-9700
Fax (510) 253-3736

MECC
6160 Summit Drive North
Minneapolis, MN 55430-4003
(612) 569-1692
Fax (612) 569-1551

Media Resources
640 N. Puente Street
Brea, CA 92621
(714) 256-5048

Media Vision, Inc.
47300 Bayside Parkway
Fremont, CA 94538
(800) 348-7116
Fax (510) 770-8648

MicroGrafx, Inc.
1303 Arapaho
Richardson, TX 75081
(214) 234-1769

MicroProse Software
180 Lakefront Drive
Hunt Valley, MD 21030
(401) 771-1151
Fax (301) 771-1174

Microsoft Corp.
One Microsoft Way
Redmond, WA 98052-6399
(800)-426-9400
Fax (206) 883-8101

Midisoft Corporation
P.O. Box 1000
Bellevue, WA 98009
(206) 881-7176

Morgan Interactive, Inc.
160 Pine Street, Suite 509
San Francisco, CA 94104
(415) 693-9596
Fax (415) 693-9597

Multicom Publishing
1100 Olive Way, Suite 1250
Seattle WA 98101
(510) 777-1211
Fax (510) 777-1311

National Geographic Society
1145 17th Street, NW
Washington, DC 20036
(202) 857-7675

Opcode Interactive
3950 Fabian Way
Palo Alto, CA 94303
(800) 557-2633

Orange Cherry/New Media Schoolhouse
390 Westchester Avenue
Pound Ridge, NY 10576
(800) 672-6002
Fax (914) 764-0104

Pacific HiTech, Inc.
4530 Fortuna Way
Salt Lake City, UT 84124
(800) 765-8369
Fax (801) 278-2666

Panasonic Corp.
Matsushita Electric Corp. of America
One Panasonic Way
Secaucus, NJ 07094
(201) 348-7000
Fax (201) 348-7209

Paramount Interactive
700 Hansen Way
Palo Alto, CA 94304
(800) 821-1177
Fax (415) 813-8055

Parsons Technology
One Parsons Drive
P.O. Box 100
Hiawatha, IA 52233-0100
(800) 223-6925
Fax (319) 393-1002

Passport
100 Stone Pine Road
Half Moon Bay, CA 94019
(415) 726-0280

Pioneer Electronics USA, Inc.
2265 East 220th Street
Long Beach, CA 90810
(213) PIONEER
Fax (213) 952-2260

Quarterdeck Office Systems Inc.
150 Pico Boulevard
Santa Monica, CA 90405
(310) 392-9851
Fax (310) 314-4218

Sierra On-Line, Inc.
P.O. Box 485
Coarsegold, CA 93614
(209) 683-4468
Fax (209) 683-3924

Software Marketing Corporation
9830 South 51st Street
Building A-131
Phoenix, AZ 85044
(602) 893-3377
Fax (602) 893-2042

The Software Toolworks
60 Leveroni Court
Novato, CA 94949
(415) 883-3000
Fax (415) 883-0298

Sony Electronic Publishing Co.
1 Lower Ragsdale Drive, Suite 160
Monterey, CA 93940
(800) 654-8802
Fax (408) 372-9267

Spinnaker Software Corp.
201 Broadway, 6th Floor
Cambridge, MA 02139-1901
(800) 323-8088
Fax (617) 494-1219

Spirit of Discovery
5421 Avenida Encinas
Carlsbad, CA 92008
(619) 929-2010 x211
Fax (619) 929-2035

STAC Electronics
5993 Avenidas Encinas
Carlsbad, CA 92008
(619) 431-7474
Fax (619) 431-0880

Syracuse Language Systems
719 East Genesee Street
Syracuse, NY 13210-7933

Texas Caviar
3933 Steck Avenue, Suite B-115
Austin, TX 78759-8608
(512) 346-7887
Fax (512) 346-1393

Viacom New Media
648 S. Wheeling Road
Wheeling, IL 60090
(800) 877-4266
Fax (708) 459-7456

The Voyager Co.
578 Broadway, Suite 406
New York, NY 10012
(800) 446-2001
Fax (212) 431-5799

Walt Disney Computer Software, Inc.
500 S. Buena Vista Street,
Burbank Centre, 20th Floor
Burbank, CA 91521-6385
(800) 688-1520
Fax (818) 846-0454

Warner New Media
3500 West Olive Avenue, Suite 1050
Burbank, CA 91505-9808
(800) 593-6334
Fax (818) 955-6499

Waterford Institute
1590 East 9400 South
Sandy, UT 84093
(801) 572-1172

WordPerfect Publishing Corporation
270 West Center Street
Orem, UT 84057
(801) 226-5555
Fax (801) 226-8804

World Book, Inc.
525 West Monroe Street
Chicago, IL 60661

Glossary

Glossary

access time The average amount of time it takes a CD-ROM drive to find a new piece of information on the disc. Access time usually is measured in milliseconds, with lower numbers being better.

application A program designed to perform a specific function. Word processors and spreadsheets are applications, as are edutainment programs.

ATA An acronym for the Alliance for Technology Access, a nationwide network of community resource centers. ATA provides a wide variety of services for users with special needs.

audio CD The kind of compact disc you find in music stores and play on your stereo.

AUTOEXEC.BAT A batch file containing DOS commands that are executed whenever the PC starts (boots up).

average access time See **access time**.

batch file A file that contains a set of DOS commands. Instead of executing each command individually, the user (or the PC) can simply execute the batch file.

BBS An acronym for *bulletin board service*. An electronic bulletin board on which users can leave messages and upload and download files. Thousands of BBSs are in operation in the United States, the majority of which are small operations run by hobbyists.

binary The base-2 number system. We humans use the decimal (base-10) number system. Where the decimal system has 10 digits, ranging from 0 to 9, the binary number system has two digits, 0 and 1. Binary is an incredibly cumbersome system for humans, but because the two digits can be represented by a switch that is open or shut, it is an ideal number system for computers.

bit A contraction of the phrase *binary digit*. A bit is the smallest unit of data in a computer and can be set to either 1 or 0.

bit-mapped An image (including fonts) stored in the form of a bitmap.

bitmap One type of digital representation of an image. A bitmap consists of an array of pixels that correspond to the original image.

boot up The process that occurs when you first turn on a PC and run its operating system.

byte A collection of eight bits. It can hold a numeric value from 0 to 255.

CD-ROM An acronym for *compact disc–read-only memory*. A CD-ROM looks like an audio CD but is designed to hold digital data. CD-ROMs can contain more than 600M of information. Unlike a hard disk, the end user cannot change the information stored on a CD-ROM.

CD-ROM drive A device capable of reading the information stored on a CD-ROM.

CD-ROM XA An acronym for CD-ROM eXtended Architecture. A special CD-ROM format that allows sound and other data to be interleaved on the disc. It does not seem to be catching on at this time.

CGA An acronym for Color/Graphics Adapter. The CGA is an early model video card that can display low-resolution graphics as well as text.

clone A computer that runs software designed for the IBM PC or its descendants but was not manufactured by IBM. Although IBM remains one of the biggest PC manufacturers, most of the machines we think of as PCs are clones. (Even though I have written commercial software for PCs, I have never owned one that was actually manufactured by IBM.)

compact disc A plastic disc containing digital data. One disc can store up to 72 minutes of high-quality music, 650M of computer data, or a combination of the two. The information on the disc is encoded as microscopic *pits*. A laser beam can read these pits and translate their reflection patterns back into digital data.

compound device A multimedia device that requires you to specify a media file before you can run the device. A sound board is an example of a compound device. (*See also*: **simple device**.)

compression Any technique that reduces the amount of data needed to store a file is a compression technique. Compression can be either *lossy* or *lossless*. (*See also*: **compression ratio**.)

compression ratio The compression ratio is the ratio of the uncompressed size of a file over the compressed size of the file. Lossless compression techniques typically achieve compression ratios of around 2:1. Lossy techniques can achieve much higher ratios, but at a cost of reduced image quality.

CONFIG.SYS   A file that specifies the devices to be installed and the device drivers to use. This file is executed whenever the PC boots up.

conventional memory   The basic type of memory found on all PCs. A machine may have as much as 640K of conventional memory.

CPU   An acronym for *central processing unit*. The CPU is another name for the main microprocessor in a PC.

cursor   Usually a short blinking line in DOS or Windows. When the user types on the keyboard, the text he enters appears at the location of the cursor.

daisy chain   When SCSI devices are connected in a line so that they use only one SCSI port in your PC, they are connected in a daisy chain.

device   A piece of equipment connected to your computer. Your mouse and printer are devices, as are the keyboard and disk drives in your machine. Every device has a device driver that DOS uses to control it.

device driver   A program that controls a particular device. An installable device driver is a device driver that is not built into the operating system but can instead be loaded, or installed, as required. Hardware manufacturers can create nonstandard devices that interact with DOS through their own installable device drivers.

dialog box   A box that appears on-screen to provide information and to let the user choose from a limited number of options.

directory   An area on a disk that contains files and subdirectories. Dividing the disk into directories and subdirectories makes it easier to organize your work.

directory tree   A hierarchical organization of directories. A directory tree begins with one root directory and then branches off into subdirectories of that root directory and files within the root or its subdirectories.

DOS   An acronym for *disk operating system*. DOS is the software that controls the operation of your computer. DOS controls the flow of information throughout the machine and is always running, even when you are using your favorite edutainment program. Throughout this book, DOS refers both to Microsoft's disk operating system (MS-DOS) and to any of the customized versions of MS-DOS created by computer manufacturers. The term does not include any of the versions of Digital Research's disk operation system (DR-DOS) which is a competing operating system.

DOS prompt   The indication that DOS is ready and waiting for the user to enter a command. The DOS prompt usually takes the form of the current drive letter and a greater-than symbol (C>).

double-speed   Describes CD-ROM drives that can transfer 300K of data per second. Double-speed drives can also transfer data at the 150K per second rate used for audio CDs. A double-speed drive is faster than a single-speed drive.

downward compatibility   A microprocessor is downward compatible with an earlier microprocessor if it can run the same software as the earlier one, even though the newer microprocessor will have additional features or capabilities beyond those contained on the earlier product.

DRAM   An acronym for *dynamic random-access memory*. Because of the way it is designed, DRAM is less expensive and slower than static RAM (SRAM).

driver   See **device driver**.

edutainment   A concept that combines elements of both education and entertainment. In this book, edutainment means the blending of education and entertainment in such a way as to make learning more enjoyable. Frequently, edutainment involves the addition of game elements to drill programs or the addition of sound and video to reference works. As PCs have become more powerful and have gained new capabilities, such as CD-ROM storage and stereo sound, edutainment programs have evolved to take advantage of these new developments.

EGA   An acronym for Enhanced Graphics Adapter. An EGA card can display higher-resolution text and graphics than the CGA. It can also display graphics in more colors.

ESDI An acronym for Enhanced Small Device Interface. An advanced version of the ST506. Like the ST506, it has been replaced by SCSI and IDE.

expanded memory (EMS) A type of memory that gives programs access to more memory than is available in the conventional memory area. Programs using EMS can only access expanded memory in 16K chunks. EMS can be installed on virtually any PC, and can be simulated by an extended-memory manager on machines equipped with 80386 or better processors.

expanded-memory manager A program that provides a standard interface to any expanded memory installed on a PC. Each expanded-memory board requires its own expanded-memory manager. An expanded-memory manager is usually unnecessary on PCs with 80386 or better processors because the PC's extended-memory manager can simulate expanded memory.

expansion card A circuit card that, when installed in a PC, gives it additional capabilities.

extended memory (XMS) A type of memory that exists beyond conventional memory. The memory addresses occupied by extended memory start at the 1M point. Not all programs can access extended memory, and those that do usually do so through an extended-memory manager. Extended memory can only exist on PCs with an 80286 or better processor.

extended-memory manager A program that provides a standard interface to the extended memory installed in a PC.

FAT An acronym for *file allocation table*. An area on the hard disk that keeps track of where files are stored on the disk. You normally do not have to worry about the FAT.

floppy disk A magnetic disk that can store information. It is called a floppy disk because the magnetic disk itself is flexible, in contrast to the rigid disks in hard drives. Both 5 1/4-inch disks (which have flexible cases) and 3 1/2-inch disks (which have rigid cases) are considered floppy disks.

FM (Frequency Modulation) Recording An early method of storing data on a hard disk. Seriously limits the capacity of the disk.

FM synthesis A technique used to create sounds on a sound card. The hardware on the card uses two to four waveforms to modulate sounds. This results in an approximation of the desired note, but is not as realistic as waveform synthesis.

font A typeface of a particular size and shape.

format (file) The particular way in which data is stored. The format determines how the data is arranged, the compression technique to be used (if any), and anything else relevant to how the data is stored in a file, as opposed to what the data actually is.

frame buffer A type of video card. Frame buffer cards merely provide storage space (a buffer) to hold a video image (a frame). The microprocessor must compute the position of every pixel that appears on the screen. Frame buffer cards are slow but inexpensive.

freeware A copyrighted piece of software the author makes available to the public for free use. It differs from public domain software in that public domain software is not copyrighted.

full-motion video Digital video that is displayed on the monitor. At least 12 frames of video must be displayed each second. Full-motion video looks like a small movie on-screen.

gigabyte Variously considered to be one billion bytes or 1,024 megabytes.

graphics accelerator A video card that can perform certain operations itself, rather than depending on the CPU for these actions. When the appropriate Windows video driver is installed, the card receives Windows video commands that it can perform. For a variety of reasons, the video card can perform these operations much faster than the CPU. A graphics accelerator card is more expensive than a frame buffer card, but it can greatly speed Windows video operations.

GUI An acronym for *graphical user interface*. A GUI provides the capability for the user to interact with the computer by pointing and clicking on icons and other graphical elements, instead of typing arcane commands such as `XCOPY C:\*.TXT A:\FILES\*.*`.

hard disk A magnetic storage device that is much faster and holds much more data than a floppy disk. Its name comes from the fact that the magnetic disk itself is rigid, or hard. Virtually all PCs now contain hard disks as their primary long-term storage area.

hard drive Another name for a hard disk.

hard drive controller An expansion card that provides the signals that control a hard drive.

hardware The physical equipment that comprises a computer system.

HGC An acronym for Hercules Graphics Card. This card can display high-resolution monochrome text and graphics.

icon A small picture that represents an application or other objects in a GUI. (*See also:* **GUI**.)

IDE An acronym for Imbedded Drive Electronics. IDE drives have a controller built right into the drive. Some PCs have a connector for an IDE drive cable built in, which eliminates the need for an interface card.

installable device driver A device driver that can be loaded from disk.

integrated circuit A circuit that contains the equivalent of millions of individual electronic components. Using highly advanced and extremely difficult procedures, scientists have learned how to combine, or integrate, individual electronic components together on a single piece of material.

interactive Products that react to the user's input. Television is noninteractive: a show runs its course regardless of how you react to it. An edutainment program is interactive: how the action progresses in the program depends on what the user does.

interface In computer terms, the connection between two pieces of hardware. They transfer commands and data through the interface.

interleave How data is arranged on the tracks of the hard disk. Interleave is not a concern on SCSI or IDE drives.

interpolation The calculation of intermediate values between two points. Interpolation is used with video displays to smooth out the jagged edges of images. (*See also:* **jaggies**.)

jaggies Used to describe the jagged, stair-step look that bitmapped images can have when interpolation or some other smoothing scheme is not used. (*See also:* **interpolation**.)

kilobyte Equal to 1024 bytes. The fact that computers use the binary (base-2) number system internally causes prefixes such as *kilo* and *mega* to refer to different numbers than they do in the decimal (base-10) number system we humans use.

math coprocessor A specialized integrated circuit that can perform many mathematical operations much faster than the CPU with which it is associated.

MDA An acronym for *monochrome display adapter*. This is an early, text-only video card.

media sequence Consists of a media file or the contents of a simple device.

megabyte Equal to 1024 kilobytes, or 1,048,576 bytes. The fact that computers use the binary (base-2) number system internally causes prefixes such as kilo- and mega- to refer to different numbers than they do in the decimal (base-10) number system we humans use.

memory address The method used by the processor to access a particular memory location. Memory addresses are similar to your postal address: just as each house in your neighborhood has a unique address, every memory location in your PC has a unique address.

memory manager A program that makes expanded and extended memory available to applications.

MFM (Modified Frequency Modulation) Recording A more efficient method of storage than FM.

microprocessor The main integrated circuit in a PC. It is the "brain" of the system and controls the function of the other components.

MIDI An acronym for Musical Instrument Digital Interface. MIDI allows a PC to interact with synthesizers and other electronic musical instruments.

millisecond One one-thousandth of a second. Values such as disk-access time are measured in milliseconds.

modem A device that translates digital signals into sounds that can be transmitted over the phone lines. It also converts the sounds from other modems back into digital form. The term *modem* is a contraction of *modulate-demodulate*.

monitor The television-like device that provides the primary way for a user to tell what the PC is up to.

mouse A pointing device used to control the on-screen cursor or other objects. It consists of a hand-sized box with sensors on the bottom. When the mouse moves across a surface, the sensors detect the motion and convert it into signals to the PC. The PC then uses those signals to reposition the cursor. A mouse also has two or three buttons that can be pressed (clicked) to signal selection of items on-screen.

MPC An acronym for Multimedia Personal Computer. The MPC specifications define the minimum equipment required for a computer to be considered a multimedia PC. A machine that meets or exceeds these specifications is known as MPC-compliant.

multimedia The use of two or more media (sound, graphics, text, or video) in one application. Virtually all educational applications use multimedia.

Multiple-Zone Recording Fits more data onto the disk by increasing the number of sectors in the outer tracks. Requires more sophisticated drive electronics than earlier methods.

multisession A CD-ROM that has had information recorded on it in two or more sessions. This is particularly common with Photo CD discs, in which each set of photos is usually recorded as a separate session. A CD-ROM drive is multisession-compatible if it can read multisession CD-ROMs.

multitasking The capability to run multiple programs, or tasks, at the same time. When a microprocessor is multitasking, it switches back and forth between tasks, executing each one for a short time before switching to the next. If the switches are fast enough, it seems as if the tasks are actually running continuously, instead of taking turns. Microsoft Windows allows multitasking on 80386 or better machines.

operating system See **DOS**.

page (memory) All of expanded memory is divided into 16K chunks, called pages. When a program accesses expanded memory, the expanded-memory manager copies the appropriate page into, or out of, the page frame.

page frame The page frame is an area of memory set aside for use by an expanded-memory manager. The expanded-memory manager copies 16K chunks of information, called pages, to and from the page frame as required by the program accessing the expanded memory. The page frame may be located in conventional memory or in the upper-memory area.

page-flipping An animation technique that uses multiple pages of video memory. A program that uses page flipping draws on one page of the video memory while displaying another. After the drawing is complete, it flips the pages, making the new one the visible one and drawing on the old one.

parent directory The directory above the current directory. A parent directory of a particular directory is the one that contains that directory.

path Tells DOS where to look for files if they are not in the current directory.

Pentium The name for the latest microprocessor from Intel. It is the next chip after the 80486. Originally expected to be named the 80586, it was renamed to avoid trademark problems.

peripheral Any hardware device connected to the computer. Printers and modems are peripherals, as are the mouse, keyboard, and monitor.

Photo CD A technology developed by Kodak that defines a way for photographs to be scanned and stored on a compact disc. The technology has some advantages over other PC-based image storage formats but requires the proper hardware and software to use it.

pixel Abbreviation for *picture element*. A pixel is the smallest element of a digitized image.

port The point where devices connect to each other.

programmable graphics coprocessor A video card with a built-in, programmable processor. A graphics accelerator card has a fixed repertoire of functions it can perform, while a coprocessor card can be optimized for each application.

prompt See **DOS prompt**.

protocol A set of rules that define how equipment will interact. A communications protocol defines rules such as which device "talks" first, how fast they will talk, and so on.

QuickTime One of the competing formats for displaying video clips on PCs. The other major format is Video for Windows.

RAM An acronym for *random-access memory*. RAM is the temporary storage area that programs run in. When you start a program, you transfer it from the disk drive (or CD-ROM drive) into RAM.

raster See **bit-mapped**.

read/write head A device that reads information from, and transfers information to, a disc, disk, or tape.

reboot To restart your PC. A *hard boot* occurs when you reboot your machine by turning the power off and then back on. A *soft boot* occurs when you reboot by pressing the Ctrl, Alt, and Delete keys simultaneously. A soft boot puts less stress on the components in your PC.

resolution For an image, the width and depth, measured in pixels. For a monitor, the maximum number of pixels it can display in each direction. A monitor with a resolution of 800 x 600 can display all of an image that is less than or equal to 800 pixels wide by 600 pixels high.

RLL (Run Length Limited) Recording A storage method that is up to 50 percent more efficient then MFM.

root directory The initial directory in a directory tree. It is designated by a back-slash (\). All other directories are directly or indirectly subdirectories of the root directory.

scanner (for users with special needs) A scanner is a device that allows the user with limited mobility to make selections on the computer screen.

scanner (video) A device that converts an image into a digital representation of that image. Most of the realistic images seen on PCs today are converted into digital form by a scanner.

SCSI An acronym for Small Computer System Interface. SCSI is an interface standard that enables multiple SCSI devices to be connected to one SCSI port in a daisy chain.

serial port An interface that transfers data one bit at a time. PCs normally come with at least one serial port installed.

SIMM An acronym for *single inline memory module*. A SIMM consists of a group of memory chips mounted on a tiny card. Most computers now use SIMMs to hold their memory.

simple device A multimedia device that does not require you to select a file before you run the device. An audio CD player is an example of a simple device. (*See also:* **compound device**.)

single-speed A CD-ROM drive that can read data from a CD-ROM at around 300K per second.

sound card An expansion card that enables a PC to play (and often record) sounds with far greater quality and realism than that produced by the PC's built-in speaker.

ST506 The identification number for a type of hard-disk controller manufactured by Seagate. Early PC hard drives worked with this controller, but it has been replaced by SCSI and IDE in newer equipment.

subdirectory A directory located within another directory. The directory that contains the subdirectory is called the *parent* directory. All directories except the root directory are also subdirectories.

SVGA Stands for Super VGA. A generic term used to describe video that goes beyond the VGA specification. It can involve using more colors than the standard VGA, higher resolution, or some combination of the two.

track bar Represents the media selection (audio or video clip, audio CD, and so on) currently being played in the Media Player. The slider on the track bar indicates the current playing position of the selection.

transfer rate The rate at which data is moved from a hard disk (or CD-ROM) to the computer. For CD-ROM drives, the transfer rate is measured in kilobytes per second.

triple-speed A CD-ROM drive that can transfer 450K of data a second. It can also transfer data at the 150K per second rate used for audio CDs. A triple-speed drive is faster than a double-speed drive.

upper-memory area The 384K area of memory located just above (after) the 640K of conventional memory in a PC. This area is normally reserved for devices such as video cards. Expanded-memory managers may also be able to use some of this space.

vertical scan rate See **refresh rate**.

VGA An acronym for Video Graphics Array. VGA cards can display higher-resolution text and graphics than earlier standards. VGA also supports a number of 256-color video modes. A VGA card can run software that uses any of the CGA and EGA video modes. Equipment that meets the VGA specification is becoming the minimum acceptable video standard. VGA video systems can display up to 640 pixels horizontally, and 480 pixels vertically. The term can be applied to video cards and monitors.

Video for Windows One of the competing formats for displaying video clips on PCs. The other major format is QuickTime.

Windows A program that supplements DOS and replaces its many cryptic commands with graphical elements. Windows provides many features besides those just mentioned but requires significantly more powerful equipment than DOS to run effectively. Most new product development is being aimed at Windows.

Index

Symbols

... (ellipsis) in commands, 195
16-bit sound cards, 169
20th Century Video Almanac, 57-58
7th Level, 276
8-bit sound cards, 169

A

Ability Systems Corporation, 209
ABLEDATA Database of Assitive Technology, 211, 313
About Program Manager dialog box, 226
access time
    CD-ROM, 320
    hard drives, 26
adaptive access, 206
    hearing impairments, 207-208
    mobility impairments, 208
    vendors, 208-211
    vision problems, 206-207
Adventure Math, 274
Adventures with OSLO, Tools and Gadgets, 282
The Adventures of Pinocchio (CD-ROM storybook), 100-101
Aesop's Multimedia Fables, 279
Alliance for Technology Access (ATA), 211, 320
Alliance Interactive Software, 259-260
America Online, 299, 313
American Standard Code for Information Interchange (ASCII), 292
amplified speakers, 208
Amy's Fun-2-3 Adventure, 272
The Animals!, 142-143
animation
    preschool products, 107
    reference works, 51
    storybooks, 93

Annabel's Dream of Ancient Egypt (CD-ROM storybook), 97-98
Announcements 2.0 for Windows, 132
Apogee Software, Ltd., 264
Apogee Software Productions, 275
applications, 320
   Windows
      closing, 225
      exiting, 202
      running, 195-197
      troubleshooting, 227-228
   frozen applications, 229
   vendors
      DOS, 271-276
      Windows, 276-283
Applied Optical Media Corporation, 314
Arnowitz Studio, 314
Art Gallery (Microsoft), 70-71
art reference works, 70-71
Arthur's Teacher Trouble (CD-ROM storybook), 95-96
Artic Technologies, 210
ASCII (American Standard Code for Information Interchange), 292
AT-compatible modems, 289
ATA (Alliance for Technology Access), 211, 320
atlases
   Encarta encyclopedia, 56
   Small Blue Planet, 66
audio CDs, 320
audio systems, 25-26, 250
   microphones, 174
   sound cards, 168, 325
      CD-ROM interfaces, 173
      compatibility, 172-173
      MIDI, 170-172
      resolution, 169
      sampling rate, 169
   speakers, 174

AUTOEXEC.BAT file, 320
Avalon Hill Game Company, 314

B

Bad command or filename error message, 214-215
Baker & Taylor, Inc., 314
BBSs (bulletin board systems), 286, 298, 320
   calling, 302-303
   resources, 313
Beat the Bomb, 45, 275
Berlitz Think & Talk German, 144-146
Beyond Planet Earth, 64-65, 278
bitmaps, 320
bits, 320
blind users, 207
BodyWorks 3.0, 60-61
books, 312
Bookshelf '94, 58-60
booting computers, 320, 325
Braille software/hardware, 207
brain teasers, 148
   Castle of Dr. Brain, 149
   Mind Castle, 151
   Super Solvers Gizmos & Gadgets, 149-151
Brannan, Douglas M., 257-258
Braun, Jeff, 258-259
Broderbund Software Inc., 314
Brown & Co., Inc., 209
Browse dialog box (Windows), 196
Bruckheim, Allan, 61
bulletin board systems, *see* BBSs
Bureau of Electronic Publishing, Inc., 314
busses, 247-248
   video systems, 164
Busytown, 118, 274
bytes, 320

C

CAD (computer-aided architectural design), 123
Cambrix Publishing, 314
Cannot load COMMAND, system halted error message, 215-216
Castle of Dr. Brain, 149
CD-ROM interfaces, 182, 185-186
   sound cards, 173
CD-ROM Professional, 312
CD-ROM storybooks, 10-11, 92-93
   The Adventures of Pinocchio, 100-101
   Annabel's Dream of Ancient Egypt, 97-98
   Arthur's Teacher Trouble, 95-96
   A Christmas Carol, 99-100
   hotspots, 93
   My Silly CD of ABC's, 98
   options, 93-95
   Scary Poems for Rotten Kids, 101-102
   T.J. Finds a Friend, 102-103
   The Tortoise and the Hare, 98-99
CD-ROM TODAY, 312
CD-ROM WORLD, 312
CD-ROMs, 178-181, 250
   access time, 320
   audio CDs, 320
   CD-ROM XA, 185, 320
   companion CD-ROM, 269
   device drivers, 182
   drives, 181-183
      double-speed, 321
      models, 186
      single-speed, 325
      speed, 183-184
      standards, 184-185
      triple-speed, 326
   Microsoft extensions, 182-183
   multiple-product CD-ROMs, 252

multisession, 324
    optical versus magnetic media, 179-180
    Photo CD, 185, 324
    troubleshooting, 232-234
        error messages, 234-238
        sound, 238-239
CDR101 error message, 234-235
CDR103 error message, 235
CGA (Color/Graphics Adapter), 23, 320
Change System Settings command (Windows
    Options menu), 224
A Christmas Carol, 99-100, 279
Civilization, 86-87
cleaning mouse, 224
clones, 320
Club KidSoft, 312
color (video cards), 166-167
Color Wizard, 276
Color/Graphics Adapter (CGA), 23, 320
command sets (modems), 289
commands, *see* individual command names
commercial on-line services, 298-299
    resources, 313
communications software, 294
    data capture, 297
    dialing directories, 295
    file transfer protocols, 295-297
    macros, 297
    scripts, 297
    terminal emulations, 297-298
compact disks, *see* CD-ROMs
Compact Publishing Inc., 314
companion CD-ROM
    category pages, 270-271
    DOS, 269
    opening page, 269-270
The Complete Idiot's Guide to CD-ROM, 312
compound devices, 320
compressing disks, 222, 320

Compton's Interactive Encyclopedia, 51-54
Compton's New Media, 314
Compu-Teach, 314
CompuServe, 313
Computability Corporation, 209
COMPUTE, 312
Computer Entertainment News, 312
computer-aided architectural design (CAD), 123
Comtrad Industries, 314
Conexus, 277
CONFIG.SYS file, 321
Context Systems, Inc., 314
conventional memory, 21, 321
Creative Multimedia Corporation, 314
Creative Writer, 128-129
creativity tools, 12
    Announcements 2.0 for Windows, 132
    Creative Writer, 128-129
    Kid CAD, 126-127
    Kid Works 2, 127-128
    My Own Stories, 130
    options, 122-124
    Print Shop Deluxe, 125, 131
    Storybook Weaver, 130
Crowther, Karen, 259-260
cursors, 321

D

daisy chaining devices, 321
data capture (telecommunications), 297
Data error reading drive x: error message, 216
Data-Cal Corporation, 209
Davidson & Associates, Inc., 277, 315
deaf users, 207-208
DEFRAG command (DOS), 220
Delorme Mapping, 315
Delphi, 313
Detroit, 273

Devasoft, 271
device independence (Windows), 190
Device not responding error message, 235
dialing directories (communications software),
    295
dialog boxes (Windows), 321
    About Program Manager, 226
    Browse, 196
    Change System Settings, 224
    New Program Object, 198
    Program Group Properties, 198
    Virtual Memory, 227
Dinosaur Safari, 143-144
Dinosoft, Inc., 315
Dinsmore, Bill, 260
direct-connect modems, 287-288
directories, 321
    parent directories, 324
    paths, 324
    root directory, 325
    subdirectories, 325
Discis, 93
Discis Knowledge Research, Inc., 315
Discovering America, 136-137
The Discovery Channel, 315
disk operating systems, *see* DOS
disk space
    DOS, 222-223
    software requirements, 250-251
    Windows, 228-229
disks
    compressing, 222
    directories, 321
    floppy disks, 322
    hard disks, 322
        FATs, 322
        FM (Frequency Modulation) Recording,
            322

ST506 controller, 325
transfer rate, 326
Multiple-Zone Recording, 324
Don Quixote, 279
DOS (disk operating system), 16-17, 321
disk space, 222-223
error messages, 214-219
hard drives, 219-220
installing applications, 269
memory, 220-222
product vendors, 271-276
prompt, 321
versions, 18
video cards, 165
DOS=HIGH command (DOS), 222
double-speed CD-ROM drives, 321
DoubleSpace utility, 222
downloading files, 300
calling BBSs, 302-303
searching files, 303-304
setting up Terminal, 300-302
downward compatibility (microprocessors), 321
Dr. T's Music Software, Inc., 278, 315
Dr. T's Sing-A-Long Kids' Classics, 117-118, 279
DRAM (dynamic random-access memory), 164, 321
drill-and-practice products, 7-8
Kid's Typing, 45-46
Learn to Speak Spanish, 46-47
Math Blaster: In Search of Spot, 39-40
math programs, 41-45
options, 38-39
driver software (video cards), 165
drives
CD-ROMs, 181-183
interfaces, 185-186
models, 186
standards, 184-185
hard drives, 249
DOS, 219-220
dynamic random-access memory (DRAM), 164, 321

E

EA*Kids Theater Collection, 272
Eagle Eye Mysteries in London, 136
Early Math, 110-111
EBook, Inc., 279, 315
Ecology Treks, 139-140
Edmark, 315
Education Resources, 313
Educational Technology, 312
EDUCORP, 313
EduQuest/IBM, 315
edutainment, 321
advantages, 5-6
definition, 4-5
evaluation, 6-7
products, 7-14
social studies products, 134-138
telecommunications, 286-287
EGA (Enhanced Graphics Adapter), 23-24, 321
Electronic Arts, 272, 315
electronic distribution of products, 253
Electronic Entertainment, 312
ellipsis (...) in commands, 195
EMS (expanded memory), 21, 321
Encarta encyclopedia, 52, 56-57
encyclopedias, 50-57
Compton's Interactive Encyclopedia, 53-54
Encarta, 52, 56-57
New Grolier Multimedia Encyclopedia, 54-56
Enhanced Graphics Adapter (EGA), 23-24, 321
Enhanced Small Device Interface (ESDI), 322
Epic Megagames, 274

error messages
CD-ROMs, 234-238
DOS, 214-219
The ESC Newsletter, 313
ESDI (Enhanced Small Device Interface), 322
Europress Software, 315
The Exceptional Parent, 313
Exeption error #12 — press Enter to reboot error message, 216-217
Exit command (Windows File menu), 203
exiting
Terminal (Windows), 304
Windows applications, 202-203
expanded memory, 21, 322
expansion cards, 322
extended memory (XMS), 21, 322
Extensions for Independence, 209
external modems, 288-289

F

Family Doctor III, 61-62
Family Health Book (Mayo Clinic), 62
FATs (file allocation tables), 322
Fatty Bear's Birthday Surprise, 273
file transfer protocols, 295-297
files
batch files, 320
CONFIG.SYS, 321
directories, 324-325
format, 322
Find Wizard (Encarta encyclopedia), 52
First Magnitude, 275
Flight Simulator, 85-86
floppy disks, 322
Florida New Concepts Marketing, Inc., 210
FM (Frequency Modulation) Recording, 322
FM synthesis (MIDI), 171
fonts, 322

format, 322
frame buffers (SVGA cards), 162, 322
freenets, 298-300
freeware, 322
front-end communication programs, 294
full-motion video, 322
Fun School Learning Adventures with Teddy Bear, 115-116

G

games (brain teasers), 148
    Castle of Dr. Brain, 149
    Mind Castle, 151
    Super Solvers Gizmos & Gadgets, 149-151
GameTek, 272
Gaspar, Elon, 260-262
Gazelle Technologies/EDUCORP, 315
General failure reading (writing) drive x: error message, 217
General MIDI standard, 171
GEnie, 313
gigabytes, 322
glare protection screen, 206
Goferwinkel's Adventures—The Lavender Land, 279
graphics accelerator cards, 162-163, 249, 322
Great Bear Technology Inc., 315
Grolier Electronic Publishing, Inc., 315
Gross, Bill, 262-263
GUIs (graphical user interfaces), 322

H

hard disks, 322, 325-326
hard drives, 26-28, 249
hardware, 323
    audio systems, 250
    CD-ROMs, 250
    changes, 246-250
    compound devices, 320
    daisy chaining devices, 321
    devices, 321
    expansion cards, 322
    hard drives, 249
    memory, 248-249
    microprocessors, 246, 321
        busses, 247-248
        speed, 247
    modems, 287-294, 324
    mouse, 324
    MPC-1 standard, 306-307
    MPC-2 standard, 308-310
    peripherals, 324
    ports, 324-325
    scanners, 325
    video cards, 249
Hayes-compatible modems, 289
health reference works
    BodyWorks 3.0, 60-61
    Family Doctor III, 61-62
    Mayo Clinic-Family Health Book, 62
    PharmAssist, 63
hearing impairments, 207-208
HGC (Hercules Graphics Card), 23, 323
HIMEM.SYS, 221
HomePC, 312
hotspots (storybooks), 93
Humongous Entertainment, Inc., 272, 315
HyperGlot Software Co., Inc., 315

I

IBM Multimedia Publishing Studio, 315
IBM National Support Center for Persons with Disabilities, 209
icons, 323
IDE (Imbedded Drive Electronics), 323
ImagiNATION Network (INN), 253, 262, 313
ImagiSOFT, Inc., 276
Impressionism and its Sources, 280
Impressions Software, 273
In the Company of Whales, 278
Incorrect DOS version error message, 217-218
Incorrect version error message, 235-236
InfoPilot (Compton's Interactive Encyclopedia), 54
INN (ImagiNATION Network), 253, 262, 313
installing
    DOS applications, 269
    Windows, 192-193
    Windows applications, 271
InterAction, 312
InterActive Publishing Corp., 315
Interface Systems International, 210
interfaces, 323
interference (sound), 240
interleave, 323
internal modems, 288-289
Internal stack overflow, system halted error message, 218
Internet, 299-300
Interplay Productions, 273
interpolation (video systems), 323
interviews, 256-265
Invalid drive specification error message, 236-238
IVI Publishing, 316

J-K

jaggies (video systems), 323
Jazz (music reference work), 71-72
Jeopardy, 272
Journey to the Planets, 65-66

karaoke, 107
keyboard (adaptive access), 207-208

Kid CAD, 126-127, 277
Kid Works 2, 127-128
Kid's Typing, 45-46
Kid's Zoo, 114-115
kilobytes, 323
Kinetic Designs, Inc., 209
Kingmaker, 87-88
Knowledge Adventure, Inc., 262-263, 316
Knowledge Explorer (New Grolier Multimedia Encyclopedia), 55

L

Labtec Enterprises, Inc., 316
LaFrenz, Dale, 263
language products
    Berlitz Think & Talk German, 144-146
    TriplePlay French, 146-147
Lawrence Productions, Inc., 316
Learn to Speak Spanish, 46-47
The Learning Company, 316, 260
Lenny's Music Toons, 282

M

Macmillan New Media, 316
macros (communications software), 297
magazines, 312-313
The Magic of Interactive Entertainment, 312
Magic Quest, Inc., 316
magnetic media, 179-180
mail-order catalogs, 313-314
Mario Teaches Typing, 273
Math & Word Rescue, 153-154
Math Ace, 152
Math Blaster: In Search of Spot, 39-42
math coprocessors, 323

Math Flashcards, 44-45
math programs, 151-152
    Beat the Bomb, 45
    Early Math, 110-111
    Math & Word Rescue, 153-154
    Math Ace, 152
    Math Blaster: In Search of Spot, 41-42
    Math Flashcards, 44-45
    Mental Math Games, 43-44
    Mickey's 123's, 111
    Operation Neptune, 152-153
    Super Solvers OutNumbered, 42-43
Math Rescue, 275
Math Sampler, 276
maximizing windows, 202
Maxis, 75, 258-259, 316
Mayo Clinic-Family Health Book, 62
MDA (Monochrome Display Adapter), 23, 323
MECC, 263, 316
Media Resources, 316
Media Vision, Inc., 316
megabytes, 323
MEM command (DOS), 221
MEMMAKER utility, 222
memory, 20-21, 248-249
    conventional memory, 321
    DOS, 220-222
    DRAM (dyanamic random-access memory), 321
    EMS (expanded memory), 322
    memory addresses, 323
    memory managers, 323
    page, 324
    RAM (random-access memory), 325
    SIMMs (single inline memory modules), 325
    space, 22
    upper-memory area, 326

    video cards, 164-165
    Windows, 190-191, 225-226
    XMS (extended memory), 322
Mental Math Games, 43-44, 282
MFM (Modified Frequency Modulation) Recording, 323
Mickey's 123's, 111
Mickey's ABC's, 113-114
MicroGrafx, Inc., 316
microphones, 174
microprocessors, 18-20, 246, 248
    busses, 247-248
    downward compatibility, 321
    math coprocessors, 323
    multitasking, 324
    Pentium, 324
    speed, 247
    video cards, 164-168
MicroProse Software, 316
Microsoft
    Art Gallery, 70-71
    Bookshelf '94, 58-60
    CD-ROM extensions, 182-183
    Encarta encyclopedia, 52, 56-57
Microsoft CD-ROM Extensions (MSCDEX), 232
Microsoft Corp., 316
Microsystems Software Inc., 210
MicroTouch Systems, Inc., 209
MIDI (Musical Instrument Digital Interface), 170-172, 323
Midisoft Corporation, 316
Miller, Scott, 264
milliseconds, 323
Mind Castle, 151
mobility impairments, 208
modems, 287, 324
    command sets, 289
    communication software, 294-295

peripherals

internal versus external, 288-289
options, 291
speed, 288
standards, 289-291
transmitting data, 291-293
troubleshooting, 294
types, 287-288
Modified Frequency Modulation (MFM)
  Recording, 323
monitors, 168, 324
  vision problems, 206
  see also video systems
Monochrome Display Adapter (MDA), 23, 323
Morgan Interactive, Inc., 281, 316
mouse, 324
  cleaning, 224
  troubleshooting, 224
  Windows, 194-195, 224
Movie Select, 281
Mowgli's Brothers, 279
MPC (Multimedia PC), 184-185, 324
  MPC-1 standard, 306-308
  MPC-2 standard, 308-310
  Windows, 191
MSCDEX (Microsoft CD-ROM Extensions), 232
Multicom Publishing, 316
multimedia
  language products, 144-148
  music products, 147-148
  reference works, 8-9
    20th Century Video Almanac, 57-58
    art, 69-72
    Bookshelf '94, 58-60
    encyclopedias, 53-57
    features, 50, 51
    health, 60-63
    music, 69-72
    prehistoric life, 67-69
    space, 64-66

Multimedia Music: Mozart, 280
Multimedia PC, *see* MPC
Multimedia Schubert, 147-148
MULTIMEDIA WORLD, 312
Multiple-Zone Recording, 324
multisession CD-ROMs, 324
multitasking, 324
music products, 147-148
music reference works, 71-72
Musical Instrument Digital Interface (MIDI),
  170-172, 323
MVP Software, 274, 281
My First World Atlas, 273
My Own Stories, 130
My Silly CD of ABC's (CD-ROM storybook), 98

N

National Geographic Society, 316
NCMEC (National Center for Missing &
  Exploited Children), 94
NeoSoft Corporation, 271
networks, 287
New command (Windows File menu), 198
New Grolier Multimedia Encyclopedia, 51, 54-56
NEW MEDIA, 312
New Program Object dialog box, 198
newsletters, 312-313
Non-system disk or disk error message, 218
Normandy: The Great Crusade, 278
Not ready reading (writing) drive x: error
  message, 218
nView, 209

O

Oceans Below, 141-142
Odell Down Under, 80
On This Day (20th Century Video Almanac), 57

on-line edutainment, 253-254
on-line services, 298-299, 313
Opcode Interactive, 317
operating systems, 16-17
Operation Neptune, 152-153
optical media, 179-180
Orange Cherry/New Media Schoolhouse, 93, 317
The Oregon Trail, 76-79
Out of environment space error message, 218-219,
  238-240
Output Hardware and Software, 210

P

Pacific HiTech, Inc., 317
page (memory), 324
Panasonic Corp., 317
Paramount Interactive, 274, 281, 317
parent directories, 324
paths (directories), 324
Parsons Technology, 317
Passport, 317
PC Magazine, 312
PC/Computing, 313
PCs (personal computers)
  audio systems, 25-26
  CD-ROMs, 178-181
    device drivers, 182
    drives, 181-186
    interfaces, 182
    Microsoft extensions, 182-183
    optical versus magnetic media, 179-180
  hard drives, 26-27
  memory, 20-21
  microprocessors, 18-20
  operating systems, 16-17
  video systems, 23-25
Pentium microprocessor, 19, 324
peripherals, 324

personal computers, *see* PCs
PharmAssist, 63
Photo CD, 185, 324
Ping & Kooky's Cuckoo Zoo, 116
Pioneer Electronics USA, Inc., 317
pixels, 324
ports, 324-325
Prehistoria, 68-69
preschool products, 11, 106-107
    animation, 107
    Busytown, 118
    Dr. T's Sing-A-Long Kids' Classics, 117-118
    Fun School Learning Adventures with Teddy Bear, 115-116
    Kid's Zoo, 114-115
    math skills, 110-111
    Ping & Kooky's Cuckoo Zoo, 116
    reading skills, 112-114
    Sierra On-Line's Early Math, 107-110
Print Shop Deluxe, 125, 131
Prodigy, 299, 313
product distribution, 252
    electronic distribution, 253
    multiple-product CD-ROMs, 252
    shareware, 252-253, 286-287
Professor Iris, 278
Program Group Properties dialog box, 198
program groups (Windows), 198-202
programmable graphics coprocessors, 163, 325
programs, *see* applications
proprietary interfaces (CD-ROM), 185
protocols, 325
PsL News, 313
Public Brand Software, 314
Putt Putt Goes to the Moon, 272
Putt Putt Joins the Parade, 273

Q-R

Quarterdeck Office Systems Inc., 317
QuickShelf (Bookshelf '94), 58
QuickTime, 325
RAM (random-access memory), 20-22, 325
read-only memory (ROM), 20
read/write heads, 325
reading skills
    Mickey's ABC's, 113-114
    Rust & Rosy Read with Me, 112-113
Reasonable Solutions, 314
reference works, 8-9
    20th Century Video Almanac, 57-58
    art, 69-72
    Bookshelf '94, 58-60
    encyclopedias, 52-57
    features, 50-51
    health, 60-63
    music, 69-72
    prehistoric life, 67-69
    space, 64-66
refresh rate (video cards), 167
Renaissance Masters #1, 280
resolution
    sound cards, 169
    video systems, 165-166, 325
resources
    BBSs, 313
    books, 312
    magazines, 312-313
    mail-order catalogs, 313-314
    newsletters, 312-313
    on-line services, 313
RLL (Run Length Limited) Recording, 325
Rock, Rap 'n Roll, 281
ROM (read-only memory), 20
root directory, 325
RoseSoft, Inc., 209
Run command (Windows File menu), 195
running applications (Windows), 195-197
Rusty and Rosy Read with Me, 112-113, 283

S

sampling rate (sound cards), 169
ScanDisk utility, 219
scanners, 325
Scary Poems for Rotten Kids (CD-ROM storybook), 101-102
Science for Kids, Inc., 282
science products
    The Animals!, 142-143
    Dinosaur Safari, 143-144
    Ecology Treks, 139-140
    Oceans Below, 141-142
    Zoo Keeper, 140-141
screen reader software, 207
scripts (communications software), 297
SCSI interfaces (CD-ROM), 185, 325
Sea School: Math Waves, 274
searching Encarta encyclopedia, 52
serial ports, 325
shareware, 252-253, 286-287
Sharks!, 278
Sierra On-Line, Inc., 317
    Gaspar, Elon, 260-262
    INN (ImagiNATION Network), 253, 262
Sierra On-Line's Early Math, 107-110
SimCity 2000, 81-82
SimFarm, 82-83
SimLife, 84
SIMMs (single inline memory modules), 325
simulation programs, 9-10, 74-75, 84-85
    Civilization, 86-87
    Flight Simulator, 86
    Kingmaker, 87-88

Maxis, 75
Odell Down Under, 80
The Oregon Trail, 76-79
SimCity 2000, 81-82
SimFarm, 82-83
SimLife, 84
simulation software, 258
single-speed CD-ROM drives, 325
sizing windows, 202
SkiSoft Publishing Corp., 210
Small Blue Planet, 66
SMARTDrive utility, 220
social studies products, 134
    Discovering America, 136-137
    Eagle Eye Mysteries in London, 136
    Normandy, 137-138
    WHERE IN THE USA IS CARMEN SANDIEGO?, 134-135
The Software Toolworks, 317
software
    changes, 250-252
    communication software, 294-295
    design, 251
    disk space, 250-251
    distribution, 252
        electronic distribution, 253
        multiple-product CD-ROMs, 252
        shareware, 252-253, 286-287
    freeware, 322
    on-line edutainment, 253-254
    screen reader software, 207
    simulation software, 258
    speech recognition, 251-252
    system software
        MPC-1 standard, 307
        MPC-2 standard, 310
    Windows, 250
Software Creations, 276
Software Marketing Corporation, 257-258, 317

Sony Electronic Publishing Co., 317
sound, 250
    interference, 240
    preschool products, 107
    troubleshooting, 238-240
    Windows, 240
sound cards, 168, 325
    CD-ROM interfaces, 173
    compatibility, 172-173
    MIDI, 170-172
    resolution, 169
    sampling rate, 169
Sound It Out Land 2, 277
space (memory), 22
space reference works
    Beyond Planet Earth, 64-65
    Journey to the Planets, 65-66
    Small Blue Planet, 66
speakers, 25, 174
    amplified speakers, 208
special needs computing, 206
    hearing impairments, 207-208
    mobility impairments, 208
    vendors, 208-211
    vision problems, 206-207
speech recognition, 251-252
speech synthesizers, 207
speed
    CD-ROM drives, 183-184
    microprocessors, 247
    modems, 288
Spinaaker Software Corp., 317
Spirit of Discovery, 317
St. West, 210
ST506 controller, 325
STAC Electronics, 317
Star Child, 280
starting Windows, 193
stereo systems, 174

Storybook Weaver, 130
storybooks, 10-11, 92-95
    The Adventures of Pinocchio, 100-101
    Annabel's Dream of Ancient Egypt, 97-98
    Arthur's Teacher Trouble, 95-96
    A Christmas Carol, 99-100
    hotspots, 93
    My Silly CD of ABC's, 98
    Scary Poems for Rotten Kids, 101-102
    T.J. Finds a Friend, 102-103
    The Tortoise and the Hare, 98-99
subdirectories, 325
Super Solvers Gizmos & Gadgets, 149-151
Super Solvers OutNumbered, 42-43
SVGA cards, 325
    frame buffers, 162
    graphics accelerators, 162-163
    programmable graphics coprocessors, 163
    resolution, 165
Syracuse Language Systems, 317
system requirements
    MPC-1 standard, 308
    MPC-2 standard, 310
system software
    DOS (disk operating system), 321
    MPC-1 standard, 307
    MPC-2 standard, 310

T

T.J. Finds a Friend (CD-ROM storybook), 102-103
telecommunications, 286-287
    BBSs (bulletin board systems), 298
    commercial services, 298-299
    communications software, 294
        data capture, 297
        dialing directories, 295
        file transfer protocols, 295-297

macros, 297
scripts, 297
terminal emulations, 297-298
downloading files, 300
  calling BBSs, 302-303
  searching files, 303-304
  setting up Terminal, 300-302
freenets, 298-300
Internet, 299-300
modems, 287, 324
  command sets, 289
  internal versus external, 288-289
  options, 291
  speed, 288
  standards, 289-291
  transmitting data, 291-293
  troubleshooting, 294
  types, 287-288
networks, 287
on-line edutainment, 253-254
Terminal (Windows), 300
  calling BBSs, 302-303
  exiting, 304
  searching files, 303-304
  setting up, 300-302
terminal communication programs, 294
terminal emulations (telecommunications), 297-298
Texas Caviar, 93, 317
The Edutainment Company, 313
The Software Labs, 314
Timeline
  20th Century Video Almanac, 57
  Encarta encyclopedia, 57
  Microsoft Dinosaurs, 67
  New Grolier Multimedia Encyclopedia, 55
Topic Tree (Compton's Interactive Encyclopedia), 54
The Tortoise and the Hare, 98-99

totware, *see* preschool products
Trace R&D Center, 210
Trace Resourcebook, 312
track bar (Media Player), 325
transfer rate (hard disks), 326
transmitting data (modems), 291-293
triple-speed CD-ROM drives, 326
TriplePlay French, 146-147
Trivia Shell, 276
troubleshooting
  CD-ROMs, 232-234
    error messages, 234-238
    sound, 238-239
  DOS
    disk space, 222-223
    error messages, 214-219
    hard drives, 219-220
    memory, 220-222
  modems, 294
  sound cards, 239-240
  Windows
    disk space, 228-229
    frozen applications, 229
    low resources, 226-227
    memory, 225-226
    mouse, 224
    slow running applications, 227-228
    sound, 238-239
TuneLand, 277
Typewriting Institute for the Handicapped, 210

U

The Ugly Duckling, 281
upgrading
  MPC-1 standard, 308
  MPC-2 standard, 310
upper memory, 21, 326

users
  preschoolers, 106-107
    math skills, 107-111
    reading skills, 112-114
  special needs computing, 206
    hearing impairments, 207-208
    mobility impairments, 208
    vendors, 208-211
    vision problems, 206-207
utilities
  DoubleSpace, 222
  MEMMAKER, 222
  ScanDisk, 219
  SMARTDrive, 220

V

vendors
  DOS products, 271-276
  product distribution, 252
    electronic distribution, 253
    multiple-product CD-ROMs, 252
    shareware, 252-253, 286-287
  special needs computing, 208-211
  Windows applications, 276-283
VESA (Video Electronics Standards Association) standards, 167-168
VESA local bus, 164
VGA (Video Graphics Array), 24-25, 165-166, 326
Viacom New Media, 318
video systems, 23
  CGA (Color/Graphics Adapter), 23, 320
  determining type, 25
  EGA (Enhanced Graphics Adapter), 23-24, 321
  full-motion video, 322
  HGC (Hercules Graphics Card), 23, 323
  interpolation, 323

jaggies, 323
MDA (Monochrome Display Adapter), 23, 323
monitors, 168, 324
pixels, 324
QuickTime, 325
resolution, 325
SVGA cards, 162-163, 325
VGA (Video Graphics Array), 24-25, 326
video cards, 249
   busses, 164
   color, 166-167
   DOS versus Windows, 165
   driver software, 165
   frame buffers, 322
   graphics accelerators, 322
   memory, 164-165
   microprocessors, 164-168
   programmable graphics coprocessors, 325
   refresh rate, 167
   resolution, 165-166
   VESA standards, 167-168
Virtual Memory dialog box, 227
Virtual Workspace (Compton's Interactive Encyclopedia), 54
vision problems, 206-207
Vivaldi, the Four Seasons, 280
Votan PC, 210
The Voyager Co., 318
VRAM, 164

W

Wade, Ian R., 264-265
Walt Disney Computer Software, Inc., 318
Warner New Media, 318
Waterford Institute, 264-265, 282, 318
wave-table synthesis, 172
WesTest Engineering Corporation, 210
WHERE IN THE USA IS CARMEN SANDIEGO?, 134-135
Where in the World? (20th Century Video Almanac), 57
The White Horse Child, 280
Window Sources, 313
Windows, 190-192, 250, 326
   applications
      closing, 225
      exiting, 202-203
      installing, 271
      running, 195-197
   components, 193-195
   downloading files, 300
   installing, 192-193
   memory, 190-191
   mouse, 194-195, 224
   MPC (Multimedia PC), 191
   product vendors, 276-283
   program groups, creating, 198-202
   sizing windows, 202
   sound, 240
   starting, 193
Terminal
   calling BBSs, 302-303
   exiting, 304
   searching files, 303-304
   setting up, 300-302
troubleshooting
   disk space, 228-229
   frozen applications, 229
   low resources, 226-227
   memory, 225-226
   mouse, 224
   slow running applications, 227-228
   sound, 238-239
   video cards, 165
Video for Windows, 326
WINDOWS Magazine, 313
Wings Over Europe, W.W. II, 278
Word Puzzle, 274
Word Rescue, 275
Word Search, 281
WordPerfect Publishing Corporation, 318
World Book, Inc., 318

X-Y-Z

Xmodem protocols, 297
XMS (extended memory), 21, 322

Zmodem protocols, 297
Zoo Keeper, 140-141

GAMES • ENTERTAINMENT • DESKTOP PUBLISHING • MULTIMEDIA • EDUCATION

Over 800 CD-ROMs!

EDUCORP WILL BEAT ANY ADVERTISED PRICE ON CD-ROM PRODUCTS*

- Encyclopedia of Dinosaurs
- Encyclopedia of Life
- ZooGuides v.1: Butterflies/World
- ZooGuides v.2: Whales & Dolphins
- ZooGuides v.3: Mammals of Africa
- ZooGuides v.4: The Rainforest
- REMedia: Animal Alphabet
- EDUCORP Shareware CD
- Grolier's Multimedia Encyclopedia
- Microsoft: Encarta Encyclopedia
- Redshift: Definitive Astronomy
- Microsoft: Art Gallery
- Software Toolworks: Space Shuttle
- Software Toolworks: Oceans Below
- San Diego Zoo: The Animals!
- Street Atlas U.S.A.
- Where in the World is Carmen Sandiego?
- The Manhole Masterpiece
- Living Books: Arthur's Birthday
- Living Books: Ruffs Bone
- Living Books: Just Grandma & Me
- Scavenger Hunt: Africa
- A Silly Noisy House
- Word Tales

EDUCORP 1-800-843-9497

Call for your FREE CATALOG! Foreign customers send $4 postage & handling.

*Some restrictions apply. Dealer Inquiries Welcome

ECA

7434 Trade Street ■ San Diego, CA 92121-2410 ■ Info: 619-536-9999 ■ FAX: 619-536-2345

Most of the CD-ROM titles listed here are available for the Macintosh and PC.

THE MULTIMEDIA PIONEER℠ • LARGEST SELECTION • LOWEST PRICES Major credit cards accepted.

What is Club KidSoft?

It's a magazine. It's a CD. **It's a Club!**

It's a place where you and your child can try leading educational software before you buy it. Demo more than 30 titles on the CD, or read the reviews in the magazine and catalog.

It's a Club where your child can share ideas, activities, stories, and art work with other Club Members across the country.

It's peace of mind for you. All our software is pre-screened and approved by our KidSoft experts including teachers, parents, and lots of kids.

It's an easy way to shop and purchase software at the lowest prices—right now! For only $6.95 shipping and handling, you will receive a free Club KidSoft magazine and CD.

Just call 800-354-6150

FOR THE CHILD...

Adventures with OSLO: Tools and Gadgets is a showcase of five engaging games, stories, and puzzles that stimulate children 5 years and older to learn about the physical science of simple machines. Windows and Mac.

just $59⁹⁵

CD-ROM SCIENCE PROGRAMS

FOR THE CLASSROOM...

Each school program includes a Windows or Macintosh compatible CD-ROM disc, Teacher's Manual, Student Journal, and Science Lab Kit. Site, District, and Network licenses are available. Favorably reviewed by the National Science Teacher's Assn.

$289 per program

SK Science for Kids
...making Science the "S" in the three "R"s of learning

To order call 1-800-KSCIENCE

25% DISCOUNT ON DIRECT ORDERS!

35% off!

Award winning software from Waterford Institute!

Rusty and Rosy Read With Me
Learn about letters and how they sound. Ages 3-7
Volume 1 (Windows or DOS)
Volume 2 (Windows or DOS)
CD Version (Contains both Volumes 1 and 2)

Write with Me
A child's first wordprocessor.
Ages 4-10
(Windows or CD)

Prices:
Windows or DOS - ~~$49.95~~ **$32.45**
CD Rom - ~~$69.95~~ **$45.45**

Mental Math Games
Speed and accuracy with basic math facts. Seven Games
Ages 6-14
(DOS)

Memphis Math
A 3-D fractions game set in ancient Egypt.
Ages 8 to Adult
(CD only, MPC2 standard)

For more information or

TO ORDER:
Call 800-767-9976
(24 hours)

WATERFORD INSTITUTE

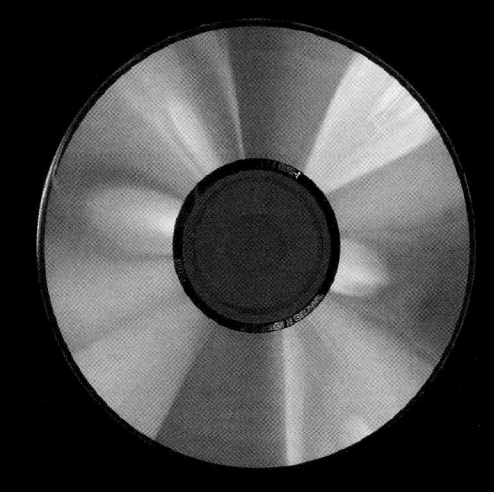

The Edutainment Comes Alive! CD-ROM

The *Edutainment Comes Alive!* CD-ROM

This CD-ROM enables you to evaluate versions of many interactive software titles. Nearly every software demo is playable, which enables you to interact with the action, sights, and sounds of each exciting product.

System Requirements

Each software title has its own set of requirements, but you should make sure that your computer meets the minimum requirements specified in the Windows and DOS sections that follow.

Windows Software

- A computer with a 386 processor (or better)
- Windows 3.1
- 2M of RAM
- Windows-compatible mouse
- VGA graphics

To fully enjoy some of the demos, you need at least 4M of RAM, a Windows-compatible sound card and speakers, and SVGA (256-color) graphics.

DOS

- A computer with a 12 MHz 286 processor (or better)
- DOS 5.0 or higher
- At least 1M of RAM
- VGA graphics

To fully enjoy many of the demos, you need at least 2M of RAM, plus a compatible sound card and speakers. Some of the demos require at least a 386 processor.

Getting Started

The organization of the CD-ROM makes it easy to navigate through the wealth of software it contains. See Appendix A, "What's on the CD-ROM," for more information on the demos and how to explore them. The appendix explains more about the menu for the DOS software and the Program Manager group created for the Windows software. If you are anxious to start right now, follow these instructions:

- **For Windows software:** From Windows, open the File menu and choose Run. In the box that appears, type

  <*drive*>\:setup

  where <*drive*> is the letter of the drive that contains the CD-ROM. This creates a Windows Program Manager group that contains icons for running and installing the Windows software.

- **For DOS software:** From the DOS prompt, type

  <*drive*>:\dosmenu

  where <*drive*> is the letter of the drive that contains the CD-ROM. This starts the DOS menu program that enables you to install and run the DOS software.

PC Compatible (DOS and Windows)

Color Gallery ONE

Multimedia Reference

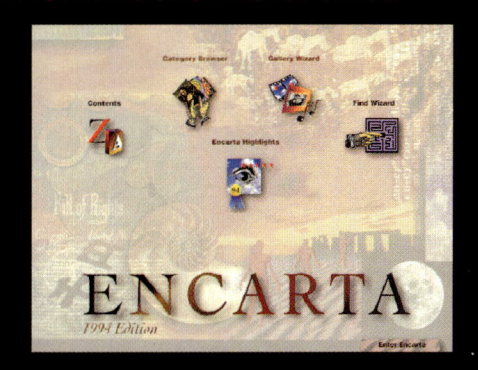

Drill and Practice

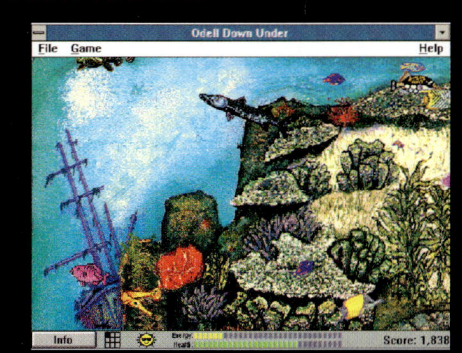

CD-ROM Storybooks

Simulations

Edutainment Comes Alive!

Drill and Practice

Drill-and-practice products have been around since the earliest days of computer education. They started out as little more than computerized versions of paper tests or flash cards. Eventually, someone hit upon the idea of rewarding good performance with something fun. Modern drill-and-practice products show what skilled developers can do with even a simple idea.

Math Blaster: In Search of Spot, from Davidson & Associates, is the latest product in the hugely successful Math Blaster series. Using an adventure theme with colorful graphics, music, and sound effects, Math Blaster: In Search of Spot is a Windows CD-ROM that weaves together a number of different math drills. The program can generate more than 50,000 different math problems. Math Blaster: In Search of Spot was a 1993 Parent's Choice Award winner.

Mental Math Games, from the Waterford Institute, contains problems covering 635 educational objectives in four categories. One of the categories is specially designed to prepare the user for tests such as the SATs or the Iowa Test of Basic Skills.

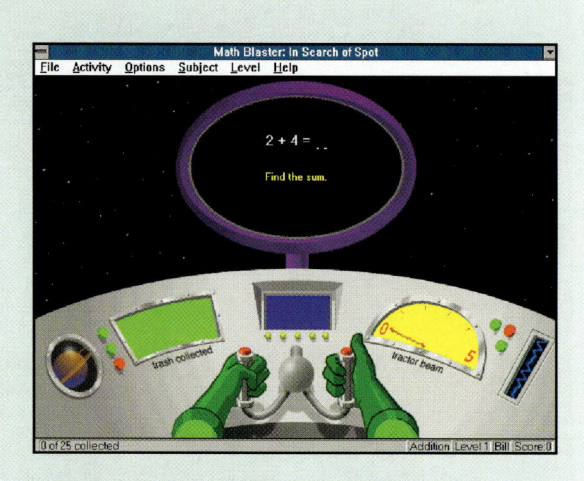

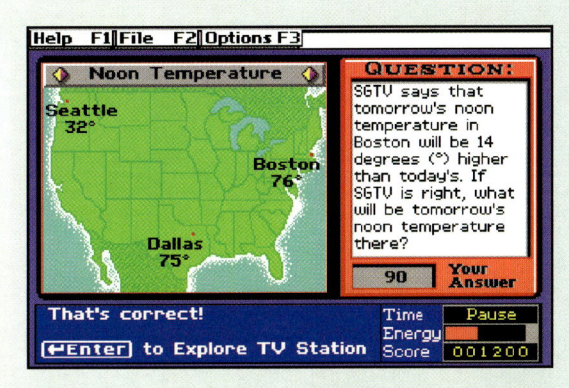

The Learning Company's Super Solvers OutNumbered! is a DOS drill-and-practice adventure game. Here the goal is to stop Morty, the Master of Mischief, from taking over the Shady Glen Television Station. The only way to do this is to solve math word problems and equations while exploring the station. A "Drill for Skill" option lets you skip all the game elements and sharpen your math skills by solving some problems.

Kid's Typing, from Sierra On-Line, is a playful typing tutor. The program introduces Spooky, a friendly ghost with an odd sense of humor. Spooky is your tutor and rewards your typing performance by haunting the house he lives in!

Multimedia Reference

Publishers of multimedia reference works take traditional reference materials and turn them into exciting computer programs. Incorporating audio and video features made possible by the new multimedia PCs, these products are more fun, and more useful, than their paper counterparts.

Microsoft took the 29-volume *Funk & Wagnalls Encyclopedia* and transformed it into Encarta, a beautiful Windows reference work on one CD-ROM. In the process, they added over 1000 new articles, hours of sound, animation, video clips, and more! Encarta is designed to take your family on a never-ending learning journey—and it succeeds.

Divided into three parts (the Encyclopedia, the Atlas, and the Timeline), Encarta gives you a number of ways, including the MindMaze question-and-answer game, to explore its wealth of information. Whatever path you choose, you eventually end up at one of Encarta's more than 25,000 topics. Each topic includes an article as well as related multimedia elements.

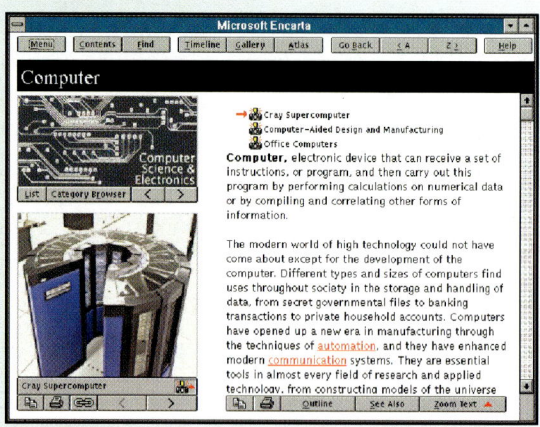

Multimedia Reference

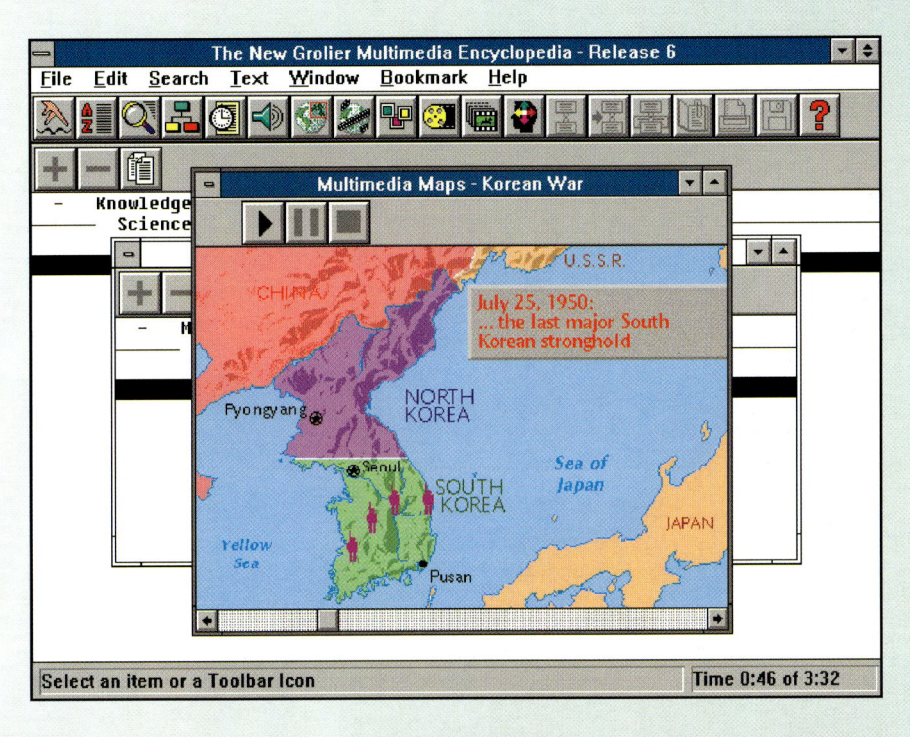

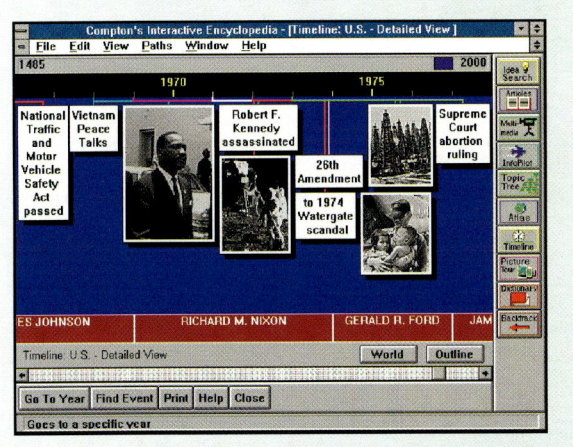

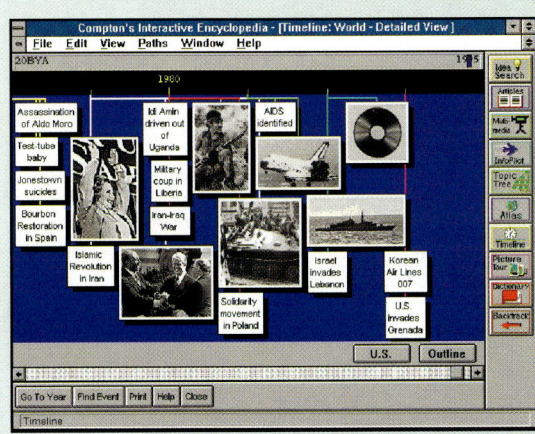

Grolier Electronic Publishing brings you the New Grolier Multimedia Encyclopedia, another CD-ROM-based multimedia reference work for Windows. Based on the 21-volume *Academic American Encyclopedia*, it contains 33,000 articles.

Compton's Interactive Encyclopedia is a powerful Windows CD-ROM from Compton's New Media. Based on the 26-volume *Compton's Encyclopedia*, it gives you nine different ways to access more than 33,000 articles. Compton's contains more than 200 multimedia clips and more than 7,000 images.

The 20th Century Video Almanac is a five-disc DOS CD-ROM reference from The Software Toolworks. Between the five discs, the Video Almanac contains thousands of photos, hundreds of video clips, and hundreds of thousands of words of text about the 20th century. One disc provides a general overview of the century; the other four discs give you an in-depth look at politics, war and disaster, sports, people, and science and technology.

Microsoft Bookshelf '94 is a complete set of reference books on one Windows CD-ROM. Updated versions of seven best-selling reference works are combined into an integrated whole with room left over for speech, maps, audio clips, music, animation, and video clips! Bookshelf '94 features QuickShelf, a floating button bar that keeps its power just a mouse click away—no matter what application you're running.

(*Astronaut and calendar page images courtesy of The Software Toolworks*)

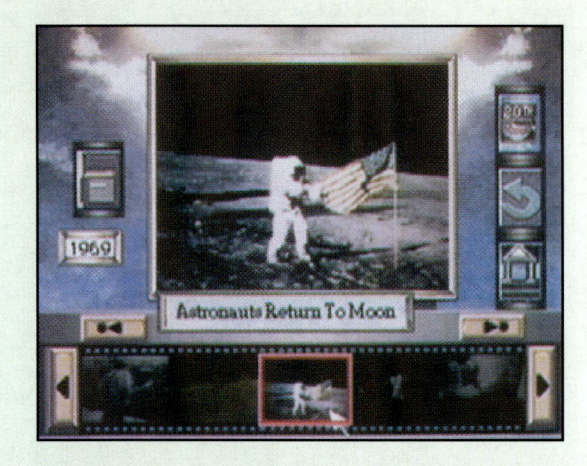

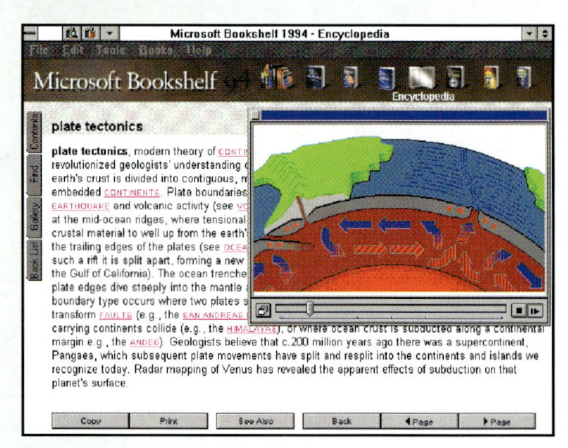

Multimedia Reference

Multimedia Reference

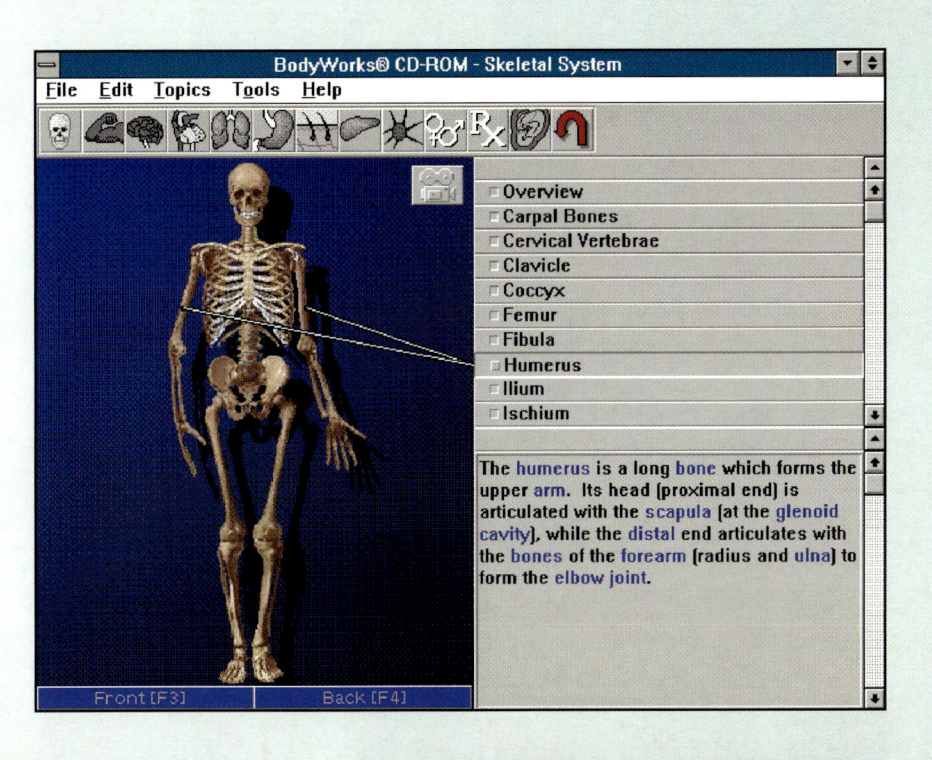

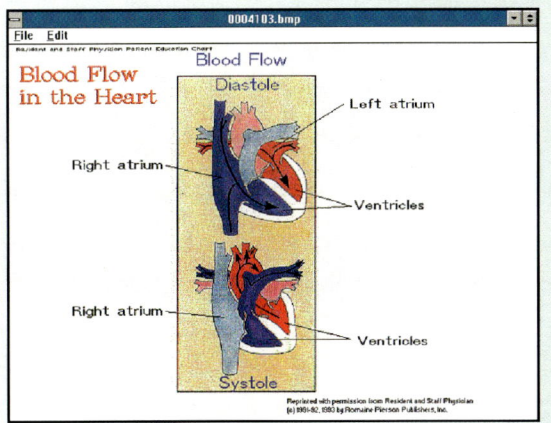

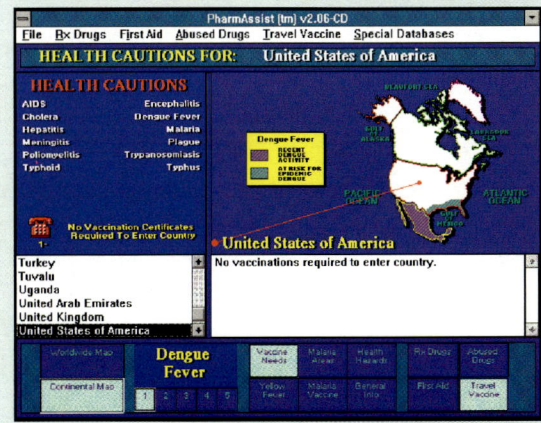

Health and the human body are popular subjects for multimedia reference works. Here are three such products, all CD-ROMs that run under Windows.

The BodyWorks 3.0 CD-ROM is an anatomy program published by the Software Marketing Corporation. BodyWorks helps you explore the systems and structures of the ultimate machine—the human body.

The Family Doctor, 3rd Edition, is a comprehensive medical reference. It was authored and edited by Allan Bruckheim, M.D., FAAFP, a syndicated medical columnist. Family Doctor III is published by the Creative Multimedia Corporation.

PharmAssist is a family health reference from the Software Marketing Corporation. The product is primarily an extensive database of prescription and non-prescription drugs, but the Windows CD-ROM version also contains other health-related information.

Multimedia Reference

Space is the last great frontier. Our machines have explored the solar system for us, returning new discoveries and spectacular pictures. A number of multimedia space reference works are available that make the beauty and wonder of space available to all of us. This book looks at three such products — all CD-ROMs that run under Windows.

Beyond Planet Earth is by Discovery Communications, Inc. Filled with footage from Discovery Channel television shows, the program addresses the most urgent questions about space exploration and planetary science.

Journey to the Planets is published by Multicom Publishing. It is an encyclopedia of the planets and other bodies in our solar system. It is filled with information about all the major bodies and includes some incredible pictures.

Now What Software brings you Small Blue Planet. It is a picture atlas of the Earth, and most of the images included in the product were generated by space-based sensors on the Space Shuttle or on orbiting satellites.

(*The "Tales from Other Worlds" image courtesy of the Discovery Channel*)

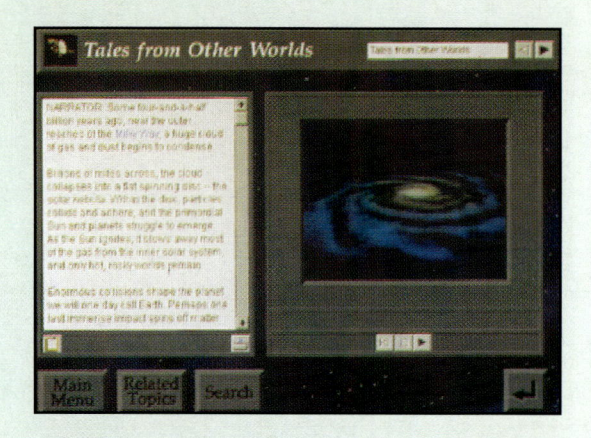

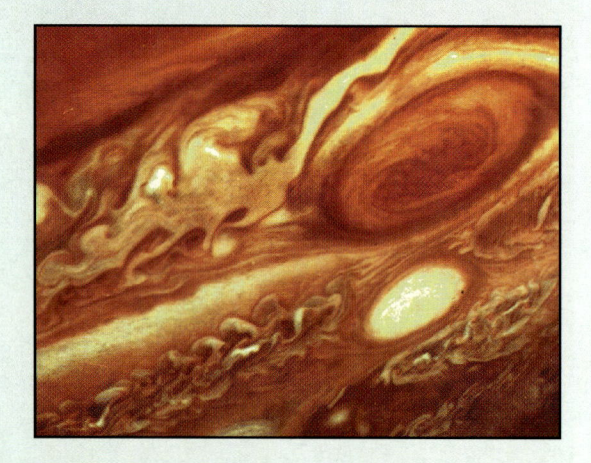

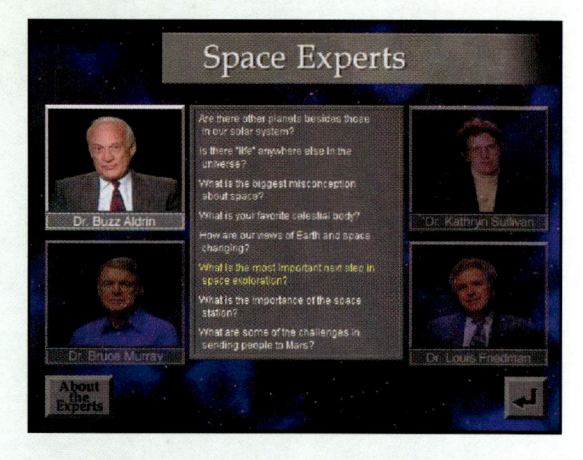

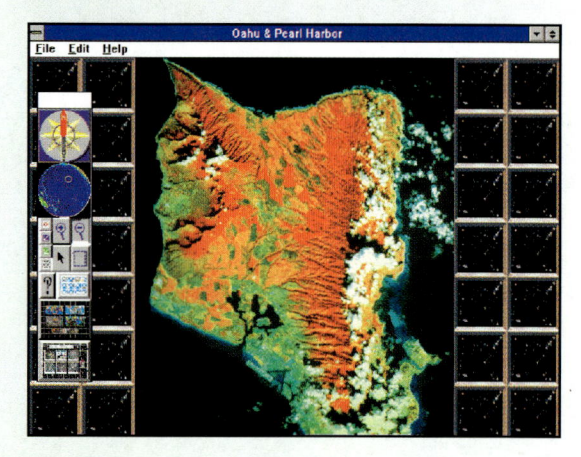

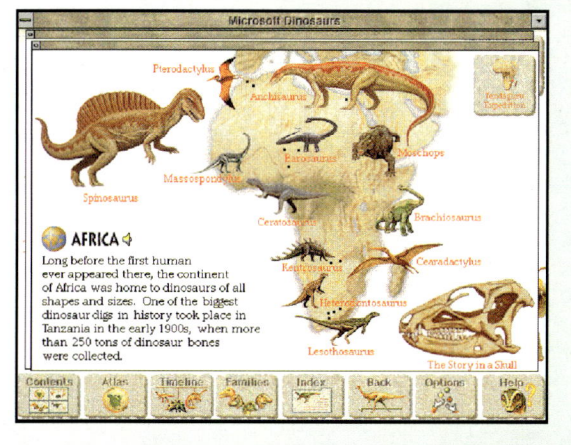

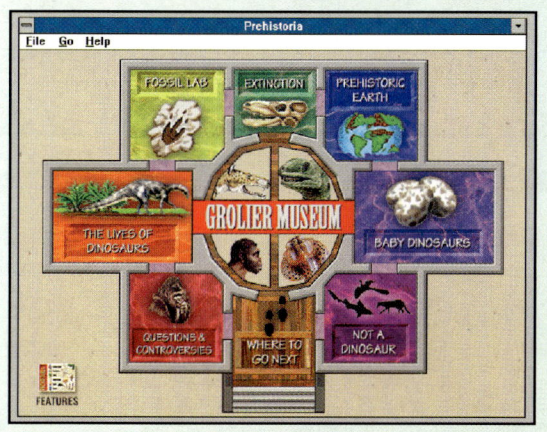

Incredible creatures, more spectacular than any alive today, once roamed the Earth. Most spectacular of all were the dinosaurs— rulers of the planet millions of years before the appearance of man. These two Windows CD-ROMs let you learn what we know about the dinosaurs and their world.

Microsoft Dinosaurs is all about dinosaurs. It combines the features of a multimedia encyclopedia and atlas with fun features such as screen savers and animated movies. The program is filled with fascinating facts and beautiful artwork.

Prehistoria, A Multimedia Who's Who of Prehistoric Life, is from Grolier Electronic Publishing. While programs like Microsoft Dinosaurs concentrate on the 160 million years when the dinosaurs ruled the Earth, Prehistoria looks at over 500 animals that lived in a time span of one-half billion years— from 250 million years before the dinosaurs until just a few thousand years ago.

Multimedia Reference

Microsoft Art Gallery is a Windows CD-ROM that contains paintings and background information from one of the world's great art collections—the National Gallery in London. Art Gallery contains reproductions of over 2000 works of art, organized by artist, subject, and other categories.

Compton's New Media publishes Jazz, a Windows CD-ROM that covers the history of jazz. Subtitled "A Multimedia History," Jazz uses text, video, and music to take you from the origins of the music to the present day.

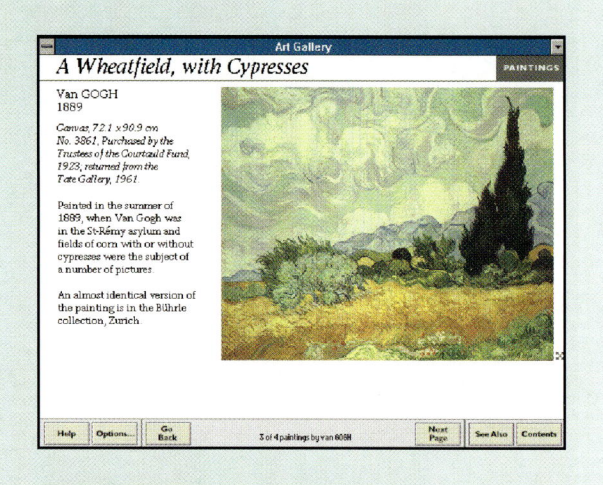

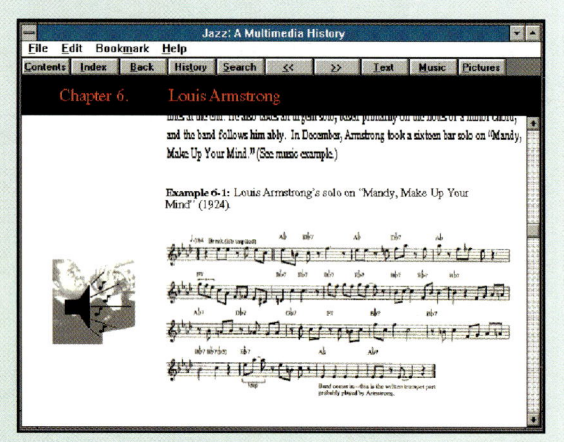

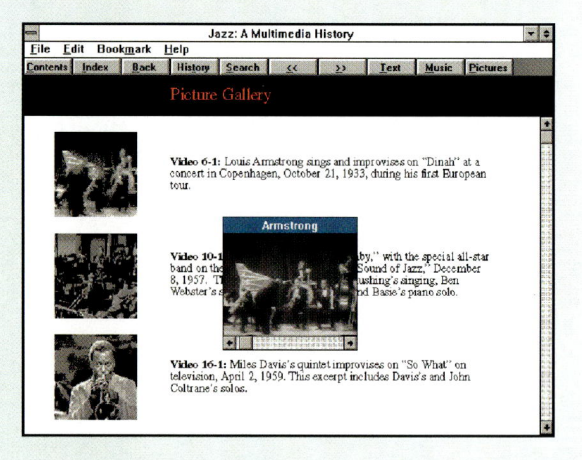

Simulations

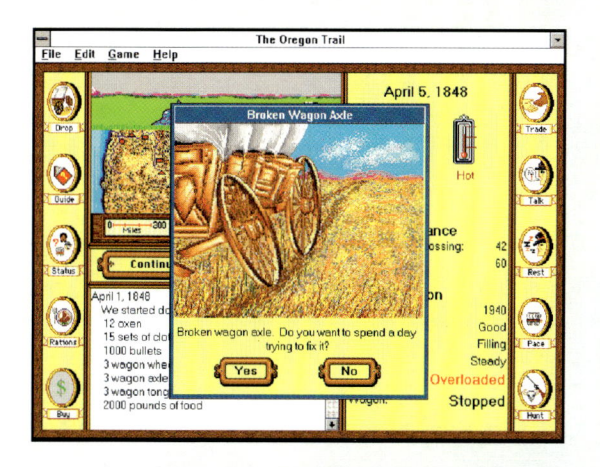

Simulation programs are an exciting form of edutainment. Simulations model aspects of the real world, with the goal of helping you understand whatever is being simulated. A simulation becomes edutainment when a complex model is turned into a game.

MECC's Oregon Trail is a simulation of the pioneers' 19th-century journey across the American West. You take the role of a pioneer leaving Independence, Missouri, for the Willamette Valley in Oregon. As leader of your party, you must make the right decisions if you are to reach the Willamette Valley safely.

SimCity 2000 is a city simulator from Maxis. You take on the role of mayor and city planner for either a brand new or existing city. Every decision you make affects the city and its citizens—sometimes for better, sometimes for worse.

(*Oregon Trail images courtesy of MECC; SimCity 2000 images courtesy of Maxis*)

MECC's Odell Down Under is a Windows simulation of life on Australia's Great Barrier Reef. You take on the role of one of more than 70 different life forms that inhabit the reef, and you try to stay alive in its natural habitat.

Microsoft's Flight Simulator is a DOS-based, real-time flight-simulation program. By combining detailed graphics with realistic simulation models and sound effects, Flight Simulator turns a PC into the cockpit of an aircraft. It even uses digitized images of the instrument panels of real aircraft.

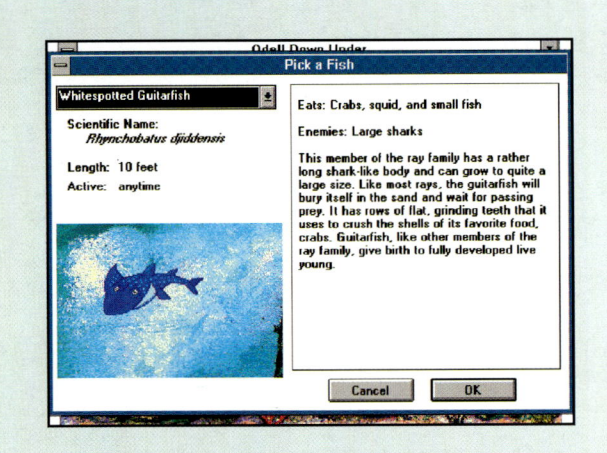

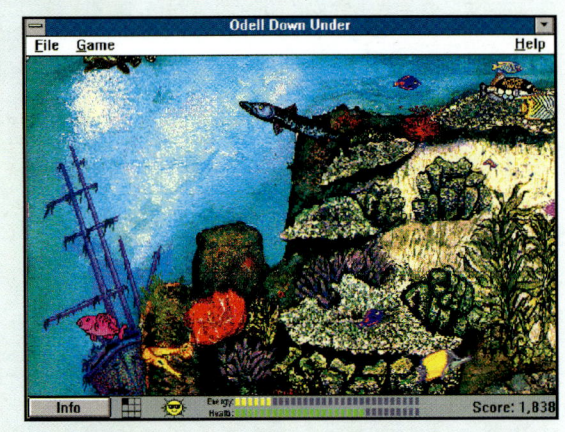

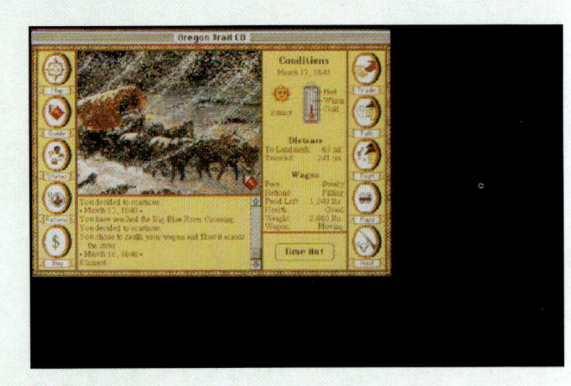

Simulations

Simulations

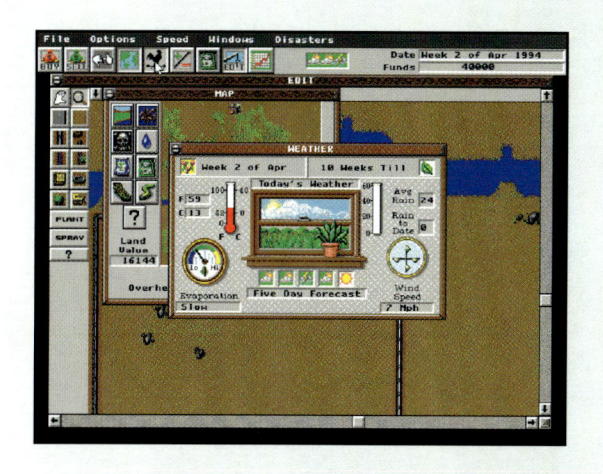

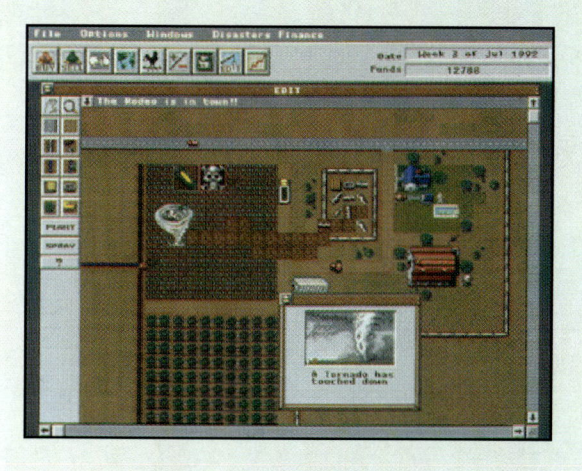

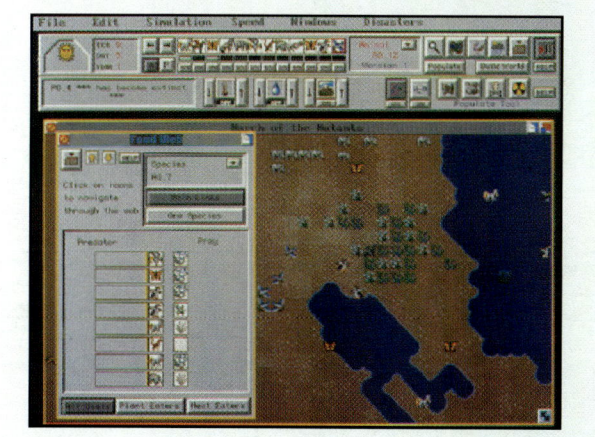

SimFarm is another simulation program from Maxis. In SimFarm, you are a farmer, and you start out with a plot of land and a run-down farmhouse, somewhere in the USA. Growing crops or raising livestock, the fate of the farm hangs on your decisions.

Maxis also publishes SimLife, subtitled "The Genetic Playground." With this program, you can create and genetically alter simulated lifeforms. You can design your own ecosystem, tailoring life to fit, or you can let evolution take its course and see what happens.

(*SimFarm and SimLife images courtesy of Maxis*)

CD-ROM Storybooks

CD-ROM Storybooks are computerized versions of children's picture books. Taking advantage of the power of multimedia PCs and the storage capacity of CD-ROMs, these products make stories come alive on the screen.

Arthur's Teacher Trouble, from Broderbund, is the story of Arthur and his new teacher, Mr. Ratburn. Mr. Ratburn is so tough he even gives homework on the first day of class! Every screen is full of music and animation, and it only takes a mouse click to start the action.

Annabel's Dream of Ancient Egypt is published by Texas Caviar. It is an original story about Annabel, a cat who must learn to deal with her annoying sisters. Her dreams take her to ancient Egypt, where she learns to cope with her anger and with her teasing sisters.

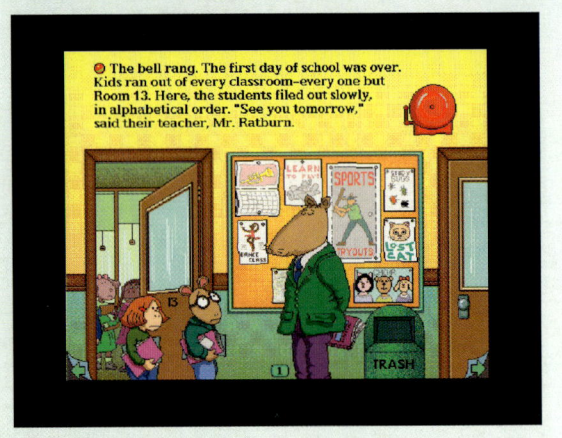

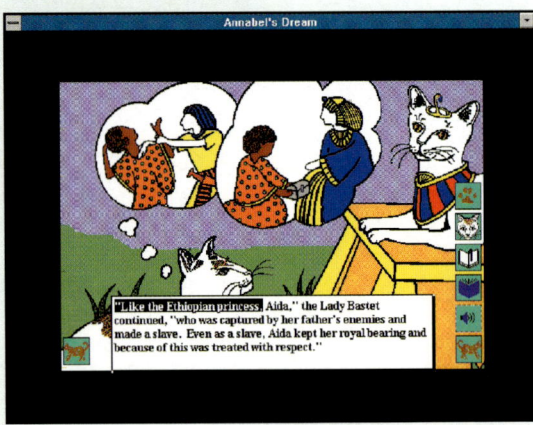

CD-ROM Storybooks

T.J. Finds a Friend was produced by Artists for Multimedia and is distributed by Media Resources. It is a fundraiser for the National Center for Missing and Exploited Children (NCMEC). Twenty percent of the proceeds from the sale of the product go directly to the NCMEC for discovery and educational programs.

The Tortoise and the Hare is another story from Broderbund. It is a computerized retelling of Aesop's fable of the same name. Every page includes clever animation, with music and sound effects.

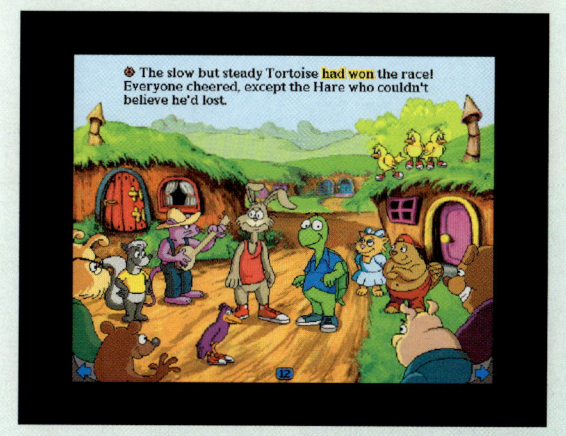

A Christmas Carol, from EBook, was created for somewhat older readers. It is the unabridged, original tale, just as Charles Dickens wrote it. It tells the story of Ebenezer Scrooge, who discovers the true meaning of Christmas.

The Adventures of Pinocchio is distributed by Orange Cherry New Media. It is an adaptation of the original story, adding new adventures and new characters. The story is almost 300 pages long.

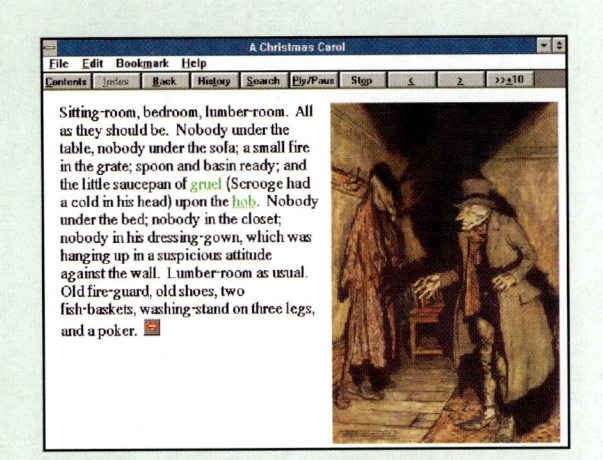

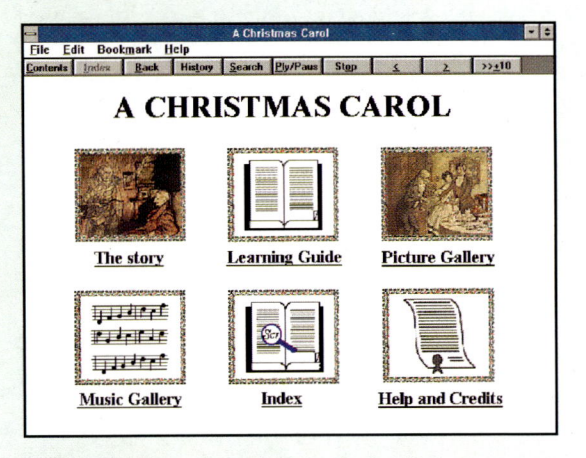

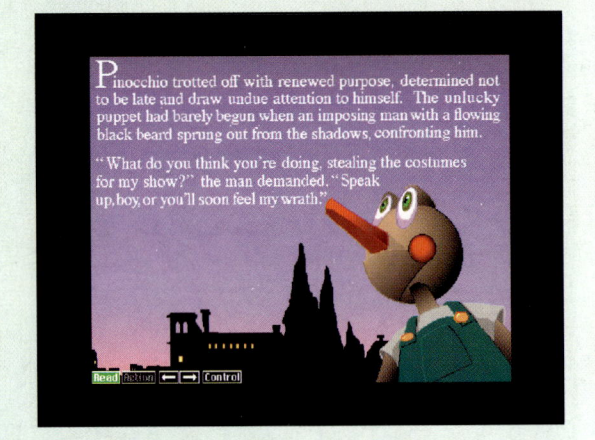

CD-ROM Storybooks

Color Gallery TWO

Preschool

Creativity Tools

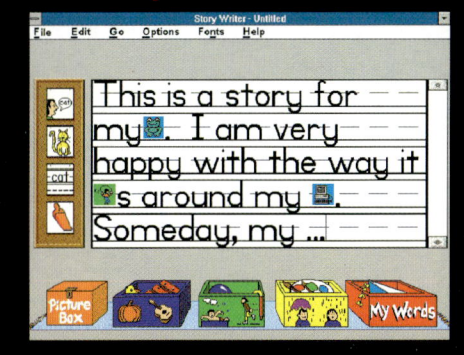

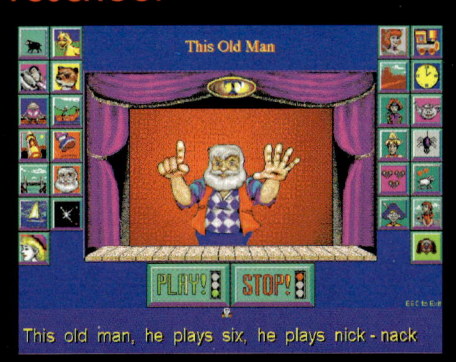

General Edutainment

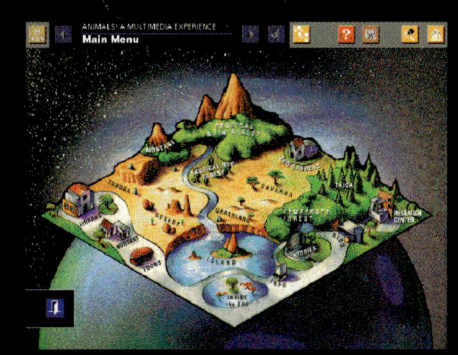

Edutainment *Comes Alive!*

Preschool products are edutainment programs designed for children as young as two. They introduce children to basic concepts, keeping them interested with interactivity, bright colors, music, and sound effects. Most preschool programs contain friendly animated characters that youngsters can relate to.

Early Math, from Sierra On-Line, is a Windows-based math and numbers program. The child's friend and tutor is Loid, an intelligent, talking, purple alien. The program contains six games that provide a progression of learning activities.

Disney Software publishes Mickey's 123's. A DOS program, Mickey's 123's is designed to introduce children to such basic concepts as number recognition, counting, quantities, and sequencing.

Preschool

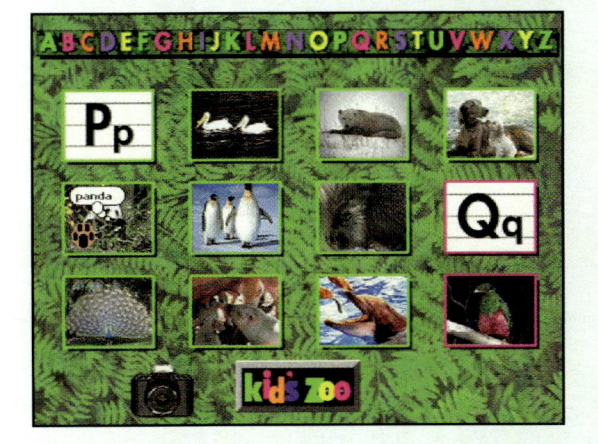

The Waterford Institute brings you Rusty & Rosy Read with Me, Volumes 1 and 2. These Windows products were developed with the help of the students at the Institute's school in Utah. The programs teach basic skills using language concepts.

Kid's Zoo is published by Knowledge Adventure. The program is designed to empower children with a sense of control over the learning experience. The activities cover a range of skills and age levels, so that Kid's Zoo keeps pace with the child's intellectual growth.

Fun School Learning Adventures with Teddy Bear is a DOS program from Europress Software. It contains six different educational games covering a broad range of skills, including pre-reading, vocabulary, counting, estimation, and creative thinking.

Ping & Kooky's Cuckoo Zoo is a Windows edutainment product from Electronic Arts. It contains a zoo with five different areas, all tied together by a fun train. Four of these areas are ecologically correct environments populated by singing, dancing, and talking animals, while the fifth area is a stage where the child can create music.

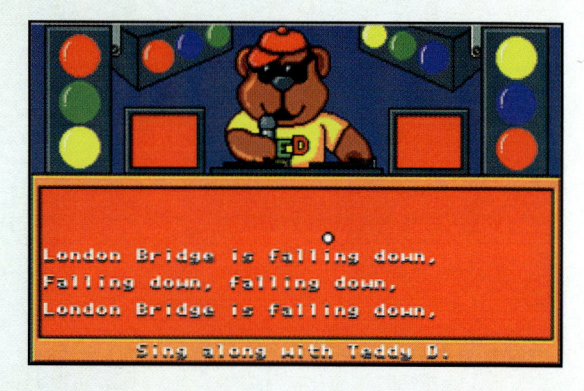

Preschool

Preschool

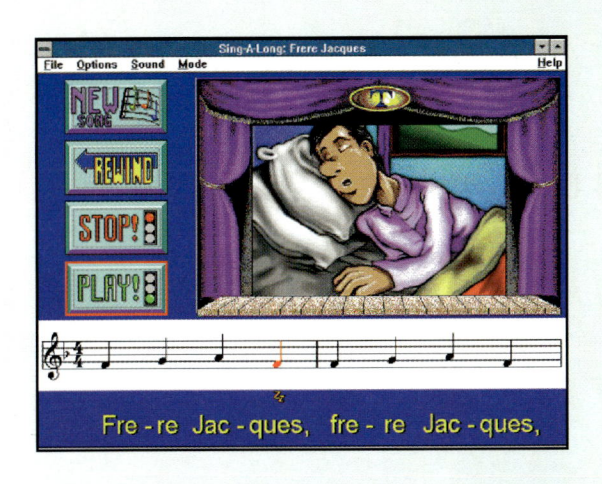

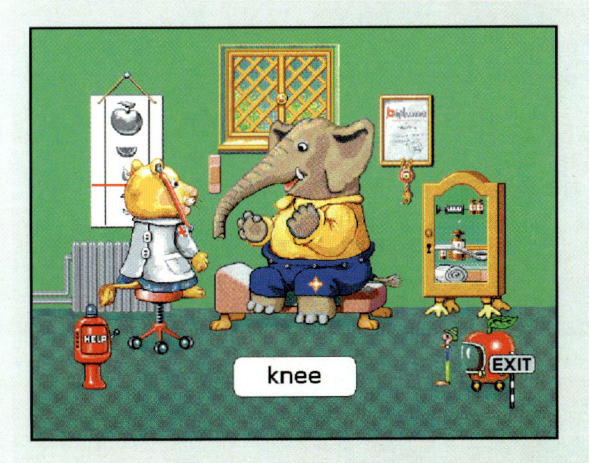

Dr. T's Sing-A-Long Kids' Classics is a music and reading skills program from Dr. T's Music Software. Running under Windows, this program combines music, animation, song lyrics, and musical notation into a singing experience for you and your children.

Busytown is a DOS CD-ROM published by Paramount Interactive. This 1993 Parent's Choice Award winner is based on Richard Scarry's Busytown book series. It is filled with exciting playgrounds that combine play with the teaching of educational skills.

Creativity Tools

Creativity tools take advantage of the power of multimedia PCs to help you explore a creative medium. Since there are no right or wrong answers with this type of product, you are encouraged to experiment to your heart's content.

Davidson's Kid CAD is a computer-aided design program for children. Running under Windows, it encourages the child to design and build houses, castles, and other structures right there on the computer screen. After they are built, the structures can be furnished and the grounds landscaped. Kid CAD is an innovative program that won a 1993 Parent's Choice Award.

Kid Works 2, another creativity tool from Davidson, is a story-creation program. It enables kids to write and illustrate their own stories. Equipped with a number of tools to help in the story-creation process, the program can even read the completed story aloud!

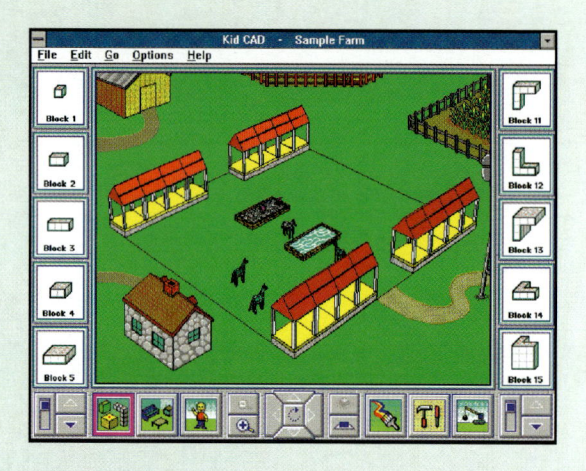

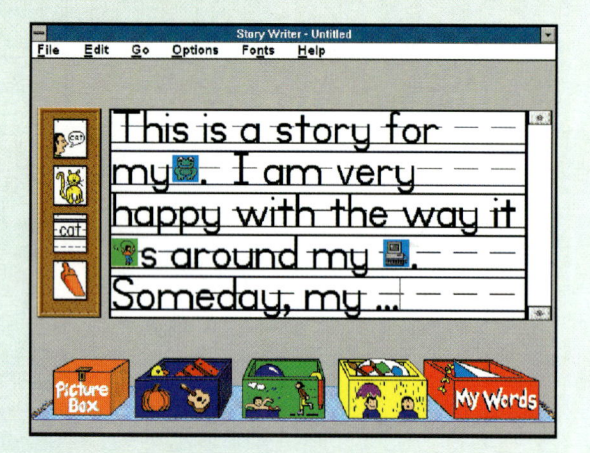

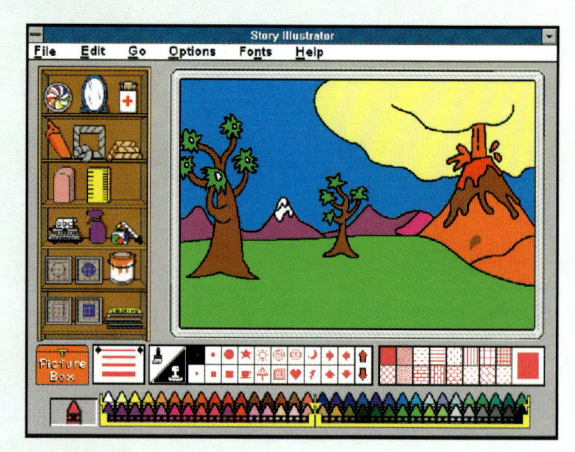

Creativity Tools

Microsoft's Creative Writer is a crazy desktop publishing application for Windows. With the help of Maggie, Max, and McZee, a child can create illustrated stories, banners, cards, and newspapers.

MECC brings you Storybook Weaver and My Own Stories—sister programs for writing and illustrating storybooks. Storybook Weaver draws from the folklore of many cultures around the world, while My Own Stories is set in the here and now.

Creativity Tools

The Print Shop Deluxe CD Ensemble is a powerful Windows package from Broderbund. You can use it to create a wide variety of personalized printed material. Combining Print Shop Deluxe with four add-on products, this package can create five different types of projects and includes over 1000 clip-art images! Print Shop Deluxe won a Parent's Choice Award in 1993.

Announcements 2.0 for Windows, from Parsons Technology, is another Windows printing package. It provides some of the power and flexibility of Print Shop Deluxe, but at a lower price.

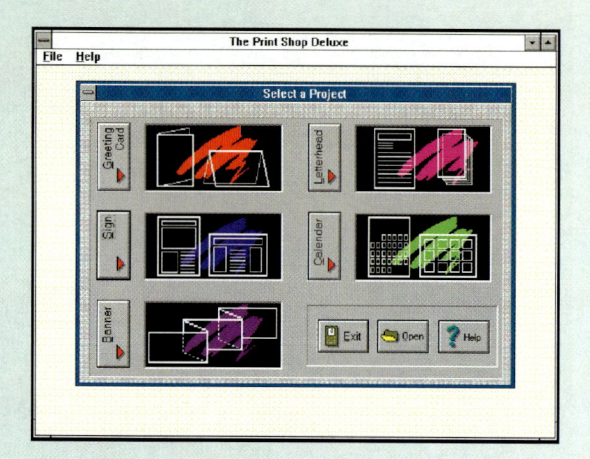

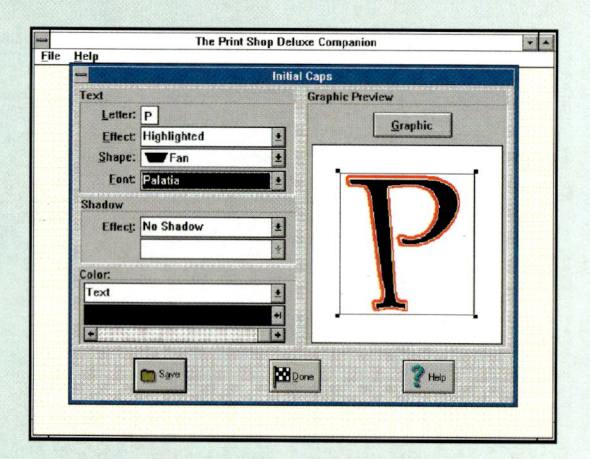

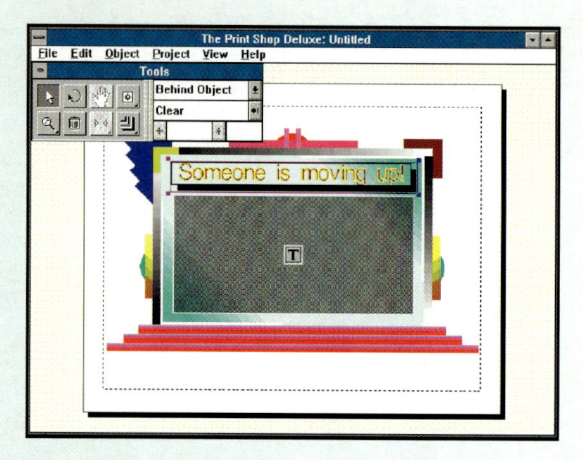

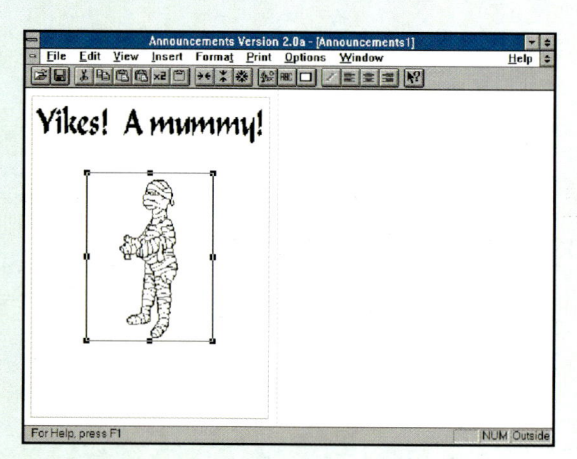

General Edutainment

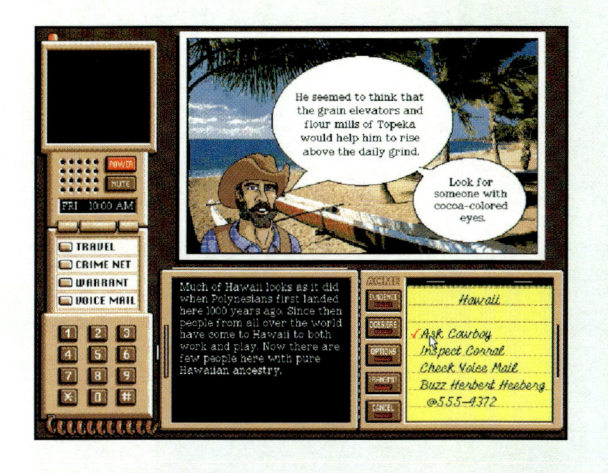

The General Edutainment category is the home for all those products that don't fit into any of the other categories of edutainment. All sorts of products fit in here, covering the spectrum from primarily educational products with some entertainment value, to primarily entertainment products with some educational value.

The Carmen Sandiego series from Broderbund is justifiably famous. This installment, WHERE IN THE USA IS CARMEN SANDIEGO? Deluxe, teaches U.S. geography, history, and culture, while helping a child improve research and problem-solving skills.

The Eagle Eye Mysteries series comes from EA*Kids, a division of Electronic Arts. The latest version takes place in London and teaches scientific and cultural facts, while emphasizing reading, reasoning, and interpretation skills.

General Edutainment

Lawrence Productions' Discovering America is an adventure game that covers the Spanish exploration of North America in the 1500s. It is designed to teach early American history, reading, and thinking skills, and to expose the player to multicultural experiences.

Normandy, from Discovery Communications, is the story of the Allied invasion of Europe. The program resembles an interactive documentary, in which you can stop the action and explore any segment you wish.

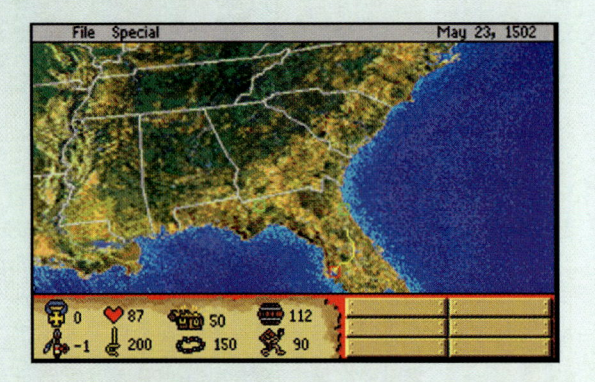

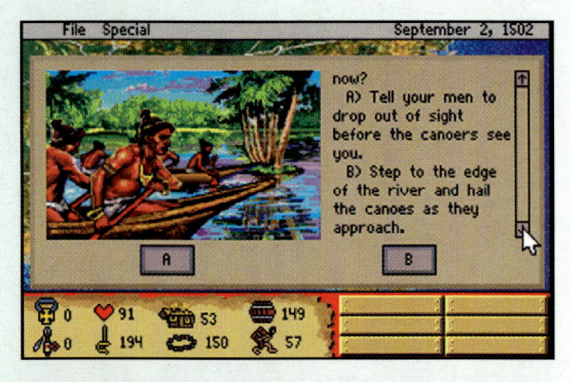

General Edutainment

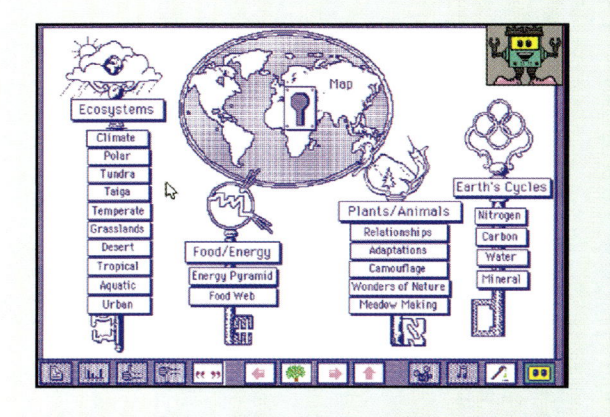

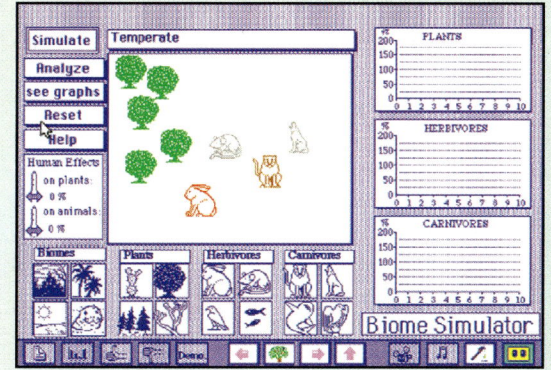

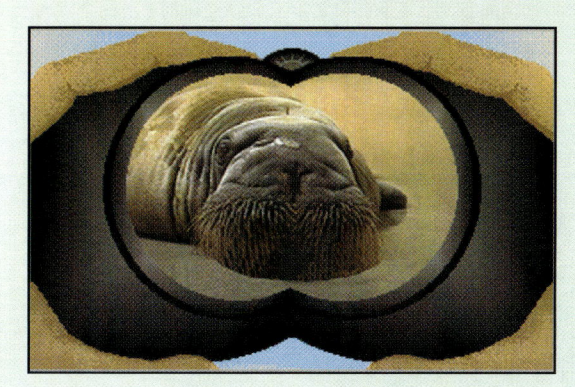

Ecology Treks is a product of Magic Quest (which is being acquired by Sanctuary Woods as this is written). It is designed to be "the program that turns kids on to ecology," while at the same time developing critical thinking, recall/memory, research, and other skills.

Zoo Keeper, from Davidson, teaches you about animals and the importance of protecting endangered species. To win, you must take care of World Zoo while the staff is off releasing an animal into the wild. To complicate your life, troublemakers are disrupting things throughout the zoo. Zoo Keeper won a Parent's Choice Award in 1993.

Oceans Below is a "virtual underwater adventure" from The Software Toolworks. It turns you into a scuba diver exploring undersea locations around the world, learning about the ocean, and searching for sunken treasure.

The Animals! is also published by The Software Toolworks. This program is a multimedia exploration of the plant and animal life in the San Diego Zoo and is modeled on the zoo's long-range plans. Someday, the creatures in the zoo will be grouped together in natural habitats called *biomes*.

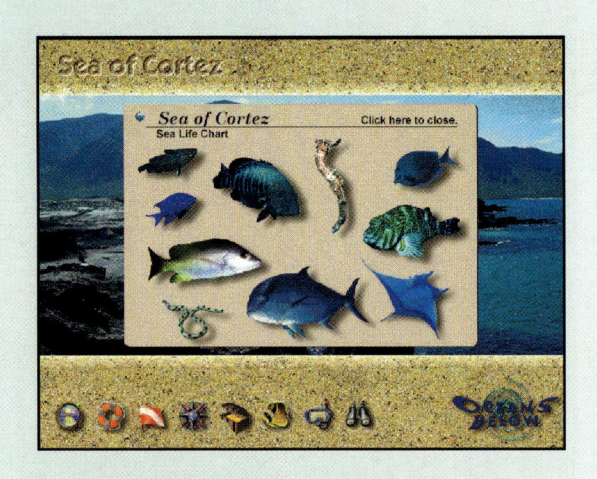

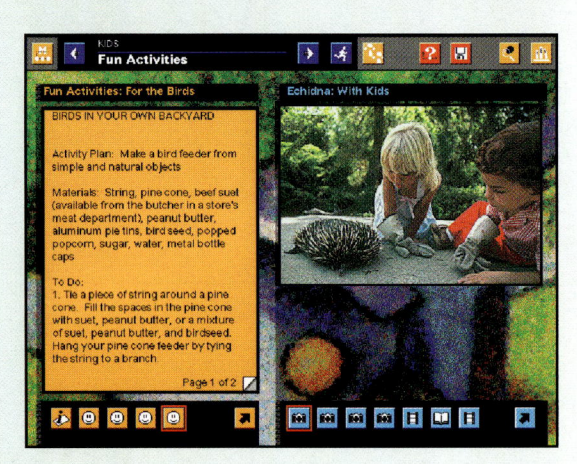

General Edutainment

General Edutainment

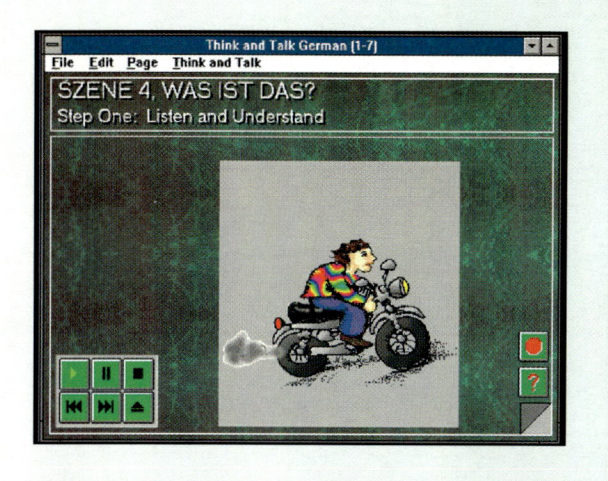

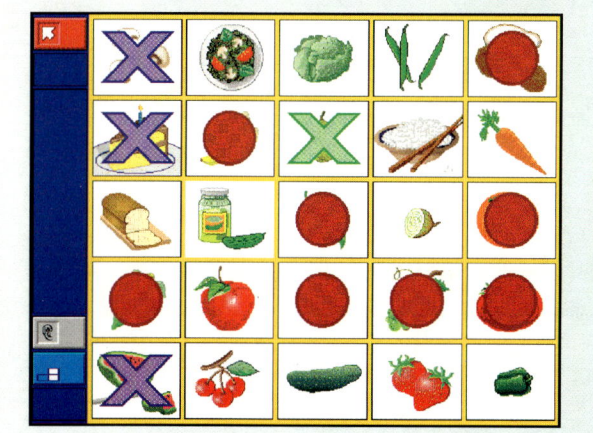

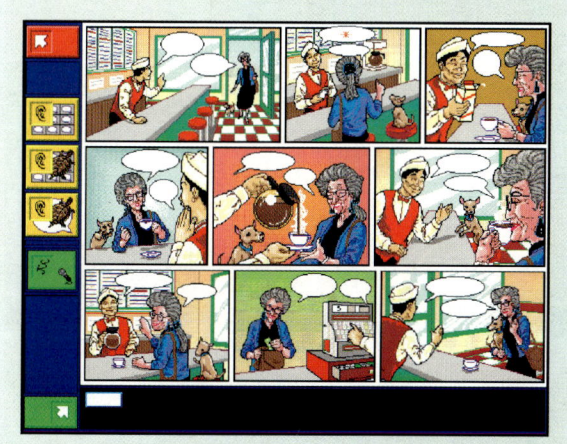

Berlitz Think & Talk German is a nine-disc CD-ROM language program published by Hyper-Glot. It is a computerized version of the Berlitz Method, which teaches a language without the translation and memorization required by most techniques.

TriplePlay French is part of the Playing With Language series from Syracuse Language Systems. It utilizes the multimedia language immersion method developed by researchers at Syracuse University and teaches French without formal lessons or vocabulary lists.

Microsoft's Multimedia Schubert is part of its CD-ROM-based multimedia composers series for Windows. An exploration of Schubert's "Quintet in A Major," also known as the "Trout Quintet," it is designed to help you understand this beautiful piece and to find out more about the man who created it.

Super Solvers Gizmos & Gadgets is part of the Super Solvers series from The Learning Company. It is designed to teach science and thinking skills, and it accomplishes that task with enjoyable sounds and graphics.

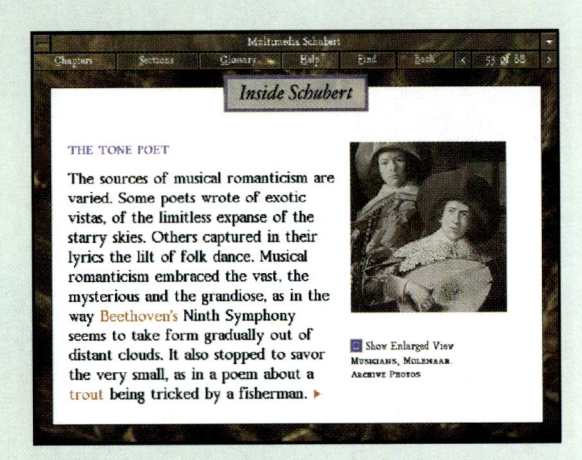

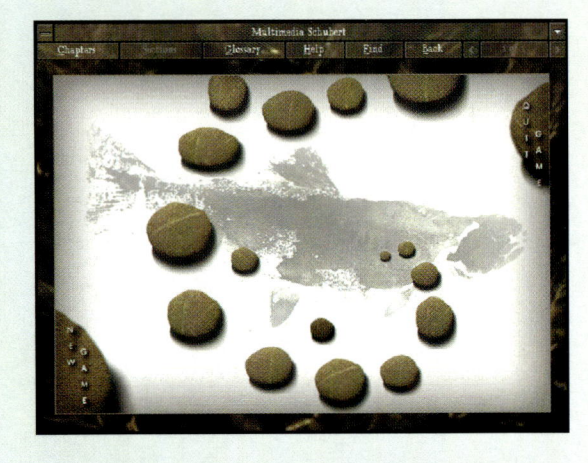

General Edutainment

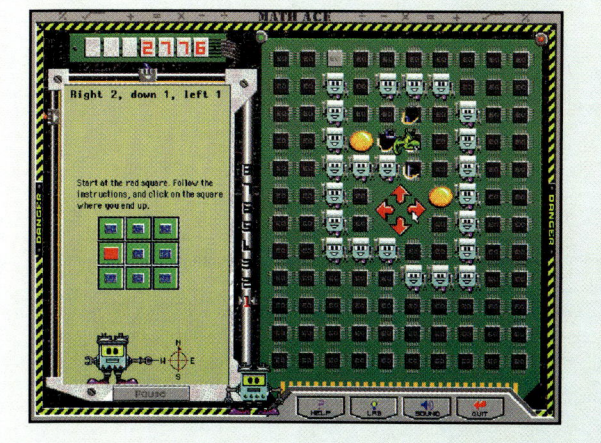

Mind Castle, The Spell of the Word Wizard, is a word-puzzle game from Lawrence Productions. The action takes place in a spooky old castle where answering spelling questions is the only thing that can save you. A Parent's Choice Award was granted to this program in 1993.

Math Ace is a "math adventure" from Magic Quest (Magic Quest is being acquired by Sanctuary Woods at the time of this writing). It takes a number of different approaches to teaching math in order to develop critical-thinking, problem-solving, and reasoning skills, as well as to stimulate a child's curiosity and interest in math.

(*Trophy room image courtesy of Lawrence Productions*)

General Edutainment

Operation Neptune is a DOS CD-ROM from The Learning Company. It is an undersea math adventure that teaches pre-algebra and problem-solving skills, while a child tries to save the Earth's oceans and retrieve secret data canisters. Operation Neptune was a 1992 Parent's Choice Award winner.

Math Rescue and Word Rescue are shareware products published by Apogee Games. Math Rescue is designed to teach basic math to children, and Word Rescue teaches basic reading to children. Both products combine learning with arcade-style action.